Lecture Notes in Computer Science 682
Edited by G. Goos and J. Hartmanis

B. Bouchon-Meunier L. Valverde
R. R. Yager (Eds.)

IPMU '92 – Advanced Methods in Artificial Intelligence

4th International Conference
on Information Processing and Management
of Uncertainty in Knowledge-Based Systems
Palma de Mallorca, Spain, July 6-10, 1992
Proceedings

Springer-Verlag
Berlin Heidelberg New York
London Paris Tokyo
Hong Kong Barcelona
Budapest

Series Editors

Gerhard Goos
Universität Karlsruhe
Postfach 69 80
Vincenz-Priessnitz-Straße 1
D-76131 Karlsruhe, FRG

Juris Hartmanis
Cornell University
Department of Computer Science
4130 Upson Hall
Ithaca, NY 14853, USA

Volume Editors

Bernadette Bouchon-Meunier
CNRS-LAFORIA-IBP, University Paris 6, Boîte 169
4 place Jussieu, F-75252 Paris Cedex 05, France

Llorenç Valverde
Dept. of Mathematics and Computer Science, University of the Balearic Islands
Cra. de Valldemossa, E-07071 Palma, Spain

Ronald R. Yager
Machine Intelligence Institute, Iona College
New Rochelle, NY 10801, USA

CR Subject Classification (1991): I.2.3-6, I.2.1, H.1.1, H.4

ISBN 3-540-56735-6 Springer-Verlag Berlin Heidelberg New York
ISBN 0-387-56735-6 Springer-Verlag New York Berlin Heidelberg

Printed in Germany

Typesetting: Camera ready by author
Printing and binding: Druckhaus Beltz, Hemsbach/Bergstr.
45/3140-543210 - Printed on acid-free paper

Foreword

The papers in this volume are extended versions of presentations at the fourth International Conference on Information Processing and Management of Uncertainty in Knowledge-Based Systems (IPMU Conference), which was held in Palma de Mallorca, July 6-10, 1992.

The conference focused on issues related to the acquisition, representation, management, and transmission of information in knowledge-based and decision-making systems. Because of the large range of presentations, we have chosen to focus this book on the methodologies which are related to artificial intelligence. We present both theoretical and applied papers.

The first section of the book is devoted to non monotonic reasoning and the management of default knowledge. The second section deals with methods using non-classical logics to deal with imperfect knowledge and to represent its spatial and temporal components. The third section presents various methods for the acquisition of uncertain and imprecise knowledge. The fourth section is concerned with the use of qualitative, uncertain, temporal, and ambiguous pieces of information in knowledge-based systems, expert systems, and process controllers. The last section contains papers using artificial neural network methodologies.

The previous IPMU Conferences have results in three other volumes of the series Lecture Notes in Computer Science, *Uncertainty in Knowledge-Based Systems* (LNCS 286), *Uncertainty and Intelligent Systems* (LNCS 313), *Uncertainty in Knowledge Bases* (LNCS 521).

April 1993

B.Bouchon-Meunier
L. Valverde
R.R. Yager

Contents

3. Acquiring Knowledge

4. Knowledge Based Systems

1. Non Monotonic Reasoning

Possibilistic Abduction

Didier Dubois – Henri Prade
Institut de Recherche en Informatique de Toulouse (I.R.I.T.)
Université Paul Sabatier, 118 route de Narbonne
31062 Toulouse Cedex – France

1. Introduction

The following pattern which from the two premises " if **h** then **e**" and "**e** is observed to be true" infers the conclusion "**h** is plausible", where **h** stands for an hypothesis and **e** for a piece of evidence, is generally considered as the simplest pattern of abductive reasoning (Peirce [35]). This pattern can be contrasted with the deductive pattern which from "if **h** then **e**" and "**h** is true" infers that "**e** is true".

The abductive pattern although considered by many authors (e.g. Pólya [39]), has not been given any logical or numerical formalization until recently, if we except the Bayesian model (where we compute the a posteriori probability of **h** when **e** is observed), and some heuristic, numerically quantified attempts (e.g. Friedman [20], Bandler and Kohout [3], Hall [23]). Abduction is often related to the handling of causation in diagnosis problems. Pearl [32] rather distinguishes between expectation-evoking and explanation-evoking rules. With our above notations, it comes down to consider the rule "if **h** then **e**" with the interpretation "if **h** is true then **e** is expected" (deduction) and the companion rule "if **e** then **h**" understood as "the observation of **e** suggests **h** as a possible explanation" (abduction). More recently, Pearl and Verma [34] have proposed a minimal-model semantics of causation, based on directed acyclic graphs.

Clearly a key problem in abduction is to provide some status to the abductive conclusion "**h** is plausible" and maybe to assign some plausibility degree to **h**. Thus we may be able to rank possible causes of an observed state of facts according to their respective plausibilities. In the following we briefly review three approaches to abductive reasoning which come from different research areas, namely

- the relational approach where a (possibly fuzzy) relation relates causes and observations;
- the conditional approach where the rule "if **h** then **e**" is understood in terms of a conditional measure and where an a posteriori measure is computed for **h** (a probability or a possibility);
- the logical approach which looks for minimal set(s) of hypotheses which makes **e** true.

In each case we suggest how a possibility theory-based model can be used. However a comparative and unified view of these three approaches is beyond the scope of the paper.

2. Relational Approach

2.1. General Principles

In the relational model, a set of potential causes $\mathcal{H} = \{\mathbf{h}_1,\dots, \mathbf{h}_i,\dots, \mathbf{h}_m\}$ is related to a set of potential observations (or more precisely of observable effects) $\mathcal{E}$ =

$\{e_1,\ldots, e_j,\ldots, e_n\}$. The h_i's are assumed to be logically independent, i.e. each h_i can be present or absent independently of the presence or absence of others h_j. In the simplest case, a classical binary relation R defined on $\mathcal{H} \times \mathcal{E}$ encodes the fact that if the cause h_i is present then the effect e_j follows, under the form $(h_i,e_j) \in R$. Then $(h_i,e_j) \notin R$ means that e_j cannot be caused by h_i; i.e. we have a complete knowledge about the possible causes of an effect. More generally, we may consider a relation R defined on $2^{\mathcal{H}} \times \mathcal{E}$, if the *conjunction* of causes is meaningful in the production of effects; for instance in case some effect can be obtained only if a particular conjunction of causes is present. For convenience R may then the defined on $2^{\mathcal{H}} \times 2^{\mathcal{E}}$. The problem is then, given a set $E \subseteq \mathcal{E}$ of observations, to find out the plausible set(s) of causes which entail(s) E.

The relational model has been used by Reggia et al. [40], Peng and Reggia [37] who advocate for the search of so-called *parsimonious covering* solutions, i.e. the smallest (in the sense of cardinality), minimal (i.e. irredundant) subset(s) of $\mathcal{H}$ which explain(s) all the effects in E. Indeed minimal subsets of $\mathcal{H}$ are such that if one cause is removed, there is at least an effect in E which is no longer explained, and there may be several such minimal subsets (which are not comparable with respect to set inclusion by construction) with different cardinalities. Note that these parsimonious minimal subsets are still allowed to have effects outside E: the conjunction of their elements explains all effects in E and perhaps causes other effects. This raises several questions about the proper interpretation of E and R. Does E represent all the observable effects or only a part of them ? In other words, if $e_j \notin E$, does it mean than e_j *cannot* be observed or has not been observed (because for instance, e_j is costly to observe and that one looks for it only if necessary) ? Does $(h_i,e_j) \in R$ really mean "if h_i then *certainly* e_j" (and then $(h_i,e_j) \notin R$ only means "it is not known if e_j can be caused by h_i"), or only "if h_i then *possibly* e_j" ?

2.2. Fuzzy Relational Model

In the late seventies Sanchez [43] developed a diagnosis method based on a fuzzy relational model where, i) R is a fuzzy relation: the degree of association $\mu_R(h_i,e_j) \in [0,1]$ may account for the uncertainty that e_j follows from h_i, or for the intensity of the effect e_j (if the strongness of the effect can be graded on a scale) when h_i is present; ii) E is a fuzzy set of observations, again the degree of membership $\mu_E(e_j) \in [0,1]$ may account for the uncertainty pervading the observation of e_j or for the intensity of e_j. See Sanchez [44] for the case where R is defined on $2^{\mathcal{H}} \times 2^{\mathcal{E}}$. Fuzzy relation-based models for diagnosis have not been widely used until now; let us however mention (Asse et al. [2], Kitowski and Bargiel [28], Gmytrasiewicz et al. [22]; see also Arigoni [1]) among recent works. Besides, fuzzy relation equations are also at the core of explanation systems designed for expert systems handling uncertainty in the framework of possibility theory (Farreny and Prade [16], [17]).

Basically the problem is to find some subset $H \subseteq \mathcal{H}$ of causes such that the composition of H with R yields E, i.e. $H \circ R = E$, which is extended to the fuzzy case by $\max_i \min(\mu_H(h_i), \mu_R(h_i,e_j)) = \mu_E(e_j), \forall j$. This equation where H is unknown may have no solution. If several solutions exist, the solution(s) which is(are) minimal (in the sense of set inclusion, defined by $F \subseteq G \Leftrightarrow \mu_F \leq \mu_G$ for fuzzy set(s)), is(are) worth considering; see Pappis and Sugeno [30]. If the equation $H \circ R = E$ has no solution, we have to relax it into $H \circ R \subseteq E$ or $H \circ R \supseteq E$. In the first case we look for an explanation of a subset of observations, while in the second case the set of potential causes H should explain all the observations but is allowed to have some unobserved effects also. This leads to consider various (fuzzy) sets of interest in $\mathcal{H}$. Namely, there are three kinds of set of causes which are worth considering

- the set of causes whose effects lie in E is defined in the non-fuzzy case by $\hat{H} = \{\mathbf{h}_i \in \mathcal{H} | R(\mathbf{h}_i) \subseteq E\}$ where $R(\mathbf{h}_i) = \{e_j, (\mathbf{h}_i, e_j) \in R\}$. $\hat{H}$ is still obtained in the fuzzy case as the largest solution of the equation $H \circ R \subseteq E$. This is also the largest solution of $H \circ R = E$ when a solution exists. The membership function of $\hat{H}$ is then given by $\mu_{\hat{H}}(\mathbf{h}_i) = \min_j \mu_R(\mathbf{h}_i, e_j) \rightarrow \mu_E(e_j)$ where $\rightarrow$ denotes the so-called Gödel implication, i.e. $\alpha \rightarrow \beta = 1$ if $\alpha \leq \beta$ and $\alpha \rightarrow \beta = \beta$ if $\alpha > \beta$. Since $\hat{H}$ may gather several distinct explanations of a subset of the observations, it is then interesting to look for minimal solution(s) of the equation $H \circ R = \hat{H} \circ R$ where H is unknown; see Di Nola et al. [6] for algorithms for computing these solutions (there may be several which cannot be compared with respect to set inclusion). Such a minimal solution is made of a set of causes which are sufficient to explain the greatest subset of observations in E which is explanable according to R, namely $\hat{H} \circ R$, and which has no effect outside E.
- the set of causes such that each of them *alone* explains all the effects in E (and may be produces some others), i.e. with crisp sets, the set $H_* = \{\mathbf{h}_i \in \mathcal{H} | R(\mathbf{h}_i) \supseteq E\}$. H_* is defined in the fuzzy case by $\mu_{H_*}(\mathbf{h}_i) = \min_j \mu_E(e_j) \rightarrow \mu_R(\mathbf{h}_i, e_j)$. Obviously H_*, as $\hat{H}$, may be empty. If H_* is empty, we may look for 2-element sets $\{\mathbf{h}_i, \mathbf{h}_k\}$ such that $\{\mathbf{h}_i, \mathbf{h}_k\} \circ R \supseteq E$ (note that $\{\mathbf{h}_i, \mathbf{h}_k\} \circ R = R(\mathbf{h}_i) \cup R(\mathbf{h}_k)$), and more generally for subsets of causes with a given number of elements which *altogether* explain E (and maybe more). In the case of 2-element sets, it is extended to the fuzzy case by the following expression $\mu_{H_*}(\{\mathbf{h}_i, \mathbf{h}_k\}) = \min_j [\mu_E(e_j) \rightarrow \max(\mu_R(\mathbf{h}_i, e_j), \mu_R(\mathbf{h}_k, e_j))]$ where $\mu_{H_*}(\{\mathbf{h}_i, \mathbf{h}_k\})$ estimates to what extent the pair $(\mathbf{h}_i, \mathbf{h}_k)$ provides an explanation of all the observations in E. Yager [46], [47] has proposed a slightly different index based on Lukasiewicz implication rather than Gödel's which, in a fuzzy set framework, provides an estimate of the extent to which a (fuzzy) set of causes D explains all the observations in E. Its expression is $\text{Explain}(E / D) = \min_j [\mu_E(e_j) \rightarrow \mu_{D \circ R}(e_j)]$ where the fuzzy set $D \circ R$ is defined by the max-min composition. It can be easily checked that $\text{Explain}(E / \{\mathbf{h}_i, \mathbf{h}_k\})$ is nothing but $\mu_{H_*}(\{\mathbf{h}_i, \mathbf{h}_k\})$ defined above. The quantity Explain(E / D) estimates to what extent $H = D$ can be considered as a solution of the equation $H \circ R \supseteq E$.
- the set of causes whose effects are partly in E, which is defined in the crisp case by $H^* = \{\mathbf{h}_i \in \mathcal{H} | R(\mathbf{h}_i) \cap E \neq \emptyset\}$, and in the fuzzy case by $\mu_{H^*}(\mathbf{h}_i) = \max_j \min(\mu_R(\mathbf{h}_i, e_j), \mu_E(e_j))$. Technically speaking, H^* is the upper image of the fuzzy set E induced by R, while H_* and $\hat{H}$ defined above are respectively the lower and the lower inverse image of E induced by R; see [9]. Clearly, H^* which is usually much

larger than H* or H, gathers all the causes of potential interest with respect to the set of observations E; however the set of effects of causes in H* does not necessarily cover E, nor is included in E.

Other worth-considering (fuzzy) subsets of causes can be defined in the framework of possibility theory, in particular the subset of causes which alone explain the most *important* effects in E, or *most* of the effects in E [9]. The fuzzy subset of causes which alone explain the most important effects in E is obtained by weighting μ_E in a way which is in agreement with possibility theory. Let $w_j \in [0,1]$ be the importance rate of observation $\mathbf{e}_j$; if $w_j = 1$ the effect $\mathbf{e}_j$ is definitely important (and thus has to be explained), if $w_j = 0$ the effects has no importance (and we have not to look for its cause). Then the fuzzy subset of causes $H^W{}_*$, which alone explains the most important effects in E is defined by substituting $\mu_{E^W}(e_j) = \min(w_j, \mu_E(e_j))$ to $\mu_E(e_j)$ in the above expressions of μ_{H_*}. Indeed E^W represents the fuzzy set of important observations; in order to keep this subset normalized, we should have $\max_j w_j = 1$. Note that in case E is an ordinary subset, i.e. $\mu_E(e_j) = 0$ or 1, and then weighting the importance of the observations is nothing but substituting w_j to $\mu_E(\mathbf{e}_j)$ when $\mathbf{e}_j$ is observed. Clearly $H^W{}_*$ is larger than H_*, in the sense of fuzzy set inclusion. In this framework, modelling a quantifier like "most" comes down to assigning a high degree of importance to k effects, arbitrarily chosen in E, with k "close to" the number of observed effects in E (this can be defined as a fuzzy set defined on the set of integers). In order to estimate to what extent the cause $\mathbf{h}_i$ explains "most" of the effects in E, we compute the maximum of $\mu_{H^W{}_*}(\mathbf{h}_i)$ on all the permutations σ of $[\![1,n]\!]$, i.e. we compute $\max_\sigma \min_j (\min(w_{\sigma(j)}, \mu_E(\mathbf{e}_j)) \to \mu_R(\mathbf{h}_i,\mathbf{e}_j)]$ where $w_{\sigma(j)} = 1$ if $\sigma(j) \in [\![1,k]\!]$ and $w_\sigma(j) = 0$ otherwise; we get the set of causes which alone explain at least k effects in E. This readily extends to subsets of causes of a given cardinality. In the general case, the weights $w_{\sigma(j)}$ may lie in [0,1] and capture the idea to take k as a fuzzy number.

3. Conditional Approach

We turn now to the conditional approach and we first briefly recall the Bayesian view, where the rule "if **h** then **e**" is understood in terms of conditional probabilities. From $P(\mathbf{h} \wedge \mathbf{e}) = P(\mathbf{e}|\mathbf{h}) \cdot P(\mathbf{h}) = P(\mathbf{h}|\mathbf{e}) \cdot P(\mathbf{e})$ we get the a posteriori probability $P(\mathbf{h}|\mathbf{e})$ of **h** when **e** is observed, namely

$$P(\mathbf{h}|\mathbf{e}) = \frac{P(\mathbf{e}|\mathbf{h}) \cdot P(\mathbf{h})}{P(\mathbf{e}|\mathbf{h}) \cdot P(\mathbf{h}) + P(\mathbf{e}|\neg\mathbf{h}) \cdot P(\neg\mathbf{h})} = 1 \Big/ \left(1 + \frac{P(\mathbf{e}|\neg\mathbf{h})}{P(\mathbf{e}|\mathbf{h})} \cdot \frac{P(\neg\mathbf{h})}{P(\mathbf{h})}\right).$$

Thus $P(\mathbf{h}|\mathbf{e})$ is all the larger as the a priori probability of **h** is larger than the one of $\neg\mathbf{h}$ and **e** is more probable in the context **h** than in the context $\neg\mathbf{h}$, which is intuitively satisfying. Moreover **e** will confirm **h** ($P(\mathbf{h}|\mathbf{e}) > P(\mathbf{h})$) whenever $P(\mathbf{e}|\mathbf{h}) > P(\mathbf{e}|\neg\mathbf{h})$, if $P(\mathbf{h}) \neq 0,1$.

A natural question is to know if it can exist a similar machinery in other uncertainty frameworks. In the following we briefly consider the situation in possibility theory where possibility measures are governed by the characteristic axiom $\Pi(\mathbf{a} \vee \mathbf{b}) = \max(\Pi(\mathbf{a}),\Pi(\mathbf{b}))$ (Zadeh [48]). Conditional possibility can then be defined from the relation $\Pi(\mathbf{h} \wedge \mathbf{e}) = \min(\Pi(\mathbf{e}|\mathbf{h}), \Pi(\mathbf{h}))$ first proposed by Hisdal [24]. It leads to the following expression for $\Pi(\mathbf{e}|\mathbf{h})$, if we obey the minimal specificity principle which allocates the greatest possibility degrees in agreement with the constraint(s), here expressed by the above relation,

$$\Pi(\mathbf{e}|\mathbf{h}) = 1 \text{ if } \Pi(\mathbf{h}) = \Pi(\mathbf{h} \wedge \mathbf{e})$$
$$= \Pi(\mathbf{h} \wedge \mathbf{e}) \text{ if } \Pi(\mathbf{h} \wedge \mathbf{e}) < \Pi(\mathbf{h}).$$

The duality relation between possibility and necessity leads to define conditional necessity measures as $N(\mathbf{e}|\mathbf{h}) = 1 - \Pi(\neg\mathbf{e}|\mathbf{h})$ which expresses that, in the context **h**, **e** is all the more certain as $\neg$**e** is more impossible. Then taking advantage of the characteristic axiom of possibility measures, we get the following relation between $N(\mathbf{e}|\mathbf{h})$ and $N(\mathbf{h} \to \mathbf{e})$ where $\to$ denotes the material implication ($\mathbf{h} \to \mathbf{e} \equiv \neg\mathbf{h} \vee \mathbf{e}$)

$$N(\mathbf{e}|\mathbf{h}) = 0 \text{ if } \Pi(\mathbf{h} \wedge \neg\mathbf{e}) \geq \Pi(\mathbf{h} \wedge \mathbf{e})$$
$$= N(\mathbf{h} \to \mathbf{e}) > 0 \text{ if } \Pi(\mathbf{h} \wedge \neg\mathbf{e}) < \Pi(\mathbf{h} \wedge \mathbf{e}).$$

We see that we are at least somewhat certain that **e** is true in the context **h** if and only if we consider that '**h** with **e**' is strictly more possible than '**h** without **e**' true. Note that when $\Pi(\mathbf{h}) = 0$, $\Pi(\mathbf{e}|\mathbf{h}) = \Pi(\neg\mathbf{e}|\mathbf{h}) = 1$, i.e. an impossible cause may lead to anything. An alternative view is to restrict the above definition when $\Pi(\mathbf{h}) > 0$ and to consider that $\Pi(\mathbf{e}|\mathbf{h}) = \Pi(\neg\mathbf{e}|\mathbf{h}) = 0$ if $\Pi(\mathbf{h}) = 0$. It is worth noticing that in this last case the statement $N(\mathbf{e}|\mathbf{h}) > 0$ has all the properties of a well-behaved non-monotonic consequence relation $\mathbf{h} \mathrel{|\!\sim} \mathbf{e}$; see Dubois and Prade [13].

Here we shall assume that $\min(\Pi(\mathbf{h}),\Pi(\neg\mathbf{h})) > 0$, i.e. **h** is not a priori certain (which would require $N(\mathbf{h}) = 1$ or $N(\neg\mathbf{h}) = 1$, i.e. $\Pi(\neg\mathbf{h}) = 0$ or $\Pi(\mathbf{h}) = 0$). $\Pi(\mathbf{h}|\mathbf{e})$ and $\Pi(\neg\mathbf{h}|\mathbf{e})$ are only related by the normalization condition $\max(\Pi(\mathbf{h}|\mathbf{e}), \Pi(\neg\mathbf{h}|\mathbf{e})) = 1$. Moreover we also have $\max(\Pi(\mathbf{h}),\Pi(\neg\mathbf{h})) = 1$. These two conditions are immediate consequences of the basic axiom of possibility theory, assuming that the possibility of a tautology should be equal to 1. The possibilistic version of Bayes theorem then reads: $\min(\Pi(\mathbf{h}|\mathbf{e}),\Pi(\mathbf{e})) = \min(\Pi(\mathbf{e}|\mathbf{h}),\Pi(\mathbf{h}))$; $\min(\Pi(\neg\mathbf{h}|\mathbf{e}),\Pi(\mathbf{e})) = \min(\Pi(\mathbf{e}|\neg\mathbf{h}), \Pi(\neg\mathbf{h}))$. Product can be used instead of min in the above equations as discussed in [12]; it then corresponds to a conditional possibility close to the one used in Shafer's evidence theory. Taking advantage of $\Pi(\mathbf{e}) = \max(\Pi(\mathbf{e} \wedge \mathbf{h}), \Pi(\mathbf{e} \wedge \neg\mathbf{h})) = \max[\min(\Pi(\mathbf{e}|\mathbf{h}),\Pi(\mathbf{h})), \min(\Pi(\mathbf{e}|\neg\mathbf{h}),\Pi(\neg\mathbf{h}))]$, we can compute the a posteriori possibilities $\Pi(\mathbf{h}|\mathbf{e})$ and $\Pi(\neg\mathbf{h}|\mathbf{e})$.

Namely the qualitative counterpart of Bayes theorem is obtained applying the principle of minimal specificity to the equations: $\min(\Pi(\mathbf{h}|\mathbf{e}), \max(A,B)) = A$; $\min(\Pi(\neg\mathbf{h}|\mathbf{e}), \max(A,B)) = B$ where $A = \min(\Pi(\mathbf{e}|\mathbf{h}), \Pi(\mathbf{h}))$ and $B = \min(\Pi(\mathbf{e}|\neg\mathbf{h}), \Pi(\neg\mathbf{h}))$ and thus $\max(A,B) = \Pi(\mathbf{e})$. It leads to compute the greatest solutions:

$$\Pi(\mathbf{h}|\mathbf{e}) = \min(\Pi(\mathbf{e}|\mathbf{h}), \Pi(\mathbf{h})) \text{ if } \min(\Pi(\mathbf{e}|\mathbf{h}), \Pi(\mathbf{h})) < \min(\Pi(\mathbf{e}|\neg\mathbf{h}), \Pi(\neg\mathbf{h}))$$
$$= 1 \text{ otherwise}$$

and the same for $\Pi(\neg\mathbf{h}|\mathbf{e})$ changing **h** into $\neg$**h**. More specifically it is easy to verify that

- if $A < B$, $\Pi(\mathbf{h}|\mathbf{e}) = \min(\Pi(\mathbf{e}|\mathbf{h}), \Pi(\mathbf{h}))$; $\Pi(\neg\mathbf{h}|\mathbf{e}) = 1$
  which corresponds to a possible confirmation of $\neg$**h**
- if $A > B$, $\Pi(\mathbf{h}|\mathbf{e}) = 1$; $\Pi(\neg\mathbf{h}|\mathbf{e}) = \min(\Pi(\mathbf{e}|\neg\mathbf{h}), \Pi(\neg\mathbf{h}))$
  which corresponds to a possible confirmation of **h**
- if $A = B$ then $\Pi(\mathbf{h}|\mathbf{e}) = \Pi(\neg\mathbf{h}|\mathbf{e}) = 1$
  which corresponds to a contraction effect (in the sense of Gärdenfors; see Dubois and Prade [14]) where **h** and $\neg$**h** become equally uncertain, i.e., we are lead to ignorance since $A = B$ means $\Pi(\mathbf{h} \wedge \mathbf{e}) = \Pi(\neg\mathbf{h} \wedge \mathbf{e})$ (just as equirepartition of

probabilities, i.e. $P(\mathbf{h}|\mathbf{e}) = P(\neg\mathbf{h}|\mathbf{e}) = 1/2$ is obtained in the probabilistic model when $P(\mathbf{e}|\mathbf{h}) \cdot P(\mathbf{h}) = P(\mathbf{e}|\neg\mathbf{h}) \cdot P(\neg\mathbf{h})$).

Let us check the conditions under which hypothesis **h** is confirmed. There are two types of confirmation: i) **h** is already certain to some extent and its certainty increases; ii) **h** is believed to be implausible and becomes less implausible or even certain to some extent.

i) $\Pi(h) = 1;\ \Pi(\neg h) < 1$

Then confirmation of **h** means $\Pi(\neg\mathbf{h}|\mathbf{e}) < \Pi(\neg\mathbf{h})$. Clearly in this case we have A > B, which leads to the two conditions $\Pi(\neg\mathbf{h}) > \Pi(\mathbf{e}|\neg\mathbf{h})$ (otherwise no updating takes place) and $\Pi(\mathbf{e}|\mathbf{h}) > \Pi(\mathbf{e}|\neg\mathbf{h})$ which expresses A > B in this case. This means that **e** must be more possible in the presence of **h** rather than ¬**h**. Moreover **h** must not be too much certain a priori. Indeed if **h** is already sure enough we would obtain $\Pi(\neg\mathbf{h}|\mathbf{e}) = \Pi(\neg\mathbf{h})$ if $\Pi(\mathbf{e}|\neg\mathbf{h}) \geq \Pi(\neg\mathbf{h})$, i.e. no updating takes place.

ii) $\Pi(h) \leq 1,\ \Pi(\neg h) = 1$

Then confirmation of **h** means $\Pi(\mathbf{h}|\mathbf{e}) > \Pi(\mathbf{h})$. From the above analysis, we must have $\Pi(\mathbf{h}|\mathbf{e}) = 1$, and the condition A > B yields the two conditions $\Pi(\mathbf{e}|\mathbf{h}) > \Pi(\mathbf{e}|\neg\mathbf{h})$ again and $\Pi(\mathbf{h}) > \Pi(\mathbf{e}|\neg\mathbf{h})$, i.e. **h** although not sure at all must not be too much implausible, otherwise no updating takes place.

On the whole the condition under which **h** can get confirmed by the observation of evidence **e** is $\Pi(\mathbf{e}|\mathbf{h}) > \Pi(\mathbf{e}|\neg\mathbf{h})$, i.e. is similar to the probabilistic case (see also Zwirn and Zwirn [49] for a systematic analysis of possibilistic relative confirmation and its link to non-monotonic reasoning). An actual modification of the prior possibility actually occurs if and only if $\min(\Pi(\mathbf{h}),\Pi(\neg\mathbf{h})) > \Pi(\mathbf{e}|\neg\mathbf{h})$, i.e. no strong a priori opinion is held in favor or against **h**. This condition also reads $\max(N(\mathbf{h}),N(\neg\mathbf{h})) < N(\neg\mathbf{e}|\neg\mathbf{h})$, that is, our certainty of either antagonistic hypotheses is outranked by our certainty of not observing **e** if **h** is false (in other words, our certainty that only **h** can produce **e**). If our a priori opinion is strongly committed to one alternative, observing **e** will not modify our state of beliefs. This behavior of the possibilistic Bayesian-like abductive inference was first noticed by Garbolino [21].

Hence, the above possibilistic model of abduction, due to its purely qualitative setting, has two limitations from a progressive learning point of view

- the impossibility to modify strongly entrenched a priori opinion. This rigidity appears in the probabilistic model only when $P(\mathbf{h}) = 1$ or 0
- the convergence of the learning process in one step when the same evidence e repeatedly appears. This is due to the idempotence of min.

These limitations disappears if we define conditional possibility by means of Dempster rule of conditioning, i.e. $\Pi(\mathbf{e}|\mathbf{h}) = \Pi(\mathbf{e} \wedge \mathbf{h}) / \Pi(\mathbf{h})$. Then

$$\Pi(\mathbf{h}|\mathbf{e}) = \min\left(1, \frac{\Pi(\mathbf{e}|\mathbf{h}) \cdot \Pi(\mathbf{h})}{\Pi(\mathbf{e}|\neg\mathbf{h}) \cdot \Pi(\neg\mathbf{h})}\right).$$

Then it is easy to see that $\Pi(\mathbf{e}|\mathbf{h}) > \Pi(\mathbf{e}|\neg\mathbf{h})$ is now necessary and sufficient for the actual confirmation of **h** under observing **e**. Moreover learning becomes progressive when **e** is repeatedly observed.

A further step of research along this line is to work with possibilistic networks whose structure expresses conditional (logical) independence assumptions, and to develop local computation methods just as Pearl [33] did in the probabilistic framework; see Fonck [18], Fonck and Straszecka [19] and Parsons [31] for preliminary attempts along this line.

4. Logical Approach

In propositional logic, a so-called abductive explanation of a formula **e** with respect to a theory $\mathcal{T}$ (e.g. in the simplest case, a collection of clauses $\neg\mathbf{h}_i \vee \mathbf{e}_j$; more generally $\mathbf{h}_i$ can be replaced by a conjunction of literals $\mathbf{h}_k$), is usually defined as a conjunction **h** of literals, such that $\mathcal{T}, \mathbf{h} \models \mathbf{e}$, where **h** is also supposed to be consistent with $\mathcal{T}$. See (Marquis [29]) for an extension of this definition to first order logic. The problem is then to compute (a) conjunction(s) **h** which is/are minimal (in the sense of subsumption) and non-trivial (i.e. not such that $\mathbf{e} \models \mathbf{h}$). Methods based on the research of prime implicates or prime implicants have been proposed in the literature (Reiter [41], Reiter and De Kleer [42], Jackson [25], [26]).

Recently Jackson [27] has proposed to extend his prime implicate-based approach to possibilistic logic. In possibilistic logic [10], classical logic formulas are weighted by lower bounds of the necessity degree with which the formula is held for certainly true. Basically, **h** is then an abductive explanation of $N(\mathbf{e}) \geq \alpha$ if $N(\mathbf{e}) \geq \alpha$ can be derived from $\mathcal{T}$, now made of weighted clauses, together with $N(\mathbf{h}) = 1$ (provided they are consistent) using the extended resolution principle of possibilistic logic ($N(\mathbf{s}) \geq \alpha$, $N(\mathbf{t}) \geq \beta \vdash N(\text{Resolvent}(\mathbf{s},\mathbf{t})) \geq \min(\alpha,\beta)$).

We are then very close to *possibilistic* Assumption-based Truth-Maintenance Systems (ATMS) [8] where labels (which are weakly consistent, sound, complete and minimal) can be computed for a proposition **e**; such a label is made of a collection of weighted sets of assumptions. See [7] for an application to a diagnosis problem. This can be related to what is done in the relational approach as suggested below.

In the framework of possibilistic logic, the composition $H \circ R$ considered in Section 2 translates into the following pattern of inference expressed in terms of a necessity measure N (using the possibilistic logic resolution rule): $N(\mathbf{h}_i) \geq \gamma_i$ and $N(\neg\mathbf{h}_i \vee \mathbf{e}_j) \geq \alpha_{ij}$ entails $N(\mathbf{e}_j) \geq \min(\gamma_i,\alpha_{ij})$. This can be applied $\forall i$, just leading to the following lower bound for the necessity of $\mathbf{e}_j$

$$N(\mathbf{e}_j) \geq \max_{i=1,n} \min(\gamma_i,\alpha_{ij}).$$

Let us now consider the following knowledge base made of uncertain implications $\mathbf{h}_i \rightarrow \mathbf{e}_j \triangleq \neg\mathbf{h}_i \vee \mathbf{e}_j$ between causes and effects, and of uncertain observations $\mathbf{e}_j$, $j = 1,k$

$$N(\neg\mathbf{h}_i \vee \mathbf{e}_j) \geq \alpha_{ij} \;,\; i = 1,m; j = 1,n \;\;;\;\; N(\mathbf{e}_j) \geq \beta_j \;,\; j = 1,k.$$

Clearly $\mu_{H*}(\mathbf{h}_i)$, i.e. here $\min_j (\beta_j \rightarrow \alpha_{ij})$ can be used as a plausibility weight for $\mathbf{h}_i$, since it estimates to what extent $\mathbf{h}_i$ alone explains all the more or less certain observations. Note that $\mu_{H*}(\mathbf{h}_i) = 1$ as soon as $\beta_j \leq \alpha_{ij}$, $\forall j$, i.e. when $N(\mathbf{e}_j) \geq \beta_j$, $j = 1,k$ is a set of valid deductions from the weighted clauses $N(\neg\mathbf{h}_i \vee \mathbf{e}_j) \geq \alpha_{ij}$ and $N(\mathbf{h}_i) = 1$. If $\forall i$, $\mu_{H*}(\mathbf{h}_i) = 0$, we shall consider to what extent a combination of causes $\mathbf{h}_{i_1},\ldots, \mathbf{h}_{i_r}$ can cause all the more or less certain observations, by the following expression $\min_j[\beta_j \rightarrow \max(\alpha_{i_1 j},\ldots, \alpha_{i_r j})]$ which corresponds, as already said, to the degree of inclusion of into E in $R(\mathbf{h}_{i_1}) \cup\ldots\cup R(\mathbf{h}_{i_r}) = R(\{\mathbf{h}_{i_1},\ldots, \mathbf{h}_{i_r}\})$; in practice, we can start with $r = 2$, i.e. looking for the possibility that the conjunction of two causes explains E (in case $\forall i$, $\mu_{H*}(\mathbf{h}_i) = 0$). This corresponds to compute, using an ATMS language, the environments of the set of weighted formulas $N(e_j) \geq \beta_j$, $j = 1,k$, with r assumptions. Obviously, in the general case we should work with a possibilistic theory $\mathcal{T}$ allowing for weighted justifications of the form $N(\neg h_{i_1} \vee \ldots \vee \neg h_{i_{s(i)}} \vee e_j) \geq \alpha_{ij}$.

5. Concluding Remarks

In this paper we have surveyed various views of abduction incorporating a fuzzy or possibilistic weighting. At the theoretical level there exist results relating possibilistic logic, conditional possibility, non-monotonic deduction, revision process à la Gärdenfors (see Dubois and Prade [13], [14]), or relating possibilistic logic, logical abduction and non-monotonic deduction (Fariñas del Cerro et al. [15]). This offers a framework for studying the differences between Bayesian-like possibilistic abduction, and logical-based possibilistic abduction, since both of them can be related to the notion of conditional possibility. Besides the apparent closeness of the relational-based approach (in the fuzzy relation style or à la Reggia et al.) with the logical-based approach is promising from an application point of view, although there are many questions still to clarify (especially we have only considered the case where R is defined on $\mathcal{H} \times \mathcal{E}$ rather than on $2^{\mathcal{H}} \times 2^{\mathcal{E}}$, where there is no intermediate entities between the disorders in $\mathcal{H}$ and the manifestations in $\mathcal{E}$, as in Peng and Reggia [36]).

Moreover, a general model should be able to take into account pieces of information concerning effects that are more or less certainly present, but also those pertaining to effects which are more or less certainly absent in order to acknowledge the incompleteness of the available information. The complement of the set of effects more or less certainly absent defines the set of effects more or less possibly present, which contains the set of effects more or less certainly present; the pair of these two latter (fuzzy) sets defines a so-called twofold fuzzy set [11]. Similarly the relation R associating causes and effects should be a twofold fuzzy relation in order to distinguish between the effects more or less certainly produced and those which are only more or less possibly produced by a cause or a cojunction of causes. Such a twofold relational model might be the basis for an approach of practical interest. Its relation to possibilistic logic where both lower bounds of necessity and of possibility degrees are stated, is an open question.

Other directions for further research are to relate these issues to model-based diagnosis concerns (e.g. Console et al. [4], Torasso and Console [45]), or to incorporate time in the diagnosis problem (e.g. Console et al. [4], Piechowiak et al. [38]).

References

[1] A.O. Arigoni: Possibility-based evidence in abductive processes. Proc. 7th Inter. Congress of Cybernetics and Systems, London, Sept. 7-11, 1987, 611-617.

[2] A. Asse, A. Maizener, A. Moreau, D. Willaeys: Diagnosis based on subjective information in a solar energy plant. In: E. Sanchez, L.A. Zadeh (eds.): Approximate Reasoning in Intelligent Systems, Decision and Control, Pergamon Press, 1987, 159-173.

[3] W. Bandler, L.J. Kohout: The four modes of inference in fuzzy expert systems. In: R. Trappl (ed.): Cybern. and Syst. Res. 2, North-Holland, 1984, 581-586.

[4] L. Console, L. Portinale, D. Theseider Dupré: Focusing abductive diagnosis. AI Communications 4(2/3), 88-97 (1991).

[5] L. Console, A.J. Rivolin, P. Torasso: Fuzzy temporal reasoning on causal models. Int. J. of Intelligent Systems 6(2), 107-133 (1991).

[6] A. Di Nola, S. Sessa, W. Pedrycz, E. Sanchez: Fuzzy Relation Equations and their Applications to Knowledge Engineering. Kluwer Academic Publ., 1989.

[7] D. Dubois, J. Lang, H. Prade: Gestion d'hypothèses en logique possibiliste: un exemple d'application au diagnostic. Proc. 10th Inter. Conf. on Expert Systems and their Applications, Avignon, May 28-June 1st, 1990, 299-313.

[8] D. Dubois, J. Lang, H. Prade: A possibilistic assumption-based truth maintenance system with uncertainty justifications, and its applications to belief revision. J.P. Martins, M. Reinfrank (eds.): Truth-Maintenance Systems (Proc. ECAI'90 Workshop), LNCS n° 515, Springer Verlag, 1991, 87-106.

[9] D. Dubois, H. Prade: Upper and lower images of a fuzzy set induced by a fuzzy relation – Applications to fuzzy inference and diagnosis. Inform. Sci. 64, 233-249 (1992).

[10] D. Dubois, H. Prade: Necessity measures and the resolution principle. IEEE Trans. on Systems, Man and Cybernetics 17, 474-478 (1987).

[11] D. Dubois, H. Prade: Twofold fuzzy sets and rough sets —some issues in knowledge representation. Fuzzy Sets and Systems 23(1), 3-18 (1987).

[12] D. Dubois, H. Prade: The logical view of conditioning and its application to possibility and evidence theories. Int. J. of Approx. Reasoning 4, 23-46 (1990).

[13] D. Dubois, H. Prade: Possibilistic logic, preference models, non-monotonicity and related issues. Proc. 12th Inter. Joint Conf. on Artificial Intelligence, Sydney, Australia, Aug. 24-30, 1991, 419-424.

[14] D. Dubois, H. Prade: Belief change and possibility theory. In: P. Gärdenfors (ed.): Belief Revision, Cambridge University Press, U.K., 1992, 142-182

[15] L. Fariñas del Cerro, A. Herzig, J. Lang: From expectation-based nonmonotonic reasoning to conditional logics. Proc. 10th Europ. Conf. on Artificial Intelligence, Vienna, Austria, Aug. 3-7, 1992, 314-318.

[16] H. Farreny, H. Prade: Positive and negative explanations of uncertain reasoning in the framework of possibility theory. In: L.A. Zadeh, J. Kacprzyk (eds.): Fuzzy Logic for the Management of Uncertainty, Wiley, 1992, 319-333.

[17] H. Farreny, H. Prade: Explications de raisonnements dans l'incertain. Revue d'Intelligence Artificielle 4(2), 43-75 (1990).

[18] P. Fonck: Building influence networks in the framework of possibility theory. Proc. RP2 1st Workshop on Defeasible Reasoning and Uncertainty Management Systems (DRUMS), Albi, France, April 26-28, 1990, 263-270.

[19] P. Fonck, E. Straszecka: Building influence networks in the framework of possibility theory. Ann. Univ. Sci. Budap., Sect. Comp. 12, 101-106 (1991).

[20] L. Friedman: Extended plausible inference. Proc. 7th Inter. Joint Conf. on Artificial Intelligence, Vancouver, 1981, 487-495.

[21] P. Garbolino: On the Plausibility of Inverse Possibility. Annali dell'Università di Ferrara, Nuova Serie, Sezione III, Filosofia, Discussion Paper n° 8, 1989, Univ. degli Studi di Ferrara.

[22] P. Gmytrasiewicz, J.A. Hassberger, J.C. Lee: Fault tree based diagnostics using fuzzy logic. IEEE Trans. on Pattern Analysis & Machine Intell. 12(11), 1115-1119 (1990).

[23] L.O. Hall: On the fuzzy logic modes of inference: confirmation and denial. Proc. 2nd Inter. Fuzzy Syst. Assoc. (IFSA) Cong., Tokyo, July 20-25, 1987, 24-25.

[24] E. Hisdal: Conditional possibilities independence and noninteraction. Fuzzy Sets and Systems 1, 283-297 (1978).

[25] P. Jackson: Propositional abductive logic. Proc. 7th Conf. of the Society for the Study of Artificial Intelligence and Simulation of Behaviour (A.G. Cohn, ed.), Pitman & Morgan-Kaufmann, 1989, 89-94.

[26] P. Jackson: Prime implicates: their computation and use. Proc. 11th Inter. Conf. on Expert Syst. & Appl., Avignon, May 27-31, 1991, Vol. 1, 53-64.

[27] P. Jackson: Possibilistic prime implicates and their use in abduction. Research Note, McDonnell Douglas Research Lab., St Louis, MO, USA, 1991.

[28] J. Kitowski, M. Bargiel: Diagnosis of faulty states in complex physical systems using fuzzy relational equations. In: E. Sanchez, L.A. Zadeh (eds.): Approximate

Reasoning in Intelligent Systems, Decision and Control, Pergamon Press, 1987, 175-194.
[29] P. Marquis: Extending abduction from propositional to first-order logic. In: Ph. Jorrand, J. Kelemen (eds.): Fundamentals of Artificial Intelligence Research (Proc. Inter. Workshop FAIR'91), LNAI n° 535, Springer Verlag, 1991, 141-155.
[30] C.P. Pappis, M. Sugeno: Fuzzy relational equations and the inverse problem. Fuzzy Sets and Systems 15, 79-90 (1985).
[31] S. Parsons: Combined modes of reasoning with uncertainty. Report ESPRIT Project DRUMS (Deliverable 4.2.2 M24), Dept. of Elec. Eng., Queen Mary & Westfield College, London, 1991.
[32] J. Pearl: Embracing causality in default reasoning. Artif. Intell. 35, 259-271 (1988).
[33] J. Pearl: Probabilistic Reasoning in Intelligent Systems: Networks of Plausible Inference. Morgan Kaufmann, 1988.
[34] J. Pearl, T.S. Verma: A theory of inferred causation. Proc. 2nd Inter. Conf. on Principles of Knowledge Representation and Reasoning, Cambridge, Mass., April 22-25, 1991, 441-452.
[35] C.S. Peirce: Abduction and induction. In: J. Buchler (ed.): Selected Philosophical Writings, 1940. Republished by Dover, 1955.
[36] Y. Peng, J.A. Reggia: Diagnostic problem-solving with causal chaining. Int. J. of Intelligent Systems 2(3), 265-302 (1987).
[37] Y. Peng, J.A. Reggia: Abductive Inference Models for Diagnostic Problem-Solving. Springer Verlag, 1990.
[38] S. Piechowiak, J. Rodriguez, P. Millot: Implémentation d'une méthode de diagnostic selon les premiers principes intégrant le temps. Proc. 12th Inter. Conf. on Expert Syst. & Natural Language, Avignon, June 1-6, 1992, Vol. 1, 269-280.
[39] G. Pólya: Mathematics and Plausible Reasoning – Vol. II: Pattern of Plausible Inference. 1st edition, 1954, 2nd edition, Princeton University Press, 1968.
[40] J. Reggia, D. Nau, P. Wang, Y. Peng: A formal model of diagnostic inference. Information Sciences 37, 227-285 (1985).
[41] R. Reiter: A theory of diagnosis from first principles. Artificial Intelligence 32, 57-95 (1987).
[42] R. Reiter, J. De Kleer: Foundations of assumption-based truth maintenance systems: preliminary report. Proc. 6th National Conf. on Artif. Intell., 1987, 183-188.
[43] E. Sanchez: Solutions in composite fuzzy relation equations: application to medical diagnosis in Brouwerian logic. In: M.M. Gupta, G.N. Saridis, B.R. Gaines (eds.): Fuzzy Automata and Decision Processes, North-Holland, 1977, 221-234.
[44] E. Sanchez: Inverses of fuzzy relations – Application to possibility distributions and medical diagnosis. Fuzzy Sets and Systems 2, 75-86 (1979).
[45] P. Torasso, L. Console: Diagnostic Problem Solving – Combining Heuristic, Approximate and Causal Reasoning. North Oxford Academic, 1989.
[46] R.R. Yager: Explanatory models in expert systems. Int. J. of Man-Machine Studies 23, 539-550 (1985).
[47] R.R. Yager: Measures of accountability and credibility in knowledge based diagnosis systems. In: A. Kandel, E. Avni (eds.): Engineering Risk and Hazard Assessment Vol. III, CRC Press, Boca Raton, Fl., 1988, 1-15.
[48] L.A. Zadeh: Fuzzy sets as a basis for a theory of possibility. Fuzzy Sets and Systems 1, 3-28 (1978).
[49] D. Zwirn, H. Zwirn: Confirmation non probabiliste. Colloque Intelligence Artificielle et Logiques Non-Classiques: Le Point de Vue Philosophique, Université de Montréal, Département de Philosophie, Oct. 17-20, 1992.

Management of Preferences in Assumption-Based Reasoning

C. Cayrol

IRIT
Université Paul Sabatier
118, route de Narbonne
31062 Toulouse, France
testemal@irit.fr

V. Royer, C. Saurel *

ONERA/CERT
2, avenue E.Belin, B.P. 4025
31055 Toulouse, France
royer@tls-cs.cert.fr

Abstract. This paper presents a methodological approach to the management of symbolic preferences in integration with classical pure logical reasoning problems. We investigate two selection modes for choosing preferred sets of assumptions: democratism and elitism.
Principally we show how to manage the optimization of democratism preference criterion in the context of coherence restoration.
The use of symbolic structures for the preferences also makes possible the translation by formal duality of democratism preference-based coherence problems into elitism preference-based explanation problems.
Finally we insist on the computational aspects by considering the pragmatics of the integration problems and proposing constructive solutions.

1 Introduction

1.1 Motivating the use of Symbolic Preferences

Classical AI applications such as planification, diagnosis, data fusion etc... involve reasoning in an incomplete or uncertain universe [15]. The reasoning systems needed for these applications must deal with knowledge which has a belief status. Typically (to face incompleteness and uncertainty) these systems must be able to select among the current knowledge some most plausible beliefs in order to support consistent and tractable reasonings. However the reasons for choosing or "preferring" some beliefs against others are in general not arbitrary but determined by specific evaluation criteria depending on the considered applications, such as for instance:

- uncertainty degrees (probability, necessity measures etc ...),
- utility degrees (for example in Decision Theory, beliefs are chosen according to their expected utility for reaching some goal),
- user preferences (for example in decision aid system, the user may impose some preferences on candidate hypothesis according to its own objectives or experience),
- pertinence with respect to some background context (for example in Diagnosis,

* ONERA-CERT participation to this work has been supported by the DRET-contract 89002.668.

the pertinence of some fault hypothesis for explaining a given symptom depends on the observation context).

The evaluation criteria for qualifying beliefs can be quite complex. In particular they can not always be formalized just as numerical metrics, but can often be given only in terms of qualitative and relative comparison orderings. Moreover, a symbolic formalization of preferences is more suitable in the perspective of dynamical knowledge and defeasible reasoning (for the definition and revision of justification / explanation tools). Here, we assume that the evaluation criteria between beliefs will be explicitely represented by symbolic binary relations called *preferability relations*.

1.2 Motivating a Methodological Approach for the Management of Preferences

In the above application context, a reasoning system must be able to manage suitably the notion of preference. More exactly, the reasoning process involves the integration of two different tasks: pure *logical reasoning* and *heuristic reasoning* aiming at choosing some "best preferred" assumptions.

Several contributions in the literature aim at integrating some notion of preference in traditional logic reasoning formalisms (preferential logics [16], prioritized circumscription [11], preferred sub-theories [3], graded default logics [5], preferential entailment in possibilistic logic [8]). The originality of our contribution is merely methodologic. First the preferential structure of the beliefs set is emphasized as a prime component of the knowledge base. Secondly, the problem is not to define what kind of preference relations could be useful to improve default reasoning (for example to solve conflicts between contradictory defaults), but to study how some given heuristic reasoning (optimization of preferences) and traditional logical reasoning can be integrated. In particular we want to go beyond the case almost exclusively considered in the literature where the preferability relation is a total (pre-)ordering. Finally we insist on the computational aspects by considering the pragmatics of the integration problems and proposing constructive solutions.

In this paper, we mainly investigate the integration problem we call "coherence" problem: restoration of coherence by choosing maximally preferred sets of beliefs (typical problem in decision making or data fusion [14]). We will show how to exploit some duality principle to solve another integration problem we call "explanation" problem: abductive reasoning and management of minimal preferred sets of supporting beliefs (typical problem in diagnosis [14]).

We propose several definitions for the coherence problem, covering different intuitions. We show that in the case of a "priority ordering" (total pre-ordering) we get a constructive characterization for these solutions. This characterization can be carried over to partial pre-orderings, but with loss of completeness. Indeed, we fail to cope with the full generality of partial pre-orderings.

2 Technical Results

2.1 Democratism, Elitism: Two Selection Modes for Choosing Preferred sets of Assumptions

Let $(E, \sqsubset)$ denote a set of assumptions (representing beliefs) together with a binary relation which represents *the preferability relation* induced by some preference criterion put on E: $a \sqsubset b$ iff a is less preferable than b according to the underlying criterion.

The point is to define a *preference relation* on $\Pi(E)$, the power set of E, *induced by the preferability relation* on E. In this paper we propose the two following aggregation policies:

democratism. Let F and G be two non-empty subsets of E, F is *democratively preferred* to G, written $G \sqsubset\sqsubset^{d} F$, iff for any element g in $G \setminus F$ there is an element f in $F \setminus G$ such that $g \sqsubset f$ and not $f \sqsubset g$.

elitism. Let F and G be two non-empty subsets of E, F is *elitistically preferred* to G, written $G \sqsubset\sqsubset^{e} F$, iff for any element f in $F \setminus G$ there is an element g in $G \setminus F$ such that $g \sqsubset f$ and not $f \sqsubset g$.

Democratism preference is also used in other works, though not called so, (it is the same relation as the preferability relation which defines perfect models in the stratifiable databases [13], or the relation used in ordered default theory [10]). Elitism is the dual selection principle. The analogy with politics (following the tradition of Arrow [1]) stems from the fact that in democratism preference everything removed is replaced by something better, while in elitism preference everything kept must be better than something removed. In particular, democratism prefers maximal (for set-inclusion) subsets while elitism prefers minimal subsets.

Transitivity seems to be a natural property for a preferability relation. So we will suppose that any preferability relation is at least a partial pre-ordering. Under appropriate finiteness condition, the induced preference relations are also partial pre-orderings.

Definition. A partial pre-ordering $\sqsubset$ on E is said *finitely chained* in E iff it has no infinite strictly increasing chain in E.

Lemma 1. Let $\sqsubset$ be a *finitely chained partial pre-ordering* on E. Then the preference relation $\sqsubset\sqsubset^{d}$ ($\sqsubset\sqsubset^{e}$) is a partial pre-ordering on the power set of E.

2.2 The Democratism Coherence Problem

Due to the compatibility between $\sqsubset\sqsubset^{d}$ and the set inclusion on $\Pi(E)$, the democratism selection mode is well suited to the "coherence" problem. In this paper, we focus on the democratism coherence problem, namely:

Let (E,$\sqsubset$) be a set of first-order formulas, together with a finitely chained preferability relation, assuming that E is K-inconsistent (inconsistent w.r.t. some knowledge base K), the *democratism coherence problem* is to find all the K-consistent subsets of E which are maximal for $\sqsubset\sqsubset^d$.

In contrast, the elitism selection mode fits better the "explanation" problem. The duality between the definitions of democratism preference and elitistism preference, and the duality between inconsistency and deduction (reductio ad absurdum), may be exploited to handle similarly the integration of elitism preference into the "explanation" problem (see [6]).

2.3 Democratism Coherence for Total Pre-ordering Preferability

This is the case where preferability is a total pre-ordering, meaning a *"priority ordering"*: d $\sqsubset$ d' means that d' has at least the same priority as d.

Maximal elements (in the set of K-consistent subsets of E) for $\sqsubset\sqsubset^d$ are called *demo-preferred* subsets of E.

Prop1. Demo-preferred subsets of E are maximal (for set-inclusion) K-consistent subsets of E.

An alternative definition of the democratism preference may be given which better captures the intuition of "priority" [3], [4]. Indeed, the priority ordering on the set E induces a *stratification* of E in the following sense:

Let E1 be the subset of the maximal elements of (E, $\sqsubset$), Ei+1 be the subset of the maximal elements of E \ (E1$\cup$ E2 $\cup$... Ei), for i≥1. As $\sqsubset$ is a total pre-ordering, each stratum Ei gathers assumptions with the same priority: for d and d' in Ei, we have d $\sqsubset$ d' and d' $\sqsubset$ d. Moreover, the set of strata is equipped with a strict total ordering, namely ...En $\propto$ En-1 . . . $\propto$ E1.

Ei $\propto$ Ej iff for each d in Ei and d' in Ej, d $\sqsubset$ d' and not d' $\sqsubset$ d.

Stratification-based preference. F being a subset of E, let Fi denote F $\cap$ Ei. F is said preferred to G iff F and G contain the same assumptions down to some priority level for which F contains more assumptions than G. We define G $\propto^d$ F iff there exists j such that Fj strictly contains Gj and for each Ei with Ej $\propto$ Ei, Fi = Gi.

Lemma2. $\propto^d$ is a strict partial ordering.

The following proposition gives a constructive characterization of $\propto^d$-preferred subsets of E.

Prop2. F (K-consistent subset of E) is maximal for $\propto^d$ iff for each i ≥ 1, (F1$\cup$ F2 $\cup$... Fi) is a maximal (for set-inclusion) K-consistent subset of (E1$\cup$ E2 $\cup$... Ei).

Prop3. Let $\sqsubset$ be a total pre-ordering on E. The relations $\sqsubset\sqsubset^d$ and $\propto^d$ are equivalent.

Thus, demo-preferred sets of assumptions may be obtained according to the above characterization with the following algorithm:

Let D1 be a maximal K-consistent subset of stratum E1,

Add as many assumptions of stratum E2 as possible, while keeping K-consistency and so on.

We also propose another algorithm, which starts from the set of conflicts, i.e. the minimal (for set inclusion) K-inconsistent subsets of E. The conflicts may be decreasingly ordered according to their minimal (in the sense of $\sqsubset$) elements, and then solved in sequence. Preferred candidates (to be retracted for solving the conflicts) are obtained by selecting one and only one assumption in each conflict among its elements of lowest priority. Demo-preferred sets are obtained by complementing the candidates.

Algorithms for both approaches can be found with detailed proofs in the full technical report [6].

The conflict resolution algorithm fits well a dynamical context, where the conflicts are produced and revised on line. When a new conflict is produced, the priority level of its minimal elements indicates exactly where the conflict must be inserted in the resolution sequence.

A similar algorithm was defined independently for restoring consistency in possibilistic knowledge bases [7].

2.4 Democratism Preference for Partial Pre-ordering Preferability

Now, we consider the case where preferability is a partial ordering[1]. As we are interested in computational techniques for preferred sets of assumptions, we also propose to follow the methodology developed for priority orderings. Indeed $\sqsubset$ induces a stratification of E (exactly as defined in the preceding section). The strict total ordering ...En $\propto$ En-1 ... $\propto$ E1 defined by this stratification[2] corresponds to completing the partial ordering (on E) to a total pre-ordering: elements from a stratum Ei are made equivalent while each element from Ei becomes higher than each element from Ej, where Ej $\propto$ Ei. Note that the completion preserves strictness: If d and d' verify d' $\sqsubset$ d and not d $\sqsubset$ d', we will find d in a stratum Ei and d' in a stratum Ej such that Ej $\propto$ Ei.

The algorithms designed for the priority ordering case may be still applied for constructing stratification-based preferred sets of assumptions (in the sense of a preference relation $\propto^d$, defined as in the preceding section). However, the relations $\sqsubset\sqsubset^d$ and $\propto^d$ are no more equivalent.

Prop4. Let $\sqsubset$ be a partial pre-ordering. We only have G $\sqsubset\sqsubset^d$ F implies G $\propto^d$ F.

---

[1]The results are presented in the case of a partial ordering but still hold in the more general case of a partial pre-ordering.

[2]This kind of stratification has been used (and called uniform stratification) in recent work on partially ordered sets of defaults [17] in order to compare differents proofs of a given formula.

Then, the proposed methodology for constructing preferred sets is not complete for the demo-preferred sets as shown by the example: E = {a, b, c, d}, b $\sqsubset$ a, d $\sqsubset$ c, and the conflicts {a, d}, {b, c}, {a, c}. E is stratified into E1={a, c} and E2 = {b, d}. The stratification-based preferred sets are {a, b}, {c, d}. But {b, d} also is maximal for $\sqsubset\sqsubset^d$.

The stratification-based approaches proposed in this paper lie in the spirit of Junker & Brewka's approach [12] where preferred sub-theories of partially ordered theories are obtained by considering successively all the total orders completing the given partial order. Indeed, we have obtained a hierarchy of preferred subsets of a partially ordered set of assumptions:
{stratification-based preferred sets} strictly included in
{Brewka-preferred sub-theories} strictly included in
{demo-preferred sets}.

3 Explanation Problems

3.1 Duality Between Democratism and Elitism

The democratism and elitism aggregation modes are dual in at least two different senses. Both duality principles exploit the duality between the preferability relation and its *inverse relation* $\sqsubset^*$, defined by: x $\sqsubset^*$ y iff y $\sqsubset$ x.

Inversion duality. Let (E,$\sqsubset$) be any partially pre-ordered set. Let F and G be two subsets of E. F $\sqsubset\sqsubset^d$ G iff G $\sqsubset^* \sqsubset^{*e}$ F.

Complementation duality. Let (E,$\sqsubset$) be any partially pre-ordered set. Let F and G be two subsets of E. F $\sqsubset\sqsubset^d$ G iff E \ F $\sqsubset^* \sqsubset^{*e}$ E \ G.

These duality principles can be used to define and solve other kinds of integration problems we call "explanation" problems: abductive reasoning and management of minimal (for set inclusion) preferred sets of beliefs. First, we consider the so-called abductive explanation problem by exploiting the inversion duality and a stratification based eli-preference.

By exploiting the complementation duality, the conflict resolution problem is shown to be dual of the so-called selective explanation problem, which is a typical problem in practical diagnosis applications. Technical details can be found in [6]. Below we just give the essential ideas.

3.2 Duality Between Coherence Problems and Abductive Explanation Problems

Let E be a K-inconsistent set of first-order formulas together with a preferability relation $\sqsubset$. Let Φ be a first-order formula representing the goal (or query) to be satisfied. The *preference-based abductive explanation* problem is to find all the K-consistent subsets of E which:

- explain Φ [3], or equivalently are K'-inconsistent where K' denotes $K \cup \{\neg\Phi\}$,
- are minimal for set inclusion,
- are eli- preferred (i.e. maximal for $\sqsubset\sqsubset^e$).

By inversion duality, we are able to define a stratification-based eli-preference. Starting from the inverse relation $\sqsubset^*$ on E, we stratify E as in section 2 except that the strict total ordering on the strata, $\propto(\sqsubset^*)$, is exactly the inverse relation $\propto^*$. According to the inversion duality principle, we define $G \propto^e F$ iff $F \propto^{*d} G$. Assuming that E is given with its minimal (for set-inclusion) K'-inconsistent subsets, called K'-conflicts, the solutions of our problem are the K-consistent $\propto^e$-preferred elements of the collection of K'-conflicts.

3.3 Duality Between Conflict Resolution Problems and Selective Explanation Problems

Let E be given in terms of a collection (Si, $i \in I$) together with a preferability relation $\sqsubset$. In a diagnosis context, each Si represents possible alternative explanations for some symptom σi (with respect to some knowledge base K). The *preference-based selective explanation* problem is to find all the consistent subsets F of E which:

- explain all the symptoms (σi , $i \in I$), that is: $F \cap Si \neq \emptyset$, for each $i \in I$,
- are minimal for set inclusion,
- are eli- preferred (i.e. maximal for $\sqsubset\sqsubset^e$).

With the above formulation, searching for selective explanations in (E, (Si, $i \in I$)) is dual to solving conflicts in E, when the sets Si are interpreted on one hand as explanation sets and on the other hand as conflict sets of E.

Formally: F is maximal for $\sqsubset\sqsubset^e$ in the set $\{G \subseteq E, \forall i \in I \;\; Si \cap G \neq \emptyset\}$ (i.e. is an eli-preferred selective explanation) iff $E \setminus F$ is maximal for $\sqsubset^* \sqsubset^{*d}$ in the set $\{G \subseteq E, \forall i \in I \;\; Si \not\subset G\}$ (i.e. is a demo-preferred conflict-free subset of E).

4 Concluding remarks

This works emphasizes a methodological approach to the management of symbolic preferences in integration with classical pure logical reasoning problems. Here principally we have shown how to manage the optimization of some preference criterion in the context of coherence restoration. Such results are particularly significant for several concrete applications of assumption-based reasoning in AI, which require reasoning about preferences, for semantical or computational reasons. Typical applications whose analysis have inspired and supported our work [15] are diagnosis, symbolic data fusion, planning. The use of symbolic structures for the preferences also makes possible the translation by formal duality of preference-based coherence problems into preference-based explanation problems (see full paper [6]). One main contribution of our work is the presentation of a formalism where specific preference criteria (depending on the considered applications) may be formalized and used to solve revision problems in the "best way" (up to some preference notion).

---

[3] S (K-consistent subset of E) explains Φ iff $K \cup S$ logically entails Φ.

Indeed the algorithm we have presented so far are somewhat incremental and well-suited for revision tasks. Another important extension for this work consists in dealing with *multi-criteria symbolic* preferences. Our work is promising for a study about general preferential non-monotonic reasoning despite general difficulties pointed out by [9].

References

1. K.J. Arrow: Social Choice and Individual Values. Yale University Press 1963.

2. F. Achard, V. Royer, C. Saurel: Management of preferences and coherence restoration. Journées nationales du PRC-IA, Plestin les Grèves, sept. 1991.

3. G. Brewka. Preferred sub-theories- An extended logical framework for default reasoning: Proc. IJCAI 1989, pp. 1043-1048.

4. C. Cayrol: Un modèle logique général pour le raisonnement révisable. Revue d'Intelligence Artificielle 6 (3), 255-284 (1992).

5. P. Chatalic, C. Froidevaux: Graded Logics: a framework for uncertain and defeasible knowledge. Proc. ISMIS 1991, Charlotte (NC).

6. C. Cayrol , V. Royer, C. Saurel: Management of Preferences in Assumption-based Reasoning. Report CERT-IRIT n° 92-13-R, University Paul Sabatier, March 1992.

7. D. Dubois, J. Lang, H. Prade: Inconsistency in possibilistic knowledge bases- To live or not live with it. In: Zadeh, Kacprzyk (eds.): Fuzzy Logic for the Management of Uncertainty. Wiley 1991.

8. D. Dubois, H. Prade: Possibilistic logic, preferential models, non-monotonicity and related issues. Proc. IJCAI 1991, pp. 419-424.

9. J. Doyle, M.P. Wellman: Impediments to Universal Preference-Based Default Theories. Proc. 1st Conf. on Principles of Knowledge Representation and Reasoning, Toronto, pp. 94-102, 1989.

10. H. Geffner: Conditional entailment: Closing the gap between defaults and conditionals. Preprints of Third International Workshop on Nonmonotonic Reasoning, South Lake Tahoe, CA, 1990.

11. V. Lifschitz: Circumscriptive theories: a logic-based framework for knowledge representation. Proc. AAAI 1987, pp. 364-368.

12. U. Junker, G. Brewka: Handling Partially Ordered Defaults in TMS. In: Kruse, Siegel (eds.): Proc. ECSQAU. Lecture Notes in Computer Science. Springer 1991, pp. 211-218.

13. T. Przymusinski: On the declarative semantics of stratified deductive databases. Proc. Foundations of Deductive Databases and Logic programming, Washington, 1986.

14. V. Royer: Le raisonnement révisable par l'expression de préférences: méthodes et outils formels. Technical Report Onera-Cert, dec. 1990.

15. C. Saurel: Applications de raisonnement révisable dans des applications d'automatique et de robotique: Logiques préférentielles et algorithmes de maintenance de vérité. Technical Report Onera-Cert, dec. 1990.

16. Y. Shoham: NonMonotonic Logics: Meaning and Utility. Proc. IJCAI 1987, pp. 388-393.

17. J. Wrzos-Kaminski, A. Wrzos-Kaminska: Explicit Ordering of Defaults in ATMS. Proc. ECAI 1990, pp. 714-719.

Appendix

Lemma1. Let $\sqsubset$ be a *finitely chained partial pre-ordering* on E. Then the preference relation $\sqsubset\sqsubset^d$ ($\sqsubset\sqsubset^e$) is a partial pre-ordering over the power set of E.

Proof: We only give the proof of transitivity for $\sqsubset\sqsubset^d$ (the proof for $\sqsubset\sqsubset^e$ is similar). Let G, H, K be three subsets of E such that G $\sqsubset\sqsubset^d$ H and H $\sqsubset\sqsubset^d$ K. We have to prove that G $\sqsubset\sqsubset^d$ K.

Let < denote the strict partial pre-ordering induced by $\sqsubset$ (x<y iff x $\sqsubset$ y and not y $\sqsubset$ x).

• Let us suppose first that G\K is empty. It means that G is included into K, so G $\sqsubset\sqsubset^d$ K is trivially true.

• Let g be some element of G\K. We must prove the property (*):

(*) There is an element k in K\G such that g<k.

• If g does not belong to H, by G $\sqsubset\sqsubset^d$ H we get an element h in H\G such that g<h. Either h belongs to K, so h is an element of K\G satisfying (*). Or h belongs to H\K and by H $\sqsubset\sqsubset^d$ K we get an element k in K\H such that g<h<k.

• Let us now suppose that g belongs to H . Then g belongs to H\K. By the hypothesis H $\sqsubset\sqsubset^d$ K, there is an element k in K\H such that g<k.

Thus we have proved that there is an element k either in K\H or in K\G such that g<k.

Let us suppose that there is no element k in K\G such that g<k. Then the set Xg = {k ∈ K\H, g<k} is non empty. Since Xg is finite, Xg has <-maximal elements. Let k' be <-maximal in Xg.

By hypothesis, k' cannot belong to K\G. Hence k' belongs to G\H. By the hypothesis G $\sqsubset\sqsubset^d$ H, there exists an element h' in H\G such that k'<h'. If h' belongs to K, h' would be a <-majorant for g in K\G, contrary to the above hypothesis. So h' belongs to H\K and by H $\sqsubset\sqsubset^d$ K there is an element k" in K\H such that h'<k". Hence k" belongs to Xg and k'<k", which contradicts the fact that k' is <-maximal in Xg.

Lemma2. The relation $\propto^d$ is a strict partial ordering.

Proof: G $\propto^d$ F iff there is j such that Fj strictly contains Gj and for each Ei with Ej $\propto$ Ei, Fi = Gi.

Nonreflexivity is obvious.

Assume that G $\propto^d$ F (with associated index j) and F $\propto^d$ G (with associated index k). As Gk $\neq$ Fk, we don't have Ej $\propto$ Ek. Similarly, as Fj $\neq$ Gj, we don't have Ek $\propto$ Ej. Then, j = k and Fj strictly contains Gj which in turn strictly contains Fj. That is impossible.

Assume that G $\propto^d$ F (with associated index j) and H $\propto^d$ G (with associated index k). Then, it is easy to see that H $\propto^d$ F with associated index min(j, k).

Prop3. Let be a total pre-ordering on E. The relations $\sqsubset\sqsubset^d$ and $\propto^d$ are equivalent. For any finite subsets F and G of E, G $\sqsubset\sqsubset^d$ F iff G $\propto^d$ F.

Proof: (->) If G is a subset of F, G $\propto^d$ F trivially holds. If G is not a subset of F, G \ F is non- empty. Recall that G $\sqsubset\sqsubset^d$ F means: "for any g in G \ F there exists f in F\ G such that g $\sqsubset$ f and not f $\sqsubset$ g". Then, the set of elements f in F \ G defined by the previous assertion is non-empty. Let Ej denote the stratum maximal for the strict total ordering $\propto$, containing such elements f. (Indeed, j is the smallest index k such that Ek contains elements f). We shall prove that:

a) Fj strictly contains Gj

b) for each Ei with Ej $\propto$ Ei, Fi contains Gi.

a) Let g $\in$ Gj = G $\cap$ Ej. If g $\notin$ F, there exists f $\in$ F \ G such that (g $\sqsubset$ f and not f $\sqsubset$ g). By definition of Ej, we are sure that f belongs to a stratum Ek, with Ej = Ek or Ek $\propto$ Ej. But, due to (g $\sqsubset$ f and not f $\sqsubset$ g) and g $\in$ Ej, f must belong to a stratum Ek with Ej $\propto$ Ek. We obtain a contradiction , then g must belong to F. The inclusion between Fj and Gj is strict since Ej is non-empty.

b) Let Ej $\propto$ Ei and g $\in$ Gi. If g $\notin$ F, we find an index k verifying (Ej = Ek or Ek $\propto$ Ej) and Ei $\propto$ Ek. Since Ej $\propto$ Ei, the same reasons (as above) show that g must belong to F.

To prove that G $\propto^d$ F, it is now sufficient to choose the smallest j (ie Ej maximal for $\propto$) verifying both a) and b).

(<-) If G $\propto^d$ F, there is j such that Fj strictly contains Gj and for each Ei with Ej $\propto$ Ei, Fi = Gi. If F strictly contains G, G $\sqsubset\sqsubset^d$ F trivially holds. Otherwise, F and G are different (since G $\propto^d$ F) and there exists g $\in$ G \ F. Let g be any element in G \ F. Let k $\geq$1 such that g $\in$ Ek; g $\in$ Gk and g $\notin$ Fk. Then, Ek $\propto$ Ej. Since Fj strictly contains Gj, there exists f $\in$ Fj and f $\notin$ Gj. Thus, we have g $\in$ Ek, f $\in$ Ej and k > j. As $\sqsubset$ is a total pre-ordering, we may conclude that (g $\sqsubset$ f and not f $\sqsubset$ g).

Prop4. Let $\sqsubset$ be a partial pre-ordering. We only have G $\sqsubset\sqsubset^d$ F implies G $\propto^d$ F.

Proof: The proof of Proposition3 (necessary condition) still holds since it does not make use of the property "total ordering" for $\sqsubset$.

Default Exclusion in a KL-ONE-like Terminological Component

P. Coupey

Laboratoire d'Informatique de Paris-Nord
Institut Galilée, U.R.A 1507-CNRS
Avenue J.B. Clément, 93430 VILLETANEUSE FRANCE
ph:(33-1) 49 40 36 09
email:pc@lipn.univ-paris13.fr

Abstract. Many theoretical studies have been made of default and exception handling but few of them can be implemented in real applications because of the hard complexity of related algorithms. However users of knowledge represention systems want the possibility expressing default informations and exceptions . We have developed KDEX, a KL-ONE-like with default and exception handling, but we have defined constraints of construction to have polynomial inheritance algorithms. In this paper, we present the default exclusion link and its interpretation in a subset of default logic (we use a "free semi-normal" default) to show the soundness of its semantics and to justify the results given by our inheritance algorithms.

1 Introduction

Many KL-ONE-like [6] knowledge representation systems have been built [5,7,19,24,28,30]. They all have a hybrid approach because they include a terminological component (T-Box) and a logic based component (A-Box). A T-Box contains limited knowledge about concepts and their analytic interrelations (taxonomic relations and roles). The specialized algorithms (propagations through the "is-kind-of" links) of the T-Box inheritance mechanism is simple and efficient. The classifier is a fundamental feature of these systems, it automatically compares the definition of a new defined concept[1] with those present in the T-Box and places it in the best position in the hierarchy. The designers of the previously mentioned hybrid systems have restricted more and more the language definition of the T-BOX to have a sound, tractable and efficient classifier (as Levesque and Brachman [7] argue). On the other hand, as Doyle and Patil [10] show, the more the language is restricted the more the utility of the classifier is reduced because the definitions of definable concepts are inexpressible and they must be entered as primitive and therefore unclassifiable. Futhermore recent works [22,25] prove that the restricted languages are still too rich for the tractability and the completeness of the classification. With regard to these arguments, our main interest is to determine the elements which we consider necessary (from the expressive power point of view) in the definition language of the T-BOX without giving one's attention to the classifier. So we developed a KL-ONE-like T-Box (called KDEX (KL-ONE with Default and EXception)). Defaults and exceptions are important in a T-Box language because in the most cases there are very

[1]There are two kinds of concepts in KL-ONE, the defined concept where its definition in the T-Box is neccessary and sufficient to determine the membership of an instance to the defined concept, and the primitive concept which is an incompletely described or undefinable concept in the language definition of the T-Box.

few strictly necessary conditions and they give a great adaptability to create knowledge bases[2]. Defaults and exceptions are desired by users of knowledge representation systems [10,20] but designers are very reticent because theoretical research in non monotonic logic shows it is very complex to envisage an implementation in real applications. But we argue there is a mean to handle the defaults and the exceptions under some conditions. One of them is the use of explicit exceptions [18,3]. KDEX offers the possibility to express "default is-kind-of" links, "default exclusion" links (those we present in this paper), "role with default number restriction" and "role with default value restriction". The exception link allows to inhibit the inheritance of these default properties.

The features of our system are:

*inheritance algorithms with polynomial complexity to be used in real applications [2,8].

*explicit negation with exclusion link and no closed world hypothesis.

*explicit exception link.

*the guarantee of non-existence of semantic ambiguity.

*use of a non monotonic logic to prove the soundness of the semantic of the objects (concepts,roles,links) and to justify the results obtained by our algorithms.

In KDEX, inherited values are computed dynamically because the system is now used for automatic enrichment from natural language analysis [2] with quick detections of inconsistencies [8].

In section 2, we expose "default exclusion" link and "exception" link on default exclusion, in section 3 we give legality conditions in KDEX that guarantee polynomial inheritance algorithms and the absence of semantic ambiguities, in section 4 we present an example, in section 5 we give the subset of default logic to translate the exclusion link (we determine a special default we call "free semi-normal") and finally, we compare our results with previous approaches in non monotonic reasoning in semantic networks [15], in non monotonic logics [27,1,18] and in object oriented languages [12,11].

2 Default Exclusion

2.1 Default Exclusion Link.

It is a link between two generic concepts and expresses an exclusion. A is in exclusion with B means that individuals of A are not individuals of B and vice-versa. This exclusion defines a constraint *"an individual of A must not be an individual of B"* but has a deductive power too" *if x is an individual of A then it is not an individual of B"*. An exclusion can be strict ("strict exclusion" link) or default ("default exclusion" link) then admits exceptions.

example:

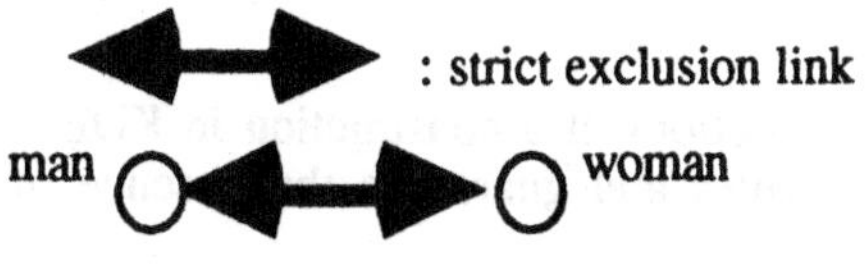

"men are not women and women are not men"

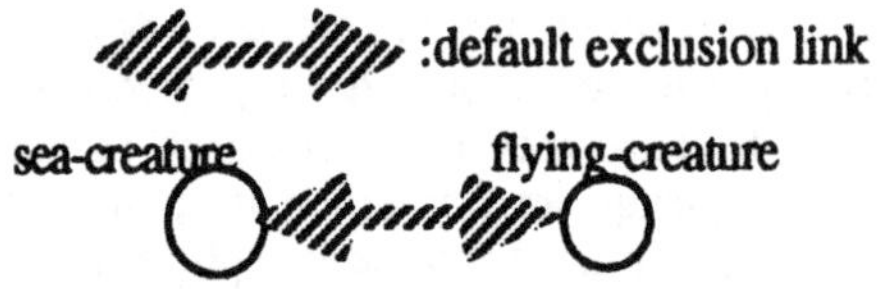

"sea creatures are generally not flying creatures and flying creatures are generally not sea creatures".

Remarks: Our exclusion link can be compared to the "is-not" link in NETL [15,13,18] but ours is symetric. Indeed it is natural[2] (as Besnard shows[1]) that the knowledge "ostriches are generally not flying creatures" brings us to think that "flying creatures are generally not ostriches".

We have not closed world hypothesis in KDEX because we have the possibility to express explicit negations with exclusion links and our current applications do not need it.

2.2 Exception Link on Exclusion Link

An exception link from a concept A to a default exclusion link blocks the inheritance of an exclusion for A.

example:

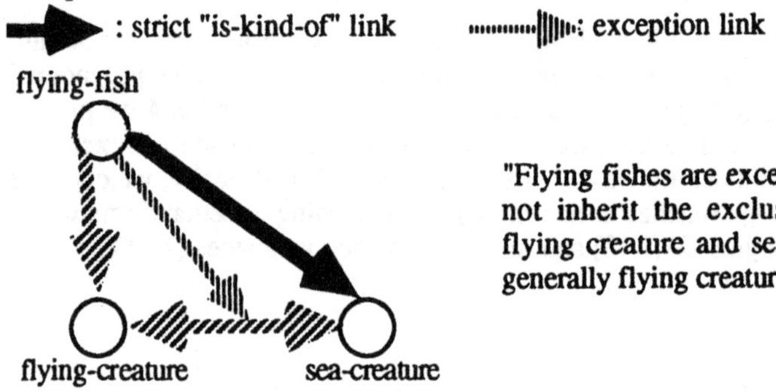

"Flying fishes are exceptional because they do not inherit the exclusion property between flying creature and sea creature and they are generally flying creatures".

Remarks: The default "is-kind-of" link from "flying-fish" to "flying-creature" is necessary to express that flying fishes are generally flying creatures and the exception link is necessary to block the inheritance of the exclusion between flying creatures and sea creatures.

In the above example, the concept "flying-creature" (still) inherits the exclusion with "sea-creature" and then represent the knowledge "flying creatures are generally not flying fishes (even flying fishes are generally flying creatures)".

3 Legal Construction

In this section we are going to develop legality notions of a construction in KDEX. These constraints clearly explicit inheritance rules and guarantee the absence of

---

[2]It is natural because KDEX(as KLONE and NETL) is used to represent classification relations.

ambiguity. As a consequence, our inheritance algorithms are polynomial that is necessary in our real applications.

Notations: Capital letters denote generic concepts.

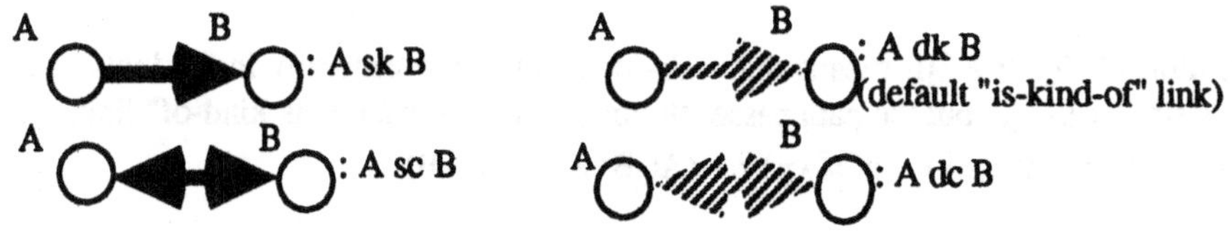

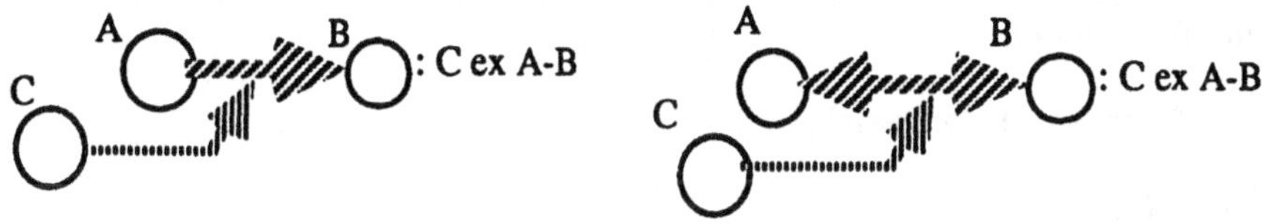

Remark: There is neither cycle through "is-kind-of" links and at least one "exception" link nor cycles through strict "is-kind-of" links in KDEX. These cases have no sense and give no extension in the associated default theory [14].

3.1 Strict subsumption($\langle_s$)

a path from "A" to "B" through strict "is-kind-of" links is noted: Cs_{AB}

$A\langle_s B$ means that all individuals of A are individuals of B.
$\forall A\ A\langle_s A$.
$\forall A,B\ A\langle_s B \Leftrightarrow \exists\, Cs_{AB}$.

3.2 Strict Exclusion($\leftrightarrow_s$)

$A\leftrightarrow_s B$ means that all individuals of A are not individuals of B.
$\forall A,B\ A\leftrightarrow_s B \Leftrightarrow \exists\, C,D\ /\ (C \text{ sc } D) \wedge (A\langle_s C) \wedge (B\langle_s D)$.
Remark: $(A\leftrightarrow_s B) \wedge (A\langle_s B)$ is rejected in KDEX.

3.3 Default Subsumption($\langle_d$)

Prerequisites:
$\forall A,B\ A\langle B \Leftrightarrow (A\langle_s B) \vee (A\langle_d B)$.

a path from "A" to "B" through "is-kind-of" links with at least a default one is noted: Cd_{AB}

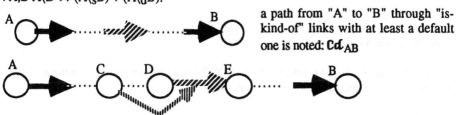

Such a path is "unusable" because the exception inhibits the default link. We use a predicate "b" which is true for this kind of path.

$b(\mathbf{Cd}_{AB}) \Leftrightarrow \exists\, C,D,E \,/\, (D \in \mathbf{Cd}_{AB}) \wedge (E \in \mathbf{Cd}_{AB}) \wedge (C \text{ ex } D\text{-}E) \wedge (A\langle C)$

Definition of "$\langle_d$": $A\langle_d B$ means that individuals of A are generally individuals of B. This is similar to "$\langle_s$" but the path passes through at least a default "is-kind-of" link.
$\forall A,B\ A\langle_d B \Leftrightarrow\ \exists\, \mathbf{Cd}_{AB} \,/\, \neg b(\mathbf{Cd}_{AB}) \wedge \neg(A\langle_s B) \wedge\ \neg(A\leftrightarrow_s B)$.

remark: $\neg(A\langle_s B) \wedge \neg(A\leftrightarrow_s B)$ means that a strict subsumption/exclusion prevails over a default subsumption.

3.4 Default Exclusion($\leftrightarrow_d$)

Prerequisites:

Such a path from "A" to "D" is noted: $\mathbf{Ce}_{ACD}$
$\forall A,C,D\ \mathbf{Ce}_{ACD} \Leftrightarrow (A\langle C) \wedge (C \text{ dc } D)$

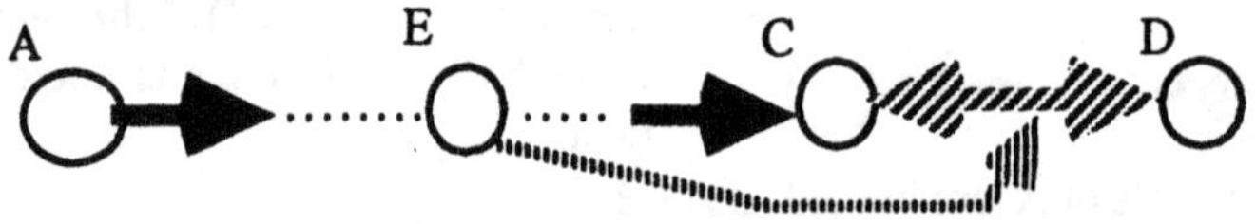

In such a path, the exception link from "E" to the exclusion link from "C" to "D" inhibits the default link. We use a predicate "c" which is true for this kind of path.
$c(\mathbf{Ce}_{ACD}) \Leftrightarrow \exists\, E \,/\, (E \in \mathbf{Ce}_{ACD}) \wedge (E \text{ ex } C\text{-}D)$

Definition of "$\leftrightarrow_d$": $A\leftrightarrow_d B$ means that individuals of A are generally not individuals of B. This is similar to "$\leftrightarrow_s$" but the exclusion link is default or the path from "A" to "C" is default ($A\langle_d B$).
$\forall A,B\ A\leftrightarrow_d B \Leftrightarrow$
a)the exclusion link from "C" to "D" is strict but the path from "A" to "C" is default

$(\exists\, C,D \,/\, (C \text{ sc } D) \wedge (A\langle_d C) \wedge (B\langle D) \wedge \neg(A\langle_s B) \wedge \neg(A\leftrightarrow_s B))$

$\vee$

b)The exclusion link from "C" to "D" is default.

$(\forall\, \mathbf{Ce}_{ACD}, \neg c(\mathbf{Ce}_{ACD}) \wedge (B\langle D) \wedge \neg(A\langle_s B) \wedge \neg(A\leftrightarrow_s B))$.

remark: $\neg(A\langle_s B) \wedge \neg(A\leftrightarrow_s B)$ means that a strict subsumption or a strict exclusion prevails over a default exclusion.

remark: $(A\leftrightarrow_d B) \wedge (A\langle_d B)$ is rejected by KDEX. It would be semantically ambiguous and corresponds to multiple world (extension) notions.

3.5 Precisions on the Non-Existence of Semantic Ambiguity

These inheritance rules guarantee the non-existence of semantic ambiguity as:

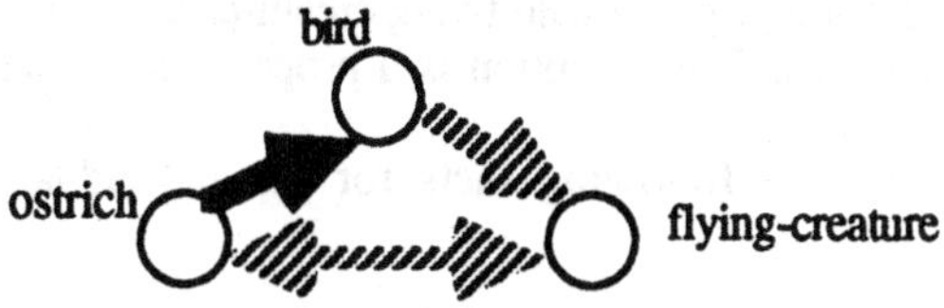

"Are ostriches flying creatures or not?".

We impose to modify the construction (for example adding an exception link) to eliminate ambiguities. This constraint can seem hard but it is necessary to have polynomial inheritance algorithms. Indeed it is not possible to keep inheritance conflicts in real applications where inherited properties are computed dynamically. On the other hand, it could be imagined that conflict resolutions could be done by external mechanisms (Truth maintenance system (TMS) based for example on specificity [26,29]) which would find the modifications to make into the construction to resolve ambiguities. By imposing to pass the TMS deductions onto the T-BOX to eliminate ambiguities (adding for instance exception links) makes a balance between the TMS and the T-BOX inferences.

4 An Example

Below example illustrates our inheritance algorithms (see [9] for details). They apply the inheritance rules of the previous section.

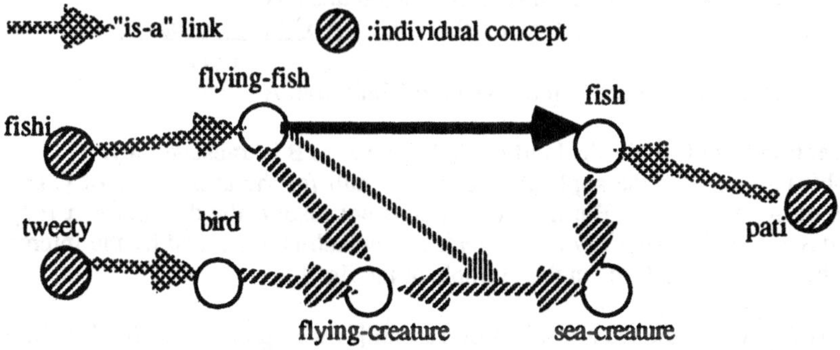

Fig. 1.

flying creatures are generally in exclusion with sea creatures,
birds are generally flying creatures,
fishes are generally sea creatures, flying fishes are fishes but are exceptional relative to the exclusion between sea creatures and flying creatures and are generally flying creatures.
pati is a fish, fishi is a flying fish,tweety is a bird.

remark: The exception link from "flying-fish" to the "exclusion" link only inhibits the "exclusion" property for flying fishes then the "is-kind-of" link from "flying-fish" to "flying-creature" is necessary to express that flying fishes are generally flying creatures.

Relatively to the second remark in section 2.2, it is for example deduced that birds are generally in exclusion with sea creatures, with fishes and with flying fishes knowing that flying creatures are generally in exclusion with sea creatures. On the other hand, flying fishes are exceptional relatively to the exclusion property with flying creatures but flying creatures are generally (still) not flying fishes. The exception is a property of flying fishes but not a property of flying creatures.

Therefore the deduction algorithms infer the following facts for the individuals "pati","fishi" and "tweety":

strict facts:

*fishi is a fish.

default facts:

*pati is a sea creature.
*pati is not a flying creature.
*pati is not a bird.
*pati is not a flying fish

*fishi is a sea creature.
*fishi is a flying creature.

*tweety is a flying creature.
*tweety is not a sea creature.
*tweety is not a fish.
*tweety is not a flying fish.

5 Default Logic Interpretation

We determine a subset of default logic [27] to clearly translate the KDEX objects. This translation is indispensable for proving the soundness of the semantics we associate to the objects. We have chosen the default logic because works demonstrate it is a priviliged tool to translate semantic networks with exceptions [18,14].

Froidevaux and Kayser propose a semi normal default to translate the "default is-kind-of" link. At each default link they associate a one place predicate which thus describes the presence or the absence of an exception on this link.

a "default is-kind-of" link from A to B is translated by:
$$\frac{A(x) : B(x) \wedge Lab(x)}{B(x)}$$
(Lab(x) is the predicate associated to the "is-kind-of" link from A to B).

Then an exception from C to the "is-kind-of" link from A to B is translated by: $C(x) \supset \neg Lab(x)$ and blocks the application of the default for the individuals of C that corresponds to our algorithms. But this default does not justify the deduction *x is by default not a A if x is (by default or strictly) not a B* which is illustrated by the infered fact "pati is by default not a bird" in the example of the fig. 1.

To justify this deduction rule we use works of Besnard[1] who proposes a "free" default (free because it has no prerequisite):

a "default is-kind-of" from A to B is translated by:
$$\frac{: A(x) \supset B(x)}{A(x) \supset B(x)}$$
As it has not prerequisite (i.e. it is always true), if $A(x) \supset B(x)$ is justified (i.e. it can not be infered it is false) one infer $A(x) \supset B(x)$ and if $A(x)$ is true then $B(x)$ is infered (ponens) but if $B(x)$ is false $\neg A(x)$ is infered (tollens).

From these two defaults we create the "free semi normal" default to interpret "default is-kind-of" and "default exclusion".

a "default is-kind-of" link from A to B is translated by:
$$\frac{: (A(x) \supset B(x)) \wedge Lab(x)}{A(x) \supset B(x)}$$
a "default exclusion" link from C to D is translated by:
$$\frac{: (C(x) \supset \neg D(x)) \wedge Lcd(x)}{C(x) \supset \neg D(x)}$$

The default logic interpretation of the construction in figure 1 is the TD=(D,T) theory with D a default set and T a theorem set:

$$D = \left\{ \frac{:(bird(x) \supset flying\text{-}creature(x)) \wedge Lbf(x)}{bird(x) \supset flying\text{-}creature(x)} ; \right.$$

$$\frac{:(sea\text{-}creature(x) \supset \neg flying\text{-}creature(x)) \wedge Lsf(x)}{sea\text{-}creature(x) \supset \neg flying\text{-}creature(x)} ;$$

$$\frac{:(flying\text{-}fish(x) \supset flying\text{-}creature(x)) \wedge Lff(x)}{flying\text{-}fish(x) \supset flying\text{-}creature(x)} ;$$

$$\left. \frac{:(fish(x) \supset sea\text{-}creature(x)) \wedge Lfs(x)}{fish(x) \supset sea\text{-}creature(x)} \right\}$$

T= { flying-fish(fishi), flying-fish(x) ⊃ fish(x), fish(pati), flying-fish(x) ⊃ ¬Lsf(x), bird(tweety) }

The TD theory admits only one extension which contains:

{flying-fish(fishi), flying-creature(fishi), fish(fishi), sea-creature(fishi), fish(pati), sea-creature(pati), ¬flying-creature(pati), ¬flying-fish(pati), ¬bird(pati), bird(tweety), flying-creature(tweety), ¬sea-creature(tweety), ¬fish(tweety), ¬flying-fish(tweety)}

and therefore justifies the results given by our algorithms.

Properties of default theory (TL) associated to a legal construction in KDEX.

The main problems with semi-normal defaults are the non existence of extension and multiple extensions. We show [9] that a theory TL is ordered according to the Etherington order [14] that guarantees at least one extension. This is true because there is no cycle through "is-kind-of" links with at least one exception link. Moreover the legality notions (cf. section 3) prevent from multiple extensions. Then a TL theory admits an unique extension.

6 Previous Works

Default and exception handling has inspired many studies in semantic network. Fahlman in NETL[16] proposes massively parallel algorithms for inheritance mechanisms. Unfortunately Etherington and Reiter [13] and Touretzky [29], show that (with an interpretation in default logic) the examples proposed by Fahlman are not sound and parallel algorithms need hard restrictions to be used. In literature we can found a lot of works concerning the conflicts handling in multiple inheritance based on the specificity[3] in semantic network [29,26,23] and in object oriented language [11,12]. The results correspond in fact in resolving inheritance conflicts by applying specificity criteria in order to explicit exceptions. But Moinard [21] proves that these mechanisms are enough efficient but have not always a semantic justification. Our works are nearer than Fikes and Nado's [17] who are interested in the implementation of inheritance algorithms to handle default and explicit exceptions. But first our system is used for automatic enrichment from natural language analysis that impose us to systematically and dynamically detect and resolve ambiguities (modifying the construction), second we clearly define inheritance rules and the constraints which guarantee an unique extension

[3]Specificity is based on an inheritance order calculation to make a choice in confictual multiple inheritance cases.

in the associated default logic theory and third we added the "exclusion" link its treatment impose us the "free semi-normal" default use to interpret it.

7 Conclusion and Future Works

Our main interest in our T-box is the possibility of expressing default properties. So we have developed KDEX with "default is-kind-of" link, "default exclusion" link, "role with default value restriction" and "role with default number restriction". In this paper, we have presented the "default exclusion" link and the "free semi normal" default to interpret it and justify our deduction algorithms. Our concerns are to benefit defaults and exceptions while having polynomial inheritance algorithms. Our future work will in part concern the TMS system. We have not spoken about it in this paper because it is now essentialy made up of an interaction component with the user who specifies the modifications in order to eliminate ambiguities. We would like to obtain efficient mechanisms (for example based on the specificity) to limit questions to the user but while still trying to have algorithms with reasonable complexity. Our second main objective is to define a classifier. Though conceptual definition which default and exception does not supply sufficient and necessary conditions for an object to be an instance of a concept, we argue that there is a mean to define a terminological language with default and explicit exception statements while allowing classification and equiped with a formal semantics. Our system is implemented in SMALLTALK on SUN workstation. It is now used as knowledge base in two projects in which we automatically create new objects (concepts, roles, links) from requirements expressed in natural language [2,3].

References

1 P. Besnard, R. Quiniou, P. Quinton: A Theorem-Prover for a Decidable Subset of Default Logic, Proc. of A.A.A.I. pp. 27-30, Washington, 1983.

2 B. Biebow, S. Szulman: Enrichment of Semantic Network for Requirements Expressed in Natural Language, IFIP 89, San Francisco, 1989.

3 B. Biebow, P. Coupey, S. Szulman: Using Exceptions in a Semantic Network for a Natural Language Application, Proc. of the 2th EUROSPEECH 89, Paris, 1989.

4 D. G. Bobrow and M. Stefik: The LOOPS Manual, Xerox Corporation, 1983.

5 A. Borgida, R. J. Brachman, D. L. McGuiness, L. A. Resnick: Classic: A Structural Data Model for Objects, Proc. of the International Conference on Management of Data, Portland, Oregon, 1989.

6 R.J. Brachman ,J.G. Schmolze: An Overview of the KLONE Knowledge Representation System, Cognitive Science vol.9 n°2 pp. 171-216, 1985.

7 R.J. Brachman, V.P. Gilbert, H.J. Levesque: An Essential Hybrid Reasoning System: Knowledge and Symbol Level Accounts of KRYPTON, Proc. of 9th I.J.C.A.I. pp. 532-539, 1985.

8 P. Coupey : A semantic Network Including a System for a quick Detection of Inconsistency, Proc. of ICNTSSD'89, International Congress on New Technologies for Software and Supercomputers development, Caracas, November 1989.

9 P. Coupey: Etude d'un Réseau Sémantique avec Gestion des Exceptions, PhD thesis, University of Paris-Nord, January 89.

10 J. Doyle, R. S. Patil: Two Theses of Knowledge Representation: Language Restrictions, Taxonomic Classification, and the Utility of Representation Services, Artificial Intelligence, Vol. 48, n° 3, April 1991.

11 R. Ducourneau, M. Habib: On some Algorithms for Multiple Inheritance in Object Oriented Programming, Proc. of ECOOP'87, pp. 243-252.

12 R. Ducournau, M. Habib: La Multiplicité de l'Héritage dans les Langages à Objets, TSI, vol.8,n°1, january 89.

13 D.W. Etherington and R. Reiter: On Inheritance Hierarchies with Exceptions, Proc A.A.A.I. 83 August 1983, pp. 104-108.

14 D.W. Etherington: Formalizing Nonmonotonic Reasoning Systems, Artificial Intelligence vol.31 n°1, pp. 41-85, January 1987.

15 S.E. Fahlman: a System for Representing and Using Real-world Knowledge, MIT Press, Cambridge, MA, 1979.

16 S.E. Fahlman: Design Sktech For a Million-Element NETL Machine, Proc. of A.A.A.I., pp. 249-252, Stanford, August 1980.

17 R. Fikes and R. Nado: Semantically Sound Inheritance for a Formally Defined Frame Language with Defaults, Proc. of A.A.A.I. vol.2 pp. 443-448, 1987.

18 C. Froidevaux et D. Kayser: Inheritance in Semantic Networks and in Default Logic, in Non-standard Logic for Automated Reasoning (P.Smets, A.Mamdani, D.Dubois, H.Prade eds.), Academic Press, pp. 179-212, 1988.

19 R.MacGregor, R.Bates: The LOOM Knowledge Representation Language, Technical Report ISI/RS-87-188, University of Southern California, Information Science Institute, Marina del Rey, Cal., 1987.

20 R. MacGregor: The Evolving Technology of Classification-based Knowledge Representation Systems, in Principles of Semantic Networks, ed. J.F. Sowa, pp.385-400.

21 Y. Moinard: La Spécificité en Logique des Défauts, Publication interne I.R.I.S.A. n°343, November 1987.

22 B. Nebel: Terminological Reasoning is Inherently Intractable, Artificial Intelligence vol. 43 n° 2, pp. 235-249, Nov. 1990.

23 Guillermo R. Simari and Ronald P. Loui: A Mathematical Treatment of Defeasible Reasoning and its Implementation, Artificial Intelligence 53, pp. 125-157, 1992.

24 K. Von Luck, B. Nebel, C. Peltason, A. Schmiedel: The Anatomy of the BACK System, TU-Berlin, Kit-Report, November 1986.

25 P. F. Patel-Schneider: Undecidability of Subsumption in NIKL, Artificial Intelligence 39, pp 263-272, 1989.

26 D.L. Poole: On the Comparaison of Theories: Preferring the Most Specific Explanation, Proc. of the 9th I.J.C.A.I. pp. 144-147, los Angeles, August 1985.

27 R. Reiter: A Logic for Default Reasoning, Artificial Intelligence vol.13 n°1-2, pp.81-132, April 1980.

28 J.G. Schmolze, W. S. Mark: The NIKL Experience, Computer Intelligence, Vol 7, n° 1 pp. 48-69, february 1991.

29 D.S. Touretzky: The Mathematics of Inheritance Systems, Doctoral dissertation, Carnegie-Mellon University, Pittburg, PA, 1984.

30 M. Vilain: The Restricted Language Architecture of a Hybrid Representation System, Proc. of 9th I.J.C.A.I. pp. 547-551, Los Angeles, 1985.

Unifying Various Approaches to Default Logic

Yves Moinard *

IRISA, Campus de Beaulieu, 35042 RENNES-Cedex FRANCE E-mail: moinard@irisa.fr

Abstract. Default logic is the most popular non monotonic formalism. We present a general framework, defining the classical default extensions as "justified pre-extensions" having a particular property, "stability". These pre-extensions have a constructive definition, contrary to classical extensions, and they give rise to a notion of "formula provable by default" which has appeared yet under several formulations in the literature. Also, we show how a less known proposal of this kind gives a very interesting "semi-constructive" definition of default extensions. Finally our framework applies to some modal translations of defaults, making precise the relations between the stability in default logic and in autoepistemic modal logic.

1 Introduction

The aim of default logic is to express concisely and naturally rules with exceptions. A great amount of literature has been published on the subject since its introduction by Reiter in 1980. Here, we show how the classical fix point definitions may be split into a constructive stage and a final test. [11] and [5] give an interesting variant of the original definitions of [10]. [3] gives a "semi- constructive" definition of extensions. Also, following [4], there are "modal simulations" of default logic [12, 13]. [6] has defined a slightly different notion which appears regularly since, in many proposals, explicitely or not [2, 12]. Here, we show how all these definitions relate together. When the final result is Reiter's extensions, we get an "equivalence" in this meaning, but here we look deeper inside the definitions to show what they have in common. This comparison allows to tell which definition is "the most constructive". However its main interest is to unify these proposals which look so different.

The next section introduces our general framework, with the notion of justified pre-extensions, which possess a "constructive definition". This unifies several proposals already made. Section 3 shows how a semi-constructive definition by [3] is an interesting application of our general framework. Also, this is very close to the well-known Lukaszewicz's variant of default logic which gives the same notion of provability by default as our pre-extensions. Section 4 shows that some modal translations of default logic can profitably be studied in our framework.

2 Pre-extensions in default logic

(W, Δ) is a default theory in the meaning of [10]. W is a set of first order formulas in an enumerable language $\mathcal{L}$, and Δ is a set of *defaults* $\delta = \frac{a : b}{c}$ where a, b and c

* This work has been supported by DRUMS, ESPRIT BRA project number 3085.

are closed formulas in $\mathcal{L}$. For the sake of simplicity we use only one *justification* b. **Notations:** $a = Pre(\delta)$, $b = Jus(\delta)$, $c = Con(\delta)$ and for a set Δ we note $Pre(\Delta) = \{Pre(\delta) : \delta \in \Delta\}$, and the same for $Jus(\Delta)$ and $Con(\Delta)$.

Definition 2.1 [11] A set Δ' of defaults is *grounded in* W when for every default $\delta \in \Delta'$, there exists a finite sequence $(\delta_1, ..., \delta_n)$ in Δ' with $\delta_n = \delta$ such that:
$W \vdash Pre(\delta_1)$, $(W \cup Con(\delta_1, \ldots, \delta_i)) \vdash Pre(\delta_{i+1})$ for $1 \leq i \leq n-1$.

A set E of formulas is *grounded in* (W, Δ) when there exists a subset Δ' of Δ which is grounded in W and such that $E = Th(W \cup Con(\Delta'))$.

Definition 2.2 A set Δ' of defaults is *justified in* W when for every default $\delta \in \Delta'$ we have $\neg Jus(\delta) \notin Th(W \cup Con(\Delta'))$.

A set E of formulas is *justified in* (W, Δ) when there exists a subset Δ' of Δ which is justified in W and such that $Pre(\Delta') \subseteq E$ and $E = Th(W \cup Con(\Delta'))$

Definition 2.3 A set E of formulas in $\mathcal{L}$ is a *pre-extension* of a default theory $T = (W, \Delta)$ iff there exists a sequence E_i with $E = \cup E_i$, $E_0 = Th(W)$ and:
$E_{i+1} = Th(E_i \cup Con(\Delta_i))$ with $\Delta_i = \{\delta \in \Delta : Pre(\delta) \in E_i, Con(\delta) \in E\}$.

A *generator set* of a pre-extension E is any subset Δ' of Δ, grounded in W, such that $E = Th(W \cup Con(\Delta'))$. $\Delta' = \cup \Delta_i$ is a generator set of the pre-extension E.

Property 2.1 A set E of formulas is a pre-extension iff there exists a subset Δ' of Δ, grounded in W and such that $E = Th(W \cup Con(\Delta'))$.

Property 2.2 A set E of formulas is a pre-extension of (W, Δ) iff E is closed for Th, $W \subseteq E$, and $\forall \phi \in E$, $\exists \delta_i$ ($\delta_i \in \Delta$ and $Con(\delta_i) \in E$) for $0 \leq i \leq n$ such that
$W \cup Con(\{\delta_0, \ldots, \delta_{i-1}\}) \vdash Pre(\delta_i)$ for $(0 \leq i \leq n)$, and
$W \cup Con(\{\delta_0, \ldots, \delta_n\}) \vdash \phi$. Then $\Delta' = \bigcup_{\phi \in E} \{\delta_0, \ldots, \delta_n\}$ is a generator set of E.

The proofs are obvious. Our pre-extensions are grounded, we are interested by the pre-extensions which are also justified. A pre-extension is justified in (W, Δ) iff it has a generator set Δ' which is justified in W. We call Δ' a *justified generator set*. [5] calls Δ' a *regular* generator set (instead of *justified*) and calls *universe* what we call a grounded set of defaults. Justified pre-extensions are called *E-sets* in [2]. They are called *approachable belief set* in [7], which gives the definition only for normal defaults; [7] gives also the corresponding definition (*m-approachable BJ-pair*) for any kind of default for his own modified default theory [6, 7], described later in this text.

Property 2.3 A set E of formulas in $\mathcal{L}$ is a justified pre-extension of (W, Δ) iff $E = \cup E_i$ with: $E_0 = Th(W)$, $E_{i+1} = Th(E_i \cup Con(\Delta_i))$ where
$\Delta_i = \{\delta \in \Delta : Pre(\delta) \in E_i, Con(\delta) \in E \text{ and } \neg Jus(\delta) \notin E\}$.
(Proof easy.) This is very close to the original definition of default extensions, here called R-extensions:

Definition 2.4 [10] E is a *R-extension of* (W, Δ) iff $E = \cup E_i$ with: $E_0 = Th(W)$, $E_{i+1} = Th(E_i \cup Con(\Delta_i))$ where$\Delta_i = \{\delta \in \Delta : Pre(\delta) \in E_i \text{ and } \neg Jus(\delta) \notin E\}$.

A modification of Reiter's definition such as the one appearing in proposition 2.3 has been proposed in [2]. Every R-extension is a justified pre-extension, the converse is false. The problem of determining when a justified pre-extension is a R-extension has been tackled by [5, 11, 12, 3, 1] among others. Thanks to our general framework, we are able to show how closely these texts relate to each other.

Before that, let us notice that we may weaken the notion of *justified*:

Definition 2.5 A *weakly justified* pre-extension E of (W, Δ) is a set of formulas closed for Th, such that $W \subseteq E$ and for every $\phi \in E$, either $W \vdash \phi$, or there exists $\delta_i \in \Delta$ with $Con(\delta_i) \in E$, for $1 \leq i \leq n$, such that $W \cup Con(\delta_1, \ldots, \delta_n) \vdash \phi$, and for $(1 \leq i \leq n)$, $W \cup Con(\delta_1, \ldots, \delta_{i-1}) \vdash Pre(\delta_i)$ and $W \cup Con(\delta_1, \ldots, \delta_n) \not\vdash \neg Jus(\delta_i)$.

Any weakly justified pre-extension is a pre-extension (take $\Delta' = \bigcup_{\phi \in E}\{\delta_1, \ldots, \delta_n\}$ as a generator set). Any justified pre-extension is weakly justified, but the converse is not guaranteed as shown by the following example, inspired by ex. 4.3 in [6]:

Example 2.1 $W = \emptyset$, $\Delta = \{\delta_i = \frac{: q_i}{a \wedge \neg q_1 \wedge \cdots \wedge \neg q_{i-1}}\}_{i=1,2,3,\ldots}$.

$E = Th(a, \neg q_1, \ldots, \neg q_i, \ldots)$ is a weakly justified pre-extension, E is not justified.

It is a pre-extension: in the definition, choose $\Delta_0 = \Delta$, thus $E_1 = Th(W \cup \{a, a \wedge \neg q_1, \ldots\}) = E$. It is a weakly justified pre-extension: $\phi \in E$ iff $(a, \neg q_1, \ldots, \neg q_{i-1}) \vdash \phi$ for some $i \geq 0$ (by compactness), that is iff $W \cup\ Con(\{\delta_i\}) \vdash \phi$, and we also have $W \cup\ Con(\{\delta_i\}) \not\vdash \neg q_i$. E is not a justified pre-extension: We cannot find any finite generator set Δ' (one δ_i would suffice, and $\neg q_i$ would not be in E). For any infinite $\Delta' \subseteq \Delta$, for any $\delta_j \in \Delta'$, there is $\delta_k \in \Delta'$ with $Con(\delta_k) \vdash \neg q_j$.

For any *finite* Δ, there is equivalence between weakly justified and justified pre-extensions. For infinite Δ, it can be argued that the notion of weakly justified pre-extension is the best one.

Property 2.4 A (weakly) justified pre-extension is unconsistent iff W itself is unconsistent. (Proof easy.)

A justified pre-extension always exists. Moreover, it is easy to give a *constructive definition* (not using the final result E in the steps used to define the successive E_i). This affirmation may seem paradoxical as the characteristic property 2.3 seems to be "less constructive" than the definition of R-extensions: the final result E appears twice instead of once only. But here is another equivalent definition:

Property 2.5 E is a justified pre-extension of (W, Δ) iff there exists two sequences $(E_i)_{i \in \mathbb{N}}$, $(F_i)_{i \in \mathbb{N}}$ of sets of formulas such that $E = \cup E_i$, $E_0 = W$, $F_0 = \emptyset$; and:
- If there is some $\delta_i \in \Delta$ such that $(Pre(\delta_i) \in E_i$ and
  for any $\phi \in F_i \cup \{Jus(\delta_i)\}$, we have $E_i \cup Con(\delta_i) \not\vdash \neg\phi)$ then
  $(E_{i+1} = E_i$ and $F_{i+1} = F_i)$ or $(E_{i+1} = Th(E_i \cup Con(\delta_i))$ and $F_{i+1} = F_i \cup \{Jus(\delta_i)\})$;
  if there is no such δ_i then $(E_{i+1} = E_i$ and $F_{i+1} = F_i)$.

(Proof easy.) This reminds some definitions appearing in the literature, e. g. [6, 1], even if it is slightly different. This characterization is not only "constructive" but of a "one default at a time" kind. However, there may be an infinite number of steps and there is undeterminism involved at each step.

We need another property if we want to obtain R-extensions.

Definition 2.6 A set E of formulas satisfying $E = Th(E)$ is *stable for* Δ iff for any default $\delta \in \Delta$: *if* $Pre(\delta) \in E$ *and* $\neg Jus(\delta) \notin E$ *then* $Con(\delta) \in E$.

Checking for stability of a given set E is called *stability test*, or *st-test*.

This property appears in several texts, moreover it is an adaptation of a property appearing in the founding paper [10]. It is clear that any R-extension is a justified pre-extension which is stable. The converse is also true. As this is a relatively well known result, we do not give the proof here. Thus we have split the definition of R-extensions into three properties: groundedness, justification and stability. Groundedness is constructive, and even it is much easier to guarantee this condition in the construction of extensions (however [11] computes R-extensions firstly without taking care of groundedness, and then making a check). Justification can easily be made constructive also: it suffices to take care of all the justifications needed at the previous steps and to respect the new justifications at each step. Stability is the only inherently non constructive property: we need the final result E to ensure stability. If we construct our pre-extensions "from below" (with growing pre-extensions), we have problems with the $\neg Jus(\delta) \notin E$ part, and if we design a construction "from above" (decreasing pre-extensions), we have problems with the $Pre(\delta) \in E$ part.

There have been several "semi-constructive" definitions of R-extensions in the literature, consisting in a first constructive stage, giving some class of pre-extensions, followed by a final "test". Generally, even when it has not been recognized, the final test is either a stability test or a more complicated test including a stability test.

3 Justified pre-extensions and Łukaszewicz defaults

For improving our definition, we may try to give the minimum work to the final stability test, constructing fewer pre-extensions. [3] gives one of the most interesting solutions in this direction. Their constructive stage is simple and natural, and it gives only a restricted sort of justified pre-extensions. We call "K-extensions" their pre-extensions, and show how they relate to the well-known Łukaszewicz' extensions.

Definition 3.1 (adaptation of a definition in [3]) E is a *K-extension* iff there exists two sequences (E_i), (F_i) of sets of formulas with $E = \cup E_i$, $E_0 = W$, $F_0 = \emptyset$, and
- for any ordinal $\alpha \neq 0$, we define $E'_\alpha = \bigcup_{i<\alpha} E_i$, $F'_\alpha = \bigcup_{i<\alpha} F_i$;
  if there is some $\delta_\alpha \in \Delta$ such that $E'_\alpha \vdash Pre(\delta_\alpha)$, $E'_\alpha \nvdash Con(\delta_\alpha)$ and
  for any $\phi \in F'_\alpha \cup \{Jus(\delta_\alpha)\}$, $E'_\alpha \cup \{Con(\delta_\alpha)\} \nvdash \neg\phi$
  then choose one such δ_α and $E_\alpha = Th(E'_\alpha \cup \{Con(\delta_\alpha)\})$, $F_\alpha = F'_\alpha \cup \{Jus(\delta_\alpha)\}$;
  if there is no such δ_α then $E_\alpha = E'_\alpha$ and $F'_\alpha = F_\alpha$.

The only two real differences with justified pre-extensions (prop. 2.5) are that if we can increase E_i here we must do it and there is the additional condition $E_i \nvdash Con(\delta)$ (only defaults of some utility are used). Thus K-extensions are justified pre-extensions, the converse being not guaranteed. An apparent third difference is that here we must consider ordinals greater than ω, in order to be sure that we do not stop too early. This complication is not needed in property 2.5 as anyway with justified pre-extensions we may "stop too early". Due to the "constructive nature" of definition 3.1, we get that any default theory has a K-extension.

Property 3.1 [3] A K-extension is a R-extension of (W, Δ) iff it is stable.

K-extensions are very close to the m-extensions of [6, 7], here called L-extensions:
Definition 3.2 [6] S and U being two sets of formulas, $\Gamma_1(S,U)$ and $\Gamma_2(S,U)$ are the smallest sets verifying: 1) $\Gamma_1(S,U) = Th(\Gamma_1(S,U))$; 2) $W \subseteq \Gamma_1(S,U)$;
3) for any $\delta \in \Delta$ such that $(Pre(\delta) \in \Gamma_1(S,U))$ and (for any $\phi \in U \cup \{Jus(\delta)\}$, $S \cup \{Con(\delta)\} \nvdash \neg\phi$), then $(Con(\delta) \in \Gamma_1(S,U)$ and $Jus(\delta) \in \Gamma_2(S,U))$.
E is a *L-extension* iff there exists a F such that $E = \Gamma_1(E,F)$ and $F = \Gamma_2(E,F)$.

We may characterize L-extensions in a way more interesting for us:
Property 3.2 E is a L-extension of $\mathcal{T} = (W, \Delta)$ iff there exists a set F and two sequences (E_i), (F_i) of sets of formulas such that $E = \cup E_i$, $F = \cup F_i$ and:
- $E_0 = W$, $F_0 = \emptyset$, $\Delta_0 = \Delta$;
- for any ordinal α other than 0, we define $E'_\alpha = \bigcup_{i<\alpha} E_i$, $F'_\alpha = \bigcup_{i<\alpha} F_i$, $\Delta'_\alpha = \bigcap_{i<\alpha} \Delta_i$,
if there is $\delta_\alpha \in \Delta'_\alpha$ such that $E'_\alpha \vdash Pre(\delta_\alpha)$ and
for any $\phi \in F'_\alpha \cup \{Jus(\delta_\alpha)\}$, $E'_\alpha \cup \{Con(\delta_\alpha)\} \nvdash \neg\phi$
then choose one of these δ_α and define
$E_\alpha = Th(E'_\alpha \cup \{Con(\delta_\alpha)\})$, $F_\alpha = F'_\alpha \cup \{Jus(\delta_\alpha)\}$ and $\Delta_\alpha = \Delta'_\alpha - \{\delta_\alpha\}$;
if there is no such δ_α then $E_\alpha = E'_\alpha$, $F_\alpha = F'_\alpha$ and $\Delta_\alpha = \Delta'_\alpha$.

This is a corollary of theorem 5.18 in [6]. In [6] there is an additional "L-stability test" (stability test for L-extensions). This test is a rewriting of the condition appearing in each stage, and, as the property is written here, it is unnecessary. Thus, there exists a "constructive" (and even a "one default at a time") definition of L-extensions.

The only difference between L-extensions and K-extensions is that in definition 3.1 there is the additional requirement $E_i \nvdash Con(\delta)$. Thus any K-extension is a L-extension, the converse is not guaranteed as shown by the following example, even if K-extensions and L-extensions are rather close together:
Example 3.1 (cf example 4.2 in [6])
$W = a$, $\Delta = \{\delta_1 = \frac{:c}{a}, \delta_2 = \frac{:b}{\neg c}\}$.
First, we look for K-extensions. $E_0 = \{a\}, F_0 = \emptyset$,
δ_1 ? no because $E_0 \vdash a$ (this is the difference with L-extensions).
δ_2 ? yes because $E_0 \nvdash \neg c$, $E_0 \cup \{\neg c\} \nvdash \neg b$. Thus $E_1 = Th(a, \neg c), F_1 = \{b\}$.
There is only one K-extension $E = E_1 = Th(a, \neg c)$. E is also a R-extension.
However there are two L-extensions $E' = Th(a)$, associated with $F' = \{c\}$ and
$E = Th(a, \neg c)$, associated with $F = \{b\}$.

The existence of non maximal extensions is a weakness of Lukaszewicz's proposal. Unfortunately, as the following example shows, some non maximal K-extensions are not eliminated by the additional requirement $E_i \nvdash Con(\delta)$ in definition 3.1:
Example 3.2 $W = \emptyset$, $\Delta = \{\delta_1 = \frac{:j_1}{a}, \delta_2 = \frac{:j_2}{a \wedge \neg j_1}\}$.
There are two K-extensions, which are also L-extensions:
$E = Th(a)$, with $F = \{j_1\}$, and $E' = Th(a, \neg j_1)$, with $F' = \{j_2\}$.
Note that here st-test eliminates E, E' being the only R-extension.

From property 2.5 it is clear that any L-extension is a justified pre-extension.
To continue our comparison with the existing literature, we study here a proposal made in [2]. We have yet signaled that they too introduce justified pre-extensions,

under the name "E-sets". Their goal was to define a "new kind" of default extensions. They came up with a kind of extensions which is very close to L-extensions. As this fact is not mentioned in their text, we precise this point now.

Definition 3.3 (adapted from [2]) Let $\mathcal{T} = (W, \Delta)$ be a default theory. Any set E which is a union of justified pre-extensions of $\mathcal{T}$ and which is closed for Th (i.e. $Th(E) = E$) is a *G-pre-extension* of $\mathcal{T}$. Any G-pre-extension of $\mathcal{T}$ which is maximal for $\subseteq$ is a *G-extension* of $\mathcal{T}$.

As justified pre-extensions are closed for Th, the only unions of justified pre-extensions which are closed for Th are the unions $\cup_{i \in I} E_i$, containing an inclusion chain $E_{j_1} \subseteq E_{j_2} \subseteq \cdots$ where $J = \{j_1, j_2, \ldots\} \subseteq I$, such that for any $i \in I$ there exists a $j \in J$ with $E_i \subseteq E_j$. As only the maximal G-pre-extensions will be considered, these unions are needed only with infinite chains of justified pre-extensions as in example 2.1 where $Th(a) \cup Th(a \wedge \neg j_1) \cup Th(a \wedge \neg j_1 \wedge \neg j_2) \cup \cdots$ is a G-extension but is not a L-extension. Anyway, the notion of "default proof" is exactly the same with [6] and [2]. This means that a given formula ϕ belongs to a L-extension iff it belongs to a G-extension. To see this, it suffices to compare the definition of a *G-proof* (definition 4 in [2]) and the characterization of *L-proofs* as given in theorem 7.7 of [6] or theorem 5.126 in [7], they coincide[2]:

Property 3.3 [6, 7] (resp. [2])
A sentence ϕ belongs to a L-extension (resp. a G-extension) of (W, Δ) iff there exists a finite sequence $\Delta_0, \cdots, \Delta_k$ of finite subsets of Δ such that: (1) $W \cup Con(\Delta_0) \vdash \phi$; (2) $W \cup Con(\Delta_i) \vdash Pre(\Delta_{i-1})$, $(1 \leq i \leq k)$;
(3) $\Delta_k = \emptyset$; (4) $W \cup \bigcup_{i=0}^{k} Con(\Delta_i) \not\vdash \neg\psi$ for any $\psi \in \bigcup_{i=0}^{k} Jus(\Delta_i)$.

Note that this result holds also with K-extensions, with justified pre-extensions, and with weakly justified pre-extensions instead of L- (or G-)extensions. Regarding the respective extensions, here are the precise relations (proofs easy):

Property 3.4 Any maximal L-extension is a G-extension. Any G-extension is either a maximal L-extension or a union of an infinite chain of L-extensions.
G-extensions coincide with maximal weakly justified pre-extensions.

Now, we examine a seemingly different proposal [12], and show that it has several profound analogies with our presention of stable justified pre-extensions.

4 Pre-extensions in modal translations of defaults

Several authors ([4, 9, 13]) have "translated" default logic into a modal formalism. [12] chooses the modal system T:

Definition 4.1 The modal system T adds to classical first order logic a modal operator L (also M is $\neg L \neg$) with the following properties: – axiom schema of necessity: $L\phi \Rightarrow \phi$; consequence: $L(\phi \Rightarrow \psi) \Rightarrow (L\phi \Rightarrow L\psi)$; Barcan: $\forall x (L\phi(x)) \Rightarrow L(\forall x \phi(x))$; – rule of necessitation: If $\vdash \phi$ then $\vdash L\phi$ (if ϕ is a tautology, so is $L\phi$).

[2] Note however that this was not readily apparent due to a mistake in theorem 7.7 in [6], not corrected before [7].

The system of [12] contains also a set of modal operators $\{H_\delta\}_{\delta \in \Delta}$ which respect only one property: $H_\delta\phi \Rightarrow \neg L \neg \phi$ (for any index δ and formula ϕ). Any term $H_\delta\phi$ is considered as another propositional variable. Here is how the authors translate a default theory $\mathcal{T} = (W, \Delta)$ (where W is supposed consistent):

Definition 4.2 ([12] adapted) $\mathcal{T}$ gives rise to $\mathcal{T}^M = \{L\phi : \phi \in W\} \cup \{La \wedge H_\delta b \Rightarrow Lc : \delta = \frac{a:b}{c} \in \Delta\}$. A consistent set E^M of modal formulas is a *modal S-extension* of $\mathcal{T}^M$ iff $\mathcal{T}^M \cup \{H_\delta b \Rightarrow \neg L \neg b : \delta = \frac{a:b}{c} \in \Delta\} \subseteq E^M$ and
1) For any default $\delta = \frac{a:b}{c} \in \Delta$, either $H_\delta b \in E^M$ or $\neg H_\delta b \in E^M$.
2) $Th_T(E^M) = E^M$: E^M is closed for the consequence relation of system T.
3) It is not possible to add another $H_\delta b$ to E^M without provoking an inconsistency.
4) E^M is a minimal set with these properties.

We are interested by the objective formulas (without modality) ϕ such that $L\phi \in E^M$. The name *S-extension* refers to this objective subset E of E^M.

Property 4.1 [12] A S-extension E is a R-extension iff E^M respects the additional condition: *For any* $\delta = \frac{a:b}{c} \in \Delta$, *if* $\neg H_\delta b \in E^M$, *then* $L \neg b \in E^M$.
We call this test the *S-test*. Moreover any R-extension can be obtained in this way.

In the original definitions there was only one operator H. Here is a strange behavior of the *S'-extensions* so defined (definition 4.2 with $H_i\phi \equiv H_j\phi$ for any i, j):
Example 4.1 $W = \emptyset$, $\Delta = \{\delta_1 = \frac{:b}{c}, \delta_2 = \frac{:b}{\neg c}\}$.

The translation respecting the original definition of [12] gives $\mathcal{T}^M = \{Hb \Rightarrow Lc, Hb \Rightarrow L\neg c\}$. As $\mathcal{T}^M \subseteq E^M$ and $E^M = Th_T(E^M)$, we get $(\neg Lc \vee \neg L \neg c) \Rightarrow \neg Hb \in E^M$. Now, $Lc \Rightarrow c$ and $L\neg c \Rightarrow \neg c$ are axioms of the system T, thus $\neg Lc \vee \neg L \neg c \in E^M$. This gives: $\neg Hb \in E^M$. Thus, the only modal S'-extension E^M of $\mathcal{T}^M$ is $Th_T(\mathcal{T}^M)$, no default is applicable: $E = Th(W) = Th(\emptyset)$.

Imagine now that we start from: $W' = \{b_1 \Leftrightarrow b_2\}$, $\Delta' = \{\delta_1 = \frac{:b_1}{c}, \delta_2 = \frac{:b_2}{\neg c}\}$.
$\mathcal{T}'^M = \{Hb_1 \Rightarrow Lc, Hb_2 \Rightarrow L\neg c\}$, giving two S'-extensions:
- We put $Hb_1 \in E_1'^M$, then we have $Lc \in E_1'^M$, thus $\neg L \neg c \in E_1'^M$ and $\neg Hb_2 \in E_1'^M$, this giving our first S'-extension $E_1' = Th(c)$.
- We put $Hb_2 \in E_2'^M$. This gives a second and last S'-extension $E_2' = Th(\neg c)$.

We consider this behavior as very contestable: these two default theories should have the same extensions. With our definition 4.2 we get the same result in each case: Both (W, Δ) and (W', Δ') have two S-extensions, $Th(c)$ and $Th(\neg c)$. Note that none S'-extension succeeeds to the S-test, there is no R-extension.

Our solution is very close to the original text, a difference appears only when two defaults have the same justification. Property 4.1 is true with S-extensions and with S'-extensions. Also, S-extensions as well as S'-extensions are justified pre-extensions. There are some analogies between S-extensions and L-extensions. In example 4.1 the two S-extensions are also the two L-extensions, and the two K-extensions.

Property 4.2 Every L-extension is a S-extension (converse false).
Every S-extension is a justified pre-extension (converse false). Thus, the notion of "default proof" is the same for S-extensions and for L-extensions.

The proof is not difficult and appears in [8]. Any example in which W is not a S-extension of (W, Δ) establishes that the converse of the second part is false. The following example establishes that the converse of the first part is false.

Example 4.2 $W = \{\neg d\}, \Delta = \{\delta_1 = \frac{:b}{c}, \delta_2 = \frac{c:b'}{d}\}$. We note H_i for H_{δ_i}.

$H_1 b \Rightarrow Lc \in T^M$, $Lc \wedge H_2 b' \Rightarrow Ld \in T^M$, $L\neg d \in T^M$. Also, $L\neg d \Rightarrow \neg Ld \in T^M$, thus $H_2 b' \Rightarrow \neg H_1 b \in T^M$. There are two modal S-extensions $E^M = Th_T(T^M \cup \{H_1 b\})$ and $E'^M = Th_T(T^M \cup \{H_2 b'\})$, which gives as our two S-extensions $E = Th(\neg d, c)$ and $E' = Th(\neg d)$. There is only one L-extension (or one K-extension) E, corresponding to $F = \{b\}$ (there is no R-extension). This example shows that there are even more non maximal S-extensions than L-extensions.

Now that we have established how closely related are S-extensions and L-extensions (they give rise to the same notion of "default proof" and they often coincide), it remains to compare the S-test to our previous tests. In fact we may say that *S-test is a translation of our familiar stability test in [12]'s formalism.*

Here are the main lines of the proof, (1) is equivalent to (2):

Here is a word to word translation of the stability test in [12]' terms:

For any $\delta = \dfrac{a:b}{c} \in \Delta$, we have ($La \notin E^M$, or $Lc \in E^M$, or $L\neg b \in E^M$) (1)

$\neg H_{\delta'} b' \in E^M$ only if $W \cup \{H_\delta b : H_\delta b \in E^M$ and $\delta \neq \delta'\} \vdash_T \neg H_{\delta'} b'$ and $\neg H_{\delta'} b'$ may be entailed iff $L\neg b' \vee (La' \wedge \neg Lc')$ is entailed. The S-test may be rewritten: for any

$\dfrac{a':b'}{c'} \in \Delta$, if ($L\neg b' \vee La' \in E^M$ and $L\neg b' \vee \neg Lc' \in E^M$) then $L\neg b' \in E^M$ (2)

We end our comparison of various presentations of default logic with the way used in [13] to define extensions thanks to a modal logic. The method has some analogies with the one in [12]. We restrict our attention to system T ([13] considers several systems, including T). [13] uses a propositional language $\mathcal{L}$, and $\mathcal{L}_L$ wich is $\mathcal{L}$ augmented by the modal operator L. [13] uses a system T, with the difference, emphasized in [12], that the notion of consequence in T, noted Cn_T, uses the *strong* necessity rule: if $\phi \in E$, then $L\phi \in Cn_T(E)$.

Definitions 4.3 (see [13]) A set E of formulas in $\mathcal{L}_L$ is a *T-expansion of a set of formulas I* iff: $E = Cn_T(I \cup \{\neg L\phi : \phi \notin E\})$. A set E of formulas in $\mathcal{L}_L$ is a *ground T-expansion of a set of formulas I* iff: $E = Cn_T(I \cup \{\neg L\phi : \phi \in \mathcal{L} - E\})$.

A set of formulas E in $\mathcal{L}_L$ is *m-stable* if it is closed for Cn_T and if for every $\phi \notin E$ we have $\neg L\phi \in E$. T-expansions and ground T-expansions are m-stable.

For any set S of formulas in $\mathcal{L}$, there is exactly one m-stable set E such that $E \cap \mathcal{L} = Th(S)$. This unique m-stable set is noted $St(S)$.

The notion of *m-stability* introduced here is the standard notion of stability in modal *autoepistemic logic* (see [4, 9]). Here is how [13] translates a default theory:

Notation 4.4 [13] For any default $\delta = \frac{a:b}{c} \in \Delta$, $emb(\delta) = La \wedge L\neg L\neg b \Rightarrow Lc$, $emb(W, \Delta) = \{L\phi : \phi \in W\} \cup \{emb(\delta) : \delta \in \Delta\}$.

Theorem 4.3 [13] E being a consistent set of propositional formulas, closed for propositional consequence, E is a R-extension of $T = (W, \Delta)$ iff:

$St(E)$ is a T-expansion of $emb(W, \Delta)$ iff:

$St(E)$ is a ground T-expansion of $emb(W, \Delta)$.

We split this definition into a constructive stage and a final test, in a natural way. Again, as final test we get a kind of stability test, which makes precise the relationship between the stability condition in default logic and m-stability.

Definition 4.5 A *T-extension of* $\mathcal{T} = (W, \Delta)$ *justified by* F $(F \subseteq \mathcal{L})$ is a consistent set E of formulas in $\mathcal{L}_L$ defined by: $E = Cn_T(emb(W, \Delta) \cup \{\neg L\neg\phi : \phi \in F\})$

Theorem 4.4 (corollary of theorem 4.3) A T-extension E of $\mathcal{T}$ justified by F is such that $E \cap \mathcal{L}$ is a R-extension of $\mathcal{T}$ iff we have: if $\phi \in \mathcal{L} - E$, then $\neg L\phi \in E$. This is called here the *T-test*. Moreover, any R-extension can be obtained in this way.

In order to compare the T-test to the stability test, we compare it to the S-test: *if* $\neg Hb \in E$ *then* $L\neg b \in E$ *for any* $b \in Y$, with $Y = \{b : \frac{a:b}{c} \in \Delta\}$, which is: *if* $L\neg b \notin E$ *then* $\neg Hb \notin E$ *for any* $b \in Y$. Due to the properties of S-extensions, it is also equivalent to: *for any* $b \in Y$, *if* $\neg b \in \mathcal{L} - E$ *then* $Hb \in E$, which with [13]'s translation of default theory gives: *for any* $b \in Y$, *if* $\neg b \in \mathcal{L} - E$ *then* $L\neg L\neg b \in E$, This in turn, due to the properties of Cn_T, is equivalent to: *for any* $b \in Y$, *if* $\neg b \in \mathcal{L} - E$ *then* $\neg L\neg b \in E$. This emphasizes the fundamental difference between S-test (and thus stability test) and T-test: the T-test must be made for any $\phi \in \mathcal{L}$, while the S-test has to be done only for any $b \in Y$. The T-test is far harder to execute to that respect. *The stability test is equivalent to a very partial T-test.*
It remains to see whether the T-test can be simplified into an ordinary stability test. The answer is that this can be done, with some caution.

Theorem 4.5 Let $\mathcal{T} = (W, \Delta)$ be a default theory. Let Y be the set of all the justifications $\{b : \frac{a:b}{c} \in \Delta\}$. If a T-extension E of $\mathcal{T}$, justified by F, is such that for any $b \in Y$ we have: if $\neg b \notin E$ then $\neg L\neg b \in E$, then $E \cap \mathcal{L}$ is a R-extension. This is the *restricted T-test*. Moreover, any R-extension can be obtained in this way.

The proof uses our treatment of S-extensions and is left to the reader. Note however that a T-extension succeeding with this test is not necessarily a T-expansion: it is not necessarily m-stable as $\phi \notin E$ does not imply $\neg L\phi \in E$. The condition needed for R-extensions is not m-stability: we need not to restrict our attention to the autoepistemic expansions, the relevant property is *"autoepistemy with respect to* $\neg Y$*"*, i.e. for any $b \in Y$, if $\neg b \notin E$ then $\neg L\neg b \in E$.

The T-test being a kind of "extended stability test", we now look closer to the first phase of our definition. The unfortunate conclusion is that this phase cannot be considered as "constructive", there are cases where T-extensions do not exist.

Example 4.3 $W = \{\neg a\}, \Delta = \{\frac{:\neg a}{a}\}$: $emb(W, \Delta) = \{L\neg a, L\neg La \Rightarrow La\}$. As $L\neg a \in E$, we get $\neg a \in E$ and also $\neg La \in E$, also, due to the properties of Cn_T, we get $L\neg La \in E$ which gives $a \in E$, thus getting a contradiction: $E = \mathcal{L}_L$.

5 Conclusion

Various presentations of default theories are very similar, not only in the final notion of "extensions" they get, but also in the notions of "pre-extension" they first define.

This was not obvious while reading the texts. These definitions consist in a first "constructive stage", followed by a stability test. The stability test is very powerful, it may be applied to sieve a large class of "pre-extensions", producing all the R-extensions and only these. As class of pre-extensions, we may use all the justified pre-extensions (which constitute a simply defined class of pre-extensions) or L-extensions of [6, 7] or some refinement of these, called here K-extensions. Also, some modal simulations of default logic were proved to be of this kind: S-extensions of [12], or even T-extensions defined so as to encompass the method of [13]. This has given the precise relationship between the classical stability test of default logic and some related notions in modal logics. The final test of [12] is equivalent to the stability test. The "autoepistemic test" used in [13] is a stability test extended to more formulas than strictly necessary (when the goal is R-extensions). A R-extension need not correspond to an autoepistemic expansion, all we need is a restricted (and easier to test) kind of autoepistemy.

The method used here allows to attribute some "degree of constructiveness" to each definition. The less pre-extensions is the better, and to that respect [3] is the best. We should refine this notion, but this classification gives an idea. For example, [11]'s method is one of the least constructive in that classification. The method extracted from [13]'s text is still worse as here the test itself is far more complicated. This may give some clues in order to improve efficiency in computing extensions.

As a by-product of our study, we have proved that the notion of "formula provable by default" is exactly the same for K-extensions of [3], G-extensions of [2], L-extensions of [6], S-extensions of [12], and justified pre-extensions. Also, all these kinds of extensions have a "constructive" definition.

References

[1] Ph. Besnard. Characterisation of extensions for default logic. *Submitted*, 1992.

[2] R.A. de T. Guerreiro, M.A. Casanova, and A.S. Hemerly. Contribution to a proof theory for generic defaults. In *ECAI*, pp 213–218, Pitmman Publ, 1990.

[3] P. J. Krause, P. Byers, and S. Hajnal. Formal Specification of a Database Extension Management System: A Case Study. *submitted*, 1992.

[4] Kurt Konolige. On the relation beween default and autoepistemic logic. *Artificial Intelligence*, 35:343–382, 1988. *Errata in Artificial Intelligence, 41:115, 1989.*

[5] F. Lévy. Computing extensions of default theories. In *Symbolic and Quantitavive Approaches to Uncertainty, in LNCS-548*, pages 219–226. Springer-Verlag, 1991.

[6] Witold Lukaszewicz. Considerations on default logic: an alternative approach. *Computational Intelligence*, 4:1–16, 1988.

[7] Witold Lukaszewicz. *Non-monotonic Reasoning: formalization of commonsense reasoning.* Ellis Horwood, Chichester, UK, 1990.

[8] Y. Moinard. Unifying various approaches to default logic. T.R. IRISA, 1993 .

[9] Victor Marek and Mirosław Truszczyński. Relating autoepistemic and default logics. In *Knowledge Representation*, pages 276–288, Toronto, 1989.

[10] Ray Reiter. A logic for default reasoning. *Artificial Intelligence*, 13:81–132, 1980.

[11] C. Schwind, V. Risch. A tableau-based characterisation for default logic. In *Symbolic and Quantitative Approaches to Uncertainty,* LNCS-548: 310–317. 1991.

[12] P. Siegel, C. Schwind. Hypothesis theory for nonmonotonic reasoning. In *Workshop on Non-standard Queries and Answers*, pp 189–210, Toulouse, jul. 1991.

[13] Mirosław Truszczyński. Modal Interpretations of Default Logic. In *IJCAI*, pages 393–398, Sydney, Morgan Kaufmann, 1991.

Using Maximum Entropy in a Defeasible Logic with Probabilistic Semantics

James Cussens[1] and Anthony Hunter[2]

[1] Centre for Logic and Probability in IT, King's College
Strand, London, WC2R 2LS, UK
email: j.cussens@elm.cc.kcl.ac.uk
[2] Department of Computing, Imperial College
180 Queen's Gate, London, SW7 2BZ, UK
email: abh@doc.ic.ac.uk

Abstract. In this paper we make defeasible inferences from conditional probabilities using the Principle of Total Evidence. This gives a logic that is a simple extension of the axiomatization of probabilistic logic as defined by Halpern's AX_1. For our consequence relation, the reasoning is further justified by an assumption of the typicality of individuals mentioned in the data. For databases which do not determine a unique probability distribution, we select by default the distribution with Maximum Entropy. We situate this logic in the context of preferred models semantics.

1 Introduction

Traditionally there has been a dichotomy between the probabilistic and logical views on uncertainty reasoning in AI. However, there does seem to be an intuitive overlap of the two views. Whilst there are logics capturing aspects of probabilistic reasoning ([1,3,6,9]), the formal relationship of defeasible logics with probability theory remains an interesting research topic. In particular, using probability theory gives us an opportunity to clarify aspects of non-monotonic logics.

Here we show how using established principles from probability theory, together with the axioms of probability, can provide a useful semantic foundation for a defeasible logic. For the logic we extend the approach of [6] to allow non-monotonic reasoning from a database of conditional probability statements and ground formulae. We justify such non-monotonic inferences by the Principle of Total Evidence. We use this when we have two or more conditional probabilities all of whose conditions are satisfied. From these, the principle selects the conditional probability with the most specific condition. The idea here is that when assessing the probability of a given event, we should calculate its probability value conditional on all the available evidence. It is clear that the probability-theoretic Principle of Total Evidence is analogous to the notion of specificity as used in defeasible logic.

If there is no conditional probability statement that matches the available evidence, then we can estimate the required probability statement by invoking the Principle of Maximum Entropy. This gives the least biased estimate given the conditional probability statements already in the database ([8,2,10]).

In the following we provide an overview of the language, form of database and consequence relation for the defeasible logic; together with an outline of the formal semantics. We also discuss how we use Maximum Entropy to support reasoning in this logic.

2 A Representation for Defeasible Reasoning

We use Halpern's language $L_1^=(\Phi)$ together with the axiomatization AX_1 for $L_1^=(\Phi)$ which is correct for finite domains. Essentially this extends first-order classical logic to give a logic of probability. We use $\vdash$ to denote the consequence relation for AX_1. We reason with two kinds of information: We have conditional probability statements that give statistical information, and we also have a scenario—a set of ground formulae.

A probabilistic database is a pair (Δ, Σ), where Δ is a finite set of conditional probability statements in the language $L_1^=(\Phi)$ and Σ, the scenario, is a finite set of closed object formulae in $L_1^=(\Phi)$. The conditional probability terms are restricted to the form, $w_x(\alpha(x)|\beta(x))$, where both α and β are formulae with x free, s.t. x is a tuple of variables, β is classically consistent and there are no further variables or function symbols in either α or β. These are called *completely bound* probability terms. The conditional probability statements are restricted to the form $w_x(\alpha(x)|\beta(x)) = \zeta$, where $w_x(\alpha(x)|\beta(x))$ is a completely bound probability term, and ζ is real. We abbreviate terms of the form $w_x(\alpha(x)|\beta(x) \vee \neg\beta(x))$ to $w_x(\alpha(x))$.

A probabilistic database (Δ, Σ) is complete w.r.t./ Φ if, for every completely bound probability term $w_x(\alpha(x)|\beta(x))$ in $L_1^=(\Phi)$, there is a ζ s.t. $\Delta \vdash w_x(\alpha(x)|\beta(x)) = \zeta$ holds. However, if a database is not complete then we can complete it using Maximum Entropy. We discuss this below.

3 A Consequence Relation for Defeasible Reasoning

Given a complete probabilistic database (Δ, Σ), we wish to ascertain a probability value for ground literals α if $\alpha \notin \Sigma$. If we use the Principle of Total Evidence, then there is only one conditional probability statement in the database that can be used. If the value of this conditional probability is greater than a certain threshold, say θ, then we defeasibly infer α. Note, we must have θ at least $1/2$ for consistency. If the value is less than $1-\theta$, then we defeasibly infer $\neg\alpha$. However, if the value is in $[1-\theta, \theta]$, then we infer neither α nor $\neg\alpha$.

We formalize an inference from a database as follows, where θ is the probabilistic threshold value, and the relation $\mid\sim$ denotes non-monotonic consequence. Let σ be a function that assigns every constant in Φ a distinct variable. Given a formula α, let α^σ be the result of replacing every constant c that appears in α by the variable $\sigma(c)$. Let $\sigma(\alpha)$ be the set of variables appearing in α^σ. The conjunct $\bigwedge(\Sigma)$ is formed from all the elements in Σ, and $\vdash$ is the consequence relation defined by Halpern for $L_1^{=}(\Phi)$:

$$(\Delta, \Sigma) \mid\!\sim \alpha \text{ iff } \Delta \vdash w_{\sigma(\Sigma)}(\alpha^{\sigma} | (\bigwedge(\Sigma))^{\sigma}) > \theta \tag{1}$$

The non-monotonic consequence relation captures the notion of reasoning from a preferred conditional probability for a query α, where it is preferred on the basis of the Principle of Total Evidence. The definition ensures the following: (1) the chosen conditional probability is greater than θ; and (2) the function σ makes the head of the conditional probability equivalent to the query and the antecedent equivalent to the scenario.

4 An Example of Defeasible Reasoning

We take the bird example, where the database (Δ, Σ) is defined as follows, and $\Phi = \{\text{bird}, \text{fly}, \text{penguin}, \text{polly}, \text{tweety}\}$

$$\begin{aligned}
\Delta = \{&w_x(\text{bird}(x)) = p_1 \\
&w_x(\text{fly}(x)) = p_2 \\
&w_x(\text{penguin}(x)) = p_3 \\
&w_x(\text{fly}(x)|\text{bird}(x)) = p_4 \\
&w_x(\text{bird}(x)|\text{penguin}(x)) = p_5 \\
&w_x(\text{penguin}(x)|\text{fly}(x)) = p_6 \\
&w_x(\text{fly}(x)|\text{bird}(x) \wedge \text{penguin}(x)) = p_7\}
\end{aligned} \tag{2}$$

$$\Sigma = \{\text{bird}(\text{tweety}), \text{bird}(\text{polly})\} \tag{3}$$

For query fly(tweety), we have: $\Delta \vdash w_x(\text{fly}(x)|\text{bird}(x)) = p_4$. Now, if $p_4 > \theta$ holds, then by AX_1 and (1), we have $(\Delta, \Sigma) \mid\!\sim \text{fly}(\text{tweety})$.

We extend the scenario to the following,

$$\Sigma' = \{\text{bird}(\text{tweety}), \text{bird}(\text{polly}), \text{penguin}(\text{tweety})\} \tag{4}$$

For query $\neg$fly(tweety) from the database (Δ, Σ'), we have the following:

$$\Delta \vdash w_x(\neg\text{fly}(x)|\text{bird}(x) \wedge \text{penguin}(x)) = 1 - p_7 \tag{5}$$

Now, if $(1 - p_7) > \theta$ holds, then by AX_1 and (1), we have $(\Delta, \Sigma') \mid\!\sim \neg\text{fly}(\text{tweety})$.

5 A Probabilistic Semantics for the Logic

To provide a semantics for the defeasible logic, we extend the type-1 semantics ([6]) which is correct with respect to the AX_1 axiomatization for finite domains—for this paper we assume all domains are finite. A type-1 probability structure is a tuple (D, π, F, μ) where D is a domain, π assigns to the predicate and function symbols in the language predicates and functions of the right arity over D (so that (D, π) is just a standard first-order structure). F is a finite algebra generated from the set of all sets definable in $L_1^=(\Phi)$, and μ is a probability function on F. We define the atoms of F, denoted $A(F)$, as the minimal non-empty sets of F. μ is determined by the values it takes on $A(F)$.

A valuation v, is a function mapping each object variable into an element of D. Given a type-1 probability structure M and valuation v, we proceed by induction to associate with every object (respectively field) term t, an element $[t]_{(M,v)}$ of D (respectively $\mathbb{R}$), and with every formula ϕ a truth value, writing $(M, v) \models \phi$ if the value true is associated with ϕ by (M, v). We write $M \models \phi$ if $(M, v) \models \phi$ for all valuations v. We also define $D_\phi = \{d \in D : (M, v[x/d]) \models \phi\}$. Finally for every probability term $w_x(\phi)$, $[w_x(\phi)]_{(M,v)} = \mu^n(D_\phi)$ where n is the number of free variables in ϕ, and μ^n is the product measure. We also add the following to the definition of satisfaction: $(M, v) \models (\Delta, \Sigma)$ iff $\forall \phi \in \Delta \cup \Sigma$: $(M, v) \models \phi$. For this definition, if $(M, v) \models (\Delta, \Sigma)$ for some valuation v, then $(M, v) \models (\Delta, \Sigma)$ for all valuations v, since (Δ, Σ) contains no free variables. So we can replace $(M, v) \models (\Delta, \Sigma)$ by $M \models (\Delta, \Sigma)$.

Using this semantics it is straightforward to define a corresponding notion of semantics for the defeasible logic consequence relation, and show correctness results. For this semantics we take the set of models for (Δ, Σ) and select a subset of models, denoted $[[\Delta, \Sigma]]$. This subset of models is the set of preferred models for the database, such that $M \in [[\Delta, \Sigma]]$ if, whenever $M \models (\Delta, \Sigma)$ and $M \models w_{\sigma(\Sigma)}(\alpha^\sigma | (\bigwedge(\Sigma))^\sigma) > \theta$, then $M \models \alpha$. Using preferred models builds on the non-monotonic logics framework initially proposed by [12]. We define preferred satisfaction as follows:

$$M \models\!\approx_\Sigma \alpha \text{ iff } M \models w_{\sigma(\Sigma)}(\alpha^\sigma | (\bigwedge(\Sigma))^\sigma) > \theta \tag{6}$$

Using this, we define preferred entailment, denoted $\models\!\approx$, as follows:

$$\forall M (M \models (\Delta, \Sigma) \Rightarrow M \models\!\approx_\Sigma \alpha) \text{ iff } (\Delta, \Sigma) \models\!\approx \alpha \tag{7}$$

We now consider properties of this form of non-monotonic reasoning. For a database (Δ, Σ), we use the notation $(\Delta, \Sigma) \vdash \alpha$ to represent $(\Delta \cup \Sigma) \vdash \alpha$.

Theorem 1. *For the consequence relation $\vdash$ for $L_1^=(\Phi)$, the entailment relation $\models$ for $L_1^=(\Phi)$, and a database (Δ, Σ), where $(\Delta \cup \Sigma) \subset L_1^=(\Phi)$, and $\alpha \in L_1^=(\Phi)$, the equivalence $(\Delta, \Sigma) \vdash \alpha$ iff $(\Delta, \Sigma) \models \alpha$ holds, since we assume finite domains.*

Proof. See [6]. □

Lemma 2. *Using the definition of preferred entailment, the following equivalence holds:* $(\Delta, \Sigma) \approx \alpha$ *iff* $(\Delta, \Sigma) \models w_{\sigma(\Sigma)}(\alpha^{\sigma}|(\bigwedge(\Sigma))^{\sigma}) > \theta$.

Proof. Assume $(\Delta, \Sigma) \approx \alpha$ holds, then choose an arbitrary M such that $M \models (\Delta, \Sigma)$. From (7), we have $M \approx_{\Sigma} \alpha$, and hence from (6), $M \models w_{\sigma(\Sigma)}(\alpha^{\sigma}|(\bigwedge(\Sigma))^{\sigma}) > \theta$. Since M was arbitrary this shows $(\Delta, \Sigma) \models w_{\sigma(\Sigma)}(\alpha^{\sigma}|(\bigwedge(\Sigma))^{\sigma}) > \theta$. So $(\Delta, \Sigma) \approx \alpha$ implies $(\Delta, \Sigma) \models w_{\sigma(\Sigma)}(\alpha^{\sigma}|(\bigwedge(\Sigma))^{\sigma}) > \theta$. Now assume $(\Delta, \Sigma) \not\approx \alpha$. From (7) there exists an M such that $M \models (\Delta, \Sigma)$, but $M \not\approx_{\Sigma} \alpha$. From (6), this implies $M \not\models w_{\sigma(\Sigma)}(\alpha^{\sigma}|(\bigwedge(\Sigma))^{\sigma}) > \theta$. Hence $(\Delta, \Sigma) \not\models w_{\sigma(\Sigma)}(\alpha^{\sigma}|(\bigwedge(\Sigma))^{\sigma}) > \theta$. So $(\Delta, \Sigma) \models w_{\sigma(\Sigma)}(\alpha^{\sigma}|(\bigwedge(\Sigma))^{\sigma}) > \theta$ implies $(\Delta, \Sigma) \approx \alpha$ and the result follows. □

Theorem 3. *For any probabilistic database* (Δ, Σ), *the equivalence* $(\Delta, \Sigma) \approx \alpha$ *iff* $(\Delta, \Sigma) \mid\sim \alpha$ *holds, where* α *is a ground literal.*

Proof. By (1) and Lemma 2, the result obtains by showing the equivalence $(\Delta, \Sigma) \models w_{\sigma(\Sigma)}(\alpha^{\sigma}|(\bigwedge(\Sigma))^{\sigma}) > \theta$ iff $(\Delta, \Sigma) \vdash w_{\sigma(\Sigma)}(\alpha^{\sigma}|(\bigwedge(\Sigma))^{\sigma}) > \theta$. This equivalence follows directly from Theorem 1. □

6 Properties of the Logic

It is of interest to draw an analogy with the Closed World Assumption (CWA), where extra assumptions can be drawn from the database under certain conditions. However, since our non-monotonic consequence relation is based on probability theory, we avoid some of the problems of the CWA. For pathological examples, such as the following database $\Gamma = \{\neg\alpha \rightarrow \alpha\}$, the equivalent formula in $L_1^{=}(\Phi)$, $w_x(\alpha(x)|\neg\alpha(x)) > \theta$ does not hold since $w_x(\alpha(x)|\neg\alpha(x)) = 0$ follows directly from probability theory.

Another interesting difference between our non-monotonic consequence relation and that of CWA is with regard to the following kind of database: For $\Gamma' = \{\neg\beta \rightarrow \alpha\}$, both $\neg\alpha$ and $\neg\beta$ follow by CWA, and the pair of inferences are inconsistent with Γ. In our approach, for a consistent database, the non-monotonic consequence relation does not allow inconsistent inferences. Indeed, it is straightforward to show that if (Δ, Σ) is satisfiable then $[[\Delta, \Sigma]]$ is non-empty, since there is no consistent (Δ, Σ) and α such that $(\Delta, \Sigma) \approx \alpha$ and $(\Delta, \Sigma) \approx \neg\alpha$.

In comparison with Gabbay's axiomatization of the consequence relation [4], cut holds if no conditional probability values deducible from Δ lie in the interval $(\theta^2, \theta]$. Similarly, cautious monotonicity holds if no conditional probability values deducible from Δ lie in the set $(\theta(1-\theta)^2, 1-\theta]$. However, in general, neither cut nor cautious monotonicity hold. Furthermore, in general, reflexivity holds and monotonicity fails.

Theorem 4. *For the consequence relation* $\mid\sim$, *with query* α *and database* (Δ, Σ), *the following property does not hold:* $(\Delta, \Sigma) \mid\sim \alpha$ *and* $(\Delta, \Sigma) \mid\sim \beta$ *implies* $(\Delta \cup \{\alpha\}) \mid\sim \beta$.

Proof. Suppose we have that $\Delta = \{w_x(\text{mammal}(x)) = 0.55, w_x(\text{egg-layer}(x)) = 0.55, w_x(\text{mammal}(x)|\text{egg-layer}(x)) = 0.2\}$ and θ is set to its lowest value: 0.5. We have $(\Delta, \emptyset) \mid\!\sim$ mammal(agatha) and $(\Delta, \emptyset) \mid\!\sim$ egg-layer(agatha) but not $(\Delta, \text{egg-layer(agatha)}) \mid\!\sim$ mammal(agatha)). □

Theorem 5. *For the consequence relation $\mid\!\sim$, with query α and database (Δ, Σ), the following property does not hold: $(\Delta, \Sigma) \mid\!\sim \beta$ and $(\Delta, \Sigma \cup \{\beta\}) \mid\!\sim \alpha$ implies $(\Delta, \Sigma) \mid\!\sim \alpha$.*

Proof. Suppose that we have $\Delta = \{w_x(\text{bird}(x)) = 0.7, w_x(\text{flies}(x)) = 0.6, w_x(\text{flies}(x)|\text{bird}(x)) = 0.9\}$ and θ is set to 0.65, then we have $(\Delta, \emptyset) \mid\!\sim$ bird(tweety) and $(\Delta, \text{bird(tweety)}) \mid\!\sim$ flies(tweety), but not $(\Delta, \emptyset) \mid\!\sim$ flies(tweety). □

Theorem 6. *For the consequence relation $\mid\!\sim$, with query α and database (Δ, Σ), the following properties do hold:*

(Left logical equivalence)

$$\frac{\vdash \alpha \equiv \beta; (\Delta, \Sigma \cup \{\alpha\}) \mid\!\sim \gamma}{(\Delta, \Sigma \cup \{\beta\}) \mid\!\sim \gamma)} \tag{8}$$

(Conjunctive Sufficiency)

$$\frac{(\Delta, \Sigma) \mid\!\sim \alpha \wedge \beta}{(\Delta, \Sigma \cup \{\alpha\}) \mid\!\sim \beta} \tag{9}$$

(Weak Conditionalization)

$$\frac{(\Delta, \Sigma \cup \{\alpha\}) \mid\!\sim \beta}{(\Delta, \Sigma) \mid\!\sim \alpha \rightarrow \beta} \tag{10}$$

(Right Weakening)

$$\frac{\Sigma \vdash \alpha \rightarrow \beta; (\Delta, \Sigma) \mid\!\sim \alpha}{(\Delta, \Sigma) \mid\!\sim \beta} \tag{11}$$

(Reasoning by Cases)

$$\frac{(\Delta, \Sigma \cup \{\alpha\}) \mid\!\sim \beta; (\Delta, \Sigma \cup \{\neg\alpha\}) \mid\!\sim \beta}{(\Delta, \Sigma) \mid\!\sim \beta} \tag{12}$$

(Correlative Monotonicity)

$$\frac{(\Delta, \Sigma) \mid\!\sim \beta; (\Delta, \Sigma \cup \{\beta\}) \mid\!\sim \alpha; (\Delta, \Sigma) \not\mid\!\sim \alpha}{(\Delta, \Sigma \cup \{\alpha\}) \mid\!\sim \beta} \tag{13}$$

(Correlative Cut)

$$\frac{(\Delta, \Sigma) \mid\!\sim \alpha; (\Delta, \Sigma \cup \{\alpha\}) \mid\!\sim \beta; (\Delta, \Sigma \cup \{\beta\}) \not\mid\!\sim \alpha}{(\Delta, \Sigma) \mid\!\sim \beta} \tag{14}$$

(Cautious $\vee$ Introduction)

$$\frac{(\Delta, \Sigma \cup \{\alpha\}) \mid\!\sim \gamma; (\Delta, \Sigma \cup \{\beta\}) \mid\!\sim \gamma; \Sigma \vdash \neg(\alpha \wedge \beta \wedge \gamma)}{(\Delta, \Sigma \cup \{\alpha \vee \beta\}) \mid\!\sim \gamma} \tag{15}$$

Proof. All of the above follow directly from the probability calculus. □

7 Completing a Probabilistic Database by Using Maximum Entropy

We can increase the applicability of this defeasible logic by providing ways of constructing a complete database from an incomplete database. A complete database fully determines a probability distribution μ over F, whereas a incomplete database only gives a set of constraints on possible probability distributions over F. Therefore to complete a database, we need to consider how to select one appropriate probability distribution from the possible distributions allowed by the incomplete database.

Here, we consider using Maximum Entropy to complete a database. This provides a unique complete database Δ^* that extends the incomplete database Δ. Essentially entropy is an inverse measure of the information contained in a probability distribution. Any probability distribution μ has an associated entropy $H(\mu)$ defined as follows, where ln equals $\log_e$.

$$H(\mu) = \sum_{B \in A(F)} \mu(B) \ln \mu(B) \tag{16}$$

Choosing the distribution with the Maximum Entropy hence corresponds to completing a database in an unbiased way ([8,2,10]). For example, consider the database $\Delta = \{w_x(\text{fly}(x)) = p_2, w_x(\text{bird}(x)) = p_3\}$ which is incomplete with respect to $\Phi = \{\text{fly}, \text{bird}\}$. To complete the database, we need to add the following conditional probability statement $w_x(\text{fly}(x)|\text{bird}(x)) = p_1$. Using Maximum Entropy, we calculate (below) that the value of p_1 is equal to the value of p_2. In this simple example, Maximum Entropy allows us to assume that the two predicates are independent.

Now consider the database $\Delta' = \{w_x(\text{fly}(x)|\text{bird}(x)) = p_1, w_x(\text{fly}(x)) = p_2, w_x(\text{bird}(x)) = p_3\}$ which is complete with respect to $\Phi = \{\text{fly}, \text{bird}\}$. Suppose we extend Φ' to $\{\text{fly}, \text{bird}, \text{sparrow}\}$, then Δ' is incomplete with respect to Φ'. Therefore we need to generate a database that include statements such as $w_x(\text{fly}(x)|\text{bird}(x) \wedge \text{sparrow}(x)) = p_4$. Using Maximum Entropy again, we can calculate that $p_1 = p_4$. In this situation, we can also see that Maximum Entropy is introducing an assumption that new properties are irrelevant to the probability distribution unless otherwise stated.

Viewing the use of Maximum Entropy as capturing a notion of relevance in probabilistic data follows the approach discussed by [11]. We can also view the use of Maximum Entropy as an inheritance principle as discussed by [5].

For example, for the database $\Delta = \{w_x(\text{fly}(x)) = p_2, w_x(\text{bird}(x)) = p_3\}$ which is incomplete with respect to $\Phi = \{\text{fly}, \text{bird}\}$, we find the value of p_1 for $w_x(\text{fly}(x)|\text{bird}(x)) = p_1$, by the use of Lagrange multipliers. The formulae in Δ provide linear constraints on any distribution satisfying Δ. For each constraint we define a function on $A(F)$, denoted f_0, f_1, and f_2 as follows:

$$f_0(A(F)) = \sum_{B \in A(F)} w_x(B(x)) - 1 = 0 \tag{17}$$

This constraint is that all the probabilities add to 1. We also have,

$$f_1(A(F)) = w_x(\text{bird}(x) \wedge \text{fly}(x)) + w_x(\neg\text{bird}(x) \wedge \text{fly}(x)) - p_2 = 0 \tag{18}$$

$$f_2(A(F)) = w_x(\text{bird}(x) \wedge \text{fly}(x)) + w_x(\text{bird}(x) \wedge \neg\text{fly}(x)) - p_3 = 0 \tag{19}$$

Entropy is maximized, subject to the above constraints, by the following scheme. For any B in $A(F)$

$$\frac{\partial H}{\partial(w_x(B(x)))} + \lambda\frac{\partial f_0}{\partial(w_x(B(x)))} + \lambda_1\frac{\partial f_1}{\partial(w_x(B(x)))} + \lambda_2\frac{\partial f_2}{\partial(w_x(B(x)))} = 0 \tag{20}$$

For each $B \in A(F)$ we differentiate to give the following:

$$-(\ln(w_x(\text{bird}(x) \wedge \text{fly}(x)) + 1) + \lambda + \lambda_1 + \lambda_2 = 0 \tag{21}$$

$$-(\ln(w_x(\text{bird}(x) \wedge \neg\text{fly}(x)) + 1) + \lambda + \lambda_2 = 0 \tag{22}$$

$$-(\ln(w_x(\neg\text{bird}(x) \wedge \text{fly}(x)) + 1) + \lambda + \lambda_1 = 0 \tag{23}$$

$$-(\ln(w_x(\neg\text{bird}(x) \wedge \neg\text{fly}(x)) + 1) + \lambda = 0 \tag{24}$$

We rewrite these as follows,

$$w_x(\text{bird}(x) \wedge \text{fly}(x)) = e^{(\lambda-1)+\lambda_1+\lambda_2} = e^{(\lambda-1)}e^{\lambda_1}e^{\lambda_2} \tag{25}$$

$$w_x(\text{bird}(x) \wedge \neg\text{fly}(x)) = e^{(\lambda-1)+\lambda_2} = e^{(\lambda-1)}e^{\lambda_2} \tag{26}$$

$$w_x(\neg\text{bird}(x) \wedge \text{fly}(x)) = e^{(\lambda-1)+\lambda_1)} = e^{(\lambda-1)}e^{\lambda_1} \tag{27}$$

$$w_x(\neg\text{bird}(x) \wedge \neg\text{fly}(x)) = e^{(\lambda-1)} = e^{\lambda-1} \tag{28}$$

Following Cheeseman, we abbreviate $e^{(\lambda-1)}$ by α_0, e^{λ_1} by α_1, and e^{λ_2} by α_2.

$$w_x(\text{bird}(x) \wedge \text{fly}(x)) = \alpha_0\alpha_1\alpha_2 \tag{29}$$

$$w_x(\text{bird}(x) \wedge \neg\text{fly}(x)) = \alpha_0\alpha_2 \tag{30}$$

$$w_x(\neg\text{bird}(x) \wedge \text{fly}(x)) = \alpha_0\alpha_1 \tag{31}$$

$$w_x(\neg\text{bird}(x) \wedge \neg\text{fly}(x)) = \alpha_0 \tag{32}$$

We could use the above three constraints to solve α_0, α_1, and α_2.

$$f_0(A(F)) = \alpha_0(\alpha_1\alpha_2 + \alpha_2 + \alpha_1 + 1) - 1 = 0 \tag{33}$$

$$f_1(A(F)) = \alpha_0\alpha_1\alpha_2 + \alpha_0\alpha_1 - p_2 = 0 \tag{34}$$

$$f_2(A(F)) = \alpha_0\alpha_1\alpha_2 + \alpha_0\alpha_2 - p_3 = 0 \tag{35}$$

However, we use an alternative way of showing $p_1 = p_2$

$$\begin{aligned} p_1 &= w_x(\mathrm{fly}(x)|\mathrm{bird}(x)) \\ &= \frac{w_x(\mathrm{bird}(x) \wedge \mathrm{fly}(x))}{w_x(\mathrm{bird}(x) \wedge \mathrm{fly}(x)) + w_x(\mathrm{bird}(x) \wedge \neg\mathrm{fly}(x))} \\ &= \frac{\alpha_0\alpha_1\alpha_2}{\alpha_0\alpha_1\alpha_2 + \alpha_0\alpha_2} \\ &= \frac{\alpha_1}{\alpha_1 + 1} \end{aligned} \tag{36}$$

Furthermore, we have $p_2 = \alpha_0\alpha_1\alpha_2 + \alpha_0\alpha_1$. However, we have $\alpha_0(\alpha_1\alpha_2 + \alpha_2 + \alpha_1 + 1) = 1 \Leftrightarrow \alpha_0(\alpha_2 + 1)(\alpha_1 + 1) = 1 \Leftrightarrow \alpha_0(\alpha_2 + 1) = 1/(\alpha_1 + 1) \Leftrightarrow p_1 = p_2$.

In this example the maximum entropy completion was straightforward. Unfortunately, in general this does not seem to be the case. Quoting from [10], 'if we accept maximum entropy,..., the problem of actually computing weights to any reasonable approximation is NP-hard and thus probably infeasible'. While noting that using maximum entropy, 'yields patterns of reasoning that parallel common discourse', Pearl also warns that its biggest shortcoming is 'its computational complexity' ([11]).

In our approach the complexity problem occurs when setting the database up, but once the database is complete, then the reasoning is tractable. The price for this tractability is that the size of a database will grow exponentially with the number of predicates in the language. This is in contrast to existing non-monotonic logics where there is no analogue to completing the database, but the reasoning is intractable—for example for default logic [7]. We therefore see a trade-off between completing a database and reasoning with a database.

8 Discussion

We can summarize the advantages of our approach: (1) We only need probabilities on the domain to represent defeasible rules; and (2) we can use a 'natural' assumption to augment probability theory in a way to allow detachment of the consequents of such rules.

To expand the second point, probability logics do not capture all of the reasoning that is done in situations of uncertainty. In particular, we are interested in addressing issues of (1) choice of reference class, (2) typicality assumptions, and (3) taking decisions. All three involve default assumptions. Our primary aim is to formalise such default assumptions.

Our approach combines the notion of preferred models with that of Halpern type-1 semantics. First, if our database is incomplete, we select a subset of the models for that database to force a completion by maximising entropy. Second, for a completed database, we take a subset of the corresponding models to force the entailment of the default inferences.

Acknowledgements. This work is currently being funded by UK SERC grants GR/G 29861 and GR/G 29854 for the Rule-based Systems project. Special thanks are due to Dov Gabbay and Donald Gillies. We also are very grateful to anonymous referees for helpful suggestions on improving previous versions of this work.

References

1. Fahiem Bacchus. *Representing and Reasoning with Probabilistic Knowledge: A Logical Approach to Probabilities.* MIT Press, Cambridge, MA, 1990.
2. P. Cheeseman. A method of computing generalized bayesian probability values. In *IJCAI'83*, pages 198–202. Morgan Kaufmann, 1983.
3. James Cussens and Anthony Hunter. Using defeasible logic for a window on a probabilistic database: some preliminary notes. In *Symbolic and Qualitative Approaches for Uncertainty*, pages 146–152. Lecture Notes in Computer Science 548, Springer, 1991.
4. Dov Gabbay. Theoretical foundations for non-monotonic reasoning in expert systems. In K. R. Apt, editor, *Proceedings NATO Advanced Study Institute on Logics and Models of Concurrent Systems*, pages 439–457. Springer, 1985.
5. B. Grosof. Non-monotonicity in probabilistic reasoning. In K. R. Apt, editor, *Uncertainty in Artificial Intelligence 3*, pages 237–249. North-Holland, 1988.
6. Joseph Y. Halpern. An analysis of first-order logics of probability. *Artificial Intelligence*, 46:311–350, 1990.
7. H. Kautz and B. Selman. Hard problems for simple default logics. *Artificial Intelligence*, 49:243–279, 1991.
8. B. Lewis. Approximating probability distributions to reduce storage requirements. *Information and Control*, 2:214–225, 1959.
9. N. Nilsson. Probabilistic logic. *Artificial Intelligence*, 28:71–87, 1986.
10. J. Paris and A. Vencovská. A note on the inevitability of maximum entropy. *International Journal of Approximate Reasoning*, 4:183–223, 1990.
11. Judea Pearl. *Probabilistic Reasoning in Intelligent Systems.* Morgan Kaufmann, 1988.
12. Y. Shoham. *Reasoning about Change.* MIT Press, 1988.

Legality in Inheritance Networks

Nacéra MADANI

LIPN - URA 1507 du CNRS. Institut Galilée. Université Paris Nord

Avenue J.B Clément 94340 Villetaneuse France

Abstract. In this paper we are interested in inheritance networks called "legal" inspired by [4], especially by the problem of maintaining network's legality during an update in order to operate on a possible ambiguity. The ambiguity known as "Nixon Diamond" [14] is resolved on inserting an exception link that inhibits the inference on one path. But as there exists many possibilities to add exception link we ask the user to settle the question. After an update the network's legality is maintened on taking out the "responsable ancestrally" cycles of the ambiguities. These cycles are called aac's (ancestor ambiguous cycles). The ambiguity's resolution at level of an aac entails the systematic resolution of ambiguous cycles having aac as ancestor. The number of aac allows to answer the question "what is the number of exception links to add to the network (or number of questions to ask to the user) in order to keep it in a legal state".

1 Introduction

Various definitions and formalizations of the notion inheritance in knowledge representation systems based on semantic networks have been developed in the artificial intelligence literature [4, 3, 15, 8, 9, 10, 6,7] and others.

Elaborate networks have multiple inheritance (i.e. a concept can have one or more immediate superiors), are heterogeneous (i.e. composed with strict and not strict links [1]) and acyclic. There are based on the principle of inserting an exception link that inhibits an inference whenever an ambiguity of the "Nixon Diamond" type arises [14]. But if there exists several possibilities we ask the user to insert such an exception link. We illustrate the intuitive notion of legality on an example described in [9].

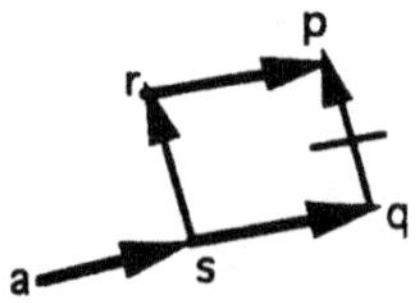

Fig.1. Inheritance network Γ

where a : Hermann,
s : native speakers of Pennsylvania Dutch,
q : native speakers of German,
r : persons born in Pennsylvania,
p : persons born in America.

[1]Links $\Rightarrow$, $\not\Leftrightarrow$ schematize respectively the inclusion relation and exclusion relation between two concepts (or class of objects).

Idem for $\rightarrow$, $\not\rightarrow$ that schematize respectively the defeasible relations IS-A and IS-NOT-A. An exception link is established on a not strict link a $\rightarrow$ b (with x) and means that x is an exception to the rule a $\rightarrow$ b(or a $\not\rightarrow$ b).

The interpretation of the network Γ is : "Hermann is a speaker of Pennsylvania Dutch, every speaker of Pennsylvania Dutch speaks German, native German speakers tend not to be born in America, speakers of Pennsylvania Dutch tend to be born in Pennsylvania and, everyone born in Pennsylvania is born in America".

An upward inheritance mechanism on Γ from the node "a" provides two interpretations (a, s, r, p), $(a, s, q, \neg p)$ that contradict each other about the country where Hermann is born. This ambiguity on birthplace of "a" is inherited from his ancestor class s. To remedy this type of situation, we propose to introduce explicitly an exception i.e. to introduce an exception link at the level of an ambiguous cycle $(s, r, p; s, q, \neg p)$ and from the ancestor (s) where ambiguity emerges. This cycle is called ancestor ambiguous cycle (aac). For getting rid of the ambiguity in Γ, we add to Γ an exception link from s to q ⟶ p

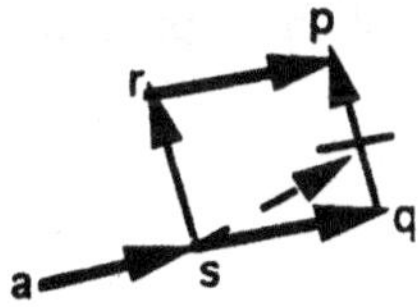

and only one interpretation is delivered, mentioning that Hermann is born in America.

Fig.2. First solution.

But we can envisage that for the special case of "a", the user wants to express that a is $\neg p$; so the systematic ambiguity resolution from the ancestor node s does not suit his intentions. In this case he/she must introduce :

- an exception link on exception,
- and an exception link on not strict positive link.

The resulting network is :

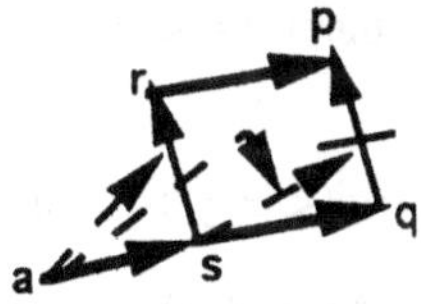

which enables to infer that Hermann is not born in America.

Fig.3. Second solution.

Networks obtained after raising the ambiguity and owning one interpretation are called "legal networks". The solution adopted in the case of several possibilities to add the exception link, is to tell the user for selecting an exception link to introduce at the network; solution according to user's intentions. This idea contradicts the attempts among which the one [13] is probably the most elaborated to guess what the user wants without to ask him/her.

Developed inheritance theories in A I literature are based on an automation of a credulous or skeptical reasoning [see synthesis developed in 6] in order to treat the ambiguity as in network Γ. In our approach we opt for a "partial" automation of reasoning i.e. in the case of an ambiguity an interaction with the user turns out sometimes necessary. On presenting the network Γ we have mentioned that an automatic introduction of an exception link is possible but there can exist several possibilities (figures 2 and 3) from which the interest to let the user making a decision.

Our objective is to get only one interpretation of a network i.e. the network must be legal. That's why after obtaining a legal network the legality is maintened during an update on decising for an incremental construction of a legal network and, on taking out the set of generated aac's after an insertion of a link.

The resolution of the ambiguity is realised as follows :

- automatic : an exception link introduction at the level of aac and,
- interactive with the user in the case where there exists several possibilities to add the exception link.

The continuation of this paper is organized as follows : section 2 introduces notation and some definitions. In section 3 we describe the construction of inheritance paths and, define the notion of valid paths and prohibited paths. The legality's maintenance is explored in section 4 with the notion of aac and extension of a legal inheritance network. We conclude in section 5 on the main results of our approach.

2 Notation and definitions

We note by :

- x, y, $z \ldots, x_1, x_2, \ldots$ concepts, $e, e_i \ldots$ exception links,
- σ a special path, Σ set of paths,
- Γ inheritance network, Φ set of strict, not strict and exception links.

Let X be a set (called set of concepts or of properties) whose elements are noted x, y, z, possibly indexed;
Let U be a subset of $X \times X$ (the links between concepts); to every element $u =< x, y >$ of U, we associate :

- its origin and its end in the usual way ($origin(< x, y >) = x$, $end(< x, y >) = y$)
- its polarity by a function $P : U \rightarrow \{0, 1\}$; a link $u \in U$ such that $P(u) = 1$ is called positive; otherwise it is called negative.

Let S be a subset of U (the strict links); its complementary is the set of not strict or defeasible links R;
Let $\mathcal{N}$ be a set of names; we associate a name to every not strict link, i.e. there exists an injection N from R into $\mathcal{N}$.
Every negative strict link possesses a symmetrical, i.e. $(\forall u)((u \in S \wedge P(u) = 0) \Rightarrow ((\exists u')(u' \in S \wedge P(u') = 0 \wedge origin(u') = end(u) \wedge end(u') = origin(u)))$
Let E be a subset of $X \times \mathcal{N}$ called the set of exception links; we extend the functions *origin* and *end* to E ($origin(< x, n >) = x$; $end(< x, n >) = n$);
we extend the injection N to E, i.e. all the exception links have names and these names are distinct from those of not strict links; we define a function type from E into $\{notstrict, exception\}$ such that $type(< x, n >) = notstrict$ iff n is the name of a not strict link and $type(< x, n >) = exception$ iff n is the name of an exception link.

Graphical representation :

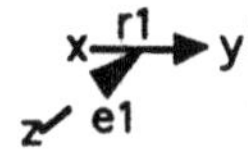

is defined by $< z, r_1 >$ where r_1 is the name of the not strict link $< x, y >$ and, e_1 is the exception link name, i.e. $N(< z, r_1 >) = e_1$.

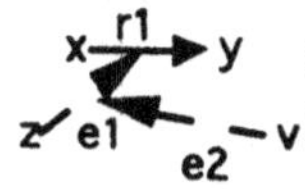

is defined by $< v, e_1 >$ where e_1 and e_2 are the names of two exception links, and $N(< v, e_1 >) = e_2$

In this study an inheritance network Γ is described by the set of nodes X, links U and exception links E and corresponds at a triplet (X, U, E) where (X, U) defining a graph and, $E \subset X \times \mathcal{N}$.

3 Construction of an inheritance path. Valid paths. Prohibited paths.

Like the approach of [8, 9, 10] the definition of a path presented here leads to an analysis of positive paths and negative paths characterizing the chains of reasoning. Each path (positive or negative) is considered as an argument for a statement : a positive path (negative path respectively) of origin x and end y corresponds a statement x are y (x are not y respectively). We construct paths as proceeding inductively and using the technical bottom-up (i.e. upward); but in the case of negative paths we can proceed on using bottom-up and top-down (i.e. downward) methods. We illustrate that on the example below.

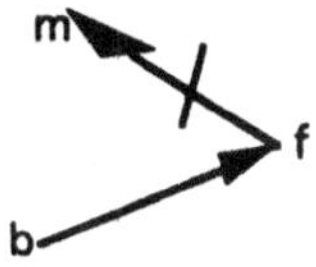

Fig.4. Γ1

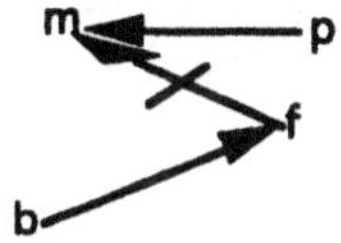

Fig.5. Γ2

Just to fix an interpretation, let b = birds, f = flying things, m = marine things and p = fishes. In Γ_1 the negative path is compound with a positive path b $\longrightarrow$ f and only at its end a direct negative link f $\not\longrightarrow$ m. This path represents an argument to "typically birds are not marine things". In Γ_2 the negative path b $\longrightarrow$ f $\not\longrightarrow$ m $\longleftarrow$ p is constructed on assembling a upward positive path b $\longrightarrow$ f, a direct negative link f $\not\longrightarrow$ m and a downward positive path m $\longleftarrow$ p. This path represents a "weak" argument to "typically birds are not fishes". This second construction of negative paths is admited in the case where "$p \cup m$ is little in the face of all universes, then we can suppose that typically $\neg m$ are $\neg p$ [11]" so in Γ_2 the universe of the discussion is that's of birds. In this paper we are restricted to negative paths constructed by the first approach.

3.1 Path or inheritance path.

The notion of path is defined in the same way as in graph theory : we call path a not empty sequence of elements $u_1, \ldots, u_m$ of U such that $(\forall i)(1 \leq i \leq m-1 \Rightarrow$ $end(u_i) = origin(u_{i+1}))$;
we extend the functions *origin* and *end* to the set Σ of paths : the origin of a path $u_1, \ldots, u_m$ is $origin(u_1)$, its end is $end(u_m)$.

A positive or negative path is said strict if all its elements are strict links; otherwise it is said not strict.

We extend the function polarity to a path $u_1, \ldots, u_m$ as follows :

- $P(u_1, \ldots, u_m) = 1$ iff $(\forall i)(1 \leq i \leq m \Rightarrow P(u_i) = 1)$
- $P(u_1, \ldots, u_m) = 0$ iff $(\forall i)(1 \leq i \leq m-1 \Rightarrow P(u_i) = 1) \wedge P(u_m) = 0$
- $P(u_1, \ldots, u_m)$ is not defined in the other cases.

3.2 Admissible Markage.

A markage M is a mapping from $X \cup \mathcal{N}$ into $\{0,1\}$. A markage M is called <u>admissible w.r.t an inheritance network Γ</u> iff
(i) $\forall x, y \in X \ (M(x) = 1 \wedge <x,y> \in S \wedge P(<x,y>) = 1) \Rightarrow M(y) = 1$
(ii) $\forall x, y \in X \ (M(x) = 1 \wedge <x,y> \in S \wedge P(<x,y>) = 0) \Rightarrow M(y) = 0$
(iii) $\forall u \in R \cup E \ ((P(u) = 1 \vee u \in E) \wedge M(origin(u)) = 1 \wedge M(N(u)) = 0) \Rightarrow M(end(u)) = 1$
(iv) $\forall u \in R \ (P(u) = 0 \wedge M(origin(u)) = 1 \wedge M(N(u)) = 0) \Rightarrow M(end(u)) = 0$

3.3 Valid paths.

A positive path $\sigma = u_1, \ldots, u_m$ is said <u>valid</u> iff
$\forall i \in [1,m] M(origin(u_i)) = 1 \wedge M(end(u_m)) = 1 \wedge M(N(u_i)) = 0$.
A negative path $\sigma = u_1, \ldots, u_m$ is said <u>valid</u> iff
$\forall i \in [1,m] M(origin(u_i)) = 1 \wedge M(end(u_m)) = 0 \wedge M(N(u_i)) = 0$.

3.4 Prohibited paths.

To base one's argument on the study [2], we introduce on examples the notion of "not natural" nets like :

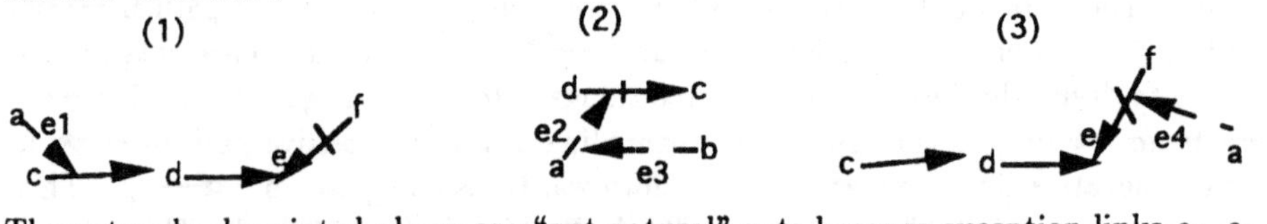

The networks descripted above are "not natural" nets because exception links e_1, e_2, e_3, e_4 have no influence on the paths (c,d,e,f), (d,c), (c,d,e,f). But the existence of such paths can lead to blocking up the inference.

Example: let Γ be an inheritance network :

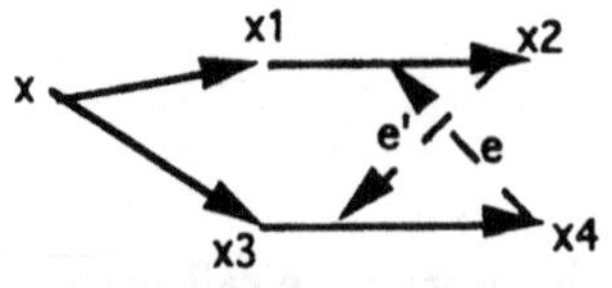

Fig.6. Prohibited paths.

In Γ we can obtain any conclusion about the concept x. This situation is produced by two prohibited paths.

A valid path $\sigma = u_1, \ldots, u_m$ is said prohibited iff $\exists \sigma' = u'_1, \ldots, u'_{m'}$ a valid path $\wedge (origin(\sigma) = origin(\sigma')) \wedge [\exists e, e', i, j, i', j', x, y, x', y'][(e \in E \wedge e' \in E) \wedge (1 \leq i, i' \leq m \wedge 1 \leq j, j' \leq m') \wedge ((x = origin(u_i) \vee x = end(u_i)) \wedge (end(e) = u'_j)) \wedge ((y = origin(u'_{j'}) \vee y = end(u'_{j'})) \wedge (end(e') = u_{i'}))]$

3.5 Assertion . Justified assertion.

The assertions are subsets of $X \times X$; this subset is divided into positive assertions noted *is-a*(x, x') and negative assertions noted *is-not-a*(x, x').
A positive assertion is called justified iff it is in form *is-a*(x, x') and there exists a not prohibited valid path σ such that $origin(\sigma) = x$, $end(\sigma) = x'$, and $P(\sigma) = 1$.
A negative assertion is called justified iff it is in form *is-not-a*(x, x') and there exists a not prohibited valid path σ such that $origin(\sigma) = x$, $end(\sigma) = x'$, and $P(\sigma) = 0$.

4 Legality's maintenance

In this section we describe the principles on which the legality's maintenance is based and, we determine the majoration of the number of aac's genereted during an update.

4.1 Cycle. Ambiguous cycle . aac.

We define a cycle as a not empty series of elements $u_1, \ldots, u_m$ of U such that $origin(u_1) = origin(u_m) \wedge (\forall i)(1 \leq i \leq m \Rightarrow (end(u_i) = origin(u_{i+1}) \vee end(u_i) = end(u_{i+1})) \vee origin(u_i) = end(u_{i+1}))$.
Example of an ambiguous cycle :

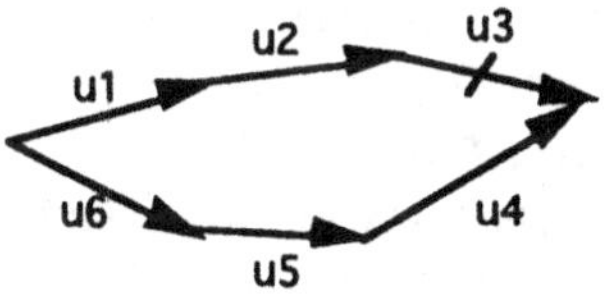

Two not prohibited valid paths $\sigma = u_1, \ldots, u_m$ and $\sigma' = u_{1'}, \ldots, u'_{m'}$ make an ambiguous cycle iff $P(\sigma) = 0$, $P(\sigma') = 1$, and the series $u_1, \ldots, u_m, u'_{m'}, \ldots, u'_1$ makes a cycle.

4.2 An ancestor ambiguous cycle aac.

Taking any inheritance network, a set of cycles can be found ambiguous and, it will be interesting to identify the cycles that are ancestrally responsible for all ambiguities. These cycles are called aac's. Our proposal is based on the fact that resolving ambiguity at an aac induces a systematical resolution of the ambiguity of cycles whose have that aac as ancestor. Since our approach consists to insert explicity an exception link for the resolution of the ambiguity and in the order to maintain the legality, we insert these links only at aac's. In order to realize this objective we partition the ambiguous cycles of an inheritance network on class identified by aac. Formally : we introduce at first

1. the notion of the end of an ambiguous cycle c as the common end of the two paths σ_c and σ'_c that constitute it : $end(c) = end(\sigma_c) = end(\sigma'_c)$

2. and a function F_{Names} delivering the set of links names composing the path σ: $F_{Names}(\sigma) = \{N(u_i)\}$.

Let be A_x the set of ambiguous cyles of an inheritance network having the same end node x :
$A_x = \{c_i = (\sigma_{c_i}, \sigma'_{c_i}) / \forall i P(\sigma_{c_i}) = 1 \wedge P(\sigma'_{c_i}) = 0 \wedge end(c_i) = x\}$
Let be c_j, c_k two subsets of A_x such that : $\sigma_{c_j} = \cap_{i \neq j} \sigma_{c_i}$ and $\sigma'_{c_k} = \cap_{i \neq k} \sigma'_{c_i}$
Two possibilities emerge to define the class of A_x according to the way to treat the ambiguity at level of an aac :

- (a) introduction of the exception link on the positive sequence of *aac*. In this case we set:
  $aac = (\sigma_{aac}, \sigma'_{aac}) = (\sigma_{c_j}, \sigma'_{c_j})$ and is defined as the upperbound of B in A_x i.e. $\forall c \in B\ c \prec caa$ iff $F_{Names}(\sigma_{aac}) \subset F_{Names}(\sigma_c)$
  with B a subset of A_x and $\prec$ a total order relation.

- (b) introduction of the exception link on the negative sequence of *aac*. In this case we set: $aac = (\sigma_{aac}, \sigma'_{aac}) = (\sigma_{c_k}, \sigma'_{c_k})$
  $\forall c \in B\ c \prec aac$ iff $F_{Names}(\sigma'_{aac}) \subset F_{Names}(\sigma'_c)$

Example 1 Let be Γ an inheritance network in which we decide to resolve the ambiguity using (a) :

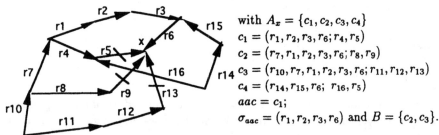

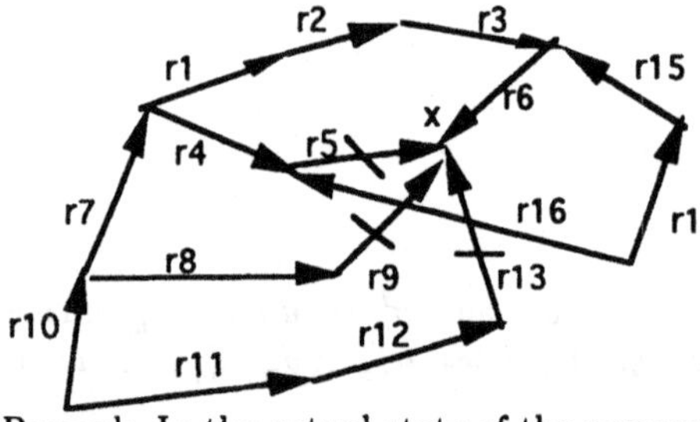

with $A_x = \{c_1, c_2, c_3, c_4\}$
$c_1 = (r_1, r_2, r_3, r_6; r_4, r_5)$
$c_2 = (r_7, r_1, r_2, r_3, r_6; r_8, r_9)$
$c_3 = (r_{10}, r_7, r_1, r_2, r_3, r_6; r_{11}, r_{12}, r_{13})$
$c_4 = (r_{14}, r_{15}, r_6;\ r_{16}, r_5)$
$aac = c_1;$
$\sigma_{aac} = (r_1, r_2, r_3, r_6)$ and $B = \{c_2, c_3\}$.

Remark. In the actual state of the progress of our study, there comes back to the user to establish criterions of preference of (a) and (b).

Proposition 1 An inheritance network Γ contains an ambiguous cycle iff it contains an aac.

4.3 Definition of a legal network. Extension.

An inheritance network Γ is called **legal** iff Γ doesn't contain an ambiguous cycle.
Extension of a legal network: An extension of an legal network Γ related to a concept x, is equal to the set of all "inferable" links from the set of strict, not strict and exception links Γ_x (Γ_x is the set of all paths having the origin of sequence equal to x) i.e. the set of assertions justified by all not prohibited valid paths of Γ_x.

4.4 Estimation of the number of ancestor ambiguous cycles.

Our purpose now is to research the number of ambiguous cycles from that we send the exception links in order to respect the network's legality. Find this number reverts to find the number of questions to ask the user in order to keep the network in a legal state. For this we apply results of graph theory at our inheritance network. Not knowing a priori the orientation of links, we assimilate the inheritance network Γ at a multigraph G with :

- n : number of nodes (concepts),
- m : number of lines (strict and not strict links),
- p : number of connected components (in our network p is equal to 1, that corresponds to a hierarchy).

Let be $\rho(G) = n - p$ and $\eta(G) = m - \rho(G) = m - n + 1$: cyclomatic number of the multigraph G. Consider the theorems 1 and 2 of [1] :

Theorem 1 The cyclomatic number $\eta(G)$ of a multigraph G is equal to the maximal number of independent cycles.

Theorem 2 Let be G a multigraph and G' a multigraph obtained from G on connecting by a new line the nodes a and b of G;
- if a and b are confounded (inexistant case in our inheritance network) or joined by a chain of G , we have : (1) $\rho(G') = \rho(G)$ $\quad \eta(G') = \eta(G) + 1$
in the contrary case, we have (2) $\rho(G') = \rho(G) + 1$ $\quad \eta(G') = \eta(G)$.

Let be Γ' obtained from the legal network Γ on adding to it a link. Let be nc the number of cycles in Γ with :
- nca the number of ambiguous cycles anteriorly,
- ncn the number of not ambiguous cycles.
The case (2) of theorem 2 is without influence in our study. Consider the case (1) i.e. case where the number of cycles increases by 1.

Case 1:

In Γ	+1 link	InΓ'
$nca \neq 0$		$ncn' = nca$
$ncn \neq 0$		$ncn' = ncn + 1$

The new cycle belongs to not ambiguous cycles of Γ'. No question to ask the user.

Case 2:

In Γ	+1 link	In Γ'
$nca \neq 0$		$nca' = nca + 1$
$ncn \neq 0$		$ncn' = ncn$

The new cycle belongs to ambiguous
cycles of Γ'. Then a new *aac* appears : one question to ask the user.

Case 3:

In Γ	+1 link	In Γ'
$nca \neq 0$		$nca' = nca + 1$
$ncn = 0$		$ncn' = 0$

Like case 2, one question to ask the user.

Case 4:

In Γ	+1 link	In Γ′
$nca = 0$		$nca' = nca + 1$
$ncn \neq 0$		$ncn' = 0$ not ambiguous cycle

In this case we ask $(ncn + 1)$ questions the user. We establish two propositions :

Proposition 2 If in a multigraph G (connected) we have n cycles in each one one line not belongs to the others then the n cycles are linearly independent.

Proposition 3 The ambiguous cycles belong to the set of linearly independent cycles of the net.

The most unfavourable case corresponds to the network configuration below :

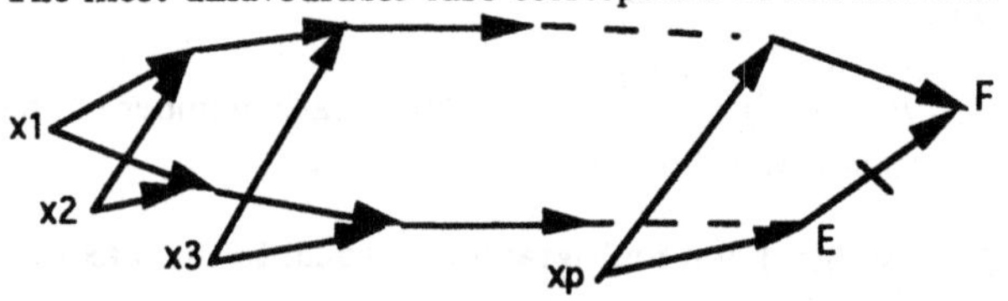

where x_i "node of ambiguity" i.e. node from which we have a valid positive path and an other valid negative path to F. Or in each cycle $(x_i, \ldots, F)$ we have two distinct lines. On applying the proposition 2, the cycles corresponding to p ambiguous cycles are linearly independent. And applying the Berge's theorem "the number of linearly independent cycles in a connected multigraph is equal to the cyclomatic number i.e. $m - n + 1$"; we obtain the theorem

Theorem 3 (1) the number of questions to ask an user is equal to the number of *aac's*.
(2) The number of *aac's* is bounded by $m - n + 1$ where

- m is the number of links in the network and n is the number of concepts in the network.

5 Conclusion

In this study, we have opted for a partial automation of reasoning i.e. in the case of an ambiguity an interaction with the user sometimes turns out to be essential.
As mentionned in the previous example, an automatic introduction of an exception link is possible, but there can be several possibilities; that is why it is useful to allow the user decide by himself. The inheritance mechanism applied to a legal network delivers always one extension using a quite simple polynomial algorithm $O(n^3)$. In return the system of legatily maintenance (based on cycles research) is NP-complete. But the fact that the number of consultations is generally highly elevated in comparison with the number of modifications is in favour of this approch. We have studied the problem to add a link in a network, but the converse operation that consists of deleting a link in a legal network is relatively simple and doesn't raise any conflit problem.

Adopting default logic [5] for a semantic interpretation of legal networks is proved to be correct and coherent with expected results [12].
The interest of our study is the possibility to use the legality maintenance system in a validation of a knowledge base, in which we admit some inconsistencies during its creation. This system is able to detect and follow incoherences during the evolution of a knowledge base.

References

1. C. Berge: Graphes et hypergraphes. Dunod. Paris, 1970.
2. P. Coupey: Etude d'un réseau sémantique avec gestion des exceptions. Interprétation logique et implantation informatique. Thèse de Docteur d'Université, LIPN, Université Paris Nord, 1989.
3. D.W. Etherington, R. Reiter: On inheritance hierarchies with exceptions. Proceedings of AAAI 83, Washington, DC 1983, pp 104-108.
4. S.E. Fahlman, D.S. Touretzky, W.V. Roggen: Cancellation in a parallel semantic network. Proceedings of IJCAI, 24-28 August 81, pp 257-263.
5. C. Froidevaux, D. Kayser: Inheritance in semantic networks and in default logic. In: P. Smets et al. (eds), Non standard logics for automated reasoning, Academic Press, New York, 1988.
6. E. Grégoire: Logiques non monotones. Programmes logiques stratifiés et théories sceptiques de l'héritage. Thèse de doctorat en sciences appliquées. Université Catholique de Louvain, Juin 1989.
7. E. Grégoire: Skeptical inheritance can be more expressive. Proc. 9th ECAI, August 90, Stockholm.
8. J.F. Horty, R.H. Thomason, D.S. Touretzky: A skeptical theory of inheritance in non monotonic semantic networks. Proceedings of AAAI 87, pp 358-363.
9. J.F. Horty, R.H. Thomason: Mixing strict and defeasible inheritance. Proceedings of AAAI 88, volume 2, pp 427-432.
10. J.F. Horty, R.H. Thomason, D.S. Touretzky: A skeptical theory of inheritance in non monotonic semantic networks. A.I., volume 42, number 2-3, March 90, pp 311-348.
11. Daniel Kayser: Cours de DEA. LIPN. Université Paris 13. Villetaneuse.
12. Nacéra Madani: Héritage dans les réseaux légaux. paper submitted to 1e J.F.J.C, Rennes 1992.
13. Y. Moinard: Donner la préférence au défaut le plus spécifique. Actes 6ème congrés AFCET Reconnaissance des Formes et Intelligence Artificielle, Antibes, 1987, pp 1123-1132.
14. R. Reiter, G. Criscuolo : On interacting defaults. Proc. IJCAI 81, pp 270-276.
15. D.S. Touretzky, J.F. Horty, R.H. Thomason: A clash of intuitions : the current state of non monotonic multiple inheritance systems. Proceedings of AAAI 87, pp 476-482.

A Note on Information Systems Associated to Termal Algebras

Miquel Monserrat*, Francesc Rosselló*† and Joan Torrens*

Dept. Ciències Matemàtiques i Informàtica, Universitat de les Illes Balears, 07071–Palma de Mallorca (Spain)

Abstract. Termal algebras have been proposed by W. Bartol as general algebraic models for systems of inference rules over incomplete data. As a step towards such interpretation, in this note we associate two different information systems (in the sense of D. Scott) to a termal algebra, in such a way that the elements of the domains generated by them turn out to have clear counterparts in the knowledge systems setting.

1 Introduction

Roughly speaking, a *termal algebra* is a partial algebra whose operations are not induced by fundamental operation symbols but by terms (compositions of fundamental operations). In particular, and due to the aforesaid partiality, the value of a term on a given tuple of arguments may be defined even though not all its subterms are defined on it. The only restriction one imposes is that if two compositions of terms (i. e., terms of terms) are defined for a given argument, and they represent the same sequence of fundamental operations, then they have to yield the same result.

In the introduction of [Ba1], Bartol explains that termal algebras could be considered as algebraic models for systems of inference rules on incomplete data: thinking of the fundamental operations as elementary deductions, termal operations would correspond to composite deductions which might yield a result although not all intermediate steps were known. This situation is frequent in common reasoning, where conclusions are usually "guessed", instead of drawn by means of a well constructed sequences of formal deductions. Notice that if two such composite deductions correspond to the same sequence of primary deductions, then they should yield the same conclusion when applied to the same instances. If we translate this observation into the algebraic language, we obtain the aforementioned restriction imposed to term operations on termal algebras.

Under such interpretation, an embedding of termal algebras could be understood as an extension of the available knowledge, and in particular the embedding of a termal algebra into a total one could be understood as a completion of the partial knowledge represented by the termal algebra. So, a termal algebra which can be embbeded into a total one (a *consistent termal algebra*) corresponds to a consistent system of deduction rules, i. e., a set of rules which form a part of some complete set of knowledge.

* Partially supported by by the DGCIyT grant PB91-0334

† Partially supported also by the UPC grant PR9014

There are also other special features of such systems of deduction rules which have clear counterparts in the termal algebras setting: for instance, the possibility of finding a complete set of knowledge containing the original system and satisfying some given conditions (which corresponds to the K*–consistency*, for K a class of total algebras); the closedness under composition (which corresponds to the *term–closedness* of the termal algebra); or the property that if some rule is valid in all complete sets of knowledge containing the system of rules and satisfying some properties, then it has to belong to this system (notion which corresponds to the K*–closedness* of the termal algebra, with K as before).

As a step towards such interpretation of a termal algebra as a model for knowledge, Bartol associates in [Ba2] to a termal algebra an information system in the sense of [Sco], relative to a variety K of total algebras. Let us recall that D. Scott's theory of information systems represents a mathematical logic approach to the theory of domains for denotational semantics. In particular, an information system "generates" such a domain.

In this paper, we propose two new different information systems associated to a termal algebra $\mathbf{A}$ and relative to a variety K, in such a way that the elements of the domain associated to one of them are exactly the K–closed, K–consistent inner extensions of $\mathbf{A}$, and the elements of the domain associated to the other one are exactly the term–closed K–consistent inner extensions of $\mathbf{A}$. (In [Ba2], Bartol does not give a characterization of the elements of the domain associated to the information system introduced therein.)

It is our behalf that such an abundance of relevant information systems associated to a termal algebra reinforces Bartol's original intuition on the relation between termal algebras and inference systems.

2 Preliminaries

We shall assume that the reader knows the basic vocabulary of partial algebras (see for instance [Bur] §§1–5). In this section we gather the definitions and properties concerning termal algebras and Scott's information systems which shall be used in this paper. Further information on both concepts can be found in [BR] and [Sco], respectively.

2.1 Termal Algebras

Let $\mathcal{F} = (F, \eta)$ be a type of algebras, i. e. let F be a set of operation symbols and $\eta: F \to \mathbb{N}$ an arity function from F into the set $\mathbb{N}$ of all non–negative integers. Let $\mathbf{T}_{\mathcal{F}}(\mathcal{X})$ be the set of all $\mathcal{F}$–terms over a fixed (countably infinite) set of variables $\mathcal{X} = \{x_i \mid i \in \mathbb{N} - \{0\}\}$.

Let $\equiv$ denote the equivalence relation on $\mathbf{T}_{\mathcal{F}}(\mathcal{X})$ defined by

> $\mathbf{t}_1 \equiv \mathbf{t}_2$ iff a permutation $\pi: \mathcal{X} \to \mathcal{X}$ exists such that $\mathbf{t}_2 = \bar{\pi}(\mathbf{t}_1)$ (where $\bar{\pi}: \mathbf{T}_{\mathcal{F}}(\mathcal{X}) \to \mathbf{T}_{\mathcal{F}}(\mathcal{X})$ denotes the unique homomorphic extension of π).

Let $\mathbf{T}_{\mathcal{F}}$ denote the quotient $\mathbf{T}_{\mathcal{F}}(\mathcal{X})/{\equiv}$. Any equivalence class $\mathbf{t} \in \mathbf{T}_{\mathcal{F}}$ represents an ***abstract*** construction of a term as a composition of operations, independent of the names of the variables. Every $\mathbf{t} \in \mathbf{T}_{\mathcal{F}}$ has a first representative w. r. t. the lexicographic order on it induced by the subscripts order on $\mathcal{X}$. We shall call it the *canonical representative of* $\mathbf{t}$.

Let $\eta^*: \mathbf{T}_{\mathcal{F}} \to \mathbb{N}$ be the function which assigns to each $\mathbf{t} \in \mathbf{T}_{\mathcal{F}}$ the number of different explicit variables of any representative element of it. We shall understand the function η^* as an arity function on $\mathbf{T}_{\mathcal{F}}$, and we shall consider $(\mathbf{T}_{\mathcal{F}}, \eta^*)$ as a new type of algebras. Let $\mathbf{T}_{\mathbf{T}_{\mathcal{F}}}(\mathcal{X})$ (which for simplicity shall be denoted henceforth $\mathbf{T}_{\mathbf{T}}(\mathcal{X})$) be the set of all terms over $\mathcal{X}$ with respect to this new type of algebras.

Every $\mathbf{t} \in \mathbf{T}_{\mathcal{F}}$ will induce a partial function

$$\mathbf{t}^{\mathbf{A}}: A^{\eta^*(\mathbf{t})} \to A$$

on any partial algebra $\mathbf{A} = (A, (f)_{f \in F})$ of type $\mathcal{F}$. Specifically, the term function associated to the canonical representative of $\mathbf{t}$.

So, to any partial algebra $\mathbf{A} = (A, (f^{\mathbf{A}})_{f \in F})$ of type $\mathcal{F}$ we can associate a partial algebra $\overline{\mathbf{A}} = (A, (\mathbf{t}^{\mathbf{A}})_{\mathbf{t} \in \mathbf{T}_{\mathcal{F}}})$ of type $\mathbf{T}_{\mathcal{F}}$ such that $\mathbf{A}$ is the $\mathcal{F}$-reduct of $\overline{\mathbf{A}}$.

Every term $\mathbf{t} \in \mathbf{T}_{\mathbf{T}}(\mathcal{X})$ has a unique decomposition into a term $\mathbf{t}^* \in \mathbf{T}_{\mathcal{F}}(\mathcal{X})$ which can be defined recurrently as follows:

- if $\mathbf{t} = x_i \in \mathcal{X}$ then $\mathbf{t}^* = x_i$
- if $\mathbf{t} = \mathbf{p}(\mathbf{t}_1, \ldots, \mathbf{t}_n)$, where $\mathbf{p} \in \mathbf{T}_{\mathcal{F}}$ with $\eta^*(\mathbf{p}) = n$, and $\mathbf{t}_1, \ldots, \mathbf{t}_n \in \mathbf{T}_{\mathbf{T}}(\mathcal{X})$ are terms whose decompositions $\mathbf{t}_1^*, \ldots, \mathbf{t}_n^* \in \mathbf{T}_{\mathcal{F}}(\mathcal{X})$ are already defined, then

$$\mathbf{t}^* = \mathbf{p}^{\mathbf{T}_{\mathcal{F}}(\mathcal{X})}(\mathbf{t}_1^*, \ldots, \mathbf{t}_n^*) \in \mathbf{T}_{\mathcal{F}}(\mathcal{X})$$

  where $\mathbf{p}^{\mathbf{T}_{\mathcal{F}}(\mathcal{X})}$ denotes the function $\mathbf{T}_{\mathcal{F}}(\mathcal{X})^n \to \mathbf{T}_{\mathcal{F}}(\mathcal{X})$ associated to $\mathbf{p}$.

A partial algebra $\mathbf{A} = (A, (\mathbf{t}^{\mathbf{A}})_{\mathbf{t} \in \mathbf{T}_{\mathcal{F}}})$ of type $(\mathbf{T}_{\mathcal{F}}, \eta^*)$ is a *termal algebra of type* $\mathcal{F}$ iff

$$\mathbf{A} \models \mathbf{t}_1 \overset{w}{\approx} \mathbf{t}_2, \qquad \forall\, \mathbf{t}_1, \mathbf{t}_2 \in \mathbf{T}_{\mathbf{T}}(\mathcal{X}) \text{ such that } \mathbf{t}_1^* = \mathbf{t}_2^*.$$

I. e., iff for every pair $\mathbf{t}_1, \mathbf{t}_2 \in \mathbf{T}_{\mathbf{T}}(\mathcal{X})$ with $\mathbf{t}_1^* = \mathbf{t}_2^*$ and for every $\underline{a} \in \operatorname{dom} \mathbf{t}_1^{\mathbf{A}} \cap \operatorname{dom} \mathbf{t}_2^{\mathbf{A}}$ it turns out that $\mathbf{t}_1^{\mathbf{A}}(\underline{a}) = \mathbf{t}_2^{\mathbf{A}}(\underline{a})$.

Observe that if $\mathbf{A}$ is a partial algebra of type $\mathcal{F}$ then the algebra $\overline{\mathbf{A}}$ of type $\mathbf{T}_{\mathcal{F}}$ associated to it, is a termal algebra. Such a termal algebra shall be called the *canonical termal algebra over* $\mathbf{A}$. It is not difficult to prove that a total termal algebra of type $\mathcal{F}$ is always the canonical termal algebra over its $\mathcal{F}$-reduct. In the sequel, we shall identify these two kinds of algebras.

We shall denote by $\mathcal{T}_{\mathcal{F}}$ the class of all termal algebras of type $\mathcal{F}$. Since $\mathcal{T}_{\mathcal{F}}$ is a class of partial algebras defined by weak equations, it turns out that it is closed under weak subalgebras, direct products and direct limits.

Remark. If K is a variety of total algebras of type $\mathcal{F}$, then the class formed of all canonical termal algebras over algebras in K is again a variety of total algebras (now of type $\mathbf{T}_{\mathcal{F}}$). We shall identify in the sequel both kinds of varieties, usually without any further comment.

Now, let $\mathbf{A}$ be a termal algebra of type $\mathcal{F}$ and K a variety of total algebras of type $\mathcal{F}$. The algebra $\mathbf{A}$ is K-*consistent* iff there exists an embedding of $\mathbf{A}$ into an algebra of K (by which we mean that there exists an embedding of $\mathbf{A}$ into the canonical termal algebra over an algebra of K). In the sequel we shall abbreviate K-consistent termal algebra by K-*c.t.a.*

Notice that the classs CT_K of all K-c.t.a.'s, with K a variety of total algebras, is closed under weak subalgebras.

The following result is a special case of a theorem of J. Schmidt (cf. [Sch]):

Theorem 1. *Let K be a variety of total algebras and let $\mathbf{A}$ be a K-c.t.a. Then there exists an algebra $\mathbf{B} \in K$ and an embedding $h: \mathbf{A} \to \mathbf{B}$ verifying the following universal property:*

> *for any $\mathbf{C} \in K$ and any homomorphism $g: \mathbf{A} \to \mathbf{C}$ there exists a unique homomorphism $\tilde{g}: \mathbf{B} \to \mathbf{C}$ such that $g = \tilde{g} \circ h$.*

Such a monomorphism $h: \mathbf{A} \to \mathbf{B}$ is unique up to isomorphism and will be called a *K-monoreflection* of $\mathbf{A}$.

Such K-monoreflections behave well under direct limits (see [BR] Th. 5'):

Proposition 2. *Let K be a variety of total algebras of a fixed type $\mathcal{F}$. Let $(\mathbf{A}_i)_{i\in I}$ be a direct system of K-c.t.a.'s, with direct limit $\mathbf{A}$. For every $i \in I$ let $h_i: \mathbf{A}_i \to \mathbf{B}_i$ be a K-monoreflection of $\mathbf{A}_i$. Then one can give to $(\mathbf{B}_i)_{i\in I}$ a direct system structure in such a way that, if $\mathbf{B} \in K$ denotes their direct limit, then*

a) The family of embeddings $(h_i)_{i\in I}$ induces an embedding $h: \mathbf{A} \to \mathbf{B}$.

b) Such $h: \mathbf{A} \to \mathbf{B}$ is a K-monoreflection of $\mathbf{A}$.

Let K be a variety of total algebras of type $\mathcal{F}$, let $\mathbf{A}$ be a K-c.t.a. with universe A, and let $h: \mathbf{A} \longrightarrow \mathbf{B}$ be a K-monoreflection of $\mathbf{A}$. We shall say that $\mathbf{A}$ is *K-closed* iff for every $\mathbf{t} \in \mathbf{T}_{\mathcal{F}}$, $\underline{a} \in A^{\eta^*(\mathbf{t})}$ and $a \in A$

$$\mathbf{t}^{\mathbf{B}}(h(\underline{a})) = h(a) \text{ implies } \underline{a} \in \operatorname{dom} \mathbf{t}^{\mathbf{A}} \text{ and } \mathbf{t}^{\mathbf{A}}(\underline{a}) = a.$$

I. e., iff the monomorphism h is full.

It is not difficult to check, using the universal property of K-monoreflections, that this definition is equivalent to: if $\mathbf{A}$ is a K-c.t.a., then $\mathbf{A}$ is K-closed iff

> for any $\mathbf{t} \in \mathbf{T}_{\mathcal{F}}$, $\underline{a} \in A^{\eta^*(\mathbf{t})}$ and $a \in A$, $\mathbf{t}^{\mathbf{C}}(g(\underline{a})) = g(a)$ for every embedding $g : \mathbf{A} \to \mathbf{C}$ of $\mathbf{A}$ into an algebra $\mathbf{C} \in K$ iff $\mathbf{t}^{\mathbf{A}}(\underline{a}) = a$

which is Definition 7 in [Ba2].

In order to simplify our notations, we shall identify in the sequel the elements of $\mathbf{A}$ with their images under any embedding $g: \mathbf{A} \to \mathbf{A}'$.

We shall say that a termal algebra $\mathbf{A}$ of type $\mathcal{F}$ is *term-closed* iff the following condition holds:

> For any $\mathbf{t} \in \mathbf{T}_{\mathcal{F}}$, if $\tilde{\mathbf{t}} = \tilde{\mathbf{t}}(x_1, \ldots, x_{\eta^*(\mathbf{t})}) \in \mathbf{T}_{\mathbf{T}}(\mathcal{X})$ is such that the class in $\mathbf{T}_{\mathcal{F}}$ of $\tilde{\mathbf{t}}^* \in \mathbf{T}_{\mathcal{F}}(\mathcal{X})$ is $\mathbf{t}$, and $\tilde{\mathbf{t}}^*$ is the canonical representative of $\mathbf{t}$, then for every $\underline{a} \in A^{\eta^*(\mathbf{t})}$ such that $\underline{a} \in \operatorname{dom} \tilde{\mathbf{t}}^{\mathbf{A}}$, it turns out that $\underline{a} \in \operatorname{dom} \mathbf{t}^{\mathbf{A}}$ and $\mathbf{t}^{\mathbf{A}}(\underline{a}) = \tilde{\mathbf{t}}^{\mathbf{A}}(\underline{a})$.

It turns out that

Proposition 3. *Let K be a variety of total algebras of type $\mathcal{F}$ and let $\mathbf{A}$ be a K-closed termal algebra. Then $\mathbf{A}$ is term-closed.*

Proof. Let $\mathbf{A} = (A, (\mathrm{t}^{\mathbf{A}})_{\mathrm{t} \in \mathbf{T}_{\mathcal{F}}})$ and $\mathrm{t} \in \mathbf{T}_{\mathcal{F}}$. Let $\tilde{\mathrm{t}} = \tilde{\mathrm{t}}(x_1, \ldots, x_{\eta^*(\mathrm{t})}) \in \mathbf{T}_{\mathbf{T}}(\mathcal{X})$ be such that $\tilde{\mathrm{t}}^*$ is the canonical representative of t. Let $\underline{a} = (a_1, \ldots, a_{\eta^*(\mathrm{t})}) \in \operatorname{dom} \tilde{\mathrm{t}}^{\mathbf{A}}$ and $\tilde{\mathrm{t}}^{\mathbf{A}}(\underline{a}) = a \in A$. In this case, if $h \colon \mathbf{A} \longrightarrow \mathbf{B}$ is a K-monoreflection of $\mathbf{A}$ then $\tilde{\mathrm{t}}^{\mathbf{B}}(\underline{a}) = a$.

Now, notice that the decomposition in $\mathbf{T}_{\mathcal{F}}(\mathcal{X})$ of $\mathrm{t} \in \mathbf{T}_{\mathcal{F}}$, considered as a term in $\mathbf{T}_{\mathbf{T}}(\mathcal{X})$ with variables $x_1, \ldots, x_{\eta^*(\mathrm{t})}$, is the canonical representative of it in our case, $\tilde{\mathrm{t}}^*$. Therefore, t and $\tilde{\mathrm{t}}$ have the same decomposition. Since $\mathbf{B}$ is a total termal algebra, it turns out that

$$\mathrm{t}^{\mathbf{B}}(\underline{a}) = \tilde{\mathrm{t}}^{\mathbf{B}}(\underline{a}) = a$$

Finally, since $\mathbf{A}$ is K-closed, it implies that $\mathrm{t}^{\mathbf{A}}(\underline{a}) = a$. □

2.2 Information Systems

Let us recall now some definitions from Scott's paper [Sco].

An *information system* is a structure

$$I = (\mathcal{D}, \Delta, Cons, \vdash)$$

where $\mathcal{D}$ is a set (the *set of propositions*), Δ is a distinguished element of $\mathcal{D}$ (the *least informative proposition*), *Cons* is a subset of $\mathcal{P}_\omega(\mathcal{D})$ (the set of *consistent finite sets of propositions*) and $\vdash \subseteq Cons \times \mathcal{D}$ is a binary relation between finite consistent sets and propositions (the *entailment relation*), satisfying the following conditions

(i) If $u \in Cons$ and $v \subseteq u$ then $v \in Cons$

(ii) If $X \in \mathcal{D}$ then $\{X\} \in Cons$

(iii) If $u \vdash X$ then $u \cup \{X\} \in Cons$

(iv) For every $u \in Cons$, $u \vdash \Delta$

(v) If $u \in Cons$ and $X \in u$ then $u \vdash X$

(vi) If $u \vdash X$ and $v \vdash Y$ for every $Y \in u$ then $v \vdash X$.

Given an information system $I = (\mathcal{D}, \Delta, Cons, \vdash)$,

a) a subset x of $\mathcal{D}$ is *deductively consistent* for I iff $\mathcal{P}_\omega(x) \subseteq Cons$ (i. e., if all its finite subsets are consistent);

b) a subset x of $\mathcal{D}$ is *deductively closed* for I iff for any $u \in \mathcal{P}_\omega(x)$ and $X \in \mathcal{D}$

$$u \vdash X \Longrightarrow X \in x;$$

c) a subset x of $\mathcal{D}$ is an *element* of I iff it is deductively consistent and closed. The set $|I|$ of all the elements of I is called its *domain*.

We may think of the objects in $\mathcal{D}$ as propositions about the elements of the domain. In this way, the sets belonging to *Cons* can be interpreted as finite sets of propositions that can be true of an element at the same time, and the entailment relation can be translated as

> $u \vdash X$ iff whenever all the propositions in u are true of an element of the domain, then X is also true of that element.

Finally, coming back to the elements, we can understand that two elements are different iff there is some proposition in $\mathcal{D}$ which is true of one of them and false of the other one. In this way, we can identify an element x with the set of propositions which are true of it, i. e.

$$x = \{X \in \mathcal{D} \mid X \text{ is true of } x\},$$

which gives an interpretation of the elements of the domain as sets of propositions.

3 An Information System Corresponding to K–Closedness

Throughout this section, K will be a variety of total algebras of some fixed type $\mathcal{F} = (F, \eta)$ and $\mathbf{A} = (A, (\mathbf{t}^{\mathbf{A}})_{\mathbf{t} \in \mathbf{T}_{\mathcal{F}}})$ will be a K–c.t.a. We shall identify K with the variety of all canonical termal algebras over algebras in it.

Set

$$\widetilde{\mathcal{D}}_{\mathbf{A},K} = \{(\mathbf{t}, \underline{a}, a) \mid \mathbf{t} \in \mathbf{T}_{\mathcal{F}},\ \underline{a} \in A^{\eta^*(\mathbf{t})} - \operatorname{dom} \mathbf{t}^{\mathbf{A}},\ a \in A\} \cup \{\emptyset\}$$

For every $x \subseteq \widetilde{\mathcal{D}}_{\mathbf{A},K}$ and every $\mathbf{t} \in \mathbf{T}_{\mathcal{F}}$ let

$$\mathbf{t}^x = \mathbf{t}^{\mathbf{A}} \cup \{(\underline{a}, a) \in A^{\eta^*(\mathbf{t})} \times A \mid (\mathbf{t}, \underline{a}, a) \in x\}$$

and consider the relational system

$$\mathbf{A}^x = (A, (\mathbf{t}^x)_{\mathbf{t} \in \mathbf{T}_{\mathcal{F}}})$$

We shall also write $\mathbf{A}^{\{\emptyset\}} = \mathbf{A}$.

Notice that, since x can be any subset of $\widetilde{\mathcal{D}}_{\mathbf{A},K}$, $\mathbf{A}^x$ need not be an algebra, and even when it is an algebra, it need not be termal.

Set

$$\mathcal{D}_{\mathbf{A},K} = \{X \in \widetilde{\mathcal{D}}_{\mathbf{A},K} \mid \mathbf{A}^{\{X\}} \text{ is a } K\text{–c.t.a.}\}$$
$$Cons_{\mathbf{A},K} = \{u \in \mathcal{P}_\omega(\mathcal{D}_{\mathbf{A},K}) \mid \mathbf{A}^u \text{ is a } K\text{–c.t.a.}\}$$

and $\Delta_{\mathbf{A},K} = \emptyset$ (notice that $\mathbf{A}^{\{\emptyset\}}$ $(= \mathbf{A})$ is a K–c.t.a., so $\emptyset \in \mathcal{D}_{\mathbf{A},K}$).

Finally, take as entailment relation $\vdash_{\mathbf{A},K}$ on $Cons_{\mathbf{A},K} \times \mathcal{D}_{\mathbf{A},K}$

> $u \vdash_{\mathbf{A},K} X$ iff either $X = \emptyset$ or $X = (\mathbf{t}, \underline{a}, a)$ and if $h_u \colon \mathbf{A}^u \to \mathbf{B}^u$ is a K–monoreflection of $\mathbf{A}^u$ then $\mathbf{t}^{\mathbf{B}^u}(\underline{a}) = a$.

Since all K–monoreflections of $\mathbf{A}$ are isomorphic (over $\mathbf{A}$), if $h'_u \colon \mathbf{A}^u \to \mathbf{B}'^u$ is any other K–monoreflection of $\mathbf{A}$ then $\mathbf{t}^{\mathbf{B}^u}(\underline{a}) = a \in A$ iff $\mathbf{t}^{\mathbf{B}'^u}(\underline{a}) = a \in A$. So, the definition of $\vdash_{\mathbf{A},K}$ is independent of the K–monoreflection.

Proposition 4. *$I_{\mathbf{A},K} = (\mathcal{D}_{\mathbf{A},K}, \Delta_{\mathbf{A},K}, Cons_{\mathbf{A},K}, \vdash_{\mathbf{A},K})$ is an information system.*

Proof. The proof that $I_{\mathbf{A},K}$ satisfies properties (i)–(v) in the definition of an information system is straightforward, and it is left to the reader. We prove here that it satisfies property (vi).

Indeed, assume that $u \vdash_{\mathbf{A},K} X$ and that $v \vdash_{\mathbf{A},K} Y$, for every $Y \in u$. If $X = \emptyset$, then v always entails it. So let us suppose that $X = (\mathbf{t}, \underline{a}, a)$. Let

$$h_u\colon \mathbf{A}^u \to \mathbf{B}^u \quad \text{and} \quad h_v\colon \mathbf{A}^v \to \mathbf{B}^v$$

be K–monoreflections of $\mathbf{A}^u$ and $\mathbf{A}^v$ respectively. Since for every $(\mathbf{p}, \underline{a}', a') \in u$ we have $\mathbf{p}^{\mathbf{B}^v}(\underline{a}') = a'$, and $\mathbf{A}$ is a weak subalgebra of $\mathbf{A}^v$, which is embedded into $\mathbf{B}^v$, there exists a monomorphism

$$f\colon \mathbf{A}^u \to \mathbf{B}^v$$

compatible with the inclusion of A into the carrier set of $\mathbf{B}^v$ given by h_v. By the universal property of K–monoreflections, there exists a morphism h from $\mathbf{B}^u$ to $\mathbf{B}^v$ such that $f = h \circ h_u$.

Now, $u \vdash_{\mathbf{A},K} (\mathbf{t}, \underline{a}, a)$ implies that $\mathbf{t}^{\mathbf{B}^u}(\underline{a}) = a$ and, because of the existence of h, $\mathbf{t}^{\mathbf{B}^v}(\underline{a}) = a$. Therefore, $v \vdash_{\mathbf{A},K} (\mathbf{t}, \underline{a}, a)$. □

Our next goal is to characterize the elements of this information system. To do that, we have to translate deductive consistency and deductive closedness into the language of termal algebras.

The part corresponding to deductive consistency is given by the following result, which is a rephrasing of Lem. 4 in [Ba2], and whose proof is left to the reader:

Proposition 5. *A subset $x \subseteq \mathcal{D}_{\mathbf{A},K}$ is deductively consistent for $I_{\mathbf{A},K}$ iff $\mathbf{A}^x$ is a K–c.t.a.*

The part corresponding to deductive closedness is given by the following result:

Proposition 6. *Let x be a subset of $\mathcal{D}_{\mathbf{A},K}$ such that $\mathbf{A}^x$ is a K–c.t.a. Then x is deductively closed for $I_{\mathbf{A},K}$ iff $\mathbf{A}^x$ is K–closed.*

Proof. First of all, since $\mathbf{A}^x$ is a K–c.t.a., $\mathbf{A}^u$ is also a K–c.t.a. for every $u \in \mathcal{P}_\omega(x)$. Let

$$h_u\colon \mathbf{A}^u \longrightarrow \mathbf{B}^u$$

be a K–monoreflection of $\mathbf{A}^u$.

Since $(\mathbf{A}^u)_{u \in \mathcal{P}_\omega(x)}$, with the natural embeddings as mappings, is a direct system with direct limit $\mathbf{A}^x$, Proposition 2 implies that $(\mathbf{B}^u)_{u \in \mathcal{P}_\omega(x)}$ form also a direct system, with direct limit some algebra $\mathbf{B}^x \in K$, and that the family of monomorphisms

$$h_u\colon \mathbf{A}^u \longrightarrow \mathbf{B}^u, \quad u \in \mathcal{P}_\omega(x)$$

induces a monomorphism $h\colon \mathbf{A}^x \longrightarrow \mathbf{B}^x$ which is a K–monoreflection of $\mathbf{A}^x$.

Assume now that x is deductively closed, and let $\mathbf{t} \in \mathbf{T}_{\mathcal{F}}$, $\underline{a} \in A^{\eta^*(\mathbf{t})}$ and $a \in A$ such that

$$\mathbf{t}^{\mathbf{B}^x}(\underline{a}) = a.$$

If $\underline{a} \in \operatorname{dom} \mathbf{t}^{\mathbf{A}}$ then $\mathbf{t}^{\mathbf{A}}(\underline{a}) = a$ (because $\mathbf{A}$ is embedded into $\mathbf{B}^x$) and, a fortiori, $\mathbf{t}^x(\underline{a}) = a$. So let us assume that $\underline{a} \notin \operatorname{dom} \mathbf{t}^{\mathbf{A}}$. It implies that $(\mathbf{t}, \underline{a}, a) \in \mathcal{D}_{\mathbf{A},K}$, because $\mathbf{A}^{\{(\mathbf{t},\underline{a},a)\}}$ is embedded into $\mathbf{B}^x$. Since $\mathbf{B}^x$ is the direct limit of $(\mathbf{B}^u)_{u\in\mathcal{P}_\omega(x)}$, there exists some $u \in \mathcal{P}_\omega(x)$ such that

$$\mathbf{t}^{\mathbf{B}^u}(\underline{a}) = a.$$

By definition, it implies that $u \vdash_{\mathbf{A},K} (\mathbf{t},\underline{a},a)$. Therefore, since x is deductively closed, $(\mathbf{t},\underline{a},a) \in x$ and thus $\mathbf{t}^x(\underline{a}) = a$. It proves that $\mathbf{A}^x$ is K–closed.

Conversely, assume that $\mathbf{A}^x$ is K–closed, and let $u \in \mathcal{P}_\omega(x)$ and $(\mathbf{t},\underline{a},a) \in \mathcal{D}_{\mathbf{A},K}$ be such that $u \vdash_{\mathbf{A},K} (\mathbf{t},\underline{a},a)$, and in particular such that $\mathbf{t}^{\mathbf{B}^u}(\underline{a}) = a$. Since $\mathbf{B}^x$ is the direct limit of the $\mathbf{B}^u$'s, we have $\mathbf{t}^{\mathbf{B}^x}(\underline{a}) = a$ which implies, since $\mathbf{A}^x$ is K–closed, that $\mathbf{t}^x(\underline{a}) = a$. Therefore $(\mathbf{t},\underline{a},a) \in x$. It entails that x is deductively closed. □

Combining the last two propositions we get the following characterization for the elements of $I_{\mathbf{A},K}$.

Theorem 7. *A subset $x \subseteq \mathcal{D}_{\mathbf{A},K}$ is an element of $I_{\mathbf{A},K}$ iff $\mathbf{A}^x$ is a K-closed, K-consistent termal algebra.*

In other words, there is a bijection between $|I_{\mathbf{A},K}|$ and the set of all K–closed inner extensions of $\mathbf{A}$.

Example 1. Let $\mathcal{F}_0 = (F_0, \eta_0)$, with $F_0 = \{f\}$ and $\eta_0(f) = 1$. Let $\mathbf{A}$ be the termal algebra of type $\mathcal{F}_0$ given by Diagram 1 below. Let T be the variety of all total algebras of type $\mathcal{F}_0$. It is not difficult to check that $\mathbf{A}$ is T–consistent, with T–monoreflection the natural embedding into the algebra $\mathbf{B} \in T$ defined by Diagram 2.

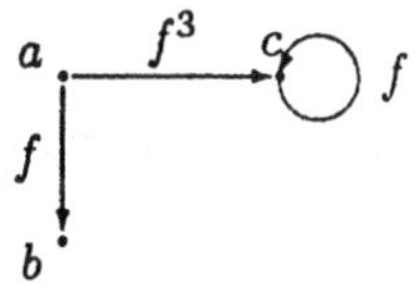

Diagram 1

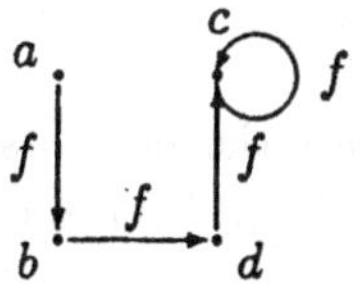

Diagram 2

In this case, it can be proved that $|I_{\mathbf{A},T}|$ has two elements:

$$x_b = \{(f^n, a, c) \mid n \geq 4\} \cup \{(f^n, c, c) \mid n \geq 2\} \cup \{(f^n, b, c) \mid n \geq 2\}$$
$$x_t = \{(f^n, a, c) \mid n \geq 2, n \neq 3\} \cup \{(f^n, c, c) \mid n \geq 2\} \cup \{(f^n, b, c) \mid n \geq 1\}$$

with $x_b \leq x_t$.

4 An Information System Corresponding to Term–Closedness

Let $\mathbf{A}$, K, $\tilde{\mathcal{D}}_{\mathbf{A},K}$, $\mathcal{D}_{\mathbf{A},K}$, $Cons_{\mathbf{A},K}$ and $\Delta_{\mathbf{A},K}$ as in the last section, and consider the following new entailment relation on $Cons_{\mathbf{A},K} \times \mathcal{D}_{\mathbf{A},K}$:

> $u \vdash_{\mathbf{A}} X$ iff either $X = \emptyset$ or $X = (\mathbf{t},\underline{a},a)$ and there exists some $\tilde{\mathbf{t}}(x_1,\ldots,x_{\eta^*(\mathbf{t})}) \in \mathbf{T_T}(\mathcal{X})$ such that $\tilde{\mathbf{t}}^*$ is the canonical representative of $\mathbf{t}$, $\underline{a} \in \operatorname{dom} \tilde{\mathbf{t}}^{\mathbf{A}^u}$ and $\tilde{\mathbf{t}}^{\mathbf{A}^u}(\underline{a}) = a$.

In the sequel, we shall commit the abuse of notation of writing "$\tilde{\mathbf{t}}^* = \mathbf{t} \in \mathbf{T}_{\mathcal{F}}$" instead of "$\tilde{\mathbf{t}}^*$ is the canonical representative of t". Moreover, and in order to simplify the exposition, given a term $\tilde{\mathbf{t}} \in \mathbf{T}_{\mathbf{T}}(\mathcal{X})$, we shall write $\tilde{\mathbf{t}}^x$ instead of $\tilde{\mathbf{t}}^{\mathbf{A}^x}$, for every $x \subseteq \tilde{\mathcal{D}}_{\mathbf{A},K}$.

Proposition 8. *$I'_{\mathbf{A},K} = (\mathcal{D}_{\mathbf{A},K}, \Delta_{\mathbf{A},K}, Cons_{\mathbf{A},K}, \vdash_{\mathbf{A}})$ is an information system.*

Proof. Again, the proof that $I'_{\mathbf{A},K}$ satisfies properties (i)–(v) in the definition of an information system is straightforward, and it is left to the reader. We prove here that it satisfies property (vi). To do that, we shall use the following fact, which can be easily proved by algebraic induction:

Lemma. *Let $u, v \in Cons_{\mathbf{A},K}$ be such that $v \vdash_{\mathbf{A}} Y$, for every $Y \in u$. Let $\tilde{\mathbf{t}} = \tilde{\mathbf{t}}(x_{i_1}, \ldots, x_{i_m}) \in \mathbf{T}_{\mathbf{T}}(\mathcal{X})$, $n \geq i_m$, $\underline{a} = (a_1, \ldots, a_n) \in \operatorname{dom} \tilde{\mathbf{t}}^u$ and $a = \tilde{\mathbf{t}}^u(\underline{a})$. Then, there exists a $\tilde{\mathbf{t}}'(x_{i_1}, \ldots, x_{i_m}) \in \mathbf{T}_{\mathbf{T}}(\mathcal{X})$, such that $\tilde{\mathbf{t}}'^* = \tilde{\mathbf{t}}^*$, $\underline{a} \in \operatorname{dom} \tilde{\mathbf{t}}'^v$ and $a = \tilde{\mathbf{t}}'^v(\underline{a})$.*

Assume that $u \vdash_{\mathbf{A}} X$ and that $v \vdash_{\mathbf{A}} Y$, for every $Y \in u$. As always, the case $X = \emptyset$ is trivial, so let us suppose that $X = (\mathbf{t}, \underline{a}, a)$. Then there exists a $\tilde{\mathbf{t}}(x_1, \ldots, x_{\eta^*(\mathbf{t})}) \in \mathbf{T}_{\mathbf{T}}(\mathcal{X})$ such that $\tilde{\mathbf{t}}^* = \mathbf{t}$, $\underline{a} \in \operatorname{dom} \tilde{\mathbf{t}}^u$ and $\tilde{\mathbf{t}}^u(\underline{a}) = a$. By the previous Lemma, there exists some $\tilde{\mathbf{t}}'(x_1, \ldots, x_{\eta^*(\mathbf{t})}) \in \mathbf{T}_{\mathbf{T}}(\mathcal{X})$ such that $\tilde{\mathbf{t}}'^* = \tilde{\mathbf{t}}^*$ (and therefore, $\tilde{\mathbf{t}}'^*$ is the canonical representative of t), $\underline{a} \in \operatorname{dom} \tilde{\mathbf{t}}'^v$ and $\tilde{\mathbf{t}}'^v(\underline{a}) = a$. It entails that $v \vdash_{\mathbf{A}} (\mathbf{t}, \underline{a}, a)$ too. □

Let us study the elements of $I'_{\mathbf{A},K}$. Since the finite consistent sets are the same in $I_{\mathbf{A},K}$ as in $I'_{\mathbf{A},K}$, Proposition 5 yields

Proposition 9. *A set $x \subseteq \mathcal{D}_{\mathbf{A},K}$ is deductively consistent for $I'_{\mathbf{A},K}$ iff $\mathbf{A}^x$ is K-consistent.*

As far as deductive closedness goes, we have

Proposition 10. *A set $x \subseteq \mathcal{D}_{\mathbf{A},K}$ is deductively closed for $I'_{\mathbf{A},K}$ iff $\mathbf{A}^x$ is term-closed.*

Proof. Let us suppose that x is deductively closed. Let $\tilde{\mathbf{t}} = \tilde{\mathbf{t}}(x_1, \ldots, x_{\eta^*(\mathbf{t})}) \in \mathbf{T}_{\mathbf{T}}(\mathcal{X})$ be such that $\tilde{\mathbf{t}}^* = \mathbf{t} \in \mathbf{T}_{\mathcal{F}}$, and let $\underline{a} \in A^{\eta^*(\mathbf{t})}$ be such that $\underline{a} \in \operatorname{dom} \tilde{\mathbf{t}}^x$ and $\tilde{\mathbf{t}}^x(\underline{a}) = a$. Since $\mathbf{A}^x$ is the direct limit of $(\mathbf{A}^u)_{u \in \mathcal{P}_\omega(x)}$, there exists some finite subset $u \subseteq x$ such that $\tilde{\mathbf{t}}^u(\underline{a}) = a$ in $\mathbf{A}^u$. Then either $\mathbf{t}^{\mathbf{A}}(\underline{a}) = a$ or $u \vdash_{\mathbf{A}} (\mathbf{t}, \underline{a}, a)$. In the first case, $\mathbf{t}^x(\underline{a}) = a$ because $\mathbf{A}$ is a subalgebra of $\mathbf{A}^x$. In the second case, since x is deductively closed, $(\mathbf{t}, \underline{a}, a) \in x$, and thus $\underline{a} \in \operatorname{dom} \mathbf{t}^x$ and $\mathbf{t}^x(\underline{a}) = a$. This proves that $\mathbf{A}^x$ is term-closed.

Conversely, let us suppose that $\mathbf{A}^x$ is term-closed, and that $u \vdash_{\mathbf{A}} (\mathbf{t}, \underline{a}, a)$ for some finite subset $u \subseteq x$ and some $(\mathbf{t}, \underline{a}, a) \in \mathcal{D}_{\mathbf{A},K}$. Then, there exists some $\tilde{\mathbf{t}} =$

$\tilde{\mathbf{t}}(x_1, \ldots, x_{\eta^*(\mathbf{t})}) \in \mathbf{T_T}(\mathcal{X})$, such that $\tilde{\mathbf{t}}^* = \mathbf{t} \in \mathbf{T}_\mathcal{F}$, $\underline{a} \in \operatorname{dom} \tilde{\mathbf{t}}^u$ and $\tilde{\mathbf{t}}^u(\underline{a}) = a$. Since $\mathbf{A}^u$ is a weak subalgebra of $\mathbf{A}^x$, it turns out that $\underline{a} \in \operatorname{dom} \tilde{\mathbf{t}}^x$ and $\tilde{\mathbf{t}}^x(\underline{a}) = a$ also. But since $\mathbf{A}^x$ is term–closed and $\tilde{\mathbf{t}}^* = \mathbf{t} \in \mathbf{T}_\mathcal{F}$, it implies $\mathbf{t}^x(\underline{a}) = a$, and thus $(\mathbf{t}, \underline{a}, a) \in x$. □

Combining the last two propositions we get the following result:

Theorem 11. *A subset $x \subseteq \mathcal{D}_{\mathbf{A},K}$ is an element of $I'_{\mathbf{A},K}$ iff $\mathbf{A}^x$ is a term–closed, K-consistent termal algebra.*

In other words, there is a bijection between $|I'_{\mathbf{A},K}|$ and the set of all K–consistent inner extensions of $\mathbf{A}$ which are term–closed.

Example 2. Let $\mathbf{A}$ and T as in Example 1. It can be proved that, in this case, $|I'_{\mathbf{A},T}|$ has as elements

$$\begin{aligned}
x_\infty &= \{(f^n, a, c) \mid n \geq 4\} \cup \{(f^n, c, c) \mid n \geq 2\}\\
y_\infty &= \{(f^n, a, c) \mid n \geq 2, n \neq 3\} \cup \{(f^n, c, c) \mid n \geq 2\}\\
y_0 &= \{(f^n, a, c) \mid n \geq 2, n \neq 3\} \cup \{(f^n, c, c) \mid n \geq 2\} \cup \{(f^n, b, c) \mid n \geq 1\}\\
x_i &= \{(f^n, a, c) \mid n \geq 4\} \cup \{(f^n, c, c) \mid n \geq 2\} \cup \{(f^n, b, c) \mid n \geq i+1\}, \quad i \geq 1\\
y_i &= \{(f^n, a, c) \mid n \geq 2, n \neq 3\} \cup \{(f^n, c, c) \mid n \geq 2\} \cup \{(f^n, b, c) \mid n \geq i+1\}, i \geq 1
\end{aligned}$$

forming a lattice with Hasse diagram

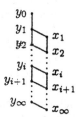

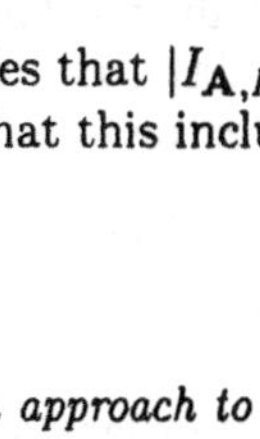

Observe that Proposition 3 implies that $|I_{\mathbf{A},K}|$ is embedded into $|I'_{\mathbf{A},K}|$, for any $\mathbf{A}$ and K. Examples 1 and 2 show that this inclusion is in general strict.

References

[Ba1] Bartol, W.; *Termal algebras—an approach to inference on incomplete data,* in *Universal and Applied Algebra, Proc. V Univ. Alg. Symp., Turawa 1988* (H. Hałkowska, B. Stawski eds.). World Scientific (1989) pp. 1–12.

[Ba2] Bartol, W.; *Information systems of termal algebras,* manuscript (1989).

[BR] Bartol, W.–Rosselló, F.; *Termal Algebras: a guided tour,* Tech. Rep. UIB-DMI-B-004 (1991).

[Bur] Burmeister, P.; *A model–theoretic approach to partial algebras,* Akademie–Verlag (1986).

[Sch] Schmidt, J. A.; *A general existence theorem on partial algebras and its special cases,* Coll. Math. 14 (1966), pp. 73–87.

[Sco] Scott, D. S.; *Domains for denotational semantics,* in: *Proc. ICALP'82* (M. Nielsen, E. M. Schmidt eds.). Lect. Notes in Comp. Sc. 140 (1982), pp. 577–613.

A Backward Chaining Resolution Process Involving Non-Monotonic Operators

D. Ferney & A. Quilliot

Université Blaise Pascal
Cust BP 206, Plateau des Cézeaux
63174 AUBIERE, FRANCE

Abstract. From a reflexion about the possible semantics of a special subset of the first order logic we extract a resolution process based upon dynamic handling through backward chaining of temporary knowledge. It leads us to the conception of an experimental declarative language, aimed at describing logical specifications, which unifies backward and forward chaining and makes easier dealing with a non monotonic behaviour of the knowledge.

Area: Automated (qualitative) reasoning; Non monotonicity.
Keywords: "Suppose" operator; Non monotonicity; Resolution process.

1 Introduction: a Case of Non Monotonicity in First Order Logic

Dealing with a goal which may be written as an implication (A -> B) usually induces two very differents possibles schemes. For instance, let us first suppose that we want to check the following statement, related to some scheduling problem:

"If the agents affected to the realization of two given tasks are the same, then the starting times of the two task may be exchanged". (1)

The true meaning of (1) is that we will get the answer to a question

? Exchange(Task1,Task2)

by reviewing both lists of agents which have been affected to respectively Task1 and Task2 and by comparing them. Here the resolution process will be as follows:

(x = Val), where Val is a term, is solution of
?($_t$ A(x,t) -> B(x,t)) (with an extraction of solution mechanism)

iff

Any solution (t = Val1) of ?(A(Val,t), where Val is taken as a constant, is also a solution of ? B(Val,t).

Its implementation may yields partial instanciation such that: "Any x which can't be written as x = f(z) and is different from ...", and be difficult to realize.

Such a process will be based upon the closed world assumption, and will make arise the classical obstacles associated with defaults and non monotonicity (see[3,18]).

Still, variants of this interpretation of the operator " -> " as a causality will prevail in many cases. For instance, we will infer that an animal A is a cameleon from a rule: *($_x$ ($_y$ Afraid(x) Support (x,y) -> Take-color(x,y)) -> Cameleon(x))*
not after performing an abstract reasoning about what does A when he is afraid, but after taking help from some experimental knowledge.

Conversely, let us consider an agent who tries to reach some goal in middle of an uncertain world and may have to handle one among N events E(i), i = 1...N.

Succeeding in it will mean for him proving any implication: (Occur(E(i)) -> Goal), i = 1...N. He will do it by successively writing, for i = 1...N :

Let us suppose Occur(E(i)); Proof of Goal ; (*)

If we suppose now that this agent will have to launch his strategy before he gets a full knowledge of the coming event, then the process will become:

Generate(event);
Prove: (Occur(event) -> Goal).

Such an intuitionistic approach, based upon the Deduction theorem:

$$Th \models (X \rightarrow Y) \text{ iff } Th \cup \{X\} \models Y$$

will also be our if we try to simulate induction in first order logic: If P is some unary predicate and D an at most countable ordered domain without any infinite decreasing chain, then the Induction Principle will be rewritten for this particular context under the following form:

{ [∀x in D (Minimal(x) -> P(x))]
[∀x in D [∀y in D (Less-than(y,x) -> P(y))] -> P(x)] } *-> P is true everywhere.*

Then we will get a proof of P by successively writing:

"Let x_0 be in D such that Minimal(x_0); Proof of P(x_0): ....";
"Let x_0 be such that if y in D is such that Less-than(y,x_0) then P(y) is true; Proof of P(x_0):......."; (**)

Both processes (*) and (**) above involve temporary knowledge. In fact, building a reasoning around sentences like: "Let us suppose (the existence of x_0 such) that P(x_0) is true ... " is part of a way to cope with an unstable or uncertain world (*non monotonicity*) or with various possibles points of view (*modality*). Of course, this problem is not unknown from the people who work on automated reasoning and logic programming, but it has most often been adressed through the introduction of explicit operators (see for instance the logics with "suppose" operators [3,16], or some problem resolution oriented languages like SNARK, ARGOS [20, 11, 15]), or through extensions of the first order calculus framework (Modal logics [1,7,12,14], Autoepistemic logics [17], logics for the analysis of modules [19]), which very often fail to provide an efficient and well-fitted associated resolution process.

Also both are backward chaining processes. When asked to answer to some situation inside an evolutive world, one first asserts his own current subjective vision of the world and next builds his decision. In such a context, any event tends to propagate itself into an enlargement or an invalidation of some part of the knowledge. Practically, such a process must be coupled with a forward propagation mechanism taking in charge the monotonic part of the evolution of the knowledge.

The fact that (*) and (**) involve problems which may typically be solved inside the first order logic framework suggests that it must be possible to cast into it the non monotonic features of the aboves reasoning schemes, and this without recurring neither to the insertion of explicit operators nor to a description of the time in order to handle suppositions and temporary knowledge.

Thus, the rest of this work will consist in dealing with the points of view expressed through (*) and (**). Namely, we will introduce a specific resolution process, defined as an extension of the usual linear input ordered resolution which works on the Horn Clauses. In order to capture the semantics of this process (the bulk of our contribution), we shall present and discuss a special subset of the first order logic which will allow us to get Soundness and Completude results. We will conclude by describing of an experimental declarative language aimed at facilitating algorithm specifications and by describing further developpements .

2 A Theoretical Framework

2.1 A Special Subset of the First Order Logic.

We define an AHE (Almost Horn Expression) as being:

- A first order atom (whose variables are free or universally quantified)

or

- An expression: ($_{variables}$ (AND AHEs) -> atom).

A closed AHE is an AHE without any free variable (we only consider closed AHE).

Examples: (for a better readibility, we specify the scope of the variables).

- Any Horn clause is an AHE;
- The set inclusion characterization: *($_{a,b}$ ($_x$ In(x,a) -> In(x,b)) -> Included(a,b))*
  Thus proving an inclusion *Included(A,B)* will come from:
  "Let $x_0 \in$ A; Let us prove that $x_0 \in$ B ".
- The translation of the statement (1) of the introduction:
  ($_{a,b}$ {($_x$ Affected (x,a) -> Affected(x,b))
  ($_x$ Affected (x,b) -> Affected(x,a)) }-> Exchange(a,b))
- The "pseudo-induction" rule ,as described above:
  ($_z$ { ($_x$ Minimal(x) -> P(x))
  ($_x$ ($_y$ Less-than(y,x) -> P(y)) -> P(x)) } -> P(z))

(This last AHE is with "depth " 2 ,while the two others are with depth 1).

Remark: Obviously not every clause of the F.O.L. is an AHE.

2.2 Interpretation.

The implicit skolemization contained in the transition from a goal like:

"Prove ($_t$ a(x,t) -> b(x,t)) "

to an other goal:

"For any x: let us consider f_0(x) such that a(x,f_0(x)); prove b(x,f_0(x))" (2)

(such a skolemization means a temporary change in the Herbrand Universe) tells us that an implication A -> B is true only if some causality explicitly connects A and B in the knowledge basis.

When proceeding according to (2) above, we may enlarge the validity domain of the antecedent part of the implication which we are trying to prove in such a way that we tend to forbid ourselves to get our result from considering the fact that x_0 may have only some special values (or none). This is precisely the kind of signification which interests us. It leads to an interpretation of the AHE and of their potential insertion inside applications essentially in terms of dynamic handling of temporary objects (mostly as in [19]) like in the case of :

- Possible trials performed during a try/test algorithm:
  (Choose(Trial)
  (Trial -> Succeed) -> Succeed)
- Strategy building through hypothesis generation:

(Generate(hypothesis) *-> perform-strategy)*
(hypothesis -> perform-strategy1)

- Instantaneous tests (learning or some diagnostic processes):
  ((Instantaneous-test -> result-test) -> Decision)
- Simulation of mathematical theorem proving.

2.3 A Resolution Process.

N.B.: In order to make our presentation more concise and easier to read, we will most often during this part of our work limit ourselves to the propositional calculus context.

The Resolution Mechanism. So let BASIS an AHE family, Q a question (atom or symbol which we want to deduce from BASIS), and let us first introduce the way we formalize the resolution mechanism for which we provided an intuitive description at the introduction.

At any time during a resolution process, the current state of our system will be summarized by :

- A current world W, i.e a stack whose every level contain a conjunction of AHE (part of the temporary knowledge) and a disjunction of negations of AHE (we say AHE-neg-clause) which is called the queue of W;
- A current goal G (AHE-neg-clause).

The following inference rules will work on this system:

Rule R1: G = NOT(A) OR T different from Queue(W)
A OR R is in BASIS {current temporary knowledge}

G := R OR T (A is a symbol,R,T are AHE-neg-clauses)

Rule R2: G = Queue(W)

Unstack(W)

Rule R3: G = NOT(B -> A) OR T different from Queue(W)
(B is a conjunction of AHE, A is a symbol, T is an AHE-neg-clause)

Stack(W,(B,T));
G := A OR T

Then a linear input proof of Q from BASIS will be a finite sequence (W(i),G(i)), i in O...n such that:

- W(0) = empty stack;
- G(n) = Nil = Empty AHE-neg-clause;
- for any i in O...n-1 ,the transition from (W(i),G(i)) to (W(i+1),G(i+1)) will be performed through one of the above rules *R1, R2, R3*.

If we are concerned with first order expressions, then rule *R1* will take into account the unification mechanism, and *R3* will be rewritten as follows:

G = NOT(B -> A) OR T

Stack(W,(B*,T))
G:= A* OR T

where B* ,A* are A and B after Skolemization (and thus incrementation of the Herbrand Universe associated with the current knowledge) of the internal variables of the implication (B -> A).

Example :

BASIS = { $(_y\,(_x$ a(x,y) -> b(x,y))
d(y)-> c(y));
$(_{x,y}$a(x,y)e(y)-> f(x,y));
$(_{x,z}$ f(x,z) -> b(x,z)) ;
d(Toto);
e(Toto); }.

Q = c(y) .

A linear input proof of Q from BASIS comes as follows :

Step 1 : G = Not c(y); W = Nil ;
Step 2 : G = Not $(_x$ a(x,y) -> b(x,y)) OR Not d(y); W = Nil ; (R1)
Step 3 : G = Not b(F(y),y) OR Not d(y) ; (F is a Skolem function)
W = a(F(y),y d(y) ; (R3)
Step 4 : G = Not f(F(y),y) OR Not d(y) ; W unchanged ; (R1)
Step 5 : G = Not a(F(y),y) OR Not e(y) Or Not d(y) ; W unchanged ; (R1)
Step 6 : G = Not e(y) Or Not d(y) ; W unchanged ; (R1)
Step 7 : G = Not d(Toto) ; W unchanged ; (R1)
Step 8 : G = Not d(Toto) ; W = Nil ; (R2)
Step 9 : G = Nil ; W = Nil; (R1)

2.4 The Search for a Linear Proof as a Backward Chaining Process.

Of course such a proof should come from some tree search (as it is the case with the Horn fomulae). In order to justify such an intuition, let us consider BASIS and Q defined as above and let us define the trees H(n), n $\geq$ 0 as follows:

- H(0) is reduced to one vertex Root, labeled with a pair (OR,Q); We set B(Root) = BASIS.
- We get H(n+1) from H(n) through the following transformation:
  - To any leaf x of H(n) with label (OR,s) (s is a symbol) ,we add as many sons y(e) with labels (AND,Premice(e)) as there exist expressions e in B(x) which admit s as consequent; For any such e, we set B(y(e)) = B(x).
  - To any leaf x of H(n) with label (AND,Premice), we add as many sons z(d) with label (OR,d) as there exist components d of Premice which are symbols, and as many sons z(d) with label (SUPPOSE,d) as there exist such components which are not symbols. In any case set B(z) := B(x).
  - To any leaf x of H(n) with label (SUPPOSE,d), we add a son z with label (OR,Consequent(d)) and we set B(z) := B(x) $\cup$ {Premice(d)}.

Then we partially mark the vertices of $H(BASIS,Q) = \bigcup_{n\geq 0} H(n)$, as follows:

Receives a marker:

- Any leaf of H(BASIS,Q) with label (AND,Nil) (Nil = empty conjunction)
- Any vertex x of H(BASIS,Q) with label (OR,-) and whose at least one son has been marked;
- Any vertex x of H(BASIS,Q) with label (AND,-) or (SUPPOSE,-) and whose all the sons have been marked.

Then it is possible to state :

Theorem I.

a) There exists a linear input proof of Q from BASIS *if and only if* the root of H(BASIS,Q) receives a marker.

b) (Soundness of the rules R1,R2,R3)
In this last case we have BASIS |= Q (in the usual sense)

N.B: Of course a similar result holds in the context of first order logic.

Sketch of proof: After extending the definition of a linear input proof of a symbol to the case of a conjunction of AHE, we check (by induction on the time at which any vertex of H(BASIS,Q) receives a marker during the process described above) that :

- If a vertex x of H(BASIS,Q) labeled (AND,Premice) has been marked, then there exists a linear input proof of Premice from B(x) and: B(x) |= Premice.
- If a vertex x of H(BASIS,Q) with label (OR,s) has been marked ,then there exists a linear input proof of s from B(x) and: B(x) |= s .
- If a vertex x of H(BASIS,Q) with label (SUPPOSE,d) has been marked,then there exists a linear input proof of d from B(x) and: B(x) |= d.

We get the reciprocal implications by induction on the length of a proof. ❑

2.5 Soundness and Completeness.

Not surprisingly, *b) of theorem 1* can't be turned into an equivalence. However, we get closer to completeness by adding to the definition of a linear input proof the following transition rule :

Rule R4: G(i) = NOT(B -> A) OR T ' OR T (T,T ' are AHE-neg-clauses)
G(j) = NOT(R) OR T , with j in 0...(i-1);
B |= R (in the usual sense) ; W(j) is a substack of W(i)

G(i+1) := T' OR T ;W(i+1) := W(i)

This way conserve the soundness, (we leave the proof to the reader), and we become able to solve :

BASIS = {((a -> b) -> a)} ; Q = a .

(Here BASIS |= Q but R4 is required in order to get it through our process)

Still we keep missing the completeness, as we can see with the following example :

BASIS = { ((a -> b) -> c), ((b -> a) -> c)} ; BASIS |= c.

moeover the rule R4 itself looks rather difficult to implement .

As a matter of fact, dealing with AHE is of higher complexity than dealing with Horn formulae. One may for instance check that while solving a satisfiability problem about Horn clauses can be done by relaxation of the associated linear integer program [10] , it is no longer possible in the case of AHE.

2.6 Formal Semantics of the AHE.

So, what semantics for the AHE will turn *b) of Theorem 1* into an equivalence? (Once again ,we limit ourselves to the propositional case).

An *AHE-interpretation* Val* of an AHE family will be defined, for any symbol a, by some distribution a(i) = Val*(i,a) , i ≥ 0, with values in {0,1};

Then the following mechanism will make possible, for any AHE D, to compute its values Val*(i,D):

- If D is a symbol a, then Val*(i,D) = 1 *iff* Val*(j,a) = 1 for any j $\geq$ i ;
- If D is an implication (A -> a) then Val*(i,D) = 1 *iff* for any j $\geq$ i we have Val*(j,a) = 1 or Val*(j,A) = 0;
- The value Val* of a conjunction (for a given i) of AHE is the product of the values Val* of its components .

Example: If BASIS = { (a -> b) -> a } and Q = a ,
and if we set : Val*(0,a) =0; Val*(i,a) = 1 for i > 0; Val*(i,b)=0 for i $\geq$0;
we get Val*(0,BASIS) = 1 *(we say that Val *is an AHE-model));*
while Val*(0,a) = 0.

Remark : The above semantics may be considered as "possible world" semantics.

It is possible to state (Completeness result):

Theorem 2 : A linear input proof of Q from BASIS exists *if and only if* there doesn't exist any AHE-model Val* of BASIS such that Val*(0,Q)=0.

Scketch of proof :
* *Part if:* We suppose that no proof of Q from B exists and we proceed in a constructive way; The vertex set of H(BASIS,Q) is at most countable, so we assign to any vertex x with label (SUPPOSE,-) some strictly positive integer number p(x) in such a way that :

- No two such vertices are assigned with a same number;
- If x and y are two such vertices such that x is between Root and y in H(BASIS,Q) then p(x) < p(y).

We extend this assignment by considering that any vertex z of H(BASIS,Q) is either under the direct scope of some vertex x as above (and then we set p(z) = p(x)) or that z is under the direct scope of Root (and then we set p(z) = 0). Then for any vertex x in H(BASIS,Q) with label (OR,s) (s is a symbol), we set : Val*(p(x),s) = 1 if x has received a marker and 0 else ; and check that Val* can be extended (by setting Val*(i,s) = 1 for any pair (i,s) which can't be writen (p(x),s) as above) in order to become an AHE-model of BASIS as required in the statement of Theorem 2.
* *Part iff:* We proceed as in Theorem 1.❑

2.7 Why the AHE and Why the Above Resolution Process ?

The above resolution process is sound but not complete. So what may be its interest since dealing with AHE could be done by turning them into usual clauses and applying the usual Robinson's resolution principle ?

The answer is two-faced

* The first side comes from semantics: breaking the AHE provokes the lost of their true meaning. Our resolution process reflects well the natural mental process which consists in generating assumptions and confronting them to the true world, thus making non monotonicity to be a natural part of any reasoning. AHE (even "false" AHE containing negative atoms) help in reproducing this mechanism).
* The second side comes from complexity: turning an AHE basis into clausal form may strongly increase the encoding length of the problem, while the effectiveness of the linear input ordered AHE resolution is lost.

3 An Illustrative Ruled Based Deduction System

The above resolution process may be implemented as an extension of the PROLOG language. Still, since any rule based inference system is a derivation of the resolution in first order logic (more specifically of the Modus Ponens rule) we want to adapt the above ideas to the design of such systems, in order to make easier the management of non monotonic knowledge.

We see that practically, any hypothesis generated through our process requires some forward propagation mechanism to be launched in order to get the immediate consequences of the hypothesis (eventually Nil, i.e a contradiction).

We also see that in some cases the way the new fact is generated needs to be explicit (it is usually the case when the system works by forward chaining.

Taking this into account we designed an experimental declarative language (aimed more at describing specifications than at really writing programs), which emphasizes on the existence of some operators built for handling supposition and temporary knowledge or controlling the search and which mixes both mechanisms into a unique formalism .

The basic objects our system works on are facts and rules (static variables and properties are also allowed), a rule being a pair : (premices -> consequents) where a premice (or a consequent) can mainly be :

- a first order atom ; Not (Atom) ; Non (Atom) ;
- a simple rule (without any operator) ;
- Nil, T ;
- Operator(arguments) .

Various operators may control the way the search is performed ('?', Solve, Propagate, Apply-rule), create or retract temporary knowledge (Pose, Suppose, Superpose, Rule-pose), perform arithmetical tests and operations and directly affect the static part of the knowledge .

The rules are run by forward chaining, and may succeed or fail . The apparition of Nil as a consequent of a rule provokes the retraction of the current world (the current hypothesis and all its consequences (which may be the current values of some static variables)).

Backward chaining can be implicitly performed through the operator ' ? ' :
if one needs to satisfy the premice A, then he looks for (something which may be unified with) A in the knowledge basis or for a rule whose first premice is ? A .

Explicit backward chaining may be commanded from the consequent level through the operator Solve. A call "Solve(A)" makes the fact Non(A) to be inserted into the knowledge basis, and this implies that Solve(A) is considered to succeed in the case where Non(A) has to be retracted.

Satisfying any premice (A -> B) means satisfaying B after inserting A inside the knowledge basis (implicit knowledge creation).

But explicit creation (or destruction) of knowledge may also be commanded through various operators. For instance the operator Suppose works as follows:

Suppose(A) |= Create a new current world (Stack) with the fact A
and next propagate
all the simples rules which may define a deduction path from A;

That means that a call "Suppose (x = 3)" where x is a static variable makes the current value of x to be saved on a stack while a call Suppose(Not(A)) provokes the freeze of the fact A (if it exists).

The way backward and forward chaining are mixed in our system makes possible at the same time a natural declarative description of Hill-Climbing-like algorithms (which are typically propagation mechanisms) and of tree search based algorithms (Branch/Bound procedures and others recursive schemes).

With this system (written in Le-Lisp on SUN Station), we tested some small examples, like those which we presented at the beginning of the paper. Let us consider for instance the following small constraint satisfaction problem:

Check the satisfiability of a task set, constrained by relations "Before" and "Disjoint", made with tasks of length 1 and supposed to be done in at most 10 time units.

We get:

R5 : (? Fail(t)
Disjoint(x,y)
(Not (Disjoint(x,y)) Before (x,y) -> Fail(t))
(Not(Disjoint(x,y)) Before(y,x) -> Fail(t)) -> T)
R1: (Before1(x,y,u) Non(Fail(u)) -> Nil);
R2: (Before1(x,x,u) -> Nil).
R3: (Before(x,y) -> Before1(x,y,1));
R4: (Before1(x,y,u) Before(y,z) -> Before1(x,z,u+1));

which will answer a question: Propagate {R1, R2, R3, R4}, Solve(Fail(10)) ;

4 Conclusion.

So part of non monotonicity (Decision making inside an evolutive world) may be adressed inside the first order logic framework.

The practical consequences may be important since most of the non standard logic models which have been designed in order to deal with modality and non monotonicity hardly produce efficient resolution algorithms.

The above ideas should help in designing rule based inference system more flexible and better adapted to dynamic knowledge handling.

References

1. M. Abadi, Z. Manna: Modal theorem proving. Proc 8th Int Conf Automated deduction, Springer -Verlag LNCS 230, pp. 172-189 (1986) .
2. K. Apt, M. Van Emden : Contributions to the theory of logic programming. JACM 29.3, pp. 941-862 (1982).
3. P. Besnard, P. Siegel : A framework for logic of "suppose" and "admit". Proc JELIA 88 ROSCOFF (1988).
4. W. Bledsoe: Non resolution theorem proving ; A.I. 9, pp. 1-35 (1977).
5. G. Bossu, P. Siegel: Saturation,non monotonic reasoning and the closed world assumption. A. I. 25(1) pp.13-65 (1985).
6. K. Bowen, T. Weinberg: A metalevel extension of PROLOG. Symp of logic Programing;BOSTON pp 48-53 (1985).
7. B. Chellas: Modal logic: an introduction. Cambrige Univ Press (1980).
8. A. Colmerauer, H. Kanoui, M. Van Caneghem: PROLOG: bases théoriques, développements actuels. TSI 2, 4 pp 271-313 (1983).
9. R. Davis : Reasoning about rules. A.I. 15, pp 223-239 (1980).
10. W. Dowling, J.H. Gallier : Linear time algorithms for testing the satisfiability of propositional Horn formulae. Jour Log Prog 1 (1984).
11. B. Fade : ARGOS II: Contribution à la réalisation d'un resolveur automatique de problèmes. Thèse de 3° cycle. Univ P.Sabatier TOULOUSE (1980).
12. M. Fitting: Proof methods for modal and intuitionistic logic. Reidel, DORDRECHT (1983).
13. D. Gabbay: Theoretical foundations for non monotonic reasoning in expert systems. RR 84 Imperial college (1984).
14. S. Kripke: Semantical considerations on modal logic. In L.Linsky (eds.): Reference and modality. Oxford Univ Press, LONDON pp. 63-72 (1971).
15. J.L. Laurière: Un langage déclaratif:SNARK. TSI 3 pp. 141-170(1896).
16. LEA SOMBE: Inférences non classiques en I.A. 2° journées Proc GRECO I.A pp. 137-230 (1988) .
17. R.C. Moore: Autoepistemic logic in P.Smets(eds): Non standard logics for automated reasoning. Acad press London pp. 105-136(1988).
18. R.C. Moore: Semantical considerations on non monotonic logic. A.I. 25(1) pp. 75-94 (1985).
19. D. Miller: A logical analysis of modules in logic programing. JLP. 7 pp. 79-108 (1989).
20. D. Pastre: MUSCADET: An automatic theorem proving using knowledge and metaknowledge in mathematics. A.I. 38(3) pp. 257-319 (1989).
21. R. Reiter: A logic for default reasoning. A.I. 13(1-2), pp. 81-131 (1980).

2. Logical Methods

ON FUZZY CONDITIONALS GENERALISING THE MATERIAL CONDITIONAL

Enric Trillas,

Departamento de Inteligencia Artificial,
Universidad Politécnica de Madrid and
Instituto Nacional de Técnica Aeroespacial.
Madrid, Spain

ABSTRACT

The paper deals with the problem of analysing if some Fuzzy Relations, widely used as Implications or Conditionals, are or are not good generalizations of the classical Material Conditionals. It is showed:

1) That Material Conditionals can be obtained from some elementary Fuzzy Preorders using special non-classical Membership Functions.

2) That other two large families of usual Fuzzy Conditionals both give the Material Conditionals only through Characteristic Functions, and that they are W-Fuzzy Preorders but neither Prod nor Min-Fuzzy Preorders.

3) That a third and very large family of Fuzzy Relations, sometimes considered in the literature as Implications, also generalizes the Material Conditionals when and only when are refined by Characteristic Functions.

4) That the family of Mamdani's (symmetrical and transitive) Fuzzy Conditionals generalize the <u>restricted</u> Material Conditionals when and only when Characteristic Functions are used.

KEY WORDS: Classical Conditionals and Material Conditionals, Fuzzy Implications, Fuzzy Conditionals and Fuzzy Preorders.

I. INTRODUCTION

1. Given a set E (of statements) and a designated non-empty subset $V \subset E$ (of <u>true</u> statements), a classical relation $\Rightarrow \subset E \times E$ is named an V-Conditional on E if it

satisfies the Meta-Rule of Modus Ponens: "If $a \in V$ and $a \Rightarrow b$, then $b \in V$". Using Characteristic Functions for V and $\Rightarrow$, respectively, such Meta-Rule is written by

If $\varphi_V(a) = 1$ and $\varphi_{\Rightarrow}(b/a) = 1$, then $\varphi_V(b) = 1$,

or by the inequality:

$$\text{Min}\,(\varphi_V(a), \varphi_{\Rightarrow}(b/a)) \le \varphi_V(b),\ \forall\,(a,b) \in E \times E,$$

equivalent to:

$$T\,(\varphi_V(a), \varphi_{\Rightarrow}(b/a)) \le \varphi_V(b),\ \forall\,(a,b) \in E \times E,\ (*),$$

for any t-norm T, because of $T \le \text{Min}$.

It is not difficult to show[1] that $\Rightarrow$ is an V-Conditional if and only if $\Rightarrow\ \subset\ \to_V$, being $\to_V = V \times V \cup (E - V) \times E$ the so-called Material Conditional associated to V. More again, given $\Rightarrow$, the class of sets $V \subset E$, $B \neq \emptyset$, such that inequality (*) holds is non-empty because of (*) is satisfied if $V = E$. Then

$$L = L\,(E, \Rightarrow) = \{V \subset E;\ V \neq \emptyset \text{ and satisfies } (*)\},$$

is the class of Logical States for $(E, \Rightarrow)$[2], and it is

$$\Rightarrow\ \subset \bigcap_{V \in L} \to_V .$$

It is clear that for each Logic State $V \in L$, $\to_V$ is the greatest V-Conditional for E, that $\to_V$ is a Preorder (a reflexive and transitive relation) and that E is the greatest Logic State for $(E,\Rightarrow)$. The class L is a non-complemented sublattice of the Boolean Algebra $\mathbb{P}(E)$ (see[1] and [2]).

As $\varphi_{\to V}(b/a) = \begin{cases} 0, \text{if } (a,b) \in V\times(E-V) \\ 1, \text{otherwise} \end{cases}$,

it is $\varphi_{\to V}(b/a) = \text{Max}\,(1-\varphi_A(a)\ \varphi_A(b))$, $\forall\,(a,b) \in E\times E$.

2. If, given $V \in L(E,\Rightarrow)$, there are in E logical connectives . (and), + (or) and ' (not) such that $a.b \in V$ iff $a \in V$ and $b \in V$; $a' \in V$ iff $a \in E-V$; and $a + b \in V$ iff $a \in V$ or $b \in V$, then it is easy to show that

$a \to_V b$ iff $a \to b \in V$,

with $a \to b = ab + a'b + a'b'$.

When in (E,.,+,') hold both the Distributive Law $x.y + x.z = x.(y + z)$, and the Excludded-Middle Law $x.(y + y') = x$, for any x, y, z in E, it is

$$a \to b = a.b + a' (b + b') = a.b + a'.$$

More again, if the Distributive Law $x.y + z = (x+z).(y+z)$ also holds, it is

$$a \to b = (a + a').(b + a') = b + a'.$$

Then, in Boolean Algebras it is $a \to_V b$ iff $a' + b \in V$, and in weaker lattices it could be $a \to_V b$ iff $a' + ab \in V$ as it is the case of Quantum Mechanic's Lattices.

In a general lattice with greatest element 1, as it is $ab + a'b + a'b' \le ab + a' \le b+a'$, if $V = \{1\}$ the three implications collapse in $a'+ b \in V$.

II. THE CASE OF FUZZY PREORDERS I_ν^T.

When considering Inexact classes and relations or Fuzzy sets and Fuzzy relations, we deal with an Inexact or Fuzzy Relational Structure (E,R), with $R: E \times E \to [0,1]$.
And it is said that an Inexact class or Fuzzy set $\nu : E \to [0,1]$ is a T-Logic State for (E,R) if the inequality

$$T(\nu(a), R(b/a)) \le \nu(b) \quad (**)$$

holds for any a,b in E and some t-norm T [3][4]. It is also said that R is a T-ν-conditional for E and when T is continuous, inequality (**) is equivalent to

$$R \le I_\nu^T,$$

being I_{ν}^{T} the elementar T-Fuzzy Preorder given by

$I_{\nu}^{T}(b/a) = \text{Sup}\,\{z \in [0,1];\ T(\nu(a), z) \le \nu(b)\}$.

Like before if $L = L(E,R) = \{\nu \in [0,1]^{E};\ \nu \ne 0$ and satisfies (**)$\}$, it is

$$R \le \text{Inf}_{\nu \in L}\ I_{\mu}^{T},$$

with $R = \text{Inf}_{\nu \in L}\ I_{\mu}^{T}$ if and only if R is a T-Fuzzy Preorder[2][5].

As it is well known, $I_{\nu}^{W}(b/a) = \text{Min}\,(1,\ 1-\nu(a) + \nu(b))$ is the Łuckasiewicz Implication;

$$I_{\nu}^{Prod}(b/a) = \begin{cases} 1, & \text{if } \nu(a) = 0 \\ \text{Min}\,(1, \frac{\nu(b)}{\nu(a)}), & \text{if } \nu(a) > 0 \end{cases}$$

is the Menger-Goguen Implication; and

$$I_{\nu}^{Min}(b/a) = \begin{cases} 1, & \text{if } \nu(a) \le \nu(b) \\ \nu(b), & \text{if } \nu(a > \nu(b) \end{cases}$$

is the Gödel-Brouwer Implication.

<u>Theorem 1</u> $\quad I_{\varphi_V}^{T} = \varphi_{->_V}$

Proof. It is $I_{\varphi_V}^{T}(b/a) = \text{Sup}\,\{z \in [0,1];\ T(\varphi_V(a), z) \le \varphi_V(b)\}$, and:

* If $a \notin V$, $b \notin V$, as $T(z,0) = 0 \le 0$ it is $I_{\varphi_V}^{T}(b/a) = 1$.

* If $a \notin V$, $b \in V$, as $T(z,0) = 0 < 1$ it is $I_{\varphi_V}^{T}(b/a) = 1$.

* If $a \in V$, $b \in V$, as $T(z,1) = z \le 1$ it is $I_{\varphi_V}^{T}(b/a) = 1$.

* If $a \in V$, $b \notin V$, as $T(z,1) = z \le 0$ it is $I_{\varphi_V}^{T}(b/a) = 0$.

Then $I_{\varphi_V}^{T}(b/a) = \text{Max}\,(1-\varphi_V(a), \varphi_V(b) = \varphi_{->_V}(b/a)$. ■

<u>Theorem 2.</u> If $I_{\nu}^{T} = \varphi_{->_V}$, with T continuous, then $\nu(x) =$

$$= \begin{cases} 0, \text{ if } x \notin V \\ \alpha > 0, \text{ if } x \in V \end{cases}$$

Proof. It is $I_\nu^T(b/a) = \text{Sup}\{z;\ T(z, \nu(a)) \le \nu(b)\} = \text{Max}(1 - \varphi_V(a), \varphi_V(b))$ (1), $I_\nu^T(a/b) = \text{Sup}\{z;\ T(z, \nu(b)) \le \nu(a)\} = \text{Max}\{1-\varphi_V(b), \varphi_V(a)\}$ (2).

Then:

1) If $a \in V$, $b \in V$, from (1): $I_\nu^T(b/a) = 1$ and $T(1,\nu a) \le \nu(b)$, or $\nu(a) \le \nu(b)$. From (2), $I_\nu^T(a/b) = 1$ and $T(1, \nu(b)) = \nu(b) \le \nu(a)$.
   Consequently $\nu(a) = \nu(b)$; and $\nu(x) = \alpha \ge 0$ for any $x \in V$.
2) If $a \notin V$, $b \notin V$, from (1), $I_\nu^T(b/a) = 1$; from (2), $I_\nu^T(a/b) = 1$ and also $\nu(a) = \nu(b)$. Then $\nu(x) = \beta \ge 0$ for any $x \in \bar{V}$.
3) If $a \in V$, $b \notin V$, from (2), $I_\nu^T(a/b) = 1$ and $\nu(b) \le \nu(a)$. Then $\beta \le \alpha$; but if $\beta = \alpha$, or $\nu(x) = \alpha$ for any $x \in E$, it should be $I_\nu^T(b/a) = \text{Sup}\{z;\ T(z,\alpha) \le \alpha\} = 1$ for any a, b in E. And this is not the case, as if $a \notin V$, $b \in V$ then $\varphi_{\underset{V}{\to}}(b/a) = \text{Max}(0,0) = 0$.
   As $\beta < \alpha$ it is $0 \le \beta < \alpha$.
4) As $T \le \text{Min}$, it follows $\{z;\ \text{Min}(z, \nu a) \le \nu b\} \subset \{z;\ T(z,\nu a) \le \nu b\}$ and $\text{Sup}\{z;\ \text{Min}(z, \nu a) \le \nu b\} \le \text{Sup}\{z;\ T(z, \nu a) \le \nu b\}$ for any a, b in E. If $a \in V$, $b \notin V$, it is $\text{Sup}\{z;\ \text{Min}(z,\alpha) \le \beta\} \le \text{Sup}\{z;\ T(z,\alpha) \le \beta\}$. Then $\beta \le \text{Sup}\{z;\ T(z,\alpha) \le \beta\} = \varphi_{\underset{V}{\to}}(b/a) = 0$, and $\beta = 0$.

Consequently $\nu(x) = \begin{cases} 0, & x \notin V \\ \alpha > 0, & \text{if } x \in V \end{cases}$, are the solutions of the given equation with T a continuous T-norm.

<u>Corollary 3.</u> (1) If T is a continuous and positive t-norm, equation $I_\nu^T = \varphi_{\underset{V}{\to}}$ has solutions different from φ_V.

(2) If T is a continuous t-norm with additive generator t such that $t(0) < +\infty$, the only solution of $I_\nu^T = \varphi_V$ is $\nu = \varphi_V$.

Proof. (1) It is $T(z,\alpha) = 0$ if and only if $z = 0$. Then, if $a \notin V$, $b \in V$ it is $I^T_\nu(b/a) = \text{Sup}\ \{z;\ T(z,\alpha) \le 0\} = \text{Sup}\ \{z;\ T(z,\alpha) = 0\} = 0 = \varphi_{->_V}(b/a)$ for any $\alpha > 0$.

(2) $T(0,\alpha) = t^{(-1)}(t(0) + t(\alpha)) = 0$, or $t(0) + t(\alpha) = t(0)$, and $t(\alpha) = 0$. Then $\alpha = 1$.■

Examples

1. If $T = W$ ($t = 1-j$) and $\nu(x) = \begin{cases} 0{,}5, & \text{if } x \in V \\ 0, & \text{if } x \notin V \end{cases}$, it is, for $a \in V$, $b \notin V$:

$$I^W_\nu(b/a) = \text{Min}\ (1,\ 1-\nu a + \nu b) = \text{Min}\ (1;0{,}5) = 0{,}5,$$

that is different from $\varphi_{->_V}(b/a) = \text{Max}\ (1-\varphi_V(a),\ \varphi_V(b)) = 0$.

Then, according to Cor. 3,2, ν is not a solution of $I^T_\nu = \varphi_{->_V}$

2. If T = Prod (positive) and $\nu(x) = \begin{cases} \alpha \in (0,1), & x \in V \\ 0, & x \notin V \end{cases}$, it is, for $a \in V$, $b \notin V$.

$$I^{\text{Prod}}_\nu(b/a) = \text{Min}\ (1,\ \frac{\nu b}{\nu a}) = \text{Min}\ (1,\ \frac{0}{1}) = 0 = \varphi_{->_V}(b/a),$$

and I^{Prod}_ν fully coincides with $\varphi_{->_V}$ according to Cor. 3,1.

3. If T = Min (positive) and $\nu(x) = \begin{cases} 1/4. & x \in V \\ 0, & x \notin V \end{cases}$, it is, for $a \in V$, $b \notin V$:

$$I^{\text{Min}}_\nu(b/a) = \nu(b) = 0,$$

and $I^{\text{Min}}_\nu = \varphi_{->_V}$, according to Cor. 3.1.

Remarks. A. It should be pointed out that, surprisingly, it is possible to reach a Material Conditional $->_V$ throught and Inexact Class ν that on V may have a value α very close to 1 or very close to 0.

B. Notice that if T has a generator t such that $t(0) < +\infty$, then T is not positive. In fact, taking $x > 0$ such that $t(x) = t(0)/2$ it is $T(x,x) = \; = t^{(-1)}(t(0)) = 0$. Consequently, positive t-norms are T = Min or those T with generator t such that $t(0) = +\infty$.

III. THE CASE OF OTHER USUAL FUZZY CONDITIONALS

1. The classical operation $a \to b = a'b + a'b' + ab$ taking its values on E, suggests to consider the Fuzzy relations $R^g_\nu(b/a) = S(T(\nu(a), \nu(b)), S(T(1-\nu(a), 1-\nu(b)), T(1-\nu(a), \nu(b)))$, for a given $\nu \in [0,1]^E$, a t-conorm S and a t-norm T.

Theorem 4. It is $R^g_\nu = \varphi_{\to_V}$ if and only if $\nu = \varphi_V$.

Proof. If $\nu = \varphi_V$ it is: 1) If $a \in A$, $b \in A$, $R^g_\nu(b/a) = S(T(1,1), S(T(0,0), T(0,1))) = S(1, S(0,0)) = S(1,0) = 1$; 2) If $a \notin A$, $b \notin A$, $R^g_V(b/a) = S(0, S(1,0)) = S(0,1) = 1$; 3) If $a \notin A$, $b \in A$, $R^g_\nu(b/a) = S(0, S(0,1)) = S(0,1) = 1$; 4) If $a \in A$, $b \notin A$, $R^g_\nu(b/a) = S(0, S(0,0)) = S(0,0) = 0$. Then, $R^g_\nu = \varphi_{\to_V}$.

Reciprocally, if $R^g_\nu = \varphi_{\to_V}$ it is $S(T(\nu a, \nu b), S(T(1-\nu a, 1-\nu b), T(1-\nu a, \nu b))) = \text{Max}(1-\varphi_V(a), \varphi_V(b))$. If $b \notin V$, $a \in V$:

$$S(T(\nu a, \nu b), S(T(1-\nu a, 1-\nu b), T(1-\nu a, \nu b))) = 0,$$

and as Max ≤ S, it means

$$\text{Max}(T(\nu a, \nu b), S(T(1-\nu a, 1-\nu b), T(1-\nu a, \nu b))) = 0,$$

or $T(\nu a, \nu b) = T(1-\nu a, 1-\nu b) = T(1-\nu a, \nu b) = 0$. As

$R^g_\nu(a/b) = S(T(\nu b, \nu a), S(T(1-\nu b, 1-\nu a), T(1-\nu b, \nu a))) = \text{Max}(1-\varphi_V(b), \varphi_V(a))$, if $b \notin V$, $a \in V$:

$$S(0, S(0, T(1-\nu b, \nu a))) = 1 \text{ or } T(1-\nu b, \nu a) = 1.$$

But as T ≤ Min, it is also $\text{Min}(1-\nu b, \nu a) = 1$ or $1-\nu b = \nu a = 1$. Finally, $\nu b = 0$ and $\nu a = 1$. That is $\nu = \varphi_V$. ∎

2. The classical operation $a \to b = a' + ab$ suggests the Fuzzy relation
$R^W_\nu(b/a) = S(1-\varphi(a), T(\nu(a),\nu(b)))$, for a given $\nu \in [0,1]^E$, a t-conorm S and a t-norm T. (see [8]).

Theorem 5. It is $R^W_\nu = \varphi_{\to_V}$ if and only if $\nu = \varphi_V$.

Proof. If $\nu = \varphi_V$ it is easy to check that $R^W_\nu = \varphi_{\to}$, like in theorem 4. If $R^W_\nu = \varphi_{\to_V}$, it is $S(1-\nu(a), T(\nu a, {}^V\nu b)) =$ Max $(1-\varphi_V(a), \varphi_V(b))$, for any a,b, in E. Taking $a \in V$ and $b \notin V$, it is $S(1-\nu a, T(\nu a, \nu b)) = 0$, or Max $(1-\nu a, T(\nu a, \nu b)) = 0$. Then $1-\nu a = T(\nu a, \nu b) = 0$, or $\nu a = 1$ and $\nu b = 0$. In conclussion, $\nu = \varphi_V$. ■

3. Finally, the classical $a \to b = a' + b$ suggests the Fuzzy relation $R^{KD}_\nu(b/a) = S(1-\nu a, \nu b)$, for a given $\nu \in [0,1]^E$ and a t-conorm S. (see [8].

Theorem 6. It is $R^{KD}_\nu = \varphi_{\to_V}$ if and only if $\nu = \varphi_V$.

Proof. The same way of theorem 4 gives $R^{KD}_\nu = \varphi_{V\to}$ if $\nu = \varphi_V$. If $R^{KD}_\nu = \varphi_{\to_V}$ it is $S(1-\nu a, \nu b) =$ Max $(1-\varphi_V(a), \varphi_V(b))$. Taking $a \in V$, $b \notin V$:

$S(1-\nu a, \nu b) = 0$, and Max $(1-\nu a, \nu b) = 0$, or $1-\nu a = \nu b = 0$. That is $\nu = \varphi_V$. ■

As $S(1-\nu a, T(\nu a, \nu b)) \le S(1-\nu a, \nu b)$, for a given S, T and ν, it is $R^W_\nu \le R^{KD}_\nu$. More again, if $S = T^*$, the t-conorm dual of the t-norm T, it is $R^W_\nu = R^{KD}_\nu$ if and only if $T(\nu a, 1-T(\nu a, \nu b)) = T(\nu a, 1-\nu b)$. Then, a sufficient condition is that $T(x, 1-T(x,y)) = T(x, 1-y)$ for any x, y in [0,1]; taking $y = 1$, $T(x, 1-x) = 0$. This equation is satisfied if, f.ex., T belongs to the Łuckasiewicz familly, that is if $T = \varphi \circ W \circ \varphi \times \varphi$, with $\varphi : [0,1] \to [0,1]$ an increasing one-to-one mapping. Then, when $T = \varphi \circ W \circ \varphi \times \varphi$, it is $R^W_\nu = R^{KD}_\nu$. For example, if T = W, it is R_{ν}^{W} (b/a) = W^{*} (1-νa, W (νa, νb)) = Min (1,1-νa + Max (0, νa + νb -1)) = Min (1-Max (1,νa, μb))= Max (1-νa, νb)=R_{ν}^{KD}(b/a), for S = Max.

4. EXAMPLES

1. If T = Prod, S = T^{*} = Sum-Prod, it is:

* R_{ν}^{W} (b/a) = T^{*} (1-νa, νa.νb) = 1-νa + νa.νb (1-νa = 1-νa + $(\nu b)^{2}$ νb,
* R_{ν}^{KD}(b/a) = T^{*} (1-νa, νb) = 1-νa + νb - (1-νa) νb =1-νa + νa νb, the so-called Reichenbach's implication. [7]

2. If T = Min, S = T^{*} = Max, it is :

* R_{ν}^{W}(b/a) = Máx (1-νa, Min (νa, νb)), the so-called Willmot's implication [7]

* R_{ν}^{KD}(b/a) = Max (1-νa,νb), the so-called Kleene-Dienes' implication. [7]

3. If T = W, T^{*} = S = Min (1, Sum), it is

* R_{ν}^{W} (b/a) = Max (1-νa,νb) (Kleene-Dienes)
* R_{ν}^{KD}(b/a) = Min (1,1-νa-νb), the well known implication of Łuckasiewicz.

4. If S = W^{*}= Min (1,Sum), T = Prod, it is

R_{ν}^{g} (b/a) = W^{*} (νa.νb, W^{*} ((1-νa).(1-νb), (1,νa) νb))=
= Min (1, νa.νb + Min (1, (1-νa).1)) =
= Min (1, νa.νb + 1-νa) = 1-νa+νa.νb
(Reichenbach)

5. In general, the relations R_{ν}^{KD}, R_{ν}^{W} and R_{ν}^{g} are not ν-T-Conditionals when S = T^{*}. For example, if E = [0,1], ν = j and T = Min, with a = 0.5, b = 0.3 it is:

* $\mathrm{Min}\ (1, \mathrm{Max}\ (1-a, b)) = 0{,}5 \wedge (0.5 \vee 0.3) = 0{,}5 > 0.3 = b$
* $\mathrm{Min}\ (a, \mathrm{Max}\ (1-a, \mathrm{Min}\ (a,b))) = 0.5 \wedge (0.5 \vee (0.5 \wedge 0.3)) = 0.5 > b$
* $\mathrm{Min}\ (a, \mathrm{Max}\ (a \wedge b, (1-a) \wedge (1-b), (1-a) \wedge b)) = 0.5 > b.$

<u>Theorem 7</u> If $S = W^* = \mathrm{Min}\ (1, \mathrm{Sum})$, both relations R_ν^W and R_ν^{KD} are W-ν-conditionals.

Proof.

As it is $S^* = W$, then:

$S^*(\nu(a), R_\nu^W(b/a)) \leq S^*(\nu(a), R_\nu^{KD}(b/a)) = W(\nu(a), R_\nu^{KD}(b/a)) = \mathrm{Max}\ (0, \nu(a) + W^*(1-\nu a, \nu b) - 1) =$
$= \mathrm{Max}\ (0, \nu(a) + \mathrm{Min}\ (1, 1 - \nu a + \nu b) - 1) =$
$= \mathrm{Max}\ (0, \mathrm{Min}\ (\nu(a), \nu(b))) = \mathrm{Min}\ (\nu(a), \nu(b)) \leq \nu(b).$ ∎

Then, both $R_V^W(b/a) = \mathrm{Max}\ (1-\nu(a), \nu(b))$ and $R_\nu^{KD}(b/a) = \mathrm{Min}\ (1, 1-\nu a+\nu b)$ are W-ν-Conditionals.

6. The general lack of conditionality for the relations R^g, R^W and R^{KD} motivates the study of its possible character of Fuzzy Preorders. In fact, if R is a T-transitive relation it suffices to take $\mu_a(x) = R(x/a)$, for each $a \in E$, and:

$T(\mu_a(b), R(c/b)) = T(R(b/a), R(c/b)) \leq R(c/a) = \mu_a(c)$

for any b, c in E; then R is a μ_a-T-Conditional, for each $a \in E$.

<u>Lemma 8</u> If T is a t-norm such that, for any x, y, z in [0,1]:

$$T(x, 1-z) \leq T(x, 1-y) + T(y, 1-z),$$

then $W \leq T$.

Proof. With $z = 0$ we get $x \leq T(x, 1-y) + y$, or $x-y \leq$ $\leq T(x, 1-y)$. Then,

$\mathrm{Max}\ (0, x-y) = \mathrm{Max}\ (0, x + 1-y-1) = W(x, 1-y) \leq T(x, 1-y)$, for any x, y in [0,1]. Then, $W \leq T$. ∎

Lemma 9. If T is both a t-norm and a copula, then

$$T(x, 1-z) \le T(x, 1-y) + T(y, 1-z)$$

for any, x, y, z in [0,1].

Proof. If $y < z$, as $1-z < 1-y$ it is $T(x, 1-z) \le T(x, 1-y) \le T(x, 1-y) + T(y, 1-z)$, for any $x \in [0.1]$. Let it be $z \le y$. With $t = 1-z$, $r = 1-y$ the inequality becomes

$$T(x, t) - T(x, r) \le T(1-r, t).$$

But $z \le y$ implies $r \le t$ and (see [6]) $T(x,t) - T(x,r) \le t - r$. As $W \le T$[6], it is $t - r = \text{Max}(0, t-r) = \text{Max}(0, 1-r + t-1) = W(1-r, t) \le T(1-r, t)$. Then $T(x,t) - T(x,r) \le t-r \le T(1-r, t)$. ∎

Theorem 10. If S^* is both a t-norm and a copula, $R_\nu^{KD}(b/a) = S(1-\nu a, \nu b)$ is W-transitive.

Proof. $W(R_\nu^{KD}(b/a), R_\nu^{KD}(c/b)) = \text{Max}(0, S(1-\nu a, \nu b) + S(1-\nu b, \nu c) -1) = \text{Max}(0, 1-(S^*(\nu a, 1-\nu b) + S^*(\nu b, 1-\nu c))) \le \text{Max}(0, 1 - S^*(1-\nu c, \nu a)) = \text{Max}(0, S(1-\nu a, \nu c)) = S(1-\nu a, \nu c) = R_\nu^{KD}(c/a)$. ∎

Consequently, the relation

$$\hat{R}_\nu^{KD}(b/a) = \begin{cases} 1, & \text{if } a = b \\ R_\nu^{KD}(b/a), & \text{otherwise,} \end{cases}$$

is a W-Preorder. And for any $\mu_a(x) = R_\nu^{KD}(x/a) = S(1-\nu a, \nu x)$, is a μ_a-W-Conditional, provided that S^* is a t-norm and a copula. If it exists $a \in E$ such that $\nu(a) = 1$, it is $\mu_a(x) = \nu(x)$ and R_ν^{KD} is a W-ν-Conditional. Obviously, theorem 10 holds for $S^* = W$, Prod and Min.

Lemma 11. If T is both a t-norm and a copula, then

$$T(x, 1-T(x,z)) \le T(x, 1-T(x,y)) + T(y, 1 - T(y,z)),$$ for any x, y, z in [0,1].

Proof. With $\Delta = T(x, 1- T(x,z)) - T(x, 1-T(x,y)) - T(y, 1 - T(y, z))$, it should be proved that $\Delta \le 0$. 1) If $y < z$, it is $1 - T(x, z) \le 1 - T(x,y)$ and:

$T(x, 1-T(x,z)) \leq T(x,1-T(x,y)) \leq T(x, 1-T(x,y)) + T(y, 1-T(y,z))$, for any $x \in [0,1]$. 2) If $z \leq y$, it is $1-T(x,y) \leq 1-T(x,z)$. Then:

$$\Delta \leq (1-T(x,z))-(1-T(x,y)) - T(y,1-T(y,z)) =$$
$$T(x,y) - T(x,z) - T(y,1-T(y,z)) \leq y-z-T(y,1-T(y,z)) =$$
$$T(y,1) - T(y, 1-T(y,z)) - z \leq 1-(1-T(y,z)) - z =$$
$$= T(y,z) - z \leq 0.$$

Then, for any x, y, z in [0,1] it is $\Delta \leq 0$. ∎

<u>Theorem</u> <u>12.</u> If $S^* = T$ is both a t-norm and a copula, then $R_\nu^W(b/a) = T^*(1-\nu a, T(\nu a, \nu b))$ is W-transitive.

Proof. $W(R_\nu^W(b/a), R_\nu^W(c/b)) = \text{Max}(0, 1-T(\nu a, 1-T(\nu a, \nu b)-T(\nu b, 1-T(\nu b,\nu c)) \leq \text{Max}(0, 1-T(\nu a, 1-T(\nu a,\nu c))) =$ $= \text{Max}(0, T^*(1-\nu a, T(\nu a, \nu c))) = T^*(1-\nu a, T(\nu a, \nu c) =$ $= R_\nu^W(c/a)$. ∎

Consequently, the relation

$$\hat{R}_\nu^W(b/a) = \begin{cases} 1, & \text{if } a = b \\ T^*(1-\nu a, T(\nu a,\nu b)), & \text{otherwise,} \end{cases}$$

is a W-Preorder. And for any $\mu_a(x) = T^*(1-\nu a, T(\nu a, \nu x))$, is a μ_a-W-Conditional, provided that T is both a t-norm and a copula. If it exists $a \in E$ such that $\nu(a) = 1$, is $\mu_a = \nu$ and R_ν^W is a W-ν-Conditional. Obviously, the theorem holds for T = Min, Prod, and W.

<u>Remarks</u> A. The Fuzzy Relations, $R_\nu^{KD}(b/a) = \text{Max}(1-\nu a, \nu b)$ and $R_\nu^W(b/a) = \text{Max}(1-\nu a, \text{Min}(\nu a,\nu b))$ are ν-W-Conditionals for any $\nu \in [0,1]^E$ "having points", that is $\nu(x) = 1$ for some $x \in E$.

B. The Fuzzy Relations $R_\nu^{KD}(b/a) = \text{Max}(1-\nu a, \nu b)$, $R_\nu^W(b/a) = \text{Max}(1-\nu a, \text{Min}(\nu a, \nu b))$ and $R_\nu^r(b/a) = 1-\nu(a) + \nu(a).\nu(b)$ are neither Min-Transitivenor Prod-Transitive. In fact, taken $\nu(a) = 0.8$, $\nu(b) = 0.5$ and $\nu(c) = 0.21$, it follows:

- $R_\nu^{KD}(b/a). R_\nu^{KD}(c/b) = \text{Max}(0.2, 0.5). \text{Max}(0.5, 0,21) \geq$ $\geq 0.25 > 0.21 = \text{Max}(0.2, 0.21)$.

$- R_\nu^W (b/a).\ R_\nu^W(c/b) = 0.5 \times 0.5 > 0.21 = R_\nu^W(c/a).$

Then, they are not Prod-transitive and a fortiori they are not Min-transitive. Analogously, taken $\nu(a) = 1, \nu(b) = 1/2$, $\nu(c) = 1/4$, it is

$$- R_\nu^r (b/a).\ R_\nu^r(c/b) = \frac{1}{2} \cdot \frac{5}{8} = \frac{5}{16} > \frac{1}{4} = R_\nu^r (c/a),$$

and the Reichenbach's Conditional is not Prod-transitive and a fortiori is not Min-transitive.

C. The analysis of the possible transitivity of R_ν^g gives also, in general, a negative answer. In fact, if S = Max and T = Min, it is

$R_\nu^g(y/x) = \mathrm{Max}\ (\mathrm{Min}\ (\nu x,\ \nu y),\ \mathrm{Min}\ (1-\nu a,\ 1-\nu y),\ \mathrm{Min}\ (1-\nu x,\ \nu y))$ and, if $\nu(a) = 1$, $\nu(b) = 1/2$, $\nu(c) = 1/8$, it is

$$R_\nu^g(b/a) = \mathrm{Max}\ (1/2,\ 0,\ 0) = 1/2,$$

$$R_\nu^g(c/b) = \mathrm{Max}\ (\tfrac{1}{8}, \tfrac{1}{2}, \tfrac{1}{8}) = \tfrac{1}{2}$$

$$R_\nu^g\ (c/a) = \mathrm{Max}\ (1/8.\ 0,\ 0) = \tfrac{1}{8}.$$

Then,

$$\mathrm{Prod}\ (R_\nu^g\ (b/a),\ R_\nu^g\ (c/b)) = \tfrac{1}{4} > \tfrac{1}{8} = R_\nu^g\ (c/a).$$

Consequently, such relation is neither Prod-transitive nor Min-transitive.

Nevertheless, the analysis of the W-transitivity for some relations R_ν^g remains an open problem.

IV. THE SPECIAL CASE OF MAMDANI's CONDITIONALS

It is a serious difficulty when using the V-Material Conditional that, if $a \in E-V$ (is a false) then $a \to_V b$ for any $b \in E$. Because of that it seems better for practical purposes to use conditionals $\Rightarrow$ such that

$$\Rightarrow \subset V\times V \subset \rightarrow_V .$$

In the applications of Fuzzy Logic to Control it is widely used [7] the so-called Mamdani's implication

$$R^m_\nu(b/a) = \mathrm{Min}\ (\nu(a),\ \nu(b)),$$

belonging to the family of Inexact Relations

$$R^T_\nu\ (b/a) = T\ (\nu(a),\ \nu(b)),$$

for any t-norm T. Obviously, those relations are symmetrical and verify

$$R^g_\nu\ (b/a) \le S\ (T\ (\nu a, \nu b),\ 0) = R^T_\nu(b/a),$$

for the selected t-norm T.

<u>Theorem</u> <u>13</u>. Every R^T_ν is a T'-ν-Conditional for any t-norm T'.

Proof. $T'(\nu a,\ R^T_\nu\ (b/a)) \le \mathrm{Min}\ (\nu a,\ T(\nu b)) \le \mathrm{Min}\ (\nu a, \nu b) \le$ $\le \nu b.$ ■

<u>Theorem</u> <u>14</u>. It is $R^T_\nu = \varphi_{\ V\times V}$ if and only if $\nu = \varphi_V$.

Proof. If $\nu = \varphi_V$, $1 = R^T_V\ (b/a) = T(\nu a,\ \nu b)$ implies Min $(\varphi_V$ $(a),\ \varphi_V\ (b)) = 1$ or $\varphi_V\ (a) = \varphi_V\ (b) = 1$, and $(a,b) \in V\times V$; then $R^T_\varphi = \varphi_{V\times V}$. Reciprocally, if $R^T_{\varphi_V} = \varphi_{V\times V}$, it is

$$T\ (\nu a, \nu b) = \mathrm{Min}\ (\varphi_V(a),\ \varphi(b))$$

for any a,b in E. Then, for a fixed $a \in V$ it is $T\ (\nu a, \nu b) =$ $\varphi_V\ (b)$ for any $b \in V$; in particular, for any $b \in V$ it is T $(\nu a, \nu b) = 1$ or $\nu a = \nu b = 1$, and $\nu(x) = 1$ for any $x \in V$. Analogously, for any $a \notin V$ it is $T(\nu a, \nu b) = 0$ for any $b \in$ E; in particular, if $b \in V$ it is $T(\nu a,\ 1) = \nu a = 0$, and $\nu(y) = 0$ for any $y \notin V$. Finally, $\nu = \varphi_V$. ■

<u>Theorem</u> <u>15</u>. If $T \ge W$, R^T_ν is W-transitive.

Proof. $W\ (R^T_\nu(b/a),\ R^T_\nu\ (c/b)) = W\ (T\ (\nu a, \nu b),\ T\ (\nu b, \nu c)) \le$ $\le W\ (\nu a, \nu c) \le T(\nu a, \nu c) = = R^T_\nu(c/a).$ ■

Theorem 16. For any t-norm T, R_{ν}^{m} is T-transitive.

Proof. T $(R_{\nu}^{m}$ (b/a), R_{ν}^{m} c/b) $\leq$ Min (Min (νa, νb), Min (νb, νc)) = Min (νa, νb, νc) $\leq$ Min (νa, νc) $= R_{\nu}^{m}$ (c/a). ■

Consequently [5],

- The Fuzzy Relation $\hat{R}_{\nu}^{m}(b/a) = \begin{cases} 1, & \text{if } a = b \\ \text{Min}(\nu a, \nu b), & \text{otherwise} \end{cases}$,

  is a T-indistinguishability Operator for any t-norm T.

- The Fuzzy Relations $R_{\nu}^{T}(b/a) = \begin{cases} 1, & \text{if } a = b \\ T(\nu a, \nu b), & \text{otherwise} \end{cases}$,
  are W-indistinguishability Operators.

REFERENCES

[1] E. Trillas, (1992), "On Exact Conditionals" to in STOCHASTICA, XIII-1, 137-143.

[2] E.Trillas, and S. Cubillo, (1992), "On Monotonic Fuzzy Conditionals", submitted to the JOURNAL OF APPLIED NON-CLASSICAL LOGICS.

[3] E. Trillas, and C. Alsina, (1993); "Logic: going farther from Tarski?" FUZZY SETS AND SYSTEMS, 53, 1-13.

[4] C. Alsina and E. Trillas, (1991) "Some Remarks onApproximate Entailment", INTERNATIONAL JOURNAL OF APPROXIMATE REASONING, (6), 525-533.

[5] Ll. Valverde, (1985) "On the Structure of F-indistinguishability operators", FUZZY SETS AND SYSTEMS, 17, 313-328.

[6] B. Scheweizer, and A. Sklar, (1983), PROBÁBILISTIC METRIC SPACES, North-Holland.

[7] B. Bouchon-Meunier and Yao Jia (1992) "Linguistic Modifiers and Imprecise Categories", INTERNATIONAL JOURNAL OF INTELLIGENT SYSTEMS, 7, 25-36.

[8] C. Alsina and E. Trillas, (1984) "Sobre operadors d'implicació en lògica polivalent", ACTES DEL TERCER CONGRÉS CATALA DE LOGICA MATEMATICA, 59-61.

Integrating resolution–like procedures with Łukasiewicz implication*

Guglielmo TAMBURRINI ° *and Settimo TERMINI* °,•
° Istituto di Cibernetica del C.N.R., Arco Felice (Napoli)
• Dipartimento di Matematica dell'Università di Palermo

Abstract

We discuss some conceptual and technical problems raised by the attempt of integrating resolution-like procedures with the use of Łukasiewicz implication $Min\{1, 1 - [a] + [b]\}$ in an environment of approximate reasoning modelled by fuzzy logics.

1 Motivations

Uncertainty, imprecision, vagueness, partial and revisable information, all play a crucial role in AI and Cognitive Science. This fact suggests a clear motive of interest for the development of comprehensive formal theories capturing the relevant nuances of uncertainty and related notions. However, work in this direction has been piloted by a justifiable emphasis on working applications – which may only need ad hoc hypotheses and techniques suitable for treating uncertainty in restricted domains – as a consequence of the difficulty of constructing a theory providing both a general conceptual framework and technical tools to be used in specific situations. One is confronted with this situation also in the domain of approximate inference: (partial) conceptual analyses must proceed on a par with the development of technical tools for specific domains. It is this general perspective that we adopt here, presenting some initial developments of resolution–like techniques in a fuzzy logic with Łukasiewicz implication, in the framework of more general considerations on the roles that Kleene and Łukasiewicz systems may play in an overarching theory of uncertainty and vagueness.

---

*We are grateful to an anonymous referee for some useful suggestions. The work of the second author was partially supported by C.N.R. with grant n. 91.04096.CT12.

The problem of finding a many-valued version of the resolution principle was first studied by Lee [1]. Even though the technical result is purely based on properties of the connectives of a many-valued logic, this work can be viewed as an early attempt at providing automated reasoning tools for the (then) recent proposal of Lotfi Zadeh [2] of modelling vagueness through fuzzy sets. More recently, Mukaidono [3] has further developed this idea paving the way for a definition of a fuzzy prolog. These proposals use the so-called Kleene implication ($a \rightarrow b \;\; iff \;\; \neg a \vee b$), which is the most straightforward generalization of classical implication.

It is well known that several other implication connectives, which formalize different nuances of many-valued logics, have been introduced and used. A central role among them is played by the implication $a \rightarrow_{\text{Ł}} b$, defined semantically as $[a \rightarrow_{\text{Ł}} b] = Min\{1, 1 - [a] + [b]\}$, where $[x]$, a number in the interval [0, 1] of the real line, is the truth value assumed by x. This connective was introduced by Łukasiewicz on the basis of the observation that the straightforward extension of the classical implication ($a \rightarrow b \;\; iff \;\; \neg a \vee b$) to the many-valued case does not preserve the tautologousness of $a \rightarrow a$, for propositions assuming truth values different from 0 and 1, if the other connectives are interpreted in the usual way.

A wide variety of considerations suggests the conceptual significance of Łukasiewicz logic. In this context we just recall that it plays an important role in standard developments of fuzzy logic and, at a more theoretical level, that Pavelka [4] has shown that it is the only many-valued logic satisfying some highly desirable properties. Moreover, it is well known that systems of many-valued logics with different implications capture different nuances of approximate reasoning: it has been suggested, for example, that Kleene's system could more reasonably capture (at least in its original three valued form) aspects of situations, intrinsically classical but incompletely known, whereas Łukasiewicz system could grasp situations characterized by the presence of more ineradicable vagueness.

In this context, the idea that different implications can capture various nuances of approximate reasoning can be brought out by considering as the "degree of reliability" – with which a certain formula b, having a truth value $[b]$, has been inferred – the truth value of the conjunction of all the formulas used to infer it. Thus, for instance, if b was derived by modus ponens from a and ($a \rightarrow b$), its "degree of reliability" is given by $[a \wedge (a \rightarrow b)]$, and if b is the resolvent of the parent clauses A and C, then its "degree of reliability" is given by $[A \wedge C]$. As is to be expected, one can easily check that the "degrees of reliability" of formulas derivable in Kleene's system and in Łukasiewicz system do not, in general, coincide. Also in the light of this semantical consideration, the development of a relatively efficient calculus for Lukasiewicz system seems desirable. In particular, the widespread use of resolution in automated theorem proving and its relatives (e.g. Prolog and Logic Programming), and the central role that Lukasiewicz implication plays in all the developments and applications of fuzzy logics, suggest that their possible integration, in addition to a clear theoretical interest, can provide a useful framework for the development of programming tools in approximate environments.

In what follows we discuss some preliminary problems presented by the introduction of a variant of the resolution principle [5] for a Lukasiewicz many-valued logic. For a standard presentation of resolution techniques see, e.g., [6].

2 Formal issues

The resolution principle in classical logic relies on the fact that $a \rightarrow b$ *iff* $\neg a \vee b$. It is then natural that the first attempt at finding versions of the resolution principle in many-valued logics made use of Kleene implication which straighforwardly generalizes the classical connective. In this section, after fixing the formalism and presenting some preliminaries, we explore the possibility of integrating a resolution-like procedure with Lukasiewicz implication.

2.1 Notations

Let L be a set of logical formulas generated by a (finite) set of atomic propositions, closed under the logical operations of union, intersection, negation and implication, semantically defined as follows:

1) $[a \vee b] = Max\{[a],[b]\}$ (disjunction)

2) $[a \wedge b] = Min\{[a],[b]\}$ (conjunction)

3) $[\neg a] = 1 - [a]$ (negation)

4a) $[a \rightarrow_K b] = Max\{1 - [a],[b]\}$ (Kleene implication)

or, alternatively:

4b) $[a \rightarrow_{\mathrm{L}} b] = Min\{1, 1 - [a] + [b]\}$ (Lukasiewicz implication)

where [ ] is a mapping from L to the interval [0, 1] of the real line and $[x]$ is interpreted as the truth value of the formula x, satisfying the above definitions.

A propositional system of logic in which the connectives $\neg, \wedge, \vee, \rightarrow$ are interpreted according to 1-3 and 4a (resp.: 4b) is called a many-valued Kleene (resp.: Lukasiewicz) logic, which will be denoted by L_K (resp.: L_{L}). Roughly speaking, one can say that if one justifies an inference procedure using implication 4a one is working in the setting of a Kleene (many-valued) logic, whereas if one justifies an inference procedure using implication 4b, one is working in the setting of a Lukasiewicz (many-valued) logic.

2.2 The case of Łukasiewicz implication

Since the resolution principle assumes the equivalence between $a \rightarrow b$ and $\neg a \vee b$ it is clear that the problem of finding a variant of this principle in thc setting of Lukasiewicz logic is far from being reducible to a more or less straightforward translation of classical properties into a many-valued setting. In what follows we shall outline some preliminary ideas for addressing this problem. Our starting point is the simple observation that the truth value of the (Łukasiewicz) implication $a \rightarrow_{\mathrm{L}} b$ which is given by $Min\{1, 1 - [a] + [b]\}$ can be equivalently written, by using the limited subtraction $[a] \dot{-} [b] = Max\{0, [a] - [b]\}$, as $Max\{1 - ([a] \dot{-} [b]), b\}$. The latter has a structure resembling (4a), but instead of the truth value of the antecedent a, one finds the value $[a] \dot{-} [b]$. We could then try to parallel the formalism of the resolution procedures by introducing, for Lukasiewicz logic, a new type of formula aMb, whose semantical interpretation is given by $[aMb] = [a] \dot{-} [b]$. aMb can be regarded as a measure of how much a "majorates" b and we shall then call it the "a-majorant of b". From the semantical definition, it follows that Lukasiewicz implication is also equivalent to $1 - ([a] \dot{-} [b])$, that is to $1 - [aMb]$.

Lukasiewicz implication is not reducible to the other classical connectives, unlike Kleene's. And this irreducibility, though semantically justifiable, complicates the calculus. As a first step towards a variant resolution, let us notice that for any formula a of L_{L} one can find a semantically equivalent translation a^* containing only negations, conjunctions, disjunctions and majorants (by assuming the equivalence $a \rightarrow_L b \ iff \ \neg(aMb)$).

Let us list now some properties of the connective M:

1) $[\neg\neg(aMb)] = [aMb]$

2) $[aM(b \vee c)] = [(aMb) \wedge (aMc)]$

3) $[(a \vee b)Mc] = [(aMc) \vee (bMc)]$

4) $[aM(b \wedge c)] = [(aMb) \vee (aMc)]$

5) $[(a \wedge b)Mc] = [(aMc) \wedge (bMc)]$

6) $[aMb] = [\neg bM\neg a]$.

These properties, together with the classical properties of $\neg$, $\wedge$, $\vee$, enable one to reduce each a^* into an "extended" conjunctive normal form, i.e. one which allows also for the presence of majorants and their negations.

Let us immediately observe that from (6) it follows straightforwardly that the contrapositive property of implication in its standard form, $a \rightarrow_L b$ *iff* $\neg b \rightarrow_L \neg a$, holds.

Let us now briefly sketch a possible resolution-like procedure for formulas in extended conjunctive normal form. The classical simplification rule of resolution is admitted; moreover:

1) MP: If F and G are two clauses such that F contains a and a formula in G contains $\neg(aMb)$ as a subformula, then erase a from F and $\neg(aMb)$ from G, writing b in its place. Finally, in accordance with the resolution procedure, take the union of the resulting clauses F' and G'.

2) MT: if F contains $\neg b$ and $\neg(aMb)$ is a subformula of a formula in G, one is allowed to cancel them both and to write $\neg a$ in the place of $\neg(aMb)$. Finally, in accordance with the resolution procedure, one takes the union of the resulting clauses F' and G'.

Let us observe that in the light of (6), the rule MT is redundant since, by transforming aMb into $\neg bM\neg a$, rule MP is immediately applicable to the modified premises and yields the same result as MT applied to the (unmodified) set of premises. MP, when applicable, allows one to reduce the possible nestings of M-operators.

3 Semantical issues

It is well known that the management of truth values is a central issue in many valued logics in general, and in the particular use which is made of them as a technical tool for modelling approximate reasoning. It is this second aspect that induced us to consider the possibility of developing resolution–like procedures also in the case in which Lukasiewicz implication is involved. Indeed, different implications in a many valued setting capture various facets of the vagueness (imprecision, approximation, etc.) present in the description of states of affairs. This point was briefly touched upon in the introduction. For a general discussion see, e.g., [8].

A conceptual analysis of the type of uncertainty associated to given states of affairs should motivate the choice of a certain implication. The adequacy of this choice should be evaluated by considering the relations obtaining between the truth values of such descriptions of states of affairs and the truth values of their syntactical consequences (which obviously depend also on the chosen type of implication).

In this connection, we limit ourselves to make the following two remarks:

(a) The "degree of reliability" of a derivation of a given formula from certain premises, if measured according to the criteria stated in section 1, is in general not the same if different implications are used, as was already observed there. Although the proposed way of measuring the degree of reliability seems very natural, it remains an open problem to see whether other measures can be fruitfully used, and which form these measures can in general assume.

(b) In using many valued logics as a tool for the modelling of approximate reasoning, it is also useful to have a sort of control on the truth–value assumed by the conclusion, once the truth–values of the premises are given. This point is of course related to (a) above, but is also of some independent interest.

For example, as concerns (b), in his study of the properties of Klenee's implication, Lee [1] showed that the truth value of the resolvent is always greater than 0.5 in the case in which the truth values of the parent clauses are also greater than 0.5. This result is no more valid, as one can easily check, if Lukasiewicz's implication is considered. However, one may study the more general and quite open problem of which semantic relations hold between the premises and the conclusions of arbitrary systems of many valued logic, and in the case of Lukasiewicz's implication, one may look for semantic properties similar to those found by Lee. Just to give an example, if $[\neg(aMb) \vee s] \geq \alpha$, and $[a \vee r] \geq \beta$ then the clause obtained in our calculus by MP satisfies the following relation:

$$[b \vee r \vee s] \geq Max(0, \alpha + \beta - 1) \qquad (*)$$

To check this relation, it is enough to observe that:

(i) if $[s] \geq \alpha$ or $[r] \geq \beta$, then $(*)$ follows by the fact that $[b \vee r \vee s] \geq \gamma$ and $\gamma \geq \alpha + \beta - 1$ (where γ is, in the two possible cases, respectively equal to α or to β).

(ii) If the conditions of (i) are not verified, then we must have both $[\neg(aMb)] \geq \alpha$ and $[a] \geq \beta$. So, if $[b] \geq [a]$, we have that $[b] \geq [a] \geq \beta$ and $(*)$ follows. Otherwise, if $[a] > [b]$, then $[\neg(aMb)] = 1 - ([a] \dot{-} [b]) = 1 - ([a] - [b]) \geq \alpha$; by using the fact that $[a] \geq \beta$, we have then $[b] \geq \alpha + \beta - 1$, from which $(*)$ follows.

The problem of operating the appropriate selection between various implications, and thus between various calculi, has been often given a rather restrictive interpretation: choose a unique implication for the many valued setting and formalize by means of this connective any conditional proposition characterized by the presence of some form of uncertainty or vagueness. Another approach is suggested by various remarks made here: the choice of appropriate implications is context dependent; different implication operators definable in many valued logics correspond to different forms of vagueness or uncertainty. Let us briefly discuss this general point in connection with the two types of implications considered in this paper.

Kleene infinite valued system is a generalization of the three valued system introduced by Kleene [7] in his treatment of partial recursive predicates. The three valued system admits the truth values T, F, and U, which stands for "Undefined." The tautologousness of $p \rightarrow p$, it was pointed out above, is not preserved in this system. Furthermore, if a tautology is a w.f.f. which assumes the truth value T for any assignment of truth values to its propositional letters, then this three valued system does not admit any tautology. Indeed, no w.f.f. of Kleene's system is true under all interpretations, and the set of w.f.f.'s that are never false (either true or undefined) coincides with the set of tautologies in the classical propositional calculus. This fact may appear counterintuitive, but a reasonable interpretation of it can be given if one understands U as the assertion that we are presently (or sometimes even permanently) incapable of determining a truth value for a certain proposition p. This interpretation does not entail that the truth value of p must or even can be different from T or F. "The third 'truth value' U – Kleene observed – is... not on a par with the other two T and F in our theory."

While Łukasiewicz's scheme can be viewed as an attempt at capturing some *structural* aspects of vague propositions, Kleene's scheme seems suitable for describing situations that are intrinsically classical but characterized by the presence of incomplete knowledge – situations in which such knowledge enables one to isolate contradictions but prevents one from isolating a corpus of indubitable propositions (the classical tautologies).

References

[1] R.C.T. LEE (1972), Fuzzy Logic and the Resolution Principle, *Journal A.C.M.* **19**, 109-119.

[2] L.A. ZADEH (1965), Fuzzy Sets, *Information and Control* **8**, 338-353.

[3] M. MUKAIDONO et al. (1989), Fundamentals of Fuzzy Prolog, *International J. of Approximate Reasoning* **3**, 179-193.

[4] J. PAVELKA (1979) On Fuzzy Logic, I, II, III *Zeitschrift für Mathematische Logik und Grundlagen der Mathematik* **25**, 45–52, 119–134, 447–464.

[5] J.A. ROBINSON (1965), A Machine-oriented Logic Based on the Resolution Principle *Journal A.C.M.* **12**, 23-41.

[6] C.L. CHANG and R.C.T. LEE (1973), *Symbolic Logic and Mechanical Theorem Proving*, Academic Press, New York.

[7] S.C. KLEENE (1952), *Introduction to Metamathematics*, Noordhoff, Groningen.

[8] H.J. SKALA, S. TERMINI and E. TRILLAS (1984), *Aspects of Vagueness*, D. Reidel, Dordrecht.

The Development of a "Logic of Argumentation"

Paul Krause‡, Simon Ambler† and John Fox‡

‡ Imperial Cancer Research Fund, Lincoln's Inn Fields
London, WC2A 3PX

† Department of Computer Science and Statistics, Queen Mary and Westfield College
London, E1 4NS

Abstract. A recurring problem with the development of decision support systems in medicine is the difficulty of eliciting precise numerical uncertainty values for large fragments of the domain. A prototype information system for general practitioners, the Oxford System of Medicine (OSM), addressed this problem by using an informal mechanism of argumentation. Arguments supporting and opposing the propositions of interest were identified when numerical uncertainty values where unavailable. We propose, in this paper, a proof theoretic model for reasoning under uncertainty which is motivated by the need to provide a formal underpinning for the OSM inference engine. As well as giving a presentation of a "Logic of Argumentation" (LA) as a labelled deduction system, we also discuss the development of a category theoretic semantics for LA.

1 Introduction

Probability then is a likeness to be true. The very notation of the word signifying as much, and from its derivation may thus be defined: "Probabile est quod probari potest," i.e., a proposition for which there be arguments or proofs to make it pass or be received for true. (John Locke, 1671 [17]).

One recurring problem with the development of decision support systems for large scale applications is the difficulty of eliciting, or the unavailability of, precise numerical coefficients for uncertain rules or facts. However, there is evidence that the identification of the factors which are relevant to a problem is actually more important than the precise numerical values used [3, 4]. Can we exploit this in designing a method for reasoning under uncertainty which is not dependent on the availability of precise numerical coefficients?

Rather than modelling reasoning by a pre-identified network of probabilistic links between propositions or inference rules directly relating propositions, we suggest that a more general model of commonsense reasoning is that of identifying and appraising *arguments* using whatever sources of information are available or relevant to the problem at hand [8]. For example, we may use general knowledge about living cells to construct a default argument that a cell in an organism will be growth limited by some mechanism. However, given the more specific information that the cell under study is a tumour cell we can construct a further argument that the cell will not be growth limited. We may appraise these arguments on the basis of the nature of the information used to construct them, perhaps preferring arguments which use the most specific information. A comparison of the relative merits of these two arguments would suggest that the cell is not growth limited is the correct conclusion.

A version of this model has been employed in a prototype information system for General Practitioners; the *Oxford System of Medicine* (OSM) [6]. The work reported here was motivated by a need to produce a formal model of the inference engine used in the OSM. However, we believe it has much wider application as a model for reasoning under uncertainty.

In this paper we propose a *proof theoretic* model for reasoning under uncertainty in which propositions are annotated with a succinct representation of their proofs. These proofs are *contingent proofs*. They may fail to establish the conclusion, perhaps because the link between the premise and the conclusion is uncertain in some way, or perhaps because the premise itself is uncertain. For this reason, we use the less categorical term "argument"; arguments are proofs which can fail. We define an inference mechanism in which propositions are labelled with a succinct representation of the arguments which support their validity. Identifying further *distinct* arguments for a proposition will in general increase the support for that proposition.

This inference procedure will enable the identification of arguments supporting, or opposing, the truth of various propositions. These arguments may then be treated as objects in themselves and reasoned about at the meta-level. We may for example; assign a subjective measure of confidence to the arguments, simply count up supporting arguments, or perhaps assign a preference on the basis of the specificity of the information used in constructing the arguments.

The reference to the "meta-level" in the previous paragraph identifies an important component of our model for reasoning under uncertainty; having identified arguments, we need to reason *about* them. Arguments are derived at the object level. We reason about those arguments, aggregate arguments, resolve inconsistencies between arguments, at the meta-level. Uncertainty or probability is a meta-level concept derived from an evaluation of the arguments concerning the propositions of interest.

2 A Logic for Identifying Arguments

We now present a formal model of "argumentation". Broadly, argumentation can be decomposed into two components; the construction of arguments themselves, and the reasoning about arguments at the meta-level. We will present a logical model for the construction of arguments in this section, and outline how this may be turned into a mechanical procedure in the next section. Aspects of meta-level reasoning will be covered less extensively in this paper.

In fact, the proposal is not so much to generate a new logic as to augment an existing logic; we wish to annotate propositions with a succinct representation of their proofs. That is, we wish to use a labelled deductive system [9], where the labels are representations of the arguments supporting the subject of the deduction.

What logic should we use to represent the underlying reasoning process? We may construct arguments for a proposition, and we may construct arguments for its negation. However, in the absence of information, we will have no prior belief in the proposition or its negation. This denial of the law of the excluded middle means that we will only accept "constructive" proofs; not proofs by contradiction. That is, the logic underlying argumentation is intuitionistic logic [12]. For the present, attention will be restricted to that fragment of intuitionistic logic which uses only the logical operators conjunction and implication. We next need to augment the logic by labelling propositions with a succinct representation of the arguments which support those propositions. This enables us to reason about the arguments themselves. Perhaps the simplest form of reasoning is merely to count arguments and obtain conclusions such as, "proposition P_1 has more supporting arguments than proposition P_2" (the improper linear model). Alternatively, one may have sufficient information to be able to assign a confidence measure to the argument.

The first requirement for any formal theory of argumentation is that we be able to identify some criteria for judging when arguments are distinct. This is a weaker condition than the requirement for arguments to be independent, which we may also need, but is a necessary first step. For example, in order to conclude whether $A \supset B$ is derivable from a knowledge base containing the axiom $A \supset B$, I may just say; "I know $A \supset B$; it is an axiom" (we use $\supset$ here to represent implication). Alternatively, I may assume A, then apply the axiom $A \supset B$ to it to conclude B. Then discharging the assumption A, I conclude $A \supset B$. Both proofs have used essentially the same information, but in a slightly different way. Are they the same, or are they different arguments? The development of an equational theory over proofs has received a great deal of thought from logicians, and there is a well established body of work on typed proof theory which may be applied to this problem [11, 13].

We use typed lambda terms as proof terms to give a concise representation of arguments. This gives us an equational theory over proof terms which has a formal agreed basis, so that we can say when two arguments are equal (are reducible to the same normal form). In this proof theoretic view of logic, a proof x of a formula A is equivalent to saying that the 'proof term' x is of type A (written $x{:}A$). Then if we have a proof $x{:}A$ and a proof $y{:}B$ for example, pairing x with y will yield a proof $pair(x,y){:}\ A \wedge B$ of the conjunction. The functional view of proofs first becomes apparent on considering a proof of an implication. By stating that $f{:}\ A \supset B$ we are saying that f is a function which takes a proof term of type A as argument and returns a proof term of type B.

Returning to the question of equivalence between two arguments posed above, the second argument is an example of hypothetical reasoning. By assuming A we generate a proof of B, and so conclude $A \supset B$. By the above, we would expect the proof term corresponding to the conclusion to be a function and this is where the notation of the lambda calculus comes into play. From the assumption $x{:}A$ a proof $v{:}B$ is derived. The lambda-term $\lambda x.v$ denotes a function which takes a single argument u of type A and returns a term $[u/x]v$ of type B (in which all occurrences of x in v are substituted by u). That is $\lambda x.v$ is the lambda abstraction of the proof of B; lambda abstraction corresponds to the discharging of assumptions. In our specific example, if $f{:}\ A \supset B$ then $\lambda x.apply(f,x)$ is also of type $A \supset B$. But by eta-conversion, [13], $\lambda x.apply(f,x)$ reduces to f; both arguments reduce to the same normal form.

We will now give a *sequent calculus* presentation of the "logic of argumentation". A sequent is usually written as an expression $\underline{A} \Rightarrow \underline{B}$; where $\Rightarrow$ represents an entailment relation, $\underline{A}$ and $\underline{B}$ are finite sequences of formulae [10]. A naive interpretation of a sequent is that the conjunction of the formulae in $\underline{A}$ implies the disjunction of the formulae in $\underline{B}$. In our presentation, the sequents are of the form:

Context $\Rightarrow$ Term: Formula

This may be read informally as "an argument, *Term*, for *Formula* can be constructed from the arguments for the formulae in *Context*". These arguments may be generated by a sequence of rule applications using the set of inference rules presented in Figure 1. In these rules Γ is a multiset of declarations $x{:}\ A$ (x is a variable of type A) and 'Γ, $x{:}A$' denotes the multiset Γ extended by $x{:}A$. The rule labelled '$\Rightarrow$ &' may be read, for example, as; "if x is an argument for A and y is an argument for B, derivable from a

Axiom $$\frac{}{\Gamma, x: A \Rightarrow x: A}$$

(& ⇒) $$\frac{x: A, y{:}B, \Gamma \Rightarrow u: C}{\Gamma, z: A \,\&\, B \Rightarrow [fst(z)/x][snd(z)/y]u: C}$$

(⇒ &) $$\frac{\Gamma \Rightarrow s: A \qquad \Gamma \Rightarrow t{:}B}{\Gamma \Rightarrow pair(s,t): A \,\&\, B}$$

(⊃ ⇒) $$\frac{\Gamma, f: A \supset B \Rightarrow s: A \qquad x: B, \Gamma \Rightarrow u: C}{\Gamma, f: A \supset B \Rightarrow [apply(f, s)/x]u: C}$$

(⇒ ⊃) $$\frac{x: A, \Gamma \Rightarrow t{:}\, B}{\Gamma \Rightarrow \lambda x.t{:}\, A \supset B}$$

Fig. 1. Rule set defining the construction of arguments with their associated proof terms. (By [u/x]v, we mean the term generated by substituting u for x in v).

context Γ, then *pair(x,y)* is an argument for *A & B* from the same context". Note that there are no explicit rules for negation; we translate $\neg A$ into $A \supset \bot$ before applying the rules. In addition, ⊥ should be read as "contradiction", which is intended as a slightly weaker concept than the usual logical reading as *falsum*. A knowledge base which enables support for the contradiction to be derived is not necessarily pathological; consequently we do not admit a rule which propagates support for ⊥ to all propositions.

3 Outline of the Argumentation Theorem Prover (ATP)

An abstract formalism is very fine, but can we turn this into an implementation which is sound and complete with respect to this model? This is certainly possible in the propositional case, and we will give an outline of the argumentation theorem prover (ATP) here.

With a given context, Γ, and a formula *C* to be proven, the general strategy is to run the rules of Figure 1 backwards to generate the proof term which corresponds to an argument from Γ supporting *C*. Unfortunately, application of '⊃ ⇒' will not necessarily result in simpler sub-formulae. For example, in attempting to construct an argument supporting *A* from a context Γ = {*r1*: *A*⇒*B*, *r2*: *B*⇒*A*} (which should fail) a non-terminating recursive loop will be generated through this rule. There are two strategies for eliminating this problem. One could use a programming solution and incorporate some form of loop checking into the theorem prover. Or one can use a modified rule set which is known to allow the same set of theorems, but which avoids the use of the problematic rule '⊃ ⇒' [5]. We have versions of the 'ATP' which use each of these approaches.

One needs to do a bit more work than just to apply the rule set in its raw form. The theorem prover should return all *distinct* arguments. So, having used the rule set to generate a proof term as a representation of an argument, it now needs to be reduced to its normal form. Then the distinct normal forms correspond to the distinct arguments which we require. This reduction can be achieved by applying the following rules. The term will be in normal form if it cannot be further reduced by applying any of these rules to the term itself or to any of its sub terms:

fst(pair(*u*,*v*)) » *u* snd(pair(*u*,*v*)) » *v*

apply(λ*x*.*v*,*u*) » [*u*/*x*]*v* pair(fst(*t*), snd(*t*)) » *t*

λ*x*.apply(*t*,*x*) » *t* (*x* not free in *t*)

It is a consequence of the *Church-Rosser property* and the *strong normalisation theorem* [13] that a reduction using these rules will always terminate with the unique normal form. As with the generation of the term in the first place, one needs to do a little more work to run this part of the program effectively. In particular, we use the de Bruijn notation for lambda calculus to keep track of variables in the terms [2].

4 Aggregation of Arguments and Semi-lattice Enriched Categories

As information becomes available arguments will be identified which support, or oppose, the propositions of interest. In the absence of any confirming arguments, we then need to aggregate support from these arguments. A simple approach is to count the number of supporting arguments and subtract the number of negating arguments for each hypothesis. This sounds a bit cavalier, but such a counting of pros and cons (technically, an improper linear model with uniform weighting) is intuitive and effective [4, 18]. However, we may be able to refine the aggregation procedure further by associating a measure of *confidence* to the arguments. We will outline the formal basis of this refinement in this section.

To do this we need to take a more algebraic view of argumentation. We give the semantics of the logic of argumentation (LA) a precise mathematical meaning by giving a category theoretic account of arguments [1]. In category theory, a category C has an associated set of 'objects' and a set of 'arrows'. In particular, a *deductive system* may be modelled as a category where the objects are propositions (A, B, ...) and the arrows ($f, g, \ldots$) correspond to proofs [15]. For example, the arrow f: A $\rightarrow$ B corresponds to a proof of A $\vdash$ B. We may compose arrows, so that if f corresponds to a proof of B from A, and g corresponds to a proof of C from B, then the composition gf will correspond to a proof of C from A. That is, the deductive system has the following rule of inference:

$$\frac{f\colon A \rightarrow B \qquad g\colon B \rightarrow C}{gf\colon A \rightarrow C}$$

Further discussion of the conditions under which a deductive system is a category can be found in, for example, [15]. In the case of LA, (sets of) arguments are modelled as the arrows of a semi-lattice enriched category [14]. The epithet of "semi-lattice enriched" means that the category structure is enriched with some ordering information on the arrows.

In the case of intuitionistic logic, there is a well trodden route to the development of a categorical semantics. The link we have used in Section 2 between proofs and typed lambda-terms is formally established by the Curry-Howard isomorphism [11]. Then the relationship between typed λ-calculus and cartesian closed categories, [15], completes the mapping of formulae to the objects, and (equivalence classes of) proofs to the arrows, of a cartesian closed category. However, we need to extend this work; we wish to make the idea of aggregation primitive to the logic. In this case, we wish arrows of the "category of arguments" $\mathcal{A}$ to correspond to sets of arguments between two propositions. Then we define an aggregation operation in terms of a least upper bound, or *supremum*, which says that the aggregation $f \vee g$ contains at least as much information as either of the two sets of arguments on their own. That is, there is an order imposed on the arrows of $\mathcal{A}$ such that $f \leq f \vee g$ and $g \leq f \vee g$. For any two propositions A and B there is also a least arrow '0' corresponding to the vacuous argument from A to B. And so the arrows from A to B form a join semi-lattice $\langle \mathcal{A}(A,B), \vee, 0 \rangle$.

In addition, we would expect the following distributive laws to hold for the arrows shown in figure 2:

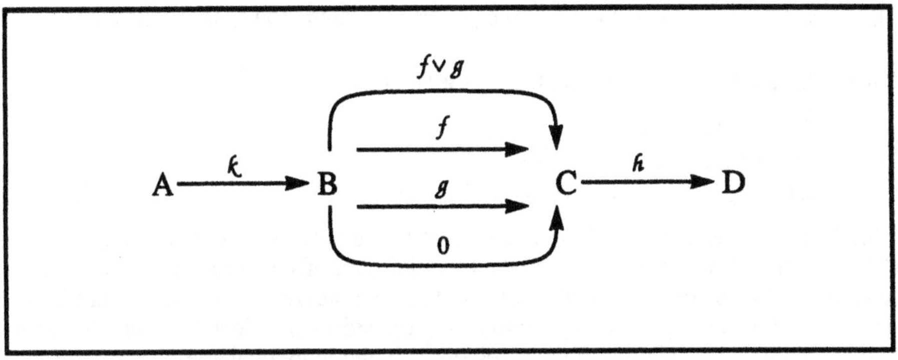

Fig. 2.

$$h(f \vee g) = hf \vee hg \qquad (f \vee g)k = fk \vee gk$$
$$h0 = 0 \qquad 0k = 0$$

That is, $\mathcal{A}$ should be a semi-lattice enriched category.

A measure of the *strength* of an argument may then be defined which maps arguments to one of a number of possible 'dictionaries'. We may model a variety of qualitative, semi-qualitative, and numerical uncertainty calculi. For example, if f is the proof term corresponding to an argument from A to B, we may have:

$$s_{A,B}(f) \in \begin{cases} \{0, +, ++\} \\ \aleph^{\infty} \\ [0, 1] \end{cases}$$

In the first case, we have confirmation or proof (++), support (+), or the vacuous argument concerning a proposition (0). This results in a very simple theory preference model which we used by way of example in Section 1. The second case, the natural numbers augmented with infinity, corresponds to a slight refinement of the improper linear model with uniform weighting [4]; basically the counting up of arguments. There are several approaches which may be taken to defining a mapping to the unit interval which we can outline here. A rigorous discussion of them can be found in [1].

A first step in the definition of an argument strength mapping is to define a *confidence measure* on arguments. The ordering of the arrows in the category of arguments $\mathcal{A}$ can be thought of as a "content ordering". We would expect that the ordering on the confidence values would respect the content ordering of the arguments themselves. Thus if $\mathcal{A}(A,B)$ denotes the semi-lattice of arguments from A to B, a confidence measure c gives rise to a family $c_{A,B}$: $\mathcal{A}(A,B) \rightarrow \mathcal{M}$ of semi-lattice homomorphisms into some suitable dictionary $\mathcal{M}$. Let **SLat** denote the category of (join) semi-lattices and semi-lattice homomorphisms between them. We require that $\mathcal{M}$ be a commutative monoid in **SLat** such that **1** is a top element and multiplication distributes over join. Then:

Defn.

A measure of confidence on $\mathcal{A}$ (valued in $\mathcal{M}$) is a family $c_{A,B}$: $\mathcal{A}(A,B) \rightarrow \mathcal{M}$ of maps in **SLat** such that

(i) $c(\zeta) = \mathbf{1}$ for all logical ζ.

(ii) $c(f) \bullet c(g) \leq c(fg)$ for all composable f and g.

(iii) $c(f \otimes \mathbf{1}) = c([\mathbf{1}, f]) = c(f)$ (See [1] for an explanation of this condition).

Concrete examples of suitable candidates for $\mathcal{M}$ are:

$\mathcal{M} = \langle [0,1], \min, \mathbf{1} \rangle$

$\mathcal{M} = \langle [0,1], *, \mathbf{1} \rangle$

$\mathcal{M}$ = a boolean algebra of 'propositions'.

The first of these corresponds to an evaluation of arguments in terms of their 'weakest link'. For a given argument, we take the minimum of the confidences assigned to the axioms used in constructing the argument to give the overall confidence in that argument. As further arguments concerning a proposition are identified, we aggregate them by taking the maximum of the confidences in the individual arguments.

The second corresponds to an evaluation of arguments by a "shortest path" type of approach. The more axioms that are used in constructing an argument, the more the confidence in that argument will be attenuated by multiplying together the confidences assigned to the axioms. Again, as further arguments concerning a proposition are identified, we aggregate them by taking the maximum of the confidences in the individual arguments.

The final example can be thought of as a preliminary stage in a "probabilistic" appraisal of arguments. We can employ a stronger ordering on the relative confidences in arguments if we explicitly take into account the dependencies between arguments as we aggregate their confidence values. We have the following definition:

Defn.

A *probability valuation* on a distributive lattice $\mathcal{D}$ is a monotone function $p: \mathcal{D} \to [0,1]$ s.t.

(i) $p(0) = 0$

(ii) $p(\top) = 1$

(iii) $p(x \vee y) = p(x) + p(y) - p(x \wedge y)$

We note in passing that this is a slightly more rigorous definition of the rule which Bernoulli gave for the combination of "pure" arguments [19].

If we now compose a confidence measure valued in $\mathcal{D}$ with a probability valuation p we will obtain an "argument strength" mapping s valued in [0,1]. If we consider all possible arguments for a proposition A and take the supremum of their strengths, then we obtain a "probability of provability" for A. As noted in [20], this gives a generalisation of Dempster-Shafer belief to non-classical logic.

5 Some Simple Examples

In the previous section, we outlined the category theoretic framework which underpins the logic of argumentation and several approaches to evaluating and appraising arguments. We will now present a few simple examples to demonstrate the argumentation theorem prover and some of the aggregation modules in use.

Let us first place this discussion in the context of the motivating domain of application. As we have metioned, the work reported here was initiated to provide a formal foundation for the inference engine used in a prototype medical application; the *Oxford*

System of Medicine (OSM). The OSM is a medical information system targeted for use in primary care [6, 7]. A requirement that the system cover the whole of general medicine and that the domain knowledge be reusable in the contexts of diagnosis, investigation, treatment and referral put major demands on the technology required to develop the system. The inference engine should be robust, in that it should be able to continue reasoning over sparse sub-domains of the knowledge base where numerical certainty coefficients are unreliable at best, or may simply be unavailable. In addition it should be flexible both in enabling domain knowledge to be reused in different problem solving contexts, and allowing the users to select different aggregation procedures depending on their requirements or the requirements of the specific problem solving context.

The OSM used an informal model of argumentation as its inference engine. The argumentation system consisting of LA and the various aggregation procedures described in this paper, provides a formal, and mathematically coherent, specification of a revised inference engine. The underlying logical knowledge representation allows us at least to identify whether a proposition is supported or opposed (its negation supported) in a given context, even in the complete absence of any numerical confidence values. So, given a context, Γ, which contains the inference rule r1: *elderly* $\supset$ *cancer* (amongst others), when an elderly patient presents, the possibility of them suffering from cancer is at least supported (along with several other possibilities, of course). Note the reading of this as a primitive argument; "if *elderly*, this argues for *cancer*". The force of this argument is weaker than certainty.

Confidence coefficients may, however, be assigned to the axioms in the context. For example, we may have the axioms with labels r1 and r2 in a context, where:

r1: *elderly* $\supset$ *cancer*	(0.1)
r2: *elderly* $\supset$ *arthritis*	(0.2)

With the axiom f1:*elderly* in the context with an associated confidence of 1, any one of the aggregation procedures of the previous section will assign a strength of 0.1 to the argument *apply(r1,f1)* supporting cancer, and a strength of 0.2 to the argument *apply(r2,f1)* supporting arthritis. That is, these arguments confer confidences of 0.1 and 0.2 in the conclusions cancer and arthritis, respectively.

The patient complains of weight loss and of suffering pain after meals. The context also contains the rules:

r3: *weight_loss* $\supset$ *cancer*	(0.3)
r4: *weight_loss* $\supset$ *gastric_ulcer*	(0.3)
r5: *delayed_pain* $\supset$ *gastric_ulcer*	(0.3)

We will now just focus on the arguments for cancer and for gastric ulcer. Suppose we were doubtful for some reason about the independence of the various arguments, or not willing to entail the computational overhead of the more complex "probability valuation". Then the confidences of the two arguments concerning each of the options should be aggregated using the simple *max* operator. This would give a confidence of 0.3 for both of the options cancer and gastric ulcer; we cannot discriminate between the two.

However, we have two relatively "good" arguments for gastric ulcer and given that they are based upon independent information, we would expect that the two could *reinforce* our confidence over and above that of the best one. The probability valuation allows this to be achieved in a coherent way by taking into account common variables in arguments as they are aggregated (although there are none in this particular example). Using the probability valuation, we obtain confidences of 0.28 and 0.51 for cancer and for gastric ulcer respectively. The aggregate of the two arguments for gastric ulcer is clearly more convincing than that for cancer.

The following points should be noted:

- These are all to be considered as pure arguments. That is, they only argue for their relevant claim. They are completely agnostic about any alternative claim.
- In the motivating domain of application we do not *a priori* know what all the relevant options are, which beliefs are alternatives and which beliefs may be held concurrently. For example, patients can, often do, suffer from more than one pathology simultaneously.

It is primarily for these reasons that we wish to weaken the impact of contradiction in the logic, and to avoid the use of normalisation in the aggregation of arguments. We wish to see which propositions, or claims, are a logical consequence of a state of knowledge (context) and allow some measure of conviction to be conferred on those claims by (purely subjective) measures of confidence in the arguments which support them.

6 Discussion

The early motivation for this work was to produce a formal model for the inference engine in a prototype application (the OSM). However, we believe that this model has much wider generality. In many practical situations the basis of uncertain reasoning is the identification and appraisal of arguments concerning the propositions or events under consideration. We have defined a 'logic of argumentation'. This is a variant of the $\wedge, \supset$ fragment of propositional intuitionistic logic in which propositions are labelled with a succinct representation of the arguments supporting their validity. The probability of a proposition is then a function of the strength and number of arguments supporting it. That is, uncertainty is evaluated by reasoning at the meta-level *about* the arguments which have been generated at the object level.

This is taking a much older and more general view than Bayesian probability; of probability as an epistemic notion. It may be that one's knowledge includes information about the chances of occurrence of an event, in which case the statistical view of probability is the appropriate one to take. However, in the case when one does not know the chances, one may argue for and against the propositions of interest using whatever sources of evidence are available. Epistemic probability is an attribute of opinion and is derived from the evaluation of arguments. The proof theoretic model of reasoning under uncertainty described in this paper offers a formal basis for this interpretation of probability.

Acknowledgements

We would like to thank our colleague Mike Clarke of Queen Mary and Westfield College for many helpful discussions on this work.

The first two authors are supported under the DTI/SERC project 1822: a Formal Basis for Decision Support Systems. This work has received an added stimulus with our involvement in and support from the Esprit Basic Research Programme 3085, DRUMS.

References

1. S. Ambler: A Categorical Approach to the Semantics of Argumentation. Department of Computer Science Report, Queen Mary College, London (1992)
2. N. G. de Bruijn: Lambda Calculus Notation with Nameless Dummies, a Tool for Automatic Formula Manipulation, with Application to the Church-Rosser Theorem. Indagationes Mathematicae 34, 381-392 (1972)
3. T. Chard: Qualitative probability versus quantitative probability in clinical diagnosis: a study using a computer simulation. Medical Decision Making 11, 38-41 (1991)
4. R.M. Dawes: The robust beauty of improper linear models in decision making. American Psychologist 34, 571-582 (1979)
5. R. Dyckhoff: Contraction-free Sequent Calculi for Intuitionistic Logic. J. Symbolic Logic (to appear, 1992)
6. J. Fox, A.J. Glowinski, C. Gordon, S.J. Hajnal, M.J. O'Neil: Logic engineering for knowledge engineering. Artifical Intelligence in Medicine 2, 323-339 (1990)
7. J. Fox, D.A. Clark, A.J. Glowinski, M.J. O'Neil: Using predicate logic to integrate qualitative reasoning and classical decision theory. IEEE Trans. on Systems, Man, and Cybernetics 20, 347-357 (1990)
8. J. Fox, M. Clarke: Towards a formalisation of arguments in decision making. Proc. Stanford Spring Symposium on Argumentation and Belief. 92-99 (1991)
9. D. Gabbay: Labelled Deductive Systems. CIS Technical Report 90-22, University of Munich 1990
10. J.H. Gallier: Logic for Computer Science. Chichester: John Wiley 1987
11. J. Girard, P. Taylor, Y. Lafont: Proofs and Types. Cambridge: Cambridge University Press 1989
12. A. Heyting: Intuitionism. An Introduction. Amsterdam: North-Holland Publ. Co 1956
13. J.R. Hindley, J.P. Seldin: Introduction to Combinators and λ-Calculus. Cambridge: Cambridge University Press 1986
14. G.M. Kelly: Basic Concepts of Enriched Category Theory. London Math. Soc. Lecture Note Series 64. Cambridge: Cambridge University Press 1982
15. J. Lambek, P.J. Scott: Introduction to higher order categorical logic. Cambridge: Cambridge University Press 1986
16. S.L. Lauritzen, D.J. Spiegelhalter: Local computations with probabilities on graphical structures and their application to expert systems. J. R. Statist. Soc. B. 50, 157-224 (1988)
17. J. Locke (1671). See: R.I. Aaron, d J. Gibb (eds): An early draft of Locke's Essay. Oxford: Oxford University Press 1936
18. M. O'Neil, A.J. Glowinski: Evaluating and validating very large knowledge-based systems. Med. Inform. 15, 237-251 (1990)
19. G. Shafer: Non-additive Probabilities in the Work of Bernoulli and Lambert. Archive for History of Exact Sciences 19, 309-370 (1978)
20. P.N. Wilson: Justification, computational efficiency and generalisation of the Dempster Shafer Theory. Research Report no. 15, Dept. of Computing and Math. Sciences, Oxford Polytechnic 1989 (also to appear in *Artificial Intelligence*)

From "and" to "or"

Thierry ARNOULD[1] and Anca RALESCU[2,3]

Laboratory for International Fuzzy Engineering Research
E-mail : arnould@fuzzy.or.jp, anca@fuzzy.or.jp
Fax : (81) 45 212 8255 Phone : (81) 45 212 8237 - (81) 45 212 8239
Siber Hegner Bldg. 4Fl., 89-1 Yamashita-cho, Naka-ku, Yokohama 231 JAPAN

Abstract. In this paper we consider the issue of aggregation of predicates. This issue appears especially in connection with fuzzy predicates. We give a probabilistic interpretation of an aggregation in terms of the possibility of a statement containing these predicates, and using "and"/"or" operators.

1 Introduction

It is well-known that the issue of aggregation arises in connection with evaluation of statements containing imprecise (fuzzy) predicates. This issue has been explored from different view points in several papers [1], [2], [3], [4].

In this paper we consider premises of the form "X_i *is* A_i", i=1,...,n, where X_i denotes a variable, and A_i denotes a fuzzy set of the universe of discourse in which X_i takes values. Thus "X_i *is* A_i" specifies a possibility distribution for X_i. For ease of notation, the label of a fuzzy set, its membership function and, later in this paper, the value of the membership function evaluated at some particular data will be represented by the same symbol A_i. Typical examples of such premises include statements of the form "*the weight is heavy, the height is tall, the age is old*".

In what follows, we focus our attention on expressions S= S("X_i *is* A_i", n, $\wedge$, $\vee$), that can be formed with n premises "X_i *is* A_i", and where "$\wedge$" and "$\vee$" denote conjunction and disjunction operators respectively. We start our study by evaluating the possibility of S. We choose the standard conjunction and disjunction operators that is, min. and max. respectively. At this point, we make no assumption on the way we write the expressions S, that is, on the order in which conjunctions and disjunctions appear, or on the use of parentheses.

We know that in the case of fuzzy predicates, $\min_{i=1,n}(A_i)$ is the largest conjunction (intersection) operator, while $\max_{i=1,n}(A_i)$ is the smallest disjunction (union) operator. It is also obvious that the possibility of any expression S, when S contains a mixture of "and"/"or" operators, lies in the interval $[\min_{i=1,n}(A_i), \max_{i=1,n}(A_i)]$. The values in this interval are usually obtained by aggregating the individual values A_i, i=1,2,...,n. An aggregation function $h(A_1,...,A_n)$ is defined for this purpose.

---

[1] On leave from Rhône-Poulenc Industrialisation, Courbevoie, FRANCE.

[2] On leave from the Computer Science Department, University of Cincinnati, USA. All correspondence about the paper should be directed to this author.

[3] This work was partially supported by NSF Grant INT-08632.

Aggregations are usually introduced by axioms which state the properties and boundary conditions that an aggregation operator must satisfy. A notable class of widely used aggregations is that of averages (or more generally convex combinations). However, while we know the statements which are modeled by any mixture of the intersection and union operators (conjunctions, disjunctions, or mixtures of these), it is not clear what could be the statement behind an aggregation. For example, what can be the statement whose possibility value is *1/3(heavy(x) + tall(y) + old(z))* ?

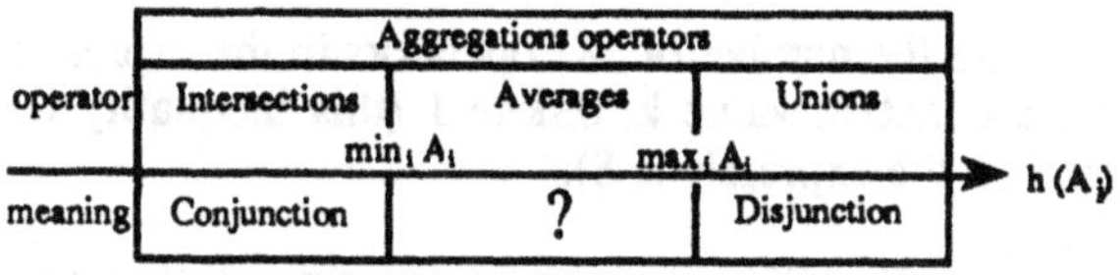

Fig. 1. Aggregation operators

Let us now consider the reciprocal problem : we restrict our attention to the interval $[\min_{i=1,n}(A_i), \max_{i=1,n}(A_i)]$ and ask ourselves about a characterization of this interval in terms of S expressions. It is clear that, since the possibility of such an expression S is always one of its premises, A_i, evaluated at some particular data, there are points in the interval $[\min_{i=1,n}(A_i), \max_{i=1,n}(A_i)]$ which do not correspond to the possibility of such expressions. However, given an aggregation operator, any point of the above interval will correspond to some particular aggregation of the A_i's. Considering the above, we will show that the possibility of all S expressions corresponds to a probability distribution on the A_i's, and that there is a connection between this distribution and previously derived aggregations.

Throughout this paper, and for the purpose of illustration, we will consider the case of aggregating the three premises *"height is tall"*, *"weight is heavy"* and *"age is old"*.

2 Possibility of a Statement Containing a Fixed Number of "$\wedge$" Operators

We start our study by considering a particular kind of expressions : all the "$\wedge$" operators are written before the "$\vee$" operators, no parentheses are allowed and the expressions are evaluated from left to right. This assumption obviously restricts the scope of this study, and its results, but our aim is to study if it is possible to attach a meaning to the result of an aggregation operator. The restriction of our assumption will eventually be reflected in that not all aggregations will have an interpretation in terms of these statements.

When an aggregation is performed, the n premises "*X_i is A_i*" are evaluated for some particular data $(x_{1o}, x_{2o}, \ldots, x_{io}, \ldots, x_{no})$, leading to the n values to be aggregated. More precisely, each value is the membership degree, $A_i(x_{io})$, of the data x_{io} to the set A_i, which, for ease of notation, we will now denote A_i (from now on, A_i will designate a membership degree, that is, a value, and no longer a fuzzy set nor a membership function). From now on, and without loss of generality, we assume that the A_i's are ordered, such that $1 > A_1 > A_2 > \ldots > A_{n-1} > A_n > 0$.

In our example, the three fuzzy sets are "*tall*", "*heavy*" and "*old*", and they are evaluated for a particular value of the *height*, *weight* and *age*, respectively. After ordering the three membership degrees, we denote them A_1, A_2 and A_3. We can assume that the three values have been ordered such that "*heavy*" > "*old*" > "*tall*" (once again, it must be kept in mind that "*heavy*", "*old*" and "*tall*" now denote the membership degrees of the data for the *weight, age, height* to the corresponding fuzzy sets).

In addition, let A denote the number of "$\wedge$" operators in the expressions S and let us assume that A has a constant value k, $0 \le k \le n-1$ (this inequality follows from the previous assumption on the expressions S).

We study the possibility, Poss(S,k,$\wedge$), of each expression S that we can write using the n premises and k "$\wedge$" operators. If we consider all the expressions S, the result proves out to be one of the A_i's, $1 \le i \le k+1$. An interesting point here is that the values $A_{k+2}, \ldots, A_n$ cannot be reached if we use exactly k "$\wedge$" operators.

More precisely, we have :

$$Poss(S,k,\wedge) = \begin{cases} A_1 & \text{if } k=0 \\ \begin{cases} A_i \quad \text{in } C_{n-i}^{k-i+2} \quad \text{cases, for } 1 \le i \le k \\ A_{k+1} \quad \text{in } C_{n-k}^{1} \quad \text{cases} \end{cases} & \text{if } 0 < k < n-1 \\ A_n & \text{if } k = n-1 \end{cases} \tag{1}$$

Note that, in the second part of (1), when 0<k<n-1, the total number of expressions is equal to C_n^{k+1} (choices, among n premises, of the k+1 premises that are the arguments of the k "$\wedge$" operators).

In our example, the result is :

$$\begin{cases} heavy & & \text{when } k=0 \\ \begin{matrix} heavy & \text{in 1 case} \\ old & \text{in 2 cases} \end{matrix} & \text{(3 cases)} & \text{when } k=1 \\ tall & & \text{when } k=2 \end{cases} \quad \text{and} \quad \begin{cases} Poss(heavy \vee old \vee tall) = heavy \\ \begin{cases} Poss(heavy \wedge old \vee tall) = old \\ Poss(heavy \wedge tall \vee old) = old \\ Poss(tall \wedge old \vee heavy) = heavy \end{cases} \\ Poss(heavy \wedge old \wedge tall) = tall \end{cases}$$

2.1 Conditional Probability Distribution Defined on Poss(S)

We previously showed that the value of the possibility of an expression is always one of the A_i's, $1 \le i \le k+1$. Next, we can consider the problem from a probabilistic point of view : what is the probability that the value of the possibility of a statement S is one of the A_i's ? In fact, since the possibility of a statement S depends on the number of "$\wedge$" operators used, it follows that we must consider conditional probabilities.

Consequently, we define q_i^k as the probability that the possibility of a statement S is equal to A_i, given that the number of "$\wedge$" operators, A, is equal to k. It is easy to check that the $\left(q_i^k\right)_i$ define a probability distribution.

More precisely, we have $q_i^k = Prob(Poss(S) = A_i | A = k)$ and $\mathbf{Q} = (q_i^k)_{i,k}$.

We have to point out that, once the value of n is chosen, the matrix **Q** is automatically determined. However, the assumption we made at the beginning of our study, and concerning the way the expressions S were written, will have an influence on the matrix **Q**, but only on the matrix **Q**. Had we chosen to consider other kinds of expressions, only the matrix **Q** would have been different.

It follows directly from the definition of q_i^k that :

$$q_i^k = \begin{cases} 1 & \text{if } i = 1 \\ 0 & \text{if } i > 1 \end{cases} \quad \text{if } k = 0 \qquad q_i^k = \begin{cases} \dfrac{C_{n-i}^{k-i+2}}{C_n^{k+1}} & \text{if } 1 \le i \le k \\ \dfrac{C_{n-k}^{1}}{C_n^{k+1}} & \text{if } i = k+1 \\ 0 & \text{if } i > k+1 \end{cases} \quad \text{if } 0 < k < n-1 \tag{2}$$

$$q_i^k = \begin{cases} 1 & \text{if } i = n \\ 0 & \text{if } i < n \end{cases} \quad \text{if } k = n-1$$

In our example, $\mathbf{Q} = \begin{pmatrix} 1 & 1/3 & 0 \\ 0 & 2/3 & 0 \\ 0 & 0 & 1 \end{pmatrix}$

For instance, since we assumed "*heavy*" > "*old*" > "*tall*", $q_2^1 = 2/3$ means that the probability that the possibility of S is given by "*old*" (A_2), when S contains only one "$\wedge$" operator (*A*=1), is equal to $2/3$. Similarly, there is a probability equal to $1/3$ that the possibility of S is given by "*heavy*" (A_1) when we use only one "$\wedge$" operator (*A*=1).

2.2 Conditional Expected Value of Poss(S)

Having defined the conditional probability distribution of Poss(S), given *A*=k, we consider its conditional expected value B_k, that is :

$$B_k = E(Poss(S) | A = k) = \sum_{i=1}^{n} A_i q_i^k \tag{3}$$

Fact 1 : Each of the B_k's corresponds to an aggregation operator (OWA operator [4]), on the k+1 greatest predicates

Indeed, we obtain using (2) :

$$B_k = \begin{cases} A_1 = Max_{i=1,n}(A_i) & \text{if } k = 0 \\ \sum_{i=1}^{k+1} A_i q_i^k & \text{if } 0 < k < n-1 \\ A_n = Min_{i=1,n}(A_i) & \text{if } k = n-1 \end{cases} \tag{3'}$$

In matrix notation, we have :
$\mathbf{B}' = (B_0, B_1, \dots, B_{n-1})$, $\mathbf{A}' = (A_1, A_2, \dots, A_n)$ and $\mathbf{B}' = \mathbf{A}' * \mathbf{Q}$

For our example, we get $B_k = \begin{cases} heavy & \text{if } k=0 \\ \frac{1}{3}(heavy + 2old) & \text{if } k=1 \\ tall & \text{if } k=2 \end{cases}$

Thus, when k=1 (one "∧" operator and one "∨" operator), the expected value of S becomes " $\frac{1}{3}(heavy + 2tall)$". When we use only "∧" operators (respectively "∨" operators), the result is obviously "*tall*" (respectively "*heavy*").

2.3 Interpretation of the B_k Operators

As mentioned before, the two extreme values k=0 and k=n-1 lead to particular B_k operators, as we get the min. and max. operators respectively.

However, for 0<k<n-1, we also get particular B_k operators. Indeed, writing k=n-j (1<j<n) :

$$q_i^k = \frac{C_{n-i}^{n-j+2-i}}{C_n^{n-j+1}} = \frac{j-1}{n(n-1)\dots(n-j+2)}(n-i)(n-i-1)\dots(n-i-(j-3)) \qquad \text{if } 1 \le i \le k$$

$$q_i^k = \frac{C_j^1}{C_n^{n-j+1}} = \frac{j-1}{n(n-1)\dots(n-j+2)} j(j-2)! \qquad \text{if } i = k+1$$

$$q_i^k = 0 \qquad \text{if } i > k+1$$

As the q_i^k define a probability distribution, we know that $\sum_{i=1}^{k+1} q_i^k = 1$.

Now, let us define, for *all* i, 1≤i≤n, λ_i^k by :

$$\lambda_i^k = \frac{j-1}{n(n-1)\dots(n-j+2)}(n-i)(n-i-1)\dots(n-i-(j-3))$$

(this formula is the same as for the q_i^k, 1≤i≤k, but is now defined for *all* the values of i, 1≤i≤n).

As a consequence of this definition, for n-(j-3)=k+3≤i≤n, we have $\lambda_i^k = 0$ and then :

$\sum_{i=1}^{n} \lambda_i^k = \sum_{i=1}^{k+2} \lambda_i^k = \sum_{i=1}^{k} \lambda_i^k + \lambda_{k+1}^k + \lambda_{k+2}^k$ which becomes, using $\lambda_i^k = q_i^k$ for 1≤i≤k :

$$\sum_{i=1}^{n} \lambda_i^k = \sum_{i=1}^{k} q_i^k + \frac{j-1}{n\dots(n-j+2)}(j-1)(j-2)\dots 2 + \frac{j-1}{n\dots(n-j+2)}(j-2)(j-3)\dots 1$$

$$\sum_{i=1}^{n} \lambda_i^k = \sum_{i=1}^{k} q_i^k + \frac{j-1}{n\dots(n-j+2)} j(j-2)! = \sum_{i=1}^{k+1} q_i^k = 1.$$

This shows that the λ_i^k define a real weighting vector and, if C_k is the aggregation operator (OWA operator) associated with this weighting vector and defined by

$C_k(A_1,\ldots,A_n)=\sum_{i=1}^{n}A_i\lambda_i^k$, we have that $B_k=C_k(A_1,A_2,\ldots,A_{k-1},A_k,A_{k+1},A_{k+1},\ldots,A_{k+1})$
The values A_i, $k+1\leq i\leq n$, are all replaced by A_{k+1}, the corresponding coefficients are added and their sum is assigned to A_{k+1}.

Examples :

- For k=n-2 (j=2), we have $\lambda_i^k=\frac{1}{n}$ and then :

$$B_{n-2}=\frac{1}{n}(A_1+A_2+\ldots+A_i+\ldots+A_{n-2}+A_{n-1}+A_{n-1})$$

- For k=n-3 (j=3), we have $\lambda_i^k=\frac{2}{n(n-1)}(n-i)$ and then :

$$B_{n-3}=\frac{2}{n(n-1)}\left[(n-1)A_1+(n-2)A_2+..+(n-i)A_i+..+4A_{n-4}+3A_{n-3}+2A_{n-2}+1A_{n-2}\right]$$

- For k=n-4 (j=4), we have $\lambda_i^k=\frac{3}{n(n-1)(n-2)}(n-i)(n-i-1)$ and :

$$B_{n-4}=\frac{3}{n(n-1)(n-2)}\left[\sum_{i=1}^{n-4}(n-i)(n-i-1)A_i+3*2A_{n-3}+2*1A_{n-3}\right]$$

3 Possibility of a Statement Given a Probability Distribution on the Number of "∧" Operators

We consider now the same problem as in Section 2, but we let A vary : in Section 2 we assumed that A had a constant value k, $0\leq k\leq n-1$, we now consider that A is a random variable taking on the values 0, 1, 2,.., n-1. Similarly, we define the random variable $\boldsymbol{O}$, the number of "∨" operators contained in the statement S. We have that $\boldsymbol{A}+\boldsymbol{O}=n-1$.

3.1 Unconditional Probability Distribution Defined on Poss(S)

Next, let w_k denote the probability that A takes on the particular value k. This probability distribution and the knowledge of the conditional probability distribution $(q_i^k)_{i,k}$ naturally leads us to consider the unconditional probability distribution of Poss(S). Let $(b_i)_i$ denote this probability distribution.

More precisely, we have $w_k=Prob(A=k)$ and $b_i=Prob(Poss(S)=A_i)$

It follows that $b_i=\sum_{k=0}^{n-1}q_i^k w_k$ (4)

Thus, we have $b_i=\begin{cases}\sum_{k=i-1}^{n-2}q_i^k w_k & \text{if } i<n\\ w_{n-1} & \text{if } i=n\end{cases}$ (4')

In matrix notation, we have $\mathbf{b}' = (b_1,\dots,b_n)$, $\mathbf{w}' = (w_0,\dots,w_{n-1})$ and $\mathbf{b} = \mathbf{Q} * \mathbf{w}$

For our example, we get $b_i = \begin{cases} w_0 + \frac{1}{3}w_1 & \text{if } i = 1 \\ \frac{2}{3}w_1 & \text{if } i = 2 \\ w_2 & \text{if } i = 3 \end{cases}$

For example, according to this result, we have that the probability for the possibility of S to be "*heavy*" (A_1) is the probability that *A* is equal to 0 (w_0) plus one third of the probability that *A* is equal to 1 (w_1).

3.2 Expected Value of Poss(S)

Next we consider the expected value of Poss(S). From the definition of the expected value it follows that :

Fact 2 : $E(Poss(S)) = \sum_{i=1}^{n} A_i b_i$ is an aggregation operator (OWA operator) on *all* A_i's.

Using (2), (3), and (4) we also have another expression for E(Poss(S)), in terms of B_k, w_k:

$$E(Poss(S)) = \sum_{k=0}^{n-1} B_k w_k = \sum_{i=1}^{n}\sum_{k=0}^{n-1} A_i q_i^k w_k = \mathbf{A}' * \mathbf{Q} * \mathbf{w} \tag{5}$$

It follows that the OWA operator E(Poss(S)) can be defined using, either the predicates A_i and the probability distribution $(b_i)_i$, *or* the OWA operators B_k and the probability distribution $(w_k)_k$. However, the expected value of the variable Poss(S) *cannot* be computed using simultaneously the premises A_i and the probability distribution w_k. This means that, *at least in our study*, the OWA operators $\sum_{i=1}^{n} A_i w_{i-1}$ as defined in [4] have no particular interpretation. In fact, as we shall show later, the OWA operators as introduced in [4] are rather ad-hoc.

For our example, we get $E(Poss(S)) = (w_0 + \frac{1}{3}w_1)A_1 + \frac{2}{3}w_1 A_2 + w_2 A_3$, whereas from [4] it would be $w_0 A_1 + w_1 A_2 + w_2 A_3$.

4 Interpretation of the Random Variable *A*. Definition of the Degree of Orness

We consider now the interpretation of the random variable *A* and the associated random variable *O*. We define the degree of "*orness*" ***DO***, based on the proportion of "$\vee$" operators among the n-1 operators used to write the statement S. To this, we associate a probability distribution, $(z_k)_k$, closely related to $(w_k)_k$, as follows :

$$DO = \frac{O}{n-1} = \frac{n-1-A}{n-1} \text{ and } z_k = Prob\left(DO = \frac{k}{n-1}\right) = Prob(A = n-i-k) = w_{n-k-1} \tag{6}$$

Given the probability distribution of ***DO***, we can easily compute its expected value which in fact is the degree of orness as defined by Yager in [4] :

$$E(DO) = \sum_{k=0}^{n-1} \frac{n-k-1}{n-1} w_k \tag{7}$$

Thus we have shown that, given the type of statements S considered here and a probability distribution $(w_k)_k$ on the number of "$\wedge$" operators in S, we can induce the probability distribution of the possibility of S on the values $A_1, ..., A_n$. The expected value of the possibility of S, with respect to the probability distribution $(b_i)_i$ induced by the initial probability distribution $(w_k)_k$ is an aggregation operator on $A_1, ..., A_n$.

In addition, we can associate to the probability distribution $(w_k)_k$ an expected degree of orness *DO*. However, contrary to what is suggested in [4], we showed that it is not possible to use the same probability distribution to define the OWA operator (for which we use the distribution $(b_i)_i$) and the expected degree of orness (for which we use the distribution $(w_k)_k$). Then, the degree of orness defined in [4] to evaluate the degree to which an OWA operator $\sum_i A_i w_{i-1}$ is an "or"-like operator is not suitable, as we can not refer to the same probability distribution for the definition of the degree of orness and for the definition of the OWA operator.

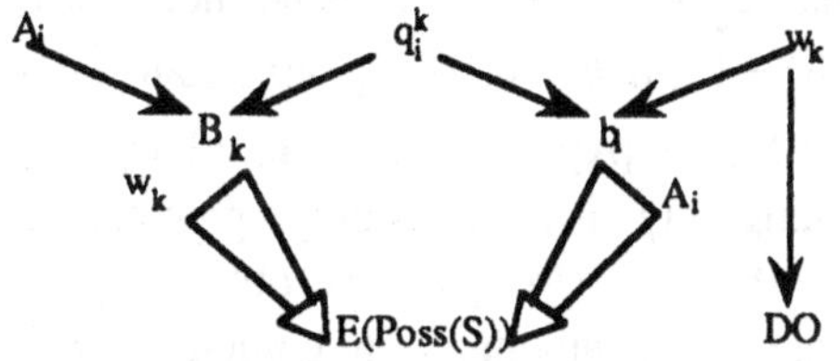

Fig. 2. Premises, OWA operators and probability distributions

5 Probability Distribution on the Number of "$\wedge$" Operators Induced by an Averaging Aggregation

Next we consider the converse problem : given an averaging aggregation (OWA operator) can we derive the probability distribution of *A*, such that the aggregation in question is the expected value of the possibility of a statement S, with respect to a probability distribution induced by that of *A* ? Note that, to specify the averaging aggregation means, in fact, to specify the probability distribution $(b_i)_i$. Then, we can prove the following :

Fact 3 : An averaging aggregation induced by a probability distribution $(b_i)_i$ induces a probability distribution $(w_k)_k$ on *A* if and only if the following condition holds :

$$\forall 0 \le k \le n-1, w_k = \sum_{i=1}^{n} \tilde{q}_i^k b_i \ge 0 \tag{8}$$

where the $\tilde{q}_i^k$ are the elements of $\tilde{Q}$,the inverse matrix of Q.

Proof : According to the previous discussion we must solve the matrix equation $\mathbf{b} = \mathbf{Q} * \mathbf{w}$ for $\mathbf{w}$. Since Q is an upper triangular matrix with diagonal elements different from 0, we are sure that w exists and is unique. In addition, we must show that $(w_k)_k$ satisfies the following conditions :

$$\forall 0 \le k \le n-1, 0 \le w_k \le 1 \text{ and } \sum_{k=0}^{n-1} w_k = 1$$

We have, using (4), $\sum_{i=1}^{n} b_i = \sum_{i=1}^{n}\sum_{k=0}^{n-1} q_i^k w_k = \sum_{k=0}^{n-1}\left(w_k \sum_{i=1}^{n} q_i^k \right) = \sum_{k=0}^{n-1} w_k$

The fact that $(b_i)_i$ is a probability distribution ensures that the sum of the w_k's is equal to 1. Then the w_k's will define a probability distribution if and only if $w_k \ge 0$, $0 \le k \le n-1$. In that case, as the sum of all the w_k's is equal to 1, each value will necessarily be smaller than 1. Since the w_k's are given by $w_k = \sum_{i=1}^{n} \tilde{q}_i^k b_i$, we get the previous necessary and sufficient condition.

Remarks:

(1) if $\tilde{q}_i^k \ge 0, \forall i,k$, then (8) holds for any probability distribution $(b_i)_i$. Using our method, it is then possible to give a probabilistic interpretation to all aggregation operators.

(2) if $\exists (i_0, k_0)$ such that $\tilde{q}_{i_0}^{k_0} < 0$, then (8) does not necessarily hold. Indeed, if we choose $(b_i)_i$ such that $b_{i_0} = 1$ and $b_i = 0, \forall i \ne i_0$, we obtain $w_{k_0} < 0$.

(3) If $b_1 = 1, b_i = 0, \forall i \ne 1$ ($\mathrm{Max}_i A_i$), we obtain $w_o = 1, w_k = 0, \forall k \ne 0$. This means that a statement containing only disjunctions of the predicates A_i is always possible. Similarly, if $b_n = 1, b_i = 0, \forall i \ne n$ ($\mathrm{Min}_i A_i$), we obtain $w_{n-1} = 1, w_k = 0, \forall k \ne n-1$, which means that a statement containing only conjunctions of the predicates A_i is always possible.

For our example, we get $\begin{pmatrix} w_0 \\ w_1 \\ w_2 \end{pmatrix} = \begin{pmatrix} 1 & -\frac{1}{2} & 0 \\ 0 & \frac{3}{2} & 0 \\ 0 & 0 & 1 \end{pmatrix} \begin{pmatrix} b_1 \\ b_2 \\ b_3 \end{pmatrix}$ (and more generally $\mathbf{w} = \mathbf{Q}^{-1}\mathbf{b}$).

This equation clearly shows the conditions the b_i's must fulfill for the w_k's to define a probability distribution. Then, given an averaging aggregation operator defined by a probability distribution $(b_i)_i$, we can easily compute the probability distribution $(w_k)_k$ on the random variable *A*.

At this point *only*, the probability distribution $(w_k)_k$ enables us to give an interpretation of the aggregation operator, a reference to the order of the n fuzzy sets being no longer necessary. As our method leads to the definition of a probability distribution, the interpretation corresponds to stating a probability distribution on *all* the possible statements that can be written using the A_i's and the conjunction and disjunction operators.

For instance, let us consider one of the most widely used aggregation operators, that is, the arithmetic mean. For our example we get $b_i = 1/3$, i=1,3. The corresponding probability distribution $(w_k)_k$ is then given by :

$$w_k = \begin{cases} \frac{1}{6} & \text{if } k=0 \\ \frac{1}{2} & \text{if } k=1 \\ \frac{1}{3} & \text{if } k=2 \end{cases}$$

Now, using the w_k's, it becomes possible to give an interpretation of the initial aggregation operator $\frac{1}{3}(heavy(x_0)+old(y_0)+tall(z_0))$ as follows :

- ("*heavy*" ∨ "*old*" ∨ "*tall*") with a probability equal to 1/6 (A=0),
- ("*heavy*" ∧ "*old*" ∨ "*tall*") or ("*heavy*" ∧ "*tall*" ∨ "*old*") or ("*old*" ∧ "*tall*" ∨ "*heavy*") with a total probability equal to 1/2 (A=1),
- ("*heavy*" ∧ "*old*" ∧ "*tall*") with a probability equal to 1/3 (A=2).

In terms of the premises, the statement that can be attached to the OWA operator is :

- ("*the weight is heavy*" or "*the age is old*" or "*the height is tall*") with a probability equal to 1/6,
- ("*the weight is heavy*" and "*the age is old*" or "*the height is tall*") or ("*the weight is heavy*" and "*the height is tall*" or "*the age is old*") or ("*the age is old*" and "*the height is tall*" or "*the weight is heavy*") with a probability equal to 1/2,
- ("*the weight is heavy*" and "*the age is old*" and "*the height is tall*") with a probability equal to 1/3.

6 Conclusion

We studied an alternative interpretation of aggregations, such as OWA operators, and we showed that some of these operators can be represented in terms of expected values. We showed that there is a close relation between averaging aggregations and the probability distribution on A, the number of "and" operators in a statement. Intuitively, the results of this research can be summed up as follows : "Between *all* (and) and *at least one* (or), there are *probable some* (aggregations)". The notion of degree of "orness" was studied, and defined in a manner consistent with the meaning of the aggregation. More work is needed to investigate the case when (8) does not hold, more general statements S and particular probability distributions $(b_i)_i$, $(w_k)_k$.

References and Related Bibliography

1. D. Dubois and H. Prade, "A Review of Fuzzy Sets Aggregation Connectives", *Information Sciences*, (1985).
2. G. J. Klir and T. A. Folger, "Fuzzy sets, uncertainty and information", Prentice Hall (1988).
3. A. Ralescu, "A note on rule interpretation in expert systems", *Information Sciences* 38 (1986).
4. R. R. Yager, "On ordered weighted averaging aggregation operators in multicriteria decision making", *IEEE Transactions on Systems, Man and Cybernetics* 18 (1988) 183-190.
5. L. A. Zadeh, "Fuzzy Sets as a basis for a theory of possibility", *Fuzzy Sets and Systems* 1 (1978) 3-28.

Representing Spatial and Temporal Uncertainty

Eugene Eberbach and André Trudel

Jodrey School of Computer Science
Acadia University
Wolfville, Nova Scotia, Canada, B0P 1X0

Abstract. We present a first order logic that can represent both spatial and temporal uncertainty at a point. We also extend this logic so as to represent uncertain interval knowledge in terms of the uncertain knowledge at the interior points.

1 Introduction

Imperfect domain knowledge and imperfect case data are two main sources of uncertainty in AI systems [3]. Imperfect domain knowledge means the domain is incomplete, erroneous, or too complex to consider all cases. Incomplete domain knowledge can be represented with a function that takes on only two possible values: 0 and 1. Zero represents false and unity represents true. Incompleteness arises at a point when the function is undefined at that point. For example in Fig. 1, the function is represented by the horizontal solid line. The function has a value of zero (i.e., false) between 0 and 8, a value of one (i.e., true) between 12 and 17, and is undefined (i.e., we don't know its value) between 8 and 12, and beyond 17. The X–axis can be discrete or continuous. Also, the X–axis can represent time or space. For example, if the X–axis is time, then the function can represent the truth value of running at a point. If the X–axis is space, then each point on the X–axis can represent a patient and the function can represent whether or not a patient has cancer.

The second source of uncertainty, imperfect case data, means that data may be imprecise or unreliable. We represent imperfect case data with a function that takes on all continuous values in the range 0–1. Once again, zero represents false and unity represents true. Values between 0 and 1 represent different degrees of truth. An example is shown in Fig. 2. Once again, the X–axis can either be discrete or continuous, and, time or space.

It is also possible to define a function which captures both types of uncertainty. For example at different times, the function may equal 1, equal 0, be undefined, or range between 0 and 1.

We present a first order logic that can represent both types of uncertainty. In this logic, the X–axis is the real numbers. In the next section, we give its syntax and semantics. We then show how uncertain knowledge about an interval can be derived from uncertain knowledge at the interior points. We then discuss how to modify the logic so that the X–axis is discrete (e.g., the integers). We conclude with a solution to the persistence (frame) problem.

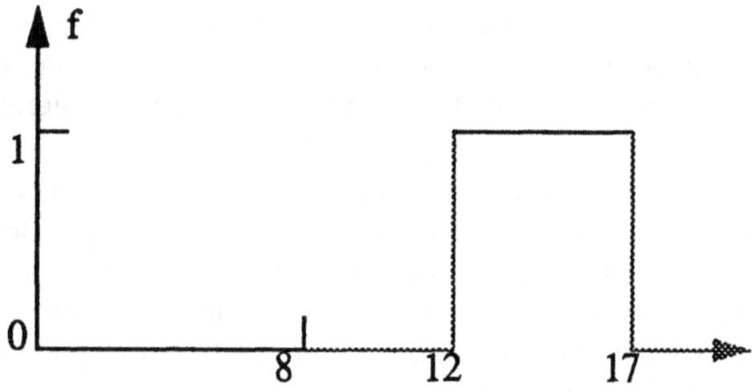

Fig. 1. Imperfect domain knowledge

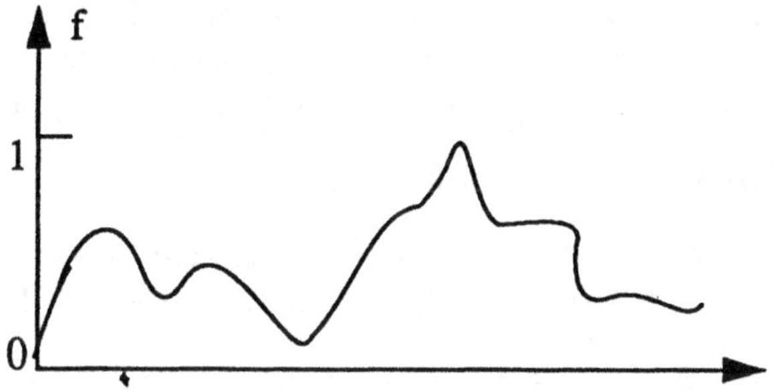

Fig. 2. Imperfect case data

2 Logic

We present a logic called UGCH which is based on the logic presented in [2]. Information at a point is represented with a real valued function which takes on values between 0 and 1 inclusive. Zero represents false and unity represents true. For example, if at time 3 the book is on the table, we write $on(book, table, 3) = 1$. If at time 4, we are fairly certain that the book is on the table then we can write $on(book, table, 4) = 0.75$. The book is no longer on the table at time 5 is written as $on(book, table, 5) = 0$.

In [2], Goodwin et. al. only consider functions that take on values of 0 and 1 exclusively. One reason for their restriction is that the integration of the functions over an interval gives the length of time the function is true over the interval. Since we do not restrict our functions to 0 and 1 values, the integration may not yield useful results. In Section 3, we define useful integral based interval measures.

We conclude this section with UGCH's syntax and semantics. The syntax and semantics are almost identical to those presented in [2]. Besides restricting their functions to be 0–1 valued, Goodwin et. al. [2] have an additional class of functions for representing quantitative information. For example, they can define a function for velocity that can take on any real value. Quantitative functions are not needed for the types of problems we are considering.

2.1 Syntax

Given a set of constant symbols C, variable symbols V (where $t \in$ V), and function symbols F, terms are defined as:

- All members of C and V are terms.
- If $f \in$ F is an n-ary ($n \geq 1$) function symbol, and $r_1, \ldots, r_{n+2}$ are terms, then $f(r_1, \ldots, r_n)$ and $\int_{r_{n+1}}^{r_{n+2}} f(r_1, \ldots, r_{n-1}, t)dt$ are terms.
- If r_1, r_2 are terms, then $(r_1 + r_2)$, $(r_1 - r_2)$, and $(r_1 \times r_2)$ are terms.

Well-formed formulas (wffs) are defined as:

- If π_1 and π_2 are terms then $\pi_1 < \pi_2$, $\pi_1 \leq \pi_2$, $\pi_1 > \pi_2$, $\pi_1 \geq \pi_2$, and $\pi_1 = \pi_2$ are wffs. The predicate symbols $<, \leq, >, \geq, =$ are the only ones defined in the logic.
- If ϕ_1, ϕ_2 are wffs, and $z \in$ V then $[\phi_1 \wedge \phi_2]$, $[\phi_1 \vee \phi_2]$, $[\phi_1 \rightarrow \phi_2]$, $[\phi_1 \leftrightarrow \phi_2]$, $[\neg\phi_1]$, $[\forall z \,.\, \phi_1]$, and $[\exists z \,.\, \phi_1]$ are wffs.

When there is no ambiguity, parentheses and square brackets are sometimes omitted.

2.2 Semantics

The semantic domain or ontology is $\mathbb{R}$. An interpretation for UGCH is a tuple $I = \langle$MC, SF, MF$\rangle$ where:

- MC: C $\mapsto \mathbb{R}$.
- SF $= \{f | f$ is an n-ary piece wise continuous function and $f : \mathbb{R}^n \mapsto [0, 1]\}$.
- MF: F $\mapsto$ SF.

A variable assignment for UGCH is a function VA: V $\mapsto \mathbb{R}$. The function TA assigns an element of $\mathbb{R}$ to each term as follows:

- If $x \in$ C then TA(x) = MC(x).
- If $x \in$ V then TA(x) = VA(x).
- If $f \in$ F is an n-ary ($n \geq 1$) function symbol, and $r_1, \ldots, r_{n+2}$ are terms, then:

$\text{TA}(f(r_1, \ldots, r_n)) = \text{MF}(f)(\text{TA}(r_1), \ldots, \text{TA}(r_n))$,
$\text{TA}(\int_{r_{n+1}}^{r_{n+2}} f(r_1, \ldots, r_{n-1}, t)dt) =$
$$\int_{\text{TA}(r_{n+1})}^{\text{TA}(r_{n+2})} \text{MF}(f)(\text{TA}(r_1), \ldots, \text{TA}(r_{n-1}), t)dt.$$
Note that the above definite integral is always defined because the integrand is a piece wise continuous function.

- If r_1, r_2 are terms, then:
  $\text{TA}((r_1 + r_2)) = \text{TA}(r_1) + \text{TA}(r_2)$,
  $\text{TA}((r_1 - r_2)) = \text{TA}(r_1) - \text{TA}(r_2)$,
  $\text{TA}((r_1 \times r_2)) = \text{TA}(r_1) \times \text{TA}(r_2)$.

The interpretation $I = \langle$ MC, SF, MF $\rangle$ and variable assignment VA satisfy a formula φ of UGCH (written $\models_I \varphi$ [VA]) under the following conditions (π_1 and π_2 are terms, φ_1 and φ_2 are wffs):

- $\models_I \pi_1 < \pi_2[\text{VA}]$ iff $\text{TA}(\pi_1) < \text{TA}(\pi_2)$.
- $\models_I \pi_1 \leq \pi_2[\text{VA}]$ iff $\text{TA}(\pi_1) \leq \text{TA}(\pi_2)$.
- $\models_I \pi_1 > \pi_2[\text{VA}]$ iff $\text{TA}(\pi_1) > \text{TA}(\pi_2)$.
- $\models_I \pi_1 \geq \pi_2[\text{VA}]$ iff $\text{TA}(\pi_1) \geq \text{TA}(\pi_2)$.
- $\models_I \pi_1 = \pi_2[\text{VA}]$ iff $\text{TA}(\pi_1) = \text{TA}(\pi_2)$.
- $\models_I [\varphi_1 \wedge \varphi_2][\text{VA}]$ iff $\models_I \varphi_1[\text{VA}]$ and $\models_I \varphi_2[\text{VA}]$.
- $\models_I [\varphi_1 \vee \varphi_2][\text{VA}]$ iff $\models_I \varphi_1[\text{VA}]$ or $\models_I \varphi_2[\text{VA}]$.
- $\models_I [\varphi_1 \rightarrow \varphi_2][\text{VA}]$ iff $\models_I [\neg\varphi_1 \vee \varphi_2][\text{VA}]$.
- $\models_I [\varphi_1 \leftrightarrow \varphi_2][\text{VA}]$ iff $\models_I [\varphi_1 \rightarrow \varphi_2][\text{VA}]$ and $\models_I [\varphi_2 \rightarrow \varphi_1][\text{VA}]$.
- $\models_I [\neg\varphi][\text{VA}]$ iff $\not\models_I \varphi[\text{VA}]$.
- $\models_I [\forall z \,.\, \varphi][\text{VA}]$ iff $\models_I \varphi[\text{VA}']$ for all VA$'$ that agree with VA everywhere except possibly on z.
- $\models_I [\exists z \,.\, \varphi][\text{VA}]$ iff $\models_I \varphi[\text{VA}']$ for some VA$'$ that agrees with VA everywhere except possibly on z.

3 Measures of Uncertainty

Given a function $f : \mathbb{R}^n \mapsto [0, 1]$, we define four measures of uncertainty based on f:

1. lower uncertainty approximation (LUA_f),
2. upper uncertainty approximation (UUA_f),
3. uncertainty ratio (ρ_f), and
4. truth over an interval (avg_f).

The exact value of the function f may not be known at a point. The LUA_f (UUA_f) is a lower (upper) bound on the function f (see Fig. 3). For all $y \in \mathbb{R}$, we have the following inequality between LUA_f, UUA_f, and f:

$$0 \leq LUA\_f(r_1, \ldots, r_{n-1}, y) \leq f(r_1, \ldots, r_{n-1}, y) \leq UUA\_f(r_1, \ldots, r_{n-1}, y) \leq 1.$$

If the exact value of f is known at a point y, then:

$$LUA\_f(r_1,\ldots,r_{n-1},y) = f(r_1,\ldots,r_{n-1},y) = UUA\_f(r_1,\ldots,r_{n-1},y).$$

If LUA_f (UUA_f) is unknown then we approximate LUA_f (UUA_f) with 0 (1).

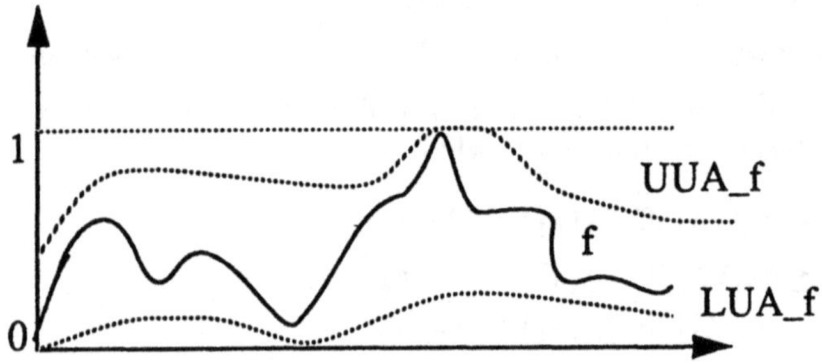

Fig. 3. Upper and lower bounds

The uncertainty ratio $\rho\_f(r_1,\ldots,r_{n-1},a,b)$, $a \neq b$, is defined as:

$$\rho\_f(r_1,\ldots,r_{n-1},a,b) = \begin{cases} 1 & \text{if } \forall x \in [a,b], \\ & \text{UUA\_f}(r_1,\ldots,r_{n-1},x) = 0, \\ \frac{\int_a^b LUA\_f(r_1,\ldots,r_{n-1},x)\ dx}{\int_a^b UUA\_f(r_1,\ldots,r_{n-1},x)\ dx} & \text{otherwise.} \end{cases}$$

From the definitions of LUA_f and UUA_f, we have:

$$0 \leq \rho\_f(r_1,\ldots,r_{n-1},a,b) \leq 1.$$

Precisely defined domains will have $\rho\_f(r_1,\ldots,r_{n-1},a,b) = 1$ and totally imprecise domains will have $\rho\_f(r_1,\ldots,r_{n-1},a,b) = 0$. Generally, uncertain domains have:

$$0 \leq \rho\_f(r_1,\ldots,r_{n-1},a,b) < 1.$$

The uncertainty ratio is useful when dealing with imperfect domain knowledge.

We also define an interval version of the function f called

$$avg\_f(r_1,\ldots,r_{n-1},a,b), \quad \text{where} \quad a \neq b,$$

which is defined as:

$$avg\_f(r_1,\ldots,r_{n-1},a,b) = \frac{\int_a^b f(r_1,\ldots,r_{n-1},x)dx}{b-a}.$$

Note that $0 \le avg\_f(r_1, \ldots, r_{n-1}, a, b) \le 1$. Also note that if the function f takes on only 0 and 1 values, then the avg_f function will usually have a value between 0 and 1. Thus, systems that are precisely defined at the point level, become imprecise at the interval level.

4 Discrete Version of the Logic

It is easy to define a discrete version of UGCH. In the syntax, we would have to replace integration with summation. In the semantics, the semantic domain would be changed from the real numbers to the integers (or some other discrete structure).

Since a discrete version of UGCH would not have any integration, we would re-define ρ_f and avg_f as follows:

$$\rho\_f(r_1, \ldots, r_{n-1}, a, b) = \begin{cases} 1 & \text{if } \forall x \in [a,b], \\ & \text{UUA\_f}(r_1, \ldots, r_{n-1}, x) \\ & = 0, \\ \frac{\sum_{x \in [a,b]} LUA\_f(r_1, \ldots, r_{n-1}, x)}{\sum_{x \in [a,b]} UUA\_f(r_1, \ldots, r_{n-1}, x)} & \text{otherwise,} \end{cases}$$

$$avg\_f(r_1, \ldots, r_{n-1}, a, b) = \frac{\sum_{x \in [a,b]} f(r_1, \ldots, r_{n-1}, x)}{cardinality([a,b])} .$$

5 Application: The Persistence Problem

Our measures of uncertainty can be used to solve the persistence problem (also called the frame problem in the situation calculus). For example, let the function f be defined over some interval (a, b), and nowhere else. To compute values for f outside the range (a, b), we approximate f with exponential decay functions. It is reasonable to assume, that the extrapolated function takes on values near f when close to the interval [a,b], and should approach zero as we move away from the interval (i.e., towards $\pm\infty$). Note that the extrapolation is done both into the past (i.e., before a) and into the future (i.e., after b). Most solutions to the persistence problem only deal with persistence into the future. This is an unnecessary restriction. There is no reason to treat the past differently from the future. For example, if we visit a city for the first time and observe a building, it is equally reasonable to assume that the building was there the previous day as it will be there the following day.

We define two extrapolating functions: f^* and f^{**}. The extrapolating function f^* is defined as:

$$f^*(r_1, \ldots, r_{n-1}, x) = \begin{cases} avg\_f(r_1, \ldots, r_{n-1}, a, b)\, e^{-r(x-b)} & \text{if } x > b \ , \\ f(r_1, \ldots, r_{n-1}, x) & \text{if } a \le x \le b \ , \\ avg\_f(r_1, \ldots, r_{n-1}, a, b)\, e^{r(x-a)} & \text{if } x < a \ , \end{cases}$$

where $r \in \mathbb{R}$ is a parameter that depends on the particulai application. We use f^* as an approximation to f outside the interval (a, b). Figure 4 shows the general shape of the f^* function. Before a and after b, f^* is an exponential decay function.

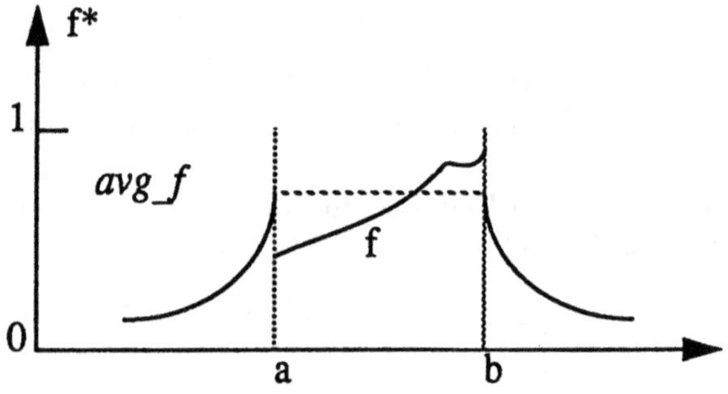

Fig. 4. Extrapolation f^*

The extrapolating function f^{**} is defined as:

$$f^{**}(r_1, \ldots, r_{n-1}, x) = \begin{cases} f(r_1, \ldots, r_{n-1}, b)\; e^{-r(x-b)} & \text{if } x > b \ , \\ f(r_1, \ldots, r_{n-1}, x) & \text{if } a \leq x \leq b \ , \\ f(r_1, \ldots, r_{n-1}, a)\; e^{r(x-a)} & \text{if } x < a \ , \end{cases}$$

where $r \in \mathbb{R}$ is a parameter that depends on the particular application. An example of the f^{**} is given in Fig. 5.

The advantage of the f^* function is that outside the range $[a, b]$, its value depends on the values of f throughout the interval $[a, b]$ (i.e., $avg\_f(r_1, \ldots, r_{n-1}, a, b)$). Outside the range $[a, b]$, the f^{**} depends on the endpoints of f (i.e., $f(r_1, \ldots, r_{n-1}, a)$ and $f(r_1, \ldots, r_{n-1}, b)$). The advantage of the f^{**} function is that there is no jump in values at the points a and b between f and the extrapolated exponential decay functions. Depending on the domain, the user must choose to use either f^* or f^{**}.

Our solution to the persistence problem can also be applied to non-temporal domains where the points in the domain are linearly ordered. We are not aware of any other work which applies a persistence approach to spatial domains.

Dean and Kanazawa [1] model persistence with linear or exponential decay functions that assume we know when events started. A truck arrives, for example, and the decay function tells us that the probability it remains decays by 5% every 15 minutes. The approach presented in [1] only works for discrete temporal ontologies and persistence in the forward direction. Our approach is more general because it works in the continuous case, works both into the past and future, and only relies on uncertain knowledge over an interval.

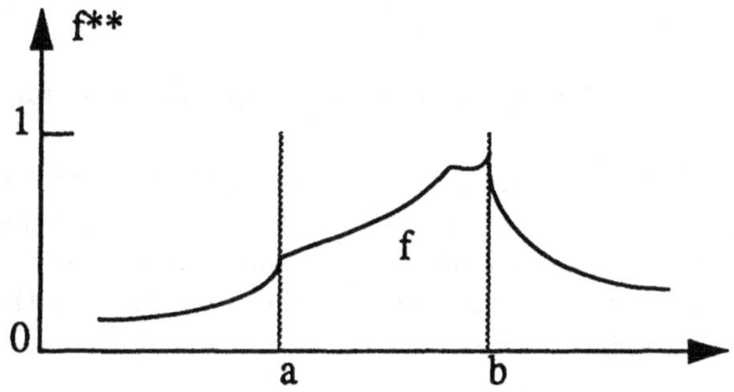

Fig. 5. Extrapolation f^{**}

6 Relationship with Bayesian Probabilities and Fuzzy Logic

UGCH can be extended and used as a research vehicle to compare standard approaches to uncertainty. In the following sections, we retain UGCH's syntax but change its semantics to coincide with Bayesian probabilitities and fuzzy logic. Our approach can also be extended to approximate the theory of evidence. This is left as a problem for future research.

6.1 Relationship with Bayesian Probabilities: Bayesian Probability UGCH

To obtain a Bayesian version of UGCH, we modify UGCH's syntax by adding $(\varphi_1|\varphi_2)$ as a wff. The semantics are changed to the following. The function p is defined to be an n-ary piece wise continuous function, called a *probability function,* which maps formulas of UGCH to elements of the set $[0, 1]$. p also has the property that the value of its integral from minus to plus infinity equals 1. p directly assigns a number between 0 and 1 inclusive to atomic formulas. For non-atomic formulas, p is defined recursively as follows:

- $p(\varphi_1 \vee \varphi_2) = p(\varphi_1) + p(\varphi_2) - p(\varphi_1 \wedge \varphi_2)$.
- $p(\varphi_1 \wedge \varphi_2) = p(\varphi_1|\varphi_2) * p(\varphi_2)$.
- $p(\varphi_1|\varphi_2) = \frac{p(\varphi_2|\varphi_1)*p(\varphi_1)}{p(\varphi_2)}$,
  Or a more general form of the above Baye's Rule:
  $p(\varphi_1|\varphi_2 \wedge \ldots \wedge \varphi_k) = \frac{p(\varphi_2 \wedge \ldots \wedge \varphi_k|\varphi_1)*p(\varphi_1)}{p(\varphi_2 \wedge \ldots \wedge \varphi_k)}$.
- $p(\neg\varphi_1) = 1 - p(\varphi_1)$.
- $p(\varphi_1 \rightarrow \varphi_2) = p(\neg\varphi_1 \vee \varphi_2)$.
- $p(\varphi_1 \leftrightarrow \varphi_2) = p((\varphi_1 \rightarrow \varphi_2) \wedge (\varphi_2 \rightarrow \varphi_1))$.
- $p(\forall z.\varphi_1) = p(\wedge_z \varphi_1)$, $z \in \mathbb{R}$.

- $p(\exists z.\varphi_1) = p(\bigvee_z \varphi_1)$, $z \in \mathbb{R}$.

In general, we will not be able to compute a specific value for formulas that contain quantified variables.

Note that the *avg_f* function from a previous section obtains a nice interpretation as an expected value of f in the interval $[a, b]$. We can use either f^* or f^{**} to extrapolate a probability function outside a known interval. Care should be taken to ensure that the parameter r satisfies the condition that the integral from minus to plus infinity is one.

6.2 Relationship with Fuzzy Logic: Fuzzy UGCH

To obtain a fuzzy logic version of UGCH which we call *fuzzy UGCH,* we retain UGCH's syntax and change the semantics to the following. The function f is defined to be an n-ary piece wise continuous function, called a *characteristic function,* which maps formulas of UGCH to elements of the set $[0, 1]$. f directly assigns a number between 0 and 1 inclusive to atomic formulas. For non-atomic formulas, f is defined recursively as follows:

- $f(\varphi_1 \vee \varphi_2) = \max(f(\varphi_1), f(\varphi_2))$.
- $f(\varphi_1 \wedge \varphi_2) = \min(f(\varphi_1), f(\varphi_2))$.
- $f(\neg\varphi_1) = 1 - f(\varphi_1)$.
- $f(\varphi_1 \rightarrow \varphi_2) = f(\neg\varphi_1 \vee \varphi_2)$.
- $f(\varphi_1 \leftrightarrow \varphi_2) = f((\varphi_1 \rightarrow \varphi_2) \wedge (\varphi_2 \rightarrow \varphi_1))$.
- $f(\forall z.\varphi_1) = f(\bigwedge_z \varphi_1)$, $z \in \mathbb{R}$.
- $f(\exists z.\varphi_1) = f(\bigvee_z \varphi_1)$, $z \in \mathbb{R}$.

In general, we will not be able to compute a specific value for formulas that contain quantified variables.

We can use the extrapolation functions from Section 5 to extrapolate the characteristic functions outside known intervals.

6.3 Example

We present an example to contrast the different versions of UGCH. Assume that at time 5, Irene is crying with a certainty of 0.6 and walking with a certainty of 0.1. In UGCH we write:

$$crying(5) = 0.6 \wedge walking(5) = 0.1 \ .$$

The above conjunction evaluates to true.

In the Bayesian probability UGCH we write:

$$\begin{aligned} &p(crying(5) = 0.6 \wedge walking(5) = 0.1) = \\ &\quad p(crying(5) = 0.6 | walking(5) = 0.1) * p(walking(5) = 0.1) = \\ &\quad p(crying(5) = 0.6) * p(walking(5) = 0.1) = 0.6 * 0.1 = 0.06 \ , \end{aligned}$$

since crying and walking are independent. We assume that we are given that p(crying(5) = 0.6) = 0.6 and p(walking(5) = 0.1) = 0.1.

In the fuzzy UGCH we have:

$$f(crying(5) = 0.6 \wedge walking(5) = 0.1) =$$

$$min(f(crying(5) = 0.6), f(walking(5) = 0.1)) = 0.1 \ .$$

We also assume that f(crying(5) = 0.6) = 0.6 and f(walking(5) = 0.1) = 0.1.

Note that the values obtained for the conjunction in the Bayesian and fuzzy versions of UGCH are different. Although UGCH is simpler than both its fuzzy and Bayesian versions, it has the drawback that it does not assign any uncertainty to formulas. All formulas in UGCH evaluate to either true or false.

7 Conclusion

We presented a general approach for representing uncertainty in both temporal and spatial domains. We formalize our approach as a logic and present examples of its use. Also, we discuss the relationship between our approach and Bayesian probabilities, and fuzzy logic.

Acknowledgements

The research of both authors is partially supported by operating grants from the Natural Sciences and Engineering Research Council of Canada, OGP0046501 and OGP0046773 respectively.

References

1. T. Dean and K. Kanazawa. Probabilistic Causal Reasoning. In *Seventh Biennial Conference of the Canadian Society for Computational Studies of Intelligence (CSCSI'88)*, pages 125-132, Edmonton, Canada, May 1988.
2. S.D. Goodwin and E. Neufeld and A. Trudel. Temporal reasoning with real valued functions. In *Pacific Rim International Conference on Artificial Intelligence (PRICAI'92)*, pages 1266–1271, Seoul, Korea, Sept 1992.
3. P. Jackson. *Introduction to expert systems*. Addison Wesley, 2nd edition, 1990.

An Analysis of the Temporal Relations of Intervals in Relativistic Space-Time

Rita V. Rodriguez and **Frank D. Anger**

The University of West Florida, Division of Computer Science
Pensacola, Florida, USA 32514
(904)474-3065, 3022, Fax:(904)474-3129, fa@ufl.edu

Key Words. *Atomic Relation, Consistency, Distributed System, Incomparable Events, Interval Temporal Model, Non-Determinism, Relativistic Space-Time, Temporal Relation Algebra.*

Abstract. Concurrent systems are subject to a form of temporal uncertainty due to the non-deterministic order of execution. Distributed systems cause additional uncertainty by the lack of a common clock and the communication delays. Adequate methods for checking the specification and design of such systems must allow for sound reasoning about asynchronous activities, while automated methods should perform the reasoning in polynomial time. This paper presents the basis for such deductive systems through a very general temporal relation algebra which can be used with constraint propagation techniques. Based on intervals in relativistic space-time, it naturally incorporates the expression of uncertain and ambiguous temporal relations, as well as concurrent actions. The possible temporal relations are analyzed and named consistently with earlier work of the authors, followed by an explanation of the calculation of compositions of the atomic temporal relations. The resulting table of compositions is the cornerstone of a temporal constraint-based reasoner that presently supports a prototype concurrent system debugger by deducing from partial run-time information the existence of temporal behavior inconsistent with specifications.

1 Introduction

Program semantics impose certain limits on the non-deterministic order of execution of concurrent processes. Checking the correctness of such programs is usually a matter of comparing output to expected results; nonetheless, this method does not assure that program execution actually followed the desired pattern. A more significant test compares actual temporal relations between process executions against supposed behavior, creating a form of uncertainty management. Program verification techniques require proving that the semantics imply the required behavior despite the uncertainty of execution order. Time-dependent errors easily elude standard program verification and testing methods. The problem lies in showing that all the temporal sequences which are semantically possible for a given program satisfy some particular set of temporal constraints. An efficient reasoner which can utilize partial knowledge about the possible temporal behavior of a concurrent program to check for potential time-dependent errors is being constructed based on the theory presented herein [13]. Even in the worst case of a distributed system with no common clock and operations each of which executes over a non-zero interval of time, the model obtained enables the use of constraint propagation and related methods for resolving a class of consistency and correctness issues in polynomial time. A sound, but not complete, constraint propagation reasoner can determine (perhaps in conjunction with other less efficient but complete algorithms) if the specifications as given are *path consistent*—hence whether it is likely that the system can be built; or if any of a class of temporal errors exist in an algorithm—hence whether the system is likely to work as required.

Several alternative temporal models not based on time points have been offered by Allen (linear [2]), Lamport (axiomatic [8]), Anger, Ladkin, and Rodriguez (branching-time [5]) and others. Whereas the compositions of the linear and branching time relations were calculated by hand, in the dense-relativistic-interval model, the number of possible atomic relations increases considerably [12].

While earlier assaults on the classification of the temporal relations of relativistic intervals have been made [3,12,6], they have been based on more abstract models which do not provide any obvious way to facilitate the construction of the table of compositions, so vital to any automated temporal constraint propagation mechanism. Using a specially selected coordinate representation of interval endpoints, a programmatic calculation of the compositions is achieved.

The definition of space-time and the temporal *point* relations follows in Section 2 where the composition of *pointwise* relations is calculated. Section 3 defines intervals in space-time and obtains all the atomic relations that can exist between two such *intervals*, classified according to the point relations between endpoints. Section 4 presents a portion of the table of compositions of the relativistic-time relations and discusses the program which generates such a table. Section 5 summarizes the presentation.

2 Fundamentals and Point Relations

A variety of temporal models have been applied to the study of concurrency [1,9,11, 18,13]. The absence of a common clock and the speed of the events in distributed computing systems dictate a flexible temporal model. For executions taking place over a period of time, intervals (t_1, t_2) are more appropriate than single time points, whereupon the order properties become considerably more interesting [10], albeit less tractable: reasoning about possible relations among the totally ordered points of a time line can be accomplished efficiently; just determining if a set of temporal constraints on intervals is satisfiable, on the other hand, is NP-hard. A partial remedy to the situation is afforded by constraint-propagation methods. A system with knowledge of the compositions of all *atomic* or *irreducible* temporal relations can derive implied temporal restrictions in n^3 time (n = number of events) in a

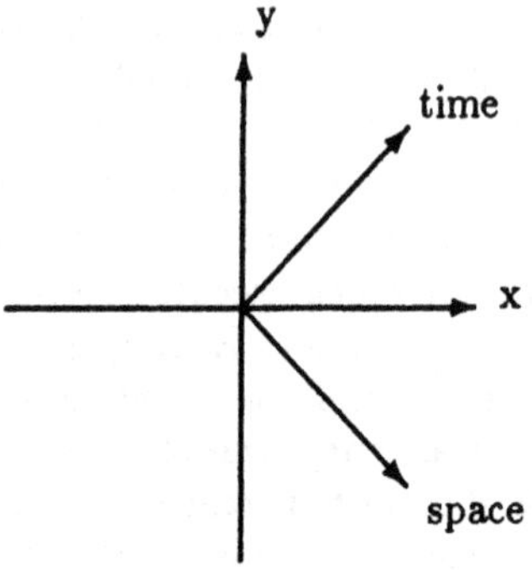

Figure 1: Two Dimensional Representation of Relativistic Space-Time

Table 1: Basic Order Composition Table

	$<$	$>$	$=$
$<$	$<$	1	$<$
$>$	1	$>$	$>$
$=$	$<$	$>$	$=$

sound manner. (A relation is *atomic* if it cannot be expressed as a disjunction of more specific relations: for example $\leq$ is not atomic, being the disjunction "$<$ or $=$.") Einstein's relativistic space-time is used as the basis of an interval model of time. In this rather complex system, the atomic temporal interval relations are determined and the required compositions calculated.

In *relativistic space-time*, which we represent with only two dimensions—one for time and one for space—there is only a *partial order*: a natural representation of concurrent events. Two axes—x and y—and a scale are chosen, as in Figure 1, such that the *time* dimension points into the first quadrant, and such that the future cone of the origin *is* the first quadrant [7].

For points $A = (A^1, A^2)$, $B = (B^1, B^2)$, a relation $(r,\ s)$ can be defined for any real-number relations r and s by $A\ (r,\ s)\ B$ iff $A^1 r B^1$ *and* $A^2 s B^2$. The atomic relations in the relation algebra so generated are essentially the 9 relations $(r,\ s)$ with r and s atomic: $<$, $>$, or $=$; however, it is pointless to distinguish between $(r,\ s)$ and $(s,\ r)$. The 6 resulting atomic relations are defined in Table 2. A useful non-atomic relativistic point relation, $\leq$, can be expressed as a disjunction of atomic relations: $\leq\, = (\prec + \ll + =)$, while strict precedence, $<$, is given by $\prec + \ll$. Intuitively, the *future* of the point A consists of all points B satisfying $A < B$ under this definition. $A \ll B$ corresponds to the case that B lies precisely on the boundary of the future time cone of A, or that a signal sent from A at the speed of light will arrive exactly at B; hence the terminology *A projects to B*. The other relation, $A \prec B$, or *A reaches*

Table 2: Definitions of the Relativistic Point Relations

Relation	Symbol	Name
$(<, <)$	$\prec$	reaches
$(<, =) + (=, <)$	$\ll$	projects to
$(<, >) + (>, <)$	$\Vert$	incomparable
$(>, =) + (=, >)$	$\gg$	projected to
$(>, >)$	$\succ$	reached by
$(=, =)$	$=$	equal

Table 3: The Point-Relation (PR) Composition Table in Space-Time ("=" is omitted)

PR	$\prec$	$\ll$	$\Vert$	$\gg$	$\succ$
$\prec$	$\prec$	$\prec$	$\not\succeq$	$\not\succeq$	1
$\ll$	$\prec$	$\prec + \ll$	$\not\succeq$	$\not\prec \& \not\succ$	$\not\preceq$
$\Vert$	$\not\succeq$	$\not\succeq$	1	$\not\preceq$	$\not\preceq$
$\gg$	$\not\succeq$	$\not\prec \& \not\succ$	$\not\preceq$	$\succ + \gg$	$\succ$
$\succ$	1	$\not\preceq$	$\not\preceq$	$\succ$	$\succ$

Notation: "+" means "or"; "$\not\succeq$" means "$\prec + \ll + \Vert$"; "$\not\preceq$" means "$\Vert + \gg + \succ$"; "1" represents the ***universal relation***, i.e., no information.

B, corresponds to two points such that it is physically possible for a body with mass to travel (at less than the speed of light) from A to B. (It is interesting to note that, although the convenient choice of coordinates gives a pleasant analytic description of $\prec$ and $\ll$, these are, in fact, invariant properties of the space-time point pairs under the theory of relativity.) The remaining relations are the converses of $\succ$ and $\gg$, and ***incomparable***, $\Vert$. Two points are ***incomparable*** or ***unrelated*** if neither is in the future cone of the other (neither precedes the other), as for example the origin and any point in the second or fourth quadrant. Note that $=$ and $\Vert$ are self-converse. The compositions of the six point relations which generate a ***relation algebra*** of $2^6 = 64$ temporal point relations, (PR Table), appears as Table 3. [14] presents proofs and details about relation algebras.

3 Interval Events and Interval Relations

When reasoning about concurrent programs, there are several sources of uncertainty. By design, concurrent processes execute in *non-deterministic* order with respect to one another. If, in addition, the processes are distributed over more than one processor, it is possible for the processes to execute simultaneously. Finally, if the processors share no clock and no memory, there may be no way to establish the actual order of execution of concurrent tasks with certainty. Together with the fact that the *events* of interest which take place in a distributed system are executions of instructions or procedures, events are better modeled as intervals than as points. No obvious way exists, in the presence of uncertainty, to use a network of temporal constraints on the endpoints of the intervals to reason about the possible relations between the intervals: the actual relations between the intervals themselves must be classified, starting from the relations between the endpoints. Several algorithms have been designed to deduce temporal information from networks of temporal relations. Vilain and Kautz [19] have shown that the problem of determining the consistency or satisfiability of a constraint system on intervals is NP-complete; however, Allen's constraint propagation approach determines *path consistency*—a special case of consistency—in time proportional to n^3 [2]. Van Beek recently obtained an $O(n^4)$ algorithm which is sound and complete for the *point* relations [16] and an algorithm for interval relations which is relatively efficient in the average case [17], based on considering first the *pointizable* relations.

Whereas Section 2 presented the point relations, the theory of the space-time relations between "interval events" is the subject of this section. An *interval event* is an event, E, which evolves over time and space, having a fixed starting point, E_s, and a fixed finish point, E_f.

Definition 1: An (*interval*) *event*, E, is a pair of points, $E_s = (E_s^1, E_s^2)$ and $E_f = (E_f^1, E_f^2)$ in space-time (as represented in Section 2) satisfying $E_s \prec E_f$. (That is, $E_s^1 < E_f^1$ and $E_s^2 < E_f^2$.)

Just as in the linear-time model, the possible relations between two processes can be characterized by the possible relations between the endpoints of one interval and the endpoints of the other. Now, nonetheless, there are 6 possibilities for each of the 4 possible pairs of coordinates, leading to potentially $6^4 = 1296$ relations; again, as in the linear case, most are ruled out by the fact that $E_s \prec E_f$ for each event, E. Next, all the possible distinct, atomic relations between two processes, or intervals, in relativistic space-time are found and described. (See [14] for proof of Theorem 1.)

Theorem 1: There are exactly 82 atomic temporal relations between events (intervals) in relativistic space-time as defined in Section 2 and generated by the relations induced by the pair of end-point relations (Table 3). These relations are all inclusive and mutually exclusive: any two events (intervals) must be in precisely one of these relations to one another.

The atomic relations can be named according to a scheme which takes the form A r:s B, where r captures what "A looks like to B" by projecting the interval A onto a "world line" through B. Similarly s captures what "B looks like to A" by projecting B onto a world line through A. r and s are therefore linear-time interval relations obtained, by mapping the four relations A_s-B_s, A_s-B_f, A_f-B_s, and A_f-B_f into two total orders, each determined by one of the events. The resulting linear-time interval relations could be named via the scheme in [2]; however, the con-

Table 4: Linear Interval Relation Names and Extended Definitions

	REL	ABBR	DEFINITION	EXTENDED DEF
1.	before	*bef*	$A_f < B_s$	$A_f \prec B_s$
2.	meets	*m*	$A_f = B_s$	$A_f = + \lll B_s$
3.	overlaps	*o*	$A_s < B_s < A_f < B_f$	$A_s \prec B_s, A_f \prec B_f, A_f \not\lesssim B_s$
4.	during	*d*	$A_s > B_s, A_f < B_f$	$A_s \not\lesssim B_s, A_f \prec B_f$
5.	contains	*cn*	$A_s < B_s, A_f > B_f$	$A_s \prec B_s, A_f \not\lesssim B_f$
6.	surpasses	*su*	$B_s < A_s < B_f < A_f$	$A_s \not\lesssim B_s, A_s \prec B_f, A_f \not\lesssim B_f$
7.	starts	*s*	$A_s = B_s, A_f < B_f$	$A_s = + \lll B_s, A_f \prec B_f$
8.	finishes	*f*	$A_s > B_s, A_f = B_f$	$A_s \not\lesssim B_s, A_f = + \lll B_f$
9.	projects to	*p*	$A_s = B_s, A_f = B_f$	$A_s = + \lll B_s, A_f = + \lll B_f$
10.	extends	*e*	$A_s = B_s, A_f > B_f$	$A_s = + \lll B_s, A_f \not\lesssim B_f$
11.	pre-extends	*pe*	$A_s < B_s, A_f = B_f$	$A_s \prec B_s, A_f = + \lll B_f$
12.	follows	*fol*	$A_s = B_f$	$A_s = + \lll B_f$
13.	after	*aft*	$A_s > B_f$	$A_s \not\lesssim B_f$

verse relations, such as *overlaps/overlapped-by* are not true converses in relativistic time. The names of the former converses have accordingly been replaced by other descriptive names: *surpasses* for *overlapped-by*, *pre-extends* for *finished-by* etc. (See Definition 2.) It is a simple matter to retrieve from the "*r:s*" description the four endpoint relations—hence the naming scheme is sufficient (allows the recapturing of the end-point relations), suggestive of experience (tells how each event views the other), and convenient (gives a more intuitive naming scheme for the relations). The notation "*r:s*" also possesses the properties: $(r : s)^{\smile} = s : r$, and $r : s = r \& s^{\smile}$, for r and s any (of 2^{13} possible) linear-time interval relations.

Definition 2: Table 4 displays the names that are used for the atomic or irreducible *linear-time* interval relations as described in terms of the endpoints of the intervals $A = (A_s, A_f)$ and $B = (B_s, B_f)$. The rightmost column, referred to as the "basic" relations, indicates how the linear-time name r is extended to mean r:1 in relativistic time. The extended relations are no longer atomic, however, except for $bef = bef$:1 $= bef : aft$.

4 Determination of Compositions

The program to generate the table of compositions of the atomic interval relations follows the chain of definitions presented in Sections 2 and 3, starting with the simple compositions of the three atomic (order) relations $<$, $>$, and $=$ given by Table 1. Table 3 is generated using the definitions summarized in Table 2. For example, $\prec \circ \lll$ is calculated as

$$(<,<) \circ [(<,=)+(=,<)] = (< \circ <, < \circ =) + (< \circ =, < \circ <) = (<,<) + (<,<) = \prec .$$

From Table 3, it is then possible to calculate the compositions of the atomic interval relations in two steps:

(1) Represent each atomic interval relation as a 2 by 2 array of endpoint relations in the form

$$\begin{pmatrix} R_{ss} & R_{sf} \\ R_{fs} & R_{ff} \end{pmatrix}$$

where, for example, R_{sf} is the point relation between the start of the first event and the finish of the second event. Now use the formula

$$R1 \circ R2 \subseteq \begin{pmatrix} R1_{ss} \circ R2_{ss} \& R1_{sf} \circ R2_{fs} & R1_{ss} \circ R2_{sf} \& R1_{sf} \circ R2_{ff} \\ R1_{fs} \circ R2_{ss} \& R1_{ff} \circ R2_{fs} & R1_{fs} \circ R2_{sf} \& R1_{ff} \circ R2_{ff} \end{pmatrix}$$

to obtain the constraints imposed on the endpoint relations of the composition.

(2) Test whether each atomic relation, represented by a similar 2 by 2 array, is contained in the resulting array. The composition is the disjunction of those atomic operations successful in (2). As the resulting table is very large, consisting of 6724 entries, each made up of a disjunction of as many as 82 atomic relations, it is neither practical nor informative to present entirely; however, analysis of the results yields a number of interesting patterns and a way to describe the results more succinctly than directly in terms of disjunctions of atomic relations. A sample of the compositions is given in Table 5 using abbreviations based on the following discussion.

In order to describe both the *legal* (non-empty) relations $r : q$ and the compositions of these relations, we introduce a partial order on the temporal relations. The "intervals" of the resulting lattice concisely represent the disjunctions required.

Definition 3: For relativistic temporal interval relations r and q define $r \rightsquigarrow q$ to mean that the following conditions hold:

(1) $r \& q = \emptyset$ (Equivalent to $r \neq q$ in the case that r and q are atomic.), and there exist intervals A, B, and C such that

(2) $A\ r\ C$ and $B\ q\ C$ and

(3) $A_s \leq B_s$ and $A_f \leq B_f$

(The $\leq$ is taken in the relativistic sense of Section 2.)

That the $\rightsquigarrow$ relation is a partial order is not immediate: irreflexivity follows from (1); transitivity is an easy consequence of the Lemma below. First another definition:

Definition 4: Define an interval I to be *between* intervals A and B iff either

$$A_s \leq I_s \leq B_s \text{ and } A_f \leq I_f \leq B_f \text{ or } A_s \geq I_s \geq B_s \text{ and } A_f \geq I_f \geq B_f.$$

We are now ready for the Lemma; the proof is omitted.

Lemma: If $r(\rightsquigarrow + =)u(\rightsquigarrow + =)q$ or $q(\rightsquigarrow + =)u(\rightsquigarrow + =)r$, then there exist intervals A, I, B, and C such that I is between A and B and $A\ r\ C$, $I\ u\ C$, and $B\ q\ C$.

Theorem 2: If r and q are chosen from the 13 "basic" relativistic temporal relations and if ri represents the *linear* converse of r, then $r : q$ *makes sense* (is *non-empty*) if and only if $ri(\rightsquigarrow + =)q$ (i.e. $ri = q$ or $ri \rightsquigarrow q$).

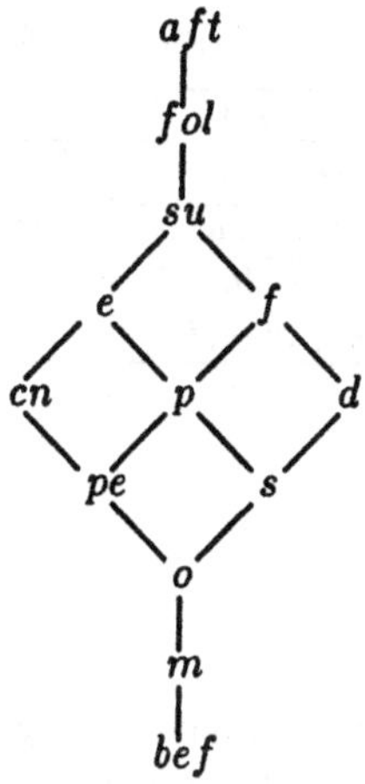

Figure 2: The Lattice of Linear-Time Interval Relations

Proof: In linear time, r and q would be atomic, ri would be $r^{\smile}$, and $r : q = r$ & $q^{\smile} \neq \emptyset$ iff $q^{\smile} = r$, which is equivalent to $ri = q$. In relativistic time, if $A\ r : q\ B$, we have $A\ r\ B$ and $B\ q\ A$: intuitively, we can find an interval, $\hat{B}$, which is *colinear* with A, which projects to B, and such that $A\ r\ \hat{B}$, or equivalently $\hat{B}\ ri\ A$. Since $\hat{B}$ projects to B, the intervals $\hat{B}$, B, and A play the roles of A, B, and C in Definition 3 and satisfy (2) and (3) with ri in place of r. Finally, q and ri, being two of the basic 13, are either equal or satisfy (1). In the former case, $ri = q$; in the latter case, $ri \rightsquigarrow q$.

It should be pointed out that, in the naming scheme presented, $befi = aft$, $mi = fol$, $oi = su$, etc. Utilizing the partial order $\rightsquigarrow$, the 13 basic relations can be seen to form a *lattice* (each pair of relations has a greatest lower bound and least upper bound among the 13) as shown in Figure 2, where $r \rightsquigarrow q$ iff there is an upward path from r to q in the figure (known as the *Hasse Diagram* of the lattice).

An *interval* in a lattice, much like the familiar intervals on the real number line, is determined by two elements of the lattice—the *infimum* (or *greatest lower bound*) and the *supremum* (or *least upper bound*)—and consists of all the lattice elements x such that $inf \leq x \leq sup$. For example, in the lattice of Figure 2, $o+pe+s+p+f+d$ is a disjunction over the interval $\langle o, f\rangle$, whereas $m+o+s+p$ is not over an interval because $m < pe < p$ but pe is not in the disjunction.

It was observed that there are only 751 different compositions in the complete table, which can be written in the form $r{:}s$ for some—not necessarily basic—relations r and s. The relations that appear on each side of the colon (:) are, of course, disjunctions of the 13 basic relations of Table 4. Moreover, each disjunction takes place over an interval in the lattice of relations as pictured in Figure 2. Table 5 uses uniformly the notation $\langle r, s\rangle$ to denote the interval from r to s.

Table 5: Atomic Relativistic Temporal Compositions: A Sample

	$bef : aft$	$o : fol$	$cn : d$	$e : f$
$bef : aft$	$bef : aft$	$bef : aft$	$bef : aft$	$bef : aft$
$o : fol$	$bef : aft$	$\langle bef,o\rangle : aft$	$\langle bef,cn\rangle : aft$	$\langle m,cn\rangle : \langle fol,aft\rangle$
$cn : d$	$\langle bef,cn\rangle : \langle d, aft\rangle$	$\langle o,cn\rangle : \langle d,su\rangle$	$cn : d$	$cn : d$
$e : f$	$\langle bef,cn\rangle : aft$	$\langle o,cn\rangle : \langle su,fol\rangle$	$cn : d$	$\langle cn,e\rangle : \langle d,f\rangle$

5 Conclusion

A temporal scheme useful for expressing and managing temporal uncertainty has been presented, bringing together ideas from temporal logic (Goldblatt), relativistic physics (Einstein), order relations on intervals (Allen), distributed system modeling (Lamport), and the recent work of Anger and Rodriguez to classify possible atomic space-time relations between intervals in a dense, infinite, relativistic space-time model. In the model discussed, all the atomic relations are found, classified, and named. A program based on the model presented was developed to calculate the table of compositions of all atomic relations in relativistic space-time; the steps followed by the program were discussed to clarify the process and definitions. The resulting compositions serve as a basis for a constraint-propagation reasoner [12] which can be used by itself efficiently to determine path consistency, or combined with slower methods to determine full consistency. Given temporal specifications of a distributed system, the method can be used to test the consistency of the specifications or to test the behavior of the actual system to see if it meets the specifications. Combined with techniques for reasoning about time measurements [4], the consistency of distributed real-time specifications can also be checked [13]. Uncertainty in specifications or about observed behavior can be managed easily using disjunctions of relations, provided that the correct relation is among the disjuncts. As tools supporting the verification of concurrent systems are still very limited,application of such temporal reasoners holds significant potential for industrial and scientific programmers opening a new direction in testing for distributed, concurrent, and parallel systems.

Acknowledgments. The program to produce the atomic compositions was implemented by the authors' student, Gregory Walrath. The work was partially supported by a *Florida High Technology and Industry Council* Applied Research Grant and by the *Center for High Performance Computing.*

References

[1] Abraham, U., Ben-David, S. & Magidor, M. On Global-Time Interprocess Communication. In *Semantics for Concurrency*, M. Kwiatkowska, M. Shields & R. Thomas, eds., Springer-Verlag, Leicester, 1990.

[2] Allen, J. Maintaining Knowledge about Temporal Intervals. *Comm. of ACM 26*, 11 (1983), pp. 832-843.

[3] Anger, F. On Lamport's Interprocessor Communication Model. *ACM Trans. on Prog. Lang. and Systems 11*, 3 (July 1989), pp. 404-417.

[4] Anger, F., Rodriguez, R., and Hadlock, F. Temporal Consistency Checking of Natural Language Specifications. *Applications of Artificial Intelligence VIII, SPIE*, Orlando, (April 1991), pp. 572-580.

[5] Anger, F., Ladkin, P. & Rodriguez, R. Atomic Temporal Interval Relations in Branching Time: Calculation and Application. *Applications of AI IX, SPIE*, Orlando, (April 1991), pp. 122-136.

[6] Anger, F. and Rodriguez, R. Time, Tense, and Relativity Revisited. In *Lecture Notes in Computer Science*, Bouchon-Meunier, B., Yager, R., and Zadeh, L., eds, Springer-Verlag, Heidelberg, Germany, 1991, pp. 286-295.

[7] Goldblatt, R. Diodorean Modality in Minkowski Spacetime. *Studia Logica 39*, 2/3 (1980), pp. 219-236.

[8] Lamport, L. The Mutual Exclusion Problem: Part I–A Theory of Interprocess Communication. *Journal ACM 33*, 2 (April 1986), pp. 313-326.

[9] Manna, Z. and Wolper, P. Synthesis of Communication Processes from Temporal Logic Specifications. *ACM Trans. Prog. Lang. & Syst. 6*, 1 (Jan.1984), pp. 68-93.

[10] Pelavin, R. and Allen, J. A Model for Concurrent Actions having Temporal Extent. *Proceedings of the Sixth National Conference on Artificial Intelligence*, Seattle, WA, (July 1987), pp. 246-250.

[11] Pnueli, A. The Temporal Semantics of Concurrent Programs. *Proceedings of the 18th Symposium on the Foundations of Computer Science*, IEEE, Providence, (Nov 1977), pp. 46-57.

[12] Rodriguez, R., Anger, F., and Ford, K. Temporal Reasoning: A Relativistic Model. *International Journal of Intelligent Systems 6*, (Jun 1991), pp. 237-254.

[13] Rodriguez, R., Anger, F., and Walrath, G. Implementation Aspects of a Minimally Intrusive Debugger for Concurrent Systems. *Software Engineering Research Forum*, Melbourne FL (Nov 1992), pp. 223-231.

[14] Rodriguez, R. A Relativistic Temporal Algebra for Efficient Design of Distributed Systems. *Journal of Applied Intelligence 3*, 1 (1993), pp. 31-45.

[15] Rodriguez, R. and Anger, F. Prior's Legacy in Computer Science. In *Logic and Reality: Essays in Pure and Applied Logic, In Memory of Arthur Prior*, J. Copeland, ed., Oxford University Press, Oxford, 1993.

[16] van Beek, P. Approximation Algorithms for Temporal Reasoning. In *Proceedings of the Eleventh International Joint Conference on Artificial Intelligence*, (1989), pp. 1291-1296.

[17] van Beek, P. *Exact and Approximate Reasoning about Qualitative Temporal Relations.* PhD Thesis, University of Alberta, 1990.

[18] van Benthem, J. *A Manual of Intensional Logic*, CSLI/SRI International, Menlo Park, CA, 1988.

[19] Vilain, M. and Kautz, H. Constraint Propagation Algorithms for Temporal Reasoning. *Proceedings of the Fifth National Conference of AAAI*, Pittsburgh, PA, (Aug 1986), pp. 377-382.

Accumulation and Inference over Finite-Generated Algebras for Mapping Approximations

Jaume Casasnovas and Jose J. Miro-Julia

University of the Balearic Islands,
Departament de Matemàtiques i Informàtica
Crra. Valldemossa Km 7.5
07071 Palma de Mallorca, Spain
e-mail: dmijcc8@ps.uib.es dmijmj0@ps.uib.es

Abstract. In this paper we propose a generalization of Belnap's method in which we assign values to the elements of a Boolean Algebra of Propositions to represent the partial knowledge known of a valuation over the algebra. This generalizations includes mappings that are not a homomorphism respect to all the operations, but only respect to some, like the measures of possibility or of necessity. We also propose the generalization of the method by which we can refer to and *accumulate* all the available information of a set of generators. This will let us make *inferences* of valid approximations.

1 Introduction

The use of certain algebras to express approximate knowledge of a mapping that assigns values from a set to sentences or elements of another algebra was introduced by Belnap in [1]. He uses four values (0, 1, NONE, BOTH) to express what is known of a binary valuation defined over a Boolean algebra of sentences. A similar system, with somewhat modified values, called *information lattice* is introduced by Driankov [3]. On the other hand, J. Miro-Julia in [6] uses four similar values (0, 1, *, κ) to express what is known about the presence or absence of attributes or properties on elements of a certain domain. Finally, J. Casasnovas in [2] uses a set of subintervals of [0 1] to express approximate knowledge of a measure of possibility with values in the interval [0 1] and defined over either a boolean algebra, or an algebra with less axioms than the boolean one [4, 5].

It is possible to define, in a more general manner, the set of values of the range of the approximate knowledge of a mapping $f : \hat{R} \rightarrow B$ where $\hat{R}$ is a boolean algebra and whose values are on a totally ordered lattice with negation B, for instance $\{0, 1\}$, the three-valued algebra of Lukasiewicz, Post's algebra, the interval [0 1],..., so that it will include and generalize, after the necessary isomorphisms, all the cases cited above. These values are the 'subintervals' of a totally ordered lattice.

In these sets of values two lattice structures, with different negations, can be defined through two *kinds of operations.* These structures generalize respectively the algebras called A4 and L4 in [1]. The generalization of A4 is the consequence of an adequate use of the standard *union, intersection,* and *complementation,* and is suited to create the *accumulation* and *aggregation* of several approximations to the same mapping. The generalization of L4 is done in such a way that if approximations to the values of a mapping over two values a and b are known, you can ***build*** valid approximations of the value of the mapping over $a \vee b, a \wedge b, \neg a, a \rightarrow b, \ldots$ as long as the approximate mapping is a ***morphism*** respect to these operations. The defined operations determine a structure that is a De Morgan's lattice, with a maximal and a minimal element. Such a structure is called a ***quasi-boolean*** algebra by Rasiowa in [7].

We will also show a generalization of the methods established in [6, 2] to accumulate all the information that refers to a mapping, even if the information refers to different elements of the domain.

Finally, we will develop a ***systematic method*** to let ***decide***, from the premises and data available, whether or not an information is valid. To do so it is necessary to study the effect produced by adding the proposed approximation to the accumulation done over the generators of the existing information.

2 Mappings which Are Morphisms with Respect to Only Some Operations

Let $R = \{r_1, \ldots, r_n\}$ be a set of properties that are susceptible of being attributed to the elements of a certain domain D. We can consider a mapping $f : R \longrightarrow \{0, 1\}$ such that

$$f(r_i) = \begin{cases} 1 \text{ If some element in } D \text{ satisfies the property } r_i \\ 0 \text{ Otherwise} \end{cases}$$

If we consider the boolean algebra $\hat{R}$ generated by the elements of R and the operations $\vee, \wedge, \neg$ we see it is formed [7] by all the finite join of the finite meet of all the elements in R. It makes sense then to ask if an element $r \in \hat{R}$ is satisfied by some element of the domain D as it can be immediately defined as:

$r \wedge r\prime$ is satisfied by some element in D if and only if some element in D satisfies both r and $r\prime$

$r \vee r\prime$ is satisfied by some element in D if and only if some element in D satisfies either r or $r\prime$ or both

$\neg r$ is satisfied by some element in D if and only if some element in D does not satisfy r

Considering in $\{0, 1\}$ its boolean algebra structure, and representing by $\wedge, \vee, \neg$ the operations defined over it we see that the mapping f satisfies:

$$f(r \vee r\prime) = f(r) \vee f(r\prime) \ .$$

On the other hand it does not satisfy $f(r \wedge r\prime) = f(r) \wedge f(r\prime)$ as there might be some element in D that satisfies r, some other that satisfies $r\prime$, but none that satisfies both. In the same way, the equality $f(\neg r) = \neg f(r)$ does not hold either as there might be some element in D that satisfies r and some that does not.

This is an example of a mapping defined over a boolean algebra that is a *morphism respect to one of the operations of the algebra, but not respect to the others.*

Other possible examples are the *measures of possibility* [4] that satisfy $\Pi(a \vee b) = \Pi(a) \vee \Pi(b)$ but in general do not satisfy neither $\Pi(a \wedge b) = \Pi(a) \wedge \Pi(b)$ nor $\Pi(\neg a) = \neg \Pi(a)$. On the other hand the *measures of necessity* satisfy $N(a \wedge b) = N(a) \wedge N(b)$ and do not satisfy $N(a \vee b) = N(a) \vee N(b)$ and $N(\neg a) = \neg N(a)$.

On the other hand the measures of possibility and necessity may be defined over a Boolean Algebra of sentences and with values in the interval $[0 \quad 1]$ satisfying:

$$\begin{aligned} \Pi(a \vee b) &= \max\{\Pi(a), \Pi(b)\} \\ N(a \wedge b) &= \min\{N(a), N(b)\} \end{aligned}$$

and constitute examples of mappings that are morphisms between algebras with structures that are not exactly alike.

If we are going to study a mapping that is a morphism respect to a binary operation, we will be interested in those algebras that might be *finite generated with respect to this operation*. For instance, if we continue with the case of properties satisfied by some element of the domain D, all the elements of the algebra $\hat{R}$ might be expressed as a finite join of elements of the form $r_1^{s_1} \wedge \ldots \wedge r_n^{s_n}$, where:

$$\begin{aligned} r_i^{s_i} &= r_i \text{ if } s_i = 0 \\ r_i^{s_i} &= \neg r_i \text{ if } s_i = 1 \end{aligned}$$

These kind of algebras have an important property: *the determination of the value of the mapping over the generators define the mapping over the whole algebra.*

If we call $\{m_1, \ldots, m_n\}$ to the set of the generators respect to the join, as we have defined above, we will have that for every $r \in \hat{R}$

$$r = \bigvee_j \delta_j^r m_j \ : j = 1, \ldots, 2^n$$

where δ_j^r are coefficients with value 0 or 1 and are characteristics of the element r.

Then, thanks to it being a morphism, we can define

$$f(r) = \bigvee_j \delta_j^r f(m_j)$$

3 Approximations to a Mapping

Let's suppose that a certain mapping $f : \hat{R} \rightarrow \{0,1\}$ is not completely known. We can represent this fact by another mapping $F : \hat{R} \rightarrow \{0,1,*\}$ where

$F(r) = 1$ means *we know that* $f(r) = 1$

$F(r) = 0$ means *we know that* $f(r) = 0$

$F(r) = *$ means *we do not know the value of* $f(r)$

In the case we have a mapping that is $f : \hat{R} \rightarrow [0 \quad 1]$, then a mapping such as: $F : \hat{R} \rightarrow \{\text{subintervals of } [0 \quad 1]\}$ such that $F(r) = [a \quad b]$ means *we know that* $f(r) \in [a \quad b]$ will be called an *approximation*.

These two definitions can be summarized into one if we consider the totally ordered set {0,1} as an interval. In this case we will have:

$$\{1\} \equiv [1 \quad 1] \quad \{0\} \equiv [0 \quad 0] \quad * \equiv [0 \quad 1]$$

and the mapping F would have the same definition as in the case of the real interval $[0 \quad 1]$.

In a more general case we can add to the set of values of the approximation the value $\emptyset$, that means *with the available information $f(r)$ cannot take any value.*

The properties of the approximate mapping and of the considered binary operations determine the following fact: if $f(r) \in [a \quad b], f(r\prime) \in [c \quad d]$ we can assure that:

$$f(r \vee r\prime) \in [a \vee c \quad b \vee d] = \{x \vee y \mid x \in [a \quad b], y \in [c \quad d]\} = [a \quad b] \vee_i [c \quad d] \quad (1)$$

This operation induced over the set of subintervals by the 'join' operation in $[0 \quad 1]$ has the following table in the case of {0,1}:

	0	1	*	$\emptyset$
0	0	1	*	$\emptyset$
1	1	1	1	1
*	*	1	*	1
$\emptyset$	$\emptyset$	1	1	$\emptyset$

which is the *least upper bound* in the following lattice scheme:

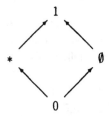

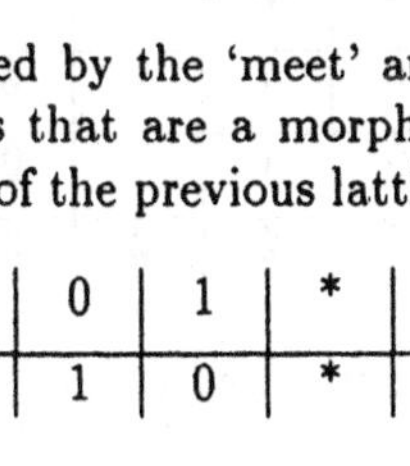

The other operations induced by the 'meet' and the 'negation' that would be usable in the case of mappings that are a morphism respect to these operations define the *greatest lower bound* of the previous lattice scheme, and for the negation:

x	0	1	*	$\emptyset$
-x	1	0	*	$\emptyset$

As a consequence of (1) we can state:

Proposition 1. *Let $F(r), F(r\prime)$ be approximations to the values $f(r), f(r\prime)$. If the approximated mapping in a morphism with respect to the join* (resp. *meet*)*, the subinterval $F(r) \vee_i F(r\prime)$* (resp. *$F(r) \wedge_i F(r\prime)$*) *is a good approximation to the value $f(r \vee r\prime)$* (resp. *$f(r \wedge r\prime)$*). *And also if $(f \neg r) = \neg f(r\prime)$, then $\neg_i F(r)$ is a good approximation to the value $f(\neg r)$.*

Corollary 2. *If f is a morphism with respect to the join and if we know approximations $F(m_j), j = 1, \dots, 2^n$ for each generator respect to the join, we can calculate an approximation $F(r)$ to the value $f(r)$ for each element r of the algebra.*

Proof. If $r = \bigvee_j \delta_j^r m_j; j = 1, \dots, 2^n$ then $\bigvee_i \delta_j^r F(m_j); j = 1, \dots, 2^n$ is a good approximation to the value of $f(r)$.

4 Accumulation

If we have several informations, i.e. several approximations by intervals of one mapping, we will need to take them all into account at the same time. Given that if we are informed that $f(r)$ belongs to two different intervals we can be sure that it belongs to the intersection, we will define:

> Given two approximations $F, G : \hat{R} \rightarrow$ {subintervals of $[0 \quad 1]$} of the same mapping $f : \hat{R} \rightarrow [0 \quad 1]$, we will call *accumulation* to the approximation that results from awarding to each element of $\hat{R}$:

$$(F \propto G)(r) = F(r) \cap G(r)$$

In this way the properties of this accumulation operation over the approximations will derive from the well known properties of the intersection of sets or, in this case, of subintervals.

Remark. In the case of a mapping $f : \hat{R} \rightarrow \{0, 1\}$ with the identification stated above of the subsets of {0,1} with the subintervals of $[0 \quad 1]$ considered as a totally ordered lattice, the operation of *accumulation* defined above is defined by the following table:

	0	1	*	∅
0	0	∅	0	∅
1	∅	1	1	∅
*	0	1	*	∅
∅	∅	∅	∅	∅

This constitutes the *greatest lower bound* operation in the following lattice

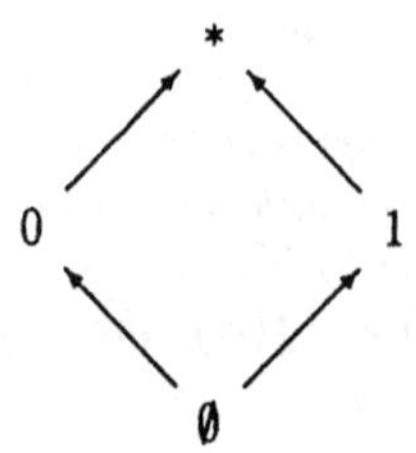

Remark. Given two approximations F and G, that assign subintervals for the generators $m_1 \ldots m_{2^n}$, we have seen that with every approximation we could compute approximate values for all the elements in the algebra $\hat{R}$. For example, let $r = m_1 \vee m_3$; we would have:

$$F(r) = F(m_1) \vee_i F(m_3)$$
$$G(r) = G(m_1) \vee_i G(m_3)$$

and therefore the total information is:

$$(F \propto G)(r) = (F(m_1) \vee_i F(m_3)) \cap (G(m_1) \vee_i G(m_3))$$

while, had we done the accumulation over the generators we would have:

$$(F \propto G)'(m_1) = F(m_1) \cap G(m_1)$$
$$(F \propto G)'(m_3) = F(m_3) \cap G(m_3)$$

and therefore

$$(F \propto G)'(r) = (F(m_1) \cap G(m_1)) \vee_i (F(m_3) \cap G(m_3))$$

and in general

$$(F \propto G)'(r) \subset (F \propto G)(r) \ .$$

The best approximation to $f(r)$ is therefore obtained by accumulating over the generators and using the induced operation afterwards.

5 Approximations Created Through Available Data Respect to the Mapping

In a general situation the available data does not refer to *the value of the mapping over the generators* but to any element, or even to relationships between several elements of $\hat{R}$. For instance

1. Case $f : \hat{R} \rightarrow \{0, 1\}$
   Data point: *If an element of the domain D satisfies the property r, then it does not satisfy the property r′*
   where r and $r\prime$ are elements of $\hat{R}$
   An example could be:

   $$r = r_1 \wedge r_3; r\prime = r_2 \vee \neg r_4$$

   where r_1, r_2, r_3, r_4 are properties that can be assigned to elements of the domain D.
   This data can be expressed as: *No element of D satisfies simultaneously both r and r′*. In terms of the mapping $f : \hat{R} \rightarrow \{0, 1\}$ this is expressed as:

   $$f(r \wedge r\prime) = f((r_1 \wedge r_3) \wedge (r_2 \vee \neg r_4)) = 0$$

So in general the data relative to the mapping $f : \hat{R} \rightarrow \{0,1\}$ will be of the form $f(p) = 1$ or $f(q) = 0$ where $p, q \in \hat{R}$, that is, in general the data are precisely the exact knowledge of the mapping over some elements of the algebra $\hat{R}$.
If we represent by $m_i \in q$ the fact that the generator can be found in the finite union of the generators in which we can express the element q, and $m_i \notin q$ as the contrary case, we have:

$$f(q) = 0, \text{ means directly that } f(m_i) = 0, \forall m_i \in q$$
$$f(p) = 1, \text{ means that the mapping } f \text{ is any of the mappings that assign a value of 1 to one or more of the generators } \{m_j\} \text{ such that } m_j \in p$$

How is the accumulation of this kind of data?

a) Some generators over which the mapping has a value of 0 inequivocally (because some of the information we have so says)

b) Some subsets of the total set of generators over each of which we can be sure that the mapping has the value 1.
It is evident that no generator of a) belongs to any subset of b) (as the final result of the accumulation).

Example 1. Let's suppose an information which allows us:
a) $f(m_1 \vee m_6 \vee m_8) = 0$
and other two informations:
b) $f(m_3 \vee m_6 \vee m_7) = 1$
c) $f(m_2 \vee m_6) = 1$.
Then, over the generators we have:

by a) $f(m_1) = 0; f(m_6) = 0; f(m_8) = 0$

by b) f can be any of the mappings $g(m_j) = 1$ where j is in any non-empty subset of {3, 6, 7}.

by c) f can be any of the mappings $h(m_k) = 1$ where k is in any non-empty subset of {2, 6}.

If we accumulate over the generators we obtain:

$$f(m_1) = 0$$
$$f(m_6) = 0$$
$$f(m_8) = 0$$
$$f(m_3 \vee m_7) = 1$$
$$f(m_2) = 1$$

2. Case $f : \hat{R} \rightarrow [0 \quad 1]$, the data point $f(p)$ determines that the mapping is any of the mappings g such that $g(m_j) \leq f(p), \forall m_j \in p$.

Example 2. Let's suppose that three informations have been taken into account:
a) $F(m_1 \vee m_6 \vee m_8) = [0 \quad 0.6]$
b) $F(m_3 \vee m_6 \vee m_7) = [0.8 \quad 1]$
c) $F(m_2 \vee m_6) = [0.7 \quad 0.9]$
Then, over the generators:

by a) $f(m_1) \leq 0.6; f(m_6) \leq 0.6$

by b) f can be any of the mappings $g(m_j) \geq 0.8$ where j is in any non-empty subset of $\{3, 6, 7\}$.

by c) f can be any of the mappings $h(m_k) \geq 0.7$ and $h(m_k) \leq 0.9$ where k is in any non-empty subset of $\{2, 6\}$.

If we accumulate over the generators:

$$\begin{array}{rl} f(m_1) \leq 0.6 & \text{i.e.: } F(m_1) = [0 \quad 0.6] \\ f(m_6) \leq 0.6 & \text{i.e.: } F(m_6) = [0 \quad 0.6] \\ f(m_8) \leq 0.6 & \text{i.e.: } F(m_8) = [0 \quad 0.6] \\ f(m_3 \vee m_7) \geq 0.8 & \text{i.e.: } F(m_3 \vee m_7) = [0.8 \quad 1] \\ 0.7 \leq f(m_2) \leq 0.9 & \text{i.e.: } F(m_2) = [0.7 \quad 0.9] \end{array}$$

6 Inference

Any approximation of the mapping that can be inferred from the data (once they have been accumulated) will be the result of applying the induced operation respect to which the approximated mapping is a morphism. This can be resumed in a simple set of rules:

Let d be an element of $\hat{R}$.

1. **a)** If any of the subsets of generators over which the mapping has a value of 1 is contained in the set of generators $\{m_i \in d\}$ then we can assure that $f(d) = 1$.

   b) if the set of generators $\{m_i \mid m_i \in d\}$is contained in the subset of generators where the mapping has a value of 0, we can assure that $f(d) = 0$.

   c) In the rest of cases we cannot assure what value does the mapping take over an element $d \in \hat{R}$.

   For instance, continuing with Example 1:

   a) If $d = m_2 \vee m_5 \vee m_7$ then we can assume $f(d) = 1$ because $f(m_2) = 1$ and the following is a good approximation:

$$\begin{aligned} F(d) &= F(m_2 \vee m_5 \vee m_7) = F(m_2) \vee_i F(m_5) \vee_i F(m_7) \\ &= [1 \quad 1] \vee_i [0 \quad 1] \vee_i [0 \quad 1] = [1 \quad 1] \end{aligned}$$

   b) If $d = m_1 \vee m_8$ then we can assure $f(d) = 0$ because $f(m_1) = f(m_8) = 0$

   c) If $d = m_3 \vee m_5$ then we cannot assure the value of $f(d)$ because over the generators we have $F(m_3) = F(m_5) = [0 \quad 1]$, and we can only build $F(m_3) \vee_i F(m_5) = [0 \quad 1] \vee_i [0 \quad 1] = [0 \quad 1]$

   If $d = m_1 \vee m_7$ we would have $F(m_1) = [0 \quad 0], F(m_7) = [0 \quad 1]$ and we can only build $F(m_1) \vee_i F(m_7) = [0 \quad 1] \vee_i [0 \quad 1] = [0 \quad 1]$

2. **a)** If the subset of generators M for which

$$F(\bigvee_i m_j \mid m_j \in M) = F(M) = [s \quad t]$$

   is contained in $\{m_i \mid m_i \in d\}$ then $F(d) = [s \quad 1]$, that is $f(d) \geq s$.

   b) If $\{m_i \mid m_i \in d\}$ is contained in the subset M then we can assure that $F(d) = [0 \quad t]$, that is, $f(d) \leq t$.

c) In any other case we cannot state an approximation to the value $f(d)$ better than $F(d) = [0 \quad 1]$.

For instance, and continuing with Example 2:

a) If $d = m_2 \vee m_5 \vee m_7$, then we can assure that $f(d) \geq 0.7$ because we can approximate:

$$F(d) = F(m_2) \vee_i F(m_5) \vee_i F(m_7)$$
$$= [0.7 \quad 0.9] \vee_i [0 \quad 1] \vee_i [0 \quad 1] = [0.7 \quad 1]$$

b) If $d = m_1 \vee m_8$, then we can assume $f(d) \leq 0.6$ because the following is a good approximation:

$$F(d) = F(m_1) \vee_i F(m_8) = [0 \quad 0.6] \vee_i [0 \quad 0.6] = [0 \quad 0.6]$$

c) If $d = m_3 \vee m_5$ we would have

$$F(m_3) \vee_i F(m_5) = [0 \quad 1] \vee_i [0 \quad 1] = [0 \quad 1]$$

If $d = m_1 \vee m_7$ we would have:

$$F(m_1) \vee_i F(m_7) = [0 \quad 0.6] \vee_i [0 \quad 1] = [0 \quad 1]$$

7 Conclusion

The generalization of Belnap's method allows a unitary treatment for partial or approximate knowledge of diverse kind of mappings, from binary valuations over a boolean algebra to measures of necessity or possibility over Boolean, or even multivalued, algebras. In the case of a Boolean subalgebra of which a set of generators is known, it is possible to refer *all* the information to the approximation over these generators and, from here, infer valid conclusions without having to go through a formal deduction process. This inference lets us *decide* which approximations *are deductible* (whether true or false) and which *are not*.

References

1. N.D. Belnap, Jr. ' A useful four-valued logic. In G. Epstein, editor, *Modern Uses of Multiple Valued Logic*, pages 8 – 40. Boston, MA, 1977.
2. Jaume Casasnovas. *Contribución a una Formalización de la Inferencia Directa.* PhD thesis, Universitat de les Illes Balears, Palma de Mallorca, Spain, 1989.
3. D. Driankov. Towards a many-valued logic of quantified belief: The information lattice. *International Journal of Intelligent Systems*, 6:135 – 166, 1991.
4. D. Dubois and H. Prade. Properties of measures of information in evidence and possibility theories. *Fuzzy Sets and Systems*, 24:161 – 182, 1987.
5. D. Dubois and H. Prade. The treatment of uncertainty in the knowledge-based systems using fuzzy sets and possibility theory. *International Journal of Intelligent Systems*, 3:141 – 165, 1988.
6. José Miró-Juliá. *Contribución al Estudio de la Demostración Automática.* PhD thesis, Universitat de les Illes Balears, Palma de Mallorca, Spain, July 1988.
7. Helena Rasiowa. *An Algebraic Approach to Non-Classical Logics.* North Holland, Amsterdam, 1974.

3. Acquiring Knowledge

Similarity Measures for Case-Based Reasoning Systems

Piero P. Bonissone, Saad Ayub
Artificial Intelligence Laboratory
GE Research and Development Center
Schenectady, NY 12301
e-mail: bonissone@crd.ge.com ayub@crd.ge.com

Abstract

A case-based reasoning (CBR) system is only as good as the cases within its Case Base and its ability to retrieve those cases in response to a new situation. In this paper we focus on the case retrieval problem and on the computation of similarity measures between cases. We illustrate this problem by showing an application of our CBR system, named CARS, Combining Approximate Reasoning Systems, in the domain of Mergers and Acquisitions.

We define a case as a situation/solution pair, indexed by surface (observed) and abstract (derived) features. The mapping from surface to abstract features, based on fuzzy predicates and plausible rules implemented in Plausible ReasonIng MOdule (PRIMO), allows us to represent the situation descriptor of the case in a more robust feature space.

The similarity of each abstract feature is computed as the complement of the distance between the fuzzy numbers representing the feature values. The abstract features similarities are aggregated hierarchically, according to a semantic taxonomy. The aggregation is based on T-norms, averaging operators, and T-conorms.

1 Introduction

Case-based reasoning (CBR) is the process of using previously acquired solutions to problems as the basis for computing new solutions to new problems. The stored problem descriptions and solutions are *cases*. CBR has been applied to problem solving in many different application areas, for example legal [Ash88, OWSB89, RS89], medical [Kot88], financial [BD90] and engineering [HH91, Gte89].

Case-based reasoning can provide an alternative to rule-based expert systems, and is especially appropriate when the number of rules needed to capture an expert's knowledge is unmanageable or when the domain theory is too weak or incomplete. Historically, CBR has shown its greatest success in areas where individual cases or precedents govern the decision-making processes, as in case law.

CBR Reasoning Process: In general, CBR systems comprise a case-memory, indexing, matching and retrieval mechanisms, and a reasoning component. The matching and retrieval mechanisms, driven by the current context (reasoner's goal and probe), return the most similar cases from the case memory. Similarity among cases is based on an evaluation of salient and relevant features. In some CBR systems the output of the matching process provides a complete solution to the input problem without requiring additional reasoning. In others, the reasoning component will process the retrieved cases, adapting their solutions (plans, explanations, interpretations) to apply in the current situation.

Uncertainty in CBR: Uncertainty and incompleteness pervade the CBR reasoning process. Uncertainty is present in the semantics of *abstract features* used to index the cases, in the evaluation of the *similarity measures* computed across these features, in the determination of *relevancy and saliency* of the similar cases, and in the solution adaptation phase.

Incompleteness is present in the partial domain theory used in the indexing and retrieval, in the (usually) sparse coverage of the problem space by the existing cases, and in the description of the probe.

Focusing on Retrieval: We believe that case retrieval is of primary importance to the overall effectiveness of any CBR system, for the following reasons:

1. Retrieving the case that will yield the best solution to a new problem ensures the best solution within the system's capability. This may or may not be the case that matches the new problem the most with respect to superficial (i.e., surface or "raw") features.

2. Retrieving the case or cases that yield the best solution to a new problem must include some computation of the similarities and differences between the input problem and the retrieved cases. All subsequent case modification uses this computation as a basis.

For this reason we focus our presentation on the retrieval problem and on its underlying similarity measure computation. We illustrate this problem within the context of our CBR system named **CARS**, Combining Approximate Reasoning Systems.

Paper Structure: In the next section we define the structure of a case as the pair situation/solution, introduce the case representation language used in our CBR, and emphasize the mapping from surface to abstract features. This mapping, based on fuzzy predicates and plausible rules implemented in Plausible ReasonIng Module (PRIMO) [Bon89, ABS90], allows us to represent the situation descriptor of the case in a more robust feature space.

In Section 3 we define the similarity measure between two cases. First, we compare the linguistic values assigned to each abstract feature and we compute the distance between their corresponding fuzzy sets. The similarity measure, obtained as the complement of this distance [Zad71, Rus91], is translated into a label taken from a termset defining different degrees of matching. The similarity measures of the abstract features are aggregated hierarchically, according to a semantic taxonomy. The aggregation is based on T-norms, Averaging Operators, and T-conorms [DP84].

Throughout Section 3 we provide examples from the domain of Mergers and Acquisitions to illustrate the indexing, matching, similarity evaluation, and retrieval process.

2 Organization of Case Memory

The case memory has been designed to represent cases consisting of the top-level goal(s) and information about the states and events. This information can be obtained from two basic sources: world observers and domain experts. *World observers* are capable of recording the *state* at any time, and of recognizing the execution of state changing *actions* in the world. Domain experts are capable of *interpreting/relating* these states and actions to the behaviors of an agent(s) attempting to achieve the top level goal(s) of the case.

The case memory is organized around two types of knowledge: conceptual knowledge and case representation. **Conceptual Knowledge** is the information about the objects, actions, goals. **Case Representation** follows the notion that a case can be represented as situation/solution pair. The situation consists of the top-level goals and starting states of the agents. The solution consists of the representation of the observable portions of the executions of actions by the agents and their effects on the states of world.

2.1 Conceptual Knowledge

The domain knowledge available to CARS is organized into three hierarchies: **Object hierarchy, Action hierarchy**, and **Goal hierarchy**.

All objects used in representing the cases are part of the IS-A **Object hierarchy**, which describes the objects of the domain and their relationships.

The actions represent the state changing operations on the objects in the domain. The IS-A **Action hierarchy** abstracts from special actions (with more restricted preconditions and effects) to more general actions. The instances of a particular action class are parts of executed plan actions in the stored cases.

The **Goal hierarchy** represents the partial knowledge of the domain theory and provides an initial, albeit incomplete goal decomposition. Its incompleteness is the reason for resorting to case-based reasoning and mixed reasoning paradigms. It provides a mechanism for expansion of knowledge by indexing into each new case at various suitable levels.

2.2 Case Representation

The cases in our Case Base are viewed as situation/solution pairs. Given the dynamic nature of M&A cases, we have chosen to divide each case into five phases: Initial Condition, Pretender, Tender-negotiation, Outcome and Long-term results. Within each phase, the case is represented by state-changes, goals, events, and interpretations. Each of the above five phases correspond to a top-level interpretation.

The object descriptions at various stages of the cases are stored as **States**. The initial state of each object is represented by a set of state variables (surface and abstract features) with their associated values. Each state change contains only the slots whose values have changed.

Events are objects that associate action, goal, and state information. Each event has at least two slots: the (instantiated) *action* used to achieve the goal and the *context*, i.e., the state at the time this event occurred. Additional optional slots can be used to describe goal, cost, and time duration of the event. The event's contextual understanding is provided by various links like temporal links, causal links, and enable links.

Explanations for the occurrence of sets of events can be given using **Interpretations**. The interpretations are currently used to represent the case analysis of domain experts.

The cases, interpretation and events are linked to the **goals** in the goal hierarchy. The uncertainty in links represent the belief that the cases, interpretations and events are the executed plans/strategies/plan steps for achieving the goals/subgoals.

2.2.1 Surface and Abstract Features

The representation of cases is augmented by a mapping from surface to abstract features. The mapping is based on approximate deduction from the surface features using plausible rules of inference. The surface features, typically obtained from textual description of the case, provide factual information at a very low level of granularity. Figure 1 (right window) shows an example of surface and abstract features for the Probe Target company.

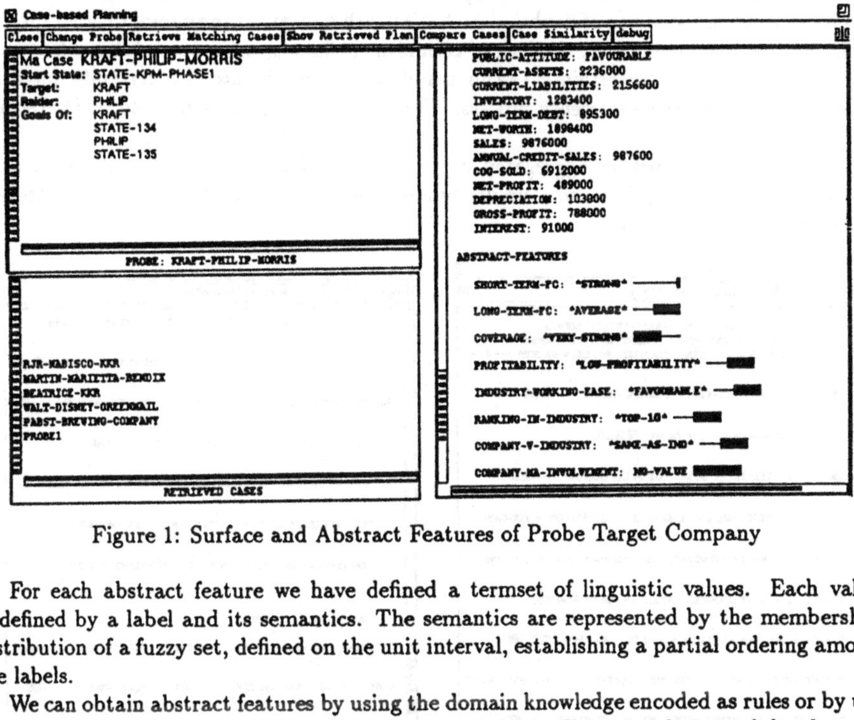

Figure 1: Surface and Abstract Features of Probe Target Company

For each abstract feature we have defined a termset of linguistic values. Each value is defined by a label and its semantics. The semantics are represented by the membership distribution of a fuzzy set, defined on the unit interval, establishing a partial ordering among the labels.

We can obtain abstract features by using the domain knowledge encoded as rules or by using the conceptual knowledge about the objects in the case. For example, one of the abstract features in our domain is `Short Term Financial Condition`, which is obtained from surface features such as `Receivable-Turnover`, `Cost of Goods Sold`, `Inventory Turnover`, `Current Assets`, `Current Liabilities`. This abstract feature is based on the outcome of various financial ratios which are calculated using the surface features (see section 3.1.1). This is a typical example of integration between CBR and RBR. In this case the Case-Based Reasoner activates the Rule-Based Reasoner to augment the case indexing information.

3 Similarity Measures

Similarities are defined at many levels: between individual abstract features, e.g. Target-Short-Term FC-SIM (which is the similarity between the target financial conditions in the probe and the retrieved case); and between groups of abstract features, e.g. Target-Target Similarity (which is the overall similarity between the target company in the probe and in the case).

For example, Figure 2 (A) illustrates a subset of the target abstract feature similarities (from Target-Short Term FC-SIM to Target-Company-Mgmt-Involvement-Sim) and their corresponding linguistic values. The bar following the linguistic value represents the degree of certainty for the value assignment. Certainty is defined on the [0,1] interval. The bar's lower bound is a measure of positive evidence supporting the assignment (i.e. a degree of belief). The distance between the bar's upper bound and 1 is a measure of evidence refuting the assignment (i.e., a degree of doubt). The bar's width indicates the amount of ignorance in qualifying the assignment (i.e., the lack of commitment in supporting or refuting the value assignment). PRIMO uncertainty calculi maintain and propagate the certainty interval throughout the deductive inference process. The interested reader is referred to references [Bon89, ABS90].

Similarity can be further aggregated by combining Target-Target-Similarity, and Raider-Raider-Similarity into a similarity measure for each phase. This is illustrated at the bottom of Figure 2 (B).

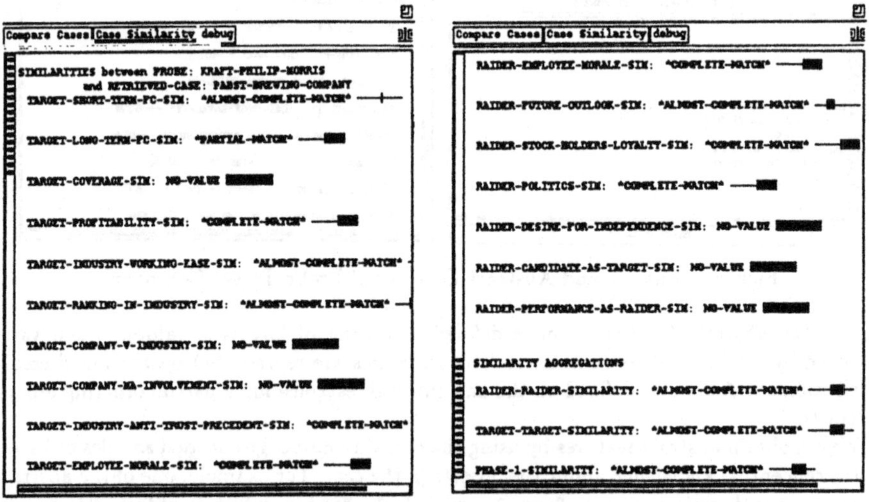

Figure 2: Abstract Features Similarity Measures: Computation (A) and Aggregation (B)

We briefly describe each of these processes next; more details on the technology can be found in [BBA90].

3.1 Similarity Module

The similarity module takes as input the cases returned by the retrieval system, the probe, and information relating to the needs of the reasoner. The retrieved cases and probe are augmented with a set of abstract features. Appropriate similarity measures are chosen and applied based on the needs of the reasoner (e.g., goal satisfaction or establishment of precedent). The most similar cases are returned.

3.1.1 Analysis of Cases

The similarity component uses domain-specific rules. These rules are specified for analyzing cases to derive abstract features. These features are assigned a value and a degree of certainty. Values for features (abstract or surface), can be raw data or lexical terms (linguistic values representing fuzzy intervals [Zad84]) chosen from feature value term-sets provided in CARS. The degree of certainty represents the extent to which the abstract features can be inferred from the surface features.

For example, let us consider `Target-Short-Term-Fc-Sim` abstract feature. Various PRIMO plausible rules are used for determining the value of this abstract feature. One such rule is `Acid-Ratio-St-Fc` which is given in Figure 3. We will now consider how the PRIMO plausible rules work and how the `Target-Short-Term-Fc-Sim` abstract feature is determined by using `Acid-Ratio-St-Fc`.

Rule Evaluation: In PRIMO, the rule *Antecedent* is a conjunction of (possibly) fuzzy predicates on object-level variables. The conjunction is implemented using T-norms [Bon87]. The result of the antecedent is the degree of applicability of the rule. The output of the antecedent and the *Rule Strength* determine the truth value of the *Rule Conclusion.* In our example we have one predicate `acid-ratio-pred`, which computes the acid ratio of the company as: $AcidRatio = \frac{CurrentAssets - Inventory}{CurrentLiabilities}$ and normalizes it with respect to the industry average acid ratio. The mapping, illustrated in Figure 4, is then used to select the term that best describes the short term financial condition of the company, given the acid ratio average of its industry sector.

In our implementation the intervals used in the mapping are actually fuzzy intervals. Therefore, the membership value of the acid ratio percentage is computed for each term in the termset. The term with the highest membership value is selected. The corresponding membership value describes the degree of confidence of this linguistic value assignment.

3.1.2 Feature Value Comparisons

By applying this process to the probe and the retrieved case, we obtain a linguistic value for each of their abstract features. It should be noted that each linguistic term has a label and a meaning. This is illustrated in the third column of Figure 4.

In the third column of Figure 4, a parametric representation is used to describe the membership distribution of each term, N_i. Using this representation we can describe a fuzzy set of a universe of discourse U as the four-tuple: (a, b, α, β). The universe U is unit interval (represented by an integer representation on the scale from 0 to 1000).

The first two parameters (a, b) indicate the interval of the universe of discourse in which the membership value is 1.0; the third and fourth parameters (α, β) indicate the left and

```
(def-rule (acid-ratio-st-fc case-based                       ; RULE NAME
                            (resources)                      ; RULE CLASS
                            (company*industry-ratios))       ; INSTANTIATION CLASS
  (?company ?industry-ratios)                                ; OBJECT-VARIABLES
  "short term financial condition using acid ratio"          ; DOCUMENTATION
  (lb-pass-threshold                                         ; CONTEXT
    (t3 (number-predicate (current-assets ?company))
        (number-predicate (current-liabilities ?company))
        (number-predicate (inventory ?company))
        (number-predicate (acid-ratio ?industry-ratios)))
    250)
  (acid-ratio-pred   (current-assets ?company)               ; ANTECEDENT
                     (current-liabilities ?company)
                     (inventory ?company)
                     (acid-ratio ?industry-ratios))
  (((short-term-fc ?company)                                 ; CONCLUSION
    ((acid-ratio-cons   (current-assets ?company)
                        (current-liabilities ?company)
                        (inventory ?company)
                        (acid-ratio ?industry-ratios))
     (i::d3 *certain* *likely* :premise) :INTERSECT))))      ; RULE STRENGTH
```

Figure 3: Rule to determine the short term financial condition of a company

right *width* of the distribution. Linear functions are used to define the slopes. Let $\mu_{N_i}(x) : X \rightarrow [0,1]$ be the membership function of the fuzzy set N_i. We can represent N_i, as the four-tuple $(a_i, b_i, \alpha_i, \beta_i)$ where:

$$\mu_{N_i}(x) = \begin{cases} 0 & \text{if } x < (a_i - \alpha_i) \\ \frac{1}{\alpha_i}(x - a_i + \alpha_i) & \text{if } x \in [(a_i - \alpha_i), a_i] \\ 1 & \text{if } x \in [a_i, b_i] \\ \frac{1}{\beta_i}(b_i + \beta_i - x) & \text{if } x \in [b_i, (b_i + \beta_i)] \\ 0 & \text{if } x > (b_i + \beta_i) \end{cases}$$

Having established the meaning of the labels used to define each abstract feature value, we now need to compute the similarity measure for each feature. This is done by executing a two-step procedure.

First we compute the distance between the fuzzy set representations of the corresponding values. For example, let us assume that the abstract feature `Target-Short-Term-Fc-Sim` has value *STRONG* in the probe and *VERY STRONG* in the retrieved case. The distance between the two corresponding fuzzy sets is computed as the absolute value of their difference. This is done using fuzzy arithmetic operations that are closed under the four-tuple parametric

Acid Ratio Percentage Interval	*Term Label*	*Term Semantics*
[0,60]	*VERY-WEAK*	(0 130 0 20)
[60,80]	*WEAK*	(170 270 20 30)
[80,90]	*BELOW-AVERAGE*	(310 410 30 30)
[90,115]	*AVERAGE*	(450 550 30 30)
[115,140]	*ABOVE-AVERAGE*	(590 690 30 30)
[140,170]	*STRONG*	(730 830 30 20)
[170, ∞]	*VERY-STRONG*	(870 1000 20 0)

Figure 4: Mapping of Percentage Acid Ratio to Terms Labels and Semantics

representation [DP79, Bon82, BD86]. Specifically, given two fuzzy numbers $X = (a, b, \alpha, \beta)$ and $Y = (c, d, \gamma, \delta)$, their difference is defined as: $X - Y = (a - d, b - c, \alpha + \delta, \beta + \gamma)$. This distance is then transformed into a degree of matching by taking the complement with respect to the unit interval. Using the same formula for the difference, by representing the unit as (1000, 1000, 0 , 0) we have the degree of matching $1 - |X - Y| = (730, 960, 30, 40)$.

The second step, referred to as linguistic approximation, consists of selecting a label (chosen from one of the similarity term-sets provided) whose meaning is the closest to that of the computed degree of matching. This semantic closeness is evaluated by a measure of set inclusion [San79]: $\frac{|P \cap D|}{|D|}$ where P is the similarity term and D is the result of complementing the set-distance. This measure, representing the degree of matching between the reference (P) and the data (D), is used as an associated certainty value for the label. The interested reader is referred to reference [DP80] (page 23-24) for a detailed study of measures of inclusions. A simple example of a seven term similarity termset is given by Figure 5.

Term Label	*Term Meaning*
NO-MATCH	(0 130 0 20)
ALMOST-NO-MATCH	(170 270 20 30)
LESS-THAN-PARTIAL-MATCH	(310 410 30 30)
PARTIAL-MATCH	(450 550 30 30)
MORE-THAN-PARTIAL-MATCH	(590 690 30 30)
ALMOST-COMPLETE-MATCH	(730 830 30 20)
COMPLETE-MATCH	(870 1000 20 0)

Figure 5: Termset For Partial Matching of Abstract Features

In the case of our example, the degree of matching was the fuzzy number $(730, 960, 30, 40)$. By using the termset described in Figure 5, we can see that the term with the closest meaning $(730, 830, 30, 20)$ is *ALMOST-COMPLETE-MATCH*. The degree of confidence in this label selection is $\frac{|(730,830,30,20) \cap (730,960,30,40)|}{|(730,960,30,40)|} = \frac{125}{265} = 0.47$. Similarly, the degree of confidence in the term *COMPLETE-MATCH* would be 0.45.

Therefore, the term *ALMOST-COMPLETE-MATCH* was used as the value for the similarity measure for the feature `Target-Short Term FC-SIM`, as shown in Figure 2 (A).

Multiple similarity term sets are provided to allow for different "views" of similarity (e.g., the lenient similarity term set has wide fuzzy intervals for the labels representing high similarity and narrower intervals for those representing low similarity. The opposite is true for the strict term set.)

3.1.3 Combinations of Similarities

The similarity measure can be aggregated or chained (using the transitivity of similarity) according to well-defined operators called triangular norms [SS63], [SS83], [Bon87]. Five uncertainty calculi based on the following five T- norms are used in PRIMO:

$$
\begin{aligned}
T_1(a,b) &= max(0, a+b-1) \\
T_{1.5}(a,b) &= (a^{0.5}+b^{0.5}-1)^2 \quad \text{if } (a^{0.5}+b^{0.5}) \geq 1 \\
&= 0 \quad \text{otherwise} \\
T_2(a,b) &= ab \\
T_{2.5}(a,b) &= (a^{-1}+b^{-1}-1)^{-1} \\
T_3(a,b) &= min(a,b)
\end{aligned}
$$

Their corresponding DeMorgan dual T-conorms, denoted by $S_i(a,b)$, are defined as: $S_i(a,b) = 1 - T_i(1-a, 1-b)$.

These five calculi provide the user with the ability to choose the desired uncertainty calculus starting from the most conservative (T_1) to the most liberal (T_3).

The use of T-norms in aggregating and chaining certainty intervals during the extraction of abstract features is extended in CARS to the aggregation of similarity measures.

This mechanism aggregates similarities by taking as input a list of similarities to be combined, their associated uncertainties, and optional weights indicating the importance of the feature in the aggregation. This mechanism is based on three aggregation operators: *T-norms*, *T-conorms*, and *Linear combinations*.

First we aggregate the low and high values of similarity: (weighted) low values are aggregated using the minimum operator (with the option of using other T-norms), while (weighted) high values are aggregated using the maximum operator (with the option of using other T-conorms). The result of these partial aggregations (multiplied by the cardinality of the aggregated values) is averaged with the intermediate values of similarity. [1]

[1]Let $\vec{X}$ and $\vec{W}$ be two nth dimensional vectors with elements in [0,1]. $x_i \in \vec{X}$ represents the similarity value of the ith abstract feature, while $w_I \in \vec{W}$ is its corresponding relevance weight. The weighted minimum WMIN($\vec{W}, \vec{X}$) is defined as

$$WMIN(\vec{W},\vec{X}) = \bigwedge_{i=1}^{n}(w_i \rightarrow x_i) = \bigwedge_{i=1}^{n} max(1-w_i, x_i)$$

Similarly, the weighted maximum WMAX($\vec{W}, \vec{X}$) is defined as

$$WMAX(\vec{W},\vec{X}) = \bigvee_{i=1}^{n} min(w_i, x_i)$$

The process normalizes the similarity values of various abstract features according to their relevance weights. Then the process penalizes bad matches and rewards good ones. Finally, the process considers tradeoffs by averaging the remaining intermediate values with the previous results. The reader is referred to reference [DP84] for a detailed study of aggregating operators.

In Figure 2 (B) we can observe two levels of aggregation of similarity measures: All the raiders abstract feature similarities (from `Raider-Industry-Anti-Trust-Precedent-Sim` to `Raider-Performance-As-Raider-Sim`) are aggregated to determine the `Raider-Raider Similarity` between probe and case. Similarly, the target abstract feature similarities are aggregated to derive the `Target-Target Similarity`. Finally, `Target-Target Similarity` and `Raider-Raider Similarity` are combined to derive the case `Phase-1-Similarity`. It should be noted that during the aggregation process of similarity, we do not account for slots with no values (denoted by the extended certainty bar).

The similarity between two cases can be computed by aggregating the *five phase similarities* in an analogous fashion. This final aggregation can be customized to reflect different goals of the retriever, as we will show in the sequel. Let us recall the definition of the five phases: (1) Initial Condition, (2) Pre-tender, (3) Tender-negotiation, (4) Outcome and (5) Long-term results.

For instance, by only aggregating phases 1, 2, and 4 we can stress the need to find successful cases with similar initial and pre-tender conditions. The result can give us the range of tender-negotiations (plans/counter-plans) which are applicable to the current situation.

Alternatively, by only aggregating phases 2, 3 and 4 we can observe the range of macroeconomic conditions to ascertain raider/target financial assessments, for which a particular (pre-tender and post-tender) plan was successful.

4 Conclusions

We have described a method for using linguistic values with fuzzy semantics to index, match and retrieve cases from a Case Base. We have built a CBR system, called CARS, that incorporates this method.

The description of cases in the Case Base is augmented by abstract features derived from the cases' observed (surface) features. Probe and cases are first compared along their abstract features, generating a linguistic value representing their corresponding similarity measure. By expressing the relevance of the various abstract features with linguistic weights, we can emphasize or de-emphasize their roles in the retrieval process.

These similarity measures are aggregated hierarchically, according to a semantic taxonomy, deriving *Target-Target, Raider-Raider* similarities, etc. The aggregation, based on T-norms, Averaging Operators, and T-conorms, generates a partial ordering on the retrieved cases.

We have tested this method by developing a M&A application that contains 90 PRIMO rules to extract 19 abstract features from 61 surface features and evaluate similarities for about 40 M&A cases.

In our system we use linguistic values (with fuzzy numbers semantics) to represent similarity and weights. Therefore, we have extended the above operations to fuzzy numbers in [0,1] using the four parameter representations and the formulae in reference [BD86].

References

[ABS90] J. K. Aragones, P. P. Bonissone, and J. Stillman. Primo: A Tool for Reasoning With Incomplete and Uncertain Information. In *Proceedings of the International Conference on Information Processing and Management of Uncertainty In Knowledge-Based Systems (Ipmu-90)*, July 1990.

[Ash88] Kevin Ashley. *Modelling Legal Argument: Reasoning with Cases and Hypotheticals.* PhD thesis, University of Massachusetts at Amherst, 1988. Computer and Information Science.

[BBA90] Piero Bonissone, Lauren Blau, and Saad Ayub. Leveraging the integration of approximate reasoning systems. In *Proceedings of the 1990 Aaai Spring Symposium In Case-Based Reasoning*, pages 1–6. Aaai, 1990.

[BD86] Piero P. Bonissone and Keith S. Decker. Selecting Uncertainty Calculi and Granularity: An Experiment in Trading-off Precision and Complexity. In L. Kanal and J. Lemmer, editors, *Uncertainty in Artificial Intelligence*, pages 217–247. North-Holland, Amsterdam, 1986.

[BD90] Piero P. Bonissone and Soumitra Dutta. Mars: A Mergers and Acquisitions Reasoning System. *Journal of Computer Science In Economics and Management*, 3:239–268, 1990.

[Bon82] Piero P. Bonissone. A Fuzzy Sets Based Linguistic Approach: Theory and Applications. In M.M. Gupta and E. Sanchez, editors, *Approximate Reasoning in Decision Analysis*, pages 329–339. North Holland Publishing Co., New York, 1982.

[Bon87] Piero P. Bonissone. Summarizing and Propagating Uncertain Information With Triangular Norms. *International Journal of Approximate Reasoning*, 1(1):71–101, January 1987.

[Bon89] Piero P. Bonissone. Now That I Have A Good Theory of Uncertainty, What Else Do I Need? In *Proceeding Fifth Aaai Workshop on Uncertainty In Artificial Intelligence*, pages 22–33. Aaai, August 1989.

[DP79] D. Dubois and H. Prade. Fuzzy real algebra. *Fuzzy Sets and Systems*, 2(4):327–348, 1979.

[DP80] D. Dubois and H. Prade. *Fuzzy Sets and Systems: Theory and Applications.* Academic Press, New York, 1980.

[DP84] D. Dubois and H. Prade. Criteria aggregation and ranking of alternatives in the framework of fuzzy set theory. In H. Zimmermann, L. Zadeh, and B. Gaines, editors, *Fuzzy Sets and Decision Analysis*, pages 209–240. North-Holland, Amsterdam, 1984.

[Gte89] Gte. Gte traffic controller. In *Proceedings of the Darpa Case-Based Reasoning Workshop*, San Mateo, May 1989. Darpa, Morgan Kaufmann Publishers.

[HH91] Daniel Hennessy and David Hinkle. Initial results form clavier: A case-based autoclave loading assistant. In *Proceedings of Case-Based Reasoning Workshop*, pages 225–232, San Mateo, Ca, May 1991. Morgan Kaufmann Publishers, Inc.

[Kot88] Phyllis Koton. Reasoning about evidence in causal explanations. In *Proceedings of the Case-Based Reasoning Workshop*, pages 260–270, San Mateo, Ca, May 1988. Morgan Kaufmann Publishers, Inc.

[OWSB89] A. Oskamp, R.F. Walker, J.A. Schrickx, and P.H. Vanden Berg. Prolexs, divide and rule: A legal application. In *Proceedings of the Second International Conference on Artificial Intelligence and Law*, 1989.

[RS89] Edwina L. Rissland and David B. Skalak. Interpreting statuatory predicates. In *Proceedings of the Second International Conference on Artificial Intelligence and Law*, pages 46–53, 1989.

[Rus91] E.H. Ruspini. On the Semantics of Fuzzy Logic. *International Journal of Approximate Reasoning*, 5(1):45–88, January 1991.

[San79] Elie Sanchez. Inverse of a fuzzy relations. applications to possibility distributions and medical diagnosis. *Fuzzy Sets and Systems*, 2(1):75–86, 1979.

[SS63] B. Schweizer and A. Sklar. Associative Functions and Abstract Semi-Groups. *Publicationes Mathematicae Debrecen*, 10:69–81, 1963.

[SS83] B. Schweizer and A. Sklar. *Probabilistic Metric Spaces.* North Holland, New York, 1983.

[Zad71] L.A. Zadeh. Similarity relations and fuzzy orderings. *Information Science*, 3:177–200, 1971.

[Zad84] Lotfi Zadeh. A computational theory of disposition. In *Proceedings of the 1984 International Conference On Computational Linguistics*, pages 312–318, 1984.

Statistical Methods in Learning

A. Sutherland 1, R. Henery 1, R. Molina 2, C.C. Taylor 3, R. King 1

1 Department of Statistics and Modelling Science, University of Strathclyde, Glasgow, Scotland.
2 Departamento de Ciencias de la Computación e I.A., Universidad de Granada, 18071 Granada, Spain.
3 Department of Statistics, University of Leeds, Leeds, England

Abstract. In this paper we describe an ESPRIT project known as 'StatLog' whose purpose is the comparison of learning algorithms. We give a brief summary of some of the algorithms in the project: linear and quadratic discriminant analysis, k nearest neighbour, CART, backpropagation, SMART, ALLOC80 and Pearl's polytree algorithm. We discuss the results obtained for two datasets, one of handwritten digits and the other of vehicle silhouettes.

1 Introduction

StatLog, is an ESPRIT project whose purpose is to compare a wide variety of learning algorithms on a wide variety of real world datasets. A 'learning algorithm' is an algorithm which extracts rules from data. In this case the data consists of a set of objects each of which is described by a number of 'attributes'. Each object belongs to one of a finite number of disjoint classes and the purpose of the algorithm is to learn how to predict the class of an object given its attributes. This process is known, in machine learning, as 'supervised learning' or, in statistics, as 'discrimination'.

In order to compare the algorithms the datasets are split up into a learning set and a test set. Each algorithm is allowed to learn rules from the learning set. It may then apply those rules to the test set and try to predict the class of each of the objects in the test set. The predictions made by the algorithm are then compared to the actual class-values and the percentage correct is measured. It is the percentage correct which is the main criterion used in comparing the algorithms.

In StatLog the learning algorithms come from the following different fields: statistics, machine-learning, neural networks. The algorithms are described in the next section. We shall consider their results when applied to a dataset of handwritten digits and a dataset of vehicle silhouettes.

⋆ This work has been supported by the Commission of the European Communities under ESPRIT project no 5170: Comparative Testing of Statistical and Logical Learning, Statlog.

2 Algorithms Description

Linear Discriminants. This is an implementation in Splus of Fisher's linear discriminant analysis. The algorithm calculates a linear combination of the attribute values for each class and assigns a new observation to the class with the largest value. The algorithm is optimal when the data are multivariate normal with a common covariance matrix. The boundaries between classes are hyperplanes in attribute space.

Quadratic Discriminants. This a variant of the above linear algorithm for the unequal covariance case. The algorithm calculates a quadratic combination of the attribute values for each class and assigns a new observation to the class with the largest value. The boundaries between classes are conic sections in attribute space. The algorithm requires to estimate many more co-efficients than linear discriminants and so will only perform well when the training set is sufficiently large

K Nearest Neighbour. (k-NN) is probably the simplest algorithm of all; it assigns each new object to the class of the majority of its k nearest neighbours in attribute space.

Naive Bayes. This is a very simple algorithm which assumes that the attributes are conditionally independent given the class. Let $A_1, A_2, \ldots, A_n$ be the n attributes. The algorithm estimates the conditional probability $P(A_i|C_j)$ for each class C_j and each attribute A_i. By Bayes' Theorem we have

$$\begin{aligned} P(C_j|A_1, A_2, \ldots, A_n) &\propto P(A_1, A_2, \ldots, A_n|C_j)P(C_j) \\ &= P(A_1|C_j)P(A_2|C_j)\ldots P(A_n|C_j)P(C_j) \qquad (1) \end{aligned}$$

by the independence of the attributes. A new observation is then assigned to the class C_j with the largest value of $P(C_j|A_1, A_2, \ldots, A_n)$.

CART. (Classification and Regression Trees) is a decision tree algorithm, which was devised by Breiman et al.[3]. The branching is determined by Gini's diversity index.

Naive Bayes and CART are part of the IND package written by various authors at Sydney University, Australia, and NASA Ames Research Centre.

Back-propagation Multi-Layer Perceptron. This is a neural network algorithm devised by Rumelhart et al.[7] which consists of a network of 'neurons' arranged in a number of layers, where each neuron is connected to every neuron in the adjacent layers. Each neuron sends a signal along the connections to the neurons in the layer above. The signals are multiplied by weights corresponding to each connection.

We used a version with three layers: an input layer, a hidden layer and an output layer. The input layer has one neuron per attribute and the output layer has one neuron per decision class. The user can decide how many neurons are in the hidden layer. The network is trained by iteratively altering the weights so that the number of mis-classifications in the training set is reduced. The weights are optimised by a gradient descent algorithm. The code was written by R.Rohwer whilst at the Centre for Speech Technology Research, Edinburgh, Scotland.

ALLOC80 - Kernel Density Estimation. ALLOC80 has been developed over a number of years, with a number of later extensions to cater for all types of (continuous and discrete) data. The program performs multigroup discriminant analysis; within each group the variability is modelled using a non-parametric density estimator, based on kernel functions. Suppose that we have to estimate the p−dimensional density function $f(x)$ of an unknown distribution. Information about f is given by n independent observations from this distribution, i.e. $Y_i = (Y_{i1}, \ldots, Y_{im}, \ldots, Y_{ip})$ with $i = 1, 2, \ldots, n$. Let $K^{(p)}(X; Y_i, \lambda)$ be a kernel function centred at Y_i and let λ denote the window width of the kernel. The estimate of $f(x)$ is given by

$$\hat{f}(x) = \frac{1}{n} \sum_{i=1}^{n} K^{(p)}(X; Y_i, \lambda)$$

Observations in the test data are then allocated to classes based on a calculation of the posterior odds by a standard Bayesian calculation. The smoothness of the kernel density estimates, as governed by the window width, is determined in a data-based manner by a pseudo maximum likelihood method. The program can handle continuous as well as mixed (discrete) data. For continuous data two models are available - one with a fixed and one with a variable smoothing parameter. In this implementation the smoothing parameter λ_i can be chosen proportional to the kth nearest neighbour distance in Y_i. It is suggested to try both, and stick to the one with better results.

Selection of variables is possible in a forward stepwise way. This is often useful in high-dimensional data and can give further insight into which variables are the most useful discriminators. However, this option is only available for continuous data and using a fixed smoothness parameter. The criterion for the selection of variables is minimisation of the error rate, or more generally, the minimisation of the estimated expected loss.

This program is computationally expensive, both in storage and CPU terms. The methods to choose the smoothing parameter automatically are not always successful, and the version in StatLog used is rather unwieldy . However, it has performed consistently well in the trials. It is expected to do better than standard methods where the data are highly non-Normal. For more bizarre datasets, such as two interlocking spirals, this method performs very well. In general, any situation where the boundaries between classes is not easily modelled by a straight line or quadratic will lend themselves well to this approach. In other trials [6]

ALLOC80 has also done well. The main difficulty, as with most nonparametric density estimators is to ensure a good choice of smoothing parameter.

SMART. SMART (Smooth Multiple Additive Regression Technique) is a collection of FORTRAN subroutines written by Friedman. It is a generalisation of projection pursuit regression PPR [4]. The regression models take the form

$$E[Y_i|x_1, x_2, \ldots, x_p] = \overline{Y}_i + \sum_{m=1}^{M} \beta_{im} f_m\left(\sum_{j=1}^{p} \alpha_{jm} x_j\right) \tag{2}$$

with $\overline{Y}_i = EY_i$, $Ef_m = 0$, $Ef_m^2 = 1$ and $\sum_{j=1}^{p} \alpha_{jm}^2 = 1$. The coefficients β_{im}, α_{jm} and the functions f_m are parameters of the model and are estimated by least squares. The criterion

$$L_2 = \sum_{i=1}^{q} E[Y_i - \overline{Y}_i - \sum_{m=1}^{M} \beta_{im} f_m(\alpha_m^T x)]^2$$

is minimised with respect to the parameters β_{im}, $\alpha_m^T = (\alpha_{1m}, \ldots, \alpha_{pm})$ and the functions f_m.

Classification is closely related. The objective here is to minimise the misclassification risk

$$R = E[\min_{1 \le j \le q} \sum_{i=1}^{q} l_{ij} p(i|x_1, x_2, \ldots, x_p)]$$

where l_{ij} is the user specified loss for predicting $Y = c_j$ when its true value is c_i ($l_{ii} = 0$). The conditional probability is reformulated using a conditional expectation which is then modelled by (2).

This algorithm performs very well whenever a cost matrix is applicable, because it (unusually) uses the cost matrix in the **training** phase as well as in the classification stage.

A problem which most inexperienced users will encounter is the appropriate choice of the dimension space (M) in which the classification will take place.

Although the training time is not competitive, the algorithm does generally produce good misclassification rates.

3 CASTLE - Conditional Probability Networks

CASTLE (Causal Structures From Inductive Learning, [1],[2]) is an implementation of the polytree algorithm defined by Pearl ([5]). Causal networks are directed acyclic graphs (DAGs) in which the nodes represent propositions (or variables), the arcs signify the existence of direct causal dependencies between the linked propositions, and the strengths of these dependencies are quantified by conditional probabilities.

The structure of a causal network can be determined in the following way: each variable in the domain is identified with a node in the graph. We then draw arrows to each node X_i from a set of nodes $C(X_i)$ considered as direct causes of X_i. The strengths of these direct influences are quantified by assigning to each variable X_i a matrix $P(X_i|C(X_i))$ of conditional probabilities of the events $X_i = x_i$ given any combination of values of the parent set $C(X_i)$. The conjunction of these local probabilities defines a consistent global model, i.e., a joint probability distribution. Once the network is constructed it constitutes an efficient device to perform probabilistic inferences. The problem of building such a network remains. The structure and conditional probabilities necessary for characterising the network could be provided either externally by experts or from direct empirical observations.

Under the Bayesian approach, the learning task in causal networks separates into two highly related subtasks, *structure learning*, that is to identify the topology of the network, and *parameter learning*, the numerical parameters (conditional probabilities) for a given network topology.

CASTLE so far is focused on learning structure rather than parameters, although obviously it also needs to do some parameter estimation in order to produce a complete causal network.

Since a model with too many links is computationally useless, as it requires too much storage and lengthy procedures to produce predictions or explanations, it is essential that we give the learning process a built-in preference toward simple structures, those that have the fewest possible parameters and embody the fewest possible dependencies.

CASTLE, currently being developed by members of the Department of Computer Science and Artificial Intelligence at the University of Granada, focuses on learning a particular kind of causal structure: polytrees (singly connected networks), networks where no more than one path exists between any two nodes. As a consequence, a polytree with n nodes has no more than $n-1$ links. It is in polytrees (and specially in trees) where the ability of networks to decompose and modularise the knowledge attains its ultimate realisation. Polytrees do not contain loops, that is, undirected cycles in the underlying network (the network without the arrows or skeleton) and this fact allows a locally efficient propagation procedure (see [5]).

Let us now more formally define the concepts of a polytree–dependent distribution. A given distribution $P(x)$ of n discrete–value variables can be represented by some unknown polytree F_0 if $P(x)$ has the form

$$P(x) = \prod_{i=1}^{n} P(x_i|x_{j_1(i)}, x_{j_2(i)}, \cdots, x_{j_m(i)}) \tag{3}$$

where $\{x_{j_1(i)}, x_{j_2(i)}, \cdots, x_{j_m(i)}\}$ is the (possibly empty) set of direct parents of the variable X_i in F_0, and the parents of each variable are mutually independent, i.e.,

$$P(x_{j_1(i)}, x_{j_2(i)}, \cdots, x_{j_m(i)}) = \prod_{k=1}^{m} P(x_{j_k(i)}) \tag{4}$$

Let us describe how CASTLE can be used in a classification problem. In any classification problem, we have a set of variables $V = \{X_i, i = 1, \ldots, n\}$ that (possibly) have influence on a certain classification variable C. The problem is, given a particular instantiation of these variables, to predict the value of C, that is, to classify this particular case in one of the possible categories of C. For this task, we need a set of examples and their correct classification, acting as training sample. In this context, the use of CASTLE is clear: in learning mode CASTLE will extract from this training sample a network structure displaying the causal relationships among the variables $\{X_i, i = 1, .., n\} \cup C$; next, in propagation mode, given a new case with unknown classification, CASTLE will instantiate and propagate the available information, showing the most likely value of the classification variable C. Let us mention that the process of building the polytree does not take into account the fact that we are only interested in classification, and so the process does not specialize on the class node. Therefore we would expect a poorer performance in classification than other classification oriented methods. However, the resulting networks may be able to display insights into the classification problem that other methods cannot.

4 Handwritten Digit Dataset

The handwritten digits dataset consists of 18,000 examples of the digits 0 to 9 gathered from postcodes on letters in one European country. The handwritten examples were digitised onto images with 16×16 pixels and 256 greylevels. The dataset was divided into a training set with 900 examples per digit and a test set with 900 examples per digit. The only algorithm that could cope with the full dataset was linear discriminants. All the others had to be provided with some form of reduced dataset. Most used a version with 16 attributes prepared by averaging over 4×4 neighbourhoods in the original images. k-NN used a version with 64 attributes prepared by averaging over 2×2 neighbourhoods. Backpropagation could use all 256 attributes but when presented with all 9000 examples in the training set took an excessively long time to train (over two CPU days). Therefore backprop used only 10% of the examples in the training and test sets.

Table 1. shows the success rate obtained by each algorithm and indicates which version of the dataset was used. The use of different versions does to a certain extent invalidate any comparisons. For example, two values are listed for linear discriminants, one for the full dataset and one for the 4×4 dataset. The difference shows the improvement due to using all the information in the full dataset. Therefore it would have been desirable that all algorithms were run on the same version of the dataset.

However, we can still draw some conclusions from these results. The fact that k-NN and backprop do so well is probably explained by the fact that they make the fewest restrictive assumptions about the data. None of them makes any assumption about the underlying probability distribution or the presence or absence of interactions between the attributes and they are able to model nonlinear aspects of the data. Discriminant analysis, on the other hand, assumes that the data follows a multi-variate normal distribution with the attributes obeying a common covariance matrix and can model only linear aspects of the data. The fact that quadratic discriminants , using a reduced version of the dataset, does better than linear discriminants, using either the full version or reduced version, shows the advantage of being able to model non-linearity. CASTLE approximates the data by a polytree and this assumption is too restrictive in this case. Naive Bayes assumes the attributes are conditionally independent. That naive Bayes does so badly is explained by the fact that the attributes are clearly not independent, since neighbouring pixels are likely to have similar greylevels.

Table 1. Accuracies for the handwritten digits dataset

algorithm	percent correct
k-NN (8×8)	98%
Backprop (10%)	95%
ALLOC80 (4×4)	93%
quadratic discriminants (4×4)	93%
linear discriminants (full)	92.6%
linear discriminants (4×4)	88.6%
Smart (4×4)	88.5%
CART (4×4)	84.6%
Castle (4×4)	82%
naive Bayes (4×4)	77.7%

5 Vehicle Silhouette Dataset

The objective of the vehicle dataset is to recognise various types of vehicle from images taken from many different angles. The dataset was created by photographing model vehicles with a digitising camera. The images were then binarised (hence 'silhouette'). A commercial image processing package HIPS was used to extract certain features such as roundness and first and second moments from the images. Eighteen such features were extracted and these form the attributes of the dataset. There were four model vehicles: two cars, Saab and Opel, and a van and a bus. These form the decision classes of the dataset. There were 846 examples in this set. The accuracy was measured using 9-fold cross-validation, in which the data was divided into 9 disjoint sets with 94 examples in each. Training and testing were performed 9 times. Each set in turn was taken as the test set with the remaining 8 sets concatenated together as the training set. The final figure for the accuracy was the average of the figures for all 9 cycles.

One would expect this dataset to be non-linear since the attributes depend on the angle at which the vehicle is viewed. Therefore they are likely to have a sinusoidal dependence.

The following results were obtained.

Table 2. Accuracies for the vehicle silhouette dataset

algorithm	percent correct
quadratic discriminants	85.0%
linear discriminants	78.4%
Smart	78.3%
Backprop	72.7%
k-NN	72.5%
CART	70.2%
ALLOC80	68.3%
Castle	45.0%
naive Bayes	44.2%

Quadratic discriminants does very well, and this is due to the highly non-linear behaviour of this data. One would have expected the backpropagation algorithm to perform well on this dataset since, it is claimed, backprop can successfully model the non-linear aspects of a dataset. However, backprop is not straightforward to run. Unlike discriminant analysis, which requires no choice of free parameters, backprop requires essentially two free parameters - the number of hidden nodes and the training time. Neither of these is straightforward to decide.

There is very little guidance in the literature as to how to choose the number of hidden nodes. Weigend [8] suggests that it be chosen so that the number of weights in the net is less than one tenth of the number of examples in the training set. In this case since there are 752 examples in the training set we should set the number of hidden nodes at no more than 3 since the number of weights would then be 66 ($3 \times 18 + 3 \times 4$).

Before running cross-validation, we split the data into a training and test set. We tried out various numbers of hidden nodes and selected the smallest that performed reasonably on this test set. This number was 5. The reason we selected the smallest was that the smaller the number the greater the generalisation ability of the network.

Selecting the training time is even more difficult. One should not let the training time be too short, otherwise the network will not reach its maximum accuracy. But one should not let the training time be too long, otherwise the network will overtrain and start to fit itself too closely to the specific training set and loose generalisation ability. However, the latter should not be a problem if the number of hidden nodes is sufficiently small (as it is in this case) because the network does not have enough free parameters to adapt to the training set.

We chose a training time of four CPU hours, because after that period the accuracy on both training and test sets seemed to have leveled off.

However, all of the above is made even more difficult by the fact that the network starts its training from a random configuration of weights. The training procedure used, conjugate gradients, is highly sensitive to local minima, so that it may simply iterate into the local minimum nearest to the random starting position. So all of one's choices of training time and hidden nodes are heavily conditional on the starting position. Ideally, one should make many training runs starting from different positions before choosing the parameters.

The above figure for backprop was obtained using 5 hidden nodes and a training time of four hours for the training time in each of the nine cycles of cross-validation. The above figure should be regarded as a minimum result for back-prop, since it is quite possible that a more expert user, taking more time to choose the number of hidden nodes and the training time, would have achieved a better result.

However, one can say that the sheer effort and time taken to optimise the performance for backprop is a major disadvantage compared to quadratic discriminants which can achieve a much better result with a lot less effort.

The poor performance of CASTLE is explained by the fact that the attributes are highly correlated. In consequence the relationship between class and attributes is not built strongly into the polytree. The same explanation accounts for the poor performance of naive Bayes.

k-NN, which performed so well on the digits dataset, does not do so well here. This is probably because in the case of the digits the attributes were all commensurate and carried equal weight. In the vehicle dataset the attributes all have different meanings and it is not clear how to build an appropriate distance measure.

6 Conclusions

In this paper we have introduced the StatLog project and described some of the algorithms within it. We have presented the results on two datasets: a set of handwritten digits and a set of vehicle silhouettes.

It would be wrong to draw general conclusions from only two datasets but we can make the following points. The proponents of backpropagation claim that it has a special ability to model non-linear behaviour. Both these datasets have significant non-linearity and it is true that backpropagation does well. However, in the case of the digits it performs only marginally better than quadratic discriminants, which can also model non-linear behaviour, and in the case of the vehicles it performs significantly worse. When one considers the large amount of extra effort required to optimise and train backpropagation one must ask whether it really offers an advantage over more traditional algorithms.

CASTLE performs poorly but this is probably because it is not primarily designed for discrimination. Its main advantage is that it gives an easily comprehensible picture of the structure of the data. It indicates which variables influence one another most strongly and can identify which subset of attributes are the most strongly connected to the decision class. However, it ignores weak connections and this is the reason for its poor performance, in that weak connections may still have an influence on the final decision class.

SMART and linear discriminants perform equally well on these two datasets. Both of these work with linear combinations of the attributes, although SMART is more general in that it takes non-linear functions of these combinations. However, quadratic discriminants performs significantly better which suggests that a better way to model non-linearity would be to input selected quadratic combinations of attributes to linear discriminants.

References

1. Acid, S., de Campos, L.M., González, A., Molina, R., Pérez de la Blanca, N.: Learning with **CASTLE**. In: R. Kruse, P. Siegel (eds.): Symbolic and Quantitative Approaches to Uncertainty. Lecture Notes in Computer Science **548**. Springer Verlag, (1991) 99–106.
2. Acid, S., de Campos, L.M., González, A., Molina, R., Pérez de la Blanca, N.: **CASTLE**: A tool for Bayesian learning, Proc. of the 1991 ESPRIT Conference (1991) 363–377.
3. Breiman, L., Friedman, J.H., Olshen, R.A. and Stone, C.J.: Classification and Regression Trees. Wadsworth. (1984)
4. Friedman, J.H. & Stuetzle, W.: Projection pursuit regression. J. Amer. Statist. Assoc. **76** (1981) 817–823
5. Pearl, J.: Probabilistic Reasoning in Intelligent Systems: Networks of Plausible Inference. Morgan and Kaufmann (San Mateo, Ca.) (1988)
6. Remme, J., Habbema, J.D.F. & Hermans, J.: A simulative comparison of linear, quadratic and kernel discrimination. J. Statist. Comput. Simul. **11** (1980) 87–106.
7. Rumelhart, D.E., Hinton, G.E. and Williams, R.J.: Learning Representations by Back-propagating Errors. Nature **323** (1986) 533–536.
8. Weigend, A.S., Huberman, B.A. and Rumelhart, D.E.: Predicting the Future: a connectionist approach. International Journal of Neural Systems **1** (1990) 193–209.

Learning from erroneous examples using fuzzy logic and "textbook" knowledge

Janusz Kacprzyk and Cezary Iwański

Systems Research Institute, Polish Academy of Sciences
ul. Newelska 6, 01-447 Warsaw, Poland

Abstract. A further development of the authors' former works ([1],[2], [3], [4], [5]) on the use of fuzzy linguistic quantifiers to devise more realistic inductive learning models is presented. As previously, the existence of errors in the classification into the positive and negative examples, in the attributes' values, etc. is assumed. Their exact number and location is assumed unknown, and their correction practically impossible. However, their "amount" may be felt by the user or analyst. A new problem formulation is considered in which a concept description is sought which covers, e.g., almost all of the positive examples and almost none of the negative ones. To safeguard against errors, first, we adopt Kacprzyk and Iwański's [5] approach in which while including particular examples in the description sought, not necessarily the existing values of the attributes are taken, but these are eventually further fuzzified to the extent dependent upon the perceived "amount" of errors in data. Possible errors in the attribute values are therefore accounted for. Moreover, to avoid disregarding (in the sense of assuming a lower degree of positiveness) examples with the attribute values (in respective selectors) out of prespecified ranges, a "textbook knowledge" is used which basically consists of a knowledge base (collection of IF – THEN rules) covering those "unusual cases". An iterative algorithm is proposed.

1 Introduction

Inductive learning (from examples) is a process of inferring a *concept description* (description, classification rule, rule,...) of a class (concept) from a collection of *positive* and *negative* examples (cf. [7]). The *examples* are described by a set of "*attribute – value*" pairs and a class description.

Two basic requirements are traditionally imposed on the inductive learning process:

- *completeness*, i.e., a concept description must correctly describe *all* the positive examples,
- *consistency*, i.e., a concept description must describe *none* of the negative examples.

Due to omnipresent errors, misclassifications, etc. such idealized requirements are usually inapplicable in practice. In most cases the number of errors and their exact location are unknown, and – even worse – they cannot be corrected (e.g., for technical or economic reasons); medicine (e.g., patients' records) is here a good example.

To overcome that difficulty, in a new approach proposed by Kacprzyk and Iwański ([1], [2], [3], [4], [5]) a concept description is sought which covers, e.g., *most, almost all, ...* of the positive examples and *at most a few, almost none, ...* of the negative examples. Notice that in such a formulation some number of records (possibly with errors) is basically not accounted for in learning, hence errors, misclassification, etc. may be somehow neglected.

This paper is a continuation of the authors' previous works ([1], [2], [3], [4], [5]) on the use of fuzzy logic in inductive learning, by introducing another error safeguarding mechanism called here *textbook knowledge*. To explain the idea and view this work in a proper perspective, we should first briefly summarize our past works. First, in [1], [2] it was made possible to account for errors, misclassifications, etc. only by neglecting some examples using the fuzzy linguistic quantifiers in the problem formulation.

However, while constructing the concept description sought (i.e., following the scheme *selectors* ⟶ *complexes* ⟶ *concept description*), the real (taken from the examples) values of the attributes were used. This increased the efficiency but, unfortunately, the possibility of errors in those values of attributes was not accounted for.

An extension was proposed in [4], [5]. As before, a concept description was sought which covered, say, *almost all* of the positive examples and *almost none* of the negative one; hence, some number of records with errors might be neglected. Then, we fuzzified the selectors included in the complexes in the concept description. Thus, we somehow "enlarged" the set of possible values of the particular attributes in the selectors involved hoping that if the values in the examples were incorrect, the new fuzzified values might "encompass" them.

The determination of how to fuzzify a set of possible values is based on such a line of reasoning. Suppose we have two formulations: find a concept description which covers:

- **most** of the positive examples and **at most a few** of the negative examples, and
- **almost all** of the positive examples and **almost none** of the negative examples

We assume now that the problem formulation (i.e., which linguistic quantifiers to use) is based on a (subjective) perception of the "amount" of errors; if we suspected more, we would use "milder" quantifiers as, e.g., *most* and *at most a few*; otherwise, if we suspected less errors, we would use more "rigid" quantifiers as, e.g., *almost all* and *almost none*. A greater fuzzification would be therefore rational in the former case, and a lower one in the latter.

Here we proceed further in trying to even more efficiently account for possible errors. Our line of reasoning is now as follows. Suppose that we have for each attribute in our examples (e.g., weight, body temperature, ...) some fuzzily specified intervals of correct (possible) values as, e.g., for the body temperature a fuzzy interval (trapezoid fuzzy number whose membership function is assumed to be piecewise linear; this will be assumed throughout the paper) given by the quadruple (34 °C, 36 °C, 41 °C, 43 °C). Suppose now that the body temperature in an example is 42 °C. This may be viewed as a possible error since the degree of membership (possibility) of 42 ° C is 0.5. Thus, an example in which 42° C appears gets a lower degree of positiveness (since we may suspect it contains an error!).

However, an improper attribute's value as above need not always lower the overall degree of positiveness. For instance, if we had in our examples an attribute *inflamation* related to an increase of the body temperature, we would not need to treat the above high temperature as a possible error which would have to lower the degree of positiveness.

Such relations of attribute values which should not affect the algorithm (in the sense of lowering the degree of positiveness) are used in our new approach, and are called here *textbook knowledge* because they may be "in the first shot" introduced from a textbook, and then refined (e.g., by determining more complex relationships); moreover, such relations represent typical situations. Notice that these relationships may range from very simple (evident) in case of no large support from the experts, to more eleborate ones in case of a larger support. In the latter case, evidently, more sophisticated situations related to errors may be accounted for.

Thus, in the algorithm if we encounter some value of an attribute that may suggest an error (because it is out of the set of normal, or feasible, values), and may lead to a lower value in the degree of positiveness, we look up our textbook knowledge base to see if there are some relations between the above value with some (combination of) other ones. If so, a degree of this relation is calculated, and then used to update the degree of positiveness (and its related degree of negativeness) of the particular example. Then, the authors' former algorithm [3], [4], [5] is used.

Fuzzy logic with linguistic quantifiers (to be more specific, its calculus of linguistically quantified proposition due to Zadeh), and elements of fuzzy arithmetic are used.

2 Linguistically quantified propositions

A *linguistically quantified proposition* as, e.g., most experts are convinced, is written as "Qy's are F" where Q is a *linguistic quantifier* (e.g., most), $Y = \{y\}$ is a *set of objects* (e.g., experts), and F is a *property* (e.g., convinced). *Importance* B may also be added yielding "QBy's are F" (e.g., *most of the important experts are convinced*). The problem is to find either truth(Qy's are F) or truth(QBy's are F).

In Zadeh's approach [9] the *fuzzy linguistic quantifier* Q is assumed a fuzzy set in $[0,1]$ as, e.g.,

$$\mu_{\text{"almost all"}}(x) = \begin{cases} 1 & \text{for } x \geq 0.8 \\ 3.33x - 1.66 & \text{for } 0.5 < x < 0.8 \\ 0 & \text{for } x \leq 0.5 \end{cases} \tag{1}$$

which may be equated with the trapezoid fuzzy number $(0.5, 0.8, 1, 1)$.

Property F is defined as a fuzzy set in Y. If $Y=\{y_1,\ldots,y_p\}$, then truth(y_i is F)$=\mu_F(y_i)$, $i=1,\ldots,p$.

Now, for the case without importance

$$r = \sum Count(F)/\sum Count(Y) = \frac{1}{p}\sum_{i=1}^{p}\mu_F(y_i)$$

$$\text{truth}(Qy\text{'s are } F) = \mu_Q(r) \tag{2}$$

and in the case of importance, B, such that $\mu_B(y_i) \in [0,1]$ is a *degree of importance* of y_i, from definitely unimportant $(= 0)$ to definitely important $(= 1)$, through all intermediate values, we have

$$r' = \sum Count(B \text{ and } F)/\sum Count(B) = \sum_{i=1}^{p}(\mu_B(y_i)\ t\ \mu_F(y_i))/\sum_{i=1}^{p}\mu_B(y_i)$$

$$\text{truth}(QBy\text{'s } \mathit{are}\ F) = \mu_Q(r') \tag{3}$$

For more details, see Zadeh's original paper [9] or Kacprzyk and Yager's [6], and for another approach – Yager's [8] or Kacprzyk and Yager's [6] works.

3 Inductive learning under imprecision and errors using "textbook knowledge

Inductive learning (*from examples*) is generally meant as to find a *concept description* R which covers *all* the *positive* examples and *none* of the *negative* ones, i.e. as to find an R such that

$$\text{"}All\ Px\text{'s are } R\text{" \& "}None\ Nx\text{'s are } R\text{"} \tag{4}$$

Since (4) may be unsolvable, it was "softened" by Kacprzyk and Iwański [1], [2],[3], [4], [5] as to find an R such that

$$Q^+\ \tilde{P}x\text{'s are } R\text{" \& "}Q^-\ \tilde{N}x\text{'s are } R\text{"} \tag{5}$$

where Q^+ is a linguistic quantifier (*almost all*, *most*,...), Q^- is a linguistic quantifier (*almost none*, (*at most*) *few*,...), $\tilde{P}$ and $\tilde{N}$ denote a *soft* (to a degree) positiveness and negativeness.

The concept description is now to satisfy:

- Q^+ – *completeness*, i.e., at least Q^+ (e.g., *almost all*) of the positive examples are to be covered,

- Q^- – *consistency*, i.e., no more than Q^- (e.g., *almost none*) of the negative examples should not be covered.

Since the number of errors is usually not known precisely, evaluation like *almost all* and *almost none* are certainly adequate; evidently, suspecting more errors, we would use "milder" quantifiers (e.g., much more than 75% and much less than 25%). This accounting for errors acts then on the whole records which may be neglected.

An example is described by "attribute–value" pairs. A single attribute–value pair is called a *selector*, $[A\ r\ `a']$, where A is an *attribute*, r is a *relation* ($=$, $\geq$, ...), a is a *value*. For instance, an example x may be described as $x =$ [height = '190 cm'][color = 'reddish'][temperature $\gg$ '100° C'].

The value of attribute A_i in a selector and in an example need not be the same as, e.g., $s_i =$ [height = '*high*'] and $x =$ [height = '190 cm']). We allow therefore for a *degree of identity* of these two values, $\mu_{s_i}(x) \in [0, 1]$. The above is crucial for Kacprzyk and Iwański's [5] approach in which the values of attributes put into the selectors are some fuzzified values of appropriate attributes in certain examples.

The fuzzification of a (possibly already fuzzy) value of an attribute which occurs in a selector has much to do with which Q^+ linguistic quantifier is used (we assume throughout this paper, for simplicity, that Q^- is related to Q^+ in that if, say, Q^+ is *almost all* then Q^- is *almost none*, etc. so that only Q^+ can be dealt with). If we have a "strict" Q^+ (not many errors are suspected), the value should be less fuzzified, otherwise, in the case of a "mild" Q^+ (more errors suspected), the value should be more fuzzified.

Suppose therefore that we have a selector $s_i =$ [height = 'v'], where v is a value (possibly fuzzy) of an attribute in an existing example defined in some universe X, and a $Q^+ = (a, b, 1, 1)$, i.e., represented as a trapezoid fuzzy number (with a piecewise linear membership function, as assumed throughout this paper). A *fuzzified value* of v is the following trapezoid fuzzy number

$$\overline{v} = [\mathrm{x} - (1-a)\phi, \mathrm{x} - (1-b)\phi, \mathrm{x} + (1-b)\phi, \mathrm{x} + (1-a)\phi] \tag{6}$$

where ϕ is a parameter (a positive real number).

Thus, if $a = b$, i.e., if Q^+ is "at least a [%], then a single valued v becomes an interval, while if $a = b = 1$, i.e, if Q^+ is "all" (no errors), then $\overline{v} = v$. For a fuzzy v, we obtain a fuzzier $\overline{v}$.

For simplicity, v and $\overline{v}$ will be used interchangeably.

A *complex*, C_j, is the con-junc-tion of se-lec-tors, $s_{j_1}, \ldots, s_{j_k}$, i.e. $C_j = s_{j_1} \cap \ldots caps_{j_k}$. The *de-gree of co-ver-ing* x by $C_j = s_{j_1} \cap \ldots \cap s_{j_k}$ is de-fined as, $\forall x \in X$,

$$\mu_{C_j}(x) = \min(\mu_{s_{j_1}}(x), \ldots, \mu_{s_{j_k}}(x)) \tag{7}$$

The *concept description* R is the alternative of the complexes, $R = C_1 \cup \ldots \cup C_m$.

The *degree of covering* x by $R = C_1 \cup \ldots \cup C_m$ is defined as, $\forall x \in X$,

$$\mu_R(x) = \max(\mu_{C_1}(x), \ldots, \mu_{C_m}(x)) \tag{8}$$

The imprecision in the classification into the positive and negative examples is represented by a *degree of positiveness* of x, $\mu_{\tilde{P}}(x) \in [0,1]$, from definitely negative to definitely positive through all intermediate values, and a *degree of negativeness*, $\mu_{\tilde{N}}(x) \in [0,1]$; $\mu_{\tilde{P}}(x) = 1 - \mu_{\tilde{N}}(x)$.

We seek now an R^* such that

$$\text{truth}(\text{"}Q^+ \ \tilde{P}x\text{'s are } R\text{" \& "}Q^- \ \tilde{N}x\text{'s are } R\text{"}) \rightarrow \max_R \tag{9}$$

i.e. an "(sub)optimal" R^* in the sense that (9) is satisfied to the highest possible extent.

In a more extended form, (9) may be written as to find an R^* such that

$$\text{truth}(Q^+ \ \tilde{P}x\text{'s are } R) \wedge \text{truth}(Q^- \ \tilde{N}x\text{'s are } R) = \overline{\mu}_{Q^+}(R) \wedge \overline{\mu}_{Q^-}(R) =$$

$$= \mu_{Q^+}\Big(\sum_{x \in X} (\mu_{\tilde{P}}(x) \wedge \mu_R(x)) / \sum_{x \in X} \mu_{\tilde{P}}(x)\Big) \wedge$$

$$\wedge \mu_{Q^-}\Big(\sum_{x \in X} (\mu_{\tilde{N}}(x) \wedge \mu_R(x)) / \sum_{x \in X} \mu_{\tilde{N}}(x)\Big) \rightarrow \max_R \tag{10}$$

where $\overline{\mu}_{Q^+}(R)$ is the *degree of completeness* and $\overline{\mu}_{Q^-}(R)$ is the *degree of consistency*.

The concept description sought, R, is built up *iteratively*, adding in each iteration a new complex to the current R, i.e., the number of examples covered by R is not decreasing. Moreover, by adding the complexes in a special way, $\overline{\mu}_{Q^+}(R)$ is increasing as quickly as possible, while $\overline{\mu}_{Q^-}(R)$ is decreasing as slowly as possible. This makes the algorithm more efficient.

The algorithm is based on the concept of a *typoid* introduced by the authors [3], [4], [5]. Suppose that $x = s_1 \ldots s_n = [A_1 = \text{'}a_1\text{'}] \ldots [A_n = \text{'}a_n\text{'}]$. Assume that A_i takes on its values in a set $\{a_{i_1}, \ldots, a_{i_q}\}$. A *typoid* is defined as an artificial example $\tau = s_1^*, \ldots, s_n^* = [A_1 = \text{'}a_1^*\text{'}] \ldots [A_n = \text{'}a_n^*\text{'}]$ such that each $s_i^* = [A_i = \text{'}a_i^*\text{'}]$ is determined by

$$\sum_{x \in X} (\mu_{\tilde{P}}(x) \wedge (1 - \mu_R(x)) \wedge \mu_{s_i = [A_i = \text{'}a_i\text{'}]}(x)) \rightarrow \max_{a_i \in \{a_{i_1}, \ldots, a_{i_k}\}} \tag{11}$$

i.e. into τ we put such consecutive selectors which are *most typical* for the examples that are *not covered* by R and *most positive*; $\mu_{s_i}(x) \in [0,1]$ is a *degree of identity* of A_i's value in s_i and in x. Evidently, the selectors taken into consideration in (and then eventually put into) the typoid are subjected to the fuzzification as formerly described.

The algorithm is now:

Step 1. To initialize, set:

Substep 1a. $R := \emptyset$ and $C := \emptyset$ to be meant that the initial R contains no complex which in turn contains no selectors.

Substep 1b. $\mu_{\tilde{P}}(x) \in [0,1]$, for each example x (evidently, $\mu_{\tilde{N}}(x) = 1 - \mu_{\tilde{P}}(x)$)

Substep 1c. For each example $x = s_1 \dots s_k$, and for each selector s_i, $i = 1, \dots, k$:

1. Calculate the degree to which the value of attribute (in fact, the one corresponding to selector) s_i satisfies its corresponding fuzzy (a trapezoid fuzzy number) feasible range, $\mu_b(s_i) \in [0, 1]$,
2. If $\mu_b(s_i) < \gamma$, where γ is a threshold, then check in the textbook knowledge base if this results from an error in data or is related to the occurence of a coincidence of conditions (e.g., a particular disease) that allow the value of s_i to exceed its related threshold, γ; if the latter occurs, then enlarge (fuzzify) appropriately the s_i's corresponding fuzzy range of feasible values (e.g., by using (6), and calculate the degree to which the value of s_i satisfies that new fuzzy range of feasible values, $\mu_{\bar{b}}(s_i)$;
3. Calculate
$$\mu_B(x) = \min(\mu_{\bar{b}}(s_1), \dots, \mu_{\bar{b}}(s_k)) \tag{12}$$
where "min" may be replaced by, e.g., a t-norm;
4. Update the value of positiveness of example x
$$\mu_{\tilde{P}'} = 0.5 + (\mu_{\tilde{P}}(x) - 0.5)\mu_B(x) \tag{13}$$
Notice that if $\mu_B(x) = 0$, then $\mu_{\tilde{P}'}(x)$=0.5, i.e. such an example will be excluded from considerations as it is insignificant; if μ_B=1, then $\mu_{\tilde{P}'}(x) = \mu_{\tilde{P}}(x)$; and $0 < \mu_B(x) < 1$ implies $0.5 < \mu_{\tilde{P}'}(x) < \mu_{\tilde{P}}(x)$; For notational simplicity, we will use $\mu_{\tilde{P}}(x)$ to denote both this and $\mu_{\tilde{P}'}$; this should not lead to confusion.

Step 2. $R := R \cup C$, i.e., "add" to the current R a currently formed C, and assume this as the new R.

Step 3. Form a typoid τ as formerly described.

Step 4. Find an example $x^* \in X$ which is both most positive and most similar to τ formed in Step 3, that is $\mu_{\tilde{P}'}(x) \wedge \text{sim}(x, \tau) \longrightarrow \max_{x \in X}$, where $\text{sim} : X \times X \longrightarrow [0, 1]$ is some function expressing the *similarity* between x and τ, from 0 for *full dissimilarity* to 1 for *full similarity* as, e.g., $\text{sim}(x, \tau) = \frac{1}{n} \sum_{i=1}^{n} \mu_{s_{i^*}}(x)$.

Step 5. Form C as follows:

Substep 5a. To initialize, set $C := \emptyset$, and $h_{max} = 0$.

Substep 5b. For each $s_i^*, i \in I'$, where I' is the set of indices of the attributes not occuring in C, (s_i^* is the i-th selector of x^* found in **Step 4**), calculate
$$h_i^* = h(\overline{\mu}_{Q^+}(R \cup (C \cap s_i^*)), \overline{\mu}_{Q^-}(R \cup (C \cap s_i^*))) \tag{14}$$
where $h : [0, 1] \times [0, 1] \longrightarrow [0, 1]$ is an averaging operator, e.g., $h(u, w) = (u + w)/2$;

Substep 5c. Find $h^* = \max_{i \in I'} h_i^*$, and i^* such that $h^* = h_{i^*}^*$;

Substep 5d. If $h^* > h_{max}$, then:

(1) $h_{max} := h^*$

(2) $C := C \cap s^*_{i_*}$
(3) $I' := I \setminus \{i^*\}$
(4) go to **Substep 5b**;
else go to **Step 6**.

Step 6. If $\min(\overline{\mu}_{Q^+}(R \cup C), \overline{\mu}_{Q^-}(R \cup C)) > \min(\overline{\mu}_{Q^+}(R), \overline{\mu}_{Q^-}(R)))$, then go to **Step 2**.

Step 7. Output the final R, and STOP.

Since a typoid is a good starting point, the algorithm is very effective and efficient in practice.

Example. Due to lack of space, we can only present Step 1c of the algorithm for a very simple case, and for how the further steps of the algorithm proceed the reader is referred to our previous works.

Suppose we have an example, x, whose degree of positiveness (corresponding to the occurence of an illness) is given as $\mu_{\tilde{P}}(x)$=0.9. in this x we have a selector (the temperature of a patient's body) given as

$$x = \ldots [\text{temperature} = \text{`42.5°C'}] \ldots$$

whose corresponding range of feasible values is specified by the trapezoid fuzzy number (34°C, 36°C, 41°C, 43°C). Thus, we obtain

$$\mu_b([\text{temperature} = \text{`42.5°C'}] = 0.25$$

Thus, due to (12) we obtain (by assuming for simplicity that this is the only selector to be taken into account) that $\mu_B(x) = 0.25$.

Suppose now that the threshold $\gamma = 0.8$. Thus, the above 0.25 is evidently too low, suggesting a possible error in the attribute value (which may lead to possibly disregarding this example by the algorithm).

We resort therefore to our textbook knowledge, and suppose that we find rule which says that in the case of the present illness (corresponding to the class of positive examples) there may be an increased temperature. This may be schematically presented as "IF illness THEN fuzzify the range of feasible values for temperature due to (6) with $\phi = 2$", i.e., the trapezoid fuzzy number of the range becomes (33°C, 35.6°C, 41.4°C, 44°C).

We obtain therefore $\mu_b([\text{temperature} = 42.5°\text{C}] = 0.58$, and due to (12) $\mu_B(.) = 0.58$. Thus, due to (13) $\mu_{\tilde{P}'}(x) = 0.5 + (0.9 - 0.5) \cdot 0.58 = 0.73$.

The new degree of positiveness of x is evidently lower than the original 0.9 intitially given because the temperature is somewhat beyond the range of feasible values. However, by resorting to texbook knowledge in which there has been found a rule allowing for such a slightly higher body temoerature in the case of the particular disease, x is not disregarded from considerations (its degree of positiveness is much higher than 0.5).

The next steps of the algorithm are analogous to those presented in the other works of the authors as, say, in [4], [5].

4 Concluding remarks

The algorithm proposed may be useful in many practical inductive learning problems in which imprecision, misclassification, inexact matching, etc. preclude the use of conventional techniques. Applications, mostly in medicine, are very promising and encouraging, and will presented in further papers.

References

1. C. Iwański, J. Kacprzyk: Machine learning from incomplete and imprecise examples. In: M. Fedrizzi and J. Kacprzyk (ads.): Proceedings of 8th Italian - Polish Symposium on Systems Analysis and Decision Support in Economics and Technology (Levico Terme, Italy, 1989), Warsaw: Omnitech Press 1990, pp. 282–297.
2. J. Kacprzyk, C. Iwański: Machine learning from misclassified and erroneous examples. In: Proc. of IPMU '90 Conference (Paris, France) 1990, pp. 213–215.
3. J. Kacprzyk, C. Iwański: Inductive learning under imprecision and errors. In: R. Lowen and M. Roubens (eds.): Proc. of 4th IFSA '91 Congress (Brussels, Belgium), Part AI, 1991, pp. 78–81.
4. J. Kacprzyk, C. Iwański: Inductive learning from incomplete and imprecise examples, In: B. Bouchon-Meunier, R. R. Yager and L. A. Zadeh (eds.): Uncertainty in Knowledge Bases, Berlin: Springer-Verlag 1991, pp. 424–430.
5. J. Kacprzyk, C. Iwański: Machine learning from incomplete and imprecise examples. In: L. A. Zadeh and J. Kacprzyk (eds.): Fuzzy Logic for the Management of Uncertainty, New York: Wiley, pp. 465–478.
6. J. Kacprzyk, R.R. Yager: Emergency-oriented expert systems: a fuzzy approach. Information Sciences 37, 147–156 (1985).
7. R.S. Michalski: A theory and methodology of inductive learning. In: R.S. Michalski, J. Carbonell and T. Mitchell (eds.): Machine Learning.Palo Alto: Tioga Press 1983, 83–133.
8. R.R. Yager: Quantifiers in the formulation of multiple objective decision functions. Information Sciences 31, 107–139 (1983).
9. L.A. Zadeh: A computational approach to fuzzy quantifiers in natural languages. Computers and Mathematics with Applications 9, 149–184 (1983).

Incremental Learning of Roughly Represented Concepts

Anio O. Arigoni
Università di Bologna
P. Porta S. Donato 5
40127 Bololgna, Italy

Cesare Furlanello
I.R.S.T.
Pantè di Povo
38100 Trento, Italy

Vittorio Maniezzo
Dep. of Electronics
Politecnico di Milano
20133, Milano, Italy

Abstract An incremental version of NIELLO, a system through which irrelevant details of the instances defining a concept are evinced, is presented in this paper. The goal is to obtain an efficient algorithm by which the irrelevant details are evinced for roughly represented concepts, as typically performed by intelligent agents.

1 Introduction

We define concepts as lists of instances called *entities* [15], i.e. as corresponding natural categories, such as "valid giustification", "nourishing food", "interesting books", etc. When one of these list is exhaustive, then the definition is said to be *extensional.*

This definition, although semantically exhaustive and not redundant, not necessarily is such from the pragmatical stand-point as well. This, because of the possible being pragmatically irrelevant of one or more details of the listed instances. Thus, the *intensional definition* of a concept, i.e. the list of its essential instances that come out upon evidencing the details that are irrelevant to the concept itself, may result quite reduced with respect to the extensional one. Because of this pragmatical redundance, instance *typicality gradient* and a consequent concept *internal structure* have to be expected, as Rosch reported to happen in human [12, 13].

The contextual dependency of the mentioned redundance, then also of typicality to a concept of the distinct instances, had been proven by us [4]. As a consequence, every new instance inherent to that concept may alter the intensional definition of the concept itself; thus, also the typicality of the instances already known as defining that concept is influenced by the new one [3]. This article treats and exemplifies the computation, both symbolic and numerical, of the considered influence in processes of incremental learning from examples.

The work described in this paper has been developed within MAIA project [16]: MAIA (acronym for "Modello Avanzato di Intelligenza Artificiale") is the main AI project under development at IRST. Its sperimental platform is an integrated system including two terminals (a "concierge" and a "librarian") and a mobile robot capable of navigating in closed environments, on the basis of a "vision" made possible by sensors of vatrious types [11].

2 Concept incremental learning

The type of learning herein considered for concept acquisition tasks consists in successively accepting instances of a concept to be learned, each one introducing a revision of the current concept description [8].

The importance of incrementally setting up the representation of a concept to be acquired has been early recognized as one of the aim to be pursued in devising machine learning systems. Already Winston's arch program fits this paradigm [17]: it encompasses operators that enable generalization and specialization of the current representation, on the basis of successively proposed instances. It is worth noticing that since incremental learning systems have been proposed (like Fisher's COBWEB [9], Carbonell's world modeller [7], Lebowitz' UNIMEM [10] and many others), incremental versions of originally non-incremental systems have been devised [14].

Several appealing properties account for this interest. The most significant to us consists in the possibility of rapidly updating knowledge with any new instance the inherence of which, to the concept, is asserted. Thus, systems that react promptly to unexperienced world stimuli and that allow an efficient use of the necessarily limited computer memory can be provided.

In the next section, the incremental algorithm and the proposal for an application to *roughly described* concept are outlined. The latter are concepts formally represented, but possibly in a redundant and partially synthesized manner; such is the usual structure of concepts elicited from humans, when questioned about. The result constitutes an extension of a non-incremental concept learning system we recently developed: the NIELLO system in which the idea of *conceptaul abstraction* [5] is utilised.

Considerations on computational complexity of the analysed algorithm as well as on its theoretical basis are outlined in the concluding section.

3 Incremental NIELLOing

The NIELLO system can be successfully used in concept inductive learning, as was reported in a previous IPMU [3]. It has a well-founded algebraic basis and allows the assessment of several descriptors upon the learned concepts, both symbolic and numerical in nature, like for instance the extraction of the *prototype(s)* of the concept, the *typicality* of its single entities, the *relevance* of each feature. The NIELLO's core is a polynomial-time algorithm for semiotic synthesis, which in fact permits deriving the intensional representation of an extensionally defined concept [4, 5].

The more practical manner of proceeding herein proposed, which avoid us the weight of some steps of the original one, is convenient in at least two situations [6]: (a) when a concept defined over many features has to be updated by the knowledge of its new instances; (b) in the case of roughly represented concepts.

Let us two entities x_α and x_β be given such that for every feature X_h, the attribute $x_{b\beta}$ of x_β, is either irrelevant, indicated by "*", or equal to its corresponding $x_{b\alpha}$ of x_α, then we say that x_α *implies semantically* x_β.; a first analysis on this subject was reported in [1, 2] and was developed in the references we cited above.

The algorithm for the incremental learning version of NIELLO is:

```
Step 1:   For each new entity x_e
                 Set NE = F
                 If  x_e implies any entity of S^m
                 then skip to next new entity
                 else set NE = NE∪x_e

Step 2:  While NE ≠ F
               Set IMPLIED = false

Step 3:        Compare each entity NE of NE with every entity
S_i^m          of S^m

Step 4:        if NE and S_i^m differ for only one significant
                 attribute X_h of S_i^m
               then  add to S^m and to NE a copy NE* of NE
with X_h             set to * and all the asterisks not in
common               substituted by the homologous
significant                                     attribute

               if  NE* is fully dominated by NE
               then set  IMPLIED = true

               If not IMPLIED then add to S^m a copy of NE
               remove NE from NE

Step 5:        Compact S^m (remove dominant entities) and
synthesize
```

The effectiveness of this procedure can be shown by the example that follows. Suppose one has already learned the concept S={**1, *1*, 1**} and the new entity x_ε=000 is asserted as inhering on S.

Since x_ε does not imply any entity of S^m, we set NE =x_ε and proceed to Step 3. The first entity of S^m compared with x_ε (= NE_1) is **1, which differs form it only for one significant attribute, X_3;; therefore the entity 00* is added to NE . Similarly, comparing x_ε with the other two entities of S^m the entities 0*0 and *00 are added to NE. Entity x_ε can be so removed and Step 3 with NE = {00*, 0*0, *00} iterated. Comparing NE_1 (=00*) with the entities of S^m, the entities 0** and *0* can be added to NE; by comparing NE_2 can further be added entity **0. Once accomplished the second iteration NE={**0, *0*, 0**} and S^m={**1, *1*, 1**,**0, *0*, 0**} can be synthesized to S^m={***}.

The proposed procedure can be applied, as a special case, to the identification of the correct minimal representation of a roughly defined concept [6]. In fact, we can consider the first entity of the representation given as the current minimal representation, and add to it, one by one, all the other entities proposed in the rough definition. Note how the procedure works both on new entities and with irrelevancies already brought into evidence in them.

This is exemplified in the following case regarding the acquisition of the concept "publications of interest for the Machine Learning (ML) community". To this purpose, we suppose to classify books, papers, etc., according to the following set of features: historical relevance; text language; considered topics; form of the overview; period of publication; nature of content.

We (suppose to) have interviewed some ML researchers, which disjunctively gave the following definition, classifying a publication as being of interest if it is historically relevant, is written in English, deals with ML topics and is either or not informal (1110**), or it has theoretical content (111**1) or it has informal but practical content (1111*0); moreover it could be of interest if is written in English, deals with ML topics, is not informal and is published recently; in the latter case, the considered publications could be either theoretical(*11011) or practical (*11010).

Within this framework, the roughly defined concept is represented as follows:R={1110**, 111**1, 1111*0, *11011, *11010}. Its roughness is patent firstly in the last two entities, which are directly synthesizable.

In order to apply our incremental algorithm to identify the minimal representation, we have to identify a subset of $\boldsymbol{R}$ which will be considered as the initial minimal representation to update; all the other members of $\boldsymbol{R}$ will be successively considered as new entities that increase the generality of the concept to learn. As in the new entities irrelevancies are already contained, we shall use the algorithm as if it were refining already synthesized data.

The subsequent phases of the algorithm are the following:

- Initially, $\boldsymbol{R}^1$={1110**};
- add 111**1 to obtain $\boldsymbol{R}^2$={1110**,111**1} where nothing can be updated
- add 1111*0 which (step 3) interacts with both the entities already present, yielding: $\boldsymbol{R}^3$={1110**, 111**1, 1111*0, 111**0, 1111**}.
- this representation can be synthesized to $\boldsymbol{R}^3$={111***}.
- add *11011 and $\boldsymbol{R}^4$={111***, *11011} is obtained.
- Finally, by adding *11010 , $\boldsymbol{R}^5$=$\boldsymbol{R}^m$={111***,*1101*} is obtained.

4 Conclusions

The adaptation of the NIELLO algorithm reported in this article supplies positive results for concept incremental learning. This can be utilized in both updating the minimal representation of a concept, at the presentation of every new entity, and identifying of the exact intensional representation of a roughly defined concept.

The evaluation of the computational complexity of the proposed algorithm and the theoretical justification for its main steps have only been sketched here and will be reported in a future full exposition. These results allow an effective application of NIELLO to the study of concepts represented through a considerable number of features. In fact, the new incremental version significantly overcomes the otherwise costly memory and time constraints of the original NIELLO procedure, due to a substantial decrease of computational complexity.

References

[1] A. O. Arigoni: "Mathematical development arising from 'semantical implication' and the evaluation of membership characteristic functions", *Fuzzy Sets and Systems*, No.4, 167-183, (1980).

[2] A. O. Arigoni: "Transformational-generative grammar for describing formal properties", *Fuzzy Sets and Systems*, No.8, 311-322 (1982).

[3] A. O. Arigoni, C. Furlanello and V. Maniezzo: "Irrelevant Features in Concept Learning", *Proceedings of the 3rd Int. Conf. on Information Processing and Management of Uncertainty, IPMU-90*, Paris, July 1990.

[4] A. O. Arigoni and V. Maniezzo: "Intensive Representation of Inductively Acquired Concepts", *10th Int. Conf. on Cybernetic and System Research*, Wien, 1990.

[5] A. O. Arigoni and V. Maniezzo: "Conceptual abstraction: a context-depending simplification of concept representations", *Working Notes of the Approximation and Abstraction of Computational Theories '92"*, San Jose, Calif. 1992.

[6] A. O. Arigoni, E. Benigni and A. Rossi: "Intensive Definition of Roughly Described Concepts", to be presented at the *11th Int. Conf. on Cybernetic and System Research*, Wien, 1992.

[7] J. G.Carbonell and G. Hood: "The world modelers project:objectives and simulators architectures", in Michalski R.S., Carbonell J.G. Mitchell T.S. (eds.): *Machine learning: a guide to current research*, Kluwer, 1986

[8] R. Elio and L. Watanabe: "An incremental deductive strategy for controlling constructive induction in learning from examples", *Machine Learning*, 7, 1991

[9] D. H. Fisher: "Knowledge acquisition via incremental conceptual clustering", *Machine Learning*, 2, 1987.

[10] M. Lebowitz: "Concept Learning in a rich input domain: generalization-based memory", in Michalski R.S., Carbonell J.G. Mitchell T.S. (eds.): *Machine learning: an artificial intelligence approach*, Morgan Kaufmann, 1986.

[11] T. Poggio and L. Stringa: "A Project for an Intelligent System: Vision and Learning" International Symposium Biological and Artificial Intelligent Systems, Rome, Sept. 2-6, 1990.

[12] E. H. Rosch: "Cognitive representation of semantic cathegories", *Jour. of Psychology: General*, 104, 192-223 (1975).

[13] E. H. Rosch: "The nature of mental codes for color cathegories, *Human Perception and Performance*, 1, 303-322, (1975).

[14] J. C. Schlimmer and D. H. Fisher: "A case study of incremental concept induction", *Proceedings of the 5th national conference on artificial intelligence*, Morgan Kauffmann, 1986

[15] R. E. Stepp and R. S. Michalski: "Conceptual clustering of Streuctured Objects", *Artificial Intelligence*, 28, 43-69, (1975).

[16] L. Stringa: " An Integrated Approach in Artificial Intelligence", IRST - Technical Report # 9012-11, Dec. 1990.

[17] P. H. Winston: "Learning structural descriptions from examples", in Winston P.H. (ed.): *The psychology of computer vision*, McGraw-Hill, 1975.

SELF-ORGANIZING QUALITATIVE MULTIMODEL CONTROL

G. NAGIB, W. GHARIEB, Z. BINDER

Laboratoire d'Automatique de Grenoble
URA C.N.R.S. N° 228, I.N.P.G. - E.N.S.I.E.G.
BP.46 - 38402 Saint-Martin-d'Hères, Cedex, FRANCE

Abstract:- Qualitative control is a promising technique for controlling dynamic systems which are ill-defined or too complex to be modelled analytically. In this paper, a Self Organizing Qualitative Control (SOQC) is proposed for controlling dynamic systems with incomplete knowledge on their parameters. This technique is based on a learning approach which uses a qualitative multimodel representation to reduce parametric uncertainty and synthesize a fine control action. The standard problems"benchmark examples" have been selected to apply the proposed control method. To show the potential of this method for controlling interconnected systems, the control of a two coupled tanks system is achieved using the same control technique. The simulation results are satisfactory for achieving tracking and regulation objectives.

1. Introduction

Qualitative Reasoning methods (**QR**) are an emerging area of artificial intelligence (**AI**) that can help control engineers model physical systems in a more abstract way. These methods are particularly attractive when it is not easy to obtain a precise numerical model with incomplete knowledge of physical systems. The original work in this domain is presented by Forbus[1], De Kleer[2] and Kupiers[3]. AI researchers have been more concerned with explaining how physical systems work and with modelling common sense reasoning. However, they have not claimed that QR is a method for control. Applications for qualitative reasoning have so far been found in process monitoring, fault detection, diagnostic and simulation [4 -7]. In order to go beyond monitoring for control, some changes have to be made. The qualitative reasoning field has concentrated on observing and modelling system behaviour, but has barely touched the notion of using these models and observations to control the system. It may be possible to reason about control of these systems within this framework. However, the qualitative reasoning framework will need to include feedback and ***learning*** capabilities and relax some of its assumptions in order to work for control [8]. It is apparent that a system that is nonlinear, or not precisely mathematically defined, is a candidate for QR techniques. How to use QR in control is not so apparent, but is a promising avenue of research. Qualitative control depends on the thorough knowledge extracted from understanding of physical systems. This knowledge is used to construct a qualitative model. A controller is taken to be qualitative if it can operate without the precise numerical parameters required for a conventional automatic controller [9].

In this paper, we present a new qualitative control method (Self Organizing Qualitative Control). This method is applied to control first and second benchmark examples which are proposed in [10]. These examples are basically proposed to test the capabilities of different adaptive controllers where system parameters are not completely defined (knowing the bounds of parameters only). For the first benchmark example, a stress test is applied for additional complexities which is proposed in [11]. This method is also applied to the two coupled tanks system. A simulation work is perfomed to show the potential of the proposed methodology.

2. Qualitative control proposed by (Abulmajid, 89)

This section presents the method of qualitative control proposed in [12]. This method concerns a single-input single-output dynamic system. The qualitative model is obtained by considering the process as a series of sub-systems, each of which is represented by a qualitative variable which has a value only from the set {-, 0, +} as the set of all possible values. Therefore, the sub-system i can be represented by qualitative variable **xi** which takes only one value of the set {-, 0, +} at any instant. The dynamic interaction between any two adjacent sub-systems can either be a monotonically increasing (M^+) or monotonically decreasing (M^-) function. Monotonically increasing means that one variable increases as the adjacent variable increases and vice versa. Monotonically decreasing means that one variable decreases as the result of the adjacent variable increasing. Figure (1) shows two sub-systems with M^+ relationship ($x2=M^+(x1)$).

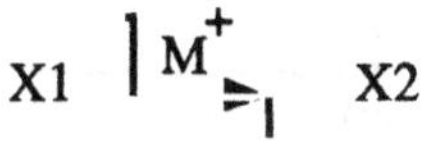

Fig. (1) Two sub-systems with M^+ relationship

The aim is to control the variable x2 by using variable x1 as a control variable. Control rules can be derived to perform the above objective knowing the current value and the desired value of x2. For example:

IF current x2 is (+) and desired x2 is (0) THEN x1 is (-)

The qualitative control law is represented by the following equation:

$$u(k+1) = u(k) \pm \Delta \quad (1)$$

Where

$\pm$ is the control tendency which is determined using the control rules

Δ is the increment change of control, which is a constant value.

Figure (2) represents the basic configuration of this method. This method is applied to the two coupled tanks system to control the level in the second tank. The dynamic performance of this controller is poor. Its response to a step change in the required value takes some time to reach the desired level and then oscillates around the required value. Changing the control increment value (Δ) can help improve the system response. IF the increment value is increased, the required level is reached faster but with greater overshoot and oscillation. A small increment size reduces the magnitude of the oscillation, but makes the system slow to respond.

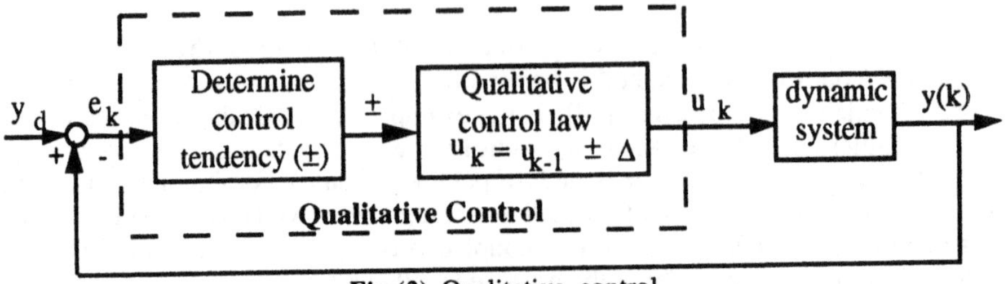

Fig.(2) Qualitative control
Fig.(2) Qualitative control

The transient and steady state behaviour can be improved by combining the basic qualitative controller with domain specific quantitative knowledge, but some experimentation is required to obtain the best possible control result. However, the qualitative controller will need to include learning capabilities (on the value of Δ) in order to obtain a satisfactory transient and steady state system behaviour.

3. Methodology of self organizing qualitative control

In this section, we propose a qualitative control methodology (Self Organizing Qualitative Control SOQC) as shown in Figure (3).

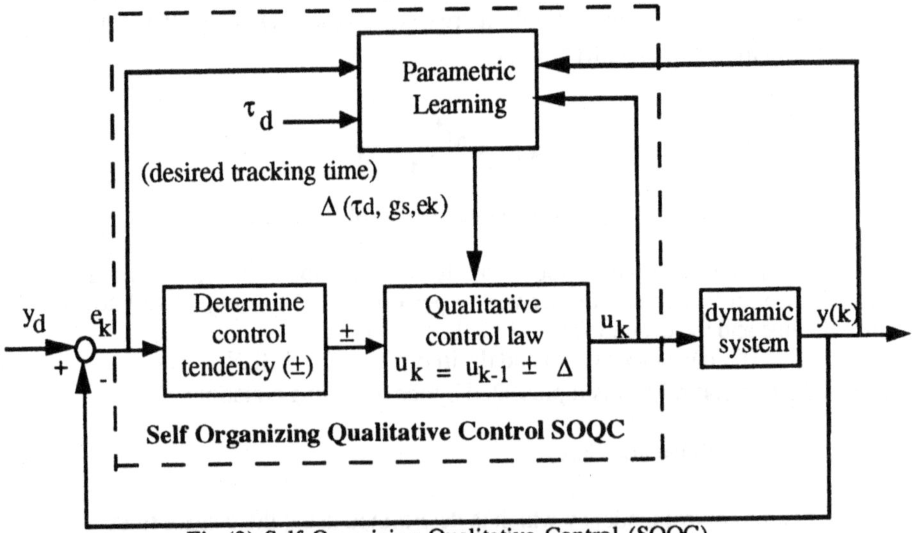

Fig.(3) Self Organizing Qualitative Control (SOQC)

The system is characterized by qualitative parameters, which means that we have certain uncertainty on parameter values (bounded parameters). For example: the zone of uncertainty for the system parameter x is $[x_{min} \;\; x_{max}]$ and x is situated between x_{min} & x_{max}.

Parametric learning:

Knowing the structure of the system and the bounds of their parameters, we can start with this knowledge to construct a qualitative multimodel. The basic idea of the qualitative multimodel is to divide all the qualitative parameters into a number of regions such that each region is represented by one qualitative model, which has a specific range of parametric uncertainty. For example, if we have a first order system described by:

$$y(k) = k1\ y(k-1) + k2\ u(k-1) \tag{2}$$

The qualitative model equation is given by:

$$[y_m(k)] = [k1]\ y(k-1) + [k2]\ u(k-1) \tag{3}$$

where:-

y(k-1) and u(k-1) are the system output and input respectively at the instant k-1.
[k1] and [k2] are qualitative parameters

If we take the different combinations between [min max] values of system parameters [k1] and [k2], we will obtain four values of $[y_m(k)]$ as follows:

$$[y_m(k)] = \begin{bmatrix} k1_{min} & k2_{min} \\ k1_{max} & k2_{min} \\ k1_{min} & k2_{max} \\ k1_{max} & k2_{max} \end{bmatrix} \begin{bmatrix} u(k-1) \\ y(k-1) \end{bmatrix} \tag{4}$$

The minimum and maximum values of the model output are used to detect its validity with respect to the system evolution.

The qualitative multimodel can be obtained by dividing the range of each parameter into two equal ranges. This gives four regions, each of which represents a qualitative model as shown in Figure (4).

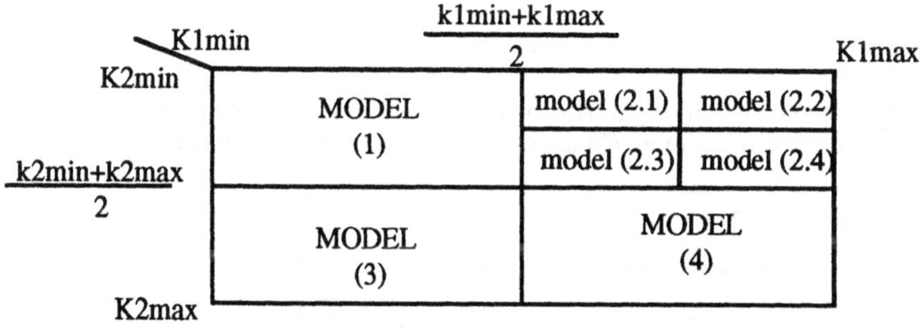

Fig. 4. Qualitative Multimodel (parametric learning in parallel)

The proposed algorithm (parametric learning) tries to reduce the parametric uncertainty to find the most accurate system parameters. Comparing the system output to the average output of each qualitative model, we can find the candidate model which gives the minimum output error. Our mechanism divides the parameter space for this model to follow parameter evolution. For example, if the second model in Figure (4) is selected, it will be divided into four new models (2.1), (2.2), (2.3) and (2.4). The mechanism will be repeated until it reduces the uncertainty of system parameters. This method is called ***parametric learning in parallel*** because we try to reduce all parameter ranges (K1 &K2) at the same time. This method is fast but the cost of models is high. We therefore propose another method called ***parametric learning in series*** using two overlapping models only . In this method, we divide the first qualitative parameter into two overlapping regions such that each region is represented by one qualitative model. The mechanism tries to reduce the range of the first parameter while other parameter ranges are fixed. After that it reduces the range of the second parameter and so on. It is not necessary to find the exact values, because if we have certain parametric errors, the controller has to compensate for them. We apply the following qualitative control law:-

$$u(k+1) = u(k) \pm \Delta \tag{5}$$

Where

- $\pm$ is the control tendency which is determined using the method proposed in [12].
- Δ is the increment change of control, which is a function of tracking error and system parameters which can be obtained by parametric learning.

The value of Δ is obtained by:

$$\Delta = \frac{T\, e_k}{\tau_d\ g_s} \tag{6}$$

Where

T: Sampling period
e_k : Tracking error at instant k
τ_d: Desired tracking time
g_s: System static gain which is a function of system parameters obtained by parametric learning

4. SIMULATION WORK

4.1. Two coupled tanks system

Our method of self organizing qualitative control is applied to the two coupled tanks system shown in Figure (5) to control the level in the second tank.

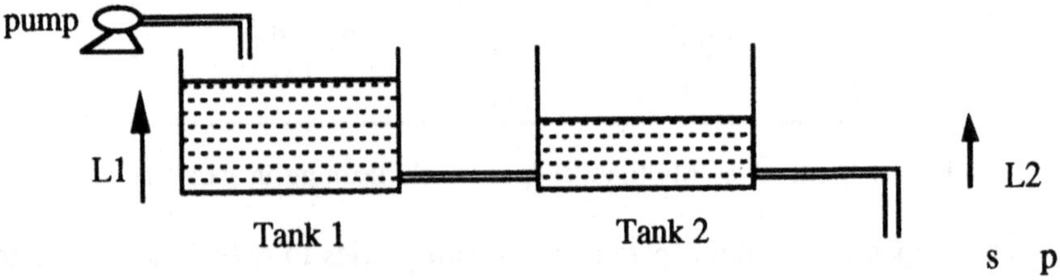

Fig. 5. The coupled tanks system

The transfer function of the system is:

$$G(s) = \frac{k}{(1+\tau_1\, s)\,(1+\tau_2\, s)} \tag{7}$$

Where k is static gain
τ_1 is the time constant of the first tank.
τ_2 is the time constant of the second tank.

Assuming that the bounds of τ_1 and τ_2 are :

$$\tau_1=[0.8 \quad 2], \quad \tau_2=[0.2 \quad 0.7]$$

The nominal transfer function is given by:

$$G(s) = \frac{k}{(s+1)(s+2)} \tag{8}$$

The qualitative transfer function

$$[G(s)] = \frac{k}{(s+[a_1])(s+[a_2])} \tag{9}$$

Where

$$k = 0.3, \quad a_1=[0.5 \quad 1.25], \quad a_2=[1.43 \quad 5]$$

The response of the level in the second tank with the (SOQC) and using a well tuned PID controller for comparison, is shown in Figure (6), while Figure (7) shows the static gain obtained by the learning approach.

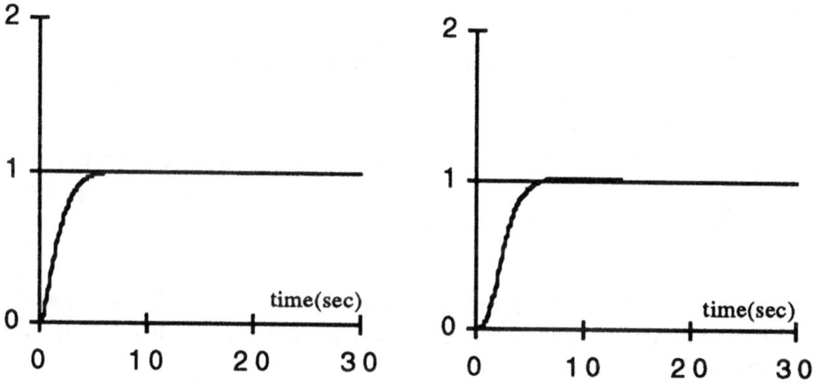

System response (PID) System response (SOQC)

Fig.6. The unit step response of the second tank level

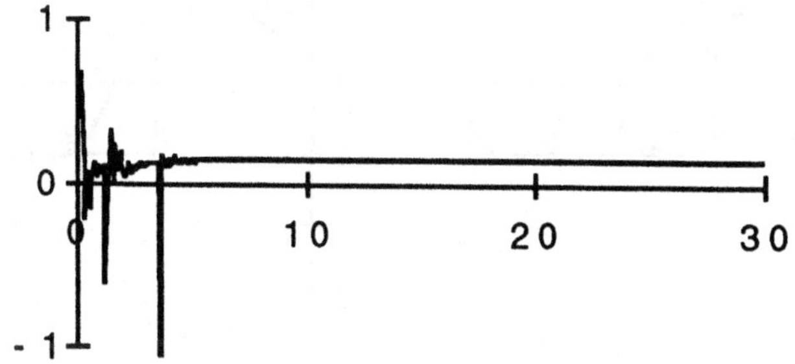

Fig.7. The system static gain

4.2. Benchmark examples

A simulation work has been performed also for the "Benchmark" examples (first and second order systems) proposed in [10]. The general format of the set-point regulator problems to be considered here is illustrated in Figure (8)

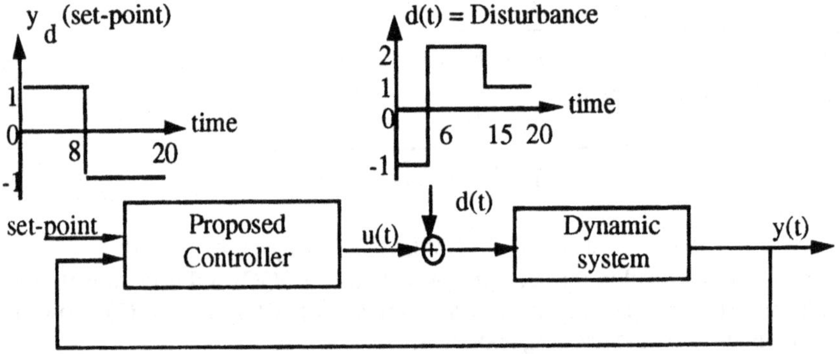

Fig. 8. General format of benchmark examples

Example(1):

The plant involved in this example is described by the transfer function:

$$G_1(s) = K/(s+a) \tag{10}$$

Where, $k=1+\Delta k$ with $-0.5<\Delta k<2$ and $a=1+\Delta a$ with $-2<\Delta a<2$. The variations are used to detect the bounds of each parameter. The derived closed loop response has been specified in terms of the following model:

$$y + y = y_d \tag{11}$$

Figure (9.a) represents the desired response of the first benchmark example, and Figure (9.b) represents the undisturbed response with SOQC controller. The response is comparable to the desired one.

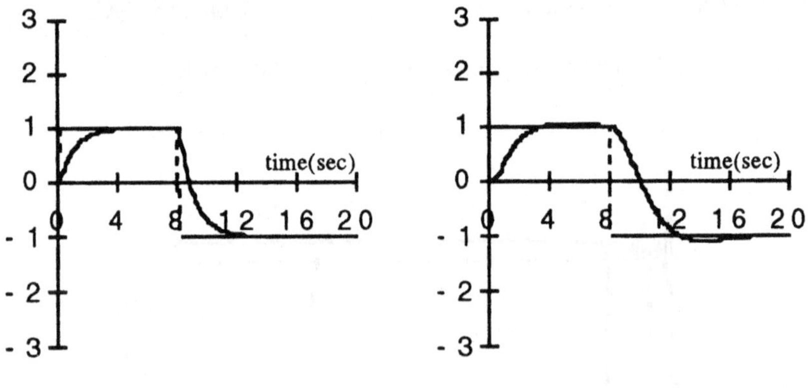

(a) Desired response (b) Undisturbed response

Fig.9. The system response using SOQC controller

A stress test is applied for additional complexities (by adding process time delay, actuator unmodelled dynamics, disturbance, sensor noise) which is proposed in [11]. Table (2) represents the stress test progression from level 0 to the maximum stress case level 3.

Level	Disturbance level (%)	Simulation time	Unmodelled dynamics time constant Ta	Time delay (s) T_d	sensor noise (RMS)
0	100%	20	0	0	0
1	10%	100	0.1	0.05	0.04
2	60%	60	0.25	0.1	0.16
3	100%	20	0.33	0.3	0.2

Tab.2. Stress test for the first order benchmark example

Figure (10) represents the system output with additional complexities.

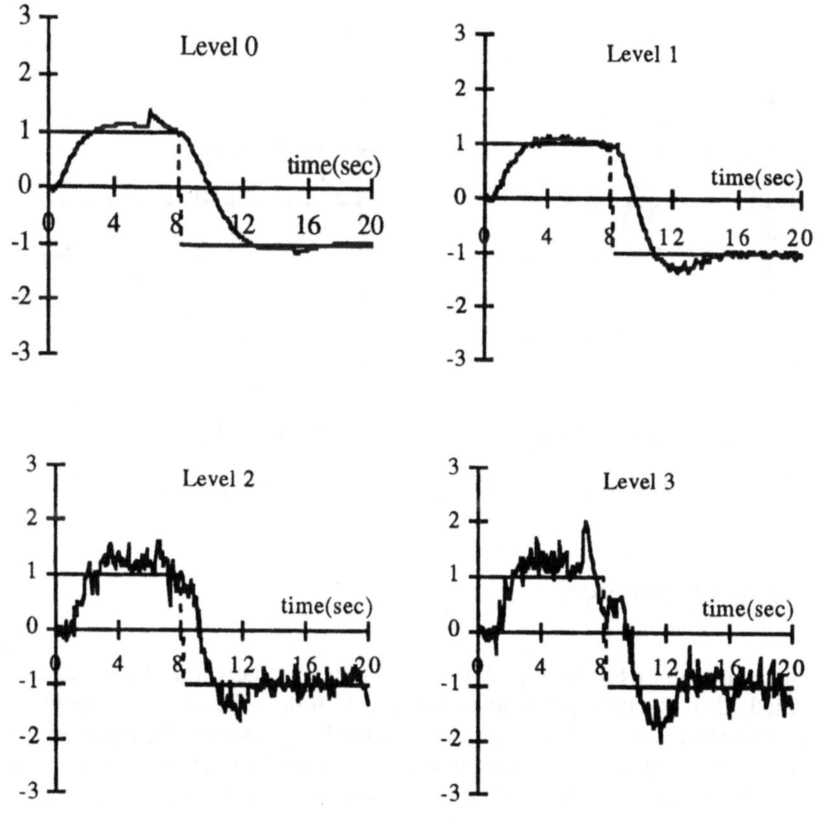

Fig.10. The system output with additional complexities

Example (2):

The plant involved in this example is described by the following transfer function:

$$G_2(s) = \frac{k}{s^2 + a_2 s + a_1} \tag{12}$$

Where

$$k = 1 + \Delta k \qquad \text{with} \quad -0.5 < \Delta k < 2,$$
$$a_2 = 1.4 + \Delta a_2 \qquad \text{with} \quad -2 < \Delta a2 < 2$$
$$a_1 = 1 + \Delta a_{1r} \qquad \text{with} \quad -3 < \Delta a1 < 3$$

The desired closed loop response has been specified by:

$$y'' + 1.4y' + y = y_d \tag{13}$$

Figure (11.a) represents the desired response and Figure (11.b) represents the undesturbed response with SOQC controller. The obtained response is comparable to the desired one.

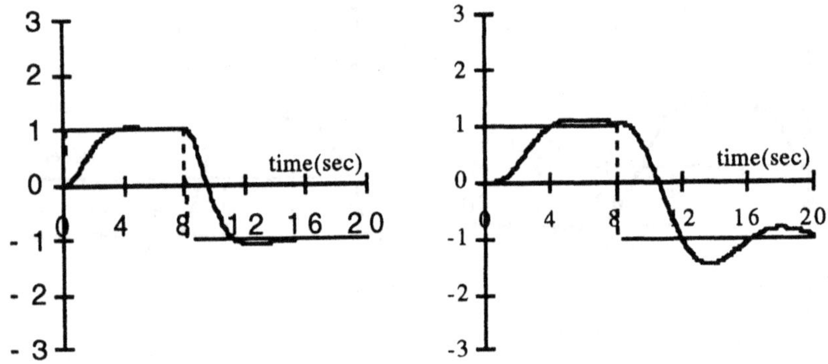

(a) Desired response (b)Undisturbed response

Fig.11. The system response using SOQC controller

5. CONCLUSIONS

A new methodology has been proposed to model and to control ill-defined systems. This method is based on a learning approach to follow the system evaluation. The simulation results showed that the proposed method is powerful enough to identify the system parameters and to achieve regulation and tracking objectives in control. This method also improves the overall system response rather than classical qualitative control.

References

1. K. Forbus: Qualitative process theory. Artificial Intelligence, Vol.24, pp.85-168,(1984)

2. J. De Kleer, J. S. Brown: A qualitative physics based on confluenc. Artificial Intelligence, Vol.24, n°.1-3, pp.7-83, (1984)

3. B.kuipers: Common sense reasoning about causality: deriving behaviour from structure.Artificial Intelligence, n°. 24, pp.169-203, (1984)

4. M.M. Kokar & J. J Reeves: Qualitative monitoring of time varying physical system", Proc. 29 th IEEE CDC, Honolulu, 1990.

5. R.C.Arkin & G. Vachtsevanos: Qualitative fault propagation in complex systems", Proc. 29 th IEEE CDC, Honolulu, 1990.

6. D. L. Dovrak, D. T. Dalle Molle, B. Kuipers and T. F. Edgar: Qualitative simulation for expert systems", 11th IFAC world congress, Vol.7, USSR, 1990, pp.204-209

7. B. Kuipers: Qualitative simulatio. Artificial Intelligence, Vol.29, 289-338, (1986)

8. J. A. Franklin: What is qualitative reasoning, and can we use it for control ?. Proc. 29th IEEE CDC, Honolulu-Hawaii, U.S.A., 1990 pp.1487-1492,

9. W. F. Clocksin, A. J. Morgan: Qualitative control. Proc. 7th European Conference on Artificial Intelligence, Brighton, U. K., Vol.1, 1986, pp.350-356

10. M. K. Masten and H. E. Cohen: A showcase of adaptive controller designs.Int. J. of Adaptive Control and Signal Processing, vol.3, pp.95-101, (1989)

11. M. K. Masten and H. E. Cohen: An advanced showcase of adaptive controller designs. Int. J. of Adaptive Control and Signal Processing, vol.4, pp.89-98, (1990)

12. B. Abdulmajid, R. J. Wynne: Initial experience in applying qualitative reasoning to Process control", Proc. 28th IEEE CDC, Florida U.S.A., 1989, pp.783-784,

MoHA, an Hybrid Learning Model

A model based on the perception of the environment by an individual

François Bordeaux, Françoise Forest, Brigitte Grau

LIMSI - CNRS
BP 133, 91403 Orsay Cedex
bordeaux@limsi.fr, forest@limsi.fr, grau@limsi.fr

Abstract. The aim of this contribution is the presentation of a dynamic model of learning. It combines the massively parallel treatment of data for the emergence of stable concepts, and the symbolic manipulation of these concepts in schemas representing the pragmatic knowledge which one can build from his experience.
Following Vygotsky, we assume that the spontaneous concepts and the pragmatic knowledge are built from the experience anyone acquires during his everyday life, both by the accumulation of material contributing to this experience and by the mean of top-down learning.

1 Introduction

We focus on the automatic acquisition of semantic and pragmatic knowledge from linguistic data. The main object of this work is to take into account the versatility of knowledge of an individual while his experience is growing. We assume that learning is not only bottom-up generalization. It also requires to relate new information to already structured knowledge which will partly lead the learning process by means of top-down interactions between different levels.
We also assume that learning is not a specific task. It's a permanent process, still active during the course of integration of new events.

To take these phenomena into account, we propose an hybrid model which combines numeric and symbolic approaches.
The first one consists in a massively parallel treatment of real-life events through their perception by one individual. They are modelized in a connectionist type network. Our purpose is to obtain emergent concepts from the accumulation of events observations.
Through the second approach, the concepts depend on high level knowledge such as schemas. An incremental learning of these schemas is performed by using symbolic treatments such as analogy, generalization and specification.

2 Few ideas from Vygotsky

What is a perception, a word, a concept, a plan and a schema, an action? How do all these notions behave together? How do they depend on the others? Can they exist without the others? Could general behavior of an individual, communication and understanding be modelized without these notions? Vygotsky [12, 13] has studied the concept formation in the childhood and argues for the central position of language in the construction of the system of concepts upon which can be built the conscious reasoning and social behavior of the adult. His approach for the representation of meaning is constructivist : "The concept appears in the process of an intellectual operation... a concept appears only because it is the result of the resolution of a problem."[1]

Although it is very simplified, our model is based on Vygotsky's approach of concept learning by the child.

2.1 The stage of complexes, based on experience

Concepts grow through experience and the use of language, that is to say the verbal interaction between the child and its social environment, especially its parents. Vygotsky makes distinction between the functional concepts, which can already be observed through the animals' behavior, and the concepts which are built through the use of language. For the later kind of concepts, the importance of the word is fundamental. Given by the adult, the word stands for the name of a family of objects and situations observed by the child; Vygotsky calls these families *complexes.*

2.2 The two roots of the construction of concepts

The two opposite directions followed during the building of a concept are *generalization* and *differentiation.* Generalization goes from the set of real situations covered by a same word, to the recognition of a similarity when a new situation appears. Differentiation involves the capacity to recognize which features allow a situation to be agreed for the use of a word and which don't. Therefore, this abstraction of isolated features is necessary to reach the stage of adult concepts.

2.3 The central place of the word

Concepts are always growing and changing. They are concepts because they take place in a system. They exist only because they are related to other concepts by mean of which they can be described by similitude or differentiation, generalization or specification. The ability of using already known concepts to build a new one, and to insert it in a structure, cannot be done without the medium of the words. This is the problem of verbalisation, consciousness and the capacity of reasoning.

---

[1]The quotation is translated from the french text [Vygotsky 85], the corresponding paragraph being absent of the english translation [Vygotsky 62].

2.4 Attention and motivation

The attention, as a tool for structuring, is present in Vygotsky's work. It focuses on special features which become central for the definition of the concept. Besides, no concept can be built without a motivation. Although this idea is not central in Vygotsky's work, it seems to us that it must be present in our model. To survive may be a motivation, but to be loved or to catch sweets can be others. They correspond to plans of actions, very well known by the child, even if he is not able to explain the successive steps of these plans.

From the perception of situations to the plans and schemas which guide the individual in his building and use of concepts, we can exhibit three main levels of integration of its knowledge.
These three different levels represent the different degrees of integration of the experience of the individual. Links are built to allow the bottom-up and top-down interactions between them. The perceptions may reinforce concepts and schemas. Already built concepts and schemas can be used to interpret or select new perceptions.

3 The three levels of MoHA

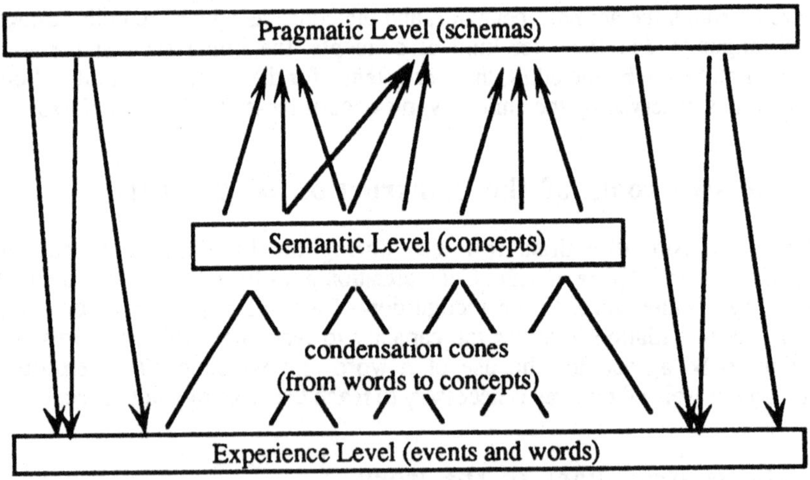

Fig. 1. Knowledge representation levels and their relations

3.1 Experience level

The individual perceives events of the real world, some of them more outstanding than others. Each primitive of perception contributes, more or less, to the building of the images of the events. We assume the primitives to be words and the images to be sets of sentences[1]. The set of images is represented by a net in which the degrees of importance are conveyed by numerical data bound to nodes and links [5].

The step of learning as it is used in neural nets is replaced, in our model, by the accumulation of perceptions of different situations, through sets of perceptions and sentences. So, the child associates perceptions and words, in reference to situations. These situations range from the simple observation of concrete objects, to very complex scenes that the child only perceives globally, associating them to a set of sensations and impressions. The phenomenon of association is modelized by a net binding the events being observed and the sensations, perceptions and words involved in the memorization of these events. At the beginning, the events only concern concrete objects, and the sentences are limited to isolated words. So, the child builds complexes around a word which stands for the family name of this category of objects. The agreement or opposition of the adults when the child uses the word helps him to find which characteristics are pertinent to group all the examples with the same name, and to reject all the others. So, the child "feels" what makes an object to be "a dog", for instance, and another one not "a dog". Next step is when the child discovers, with help of the adult, the name of those characteristics; at that time, he is developing from the stage of complexes to the stage of real adult concepts, being able of including them inside a structure, by mean of words. That leads us to put these words in an intermediate level between the experience and the semantic levels which they contribute to enrich and bind.

3.2 Semantic level

It is represented by a classic semantic network adapted from Sowa's conceptual graphs [10]. We only give here a rough description of the formalism. The semantic network is made of *a types lattice*, which represents the hierarchical structuring between the types of concepts, and *canonical graphs* which represent the default ways of linking concepts and relations together. This formalism has not been chosen according to specificities of our model, but because our model will be included in a general one which uses this representation formalism.
The concepts are bound to sets of words of the experience level which participate to their formation. As the experience is increasing, the concepts necessarily evolve. They are bound to the situations in which they appear in the upper level of pragmatic knowledge.

3.3 Pragmatic level

It consists in the set of prototypical situations which are described by a graph of schemas [7]. These situations are the generalization of particular events perceived at the experience level. Close to Shank's MOP's [11], the model allows different levels

---

[1] By choosing words to be those primitives of perception, we place ourselves at the stage of development of the child, when he "passes from primitive wordless perception to perception of objects guided by and expressed in words"[Vygotsky 62, p90].

of description (from a most general point of view to a most precise) and thus, avoids too specific descriptions. Pragmatics is then represented by a graph constituted of small units: the schemas. These ones are hierarchically related and use other schemas which are constrained by specifications that will allow us to adapt the level of the description to the situation itself.
More precisely, a schema is characterized by several elements :

- its name, which is composed of two concepts (a predicate and an object), and the case that joins them. The predicate indicates the point of view from which the object is considered. It provides a direct manner to associate a schema with a sentence.
- a set of slots, i.e. attributes. The names of the slots are CONDITION, DESCRIPTION, RESULT, TIME, PLACE, plus the names of the cases associated with the predicate. The values of these attributes can be references to a concept in the semantic net or references to other schemas. This last kind of value creates descriptive links in the graph of schemas.

A schema represents the notion of *causality*: Some slots describe the condition under which a schema will apply, the description of its contents and its results. Inside these slots, the constituents may be ordered.
Flexibility of the model is enhanced by the possibility of pointing out an order upon the schemas that fill in a slot as well as indicating if they are requested or optional.
A weight is also associated to the concepts used to describe each schema: it represents their respective importance in the described situation. These concepts will also allow us to select schemas from the literal meaning of the sentences and to give a measure of their pertinence according to the description of an event.

3.4 Conclusion

The formalisms used for the representation of the different kinds of knowledge must allow to browse from one level to another. Thus, we have adapted them in this way. At this time, we have realized a propagation mechanism which works inside SL, from SL to PL, inside PL and from PL to SL. The propagation mechanism is parameterized in order to be influenced by the kinds of relations between concepts in the canonical graphs and by the relative importance of the concepts inside a schema. Thus, the propagation may be guided if necessary.
The three levels, because of their links, allow each of them to influence the organization of the two others and give the possibility of browsing during the understanding process. This possibility is of great importance :

(i) it allows the modelling of the development of the knowledge whilst the experience is growing,
(ii) the levels represent different kinds of abstraction,
(iii) abstractions being generalizations, specific information might be lost, so backtracking to the experience level may be needed to sharpen the understanding.

4 Description of the behaviour of MoHA

One of the main functionalities of the general process which manages the interactions between cognitive levels is to ensure the duality between stability and plasticity.

Stability, because we want to use the semantic and pragmatic knowledge already acquired by the model in order to analyze the new experiences. Plasticity, because the acquired knowledge may change: when new experiences are strong enough to modify the interpretation of the previous experiences, the model must be able to reorganize the semantic and pragmatic knowledge. The other constraint for the general process is the difficulty in involving pieces of knowledge of different types in the interactions.
At last, our model has two different ways of functioning : reorganization of the semantic level and current treatment of new events.

4.1 Adaptive Resonance Theory and MoHA

The Adaptive Resonance Theory (ART) introduced by Grossberg [9] provides a suitable framework for our model. ART makes possible to recognize or build cognitive categories from a set of individual experiences. Moreover, ART has been already used in speech processing systems, which were made of several cognitive levels [3].
Against many connexionist models, as retropropagation for instance, the learning phase in ART does not precede the utilization phase. Both are simultaneous. The fact that ART can learn without any exterior supervisor is an important point in order to modelize the behaviour of a human being, who learns regularly new pieces of knowledge in his day to day life.

Among the different models developed by Grossberg et al. around the Adaptive Resonance Theory, accent has been placed in ART 3 on the implementation of several cognitive levels in cascade [2]. The levels are activated one after the other, starting from the lowest level. In our model, the lowest level corresponds to the experience level and the highest level corresponds to the pragmatic level.
The opposition stability/plasticity appears when we activate a given cognitive level from a lower one. Once we have activated all the units of the lower level, the model must find in the higher level the pieces of knowledge (i.e.,. the cognitive categories) corresponding to the lower level units. One or several units corresponding to the most plausible category are then activated in the higher level (at first, all the units of the higher level are activated in parallel, and the most activated unit remains active, following a competitive mechanism). In our model, if this category doesn't fit enough the units activated in the lower level, the Consistency Controller is the process which decides to continue sequentially the searching process and select an other unit of the higher level. Stability is reached when the system manages to find a unit on the higher level corresponding to the activation of the lower level. Otherwise, there is plasticity.
The fact that the units of the higher level are studied sequentially is not really a minus, in spite of the huge knowledge managed by the system. The biggest part of the processing is done in parallel, when we search the most plausible unit of the higher level among all the eligible units.
The Consistency Controller ensures consistency between the units activated in two consecutive levels. Taking into account a cascade of several cognitive levels, we can have, in a model inspired by ART 3, a single controller which ensures consistency in all the model.

4.2 Interactions between different levels

The interactions between cognitive levels are not as simple as they could seem at first glance, because inside the semantic and pragmatic levels, the knowledge is hierarchically organized. We consider that the concepts of the semantic level may activate non terminal schemas of the pragmatic level. Conversely, the schemas can activate concepts of the semantic level, whatever the hierarchical level of the concepts. So, although we assign only one layer to each of the three cognitive levels, we must allow extra links between units inside a given layer in order to account for the hierarchical relations inside concepts layer and inside schemas layer. We have then two types of links between units : the links which make possible competition between units (these links are necessary for ART processing, during the selection of the suitable categories), and the links which set a semantic relation (hierarchical or other) between units.

As regards the interactions between experience level and semantic level, our model differs from ART in the fact that we want it to memorize each of the individual experiences that has been "lived", and use these experiences to build knowledge of superior level. ART does not allow that kind of total memorization of experiences. A complete experience is kept in memory only if it is the only experience of its category; otherwise ART models only keep in LMT the features common to several experiences and loose the specific details.

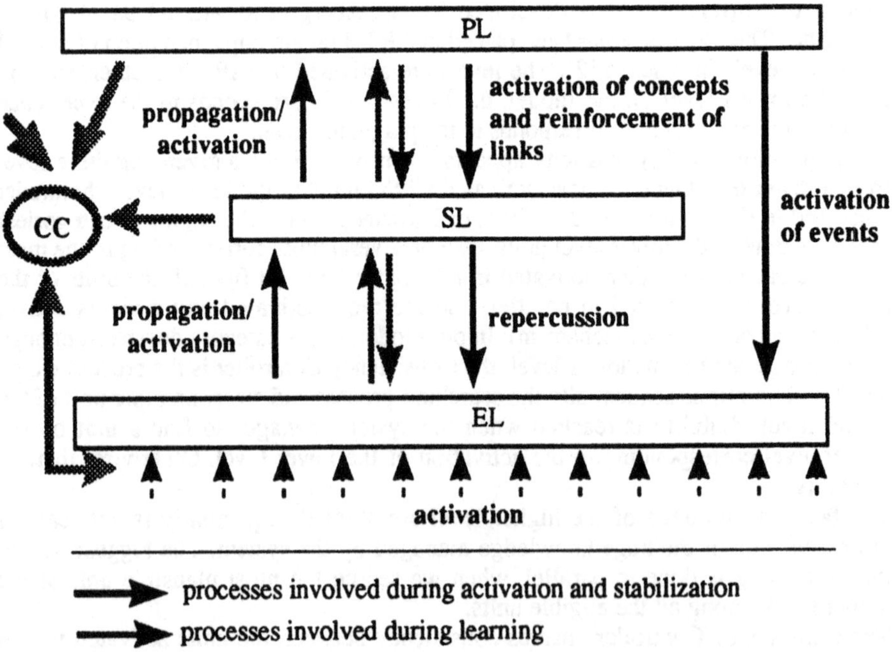

CC, consistency controller, decides what is relevant, and when learning is necessary.

Fig. 2. The processes in action while an event is perceived

Two ways of functioning. Learning can occur in both cases, stability or plasticity. When stability is reached, only minor changes can alter the content of the LMT. On the other side, when stability is not reached (i.e.,. no suitable category is found), two cases can be distinguished : adding a new category to the higher level (when there is really no similarity between the data of the lower level and the knowledge of the higher level), or reorganizing the higher level (when there are some similarities, but also too many differences). In the latter case, learning is done with a massively parallel approach, taking into account the current experience and all the previous experiences that the system has perceived).

Adding a new category. Creating a new category is very similar to what is done in ART. But, at the difference of what is done in ART, the new category has to be included in the system of concepts already built. This could imply, for instance, the creation of new hierarchical links among the new concept and the other ones. The creation of a new category may even influence the structure of schemas at the pragmatic level.

Reorganization of the semantic level. The bottom-up interactions are involved in the creation and reorganization of the semantic level. In this phase, we use a connectionist approach. Propagation of activations in the experience level leads to the detection of "attractors" which will stand for concepts. The kind of propagation is strongly bound to the numerical data involved in the perception of the events. That's why we now plan to test, both on a sequential and a massively parallel computer, how the classical data analysis and connectionist stabilization methods behave, depending on the value of those numerical data [6]. Results obtained by Crucianu & Memmi [4] about the emergence of structures will be taken into account. Psychological observations argue for non symmetric connections within the experience level. From that arises the main difficulty in the use of classical methods.

An hybrid perspective. We have already seen that the system will integrate modules which will not belong to Adaptive Resonance Theory. Other modules will be integrated to the system, especially as regards the management of the top level knowledge (i.e.,. the pragmatic level) in a symbolic way. In this hybrid perspective, ART and the symbolic modules may work in a cooperative manner.

Symbolic processes of natural language understanding are used to interpret the sentences describing the events [7].

If an interpretation is possible, some schemas are selected and a repercussion takes place towards the other levels. Concepts and relations are activated or reinforced and this modification of the activation state spreads in EL. This whole process corresponds to the stabilization phenomenon.

On the other hand, when the symbolic interpretation fails, the model is in a position of learning. Therefore, we try to create new schemas by studying activated concepts and their relations in accordance to the activated schemas and the concepts they contain. The results will lead to apply analogy, generalization or specialization processes [8] and then to possibly propose the creation of new concepts and new relations between them. This can lead to a partial reorganization of PL and SL. At this stage, we consider the possibility of an intervention of the supervisor to decide about this opportunity in the consistency maintenance purpose.

During learning, a model based on ART can be influenced by a supervisor. Several ways can be used to correct the model when it sets up his categories. The easiest of these ways is to raise or decrease the vigilance parameter, so that the system pays more or less attention to details. The behaviour of the model with regard to learning may be also determined by other processes extern to ART.
We can even consider that the vigilance parameter may be raised or decreased by the model itself, according to an "emotional" state. In situations considered as critical by the model, the vigilance level would be raised, and so the sensibility of the model would also be raised.

5 Conclusion

We have presented here the general aims and characteristics of a model for learning. We are aware of the great deal of work to do before it could realistically behaves like an individual learning from experience, even in a small domain. But it still remains for us a very fruitful challenge as far as it faces different problems well-known in computational linguistics community. The problem of automatic learning from massive data is a problem whose solution is far from easy. But some interesting works have already been done in the field of connexionism applied to the emergence of concepts from experience, although the problem of coding perception is not really satisfactory. It seems to us that such an orientation of research must be explored, as far as everybody is able of that kind of learning, and that these massive data is of an easy access for computers.
The problem of measurement of the distance between the understanding of different individuals, or between the different meanings of a sentence, depending on the individuals concerned would profit of a new approach. That is why we think that defining the notion of linguistic community from the community of experience of a set of individuals could lead us to new solutions.

References

1. Bradski G., Carpenter G.A., & Grossberg S. Working Memory Networks for Learning Temporal Order with Application to Three-Dimensional Visual Object Recognition., In Neural Computation, Vol4, NB 2, 1991

2. Carpenter G.A., & Grossberg S. , ART 3: Hierarchical Search Using Chemical Transmitters in Self-Organizing Pattern Recognition Architectures, in Neural Networks, Vol.3 (129-152), 1990

3. Cohen M.A., Grossberg S., & Stork D. Speech perception and production by a self-organizing neural network. in Y.C. Lee (Ed.), Proceedings of the International Joint Conference on Neural Networks IEEE, Washington DC, 1988

4. Crucianu M. & Memmi D., Extraction de la structure implicite dans un réseau connexionniste, Notes & rapports internes du LIMSI, Octobre 1991

5. Forest F., Le sens d'un énoncé est fondamentalement lié à l'expérience de l'individu qui le perçoit, 4ème colloque de l'ARC, Paris, 28-30 Mars 1990

6. Forest F., Le traitement massivement parallèle des données dans le domaine de la représentation du sens en langage naturel, Notes & rapports internes du LIMSI, Novembre 1991

7. Grau B., Stalking coherence in the 'topical' jungle, International conference on the fifth generation computer systems, Tokyo, 1984.

8. Grau B. & Sabah G., Vers un apprentissage automatique de connaissances pragmatiques, Cognitiva, Paris, 1985.

9. Grossberg S., Competitive learning: From interactive activation to adaptive resonance, Cognitive Science, 11, pp23-63, 1987

10. Sabah G. & Vilnat A., Flexible case structure implemented into a deterministic parser, 6th International Workshop on Conceptual Graphs, SUNY at Binghamton (NY), 1991

11. Schank R.C., Dynamic memory, Cambridge University Press, 1982

12. Vygotsky L.S., Thought and language, MIT Press, Cambridge-Mass., 1962

13. Vygotsky L.S., Pensée et langage, Editions Sociales, Paris, 1985

A New Perspective in the Inductive Acquisition of Knowledge from Examples

Gabriel Fiol   José Miró-Nicolau   José Miró-Julià

University of the Balearic Islands
Departament de Ciències Matemàtiques i Informàtica
Crra. de Valldemosa, Km. 7.5
07071 Palma de Mallorca, Spain

Abstract. In this paper we describe a new perspective in the Inductive Acquisition of Knowledge from Examples, based on three fundamental concepts: the *Object Attribute Table* (OAT), the *Base of Attributes* and *Optimality Criteria* and on a two step solution. The OAT constitutes an extensional description about some concepts to be intensionally described. To transform the knowledge from the OAT into an intensional form, the two step solution must be taken:

i. To obtain an optimal set of attributes or qualities to describe the concepts.

ii. To obtain an optimal intensional description based on the attributes obtained in the former step.

Each step is based on a optimality criterion and the two optimality criteria of the two steps are completely independent. The subset of attributes obtained in the first step is called a base of attributes.

1 Introduction

The task of the main stage of most Inductive Learning Systems is *Knowledge Acquisition from Examples* . It is in charge of the transfer of knowledge from the *Environment* to the intensional *Knowledge Base*. The knowledge received from the Environment is extensional in the form of examples, each one of which constitutes a concrete portion of information about some concepts. Knowledge Acquisition consists of transforming the information provided by the examples in order to find intensional descriptions of the concepts (this process is also called *Concept Generalization*).

From the many contributions to this subject, we summarize some of the main ones:

The AQ11 Method, proposed in [4], creates a general description from a given set of positive examples and another set of negative examples, using the language VL1 [4]. It uses the detailed description of properties of the first set not in the second one. The result is given in the form of decision rules.

The ID3 (Iterative Dicotomizer 3) Method, described in [8], generates a *decision tree* from a set of elements characterized by some attributes, using an *entropy* function to select the attributes on which to basis the decision. This method has an elegant central concept and an easy implementation.

The concept of *Rough Set*, described by Pawlak in [7] was developed through a study of approximate description of a subset, starting a whole area of research. The concept of *core*, defined in [9], is useful in finding the *reduct* of attributes to be used in the description of the subset. Although, the concept of *reduct* [6] does not always yield an optimal description of the subsets [1].

In this paper we present a new theoretical approach about the concept generalization, based on the subset descriptions [5]. In this approach some concepts are initially defined by a set of examples or specific cases of knowledge about the concepts. The generalization of a concept consists in finding a property satisfied by all the elements (or examples) which establish initially the concept and only by them; that is to say, in finding a property that allows the intensional description of the subset of elements which define originally the concept. Three concepts are essential in this approach: the *Object Attribute Table* (OAT) which defines the specification model of the specific elements of knowledge, the *Optimality Criteria* describing the characteristics of the desired solution for the particular problem, and the concept of *Base of Attributes* in terms of which the general solution is expressed.

Accordingly, the proposed problem can be stated as follows: 'Find an intensional description of some subsets of an extensionally defined domain'.

2 Formulation of the Problem and Knowledge Representation

The problem we will study can be formally described as follow:

Let $D = \{d_1, d_2, \ldots, d_m\}$ be an extensionally defined set of elements or examples and $R=\{r_1, r_2, \ldots, r_n\}$ an extensionally defined set of attributes (binary or multivalued), such that for each $d_j \in D$ the values of these attributes are known. Given the extensional subsets $D_i= \{d_a, d_b, \ldots, d_c\}$,, $i = 1, 2, \ldots, k$, $D \supseteq D_i$ we want to find an intensional description P_i, $i = 1, 2, \ldots, k$, of these subsets, $D_i = \{d_j \in D / P_i\}$, $i = 1, 2, \ldots, k$, that is *optimal* under some criterion; moreover, P_i will be expressed in terms of a subset R_x, $R \supseteq R_x$ of the attributes. Before to find an optimal intensional description P_i, one must find an optimal subset R_x of the attributes such that P_i can be expressed as a function of R_x.

The information from the examples will be stored in the *Object Attribute Table (OAT)*, defined as follows:

Definition 1. The OAT is defined as a four-tuple as follows:

OAT = <D, R, V, F>, where

$D = \{d_1, d_2, \ldots, d_m\}$ is a set of elements or concrete objects of knowledge.

$R = \{r_1, r_2, \ldots, r_n\}$ is a set of qualities or attributes.

$V = \{V_1, V_2, \ldots, V_n\}$ is a family of sets, such that V_i is the set of values of the attribute r_i adopted by the elements of D. V_i is also called the domain of r_i.

$F = \{f_1, f_2, \ldots, f_n\}$ is a set of functions that defines extensionally the values that each $d_i \in D$ takes for each attribute $r_j \in R$, that is, f_i: $D \times \{r_i\} \rightarrow V_i$, $i = 1 \ldots n$.

The Subset Definition Table (SDT), establishes, in a format compatible with that of the OAT, the subsets (or concepts) whose intensional description is desired.

Definition 2 The SDT is defined as a three-tuple as follows:

SDT = <D, C, f> where

D has the same meaning that in definition 1, C is a set of w concepts, $1 \leq w \leq m$, and the function f assigns to each element of D its corresponding concept, that is, $f: D \rightarrow C$.

The discussion of the problem becomes easier by representing graphically the OAT and the SDT, as in figure 1. We will refer to the Enlarged Object Attribute Table (Enlarged OAT); $t_i^k \in V_k$, $k = 1...n$, $i = 1...m$, is the value of the attribute r_k associated to the element d_i through the function f_k, $c_i \in C$ is the concept associated at the element $d_i \in D$, $i = 1...m$. Let us observe that the function f defines extensionally disjoint subsets of D, each one of which is composed of all the elements $d_i \in D$ establishing the same concept. They are the subsets to be intensionally described.

We use the decision-tree structure to represent the intensional description of the subsets D_i. The formal definition of a decision-tree is summarizaed in definition 3.

Definition 3. A decision-tree is a tree such that:

i. Each inner node is identified by one attribute of R and it contain as many direct descendents (or child nodes) as values are contained in its domain. That is to say, if r_i is an inner node, this node has $|V_i|$ child nodes, where $|V_i|$ is the cardinal of V_i. Each branch connecting a father node r_i with one child node is labeled by one value of V_i and it defines an equivalence class in D from V_i.

ii. Each leaf node (or terminal node) corresponds to only one concept of C.

Each inner node r_i can be interpreted as a decision. A path from the root of the decision-tree down to a leaf node is a x-tuple of attribute-value couples $((r_i, t_i), (r_j, t_j), ...,(r_k, t_k))$, where x is the number of inner nodes over which one must decide from the root of the decision-tree down to the leaf node; $r_i, r_j, ..., r_k$ are the attributes identifying the inner nodes of the path and $t_i \in V_i$, $t_j \in V_j$, ..., $t_k \in V_k$ are the results of the decisions over $r_i, r_j, ..., r_k$ respectively. Notice that a path from the root down to a leaf node defines an equivalence class over D.

Let T be a decision-tree with k leaf nodes. The number of decisions to classify all the elements of D using the tree T is:

$$DN_T = \Sigma_{i=1...k} n_i * |d_i| \qquad [2.1]$$

where d_i is the i-th leaf node, $|d_i|$ is the number of elements of D contained in the equivalence class defined by the path from the root of the decision-tree down to the leaf node d_i and n_i is the number of decisions (inner nodes) in this path.

3 Preliminary Discussion

Consider an arbitrary enlarged OAT. Each row contains the complete information about one example, represented by a (n+2)-tuple as follow: $(d_i, t_i^1, t_i^2, ..., t_i^n, c_i)$, where $d_i \in D$, $i = 1...m$, is the name or identifier of the example, $t_i^j \in V_j$, $j = 1...n$, are the values of the n attributes $r_1, r_2, ..., r_n$ respectively, and $c_i \in C$ is the concept associated at the example. This information can be interpreted in the following way: ' the example d_i has the value t_i^1 for the attribute r_1 and the value t_i^2 for the attribute r_2 and... and the value t_i^n for the attribute r_n and belongs to the concept c_i'. Since the mentioned problem in section 2 is focused exclusively on describing the concepts in terms of the attributes without taking into account the identifier of the examples, then one can forget the first term of the (n+2)-tuple, resulting the following (n+1)-tuple: $(t_i^1, t_i^2, ..., t_i^n, c_i)$. The solution of the proposed problem depends on the information provided by the 'n' attributes of the OAT being 'adequate' to describe all the subsets of D (or concepts of C).

D \ R	r_1	r_2	. . .	r_n	C
d_1	t_1^1	t_1^2	. . .	t_1^n	c_1
d_2	t_2^1	t_2^2	. . .	t_2^n	c_2
.	.	.		.	.
.	.	.		.	.
.	.	.		.	.
d_m	t_m^1	t_m^2	. . .	t_m^n	c_m

Fig. 1. Enlarged OAT

In order to define the term 'adequate', some concepts must be introduced.

Definition 4 Let $R_x=\{r_i, r_j,..., r_k\}$ be a subset of x attributes of the OAT, $R \supseteq R_x$. A (x+1)-tuple $(t_s^i, t_s^j, ..., t_s^k, c_s), 1 \leq s \leq m$, made up of the values of the attributes of R_x in the same row 's' in the enlarged OAT and the corresponding concept, is called an *instance* of R_x respect to C. Observe that this particular instance corresponds to $d_s \in D$.

Definition 5 Let $(t_s^i, t_s^j, ..., t_s^k, c_s)$ be an arbitrary instance of R_x respect to C. $(t_s^i, t_s^j, ..., t_s^k)$ is called the *left side* of the instance and (c_s) is called the *right side* of the instance.

Definition 6 Two instances of R_x respect to C are *contradictory* instances if and only if their left sides are identical whereas they have different right sides.

Definition 7 The set of all the instances of R_x respect to C is called the *Instance Set of R_x respect to C* and denoted by $IS_{R_x}{}^C$.

Possibly, the enlarged OAT will contain some identical instances of R_x respect to C, in such a case it is enough to consider only one representative instance of the class, thus $IS_{R_x}{}^C$ will be considered a set of equivalence class of elements of D.

The complete information provided by the n attributes of R respect to C is $IS_R{}^C$ and it is considered adequate to describe the concepts of C if $IS_R{}^C$ contains no couples of contradictory instances, else it is not adequate. If the information provided by $IS_R{}^C$ is not adequate then it is not possible to describe the concepts of C in terms of the attributes of R. If it is adequate there may exist more than one way to describe them.

Definition 8 For a given subset R_x, $R \supseteq R_x$, of attributes, if $IS_{R_x}{}^C$ contains no couple of contradictory instances then R_x is called a *Base of Attributes* (or simply *Base*) of R respect to C.

A basis of attributes is a subset of attributes whose instance set is adequate. Numerous bases may exist, the selection of a particular one to describe the concepts must depend on the characteristics of the particular case.

Some important properties to speed up the process to finding bases are discussed in the sequel.

Theorem 9 There exist at least one basis in R respect to C if and only if R is a basis respect to C.

Proof. →) Let $R_y=\{r_i, r_j,..., r_k\}$, $R \supseteq R_y$, a basis of y attributes respect to C. From definition 8, $IS_{R_y}{}^C$ contains no couples of contradictory instances. Each instance of R_y can be obtained from some instance of R by removing the values of the attributes which are not in R_y. Consequently, since of $IS_{R_y}{}^C$ has no contradictory instances, neither has $IS_R{}^C$.

←) It is immediate since R is a basis respect to C.

[e.o.p][1]

Theorem 10 establishes the conditions under which one can obtain directly bases from previously obtained ones.

Theorem 10 Let R_y, $R \supseteq R_y$, be a basis of attributes respect to C. Any subset R_z, $R \supseteq R_z$, such that $R_z \supseteq R_y$, is also a basis of R respect to C.

Proof. Each instance of R_y can be obtained from some instance of R_z by removing the values of the attributes which are not in R_y. Consequently, since $IS_{R_y}{}^C$ contains no contradictory instances, neither does $IS_{R_x}{}^C$.

[e.o.p]

Corollary 11 Let R_y, $R \supseteq R_y$, be a subset of attributes such that R_y is not a basis of R respect to C. Any subset R_x, $R \supseteq R_x$, such that $R_y \supseteq R_x$, is not a basis.

Proof. It is immediate, since each instance of R_x can be obtained from some instance of R_y and so, if two instances of R_y are contradictory instances then the instances of R_x obtained from them are also contradictory.

[e.o.p]

Another properties may be found in [1].

Example 1 Let us consider the following OAT and SDT:

OAT = <D, R, V, F>, where

$D = \{d_1, d_2, d_3, d_4, d_5, d_6\}$

$R = \{r_1, r_2, r_3\}$

$V = \{V_1, V_2, V_3\}$, $V_i=\{0, 1\}$, $i = 1...2$, $V_3 = \{a, b, c, d, e\}$

$F = \{f_1, f_2, f_3\}$, where f_i, $i = 1...3$, are illustrated on the enlarged OAT of figure 2.

For the SDT we have: SDT = <D, C, f>, where

D is already known; $C = \{c_1, c_2, c_3\}$ is the set of concepts and $f: D \to C$ is defined in the enlarged OAT of figure 2.

Each instance of R respect to C is a 4-tuple and the Instance Set of R respect to C, $IS_R{}^C$, is: $IS_R{}^C = \{(0, 0, a, c_1), (1, 0, c, c_3), (0, 0, d, c_1), (0, 1, a, c_3), (1, 1, b, c_2), (0, 1, e, c_3)\}$. The remaining Instance Sets[2] are:

---

[1] The term [e.o.p] indicates the end of the proof

[2] In this example we use the notation $R_{x,ij...k}$ to represent the subset of x attributes $\{r_i, r_j,..., r_k\}$, that is $R_{x,ij...k} = \{r_i, r_j,..., r_k\}$. The instance set of $R_{x,ij...k}$ is denoted by $IS_{R_{x,ij...k}}{}^C$. Thus, for example, the Instance Set of $R_{x,12} = \{r_1, r_2\}$ is denoted by $IS_{R_{x,12}}{}^C$.

• For the set of attributes $R_{1,1} = \{r_1\}$, $IS_{R_{1,1}}{}^C = \{(0, c_1), (0, c_3), (1, c_2), (1, c_3)\}$.

• For $R_{1,2} = \{r_2\}$, $IS_{R_{1,2}}{}^C = \{(0, c_1), (0, c_3), (1, c_2), (1, c_3)\}$.

• For $R_{1,3} = \{r_3\}$, $IS_{R_{1,3}}{}^C = \{(a, c_1), (a, c_3), (b, c_2), (c, c_3), (d, c_1), (e, c_3)\}$.

• For $R_{2,12} = \{r_1, r_2\}$, $IS_{R_{2,12}}{}^C = \{(0, 0, c_1), (1, 0, c_3), (0, 1, c_3), (1, 1, c_2)\}$.

• For $R_{2,13} = \{r_1, r_3\}$, $IS_{R_{2,13}}{}^C = \{(0, a, c_1), (0, a, c_3), (0, d, c_1), (0, e, c_3), (1, b, c_2), (1, c, c_3)\}$.

• For $R_{2,23} = \{r_2, r_3\}$, $IS_{R_{2,23}}{}^C = \{(0, a, c_1), (0, c, c_3), (0, d, c_1), (1, a, c_3), (1, b, c_2), (1, e, c_3)\}$.

D	R: r_1	r_2	r_3	C
d_1	0	0	a	c_1
d_2	1	0	c	c_3
d_3	0	0	d	c_1
d_4	0	1	a	c_3
d_5	1	1	b	c_2
d_6	0	1	e	c_3

Fig. 2. Graphic representation of an enlarged OAT

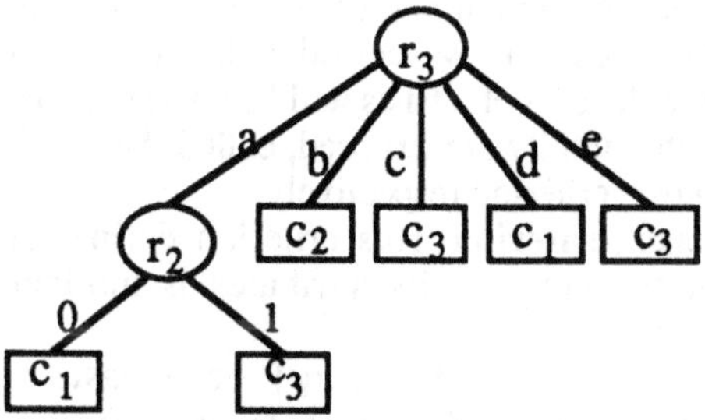

Fig. 3. A decision-tree

There exist three bases of attributes in R respect to C: the subsets of attributes $R_{2,12}$, $R_{2,23}$ and the set R of all the attributes.

A possible decision-tree constructed by using attributes r_2 and r_3 is shown in figure 3, where inner nodes are represented by circles and leaf nodes by rectangles. [e.o.e][3]

---

[3] The term [e.o.e] indicates the end of the example

4 A Two Step Solution

In order to obtain an optimal intensional description P_i, i = 1...k, for each subset (or concept) $D_i \in D$, that is, $D_i = \{d_j \in D/P_i\}$, j = 1...m, expressed in terms of a subset R_x, $R \supseteq R_x$, of attributes, two steps must be taken:

1. Find an optimal subset of attributes R_x, $R \supseteq R_x$, which will be used to describe the subsets D_i, i=1...k.

2. Once R_x has been obtained then find an optimal intensional description of D_i, i = 1...k, based on the attributes of R_x.

R_x must be a basis of attributes of R respect to C. Thus, in the first step one must obtain an optimal basis. In general, the optimality criteria of the two steps are independent: Once R_x is determined, several different descriptions, optimal under different criteria can be found without having to recompute the subset of attributes. The optimality criterion to be used and therefore the solution to be found, depends solely on the nature of the particular problem.

4.1 Optimal Base Selection Criteria

Two types of optimality criteria to select bases are introduced. One based on a *cost* associated to each attributes (what this cost might be depends on the nature of the problem); the other, on *decision-tree structural relations* existing among the attributes.

The criteria of the first type are appropiate in cases where attribute cost considerations are important. Their main features are:

- Each attribute r_i in R has associated one value, γ_i, i =1...n, which can be interpreted as the cost .
- The cost ζ_{R_x} of any basis R_x depends exclusively on the cost of each of its attributes and a basis is optimal if and only if its cost is minimum.

To facilitate the discussion we consider the cost of an attribute as an integer number and therefore the cost of a basis will be also an integer number.

Two criteria of this family are exposed, called the *minimum cost basis* criterion and the *minimum basis* criterion respectively.

Minimum cost basis criterion This criterion defines an optimal basis as that whose addition of the costs of its attributes is minimum. In definition 13 is formalized this concept.

Definition 12 Let $R_x = \{r_i, r_j, \ldots, r_k\}$ be a basis of R respect to C and $G_{R_x} = \{\gamma_i, \gamma_j, \ldots, \gamma_k,\}$ the set of costs of its attributes, such that γ_i is the cost of attribute r_i, γ_j the cost of r_j, ..., γ_k the cost of r_k. The cost of the basis R_x, ζ_{R_x}, is:

$$\zeta_{R_x} = \sum \gamma_i \, , \; \forall \gamma_i \in \Gamma_{R_x}$$

Definition 13 Let R_x a basis of R respect to C. R_x is an optimal basis if and only if there exist no other basis R_y, $R \supseteq R_y$, $R_y \neq R_x$, such that $\zeta_{R_y} < \zeta_{R_x}$.

Minimum basis criterion As a particular case of definition 12 one may assume the same unit cost for all the attributes of R, that is, $\gamma_1 = \gamma_2 = \ldots = \gamma_n = 1$. Thus, the resultant optimal bases contain a minimum number of attributes. If one takes into account the boolean nature of the intensional descriptions of the subsets D_i, then these bases have a particular significance, because they constitute a minimum subset of variables that allows describing intensionally the concept by means of a boolean expression. It is important to note that the obtained bases by applying these two exposed criteria are reducts in the sense of Pawlak [6].

The second type of criteria demand the attributes of the basis to satisfy a decision-tree relationship among them. An optimal basis is defined as the subset of attributes that satisfy a certain optimality function defined over the structure. Among the most significant criteria of this type is the *fast basis* criterion, which enables the classification of the subsets D_i with a minimum number of decisions.

Fast basis criterion With the fast basis criterion one searches for a basis which enables the classification of the subsets D_i with a minimum number of decisions.

Definition 14 Let R_x be a basis of R respect to C and $ST = \{T_{1,R_x}, T_{2,R_x}, \ldots, T_{s,R_x}\}$ the set of all the possible decision-trees fulfilling the desired task, that can be obtained from R_x. Let $T_{j,R_x} \in$ ST such that $DN_{T_{j,R_x}} \leq DN_{T_{i,R_x}}$, for all $T_{i,R_x} \in$ ST, then T_{j,R_x} is called the fastest decision-tree of R_x (FDT_{R_x}). Notice that several fast decision-tree for a certain basis R_x may exist.

Definition 15 Let R_x a basis of R respect to C. R_x is a fastest basis of R if and only if $DN_{FDT_{R_x}} \leq DN_{FDT_{R_y}}$, for any basis $R \supseteq R_y$.

In [1] has been proved that a fastest basis is not necessarily a reduct in Pawlak sense.

4.2 Some Optimal Description Criteria

Obtaining an intensional description from an optimal basis is generally a more complex process than the process of generation of an optimal base, because of the complex relations of the decision-tree structure.

Two criteria to select an optimal intensional description (or an optimal decision-tree) from the selected basis are introduced: The *minimum cost tree* criterion and the *fastest tree* criterion. With the first, the cost of the decisions to describe the subsets D_i is minimum; the second, creates a decision-tree to describe the subsets D_i with a minimum number of decisions.

The minimum cost tree criterion This criterion demands the decision-tree to satisfy certain cost considerations based on the costs defined over the attributes, as in section 4.1.

To classify an element $d_i \in$ D by using a decision-tree T, one must decide about all the attributes placed in the path from the root of the tree T down to the corresponding leaf node. If a decision-tree contain k leaf nodes $d_1, d_2, \ldots, d_k$, then it contain k paths $p_1, p_2, \ldots, p_k$ from the root down to the leaf nodes. Let p_i, i = 1...k, be the corresponding path to the leaf node d_i, $\{r_i, r_j, \ldots, r_k\}$ is the set of attributes (decisions) in this path, and $\gamma_i, \gamma_j, \ldots, \gamma_k$ the costs of these attributes, respectively. The cost λ_{p_i} of a path p_i is defined as the addition of the costs of the attributes in the path, that is to say:

$$\lambda_{p_i} = \sum \gamma_j, \quad \forall\, r_j \text{ in the path } p_i \qquad [4.2.1]$$

Definition 16 Let T a decision-tree with k paths $p_1, p_2, \ldots, p_k$, from the root down to their leaf nodes $d_1, d_2, \ldots, d_k$ respectively. The cost of this decision-tree is defined as:

$$\Psi_T = \sum_{i=1\ldots k} \lambda_{p_i} * |d_i|$$

where $|d_i|$ is the number of elements of D contained into the equivalence class defined by the path p_i.

Definition 17 A decision-tree T_i obtained from a basis R_X is a minimum cost decision-tree from R_X if and only if $\Psi_{T_i} \leq \Psi_{T_j}$, for any decision-tree T_j obtained from R_X.

A minimum cost decision-tree enables us to classify all the elements of D with a minimum cost of decisions.

The fast tree criterion A particular case of expression 4.2.1 consist of to consider the same cost for all the attributes of R, that is, $\gamma_1 = \gamma_2 = \ldots \gamma_n$. If the value of these costs is one unit, $\gamma_i = 1$, i = 1...n, then the cost Ψ_T of a tree T (see definition 16) is equivalent at the number of decisions DNT to classify all the elements of D using T, and therefore an optimal tree according to definition 17 enables us to classify all the elements of D with a minimum number of decisions. Such a tree is called a fastest decision-tree.

To obtain a fastest decision-tree from R, two procedures can be adopted:

- To obtain the fastest decision-tree directly from R.
- To obtain the fast decision-tree across the two following steps:
    i. To obtain a fastest basis R_X.
    ii. To obtain a fastest decision-tree from R_X.

Notice that if there exists at least one basis in R respect to C, then all the refered criteria concerning the two steps guarantee the existence of an optimal solution. In fact, this is true because an optimal solution is the optimal of all the possible solutions.

5 Experimental Results

A number of experiments [2] over several application environments have been realized, using the program S.A.I.C. (Inductive Ackisition of Knowledge System) [3], which is based in this new perspective. One of them [1] shows how to reduce the test circuitry needed to diagnose the system errors and how to optimize the diagnosis time to detect the errors of an electronic system. The results were compared with those provided by others methods, such as the ID3, AQ11 and ILS [9] systems, showing that the nature of the problem must be considered and an exhaustive analysis of it must be made before solving it. Another experiment about ascitic acit was realized, showing how to describe several diseases through several components of the ascitic acid of the patients.

6 Conclussions

A new perspective in the Inductive Acquisition of Knowledge from examples has been presented. It is based on three essential concepts: The Object Attribute Table (OAT) and the concepts of Base of Attributes and Optimality Criteria. The OAT constitutes an extensional description of the initial knowledge about some concepts to be intensionally described. To accoimplish this, two steps must be taken:

- An optimal subset of attributes to describe the concepts must be found.
- An optimal intensional description based on the attributes obtained in the previous step must be determined.

Each step is based on a optimality criterion and the two optimality criteria of the two steps are completely independent. The selection of the criterion to be applied depends exclusively on the nature of the problem.

The subset of attributes obtained in the first step is called a basis of attributes. We have presented three optimality criteria to obtain an optimal basis.

To represent the intensional description it has been used the decision-tree structure. Two optimality criteria to obtain an optimal intensional description have been presented.

7 Bibliography

1. Fiol, G.. *Contribución a la adquisición inductiva de conocimiento*. PhD Thesis, Universitat de les Illes Balears, Palma de Mallorca, Spain, 1991.
2. Fiol, G.. Some experiments about Knowledge Acquisition using a subset description theory. Submitted to EUROVAV'93, European Symposium on Validation and Verification of Knowledge Based Systems. 1993.
3. Fiol, G.; Miró, J.. S.A.I.C., un sistema de adquisición inductiva de conocimiento. *Revista de Ciència*. Vol. nº 7, 61-78. December, 1990.
4. Michalski, R. S.; Larson, J. B.. Selection of most representative training examples and incremental generation of VL1 hypotheses: The underlying methodology and the description of programs ESEL and AQ11. Technical Repord 867, Computer Science Department. University of Illinois at Urbana-Champaign, Urbana, IL, 1978.
5. Miró, J.. On defining a set by a property. Technical Repord, Universitat de les Illes Balears, Palma de Mallorca, Spain, 1987.
6. Pawlak, Z.. On Superfluous Attributes in Knowledge representation Systems. *Bulletin of the Polish Academy of Sciences*, 32(3-4), 1984.
7. Pawlak, Z.. Rough Sets. *International Journal on Information and Computer Sciences*, 11:341-356, 1982.
8. Quinlan, J. R.. Induction of Decision Trees. *Machine Learning*, 1:81-106, 1986.
9. Wong, J.H.. An Inductive Learning System-ILS. A thesis submitted to the Faculty of Graduate Studies and Research. University of Regina. 1986.

KNOWLEDGE REPRESENTATION THROUGH OBJECT IN THE DEVELOPMENT OF EXPERT SYSTEM CHEMICAL SYNTHESIS AND REACTION

Luque Ruiz, I.,* Cruz Soto, J.L.,† Gómez-Nieto, M.A.*

February 25, 1993

Abstract

A knowledge acquisition system is proposed to develop of inorganic chemical expert systems. The acquisition system is compose by a series of subsystems devoted specific tasks. A subsystem named Formulator carried out the acquisition of semantic knowledge through nomenclature of inorganic substance and to build a abstract data structure, named DIMS (Dynamic Internal representation of Molecular Structure), which represent all kind of knowledge corresponding inorganic substance. Others subsystem (Painter, Calculator, Nomenclator, Reactor, etc.) operates with this structure to obtain a new knowledge (physical-chemical properties, topological properties, reactions characteristic, etc.) to permits the develop of expert system in chemical inorganic area.

1 INTRODUCTION

The development of expert systems in the chemical field [2] is quite complex not only because of the nature of systems to be developed but also because there are no commercial shells available in the market for solving this kind of problems. An expert system shell oriented towards this kind of problems should have a knowledge acquisition subsystem whose characteristics would differ from those of the shells designed for the development of expert systems oriented towards control, finance, biomedicine, etc.[9, 10]

Within chemical science and specially within the field of chemical synthesis and reactions [2, 3, 10], knowledge is represented and therefore has to be acquired by the experts through symbolic representations (objects) of states and processes related to chemical substances, its properties and relations. This knowledge can be represented through different means:

*E.U.P., Avda. Menéndez Pidal s/n. Córdoba University, 14071-Córdoba (SPAIN), e-mail: ma1gonim@sun630.uco.es

†Science Faculty, Avda. S. Alberto Magno s/n. Córdoba University, 14071-Córdoba (SPAIN), e-mail:jlcruz@sun630.uco.es

The knowledge acquisition system, now being developed, covers all the modes of knowledge representation of this field mentioned above. It consist of a series of subsystems devoted to specific tasks (Figure 1). These subsystems are the following:

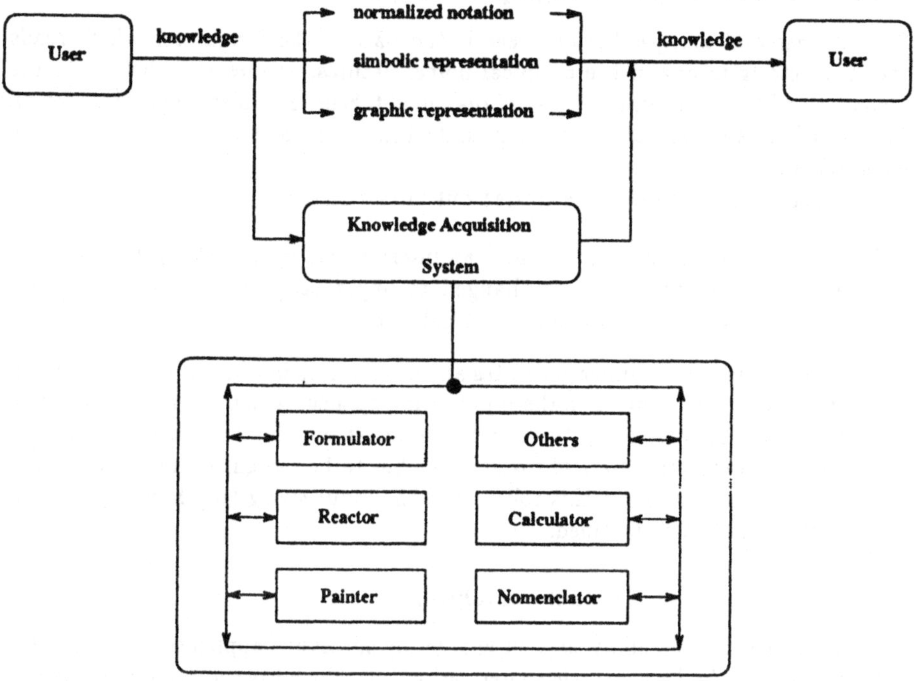

Figure 1: Knowledge acquisition system in inorganic chemical

2.1 The Formulator

The function of this subsystem is the acquisition of knowledge represented by linguistic constructions which represent chemical substances and belong to objects recognized by the system. The formulator is able to recognize expressions in any of these three standardized nomenclatures for the specification of a chemical compound (IUPAC, STOCK and CONVENTIONAL or CLASSIC). In addition to all a wide range of synonyms or trivial names in general use.

The input is a character string representing the name of an inorganic compound in any nomenclature or else its synonym or trivial name, and the output is a abstract data structure that represent the inorganic substance knowledge able to be processed by a computer program.

The system is made up of two subsystems: the scanner, which reads in the characters and generates an output which can then be operated on by the second subsystem, the parser, which uses grammatical rules to output the abstract data structure.

Both subsystems access a database holding information on chemical elements such as atomic properties, combination properties, and so on.

2.1.1 The Scanner or lexicographic analyzer

The scanner or lexicographic analyzer is the part of the formulator which reads the input string in any of the chemical nomenclatures, ensures they belong to the alphabet and builds intermediate symbols called tokens. It is also responsible for all the rest of the auxiliary and exception control functions required in the interactive translation process.[1]

The lexicographic analysis is carried out in two phases:

1. The input string is analyzed and an intermediate output string is generated in which the characters are changed to upper-case, unnecessary spaces are stripped and a check is made for illegal symbols.

2. In this phase, the scanner generates an output string in which it has replaced all of the tokens recognized in the input string by a substring delimited by special characters composed by the number associated with the token (the parser assign to each grammatical token a number to be recognized in the process), the value associated to this token, and the input string length corresponding to the morpheme identified.

2.1.2 The Parser or Syntactic analyzer

The parser or syntactic analyzer is in charge, by successive application of the rules of derivation [11], find a syntactic or derivation tree which has the grammar's axiom as a root. If this is successful, the sentence can be declared part of the grammar-generated language.

For this purpose we are used a bottom-up analyzer or LR parser. These parsers are also referred to as Shifting-Reducing parsers, since this is how they recognize the language. PCYACC [12] is an LALR parser generator, as it scans input from left to right, recognizing sentences by rightmost derivation using Look-Ahead tables, all in a bottom-up building process of the syntactic tree.

A generic series of rules, to be used for any nomenclature, and a specific set of rules, for each nomenclature and for inorganic chemical families, have been defined.

The syntactic-semantic analysis process is based on the successive reduction of the rules and the corresponding performance of their assigned functions, starting with the tokens or terminal symbols of the grammar and continuing until the main axiom is reached, that is until the rule is satisfied.

[1] The definition of a grammar (e.g. inorganic nomenclature) consist in represent every possible meaningful language sentence fragment —morpheme— by a token, the smallest information unit which would be meaningful to the syntax analyzer. Morphemes thus represent meaningful fragments of the artificial language, while tokens represent grammatical units defined by the language.

2.2 DIMS: Dynamic Internal representation of Molecular Structure

The Formulator above described translate the nomenclature representing a chemical compound into an abstract data structure (proposed by the authors) [6] called DIMS (Dynamic Internal Molecular Structure). The specification and design of the DIMS has been carried out from the point of view of object-oriented paradigm, and this terminology has been used throughout the study [1, 4, 7].

The DIMS is considered as a object type made up of active data, its to say: a set of attributes defining object properties and a set of methods that can operate it. As Figure 2 shows, the DIMS maintains an one to one relationship with a chemical compound, in this way a DIMS represents a chemical compound and vice versa. The DIMS is formed by the aggregation of four types of objects (Figure 2), each one of them describes a specific knowledge area referring to a chemical compound: The CST object (Compound Structure Table) represents knowledge about the kind of compound, subcompounds or ions that compose it, the atoms that compose the molecule and their characteristics in combination; the CPT object (Compound Properties Table) represents knowledge about the bonds, and their characteristics, between the atoms that form the compound's molecule, as well as topological information; the CRT object (Compound Representation Table) represent knowledge about the spatial geometry of the atoms which compose the molecules: and the CCL object (Compound Characteristics List) represents any type of knowledge, textual or graphic, about a substance.

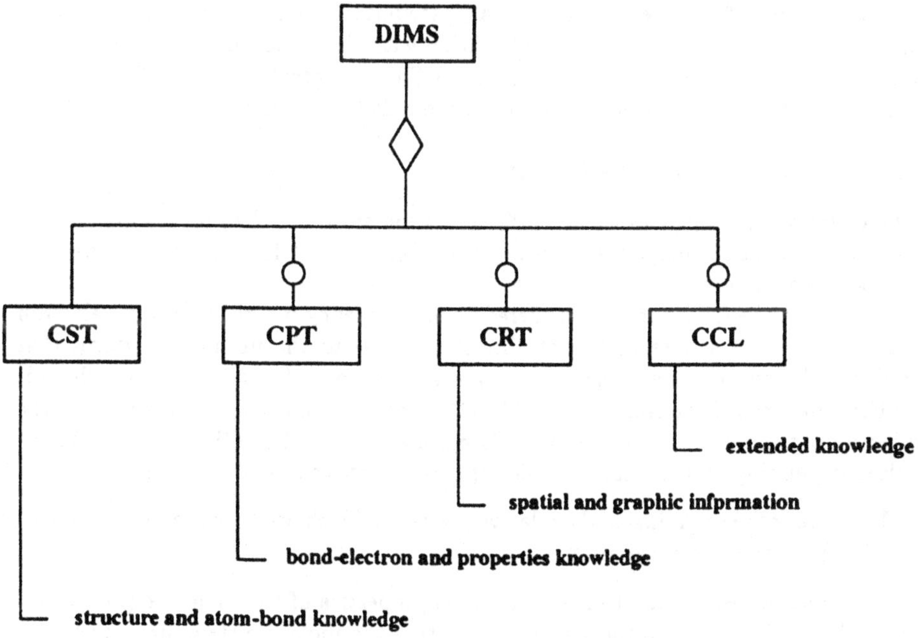

Figure 2: Structure of the DIMS

The structures and features of the each of object types that compose the DIMS object class will now be described.

2.2.1 Compound Structure Table

The Compound Structure Table, CST, is the main structure that composes the DIMS object class. This object type, the CST, is generated by interpreter subsystems from a normalized notation (i.e.; IUPAC, STOCK, Conventional) that denominates an inorganic compound [13]. Other processes generate from the CST the group of morphemes that compose a sentence that nominates a chemical compound in a normalized notation. The remaining object types that compose the DIMS (CPT, CRT and CCL) can be initialized from the information contained in the CST.

The CST keeps information about the atoms that compose a chemical substance, its stoichiometry, its combination features and the ionic composition of the substance, that is to say, the subcompounds that compose it; taking into account that a subcompound may be an ion or a neutral molecule that forms part of the molecule of a compound.

The CST is an object type formed by a collection of four attributes (CAT, CON, VAL, CHA) or simple object types which can be defined by means of simple data types.

This attributes keeps the information corresponding to the atomic number, valency and resulting charge of the atoms that compose the molecule, the number and type of subcompound that compose the molecule, and the type of the compound inorganic that CST represent.

Two values of occurrences of the CAT attribute have been defined, that allow the instances of the CST to store information with the same format as the Concise Connection Table (CCT) [8], providing the CST with great compatibility in those systems based on the representation of compounds by means of CCT.

2.2.2 Compound Properties Table

The Compound Properties Table, CPT, is a type of object that represents the nature of the relationships existing between the atoms that form part of a chemical compound structure.

Basically, the CPT can be considered as an adjacency matrix or a bond-electron matrix, as it is a square matrix of dimension equal to the number of atoms that compose the molecule and whose CPT values $(i,\ j)$ for $i \neq j$ will be zero if there is no bond between the atoms i and j. The CPT takes the maximum advantage of the directioning space of a matrix due to its non-symmetry. The CPT stores different values depending on the relative values of corresponding row and column, so:

1. Values corresponding to the relative position of each atom of the molecule with respect to the central atom.

2. Values corresponding to the topological properties of the molecule (i.e. equivalence class, level in the graph representing the molecule structure, etc.)

3. Values corresponding to the bond characteristic between the atoms that compose the molecule.

2.3 Compound Representation Table

This object is in charge to represent the spatial geometry of the molecules (inorganic substances) treated by the system. The CRT maintain information need to operate the *Painter* subsystem to representation in 2D of the 3D structure of the molecules, and operate of a interactive way with it.

2.3.1 Compound Characteristics List

This object type is defined based on the fact that in the acquisition of knowledge it is necessary to keep specific information of the chemical entities (compounds and subcompounds) of a very diverse nature; information which, because it is about a particular substance or because of being very variable, can not be modeled using rigid data structure as the CST and CPT or other authors' proposals [6, 8].

This structure allows the storage of information of a highly variable nature with respect to any chemical compound. The CCL is a double linked list: it is formed by a list which refers to the compound and all the constituent subcompounds and the elements of this list are head elements in a specific information list about each one of them.

3 OTHERS SUBSYSTEMS

To operate with the inorganic knowledge is necessary of others subsystems ables to operate with this knowledge. Has been develop a series of subsystems to carried out this function, so:

The Calculator is in charge of obtaining more information about the object (chemical substance) from the DIMS object and the exploration and firing of a set simple IF/THEN rules; it is also in change of incorporating this information to the structure.

The Painter is in charge acquiring the knowledge in the form of plain graphs representing the chemical compound. This subsystem allows for the bi-dimensional projection of a tri-dimensional structure (the chemical compound molecular structure) and for the execution of different operation on the structure.

The Nomenclator its function is to acquire knowledge symbolically and transform it into a new DIMS object for its later use. In the chemical field, it is common to represent knowledge through symbols: Atoms are represented by symbols, molecules or substances by the combination of symbols, and other elements of the system or the environment such as heat, gaseous state, solid state, etc. are also represented by symbols.

The Reactor This subsystem is in change of acquiring the specific knowledge. It allows the acquisition of elements (system objects) within certain knowledge frames, and a series of knowledge derivation rules. It is one of the complex subsystem as regards verification and validation of the acquired knowledge. A strict syntax and procedures have been designed for this purpose.

4 DISCUSSION

The knowledge acquisition system is also constituted by others subsystems that interact with the ones described above. In this system everything is an object, even the system itself. Therefore, the knowledge acquisition process consists in the definition of a series of new objects that inherit the static and dynamic properties (attributes and methods) of the types defined in the system, being these properties subject to modifications and enlargements.

The inorganic substance real world object is represent by the internal object DIMS. The DIMS object permit the representation and processing of any kind of inorganic chemical knowledge, this characteristic made up a ideal abstract data structure to operate of interface between all of subsystem of a inorganic chemical expert system.

A system based on the OOD paradigm allows for a better acquisition of the symbolic and declarative knowledge such as the one pertaining to the area of chemical synthesis and reactions in the field of inorganic chemistry.

References

[1] J. Rumbaugh, M. Blaha, et al. Object-Oriented Modeling and Design., Prentice-Hall, 1991

[2] Zdzislaw Hippe., Artificial Intelligence in Chemistry., Elservier, 1991.

[3] N.A.B. Gray., Computer-Assisted Structure Elucidation., J. Wiley and Sons., 1986

[4] J. G. Hughes., Object-Oriented Databases., Prentice-Hall., 1991.

[5] Luque Ruiz, I., Gómez-Nieto, M.A., Desarrollo de Sistemas en Entorno Windows-Actor., Actas Prode'91. Jornadas sobre programación declarativa., 1991, Málaga (España).

[6] Luque Ruiz, I.; Cruz Soto J.L.; Gómez-Nieto, M.A., Inorganic Chemical Knowledge Representation Using Dynamic Data Structures., J. Chem. Inf. Comput. Sci. (accepted for publication).

[7] E.R. Tello., Object-Oriented Programming for Windows., John Wiley and Sons, 1991.

[8] Cook-Fox, D.I., Kirby, G.H., Lord, M.R., Rayner, S.D., Computer translation of IUPAC systematic organic chemical nomenclature. Concise connection tables to structure diagrams., J. Chem. Inf. Sci., 1990, 30, 122-127.

[9] Scott, A.C. et al., A Practical Guide to Knowledge Acquisition., Diaz de Santos, 1991.

[10] Barret, J., Understanding Inorganic Chemistry. The underlying physical principles., Diaz de Santos, 1991.

[11] Aho, A.V.; Ullman, J.D. The Theory of Parsing. Translation and Compiling. Prentice-Hall. Englewood Cliffs. N.J. 1972.

[12] PCYACC/PCLEX. Abraxas Software Inc. 7033 SW Macadam Ave. Portland, OR 97219 USA.

[13] Luque Ruiz, I.; Cruz Soto J.L.; Gómez-Nieto, M.A. Computer translation of the inorganic chemical nomenclature to a abstract data structure. J. Chem. Inf. Comput. Sci. (send for publication).

4. Knowledge Based Systems

Hierarchical Representation of Fuzzy *If-Then* Rules

Ronald R. Yager

Machine Intelligence Institute, Iona College
New Rochelle, NY 10801, USA

Abstract. We introduce a hierarchical structure for the representation of fuzzy if-then rules of the type used in fuzzy systems modeling. In this structure the specificity of the rules diminishes as we go down the hierarchy. We discuss how this structure provides a natural framework for acquisition of knowledge. We introduce a new aggregation operator for combining information between levels. This operator has a saturation like component which stops aggregation when an appropriate level of specificity is reached. This saturation effect avoids the swamping of the output by less specific knowledge.

1. Introduction

In [1] Yager provides an example in which the flat representation [2] of *fuzzy if-then rules* leads to unsatisfactory results. Consider a rule base consisting to two rules

if U is 12 the V is 29 I.
If U is [10-15] the V is [25–30] II.

If U = 12 we would get V is G where G = [25 - 30]. The application of the defuzzification process leads to a selection of V = 27.5. Thus we see that the very specific instruction was not followed.

The problem with the technique used is that the most specific information was swamped by the less specific information. In this paper we shall provide for a new structure for the representation of *fuzzy if-then rules*. The representational form introduced here is called a Hierarchical Prioritized Structure (HPS) representation. Most importantly in addition to overcoming the problem illustrated in the previous example this HPS representation has an inherent capability to emulate the learning of general rules and provides a reasonable accurate cognitive mapping of how human beings store information.

2. Hierarchical Prioritized Structure

Figure 1, shows in a systematic view the of representation of the function $V = f(U)$ by this new HPS representation. The overall function f, relating the input U to the output V, is comprised of the whole collection of subboxes, denoted f_i. Each subbox is a collection of rules relating the system input, U, and the current iteration of the output, V_{i-1}, to a new iteration of the output. The output of the nth subsystem, V_n, becomes the overall output of the system, V. In the HPS the higher priority boxes, *for i < j we say that fi has a higher priority than fj*, would have less general information, consist of rules with more specific antecedents then those of lower priority. As we envision this system working an input value for U is provided, if it matches one or more of the rules in the first (highest priority) level then it doesn't bother to fire any of the less specific rules in the lower priority levels.

In the following we describe the formal operation of this HPS. As we indicated V_j denotes the output of the jth level. We shall assume $V_0 = \Phi$. In the HPS we shall use the variable $\hat{V}_j$ to indicate the **maximum membership grade** associated with the output of the jth level, V_j.

In the HPS each f_j (accept for the lowest level, j = n) is a collection of n_j rules

***When** U is $\underline{A_{ji}}$ <u>is certain</u> **and** $\hat{V}_{j-1}$ is low **then** V_j is B_{ji}* **I**

The representation and aggregation of rules at each level is of the standard Mamdani type[2], disjunction of the individual rules. If $\tilde{B}_j$ is the value obtained from the aggregation of the outputs of the collection of individual rules in I then the output of this subbox is

$$V_j = V_{j-1} \cup \tilde{B}_j.$$

In **I** a rule fires if we are certain that the input U lies in A_{ji} and $\hat{V}_{j-1}$ is low. Since $\hat{V}_{j-1}$ is the maximum membership grade of V_{j-1} it can be seen as a measure of how much matching we have up to this point. Essentially this term is saying that if the higher priority rules are relevant, $\hat{V}_{j-1}$ is not low, then don't bother using this information. On the other hand if the higher priority rules are not relevant, not to much matching $\hat{V}_{j-1}$ is low, then try using this information.

The representation of the box f_n is a collection of rules of the form

***When** U is A_{ni} **and** $\hat{V}_{n-1}$ is low **then** V is B_{ni}* **II**

plus the rule $V = V_n = V_{n-1} \cup \widetilde{B_n}$. The notable difference between the lowest priority box and the other ones is that the antecedent regarding U is certainly quality in the higher boxes. The need for this becomes apparent when the input is not a singleton.

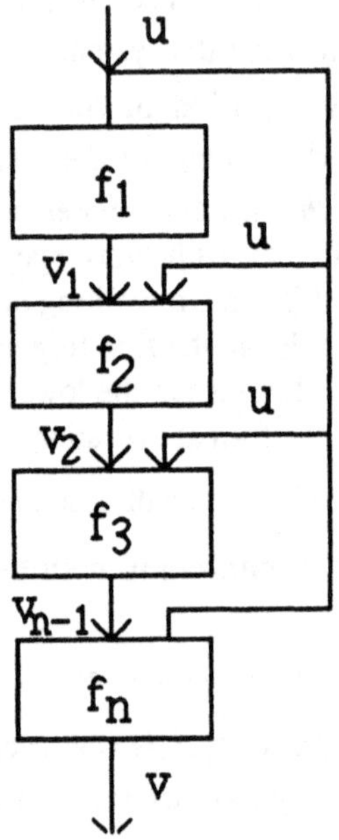

Figure 1 Hierarchical Prioritized Structure

In the HPS structure $\hat{V}_{j-1}$ is the highest membership grade in V_{j-1} and as such the term $\hat{V}_{j-1}$ is *low* is used to measure the degree to which the higher prioritized information have matched the input data. We note that low is a fuzzy subset on the unit interval. One definition for low [1] is

$$\text{low}(x) = 1 - x.$$

In [1] Yager looks at the formal operation of this kind of HPS we shall present the results obtained in [1]. We shall denote $\mathfrak{I}_{ij}$ as the degree of firing (or relevancy) of A_{ij} under the input, if the input is $U = x^*$ then $\mathfrak{I}_{ij} = A_{ij}(x^*)$. We shall denote $g_i = \text{Max}_y\, G_i(y) = \text{Poss}[G_i]$. We let $T_i = \bigcup_{j=1}^{n_i} \mathfrak{I}_{ij} \wedge B_{ij}$, the aggregation of the rules in the ith level for input U, it is essentially the contribution of the ith subsystem using the Mamdani type reasoning.. We shall let G_i be the output of the ith subbox, that is $V_i = G_i$. In [1] it is shown that

$$G_i(y) = (T_i(y) \wedge (1 - g_{i-1})) \vee G_{i-1}(y). \qquad \text{III}$$

We notice that the term $(1 - g_{i-1})$ bounds the allowable contribution of the ith subsystem to the overall output. We see that if we get at least one element y to be, a good answer (an element in G_{i-1}) we limit the contribution of the lower priority subsystems. It is this characteristic of a kind of saturation along with the prioritization that allows us to avoid the problem described earlier.

In the following we suggest a modification of the above that leads to a more suitable formulation to the aggregation between the levels of the HPS [1]. We can replace $\wedge$ by another t-norm operator product * and replace $\vee$ by another t-conorm, bounded sum, $a \boxplus b = \mathrm{Min}(1, a+b)$[3]. Thus we get

$$G_i(y) = T_i(y) * (1 - g_{i-1}) \boxplus G_{i-1}(y).$$

However we note that since $g_{i-1} = \mathrm{Max}_y G_{i-1}$ then $T_i(y) * (1 - g_{i-1}) \leq G_{i-1}(y)$ hence $T_i(y) * (1 - g_{i-1}) + G_{i-1}(y) \leq 1$ thus we can replace $\boxplus$ by +. This gives us the formulation

$$G_i(y) = T_i(y) * (1 - g_{i-1}) + G_{i-1}(y) \qquad \text{(IV)}$$

$$G_i(y) = T_i(y) * (1 - \mathrm{Poss}[G_{i-1}]) + G_{i-1}(y)$$

What is happening in this structure is that as long as we have not found one y with membership grade 1 in G_{i-1}, $\mathrm{Poss}[G_{i-1}] \neq 1$, we add some of the output of the current subbox to what we already have. Each element y, gets $1 - \mathrm{Poss}[G_{i-1}]$ portion of the contribution at that level, $T_i(y)$

We should point out that the aggregation performed in the hierarchical structure, whether we use III or IV, is not a pointwise operation. This means that the value of $G_i(y)$ doesn't only depend on the membership grade of y in G_{i-1} and T_i but on membership grades at other points. In particular through the term $\overline{g}_{i-1} = 1 - \mathrm{Max}_y\, G_i(y)$ it depends upon the membership grade of all elements from Y in Gi–1.

We should note that implicit in this structure is a new kind of aggregation. Assume A and B are two fuzzy subsets we define the combination of these sets as the fuzzy subset D, denoted $D = \gamma(A, B)$ where

$$D(x) = (1 - \mathrm{Poss}(A)) * B(x) + A(x).$$

3. Representation and Operation of the HPS

In the previous part we have described the formal mechanism used for the reasoning and aggregation process in the HPS. While the formal properties of the new aggregation structure are important a key to the usefulness of the HPS in fuzzy modeling is the semantics used in the representation of the information via this structure.

In constructing an HPS representation to model a system we envision that the knowledge of the relationship contained in the HPS structure be stored in the following manner. At the highest level of priority, i = 1, we would have the most precise (specific) knowledge. In particular we would have point to point relationships,

When U is 3 then V is 7

When U is 9 then V is 13

This would be information we know with the greatest certainty.

At the next level of priority the specificity of the antecedent linguistic variables, the A_{2j}'s, would decrease. Thus the second level would contain slightly more general knowledge.

Essentially what we envision is that at the highest level we have specific point information. The next level encompass these points and in addition provides a more general and perhaps fuzzy knowledge. We note that the lowest most level can be used to tell us what to do if we have no knowledge up to this point. In some sense the lowest level is a default value.

Example: Assume we are using an HPS representation to model a function V = f(U), where the base set for U is [0, 100]. A typical HPS representation could be as follows.

LEVEL #1

R_{11}	When U is 5 then V is 13
R_{12}	When U is 75 then V is 180
R_{13}	When U is 85 then V is 100

LEVEL #2

R_{21}	When U is "about 10" then V is "about 20"
R_{22}	When U is "about 30" then V is "about 50"
R_{23}	When U is "about 60" then V is "about 90"
R_{24}	When U is "about 80" then V is "about 120"
R_{25}	When U is "about 100" then V is "about 150"
	(we assume triangular fuzzy subsets)

LEVEL #3

R_{31}	When U is "low then V is "about 40"
R_{32}	When U is ":meet" then V is "about 85"
R_{31}	When U is "high" then V is "about 130"

LEVEL #4

R_{41} U is anything the V is 2u.

Having defined our knowledge base we now look at the performance of this system for various inputs;

Case 1: U = 75. At level one we get $T_1 = \left\{\frac{1}{180}\right\}$ hence

$$G_1(y) = \bar{g}_0 * T_1(y) + G_0(y).$$

Since $G_0 = \Phi$ then $g_1 = 1$ which give us $G_1 = T_1 = \left\{\frac{1}{180}\right\}$. We now see that $\bar{g}_1 = 0$ and hence no other rules will fire lower in the hierarchy. This system provides as its output for U = 75 that

V is 180.

Case 2: U = 80. At level one no rules fire, $\mathfrak{I}_{ij} = 0$ for all j. Thus $T_1 = \Phi$ hence

$$G_1 = \bar{g}_0 * T_1 + G_0 = \Phi$$

and therefore $\bar{g}_1 = 1$. At level two

$$G_2 = \bar{g}_1 * T_2 + \Phi = T_2.$$

For U = 80 we assume that R_{24} fires completely, $\mathfrak{I}_{24} = 1$ and that all other rules don't fire, $\mathfrak{I}_{2j} = 0$, for $j \neq 2$. Thus T_2 = "about 120" and G_2 = "about 120". Since $g_2 = 1$ then $\bar{g}_2 = 0$ and no rules at lower priority will fire thus G_2, "about 120", is the output of the system for U = 80.

Case 3: U = 20. No rule at level one will fire, hence $G_1 = G_0 = \Phi$. At level two we shall assume that R_{21} fires to degree .3 and R_{22} also fires to degree .3. Thus

$$T_2 = .3 \wedge B_1 \cup .3 \wedge B_2 = .3 \wedge (B_1 \cup B_2)$$

$$T_2(y)= .3 \wedge (B_1(y) \vee B_2(y)).$$

We note B_1 and B_2 are "about 20" and "about 30" respectively. Hence

$$G_2(y) = (1 - g_1) * T_2(y) + G_1(y) = T_2(y)$$

At level three R_{31} fires to degree 1 while R_{31} and R_{32} don't fire at all. Hence

$$T_3 = \text{"about 40"}$$

Since Max $[G_2] = .3$ thus $1 - g_2 = .7$ and therefore

$$G_3(y) = .7 * T_3(y) + G_2(y)$$

Since Max $T_3(y) = 1$ we see that the process stops here and G_3 is the output of the system.

What we see with this HPS representation is that we have our most general rule stored at the *lowest* level of priority and we store exceptions to this rule at higher levels of priority. In some cases the exceptions to general rules may themselves be rules, we would then store exceptions to these rules at still higher levels of priority. As the previous example illustrates in the HPS system for a given input we first look to see if the input is an exception, that is what we are essentially doing by looking at the high priority levels.

4.Learning in the HPS

The HPS representation is a formulation that has an inherent structure for a natural human like learning mechanism. We shall briefly describe the type of learning that is associated with this structure.

Information comes into the system in terms of point by point knowledge, data pairs between input and output. We store these points at the highest level of priority. Each input/output pair corresponds to a rule at the highest level. If enough of these points cluster in a neighborhood in the input/output space we can replace these points by a general rule (see figure 2).

Thus from the dots, input/output pairs, we get a relationship that says *if U is in A then V is B*. We can now forget about the dots and only save the new relationship. We save this at the next lowest priority in the system, in subbox 2.

We note that the introduction of the rule essentially extends the information contained in the dots by now providing information about spaces between the dots. We can also save storage because we have eliminated many dots and replaced them by one circle. One downside to this formulation is that in generalizing we have lost some of the specificity carried by the dots.

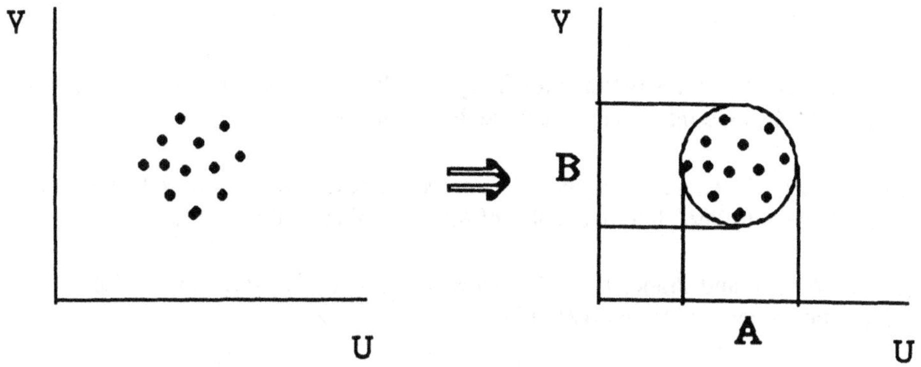

Figure 2 Formulation of Rules for Input/Output Pairs

It may occur that there are some notable exceptions to this new general rule. We are able to capture this exception by storing them as high level points.

We further note that new information enters the system in terms of points. Thus we see that the points are either new information or exceptions to more general rules. Thus specific information enters as points it filters its way up the system in rules.

We see that next that it may be possible for a group of these second level rules to be clustered to form new rules at the third level.

In figure #3 the large bold circle is seen as a rule which encompasses the higher level rules to provide a more general rule. The necessity to keep these more specific rules, thus in level 2, depends upon how good the less specific rule captures the situation.

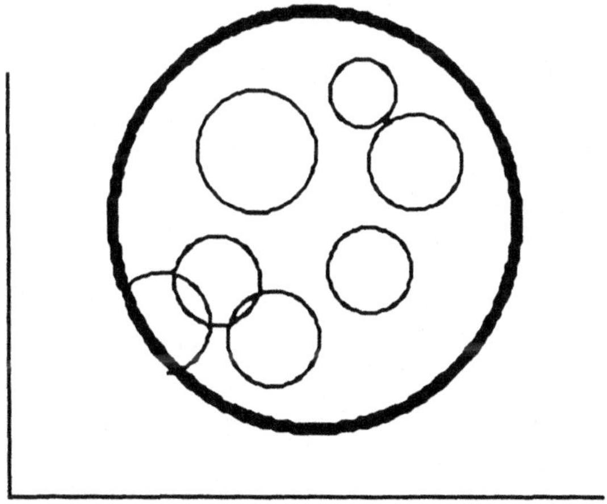

Figure 3 Aggregation of Rules into More General Rules

5. References

[1]. Yager, R. R., "On structures for fuzzy modeling and control," Technical Report MII#1213, Machine Intelligence Institute, Iona College, 1992.

[2]. Mamdani, E. H. and Assilian, S., "An experiment in linguistic synthesis with a fuzzy logic controller," International J. of Man-Machine Studies 7, 1-13, 1975.

[3]. Dubois, D. and Prade, H., "A review of fuzzy sets aggregation connectives," Information Sciences 36, 85 - 121, 1985.

Approximate Reasoning in Expert Systems : Inference and Combination Tools

A.M. SPILSKI-PÉTIEAU - D. WILLAEYS

Laboratoire d'Automatique Industrielle et Humaine
Université de Valenciennes et du Hainaut-Cambrésis
Le Mont-Houy - BP 311 - 59304 Valenciennes Cedex - France

Abstract. The purpose of the work surveyed in this paper is to provide knowledge-based systems with tools relying on the fuzzy sets and the possibility theories in order to allow them to reason on fuzzy and uncertain knowledge. First will be given a means of representation for fuzzy and uncertain facts, then an inference operation on those facts, and finally a method for combining different fuzzy properties into a single one.

1. Introduction

Knowledge-based systems, like expert systems, deal with information which is partly constituted either of experience and know-how of human experts, or of the subjective observations of human operators. As experience, know-how and sujectivity are often pervaded with fuzziness, uncertainty, inconsistency, incompleteness and/or mistakes. Those systems need appropriate and sophisticated technics to help them in their carrying out of the work they have to do on the knowledge they have at their disposal.

The characteristics of pervaded data of interest to us in this paper are fuzziness and uncertainty. These concepts can be correctly managed by means of mathematical tools provided by the Fuzzy Subsets Theory and the Possibility Theory respectively.

The purpose of the work surveyed in this paper is to provide knowledge-based systems with tools relying on these two theories and thus allowing them to reason on fuzzy and uncertain knowledge. First will be given a means of representation for fuzzy and uncertain facts, then an inference operation on those facts, and finally a method for combining different fuzzy properties into a single one.

2. Representation of imprecise and uncertain facts

Knowledge-based systems involve two types of data : facts and rules. We propound a representation for both and we now present it beginning with facts.

Let a fuzzy assertion (X is A), be represented by a membership function $\mu_A(x)$. It is associated with two possibility degrees α_A and $\alpha_{\neg A}$. The representation of the corresponding fact F, should take into account those three parameters so as not to lose any element of information.

Our work takes place in a specific case where the following hypothesis are considered :

- The proposition *X is A is α-possible* is expressed as the inequality:

$$\sup_x [\mu_A(x) * \mu_B(x)] \leq \alpha_A \tag{1}$$

to be solved for μ_B, where *X is B* is a certain, fuzzy fact and * a T-norm.
- In (1), * is the non-commutative conjunction operator associated to * as defined by DUBOIS and PRADE [1]. This gives us as a result :

$$\mu_B(y) = I_S(\mu_A(x), \alpha_A) \tag{2}$$

where $I_S(a,b) = 1 - (a * (1 - b))$ is Gödel's reciprocal implication.
- The equivalence between the propositions *X is A is α_A-possible* and *not (X is A) is 1-α_A certain* is underlain.

Additional information on the why and wherefore those hypothesis have raised can be found in [5].

According to these hypothesis and previous works [1, 2, 6, 8], we define the fact F translating the information described above, by means of two possibility distributions we call π_A and $\pi_{\neg A}$:

$$\begin{aligned} \pi_A(x) &= \text{Max}[\mu_A(x), \alpha_{\neg A}] \\ 1-\pi_{\neg A}(x) &= \text{Min}[\mu_A(x), 1-\alpha_A] \end{aligned} \tag{3}$$

The latter formula is equivalent to the former, changing A into ¬A. Nevertheless, they are not redundant. Indeed, the values of the possibility degrees α_A and $\alpha_{\neg A}$ are relatively independant. Their sum must be at least greater than one, since a piece of information constituted by an assertion and its contrary should be at least possible, but this is the only constraint they are submitted to.

This way of representation can be beared out in terms of lower and upper bounds. The pair ($1-\pi_{\neg A}$, π_A) defines the bounds of a hardly known possibility distribution π. The fact F = (μ_A, α_A, $\alpha_{\neg A}$) is thus considered as the incomplete knowledge on a possibility distribution π such as :

$$\begin{aligned} \text{Min}[\mu_A, 1-\alpha_A] \;\leq\; &\pi \;\leq\; \text{Max}[\mu_A, \alpha_{\neg A}] \\ 1-\pi_{\neg A} \;\leq\; &\pi \;\leq\; \pi_A \end{aligned} \tag{4}$$

since nothing forbids the possibility distribution of an uncertain fact to be imprecise. This approach is in the spirit of previous proposals made by SANCHEZ [9], ZADEH [14], and YAGER [13].

The linguistic interpretation of the fact represented by this method is

$$F = \begin{cases} \text{X is A is } \alpha_A\text{-possible} \\ \text{and} \\ \text{not (X is A) is } \alpha_{\neg A}\text{-possible} \end{cases}$$

This mathematical model should be useful when considering that a sentence like *Temperature is possibly close to 2000°C* does not give a complete information on the assumed state of the variable. As a matter of fact, with different little complements of information, the meaning of this sentence may be modified in different ways. For instance, adding that *...furthermore, it is hardly likely that the temperature is not close to 2000°C*, comes to prove the initial piece of information and makes it certain. Figure 1 shows a graphical interpretation of this fact using respectively .9 and .2 as numerical translations of *possibly* and *hardly likely*, the possibility degrees of the assertions.

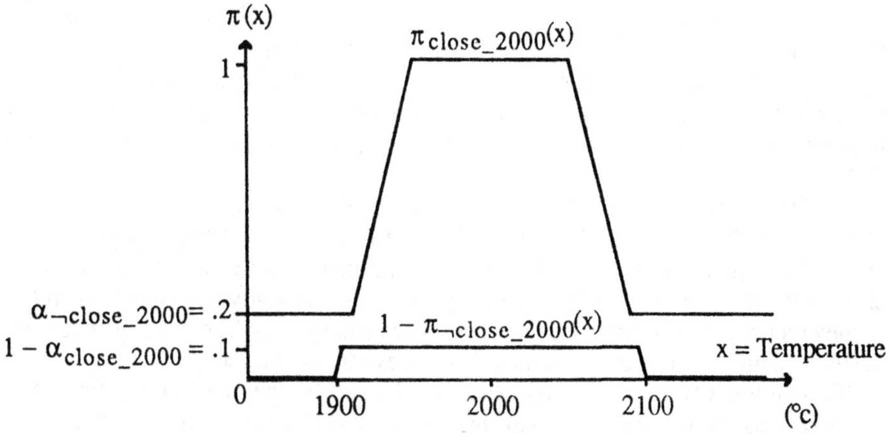

Figure 1 : An interpretation of the fact *Temperature is possibly (.9) close to 2000°C and it is hardly likely (.2) that the temperature is not close to 2000°C.*

On the contrary, making the information complete with the assertion *...but it also possibly have another value*, will lead to a sort of undetermination. Figure 2 shows a graphical interpretation of this fact. It appears that the curves of the two figures are different as well as the meaning of the sentences they are modelling.

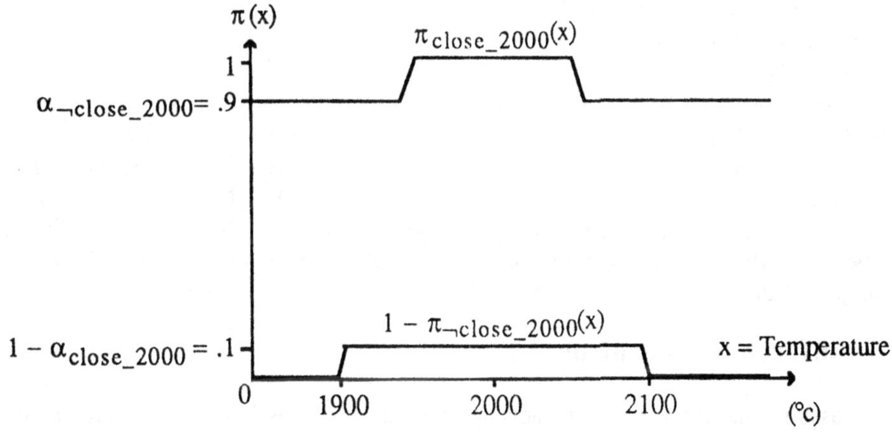

Figure 2 : An interpretation of the fact *Temperature is possibly (.9) close to 2000°C but it also possibly (.9) has another value.*

This approach allows of course to model all types of facts whenever they are precise, imprecise or fuzzy, uncertain or certain, and even undetermined.

Besides appears what we call synonymy. This notion has raised from the following remark : two different facts F1 = $(\mu_A, \alpha_A, \alpha_{\neg A})$ and F2 = $(1\text{-}\mu_A, \alpha_{\neg A}, \alpha_A)$, are both built on the same property A and the same possibility degrees. Their linguistic interpretations

$$F1 = \begin{array}{l}(X \text{ is } A) \text{ is } \alpha_A\text{-possible} \\ \text{and} \\ \text{not } (X \text{ is } A) \text{ is } \alpha_{\neg A}\text{-possible}\end{array} \quad \text{and} \quad F2 = \begin{array}{l}\text{not } (X \text{ is } A) \text{ is } \alpha_{\neg A}\text{-possible} \\ \text{and} \\ (X \text{ is } A) \text{ is } \alpha_A\text{-possible}\end{array}$$

are equivalent since the coordinating conjunction *and* does not induce any order between the assertions. In the same way, their respective possibility distributions, that is

$$\begin{array}{ll} \pi_A(x) = \text{Max}\,[\,\mu_A(x)\,,\,\alpha_{\neg A}\,] & \pi_{\neg A}(x) = \text{Max}\,[\,1\text{-}\mu_A(x)\,,\,\alpha_A\,] \\ 1\text{-}\pi_{\neg A}(x) = \text{Min}\,[\,\mu_A(x)\,,\,1\text{-}\alpha_A\,] & 1\text{-}\pi_A(x) = \text{Min}\,[\,1\text{-}\mu_A(x)\,,\,1\text{-}\alpha_A\,] \end{array}$$

are clearly equivalent as well. Then, it appears that, whenever F1 and F2 are not absolutely identical, they are linguistically and mathematically equivalent. Therefore, as they model the same idea, they are said to be synonymous. The consequence is that in some operations, either one or the other can eventually be used.

To sum up, a fact $F = (\mu_A, \alpha_A, \alpha_{\neg A})$ is defined by the membership function of the fuzzy assertion it concerns and, by the possibility degrees of the latter and its contrary. The synonym of F, which is equivalent, is $FS = (1\text{-}\mu_A, \alpha_{\neg A}, \alpha_A)$.

After the representation of a fact, let now have a look at the production rules.

Usually, a rule involving the facts *X is A* and *Y is B* is written *if X is A, then Y is B*. Here, as the facts are represented in the way above, the rule should be written *if* F_A *then* F_B. However, we assume that the uncertainty of a fuzzy and uncertain rule only bears on its conclusion. Thus we consider that the premiss is certain, that is

$$F_A = \begin{array}{l}(X \text{ is } A) \text{ is possible} \\ \text{and} \\ \text{not } (X \text{ is } A) \text{ is impossible}\end{array}$$

which can be simplified in

F_A = X is A

This is why we write *if X is A then* F_B. Consequently, $F_B = (\mu_B, \alpha_B, \alpha_{\neg B})$, F_A = (X is A) = $(\mu_A, \alpha_A{=}1, \alpha_{\neg A}{=}0)$ and the functions describing the rule are

$$\begin{array}{llll} \pi_A(x) = \mu_A(x) & \text{and} & \pi_B(y) = \text{Max}\,[\,\mu_B(y)\,,\,\alpha_{\neg B}\,] \\ 1\text{-}\pi_{\neg A}(x) = 0 & & 1\text{-}\pi_{\neg B}(y) = \text{Min}\,[\,\mu_B(y)\,,\,1\text{-}\alpha_B\,] \end{array}$$

Using rules and facts represented by this method, we have also defined an inference operation which can deduce new data from knowledge and observations. This is the subject of the next part.

3. Inference operation

Let assume that the system has facts and rules at its disposal. They are represented in the way described in the paragraph before.

Several mathematical formulas permit inference deduction. The one we propound is based on the Generalized Modus Ponens [14] and on the Extended Generalized Modus Ponens [6] and deals simultaneously with the fuzziness and the uncertainty pervading the data.

Let us consider a fact $F_{A'}$, which is represented by its two possibility distributions $\pi_{A'}$ and $\pi_{\neg A'}$, and a rule *if X is A then* F_B which is represented by two conditional possibility distributions $\pi_{Y/X}$ and $\pi_{\neg Y/X}$. $\pi_{Y/X}$ is obtained just as for the Generalized Modus Ponens, from π_A and π_B using an implication operation like the ones identified by TRILLAS and VALVERDE [10, 11], WEBER [12] or DUBOIS and PRADE [1] for example. $\pi_{\neg Y/X}$ should be calculated with the same formula as $\pi_{Y/X}$ only changing π_B into $1-\pi_{\neg B}$.

When $F_{A'}$ triggers the rule, it gives as a result a fact $F_{B'}$ defined by its two possibility distributions $\pi_{B'}$ and $\pi_{\neg B'}$:

$$\pi_{B'}(y) = \sup_x [\, \pi_{A'}(x) \wedge \pi_{Y/X}(x,y) \,]$$

$$1-\pi_{\neg B'}(y) = \sup_x [\, 1-\pi_{\neg A'}(x) \wedge \pi_{\neg Y/X}(x,y) \tag{5}$$

The first formula of (5) is a well known and much used Modus Ponens. It involves pieces of information constituted by fuzzy and uncertain assertions on the properties A, A' and B. It deduces some new information about the variable Y : $\pi_{B'}(y)$.

The second formula is an extension of this Modus Ponens to the unnormalized possibility distributions $1-\pi_{\neg B}$ and $1-\pi_{\neg A'}$. This time, what is involved is some additional information on B and A' and thus leads to additional (as well) information on Y : $1-\pi_{\neg B}$.

Considering the calculation times, (5) happens to be twice as complex as the Generalized Modus Ponens formula is. Nevertheless, it is easier to calculate than it seems to be. As a matter of fact, the only extra calculation needed, in comparison with the Generalized Modus Ponens concerns $\alpha_{B'}$, the possibility degree of the assertion *Y is B'*. This is due to the definition of the functions $\pi_?$ and $1-\pi_{\neg ?}$ that are systematically mapped on the same function : the membership function $\mu_?$, whatever the property *?* should be.

This remark leads to another one which concerns the results of the inferences and the behaviour of the rules used. The similarity between this Modus Ponens and the Generalized one entails a similarity between the results they provide. This will not surprise anyone in the least.

So, we have propound an inference operation which deals simultaneously with the fuzziness and the uncertainty of the data represented by our method. The calculations are hardly more complicated than those needed to deduce something using the Generalized Modus Ponens. The behaviour of the rules are already well known as they are identical to the behaviour obtained with the Generalized Modus Ponens, subject to the operators chosen that must be the same, of course.

Resulting from a series of such an inference, new knowledge appears. Some of the new facts may concern the same variable. If it is the case, the facts are to be combined into a single one. The last part presents an operation for fuzzy and uncertain facts combination.

4. Facts combination

Let consider that, after a series of inferences, the data contains two facts F_{A1} and F_{A2} which concern the same variable. For example :

F_{A1} = (X is A1) is α_{A1}-possible and not (X is A1) is $\alpha_{\neg A1}$-possible

F_{A2} = (X is A2) is α_{A2}-possible and not(X is A2) is $\alpha_{\neg A2}$-possible

F_{A1} and F_{A2} are not obligatorily redundant nor incompatible. If they are not too much different, they must be combined into a single fact F_A. That is why a combination operation is needed.

We consider that the data sources are independent to guarantee that the order of appearances of the facts (this means of the inferences) is not important. We do not deny yet that some applications might require the opposite constraint. Though three types of combination operations exist :

- conjunctions [3, 12] : They give advantage to precision at the detriment of certainty. They may bring inconsistencies to light, but will not resolve them.
- disjunctions [4, 7] : They give advantage to certainty at the detriment of precision and may lead to undetermination.
- compromises [15] : They are half conjunctions, half disjunctions.

We have chosen conjunctions because we find it easier to deal with inconsistency than with undetermination. Inconsistency means too much information and will lead to a choice, whereas undetermination means a lack of information which is less bearable as it is hardly dealt with.

One of the easisest and most widespread conjunction operation is the Min operation. As its efficiency has already been proved and as it is very simple, we have chosen Min to model our combination operation.

Nevertheless, combining data pervaded with uncertainty in addition to the fuzziness is a little too complicated, even linguistically. The uncertainty should not be reasonably taken apart. However, this difficulty can be overcame by involving its synonym instead of a fact if the latter is not enough possible. Let assume that

	(X is A) is hardly possible		not(X is A) is possible
$F_A =$	and	$FS_A =$	and
	not (X is A) is possible		(X is A) is hardly possible

The information *not (X is A) is possible* seems to be easier to deal with than *(X is A) is hardly possible*. Though, when combining, we consider that *not (X is A) is possible* is the actual piece of information and *(X is A) is hardly possible* is just a complement of information. That is why FS_A is used instead of F_A.

To sum up, the combination operation uses the synonym when the former assertion of the fact is less possible than the latter. For instance, let assume that $F_{A1} = (\mu_{A1}, \alpha_{A1}, \alpha_{\neg A1})$ and $F_{A2} = (\mu_{A2}, \alpha_{A2}, \alpha_{\neg A2})$ are two facts to be combined into F_A. For example, if $(\alpha_{A1} < \alpha_{\neg A1})$, then the former assertion of F_{A1} is less possible than the latter one. Though, the combination will involve F_{A1}'s synonym : $Fs_{A1} = (1\text{-}\mu_{A1}, \alpha_{\neg A1}, \alpha_{A1})$. If $\alpha_{A2} \geq \alpha_{\neg A2}$, then F_{A2} itself will be combined. Consequently, F_A will be the intersection of F_{A1}'s synonym and F_{A2} :

$$F_A = (1\text{-}\mu_{A1}, \alpha_{\neg A1}, \alpha_{A1}) \cap (\mu_{A2}, \alpha_{A2}, \alpha_{\neg A2})$$
$$(1\text{-}\mu_{A1} \wedge \mu_{A2}, \alpha_{\neg A1} \vee \alpha_{A2}, \alpha_{A1} \wedge \alpha_{\neg A2}) \qquad (6)$$

Now, let α_{A1} be greater than $\alpha_{\neg A1}$, no synonym is used anymore. So the result of the combination is :

$$F_A = (\mu_{A1}, \alpha_{A1}, \alpha_{\neg A1}) \cap (\mu_{A2}, \alpha_{A2}, \alpha_{\neg A2})$$
$$(\mu_{A1} \wedge \mu_{A2}, \alpha_{A1} \vee \alpha_{A2}, \alpha_{\neg A1} \wedge \alpha_{\neg A22}) \qquad (7)$$

It is clear that this result will be different from the one obtained in the first example. Let notice that (7), for example, results from :

$$\pi_A = \pi_{A1} \wedge \pi_{A2}$$
$$1\text{-}\pi_{\neg A} = 1\text{-}\pi_{\neg A1} \wedge 1\text{-}\pi_{\neg A2} \qquad (8)$$

provided that an approximation is done, but it has been proved that there is nothing significant about it. In actual fact, the neglected quantity does not belong to the nucleus of the resulting membership function. Besides it would disappear anyway because of the linguistic approximation.

This combination operation gives satisfying results since they do not seem to be shocking. Another advantage is its ease of use and ease of computing.

5. Conclusion

The tools we propound for simultaneous treatment of fuzziness and uncertainty in experts systems are an inference operation and a combination operation that involve facts represented by a couple of possibility distributions.

The set of tools composed of our method of representation and our inference and combination operations deal with complete information on the data as they take into account facts fuzziness, their possibility and their contraries' possibility.

Further studies of these tools should provide knowledge-based systems with powerful and easy to use tools.

References

1. D. Dubois, H. Prade : A theorem on implication functions defined from triangular norms. Stochastica, Vol. 8, n° 3, pp 267-279 (1984)
2. D. Dubois, H. Prade : Théorie des possibilités. Application à la représentation des connaissances en informatique. Edition Masson, 1985.
3. D. Dubois, H. Prade : A review of fuzzy set aggregation connectives. Information Journal of General Systems, Vol 12, pp193-226 (1986)
4. D. Dubois, H. Prade : A set of theoretic view of belief functions. Logical operations and approximations by fuzzy sets. Information Sciences, Vol 36, pp 85-121 (1985)
5. D. Dubois, H. Prade : Fuzzy sets in approximate reasoning - Part 1 : Inference with possibility distributions.Rapport IRIT/90-51/R, Octobre 1990.
6. A. Moreau : Contribution au traitement des informations subjectives dans les systèmes experts. Thèse de docteur ingénieur, Université de Valenciennes, mars 1987.
7. Oblow : A hybrid uncertainty theory. 5èmes journées internationales "Les Systèmes Experts et leurs Applications", Avignon, France, pp 1193-1201 (Mai 1985)
8. H. Prade : Sur le traitement de l'imprécis et de l'incertain en intelligence artificielle. Colloque d'Intelligence Artificielle, Toulouse, France, 1985.
9. E. Sanchez : On possibility qualification in natural languages. Information Sciences, Vol. 15, pp. 45-76 (1978)
10. Trillas, Valverde : On some functionally expressable implications for fuzzy set theory. Proc. of the 3rd Inter. Seminar on Fuzzy Set Theory, Linz, Austria, pp 173-190 (1981)
11. Trillas, Valverde : On implication and inistinguishability in the setting of fuzzy logic. Management Decision Support Systems using Fuzzy Sets and Possibility Theory (J. Kacprzyk, R.R. Yager, eds.), Verlag TÜV Rheinland, Köln, pp 198-212 (1985)

12. Weber : A general concept of fuzzy connectives, negations and implications based on t-norms and t-conorms. Fuzzy Sets and Systems, Vol 7, n°11, pp 115-134 (1983)
13. R. Yager : On a general class of fuzzy connectives. Fuzzy Sets and Systems, Vol 3, pp 235-242 (1980)
14. L. Zadeh : A theory of approximate reasoning. Memorandum n°UCB/ERL M77/58 (1977)
15. Zimmerman, Zysno : Latent connectives in human decision making. Fuzzy Sets and Systems, Vol 4, n°1, pp 37-51 (1980)

Modes of Interval-Based Plausible Reasoning Viewed via the Checklist Paradigm

Ladislav J. KOHOUT and Wyllis BANDLER

Department of Computer Science B-173, Florida State University, Tallahassee, Florida 32306, USA.

Abstract. This paper presents some further results on a theoretical semantic device called the *checklist paradigm* which gives the theoretical bounds on the performance of particular many-valued implication operators and other connectives. In its most general form, the checklist paradigm pairs the distinct connectives of the same logical type to provide the bounds for interval-valued approximate inference. After briefly reviewing the checklist paradigm fundamentals we present new theoretical results concerning four plausible modes of reasoning.

Keywords: Approximate inference, interval-valued inference, knowledge engineering, many-valued logics, informatics, fuzzy systems, relational products.

1 Introduction

The theories of relations [3],[10],[11],[5] and various kinds of fuzzy power sets [1],[2] are important structures on which the semantic-based inference in fuzzy logics cricially depends, if one attempts to go beyond propositional logics. Many-valued logic based interval-based reasoning plays increasingly important role in fuzzy and other many-valued extensions of crisp logic. In order to successfully combine these two domains one has to have a better understanding of the ways the MVL connectives used in interval inference and plausible modes of reasoning mutually interact. This investigation, however, should not be based on unmotivated algebraic manipulation and generalization of specialized abstract semigroups (e.g. t-norms and co-norms) at the peril of excluding other logical connectives that do not posses the associativity but form general groupoids. Relying, on the other hand, exclusively of the lattice residuation because it provides a convenient algebraic technical link of the PLY operator with the AND and OR logical types of connectives may also be too restrictive; in particular if one attempts to deal with modes of plausible reasoning, such as modus confirmans and modus negans.

In order to develop successful generalizations, the logical principles have to be added together with sound epistemological basis of to the basic principles on which these generalizations are based.

For this reason a formal semantics which has a sound ontological and epistemological base and is derived by means of an exact mathematical method has been urgently needed. To satisfy this need, we have developed the so called

checklist paradigm [4],[7],[9], which has given rather startling and unexpected results, shedding light not only on the semantics of the operators discussed, but also on the true methodological importance of fuzzy methods in the analysis of systems and structures. This enhances the use of triangle relational products in knowledge engineering, in particular in knowledge elicitation and representation [14],[18]. Also the semantic meaning of many-valued systems of logic used in modelling *activites and their dynamic protection* [13] is further clarified by the checklist paradigm semantics.

In its most general form, the checklist paradigm pairs the distinct connectives of the same logical type to provide the bounds for interval-valued approximate inference. The global structure imposed on the many-valued connectives by certain types of checklist paradigm contracting measures is shown to be the $\mathcal{S}_{2\times2\times2}$ group [17]. Checklist paradigm, however, is applicable not only to the components of the object language, such as logical operators and connectives, but also at the meta-level, thus providing an interval logic based semantics for various rules of inference. As shown in [9] Sec. 6, in addition to generating various multivalued interval-based extensions of the semantics for modus ponens and modus tolens rules of inference, it also provides a justification and the proofs of validity of new interval-based rules (modes) of reasoning *denial* and *confirmation* (modus negans and modus confirmans) [8]. These do not have a non-trivial analogy in Boolean crisp logic.

2 Checklist Paradigm Generated Semantics of some MVL-Operators

Let the *abstract checklist* [9] consist of n descriptive adjectives (descriptors/terms), expressing some potential features of the object to be evaluated, that are relevant to some particular class classification. The suitable formal classification criteria over the class properties provide the assertion of those terms on the checklist that apply to the object being assessed. The assessment of the object is then *summarised* by computing the total score of the object by dividing the "yes" answers by the total number of the questions (i.e. descriptor terms on the checklist). As this computation corresponds to the sigma count used in fuzzy logic, it is natural to interpret the proportion thus scored as a *fuzzy degree* of the agreement of the features of the object with the classification determined by the checklist, thus providing a fuzzy class over a finite domain of the class properties (by a class comprehension action).

Now, consider a single checklist used to give a degree of assent to two different objects A and B, where these abstract objects A, B are both some propositions. For the general case, formally, let F be any logical propositional function of propositions A and B. Where i and j can each take the value 0 or 1, let $f(i,j)$ be the classical truth value of $F(A,B)$ that corresponds to the evaluation i for A and j for B; this also must be either 0 or 1. Let $u(i,j)$ be the ratio of the number in the ij-cell of the contingency table, to the grand total. Then what we have been agreeing is that *the fuzzy assessment of the truth of the proposition*

$F(A,B)$ is

$$\left(m_1(F) = \sum_{i,j} f(i,j)u(i,j)\right). \tag{1}$$

We now have quite a satisfactory way of assigning fuzzy values to compound propositions. But *truth-functionality* has been lost. It has been employed in the construction of the fuzzy assessments of the truth of a compound proposition but it disappears in the outcome. From the point of view of general systems based theory of information, this represents the *loss of variety* in the sense of Ashby. This can be conveniently captured by a constraint table, of which the conventional contingency table of statistics is a special kind. The four interior cells of the constraint (contingency) template constitute its *fine structure*; the margins constitute its *coarse structure*. These structures are linked by the constraints $u(1,0)+u(1,1)=a$, $u(0,1)+u(1,1)=b$. The fine structure gives us the appropriate fuzzy assessments for all propositional functions of A and B; the coarse structure gives us only the fuzzy assessments of A and B themselves. Thus, this provides a genuine semantics of logics of approximation. Our central question is, *to what extent can the fine structure be reconstructed from the coarse*?

We have shown elsewhere (Bandler and Kohout [4],[7],[9],[16]) that the *coarse* structure imposes bounds upon the fine structure, without determining it completely. The solutions of the inequalities defining the constraints [4] on this structure can be conveniently summarised by means of the constraint tables [9]. Figure 1 below summarises the results.

Hence, *associated with the various logical connectives between propositions* **are** *their extreme values.* Thus we obtain the inequality restricting the possible values of m(F):

$$(contop \geq m(F) \geq conbot). \tag{2}$$

where *con* is the name of connective represented by $f(i,j)$. So there are 16 such inequalities, as there are 16 logical types of *con*, 10 of which are nontrivially two-argument.

Let us look now at some typical results [4]. Choosing for the logical type of the connective *con* the *implication* and making the assessment of the fuzzy value of the truth of a proposition by the formula $m_1(F) = 1-(\alpha_{10}/n)$ we obtain:

$$(min(1,1-a+b) \geq m_1(F) \geq max(1-a,b)). \tag{3}$$

We can see that for the *plytop* the checklist paradigm produced the Lukasiewicz implication operator, and the other bound (*plybot*) is the Kleene-Dienes operator. Note that the bounds can be directly read from Figure 1.

Imposing the restriction on (1) such that $u(0,0)=0$ always, yields $a \rightarrow_3 b \geq m_1' \geq 1$, where $\rightarrow_3$ is 'standard star' (Gödel) operator.

If for *con* type we choose an implication again, but only the evaluation "by performance" (that is, we are only concerned with the cases in which the evaluation of A is 1), we obtain

$$(min(1,b/a) \geq m_2(F) \geq max(0,(a+b-1)/a)), \tag{4}$$

1-a	0	1-a
a-b	b	a
1-b	b	1-b

MAXDIAG if b ≤ a

1-b	b-a	1-a
0	a	a
1-b	b	1

MAXDIAG if b ≥ a

1-a-b	b	1-a
a	0	a
1-b	b	1-b

MINDIAG if a+b ≤ 1

0	1-a	1-a
1-b	a+b-1	a
1-b	b	1

MINDIAG if a+b ≥ a

Figure 1: Checklist Paradigm constraint Table for Connectives.

1-a	0
1-r	r-1+a

0	1-a
1-r	r-1+a

Modus Ponens and Denial: r ≥ 1-a.

r-b	0
1-r	b

r-b	b
1-r	0

Modus Tollens an Confirmation: b ≤ r

Figure 2: Checklist Paradigm Constraint Tables for Rules of Inference.

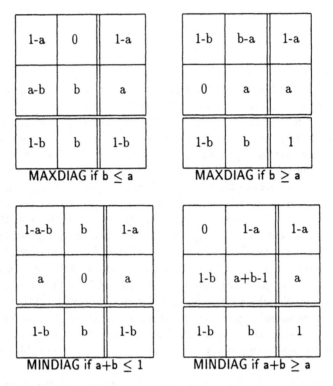

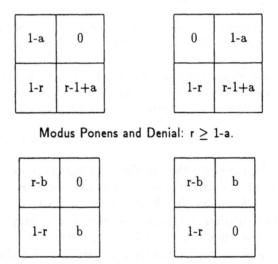

where *plytop* is in this instance the well-known G43 implication of Goguen-Gaines (cf. eg. [4]). Still another contracting measure which distinguishes the proportion of satisfactions "by performance", $u(1,1)$, and "by default", $u(0,0)+u(0,1)$ yields [4]

$$(max[min(a,b),1-a] \geq m_3(F) \geq max(a+b-1,1-a)) \,. \tag{5}$$

Choosing for $m(F)$ yet other functions we obtain a variety of other interesting results for implications bounds, the details of which cannot be discussed here. See Bandler and Kohout ([4], [9].

3 Checklist Paradigm and Four Modes of Reasoning

Rather than proceeding from propositions A and B and establishing that A *IMPLIES* B, formal reasoning in everyday situations and in Expert Systems tends to start with the premise that A *IMPLIES* B and some assertion or denial of A (or B), and proceed to a conclusion about B (or A). Elsewhere [6] the present authors have discussed the fact that in multiple-valued logic, for any fixed choice among the distinguished implication operators, to the classically valid modes of *modus ponens* and *modus tollens* are to be added fuzzily valid modes of *denial* and *confirmation* (*modus negans* and *modus confirmans*). An evaluation of the compound proposition "A IMPLIES B" and evaluation of A (or of *not*-A, or of B, or of *not*-B) leads to an evaluational conclusion.

Let us consider two of the modes, *ponens* and *confirmation*, from which the other two can be derived. *Ponens* is given information about A and seeks a conclusion about B; *confirmation* goes the other way. We now wonder, what does the Checklist Paradigm have to offer to the two attempts?

Again, we can compare the coarse structure to the fine, and see to what extent the former limits the latter. But now the coarse structure is no longer embodied in the marginal sums. Rather, we are given the measure for A *PLY* B and that for A (or B) and we seek the one for B (or A), that is, we are given the sum of the contents cells 00, 01 and 11, and the sum of row 1 (or column 1), and we wish to estimate the sum of column 1 (or row 1). Thus we get the following theorems.

Theorem 1 – Checklist Modus Ponens. *Given* $r = m(A \rightarrow B)$ *and* $a = m(A)$ *satisfying the consistency condition* $r \geq 1-a$, *the values of* $b = m(B)$ *are subject to*

$$(r-(1-a) \leq b \leq r) \,. \tag{6}$$

Proof. Subject to the constraints (1) and $u(1,0)+u(1,1)=a, u(0,1)+u(1,1)=b$, $u(i,j) \geq 0, i,j \in \{0,1\}$, modus ponens is the attempt to solve for m_p given $m_1 = r$ [cf. (1)] and $M_a = a$. Previously when proving (3), a and b were given and we were solving for m_1; now we are not told a and b, but we have the knowledge of a and r. This leaves just one degree of freedom for any changes in the fine structures, that would leave the constraints invariant. Only the transfers between the cells $u(0,0)$ and $u(0,1)$ are permitted. So, subject to the consistency condition $u(0,0)+u(0,1) \geq 0$ one obtains the inequality $0 \leq u(0,1) \leq 1-a$. Adding to this $a+r-1$ yields $a+r-1 \leq u(0,1)+a+r-1 \leq r$. From this, the bounds of this Theorem follows. Proofs of the three other theorems (Confirmation, Tollens and Denial) can be constructed in a similar manner. Constraint tables that again conveniently summarise the coarse approximating structures yielding the bounds are given in Figure 2.

Theorem 2 – Checklist Confirmation. *Given $r = m(A \rightarrow B)$ and $b = m(B)$ subject to the consistency condition $b \leq r$, the values of $a = m(A)$ are subject to*

$$(1-r \leq a \leq 1-(r-b)). \tag{7}$$

Proof. It is easy to modify the previous proof. It is, however, of independent epistemological interest to make the dynamics of permitted changes in the fine structure more explicit. Let δv denote the changes in values of v and $\neg\delta$ signify that the changes are forbidden. Then the prescribed constraints can be conceptualised as protection constraints $\neg\delta r, \neg\delta b, \neg\delta u(1,0), \neg\delta u(0,0)$. Then $u(01), u(1,1)$ are the only remaining candidates for $\delta()$. In order to complete the proof, it has to be determined if any changes on these are admissible, not violating the previously imposed constraints. If $\delta u(0,1)$ is asserted, this may generate possible changes $\delta u(0,0), \delta u(1,0), \delta u(1,1)$. It can be seen that $\delta u(1,0), \delta u(0,0)$ cannot be admitted, as it would violate the constraint $1-b = u(0,0)+u(1,0) \leq 1$ and $u(1,0) = 1-r$, respectively. So $\delta(u(0,1), u(1,1))$ is the only admissible configuration. That this is so can be seen from the fact that the changes induced by this configuration are confined to r and are also compatible with b, not violating the constraints on either of these.

Theorem 3 – Checklist Modus Tolens. *Given $r = m(A \rightarrow B)$ and $\neg b = m(not-B)$ satisfying the consistency condition $r \geq b$, the values of $\neg a = m(not-A)$ are subject to*

$$(r-b \leq \neg a \leq r). \tag{8}$$

Proof. Analogously, $\delta(u(0,1), u(1,1))$ is the only admissible configuration that does not violate the constraints, thus yielding the constraint tables (b) in Figure 2.

Theorem 4 – Checklist Denial. *Given $r = m(A \rightarrow B)$ and $\neg a = m(not-A)$ subject to the consistency condition $1-a \leq r$, the values of $\neg b = m(not-B)$ are subject to*

$$(1-r \leq \neg b \leq 2-(r+a)). \tag{9}$$

Proof. Analogously, $\delta(u(0,0), u(0,1))$ is the only admissible configuration that does not violate the constraints, thus yielding the constraint tables (a) in Figure 2.

4 Semantics of Meta-Rules for Generating Contrapositive Ply Operators

We have seen above that by means of the checklist paradigm techniques, various meta-rules can be adequately dealt with. Assertion and rejection of a proposition properly belong to the domain of meta-operations. In those logics, where the mutual duality of assertion and rejection is their meta-property, this is also reflected in the fact that the corresponding object language ply operators will be *contrapozitive.* The duality of inference rules (such as modus ponens and tolens) is assured by the contrapositive property of the ply operator involved in those rules. A ply operator is contrapositive, if its valuation satisfies the semantic equality $a \to b = \neg b \to \neg a$.

Theorem 5. *The Lukasiewicz operator* $a \to_5 b$ *is the upper contrapozitivization of the operator* $aPLYBOTb = max(a + b - 1, 1 - a)$ *of (5) above.*

Proof. Performing the contrapozitivization by $aORTOPb = min(a+b, 1)$ yields $min[max(a + b - 1, 1 - a) + max(1 - a - b, b), 1] = min[max(1 - a + b, 0), 1] = min(1 - a + b), 1)$.

This theorem complements the result of [4] Sec.5, where Klene-Dienes ply was obtained by the upper contrapozitivization of EZ, using $aORBOTb = max(a, b)$ as the contrapozitivizing connective. As EZ is generated from the constraint tables of the checklist paradigm by the contracting measure m_3 (cf. [4] (6.3)), without using statistical restrictions utilizing the expected values in the contingency tables, the inequality $a \to_5 b \geq m_1(F) \geq a \to_6 b$ represents a genuine interval formula within a general interval-based inference system.

If one employs, on the other hand, the notion of expected value within the constrain tables of the checklist paradigm, the interval bounds collapse into a single point, e.g. the inequality (3) above yields the 'point' $a \to_{5.5} b = 1 - a + ab$ (cf. [4], Th. 7.1). We indicate some typical results below, which are the additions to our previous results [4] Sec. 7, [15].

Corollary 6. *From the expected (middle) values of the checklist (cf. [9] Fig.3-2) the expected values of contracting mesure* m_2 *follow:* $expected(m_2) = em_2 = a.b/a; expected(\neg m_2) = \neg em_2 = (1 - a).(1 - b)/(1 - b)$.

Theorem 7 Values of contrapozitivized measures.

1. The upper contrapozitivization of em_2 yields:
   $em_5 = ORBOT(em_2, \neg em_2) = max(em_2, \neg em_2) = a \to_6 b$;
   $em_6 = ORTOP(em_2, \neg em_2) = min(1, em_2 + \neg em_2) = a \to_5 b$.
2. The lower contrapozitivization yields:
   $em_8 = ANDTOP(em_2, \neg em_2) = min(em_2, \neg em_2) = min(b, 1 - a)$;
   $em_9 = ANDBOT(em_2, \neg em_2) = max(0, em_2 + \neg em_2 - 1 = max(0, b - a)$.

The contracting measure m_2 is connected with G43 Goguen-Gaines ply operator, unlike the measure m_3 employed in theorem 5 above. This proves that it is important to judge the whole theory, and the whole system of connectives employed by that theory, to understand correctly the role and epistemological meaning as well as the similarities and differences of various logical systems of approximate reasoning. Our study is being currently extended to the groupoid-based many-valued Pinkava algebras used in the design of Knowledge-based and other systems [13]. This theoretical work is supplemented by empirical studies of the adequacy of various logical connectives in practical applications of fuzzy sets and relations [12].

References

1. W. Bandler and L.J. Kohout. Fuzzy relational products and fuzzy implication operators. In *International Workshop on Fuzzy Reasoning Theory and Applications*, London, September 1978. Queen Mary College, University of London.
2. W. Bandler and L.J. Kohout. Fuzzy power sets and fuzzy implication operators. *Fuzzy Sets and Systems*, 4:13–30, 1980.
3. W. Bandler and L.J. Kohout. Fuzzy relational products as a tool for analysis and synthesis of the behaviour of complex natural and artificial systems. In P.P. Wang and S.K. Chang, editors, *Fuzzy Sets: Theory and Applications to Policy Analysis and Information Systems*, pages 341–367. Plenum press, New York and London, 1980.
4. W. Bandler and L.J. Kohout. Semantics of implication operators and fuzzy relational products. *Internat. Journal of Man-Machine Studies*, 12:89–116, 1980. Reprinted in Mamdani, E.H. and Gaines, B.R. eds. *Fuzzy Reasoning and its Applications*. Academic Press, London, 1981, pages 219-246.
5. W. Bandler and L.J. Kohout. Fast fuzzy relational algorithms. In A. Ballester, D. Cardús, and E. Trillas, editors, *Proc. of the Second Internat. Conference on Mathematics at the Service of Man*, pages 123–131, Las Palmas, 1982. (Las Palmas, Canary Islands, Spain, 28 June - 3 July), Universidad Politechnica de las Palmas.
6. W. Bandler and L.J. Kohout. The four modes of inference in fuzzy expert systems. In R. Trappl, editor, *Cybernetics and Systems Research 2*, pages 581–586. North-Holland, Amsterdam, 1984.
7. W. Bandler and L.J. Kohout. Unified theory of multiple-valued logical operators in the light of the checklist paradigm. In *Proc. of the 1984 IEEE Conference on Systems, Man and Cybernetics*, pages 356–364, New York, 1984. IEEE.
8. W. Bandler and L.J. Kohout. Probabilistic vs. fuzzy production rules in expert systems. *Internat. Journal of Man-Machine Studies*, 22:347–353, 1985.
9. W. Bandler and L.J. Kohout. The use of checklist paradigm in inference systems. In C.V. Negoita and H. Prade, editors, *Fuzzy Logic in Knowledge Engineering*, chapter 7, pages 95–111. Verlag TÜV Rheinland, Köln, 1986.
10. W. Bandler and L.J. Kohout. Relations, mathematical. In M.G. Singh, editor, *Systems and Control Encyclopedia*, pages 4000 – 4008. Pergamon Press, Oxford, 1987.
11. W. Bandler and L.J. Kohout. Special properties, closures and interiors of crisp and fuzzy relations. *Fuzzy Sets and Systems*, 26(3):317–332, June 1988.

12. B. Ben-Ahmeida, L.J. Kohout, and W. Bandler. The use of fuzzy relational products in comparison and verification of correctness of knowledge structures. In L.J. Kohout, J. Anderson, and W. Bandler, editors, *Knowledge-Based Systems for Multiple Environments*, chapter 16. Ashgate Publ. (Gower), Aldershot, U.K., 1992.
13. L.J. Kohout. *A Perspective on Intelligent Systems: A Framework for Analysis and Design*. Chapman and Hall & Van Nostrand, London & New York, 1990.
14. L.J. Kohout, J. Anderson, and W. Bandler. *Knowledge-Based Systems for Multiple Environments*. Ashgate Publ. (Gower), Aldershot, U.K., 1992.
15. L.J. Kohout and W. Bandler. Axioms for conditional inference: probabilistic and possibilistic. In A. Ballester, D. Cardús, and E. Trillas, editors, *Proc. of the Second Internat. Conference on Mathematics at the Service of Man*, pages 413–414, Las Palmas, 1982. (Las Palmas, Canary Islands, Spain, 28 June - 3 July), Universidad Politechnica de las Palmas.
16. L.J. Kohout and W. Bandler. Fuzzy relational products in knowledge engineering. In V. et al. Nov'ak, editor, *Fuzzy Approach to Reasoning and Decision Making*, pages 51–66. Academia and Kluwer, Prague and Dordrecht, 1992.
17. L.J. Kohout and W. Bandler. How the checklist paradigm elucidates the semantics of fuzzy inference. In *Proc. of the IEEE Internat. Conference on Fuzzy Systems 1992*, pages 571–578. IEEE, New York, 1992.
18. L.J. Kohout and W. Bandler. Use of fuzzy relations in knowledge representation, acquisition and processing. In L.A. Zadeh and J. Kacprzyk, editors, *Fuzzy Logic for the Management of Uncertainty*. John Wiley, New York, 1992.

RULE-BASED SYSTEMS WITH UNRELIABLE CONDITIONS

L. Cardona, J. Kohlas, P.A. Monney
Institute for Automation and Operations Research
University of Fribourg
CH-1700 Fribourg (Switzerland)
E-mail kohlas@cfruni51

Abstract

This paper deals with the problem of inference under uncertain information. This is a generalization of a paper of Cardona et al. (1991a) where rules were not allowed to contain negations. In contrast, this paper discusses inference with rules involving negations. This provides more flexibility in the modeling process of knowledge, but it introduces the possibility of contradictions and the reasoning is therefore not necessarily monotone. It is well known that when the rules can be organized in a tree, computations can be performed by a simple local propagation scheme. However, when the graph of rules is not a tree, an alternative procedure to the usual Markov tree cover method called factorization is presented. This method is new in the context of evidential reasoning but it is widely used in the reliability theory of complex systems and in Bayesian networks. The whole model is placed under the unifying Dempster-Shafer theory of evidence. It has also tight connections with de Kleer's assumption-based truth maintenance systems (ATMS). The method is illustrated on an example borrowed from Pearl (1988) and translated into an evidential framework rather than a Bayesian one.

1. Introductory example.

As an illustrative example of the type of models studied in this paper, consider the alarm story described by J. Pearl (1988) in his book. There, the situation is analyzed from the classical Bayesian point of view. In contrast, we will adopt the evidential point of view or, more precisely, we will use an adaptation of the Dempster-Shafer theory of evidence to model the story. We start with the definition of a certain number of propositions occuring in the story:

a : the alarm is ringing
b : there is a burglary
e : an earthquake has occured
w : there is a phone call from Mr. Watson
g : there is a phone call from Mrs. Gibbon
d : there is a phone call from Mr. Holmes's daughter
c : there is a confirmation of an earthquake.

Besides, we need a certain number of extra propositions called *assumptions*:

a_1 : the alarm system is functioning
a_2 : an extra cause for an alarm is present
a_3 : Mr. Watson is in joke mood
a_4 : Mrs. Gibbon is deaf
a_5 : Mr. Holmes'daughter is at home
a_6 : the earthquake sensor is sensitive
a_7 : the conditions for an earthquake are present.

The difference between assumptions and the ordinary propositions involved in the story is that although it is not known which assumptions are true or false, we are in position to specify probabilities for them. In contrast, no probability information about the other propositions is assumed.

Given these definitions, the alarm system and the behaviour of Mr. Watson, Mrs. Gibbon and Mr. Holmes's daughter can be described by simple inference rules:

$$\begin{array}{llll} R_1: & b \wedge a_1 \rightarrow a & R_9: & a_4 \rightarrow \neg g \\ R_2: & e \wedge a_1 \rightarrow a & R_{10}: & \neg a \rightarrow \neg g \\ R_3: & a_2 \rightarrow a & R_{11}: & a \wedge a_5 \rightarrow d \\ R_4: & \neg b \wedge \neg e \wedge \neg a_2 \rightarrow \neg a & R_{12}: & \neg a_5 \rightarrow \neg d \\ R_5: & a \rightarrow w & R_{13}: & e \wedge a_6 \rightarrow c \\ R_6: & a_3 \rightarrow w & R_{14}: & \neg e \rightarrow \neg c \\ R_7: & \neg a \wedge \neg a_3 \rightarrow \neg w & R_{15}: & a_7 \rightarrow e \\ R_8: & a \wedge \neg a_4 \rightarrow g & R_{16}: & \neg a_7 \rightarrow \neg e. \end{array}$$

For example, the first rule states that if there is a burglary and the alarm is functioning, then the alarm will ring. We consider that these rules are certain. However, an assumption a_i has a known probability q_i to be true and $1 - q_i$ to be false, and we assume independence. Furthermore, we also dispose of factual (evidential) information. For example, there is a phone call from Mr. Watson (w), there is no call from Mrs. Gibbon ($\neg g$) and there is no call from Mr. Homes' daughter ($\neg d$). Using this information (or other information) together with the implication rules, the question to be addressed is then to determine evidence about the presence or the absence of a burglary. Then we will be in position to compute the degree of credibility (support) and the degree of plausibility that there is indeed a burglary. This example will be continued in section 5.

2. The general model.

In this section, we formalize the example described above using an adaptation of the Dempster-Shafer theory of evidence. We introduce a set of propositions $P = \{p_1, \ldots, p_n\}$ and a set of assumptions $A = \{a_1, \ldots, a_s\}$. For each element $x \in P \cup A$, let $\Theta_x = \{x, \neg x\}$ represent the frame of discernment containing the two literals x and $\neg x$ expressing the fact that either x or $\neg x$ must be true. Then an implication rule reads

$$R: \wedge_{i \in I} l_i \rightarrow l_j, \qquad (1)$$

where l_i and l_j are literals in some frames Θ_x. Expressed in this way, an implication rule has a direction, namely from the condition to the conclusion. But this direction is not essential. In fact, what really matters is the logical relation between the propositons and assumptions involved in the rule. This relation restricts the common truth values of these propositions and assumptions into the subset

$$F = \Theta_R - \{(l_i, i \in I, \neg l_j\}, \tag{2}$$

where Θ_R is the cartesian product of the frames Θ_x whose literals appear in the rule. For example, Θ_R for the rule 10 in Pearl's story is $\Theta_a \times \Theta_g$ and

$$F = \{(a, g), (a, \neg g), (\neg a, \neg g)\}. \tag{3}$$

The implication rule (1) is equivalent to the clause $\vee_{i \in I} \neg l_i \vee l_j$. This is a symmetric notation which introduces no irrelevant direction. This clause indeed represents the set F or the rule R. Whereas there are several representations of a clause as an implication rule, there is only one clause which represents a rule. In terms of clauses, the rules R_1 to R_{16} given in section 1 read as follows:

$$\begin{array}{llll} R_1: & \neg b \vee \neg a_1 \vee a & R_9: & \neg a_4 \vee \neg g \\ R_2: & \neg e \vee \neg a_1 \vee a & R_{10}: & a \vee \neg g \\ R_3: & \neg a_2 \vee a & R_{11}: & \neg a \vee \neg a_5 \vee d \\ R_4: & b \vee e \vee a_2 \vee \neg a & R_{12}: & a_5 \vee \neg d \\ R_5: & \neg a \vee w & R_{13}: & \neg e \vee \neg a_6 \vee c \\ R_6: & \neg a_3 \vee w & R_{14}: & e \vee \neg c \\ R_7: & a \vee a_3 \vee \neg w & R_{15}: & \neg a_7 \vee e \\ R_8: & \neg a \vee a_4 \vee g & R_{16}: & a_7 \vee \neg e. \end{array}$$

These clauses can be represented by a bipartite graph called the graph of the model. Its nodes are the propositions and assumptions in $P \cup A$ (the circular nodes) together with the clauses themselves (the rectangular nodes). There is an edge between a circular node $x \in P \cup A$ and a rectangular node representing a clause c if and only if x or $\neg x$ is a literal of c. The graph of the model presented in section 1 is given in fig. 1.

It remains to explain how to model the uncertainty about the assumptions. This is done using the notion of a *hint*, which is an adaptation of the notion of belief function used in the Dempster-Shafer theory of evidence. For more information about hints, refer to Kohlas, Monney, 1990 and 1991. One possibility to define a hint is to give its basic probability assignment (bpa for short). A bpa on a frame Θ_x is a mapping $m : \mathcal{P}(\Theta_x) \to [0, 1]$ such that $m(\emptyset) = 0$ and $m(x) + m(\neg x) + m(\Theta_x) = 1$ (this notion can be naturally extended to any frame of discernment). A hint (or its bpa) permits as usual to compute degrees of credibility or degrees of plausibility of hypotheses represented by subsets of Θ_x. Then our knowledge about the validity of the assumptions a_i is represented as a Bayesian (or precise) hint with bpa $m(a_i) = q_i$, $m(\neg a_i) = 1 - q_i$. Similarly, although this is not the case in the example from section 1, we can also

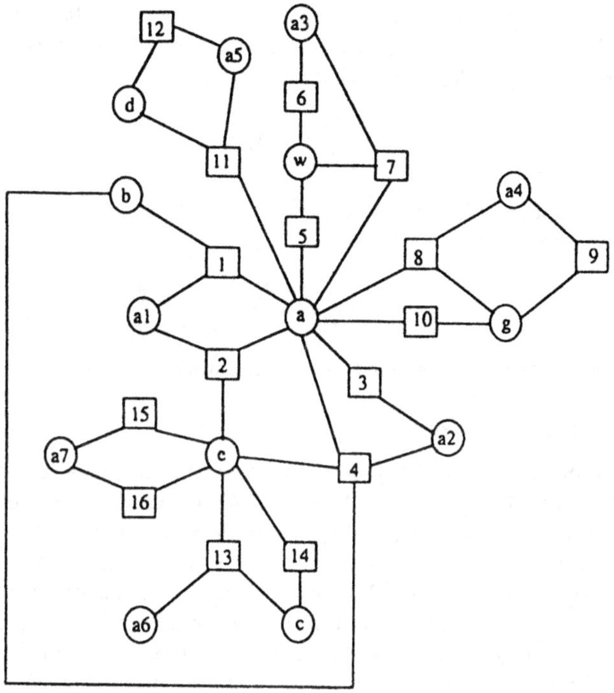

Figure 1.

consider the case where the implication rules are not fully reliable. If r denotes the reliability of the rule (1), then the hint $\mathcal{H}(R)$ with bpa $m(F) = r$ and $m(\Theta_R) = 1 - r$ represents the uncertainty about the validity of the rule. This means that if the rule is valid, then the corresponding clause is true and if not, then it can be either true or false.

If $\mathcal{H}_i$ denotes the hint for the assumption a_i and $\mathcal{R}$ denotes the set of all rules, then integrating all available information requires to compute the hint

$$\mathcal{H} = \oplus\ \{\mathcal{H}_i : i = 1, \ldots, s\} \oplus \{\mathcal{H}(R) : R \in \mathcal{R}\} \tag{4}$$

by the Dempster's rule of combination (actually, it is the bpas which are combined). This hint is relative to the overall frame $\Theta = \prod \{\Theta_x : x \in P \cup A\}$ and if we are interested in a particular proposition $p \in P$ we have to find its coarsening to the frame Θ_p. The resulting hint will be denoted by $\mathcal{H}^{\downarrow p}$. This hint is obtained by projecting the focal sets of $\mathcal{H}$ to Θ_p and this frame is called the query frame. It corresponds to Θ_b in Pearl's story.

Since we'll have to cope with contradictions during computations, it turns out that the notion of an unnormalized bpa (ubpa for short) on a frame X is important. This is a mapping $m_* : \mathcal{P}(X) \to [0,1]$ such that

$$\sum_{A \subseteq X} m_*(A) = 1. \tag{5}$$

In contrast to a bpa, $m_*(\emptyset)$ is not necessarily equal to 0. However, a ubpa m_* determines a bpa m in a canonical way:

$$m(A) = \begin{cases} \frac{m_*(A)}{1-m_*(\emptyset)} & \text{if } A \neq \emptyset \\ 0 & \text{if } A = \emptyset. \end{cases} \tag{6}$$

Conversely, a bpa can be considered as a special ubpa.

3. Computing in trees.

If the graph of the model happens to be a tree, then it is indeed a Markov tree (refer to Shafer et al. (1987) and Kohlas, Monney (1990) for a discussion of this notion). In order to compute $\mathcal{H}^{\downarrow p}$, all hints should in principle be vacuously extended to the overall frame Θ, then combined by Dempster's rule on Θ, and finally the result should be coarsened to Θ_p. But due to the Markov tree structure, this computationally difficult task can be replaced by local computations. The details on how to perform these local computations in the general case of Markov trees are presented in Shafer et al. (1987) and Kohlas, Monney (1990). However, local computations are particularly simple in this type of Markov trees involving clauses. In fact, it is clearly always possible to orient the edges of the tree in such a way that the query frame is an anti-root. Then this orientation permits to consider each clause $c = x_1 \vee \ldots \vee x_r$ as an inference rule $\wedge_{i=2}^{r} \neg x_i \to x_1$ when the arc (c, x_1) belongs to the orientation. The general local propagation scheme in Markov trees therefore reduces to the following two procedures:

(1) Propagation of evidence (hints) through an unreliable rule
(2) Combination of evidence (hints) on a frame Θ_x.

Starting from the leaves of the tree, these two operations are applied until the query frame is reached. Now let's look concretely how they can be performed in terms of ubpas. The propagation through the rule (1) corresponds to the determination of the hint

$$\mathcal{K} = \left(\oplus_{i \in I} \mathcal{H}_i \oplus \mathcal{H}(R)\right)^{\downarrow q} \tag{7}$$

if $\mathcal{H}_i$ is the hint on the frame Θ_{a_i} containing the literal $l_i, i \in I$ and Θ_q is the frame containing l_j ($\mathcal{H}_i$ can be vacuous). If m_* denotes the ubpa of $\mathcal{K}$ and m_{*i} is the ubpa of $\mathcal{H}_i$, then the following result holds.

Theorem 1. If r is the reliability of the rule R, then

$$
\begin{aligned}
m_*(l_j) &= r \prod_{i \in I} m_{*i}(l_i) \\
m_*(\neg l_j) &= 0 \\
m_*(\emptyset) &= 1 - \prod_{i \in I}(1 - m_{*i}(\emptyset)) \\
m_*(\Theta_j) &= \prod_{i \in I}(1 - m_{*i}(\emptyset)) - r \prod_{i \in I} m_{*i}(l_i)
\end{aligned} \tag{8}
$$

The proof of this theorem, like that of all theorems in this paper, can be found Kohlas, Monney (1992). Now we consider the second operation, namely combining two hints on a frame $\Theta_x = \{x, \neg x\}$. If m_{*1} and m_{*2} are the ubpas of two hints $\mathcal{H}_1$ and $\mathcal{H}_2$ on Θ_x, then we have the following result for the ubpa of the combined hint $\mathcal{H}_1 \oplus \mathcal{H}_2$.

Theorem 2.

If F equals $\{x\}$ or $\{\neg x\}$, then

$$
m_*(F) = m_{*1}(F)(m_{*2}(F) + m_{*2}(\Theta_i)) + m_{*1}(\Theta_i)m_{*2}(F) \tag{9}
$$

and $m_*(\Theta_x) = m_{*1}(\Theta_x)m_{*2}(\Theta_x)$.

Theorems 1 and 2 show explicitely how to perform local computations to determine the ubpa of the hint $\mathcal{H}^{\downarrow p}$ when the graph of the model is a tree.

4. The factorization method.

Local computations are possible in trees, but what about graphs which are not trees ? As usual, the general approach using Markov tree covers can be applied (Shafer, Shenoy, 1990). However, we propose another general method called factorization or hypothetical reasoning. The intuitive idea is to assume hypothetically that a certain event is known with certainty and to execute the inference under this hypothesis, and then to weight the obtained result according to the probability of the event. This may lead to a significant reduction of the computational effort, especially when the number of events to hypothetize about is small. This is the case in the type of models discussed here. This method is now described more formally for the model presented in the previous section, but its principle is very general. This method can be seen as a generalization of the factorization method for inference networks (Cardona et al., 1991 a, b). Note that the same idea has already been used by Pearl to treat cycles in the probabilistic, Bayesian case (Pearl, 1988).

The goal of factorization is to create trees from the original graph of the model. Factorization is always performed with respect to a hint $\mathcal{H}_i$. This hint is Bayesian and its ubpa m_{*i} satisfies $m_{*i}(a_i) + m_{*i}(\neg a_i) = 1$. Recall that we have s hints of this type in the model and suppose that we factorize on the first hint $\mathcal{H}_1$. If H equals $\{a_1\}$ or $\{\neg a_1\}$, then define the hint

$$\mathcal{H}|H = H\oplus\Big(\oplus\{\mathcal{H}_i : i = 2,\ldots,s\}\Big)\oplus\Big(\oplus\{\mathcal{H}(R) : R \in \mathcal{R}\}\Big) \tag{10}$$

where H stands for the deterministic hint focussing on H with probability 1. If $m_*^{\downarrow p}$ and $m_*^{\downarrow p}(\cdot|H)$ denote the ubpas of $\mathcal{H}^{\downarrow p}$ and $(\mathcal{H}|H)^{\downarrow p}$ respectively, the the following theorem called *factorization theorem* holds.

Theorem 3.

If A is any subset of the query frame Θ_p (including the empty one), then

$$m_*^{\downarrow p}(A) = m_{*1}(a_1)m_*^{\downarrow p}(A|a_1) + m_{*1}(\neg a_1)m_*^{\downarrow p}(A|\neg a_1). \tag{11}$$

This formula can be considered as a kind of formula of total probability. It captures the intuitive idea that we can factor or condition $\mathcal{H}$ in order to compute $\mathcal{H}^{\downarrow p}$. Note that in the general version of theorem 3, the sum extends over all focal sets of the hint used to factorize.

In the computation of $m_*^{\downarrow p}(\cdot|a_1)$, it is assumed that a_1 is definitely true. This permits to simplify the original model because each clause containing a_1 is automatically true and can therefore be eliminated from the model. Similarly, we can remove the literal $\neg a_1$ from each clause containing $\neg a_1$. These operations are very intuitive and reasonable, but their formal justification can be found in Kohlas, Monney (1992). It is interesting to remark that the graph of the reduced model no longer contains the node a_1. A similar analysis can be performed when we condition on $\neg a_1$. Again, the node a_1 no longer appears in the graph of the reduced model. For example, if the graph of the original model contains exactly one cycle and a_1 lies on it, then the graphs of the two reduced models are trees and the local computation method described in section 3 can be applied. But usually a factorization with respect to more than one hint is needed to create trees as will be seen in the next section.

5. Computing the example.

In this section, we apply the factorization method to the Pearl's story presented in section 1. Integrating the factual knowledge that Mr. Watson is calling and that neither Mrs. Gibbon nor Mr. Holmes' daughter are calling permits to reduce the original model to the following set C_0 of clauses :

$1: \neg b \vee \neg a_1 \vee a$	$7: \neg a \vee \neg a_5$
$2: \neg e \vee \neg a_1 \vee a$	$8: \neg e \vee \neg a_6 \vee c$
$3: \neg a_2 \vee a$	$9: e \vee \neg c$
$4: b \vee e \vee a_2 \vee \neg a$	$10: \neg a_7 \vee e$
$5: a \vee a_3$	$11: a_7 \vee \neg e$
$6: \neg a \vee a_4$	

In the first factorization step, we factorize on the hint $\mathcal{H}_1$. If a_1 is assumed to be true, then the first two clauses become $\neg b \vee a$ and $\neg e \vee a$ respectively. This defines a new model C_1. Similarly, if a_1 is assumed to be false, then the first two clauses in C_0 can be eliminated. This defines a new model C_1'. The graphs of C_1 and C_1' are not trees and a second factorization is necessary. This time, we factorize on the hint $\mathcal{H}_2$. The factorization of the model C_1 yields the models C_2 and C_2' depending on whether a_2 is assumed to be true or false respectively. The set C_2 is obtained from C_1 by replacing the third clause by the clause a and by eliminating the fourth clause. In the same way, C_2' is obtained from C_1 by eliminating the third clause and by replacing the fourth clause by the clause $b \vee e \vee \neg a$. The graphs of C_2 and C_2' are given in fig. 2 a) and b) respectively.

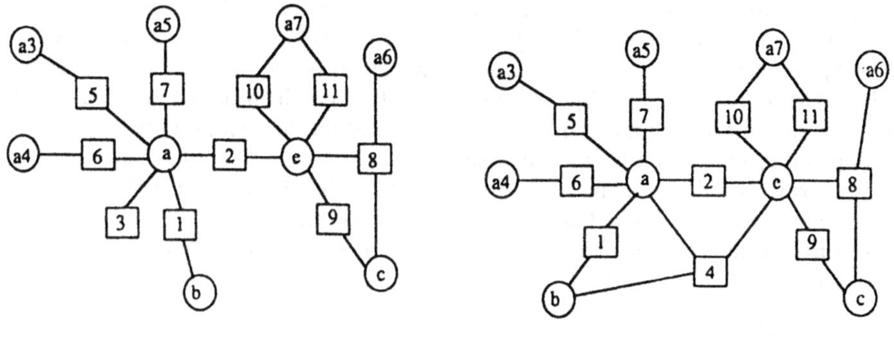

a) (0.75, 0,0,0.25)

b) (0.525, 0.174, 0.224, 0.075)

Figure 2.

The factorization of C_1' yields C_3 and C_3' whose graphs are G_3 and G_3' in fig. 3 a) and b) respectively. These models are obtained by the same procedure as the one used

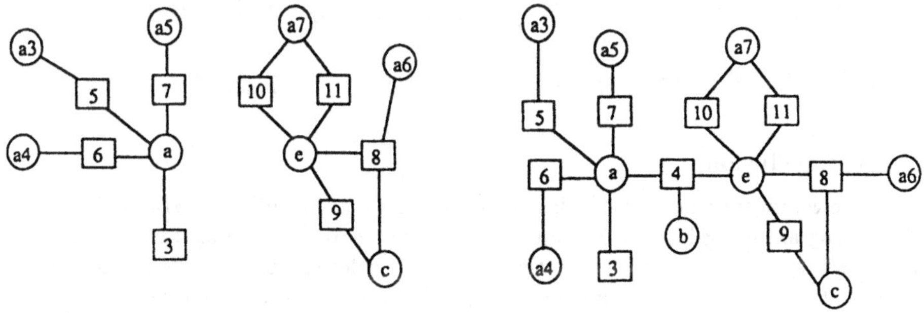

a) (0.75, 0, 0, 0.25)

b) (0.525, 0.174, 0, 0.3)

Figure 3.

to pass from C_1 to C_2 and C_2'.

Although the four graphs G_2, G_2', G_3 and G_3' are not trees, it is not necessary to factorize further because the cycles are small enough to be treated directly. Furthermore, the graph G given in fig. 4 is a subgraph of all four graphs and it is intuitively clear that it can be replaced by the single hint obtained by coarsening to Θ_e the combination of all hints in G. This is a direct consequence of a result about qualitative independence. For the same reason, this hint can itself be obtained by combining on Θ_e the hints resulting from the graphs G' and G'' (see fig. 4), which in turn are easily computed by a single factorization. If a ubpa m_* on a frame Θ_x is represented by four values (a, b, c, d) where

$$m_*(\emptyset) = a, \; m_*(x) = b, \; m_*(\neg x) = c, \; m_*(\Theta_x) = d, \tag{12}$$

then the ubpa on Θ_e coming from the graph G equals $(0, 0.001, 0.999, 0)$, assuming that the probabilities $q_i, i = 1, \ldots 7$ are $0.99, 0.01, 0.3, 0.5, 0.5, 0.99, 0.001$ respectively. In a similar way, we can group the hints on the graph given in fig. 5. Then, using theorems 1 and 2, we obtain the ubpa $(0.525, 0.175, 0.225, 0.075)$ on Θ_a. Using these values, it is then easy to compute the ubpas on Θ_b for the four graphs pictured in fig. 2 and 3 (they are given below the graphs). Then the factorization theorem permits to compute the ubpa of G_1 and G'_1 on Θ_b and then also the ubpa of G_0 on Θ_b. It is now a simple task to normalize this last ubpa to obtain the hint $\mathcal{H}^{1b}$ on Θ_b. We find that the degree of credibility that there is a burglary is 0.36 whereas the degree of credibility that there is no burglary is 0.46. These results are very reasonable in view of the available information.

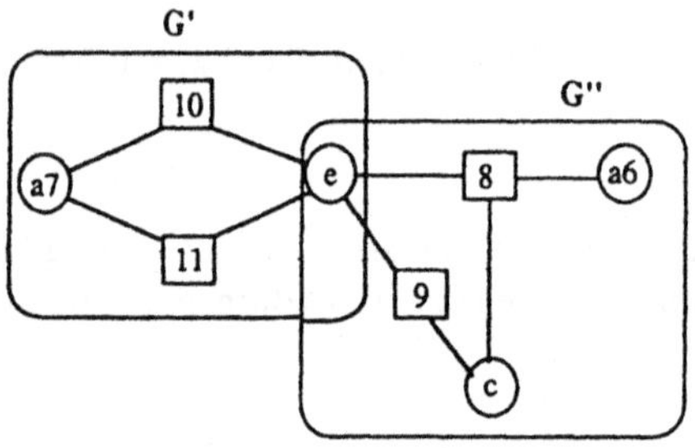

Figure 4. Graph G.

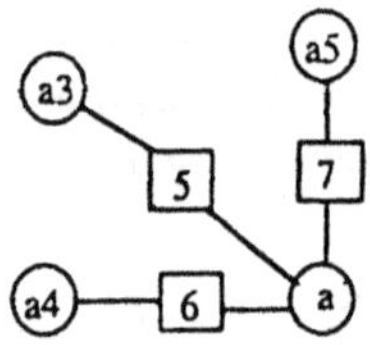

Figure 5.

6. Conclusion.

The computational method described in this paper has been integrated in a computer program using hints as the modeling tool for representing uncertainty in general rule-based systems (the only restriction is that the rules can be expressed as a disjunction of literals). The results are very promissing and current research focusses on how to incorporate the method into a backward chaining procedure yielding more and more specific hints on the query as the chaining proceeds. A precise definition of the relation "more specific" preserving Dempster's rule of combination can be given (Kohlas, Monney, 1991).

7. References.

Cardona L., Kohlas J., Monney P.A. (1991 a): Reasoning on inference nets with unreliable arguments. *Institute for Automation and Operations Research, University of Fribourg,* No. 185.

Cardona L., Kohlas J., Monney P.A. (1991 b): The reliability of reasoning with unreliable rules and propositions. *Lecture Notes in Computer Science,* **548**, Springer, 125–129.

de Kleer J. (1986 a): An assumption-based TMS. *Artificial Intelligence*, **28**, 127-162.

de Kleer J. (1986 b): Extending the ATMS. *Artificial Intelligence*, **28**, 163-196.

Kohlas J. (1991): The reliability of reasoning with unreliable arguments. *The Annals of Operations Research*, **32**, 67–113.

Kohlas J., Monney P.A. (1990): Modeling and reasoning with hints. *Institute for Automation and Operations Research, University of Fribourg,* No. 174.

Kohlas J., Monney P.A. (1991): Representation of evidence by hints. *Institute for Automation and Operations Research, University of Fribourg,* No. 186. To appear in: Fedrizzi M., Kacprzyk J., Yager R.R. (Eds.) (1993): *Advances in the Dempster-Shafer Theory of Evidence.* J. Wiley & Sons, New York

Kohlas J., Monney P.A. (1992): Rule-based systems with unreliable conditions. Extended paper. *Institute for Automation and Operations Research, University of Fribourg.*

Kohlas J., Monney P.A. (1993): Probabilistic Assumption-Based Reasoning. *Institute for Automation and Operations Research, University of Fribourg,* No. 208.

Laskey K.B., Lehner P.E. (1990): Assumptions, Beliefs and Probabilities. *Artificial Intelligence*, **41**, 65-77.

Pearl J. (1988): *Probabilistic reasoning in intelligent systems. Networks of plausible inference.* Morgan and Kaufman.

Shafer G. (1976): *A mathematical theory of evidence.* Princeton Univ. Press.

Shafer G., Shenoy P.P., Mellouli K. (1987): Propagating belief functions in qualitative Markov trees. *Intern. J. of Approximate Reasoning,* **1**, 349–400.

Shafer G., Shenoy P.P. (1990): Axioms for probability and belief-function propagation. Article in: Shachter R.D. et al. (Eds.): Uncertainty in Artificial Intelligence 4, Elsevier, 169–198.

Fuzzy Semantics in Expert Process Control

J. Quevedo[(1)], C. Gibert Oliveras[(2)], J. Aguilar-Martín[(3)]

(1) Departament ESAII, Universitat Politècnica de Catalunya, E.T.S.E.E.I.T., c/. Colom 11, 08222 TERRASSA, Spain

(2) Departament de M.i E, Universitat Politècnica de Catalunya, F.I.B, Pau Gargallo 5, 08028 BARCELONA, Spain

(3) L.A.A.S - C.N.R.S., 7 Avenue du Colonel Roche, 31400 TOULOUSE, France

> Therefore I assert as Universal System all those possible true facts,
> ....
> And because All has been named from Light and Dark, acting from their own realms,
> Thus All becomes full of Light and also of invisible Darkness,
> And both principles keep their equilibrium inasmuch as there is nothing that does not depend on them.
> **PARMENIDES**, Περι φυσεοσ.

Abstract. In Fuzzy controllers the semantics of each of the linguistic labels is a fuzzy subset defined on the range of the measured magnitudes. We adress here the theoretical aspects of this choice. A Parmenidean Paradigm is a finite set of ordered Fuzzy Linguistic Variables with trapezoidal membership functions constructed from a basic antagonism called Parmenidean pair.. A methodology is proposed in connection with a rule based regulator development tool.

1 Introduction

Nowadays the proposition of Artificial Intelligence tools in Control and Regulation is becoming more and more frequent in the scientific litterature. Nevertheless not many applications in real time and real environment are yet really implemented. The user must make an arbitrary choice to define the semantics of the linguistic terms used by the symbolic controller, this freedom is an advantage for the theoretical versatility of the method, but is a severe drawback when considering a real implementation.

For control purposes, and particularly in regulation, the type of knowledge is twofold: structure knowledge and variables knowledge.

Basic sets that can characterize variables are called *linguistic paradigms* because one element may be replaced by any other without altering the syntactic validity of the proposition. An important class of paradigms is a couple of antagonist labels as {<big>,<small>}, it has been called ***Parmenidean pair***. By introducing the concept of fuziness we extend Parmenidean pairs into Parmenidean paradigms.

2 Fuzzy Linguistic Variables

Fuzzy subsets have been defined by Zadeh as sets with imprecise boundaries. Let **a**= $[a_o,a_f]$ and **b**= $[b_o,b_f]$ be two intervals of R such that **b≥a**, and t_{ab} a mapping of R to [0,1] such that:

$$x \in R,\ t_{ab}(x)=1 \text{ if } x \in \mathbf{a},\ t_{ab}(x)=0 \text{ if } x \in \mathbf{b},$$

$$t_{ab}(x)=(x-b_o)/(a_o-b_o) \text{ if } b_o \leq x < a_o,\ t_{ab}(x)=(b_f-x)/(b_f-a_f) \text{ if } a_f \leq x < b_f$$

t_{ab} defines an *Upright Trapeze* , **a** is called *core* and **b** *base* and defines the membership function of a fuzzy set.

The use of fuzzy sets such that their membership functions are trapezoidal functions is well suited [Bonissone 86] for representing linguistic labels as SMALL, VERY LARGE, RATHER LARGE, etc.

The pair $\{\mathbf{L_i},w_i\}$ associating a word w_i, to a TFS $\mathbf{L_i}$ is a *Fuzzy Linguistic Variable* (FLV),

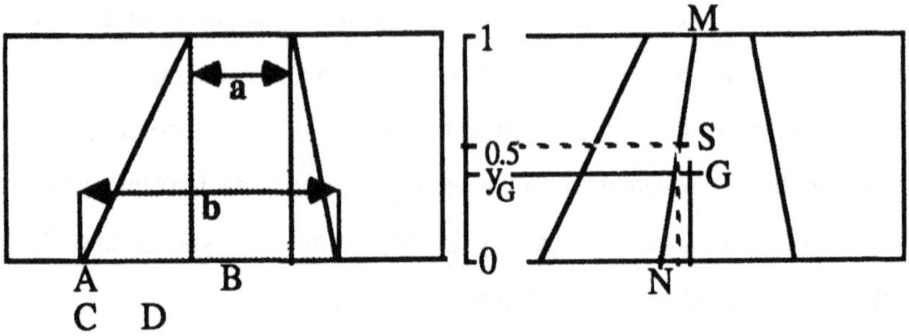

Figure 1

The following relations make reference to figure 1:

base length b = D - A, core length a = C - B

shape factor h = (b - a)/(b + a), mass m = (b + a)/2

core center abcissa M, base center abcissa N

segmental center $S = (D^2 + C^2 + B^2 + A^2)/2.(D + C + B + A)$

segmental center ordinate $y_S = 0.5$

gravity center abcissa $G = (D^2+C^2-B^2-A^2+DC-BA)/2.(D+C-B-A)$

gravity center ordinate $y_G = (3 - h)/6$

Upright trapezes are uniquely determined by 4 factors, either A, B, C, D or by other correctly chosen set of 4 features, and particularly by S, G, m, h. It shall be noted that $1/3 \leq y_G \leq 1/2$, rectangle gives $y_G = 1/2$, and triangle $y_G = 1/3$.

Two semantic features of a FLV are considered, the abcissa of the gravity center G determines the position in the range of the magnitude and the mass m, expresses the fuzziness and uncertainty. Other constraints must be imposed on the shape of the membership functions in order to determine uniquely a trapeze.

3 Semantic bases

A subset where any Fuzzy Linguistic Variable is completely determined by this two parameters is called a *Semantic Base*.

Logical operations that are necessary for the combination of FLVs when used to represent qualities related to magnitudes, are Conjunction and Disjunction.

Obviously, a parmenidean paradigm must be closed with respect to logical operations. As it is known, t-norms and t-conorms are the most general families of two place functions from $\mathbf{I}^2$ to $\mathbf{I}$ that respectively satisfy the requirements of fuzzy Conjunction and Disjunction.

Two trapezes T and T' will be *semantically equivalent* if they have the same mass and the same relative position. The semantical equivalence will be noted $T \approx T'$. It induces a partition in the set T. We shall indicate by $T/\approx$ the quotient set of T by $\approx$, and its elements will be represented as 2 dimension vectors [m,G] :

$$[m,G] = \{ T ; (m_t = m) \& (G_t = G)\}$$

Therefore in such an equivalence class a particular trapeze will be taken as representative of the class. Let T_x and T_y be two trapezes associated to GLVs X and Y, and let f be a t-norm or t-conorm mapping $\mathbf{I}^2$ to $\mathbf{I}$, then the trapeze $T_z=(f(A_x,A_y), f(B_x,B_y), f(C_x,C_y), f(D_x,D_y))$ is an upright trapeze but is not necessarily in the semantic base. An operator © (conjunction or disjuntion) between FLVs X and Y is defined in such a way that Z = X © Y is a FLV associated with the trapeze T_z. If f is a t-norm © is a conjunction and if f is a t-conorm © is a disjuntion.

As semantic bases are isomorph to subsets of the unit square $\mathbf{I}^2$, two parameters have to be preserved, i.e. the mass m and the abcissa of the gravity center G, therefore two independent parameters must be fixed. A first parameter is h, for all the elements of a semantic base S. Let us call S_h the semantic base defined by the shape factor value h, then, given T with shape factor h_t, its representative in the semantic base S_h is a trapeze $T' \in S_h$ such that $T' \approx T$ and the shape factor of T is h. .To guarantee the uniqueness of this tranformation from T to T', a fourth parameter has to be preserved, it has been proved in [Aguilar-1988] that preserving the positions of M and N, the abcissa of the segmental center S is preserved and therefore the abcissa of the gravity center is almost preserved as its maximum deviation $|G-S| \leq 1/12$, and for h=1/2 the mean value of $|G-S|$ is less than 0.03.

4 Fuzzy Parmenidean Paradigms

The construction of a semantic paradigm starts with a pair of lexical variables from a fundamental antagonism, and then refining it with intermediary lexical labels.

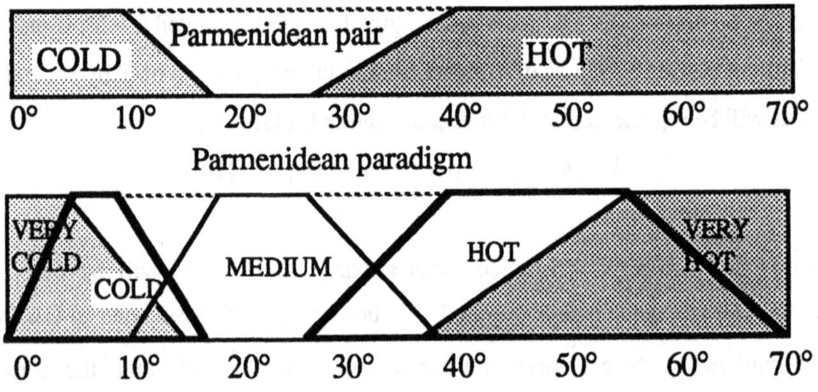

Figure 2

The only knowledge to be introduced concerns the two basic words of the initial Parmenidean pair and the limits of the certain and uncertain adequation zones. Figure 2 gives an example of Fuzzy Linguistic Paradigm, and its primary parmenidean pair is {<cold>,<hot>}.

More formally a *Parmenidean Paradigm* PP consist in:

- Two basic antagonistic words : **[a,z]** (e.g. **a**=SMALL, **z**=BIG) that form the initial parmnidean pair .
- A central word, **m**. (e.g. **m** = MEAN).
- An intensifier: (e.g. VERY, so that for **a** = SMALL , **aa** = VERY SMALL).

The resulting parmenidean paradigm will be the set of five linguisitc labels increasingly ordered: PP = {**aa, a, m, z, zz**} = {VERY SMALL, SMALL, MEAN, BIG, VERY BIG }.

A ***Fuzzy Parmenidean Paradigm*** is then a pair FPP = {L , PP} , where:

- L = $\{T_{aa}, T_a, T_m, T_z, T_{zz}\}$ is a collection of FLVs
- PP ={**aa, a, m, z, zz**}, is a Parmenidean Paradigm .

For the practical construction of FPP the following principles hold:

- The parménidian pair [**a**,**z**] is a semantic opposition and, therefore the abcissae of their gravity centers must be separated by 0.5 .

- At least three of the four vertex that define trapeze T_a must be under 0.5, and at least three of the vertex that define trapeze T_z must be over 0.5.

- Intensified labels **aa**, **zz** will be defined using the four initial values given from the parmediean pair: C_{aa} ,D_{aa} ,A_{zz} ,B_{zz} : $B_{aa} = 0$, then $A_{aa} = 0$. By analogy, $C_{zz}=1$ and $D_{zz} = 1$.

- A word **a** intensified must be defined by means of some contractive function in the interval **I** such that $G_{aa} < G_a$, a frequently used function is the square function in **I** and then $C_{aa} = C_a^2$ and $D_{aa} = D_a^2$

Symmetrically, for **z** $(1 - B_{zz}) = (1 - B_z)^2$ and $(1 - A_{zz}) = (1 - A_z)^2$

The central label exists only if $A_m = D_{aa}$ and $D_m = A_{zz}$ give rise to an upright trapeze T_m, i. e. if $C_a \leq D_{aa}$ and $A_{zz} \geq B_z$.

5 Fuzzy control

LRB is an Expert System Shell [Fernandez 91] for the design and implementation of linguistic-based control using fuzzy subsets as semantics. Linguistic variables are defined with connexion to the quantitative variables of the plant. A range is assigned to each linguistic variable, and a Parmenidean Paradigm is defined on this range so that the previous design can be applied.

An example based on the control of a first order with delay has been implemented. The plant is given by the following transfer function:

$$G(s) = \frac{K \cdot e^{-\tau . s}}{(1+Ts)}, \qquad K = \text{static gain},\ T = \text{time constant},\ \tau = \text{delay}$$

A first order with delay system has been choosen for this application because there is a number of real systems that can be modelled using this approach.The control is produced by inferences on a rule base. The rules are simply edited using standard words and linguistic values of the Parmenidean Paradigms for the problem. The general syntactical structure of such a rule is the following:

If <measure> is <value> and <measure> is <value> ...

then <contro> is <value> and <control> is <value>

The following rules are the smaller knowledge base that gives an acceptable result: (rules are expressed as LISP statements and words are in Spanish language as LRB has been developed for the control of a nuclear power plant in Argentina)

```
r(1,[f("ERROR",simplemente,"POSITIVO"),f("CAMBIO_ERROR",simplemente,"PO
SITIVO")],
[f("INC_TENSION",simplemente,"MAS")])r(2,[f("ERROR",simplemente,"NEGATI
VO"),
            f("CAMBIO_ERROR",simplemente,"POSITIVO")],
            [f("INC_TENSION",simplemente,"MENOS")])
r(3,[f("ERROR",simplemente,"POSITIVO"),f("CAMBIO_ERROR",simplemente,"NE
GATIVO")],
            [f("INC_TENSION",simplemente,"NULO")])
r(4,[f("ERROR",simplemente,"NEGATIVO"),f("CAMBIO_ERROR",simplemente,"N
EGATIVO")],
            [f("INC_TENSION",simplemente,"MENOS")])
```

In this specific knowledge base, two linguistic variables have been used as measures: "ERROR" and "CAMBIO_ERROR", and the domain of these two variables is the parmenidean paradigm {MUY-NEGATIVO, NEGATIVO, NULO, POSITIVO, MUY-POSITIVO}. control is "INC_TENSION", and its parmenidean paradigm is {MENOS, NULO, MAS}. These FPP's have been built up from the following specifications:

C(NEGATIVO)=-50; D(NEGATIVO)=-10; A(POSITIVO)=5; B(POSITIVO)=25

C(MENOS)=-40; D(MENOS)=-4; A(MAS)=4; B(MAS)=40

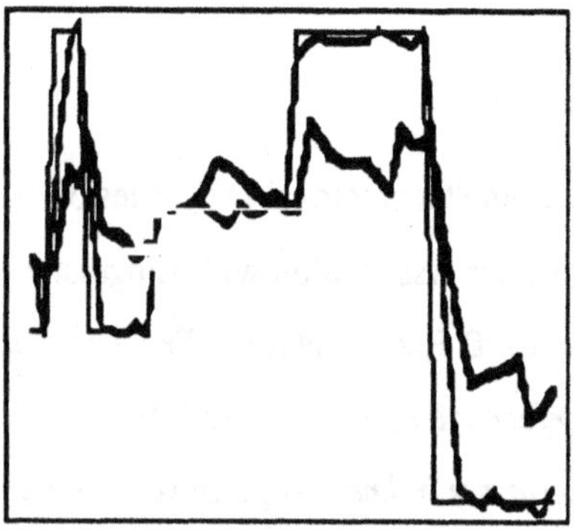

T=-0.1 K=1 delay = 0

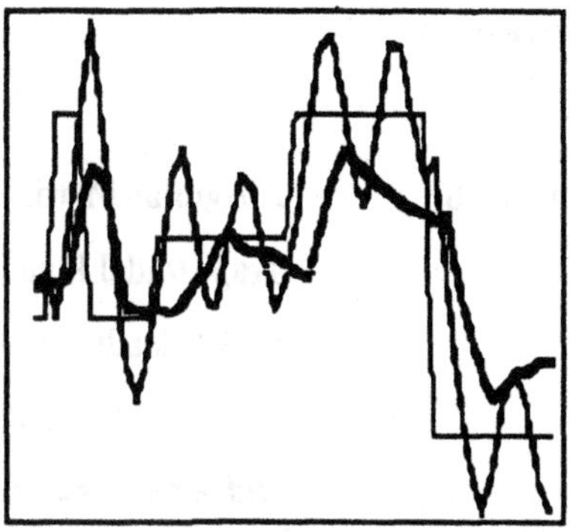

T=-0.1 K=1 delay = 1

COST	control	regul	total	control	regul	total
optim	2.3	2.0	4.3	5.0	9.8	14.8
fuzzy	0.6	8.0	8.6	0.7	9.8	10.5

Figure 3

The trajectories shown in figure 3 are obtained for a noise/signal ratio of 0.1 and for two values of the delay $\tau=0$, and $\tau=1$. It appears that applying the fuzzy control to the system with delay $\tau=0$, the cost of the control has been drastically reduced with respect to the "optimal" one, from 2.3 to 0.6, but the quality of the output regulation has been worsened 4 times (from 2.0 to 8.0), so finally the total is definetively better with the optimal, as it was expected. For a delay $\tau=1$ the "optimal" is no longer optimal, and the fuzzy control system achieves a better performance total cost for an equal regulation quality.Another advantage of fuzzy control based on this methodology is the possibility of adding a learning-like behaviour as it can adjust the commutation band based on additionnal rules that can modify the semantics of the null label by taking into account the behaviour of the error signal, this simple additional functionnality, wery hard to implement in traditional controllers could be easily added to this example.

References

[Aguilar 88] J. Aguilar-Martin (1988). Some Geometrical Properties of Trapezoidal Functions for their Association with Linguistic Labels leading to a reduced 2-D Representation, *Proceedings of the 2nd International Conference on Information Processing and Management of Uncertainty in knowledge-based systems*, Urbino-Italy, 47-54

[AM-GO-PC 91] J. Aguilar-Martin, Carina Gibert Oliveras & Nuria Piera i Carreté (1991). Fuzzy Linguistic Variables, Parmenidean Paradigms and Multivalued Logics, *Proceedings of the 1er Congreso Español sobre Tecnologías y Lógica difusas, June 17-20, 1991*, Granada-Spain.

[Bonissone 86] P. P. Bonissone (1986). Selecting Uncertainty Calculi: An Experiment in Trading-off Precision and Complexity, in *Uncertainty in Artificial Intelligence*, 217-247, L.N. Kanal and J.F. Lemmer (Editors), Elsevier Science Pub. B. V. (North-Holland)

[Dubois-Prade 89] D. Dubois & H. Prade (1989). Fuzzy Arithmetic in Qualitative Reasoning, in *Modeling and Control of Systems in Engineering, Quantum Mechanics, Economics and Biosciences.*, A. Blaquière (Editor). Lecture Notes in Control and Information Sciences, Springler Verlag, Berlin. 457-467

[Fernandez 91] Oscar Fernanfez (1991). Manual de uso de LRB, *report of Instituto Balseiro,* 8400 Bariloche, Argentina.

Qualitative Operators and Process Engineer Semantics of Uncertainty *

N. Rakoto-Ravalontsalama[(1)], A. Missier[(1)], J.S. Kikkert[(2)]

[(1)] LAAS-CNRS, 7 av Colonel Roche F-31077 Toulouse cedex, France.
[(2)] Philips TCDC, NL-5600 MD Eindhoven, The Netherlands.

Abstract

Dealing with uncertainty is one of the major topics of industrial process modelling. Indeed, it is not always possible to completely specify a given process. One alternative to cope with this problem is the introduction of qualitative representation to model the process. This paper presents a qualitative formalism, based on the process expert experience, for which a mathematical framework has been defined. It is shown that uncertainty is used at three different levels in the proposed approach of modelling. As illustration some simulation results from the manufacturing process of TV-tubes are given and then discussed.

1 Introduction

During the past few years, there has been a growing interest in using expert systems to supervise industrial processes. The first step in this complex task of supervsion is the obtention of a model. Second, the model has to be validated, after some refinements and improvements and lastly the process can be controlled. But in modeling production processes, it is often impossible to specify the knowledge available by means of quantitative relations between process and product variables.

In this paper, we will focus on the modelling of the process, more precisely on the specification and the use of qualitative operators and functions. A Qualitative calculus (Q-calculus for short) is presented that enables us to translate qualitative knowledge into formal relations.

These qualitative relations are used in conjunction with quantitative relations to establish a hybrid model of the production process. Uncertainty is introduced at three levels: first, the calculus is based on a mapping of the real numbers onto three basic symbols $\{-, 0, +\}$, as in classical sign algebra. This is the first type of uncertainty. Second, this set is then extended to a system containing all possible union of the basic symbols, that is the complete sign algebra. On this extended set of symbols, qualitative operators and functions are defined that can be used to specify qualitative relations between process and product variables. At last the introduction of a real number Δ into the definition of some functions represents the third type of uncertainty.

*this work has been partially supported by the ESPRIT-IPCES Project.

This paper is organized as follows: the next section presents the qualitative formalism while the third one shows how these relations are specified. These principles have been applied to model a complex industrial system: the manufacture of TV-tubes using the G2 Expert System shell.

2 The Qualitative Formalism

Missier has defined a general framework of Q-reasoning, the Q-spaces [11]. A Q-space S is roughly a structure of symbols which represent classes of objects in a set E (a symbol is a subset of E). These classes are defined a priori such that each subset of E maps to a unique *description* in the set of symbols S. On these structures a relation called Q-equality can be defined as follows: $A, B \in S$, $A \approx B$ if and only if $A \cap B \neq \emptyset$. This Q-relation means the *possibility of being equal*: $A \approx B$ if there exist *objects* of E represented by the symbol A as well as the symbol B. We have shown that this Q-equality is necessary to express Q-relations within the framework of Q-spaces. The aim is not to detail the theory, though we have referred to it. We would like to show its application to the analyzed process.

2.1 The Sign Algebra

A commonly used set of symbols in Q-Physics is the sign algebra set $S = \{-, 0, +, ?\}$ where the unknown symbol '?' represents the set of all reals. It has been introduced to make the addition operation being internal in the set S. Indeed, the result of $(+ \oplus -)$ cannot be expressed without the introduction of this '?' symbol. The sign algebra is the basis of most qualitative formalisms, like those introduced by Forbus [4], by De Kleer and Brown [1] or by Kuipers [10]. The main lines of these three different approaches are outlined in the table 1 below. For more details on the comparison, see [5].

	Forbus	**De Kleer & Brown**	**Kuipers**
Parameter	Quantity	Qualitative variable Quantity	Parameter
Value	Amount	Qualitative value	Value
Tendency	Derivative	Derivative	Direction of change
Quantity space	Quantity space	Quantity space	Quantity space
Parameter qual. state	Pair(amount,derivative)	Pair(value,derivative)	Qual. state
System qual. state	Situation	Situation	System qual. state
Relationships	Qual. proportionalities Influences	Confluences	Constraints
Functioning	Individual view	Qualitative state	Operating region
Qualitative behavior	Process history	History	Qualitative behavior

Table 1: Comparison of the three main qualitative formalisms

The sign algebra can be used in two different ways. First it can express the sign of a given variable. This variable will be either negative, null or positive. If this variable (say s_1) expresses the derivative of another variable (say s_2), it is clear that the interpretation of $s_1 = \{-,0,+\}$ is $s_2 = \{decreasing, steady, increasing\}$. We will see in the next sections that this sign algebra is used at different manner in our approach so that it is used to express the *qualitative influence* of a given variable.

The interest of the Q-space structure is to guarantee the existence and the unicity, for each real function f, of an associated qualitative function $[f]$, such that :

$$\begin{array}{rccl} [f]: & S & \longrightarrow & S \\ & X & \longmapsto & [f(X)] \end{array}$$

where $f(X)$ represents the *image* of X through f and $[.]$ represents the description function [1]. In fact, from a partition of the set E — the elements of this partition are called basic elements — we can build several types of Q-spaces.

The Q-operators $\oplus$ and $\otimes$ are defined as the Q-functions associated to the real operators $+$ and $\times$ (see tables 2a and 2b). Then it has been demonstrated that this sign algebra has relatively strong properties which allow Q-calculus [Dormoy84], [Missier91]:

- associativity and commutativity of $\oplus$ and $\otimes$
- 0 is the neutral element for $\oplus$
- $+$ is the neutral element for $\otimes$
- $\otimes$ is distributive with respect to $\oplus$
- $\oplus$ and $\otimes$ are Q-*inversible*:

$$a \oplus b \approx c \;\Leftrightarrow\; b \approx c \ominus a$$
$$a \otimes b \approx c \;\Leftrightarrow\; b \approx c \oslash a$$

where $\ominus$ and $\oslash$ are defined as the Q-functions associated to the real subtraction operator $(-)$ and the real division operator $(/)$ respectively.

$\oplus$	−	0	+	?
−	−	−	?	?
0	−	0	+	?
+	?	+	+	?
?	?	?	?	?

$\otimes$	−	0	+	?
−	+	0	−	?
0	0	0	0	?
+	−	0	+	?
?	?	0	?	?

Tables 2a and 2b: The basic Q-addition and Q-product operators

2.2 The Extended Sign Algebra

We have shown that the best properties with respect to associated Q-functions are obtained when the Q-space includes every possible unions of basic elements. This defines a complete Q-space. Thus an extended sign algebra can be defined : it is the set $S = \{-,0,+,[-,0],[0,+],[-,+]\}$. The semantic of these symbols is clear : $[-,0]$ represents the set of all positive or null reals, $[0,+]$ represents the set of all negative

[1] this function associates, to every subset of E its unique description in the set S.

or null reals, $[-,+]$ represents the set of all non null reals. We can note that the unknown symbol '?' is nothing else but the union of the three basic elements i.e., $[-,0,+]$.

The basic properties of sign algebra holds also for the extended set of symbols. As the union of two basic symbol $[s_1, s_2]$ expresses the logical OR operation of s_1 and s_2, the result of any operation involving such extended symbol is given by the logical OR of each result from the basic symbols. For example, if s_1, t_1, s_2 and t_2 are 4 basic symbols, the result of $[s_1, t_1] \oplus [s_2, t_2]$ will be given by $((s_1 \oplus s_2) \vee (s_1 \oplus t_2) \vee (t_1 \oplus s_2) \vee (t_1 \oplus t_1))$. This combination also holds for the Q-product operator (see tables 3 and 4).

$\oplus$	$-$	$[-,0]$	0	$[0,+]$	$+$	$[-,+]$	?
$-$	$-$	$-$	$-$	?	?	?	?
$[-,0]$	$-$	$[-,0]$	$[-,0]$	?	?	?	?
0	$-$	$[-,0]$	0	$[0,+]$	$+$	$[-,+]$	?
$[0,+]$	?	?	$[0,+]$	$[0,+]$	$+$	?	?
$+$	?	?	$+$	$+$	$+$	?	?
$[-,+]$	?	?	$[-,+]$	?	?	?	?
?	?	?	?	?	?	?	?

Table 3: The extented Q-addition operation

$\otimes$	$-$	$[-,0]$	0	$[0,+]$	$+$	$[-,+]$	?
$-$	$+$	$[0,+]$	0	$[-,0]$	$-$	$[-,+]$	?
$[-,0]$	$[0,+]$	$[0,+]$	0	$[-,0]$	$[-,0]$	?	?
0	0	0	0	0	0	0	0
$[0,+]$	$[-,0]$	$[-,0]$	0	$[0,+]$	$[0,+]$	?	?
$+$	$-$	$[-,0]$	0	$[0,+]$	$+$	$[-,+]$	?
$[-,+]$	$[-,+]$	?	0	?	$[-,+]$	$[-,+]$	?
?	?	?	0	?	?	?	?

Table 4: The extented Q-product operation

The introduction of the extended set of symbols allows to define the minus element. This one is mainly used for the subtraction operation because $s_1 \ominus s_2$ is equivalent to $s_1 \oplus (-s_2)$ where $(-s_2)$ is the minus element of s_2. The minus element of each symbol is given in the table below:

s	$-$	$[-,0]$	0	$[0,+]$	$+$	$[-,+]$	?
$(-s)$	$+$	$[0,+]$	0	$[-,0]$	$-$	$[-,+]$	?

Table 5: The minus elements of the extended set of symbols

2.3 The Proposed Qualitative Approach

Our approach is based on three basic qualitative mappings and a set of derived mappings using the qualitative addition $\oplus$ and qualitative subtraction $\ominus$ operators. These mappings express the process expert view of the system specification. A mathematical framework has been defined to validate the approach.

Three basic mappings have been defined: the first one, QPLUSP associates qualitative values to qualitative others while PLUSP and DISTP are mappings from numerical to qualitative values. For these latter, a numerical parameter Δ is introduced to express the uncertainty of the changing value. The unknown symbol '?' represents the union (or the `logical OR`) of the three basic symbols [-,0,+]. These functions are defined as follows:

- from qualitative to qualitative:

s	−	[−,0]	0	[0,+]	+	[−,+]	?
QPLUSP(s)	0	0	0	[0,+]	+	[0,+]	[0,+]

Table 6: The QPLUSP function

- from numerical to qualitative:

$$\text{PLUSP}(x,\Delta) = \begin{cases} 0, & \text{if } x \leq 0; \\ [0,+], & \text{if } 0 < x \leq \Delta; \\ + & \text{if } x > \Delta. \end{cases}$$

$$\text{DISTP}(x,\Delta) = \begin{cases} 0, & \text{if } x \leq 0; \\ ?, & \text{if } 0 < x \leq \Delta; \\ [-,+] & \text{if } x > \Delta. \end{cases}$$

Some remarks can be made about these functions. Let us for example take the second one: it is obvious that PLUSP includes the class of all real functions for which there exists a positive number x_0 inferior to Δ, such that x is constant and null before x_0, and positive after.

The choice of the name of these basic mappings expresses the process expert point of view: each mapping has the -P suffix which denotes that they associate significant images only to Positive values whether they are qualitative or numerical. The prefix Q- stands for qualitative, while PLUSP comes from the fact that the associated value is the symbol '+'. Finally DISTP denotes a notion of *disturbed* parameter i.e., a parameter that is not at the normal level, i.e., a parameter which is either at a low level, or at a high level ($[-,+]$).

Then, the association of some basic mappings allows to define some derived mappings, which are also used in the process model specification. The combination is done using the qualitative addition $\oplus$ and qualitative subtraction $\ominus$ operators. These derived mappings are PLUS, DIST and TUNE and their expressions are given in table 7 below.

Derived mappings	Expression
$\text{PLUS}(x,\Delta_1,\Delta_2)$	$= \text{PLUSP}(x-\Delta_1,\Delta_2) \ominus \text{PLUSP}(-x-\Delta_1,\Delta_2)$
$\text{DIST}(x,\Delta_1,\Delta_2)$	$= \text{DISTP}(x-\Delta_1,\Delta_2) \oplus \text{DISTP}(-x-\Delta_1,\Delta_2)$
$\text{TUNE}(x,\Delta_1,\Delta_2)$	$= \text{PLUSP}(x-\Delta_1,\Delta_2) \oplus \text{PLUSP}(-x-\Delta_1,\Delta_2)$

Table 7: Derived qualitative mappings

We can see from the qualitative formalism, and more particularly from the definitions of the basic and derived mappings that *uncertainty* is introduced at three different levels:

- First, the use of the sign algebra basic set $S = \{-, 0, +\}$, that is partitioning the real line into three symbols, represents the first level of uncertainty. Indeed it is a high level of data abstraction because the real line is clustered into only three symbols.

- A second form of uncertainty is comes by the fact that the extended set of symbols $S = \{-, 0, +, [-, 0], [0, +], [-, +], ?\}$ allows the sign algebra to be more expressive. Furthermore, they permit to give a precise semantic for the basic (and thus the derived) mappings. The unknown element '?' i.e, $[-, 0, +]$ gives no relevant information about the analyzed parameter while the unions of two basic symbols $[-, 0]$, $[0, +]$ or $[-, +]$ are more significant.

- At last, a parameter which denotes another uncertainty is Δ. It is introduced in different functions in the basic mappings as well as in the derived one. Only one parameter (Δ) is introduced to define the numerical to qualitative basic mappings like PLUSP and DISTP while the derived mappings need two parameters Δ_1 and Δ_2. These *uncertainty parameters* constitute the third level of uncertainty. Indeed, the greater is Δ, the more uncertain is the specification. The amount of such parameter can be determined heuristically, based on the process expert experience.

3 Specification of relations

The process is decomposed following the next structure: subprocess / work-cell / work-station. The work-station is the most elementary processing unit, typically consisting of one procesing tool, position or action. A given $work - station_i$ is connected to the next one ($work - station_{i+1}$) by the following relationship (about the product):

$$OutputParameter[work - station_i] = InputParameter[work - station_{i+i}]$$

So when an output parameter is no more propagated to the next work-station, it will be called *product observation*. Each work-station has the same behavioural structure. Three sets of parameters can be found, that are input, intermediate and output parameters. For more details on the process decomposition, see [9]. The output parameters are calculated by the relations using input and intermediate parameters. These relations are of three types: numerical, qualitative and hybrid.

3.1 Numerical Relations

Numerical relations are obviously used when they are avalaible. They are mostly algebraic relations or differential equations. Two example of numerical relations are TGR and HSR which calculates respectively the screen temperature (tg) and the thickness of the solution layer on the screen (hsol).

3.2 Qualitative Relations

The introduction of qualitative relations is based on the two main following reasons:

- the use of qualitative models can be viewed as a first step in obtaining more detailed knowledge. Reliable mathematical models need more time to be established and qualitative modeling (and eventually reasoning) is suitable for incomplete knowledge specification.

- some aspects of product quality are not readily expressed in physical quantities, e.g. the amount of undesirable dust on the screen (`dust quality`) or the amount of wall wetting (`qdww`). Also, a lot of physical relations -e.g. turbulence- cannot be translated into practical mathematical modes. In both cases, the only way to deal with them is by introducing qualitative relations.

Three examples of qualitative relations are described in table 8. QDUSTR gives the amount of dust on the screen (`qdust`) while QDWWR deals with the wetting of the walls of the screen. Finally the qualitative function QDABR expresses the occurrence of air bubbles in the suspension. All these three relations represent undesirable effects on the screen and the quality of the final product may be affected if they give some value different to the normal one i.e., taking the value '0'.

Q-function	Expression
QDUTSR()	= qdusti ⊕ TUNE(vrot-2.5,1) ⊕ TUNE (dtbp-13,2) ⊕ TUNE(fap-50,10)
QDWWR()	= qdwwi ⊕ PLUSP(rwet+dr,dr)
QDABR()	= qdabi ⊕ qdww

Table 8: Some qualitative functions

These qualitative functions are defined for the positive values of the time t ($t > 0$), and take the initial value, respectively `qdusti`, `qdwwi` and `qdabi`, otherwise. As illustration, the QDUSTR relation specification is given below:

$$\texttt{qdust} = \texttt{qdusti} \oplus \texttt{TUNE(vrot} - 2.5, 1) \oplus \texttt{TUNE(dtbp} - 13, 2) \oplus \texttt{TUNE(fap} - 50, 10)$$

where

- `qdust` is the amount of dust and hairs on the screen,
- `qdusti` is the initial value of `qdust` that is its last value in the previous work-station,
- `vrot` is the rotation speed of the screen,
- `dtbp` is the air blowing interval and
- `fap` is the air flow rate.

The second part (TUNE(vrot-2.5,1)), for example, comes from the fact that air is blown towards the center of the panel (screen). It is done to remove dust produced by loading the panel. A too high flow rate of the air will introduce more dust from the environment, while a too low flow rate will not be effective to remove the dust present in the panel. So, this can be represented by a TUNE relation.

3.3 Hybrid Relations

A hybrid relation is a relation that gives as output a pair of both numerical and qualitative value. A hybrid parameter is defined as a pair hp $= < x, qi >$, where `x` is the simulated numerical value and `qi` the qualitative influence on the parameter. The qualitative influence is defined in the previous qualitative formalism. For example hp

$= < 2.41, + >$ means that the simulated value of hp is 2.41 but due to qualitative influence, it is in fact higher than this reference value (hp > 2.41). We can then note that in hybrid parameters, the qualitative influences always give an information **with respect to the simulated numerical value.** The meaning of the symbols which express qualitative influences is summarized in the table 9 below where the '?' symbol which means *unknown* has not been represented.

s	–	[–,0]	0	[0,+]	+	[–,+]
	lower than	lower or equal to	equal to	greater or equal to	greater than	different from

Table 9: Interpretation of symbols for qualitative influences

4 Application

Using the G2-Expert System shell, running on Sun SparcStation, a hybrid process simulation model has been built for a complex industrial process: the manufacturing of TV-tubes. The whole process includes about a hundred different work-stations for the three colours (green, blue and red) and is defined by almost 2000 variables (input, intermediate and output). The three types of relations are easily handled in the Expert System shell. The numerical relations are obvious. As for qualitative and hybrid parameters, they are defined by some procedures which allow to manipulate both quantitative and qualitative knowledge.

A reduced part of the results in four different work-stations are given in the table 10 below. They are located in the Green Flowcoat work-cell. We can see the evolution of the three qualitative variables qdust (amount of dust on the screen), qdww (wall wetting) and qdab (air bubbles in the suspension) through the sequential work-stations, FG-02 to FG-05 (FG for Flowcoat Green). These are calculated together with other numerical variables such as tg (panel temperature) and hsol (thickness solution layer). The hybrid product parameters are not given in this table.

worksation	main task	tg(deg)	qdust	hsol(mm)	qdww	qdab
FG-02	washing	32.79	'0'			
FG-03	air cleaning	32.79	'0'	0.5904E-03	[0,+]	'0'
FG-04	sedimentation	32.72		0.5904E-03	'+'	'+'
FG-05	washing	32.65		0.1368E-03		

Table 10: Some simulation results from the Green Flowcoat work-cell

The Green Flowcoat work-cell is located at the beginning of the process. This is why only a reduced number of product (numerical or qualitative) parameters is given. Some interpretations and remaks can be made about these results:

- the screen temperature tg is expressed in centigrad degree. It has an initial value when the panel is loaded on the first work-station and its value will decrease all along the screen transformation, due mostly to the blown air and the washing water.

- at work-stations FG-02 and FG-03, qdust='0' does mean, that the value of qdust is at the normal level, i.e., the cleaning task is performing well. This parameter is not defined anymore in work-stations FG-04 and FG-05.
- qdww is the wetting of the walls due to suspension flowing into the screen. This wetting depends of the dosing flow rate, the dosing volume, angle of tilt, and spinning rate. An increase of qdww does mean more wetting than allowed.
- qdab is the occurrence of air bubbles in the suspension. It depends on the dosing flow rate and - later on - on the turbulence of the suspension being distributed over the panel (Reynold's number and amount of wall wetting). In the example, dosing is done correctly (qdab='0'), but distribution at work-station FG-04 is too fast (qdab='+').

5 Conclusions

The proposed theory about qualitative spaces, applied to the extended sign algebra, gives a method for formalizing the expression of qualitative values. This allows to obtain a qualitative model for some variables for which no numerical model is at the moment available. In our example of manufacturing process of TV-tubes, the qualitative relations which have been specified are simple examples to test the software. The introduction of uncertainty at 3 levels appears to be a suitable direction in the specification. It has to be proved now that the results will be of practical value.

The next step of this work is the modelling of the complete process, and simultaneously the refinement of the existing model specification. A process may need also information about the tendency of a parameter. This can be done by combining the (possibly hybrid) information about the level and the (possibly hybrid) information about the time-derivative into one *extended hybrid parameter* $\mathtt{hp} = < x, qi, d, qd >$ where d expresses the (quantitative) time-derivative and qd expresses the (qualitative) tendency. This *extended hybrid formalism* may be used as a basis for some prediction and some diagnosis tasks.

References

[1] J. de Kleer and J.S. Brown. A qualitative physics based on confluences. *Artificial Intelligence Journal*, 24:7–83, 1984.

[2] A. Delgado, N. Rakoto-Ravalontsalama, and J.L. de la Rosa. Esprit 2428 IPCES: Prototype 3 simulation part. Internal Report 92108, LAAS-CNRS, Toulouse, France, March 1992.

[3] J.L. Dormoy. Représentation des connaissances en physique et systèmes experts. In *Journées Internationales sur les Systèmes Experts et leurs Applications*, Avignon, France, 1984.

[4] K.D. Forbus. Qualitative process theory. *Artificial Intelligence Journal*, 24:85–168, 1984.

[5] P. Fouché, A. Charles, J.-P. Barthès and C. Melin. Qualitative physics: a survey. *Revue d'Intelligence Artificielle*, 3 (4):11–38, 1989.

[6] Gensym Corporation, Cambridge, USA. *G2 Reference Manual (Ver 2.1)*, August 1990.

[7] Gensym Corporation, Cambridge, USA. *G2 Reference Manual (Ver 3.0)*, July 1992.

[8] S. Gentil, S. Feray-Beaumont, and P. Caloud. Qualitative modelling for process supervision systems. In *1st European Meeting on Cognitive Science and Approaches to Process Control*, Paris, France, 1987.

[9] J. Kamerbeek and J.S. Kikkert. Esprit 2428 IPCES: Process description of prototype 2. Internal report, Philips (PRL and TCDC), Eindhoven, The Netherlands, December 1991.

[10] B.J. Kuipers. Qualitative Simulation. *Artificial Intelligence Journal*, 29:289–338, 1986.

[11] A. Missier. *Structures Mathématiques pour le Calcul Qualitatif, Contribution à la Simulation Qualitative.* Thèse de doctorat, LAAS-CNRS, Toulouse, France, December 1991.

[12] L. Trave-Massuyes, N. Piera, and A. Missier. What can we do with qualitative calculus today ? In *Proc. International Symposium on Advanced Information Processing in Automatic Control*, Nancy, France, July 1989.

Facing Uncertainty in the Management of Large Irrigation Systems: Qualitative Approach

S. Sawadogo, A. K. Achaibou

L.A.A.S-C.N.R.S, 7. Av. Colonel Roche, 31077 Toulouse, France
tel: () 61 33 62 00 - Telefax: 61 55 35 77 - e-mail achaibou@laas.laas.fr

F. Mora-Camino

E.N.A.C., 7. Av. Edouard Belin, 31055 Toulouse, France
tel: () 61 55 79 99 - e-mail mora@laas.laas.fr

Abstract In this paper, a management structure including supervision and control layers of large water distribution systems is investigated. The supervision layer is devoted to the efficient management on the long run of the upstream water stock •

1 The Problem Considered

Irrigation of agricultural lands is an important activity which results in increased productivity in temperate regions and turns possible cultivation in arid areas. Surface irrigation usually requires an extensive distribution system between storage and users implying in high investment costs which must be carefully planned.
At the operations level, in the short term, demand for water varies stochastically with the changing weather conditions which influence also on the long run water storage levels. In the case of larger perturbations (longuer drought periods than planned, new demands) or failures of the irrigation system, its operation must be completely revised to fulfil basic priorities.

The system considered in this paper is a stretch of canal used for water distribution and composed of the following elements :
. an upstream reservoir of unlimited capacity,
. an entry section with a flow control gate,
. a sequence of pumping stations distributed all along the canal,
. a sequence of measurement points which in general coincide with the pumping stations,
. a final exit section equiped with a flow measuring device.
Here "short term" means a period of time two or three time-lags ahead, here up to 48 hours, while "medium term" means a period of some weeks and "long term" means a period of some months.

The main objectives for the supervision of this system are:

- the efficient management on the long run of the upstream water stock,
- the guarantee of equity between users along the canal.

The current situation is assessed every week through the comparison between the current water stock levels and the estimated future needs. Qualitative rules are

used to detect this current condition of operation for the whole system (nominal, low severity restriction, medium severity restriction, high severity restriction). This leads to the regulation of the nominal inflows obtained from a control layer to get the effective inflows for the system.
The second objective implies the use of distributed control devices so that local pumped flows can be bounded in accordance with an equity principle. According with the degree of severity of the water deficit the pumping restrictions take two forms:

- for low severity conditions, water is distributed proportionally to the predicted demand, so that its deficit is balanced equally between users,
- for high severity conditions, the priority is given to the satisfaction of basic needs. In this case, the inverse adaptive control approach may suspended.

2 Qualitative Evaluation Systems State

Planned discharge curves have been used traditionally to assess the current situation of water stocks in dams devoted to irrigation. This approach relies heavily on statistics and supposes that deviations from mean values remain limited.
However, in many regions where irrigation is important, two characteristics of rain are relevant: the deficit in rain water and the irregularity of these rains.So if from one year to the next rains may change their pattern (volume and periods), the use of a mean discharge curve may be largely misleading.

Here we consider an approach which directly takes into consideration the current and future needs of the cultures. Depending of the seeding period, of the culture acreage, of the intermediate rains and volumes of drained water, at current time (a week in fact), needs for the whole irrigation sector can be estimated or their estimation can be updated for the whole remaining period of irrigation.
So an index such as $\nu(t)$ given by :

$$\nu(t) = \frac{V(t) - V_{min}}{\sum_{\tau=t}^{T} \hat{D}_\tau^t} \qquad t \leq T \tag{1}$$

where T is such as $\hat{D}_{T+\tau}^t = 0 \quad \forall \tau \geq 0$, can be estimated; with:

- V(t) is the current water stock in the barrage at the beginnig of week t,
- V_{min} is the minimum water reserve allowed in the barrage,
- $\hat{D}_\tau^t$ is the estimated demand of water at time t for period τ.

To compare two situations at different times such as ν_1 at t_1 and ν_2 at t_2, some additional hypothesis must be made.
First we see that if $\nu(t) < 1$ there is a shortage in water for irrigation while if $\nu(t) \geq 1$ the water stock seems sufficient to meet the demand until the end of the irrigation campaign.
A prolongated high deficit of water will cause damages which can be irreversible and which can ruin the whole plantation, while if the deficit is maintained within

some limits, only its yield will be diminished. In the last case, a prolongated small deficit situation will be equivalent to a severe deficit of short duration. For instance if the damage caused by water deficit grows according to weight function $g(t,T)$, then two equivalent deficits situations will be such as:

$$\sum_{\tau=t_1}^{T}(1-\nu_1)\hat{D}_{\tau}^{t_1}g(\tau,T) = \sum_{\tau=t_2}^{T}(1-\nu_2)\hat{D}_{\tau}^{t_2}g(\tau,T) \tag{2}$$

or

$$\frac{1-\nu_1}{1-\nu_2} = \frac{\sum_{\tau=t_2}^{T}\hat{D}_{\tau}^{t_2}g(\tau,T)}{\sum_{\tau=t_1}^{T}\hat{D}_{\tau}^{t_1}g(\tau,T)} \tag{3}$$

So, a deficit of ν_0 over the whole period will be considered equivalent to a deficit of $\nu(t)$ over period [t,T]. So we get deficit curves which permit the definition of different levels for the satisfaction of demand for water (Fig 1). For instance we could define:

1. High Severity conditions (HS) when : $\nu_0 \leq 0.50$
2. Medium Severity conditions (MS) when : $0.50 \leq \nu_0 \leq 0.80$
3. Low Severity conditions (LS) when : $0.80 \leq \nu_0 \leq 0.95$
4. Normal Situations (NS) when : $0.95 \leq \nu_0$

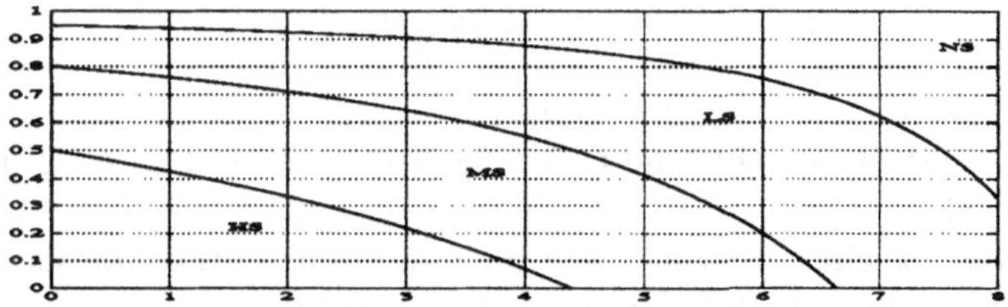

Figure 1 :

Cultures must also be classified to provide some priority ordering. We have for instance cultures classes such as:
Very essential (VE), medium essential (ME), lightly essential (LE) and secondary essential (SE). So in HS conditions irrigation water must be devoted with priority to VE cultures, and so on.

Applying a proportional-saturation rule, at the beginnig of a "week" the volume of water which is planned to be consumed during that week is given by:

$$Q^s(t) = min\ \{Q^s_{max},\ \nu(t)\hat{D}^s_t\} \tag{4}$$

where

$$\hat{D}^s_t = \sum_{j\in\mathcal{K}}\hat{D}^s_{t_j} \qquad\qquad with\ \ \mathcal{K} = \{VE, ME, LE, SE\}$$

where $\hat{D}^s_{t_j}$ is, at time t, the predicted needs of water by cultures of class j for the next week.

Membership functions can be defined for classes:

1) HS : high severity conditions 2) MS : medium severity conditions

3) LS : low severity situation 4) NS : normal situation

They are displayed in fig. 2 for a given period t:

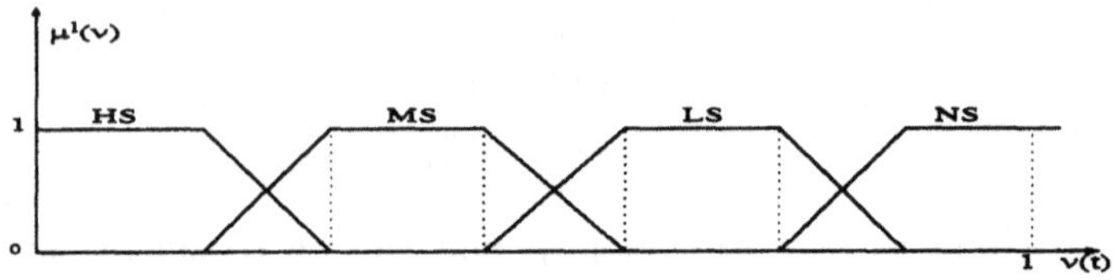

Figure 2 : membership functions for situation classes

3 Priority Assignment

However, membership functions can be considered for each category of water consumers(class of culture, industries, towns ...). Let j be one of these categories. We define the index λ_j(t) by:

$$\lambda_j(t) = P_j n_j(t) \tag{5}$$

with $0 \leq P_j \leq 1 \qquad 0 \leq n_j(t) \leq 1$, where:

P_j are the arbitrary weights and thus reflects the a priori choices of the adopted irrigation policy,

$n_j(t)$ is an index which informs about the importance of the satisfaction of water demand during period t for category j of consumers.

A KBS(Knowledge Based System) system can be used to select current values for these indexes. For cultures this KBS must integrate informations about:

. nominal needs of Water per stage of their life cycle,

. past irrigation history (chronology and volumes),

. past rain history and present precipitations over cultures during the current campaign.

For categories characterized by a permanent demand, $n_j(t)$ can be chosen constant. For instance, for human use $n_h = 0.9$ and for industrial use $n_i(t) = 0.8$

So we obtain membership functions(here independent of time) such as:

Cultures can be also classified to provide some priority ordering. The relative importance of each kind of culture may vary with the current and predicted irrigation balance(parameter ν). Here the following cultures and water consumers categories are considered: VE: Very essential, ME: Medium essential, LE: Lightly essential and SE: Secondary essential and priority weights are defined for each situation by matrix P:

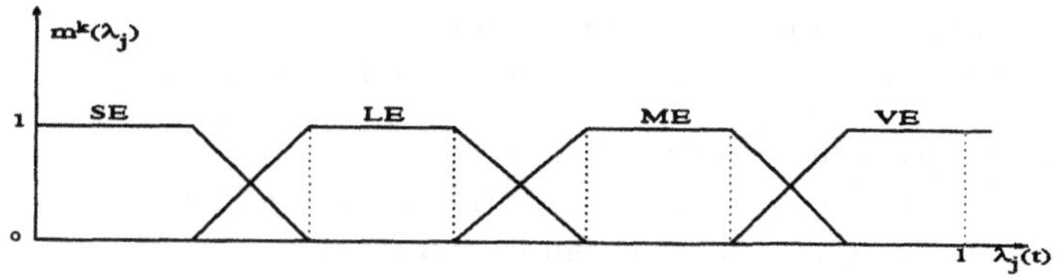

Figure 3 :

	HS	MS	LS	NS
VE	P_{VE}^{HS}	P_{VE}^{MS}	P_{VE}^{LS}	P_{VE}^{NS}
ME	P_{ME}^{HS}	P_{ME}^{MS}	P_{ME}^{LS}	P_{ME}^{NS}
LE	P_{LE}^{HS}	P_{LE}^{MS}	P_{LE}^{LS}	P_{LE}^{NS}
SE	P_{SE}^{HS}	P_{SE}^{MS}	P_{SE}^{LS}	P_{SE}^{NS}

with: $\forall$ i,j : $0 \leq P_i^j$ and $\sum_i P_i^j = 1$

Finally, we get a set of current weights for each consumer type given by the expression:

$$\Pi_j(t) = \sum_{l \in L} \sum_{k \in K} \mu^l(\nu) m^k(\lambda_j) P_k^l \tag{6}$$

with L={HS,MS,LS,NS} and K={SE,LE,ME,VE}

4 Water Allocation to Users

Once these weights are available a linear quadratic programming problem can be formulated to allocate weekly water volume to each class of culture:

$$\min_{Q_{t_j}} \sum_{j=1}^{M} \left(Q_{t_j}^s - \hat{D}_{t_j}^s\right)^2 \Pi_j(t) \tag{7}$$

subject to $\sum_{j=1}^{M} Q_{t_j}^s \leq Q_t^s$ $\quad$ *and* $\quad Q_{t_j}^s \geq 0 \;\; j = 1 \; to \; M$
œ50z Using a Lagrangian it is easily shown that the solution of this problem is given by:

$$Q_{t_j}^s = \hat{D}_{t_j}^s - \frac{[1/\Pi_j(t)]}{\sum_{k=1}^{M}[1/\Pi_k(t)]} \left(\hat{D}_t^s - Q_t^s\right) \tag{8}$$

i.e. the water deficit is allocated to each class of cultures inversely to the priority weight of that class. However if minimum volumes guaranteeing survival for some classes of cultures are taken into account, the above formulation must be completed with restrictions such as:

$$Q_{t_j}^s \geq Q_{j_{min}}^s \qquad j \in [1, \ldots, M]$$

In this case only a numerical solution will be available.

A sensitivity study can be performed in the following way:

1. If $\nu(t)$ is such that $\exists\, l \in L$:
   $0 < \mu^l(\nu(t)) < 1 \quad$ and $\quad \mu^{l+1}(\nu(t)) = 1 - \mu^l(\nu(t))$
   then two extreme situations can be considered:
   a) $\mu^l = 1 \quad$ and $\; \mu^{l+1} = 0$
   b) $\mu^l = 0 \quad$ and $\; \mu^{l+1} = 1$

2. Analyse each category of users and for each case where
   $\exists\, k \in K$ such that:
   $0 < m^k(\lambda_j) < 1 \quad$ and $\quad m^{k+1}(\lambda_j) = 1 - m^k(\lambda_j)$
   consider the two extreme situations:
   c) $m^k = 1 \quad$ and $m^{k+1} = 0$
   d)$m^k = 0 \quad$ and $m^{k+1} = 1$

So, we get $2^{(1+M)}$ possible situations to be considered. Since M is not very large, for each situation weights $\Pi_j(t)$ can be recomputed and the LQP Problem rerun to get a solution $Q^n_{t_j}$. Let

$$Q^{s_{min}}_{t_j} = \max_n \left[Q^{s(n)}_{t_j} \mid Q^{s(n)}_{t_j} \leq Q^s_{t_j} \right] \tag{9}$$

and

$$Q^{s_{max}}_{t_j} = \min_n \left[Q^{s(n)}_{t_j} \mid Q^{s(n)}_{t_j} \geq Q^s_{t_j} \right] \tag{10}$$

So, we get for each user j a possible interval for the volume of water which should be available for the next week:

$$Q^s_j(t) = [Q^{s_{min}}_{t_j}, Q^{s_{max}}_{t_j}] \tag{11}$$

Now considering the pattern of water demand during a week for each kind of culture we can get the nominal volume of water which will be allocated every day of the week to each culture.
Let Λ^k_j, $k = 1 \; to \; J$, be this pattern. We have:

$$\hat{d}^k_{t_j} = \Lambda^k_j(t) \hat{D}^s_{t_j}$$

where $\hat{D}^s_{t_j}$ is the demand of water for period t by user j.
Then a possible water delivery interval is defined as:

$$d^{k_{min}}_{t_j} = \Lambda^k_j(t) Q^{s_{min}}_{t_j} \leq \tilde{d}^k_{t_j} \leq \Lambda^k_j(t) Q^{s_{max}} = d^{k_{max}}_{t_j} \tag{12}$$

So the volume of water allocated to user j during day k of period t will be given by:

$$\begin{cases} d^k_{t_j} = \hat{d}^k_{t_j} & if \;\; d^{k_{min}}_{t_j} \leq \hat{d}^k_{t_j} \leq d^{k_{max}}_{t_j} \\ d^k_{t_j} = d^{k_{min}}_{t_j} & if \;\; \hat{d}^k_{t_j} < d^{k_{min}}_{t_j} \\ d^k_{t_j} = d^{k_{max}}_{t_j} & if \;\; \hat{d}^k_{t_j} > d^{k_{max}}_{t_j} \end{cases}$$

At the tactical level this volumes may be modified to take into account recent precipitations, so that nominal daily volumes of water for each class of culture will be given by :

$$\tilde{d}^k_{t_j} = d^k_{t_j} - \delta d^k_{t_j} \tag{13}$$

with $\delta d^k_{t_j} = r_j(\rho) d^k_{t_j}$ where ρ , $0 \leq \rho \leq 1$, indicates the importance of the precipitation and $r_j(\rho)$ is an increasing monotonic function. And the total volume for the next day is : $\sum_k \tilde{d}^k_{t_j} = \hat{\delta}$.
Now to build the hourly pattern of water which will be allocated to each user, we have to consider they demand for the following day.
Let δ^h_i be the demand of water (in m^3/s) by user i for hour h. Supposing that each user grows a unique class of culture, let S_j be the set of users which grow cultures of class j.
The total demand for hour h is given by:

$$\delta^h_{Tot} = \sum_{j=1}^{M} \left(\sum_{l \in S_j} \delta^h_l \right) = \sum_{j=1}^{M} \mathcal{D}^h_j \tag{14}$$

and the total demand for the day is then :

$$\delta = \sum_{t=1}^{24} \delta^h_{Tot}$$

The water allocated to user i during hour h will be given then by :

$$\hat{\delta}^h_i = min(\delta^h_i, \tilde{\delta}) \qquad i \in S_j \tag{15}$$

with

$$\tilde{\delta} = \tilde{d}^k_{t_j} \frac{\delta^h_i}{\mathcal{D}^h_j} \frac{\delta^h_{Tot}}{\delta} \tag{16}$$

5 The Control Layer

Let T be the receding horizon for the control of inflows which coincides with the horizon of prediction of flow demand. Actions taken at the current time t at the entrance of the canal will not influence water flows at section i until time:

$$t^i = t + \sum_{j=1}^{i} L_j \Theta(t)$$

where

$$\Theta_{t+1} = \alpha\Theta_t + \beta(Q^I_t - \bar{Q}^t_t) + (1-\alpha)\bar{\Theta}(\bar{Q}^I_t) \tag{17}$$

$0 < \alpha \leq 1 \qquad \beta < 0$
where $\bar{Q}^I_t$ is a mean flow value up to period n given by: $\bar{Q}^I_t = \sum_{m=t-N+1}^{t} Q^E_m / N$

So that events at section i will be the consequence of past decisions and of perturbations taking place upstream to this section. This gives to the problem a degree of uncontrollability which can be only overcome by an accurate prediction of the different classes of demand and perturbations. The receding horizon of control for section i is then at instant t :

$$h_i(t) = \left[t + \sum_{j=1}^{i} L_j \Theta(t), \quad t + \sum_{j=1}^{i} L_j \Theta(t) + T \right] \tag{18}$$

$i = 1, ...N$

The predicted flow at section i is given by

$$Q_i(t) = \hat{\delta}_i(t) + Q_{min} + H^{-1}(Q_{i+1}(t + L_i \Theta(t))) \tag{19}$$

$i = N, N-1, ...1$

where $\hat{\delta}_i(t)$ given by relation (15) is the flow allocated to user i during period t: H^{-1} indicates that the linear flow model is inverted to get the inflow at section i.

So, the total flow at the entrance of the canal is given finally by:

$$Q(t) = H^{-1}(Q_1(t + L_1 \Theta(t))) \qquad t \in h_1(t) \tag{20}$$

The inversion of the flow model is as follows:

For a given section of canal of length L, the value of Θ_{t+1} is obtained from relation (17), so that an estimate of the transport delay for the inflows during period $t+1$ is given by $d_{t+1} = L\Theta_{t+1}$. Then if $Q^S(t+1+d_{t+1})$ is the predicted flow at the exit section, inverting the modified Hayami's relation , we get the inflow:

$$Q^E(t+1) = max \ \{\beta_{t+1} + Q^E(t), \ \ 0\} \tag{21}$$

with

$$\beta_{t+1} = \frac{[Q^S(t+1+d_{t+1}) - \sum_{t<t+1+d_{t+1}} \beta_t \Phi(t+1+d_{t+1}, t)]}{\Phi(t+1+d_{t+1}, t+1)} \tag{22}$$

Since the flow at successive sections may vary abruptly, the inversion process leads to large variations of predicted inflows which can exceed the flow capacity of the canal.

So, at time $t+1$, the effective inflow $Q^I(t+1)$ is also submitted to capacity constraints such as:$Q_{min} \leq Q^I(t+1) \leq Q_{max}(t+1)$ where Q_{min} is a minimum inflow level related to other considerations than water distribution (protection of environment, animal life, navigation,...), while $Q_{max}(t+1)$ is related to the characteristics of the inflow control gate and to the level of water in the upstream reservoir.

6 Simulation

A 29.5km long stretch of canal with two pumping stations is considered (Fig. 4). We assume an initial steady state of $Q^I = Q^S = 0.5 m^3/s$. The desired final

outflows are given equal to $Q^* = 0.5 m^3/s$. In Fig. 5 are displayed water demands (δ_1^t , δ_2^t) by users 1 and 2 , as well as the water flows ($\hat{\delta}_1^t$, $\hat{\delta}_2^t$) allocated by the supervision level.
For this water allocated, the computed inflow is displayed in Fig.6, resulting in the outflows of Fig. 7.

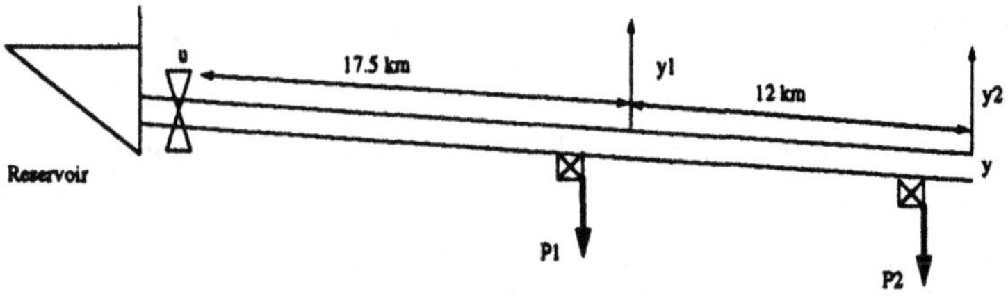

Figure 4 : The simulated system

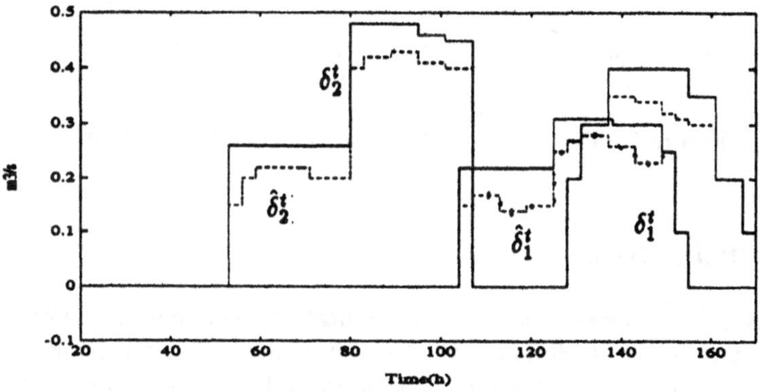

Figure 5 : The pumped flow sequence

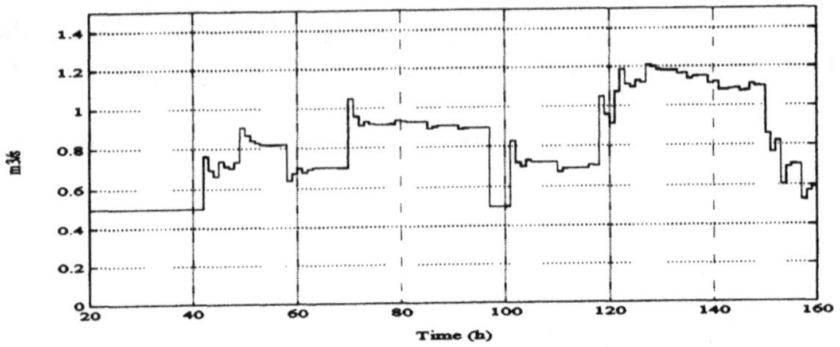

Figure 6 : Selected inflows for the controlled system

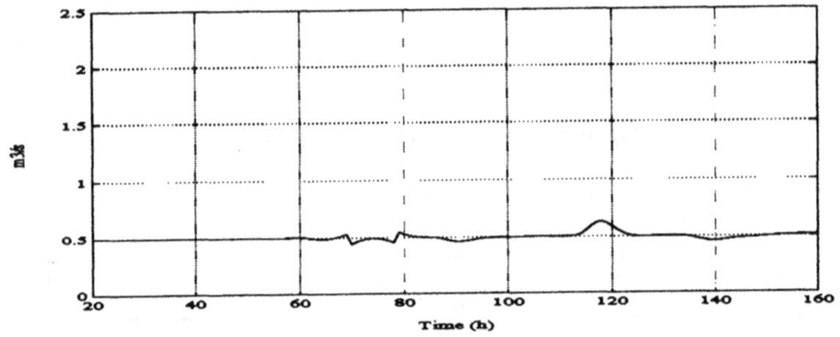

Figure 7 : Resulting outflows for the controlled system

7 Conclusion

It is an example of cooperation between qualitative techniques at the supervision level and quantitative techniques at the control level. The resulting approach, thanks to its simplicity, is compatible with normal conditions of operation.

8 References

Krijgsman A.J. and al (1988). Knowledge-based control.Proceeding, of the 27th Conference on Decision and Control, Texas, pp. 530-574.

Gentil S. and al (1987). Qualitative Modelling Process Supervision Systems. First European Meeting on Cognitive Science Approaches to Process Control. Marcoussis.

Sawadogo S., Achaibou A.K., Aguilar-Martin J. and Mora-Camino F. (1991). Output Tracking by Inverse Adaptive Control: Application to Water Distribution Systems.Proceeding of IMACS/MCTS Symposium, Lille, France, pp. 88-93.

Semantic Ambiguity in Expert Systems: The Case of Deterministic Systems

Daniel E. O'Leary

School of Business
University of Southern California
Los Angeles, CA 90089-1421
213-740-4856
oleary@mizar.usc.edu

Abstract. Typically with expert systems, the user is asked to assess or categorize evidence (E), based on data (D). The system is then responsible for matching that evidence (E) to the appropriate hypothesis (H). Throughout, the user provides the characterization of data as evidence for the system.

Unfortunately, different users may develop different categorizations of data. Based on different points of view, different users may categorize D as E or E'. This is referred to as semantic ambiguity. Such potential differences can have a major impact on the results recommended by expert systems.

This paper presents empirical results that indicate that there can be substantial ambiguity about the categorization of D as E or E'. In one situation, 50% of the subjects categorized data as E and 50% as E'. This paper also develops a probability model that is used to investigate semantic ambiguity in deterministic systems (no weights on the rules).

1 Introduction

Typically with expert systems, the user is asked to assess or categorize evidence (E), based on a set of data (D). The system is then responsible for matching that evidence (E) to the appropriate hypothesis (H). Throughout, the user interprets the data as evidence for the system.

For example, in the following rule [1, p. 512]), users of the expert system are asked to determine if the "... market followed an upward trend recently...."

If 1. the client's income tax bracket is 50%
2. the market has followed an upward trend
Then, there is evidence that the area of the investment should be high technology.

In this case, actual market performance is D, "upward trend" is E and "the area of the investment being high technology" is H.

Unfortunately, developing categorizations of data is not a straightforward task. Few probably would argue with the evidence categorization of the data (2850, 2900 and 3000) as following an "upward trend." However, the matching between the data and the meaning of terms of concern, may not be so clear in all situations. For example, does the data set (2900, 3000, 2875), follow an upward trend?

The ambiguity in the matching between E and D is referred to here as "semantic ambiguity." For each E and D there is a distribution associated with the interpretation of D as E and D as E' (not E).

1.1 Contributions of this Paper

This paper presents empirical work that suggests, depending on D and E, different users are likely to provide very different evidence assessments to the same situations. In some cases, given D, users provide the system with the assessment E, while other users provide the assessment E'.

This paper also develops an analytic model that allows us to investigate semantic interpretation. In the case where there are no weights on the rules, we can characterize and capture the probability that different assessments will be made by different users or developers for the same data set. For example, if the probability of H, given E is greater than the probability of H', given E then we could argue that only the rule linking E to H should be built in the deterministic system. However, for each user of the system to derive the same system response, that decision rule requires that under similar circumstances, each user should evaluate D as E. Thus, semantic uncertainty could result in different users, under the same circumstances, generating different system responses. As a result, if the gap between the probability of H, given E, and the probability of H, given E and D is large or costly, then it may be preferable to have the system categorize the data as evidence, rather than depending on the user.

2 Semantic Ambiguity

This paper is concerned with situations that can be characterized as follows (but also can be generalized). Assume that the user is confronted with data, D, or D' (not D) and is required to categorize that data as either E or E'. The expert system takes the user's assessment, E or E', as input, and relates that evidence deterministically with some hypothesis H. As a result, we are modeling rules of the type "If E then H," given the user assesses D as E.

P(x) is used to denote the probability of x, while $P(x|y)$ is the conditional probability of x given y. Throughout either D or D' occur and neither can be further partitioned. Either E or E' are the resulting categories, and neither can be further partitioned.

It will be said that there is semantic ambiguity in a rule "If E then H" if the probability of E given D is less than one or greater than 0 ($1 > P(E|D) > 0$). Thus, given D and no semantic ambiguity, we know that the rule "If E then H," either will or will not be executed for all users.

The problem of semantic interpretation is where one user may view D as E, with complete certainty, while another user may view D as E', also with complete certainty. (Or a user at one point in time categorizes D as E, with certainty, and at another point in time, categorizes D' as E, also with complete certainty.) At any rate, once the interpretation is made by the user, the system takes that interpretation as the only evidence, even though different users may provide completely different assessments E for the same D.

3 An Empirical Analysis

This section presents evidence that there can be substantial semantic ambiguity present in an expert system. Particular concern is given to the case where only two choices are allowed, e.g., "yes" or "no." Such binary choice situations are common in deterministic expert systems and other analysis tools, such as decision trees. Binary choices force the user to make crisp decisions. Unfortunately, these crisp decisions are often in situations where there is substantial ambiguity. The extent of that ambiguity is reflected in large percentages of the users choosing each alternative.

3.1 Tax Advisor

Tax Advisor [4] was investigated for potential semantic ambiguity. The following rules have a number of words that present the potential for semantic ambiguity. These rules were used to generate a test instrument that was used to perform an empirical analysis of the impact of semantic ambiguity in expert system situations.

Rule 142

If: 1) The *degree of financial management, experience*, and *ability of the client and/or spouse is poor,*
2) The client and/or spouse have assets that he/she is *willing to dispose of*
Then: It is definite that the client and/or spouse should invest in *low management investments.*

Rule 208

If: 1) The client and/or spouse is *willing* to consider a *low risk,* fixed dollar investment with a fixed return
2) Client and/or spouse does not have the time and/or *financial skills* to select his/her own security issues ....

Rule 175

If: ... the client has an estate that is *not liquid enough* to pay death taxes, administration, medical and funeral expenses and the immediate living expenses of the family without the sale of assets ....

Some of the ambiguous judgments are underlined in the above rules. In many cases the rules are quite extensive. As a result, these rules have been edited for presentation.

3.2 Questions and Subjects

The above rules force the users into a number of different judgments. For example, in two of those rules the user would be asked to assess "enough." What is enough insurance or what is enough liquidity? These answers are likely to vary between users and situations.

Subjects were faced with binary choices, rather than a graded choice: e.g., are the financial management skills "poor" or "not poor." An instrument was developed that required the subjects to present answers that are typical of bianry choice expert systems.

Questions were taken from the rules in Tax Advisor, discussed above, to investigate ambiguity in tax and accounting systems. The questions used in the empirical study are summarized in Table 1.

Table 1. Tax Planning Questions

A tax advisor must determine certain facts about the client in order to make recommendations related to tax planning. The following questions will present certain facts and you will be expected to rate the client (investment) attributes based on your own judgments.

Question 1 (Financial Skills)

A. The client is a well-respected attorney who specializes in trusts and estates.

His degree of financial management experience is

Poor Good

This client has the financial skills to select his own security issues.

No Yes

B. The client is a recently widowed housewife. She has been married for 28 years and has never held a compensated job. She has handled the family funds, including liquid investments totalling $250,000. She was president of the local grammar school PTA for five years.

Her degree of financial management experience is

Good Poor

This client has the financial skills to select her own security issues

No Yes

C. The client is a vice president of a large engineering firm in which he is a limited partner. He holds an M.S. in engineering as well as an M.B.A., both of which he earned when he was a young man.

His degree of financial management experience is

Good Poor

This client has the financial skills to select his own security issues

No Yes

Question 2 (Asset Questions)

A. The client currently holds assets consisting of mutual funds ($30,000), coupon bonds ($30,000), a piece of developed residential property (net fair market value of $800,000) and a family home of (fair market value of $700,000, encumbrance of $600,000).

These assets require a substantial degree of management

No Yes

The client has an estate that is liquid enough to pay death taxes, administration, medical and funeral expenses and the immediate living expenses of his spouse and two children

No Yes

B. The client currently holds assets consisting of a grantor trust which holds several variable annuities. These assets require a substantial degree of management

No Yes

The client has an estate that is liquid enough to pay death taxes, administration, medical and funeral expenses and the immediate living expenses of his spouse and two children

No Yes

C. The client currently holds assets consisting of a Southern California coin operated laundry mat and neighboring undeveloped land. These assets require a substantial degree of management

No Yes

The client has an estate that is liquid enough to pay death taxes, administration, medical and funeral expenses and the immediate living expenses of his spouse and two children

No Yes

D. The client currently has an estate which consists of several five year second trust deeds secured by residential real estate. These deeds have been issued throughout the past five year period. These assets require a substantial degree of management

No Yes

The client has an estate that is liquid enough to pay death taxes, administration, medical and funeral expenses and the immediate living expenses of his spouse and two children

No Yes

The instrument was developed and pilot tested on a faculty member and a Ph. D. student. Then the instrument was directly administered to 18 students in an advanced class in the Master of Tax program at the University of Southern California. Students are appropriate subjects since in many situations expert systems are used to delegate expertise down to lower levels in the organization. Virtually all these students were employed as professionals at the conclusion of the term in which this study was made.

3.3 Findings

The results are summarized in Table 2. An analysis of the data indicates that there apparently was substantial ambiguity. The greatest ambiguity was in question 1-C, where the respondents were equally divided between the two possible responses. A number of other situations also provided substantial semantic ambiguity. In addition, in no situation presented were the subjects unanimous in their assessment of the situation. The minimum split was with question 2 D (22.2% and 77.8%).

Table 2. Summary of Results on Tax Questions

Concept/Question			Response %	
	Poor	Good	No	Yes
Question 1 - "Financial Skills"				
A. "Financial Management"	33.3	66.7		
A. "Select Securities"			38.3	61.7
B. "Financial Management"	27.9	72.1		
B. "Select Securities"			55.6	44.4
C. "Financial Management"	55.6	44.4		
C. "Select Securities"			50.0	50.0

Question 2 - "Asset Management"

A. "Degree of Management"	66.7	33.3		
A. "Liquid Enough"			55.6	44.4
B. "Degree of Management"	50.0	50.0		
B. "Liquid Enough"			61.7	38.3
C. "Degree of Management"	55.6	44.4		
C. "Liquid Enough"			72.1	27.9
D. "Degree of Management"	22.2	77.8		
D. "Liquid Enough"			66.7	33.3

Such differences would guide the users to different parts of the rule base. Different users of the expert system would be provided with different answers to the same questions.

4 Single and Multiple Interpretations

In the development of an expert system there are at least two perspectives that guide the process of when a rule should be added to the system. Those perspectives derive from the different interpretations of the relationships between, D, E and H. First, it might be argued that there is a single correct interpretation of D as E, otherwise, expertise is lost. An expert would categorize the data in one way and expect the system to process it accordingly. In that situation, in order to capture expertise, the system must be based on a single correct interpretation of the data.

However, the empirical study in the previous section indicates that users of expert systems are likely to make multiple evidence categorizations of the same data. From a design and development perspective, there would be no "correct" answer. Because of the resulting ambiguity, generally systems are *not built* assuming multiple interpretations of the data. However, when they are *used*, there may be multiple interpretations of the same data.

Thus there is interest in determining when to add a rule to an expert system, given that it is assumed that there will be either a single interpretation (no semantic ambiguity) or multiple interpretations (semantic ambiguity).

4.1 Single Interpretation: System Design

If the expert thinks the data has an "upward trend," then it is likely that it is assumed that all must interpret the data in the same manner. Assuming a single interpretation is consistent with the notion of expertise: the expert views the world in a given manner and the system should be built to reflect that view.

If we assume a single interpretation in model design, then ideally a rule "If E then H," should be added to the system if the evidence *and* the data indicate that it is the appropriate rule. One approach to the choice of rules is to employ a probability-based decision rule. In particular, call the "evidence and data rule" the following: if $P(H|E,D) \geq P(H|x,y)$, for $(x,y)=(E,D')$, (E',D) and (E',D') then add the rule "If E then H". Although developers may not use this decision rule explicitly to design an expert system, the single interpretation assumption, results in the *effective* assumption of that decision rule.

4.2 Multiple Interpretations: System Use

Alternatively, based on the above empirical results, that users of expert systems may categorize evidence in multiple ways. There may be two feasible interpretations of D *and* D' as E (and, thus, D and D' as E'). In fact much of human communications seems to focus on these alternative interpretations.

The use of an expert system differs from the design in the relationship of the data and the evidence. In the case of semantic ambiguity, different users may employ either D or D' to develop E, which leads to H. Thus, the use of an expert system indicates that a rule "If E then H" will be employed if $P(H|E,D,D') \geq P(H|E',D,D')$.

4.3 Relationship Between Use and Design

Thus, it is assumed that the designer/developer assumes a single correct interpretation in the design and development of the system. Similarly, it is assumed that users may have multiple interpretations in the use of the system. As a result, we can see that development decision rules and use decision rules are not the same. In particular, $P(H|E,D)$ does not equal $P(H|E,D,D')$. Thus, probability models indicate that use and design perspectives result in different systems.

As a result, as the distance of $P(H|E,D)$ and $P(H|E,D,D')$ increases, we are likely to find that the use of expert systems that require the user to provide data will become more ineffective. As that distance increases (or if the cost is large), it is likely that other approaches to evidence categorization would be more appropriate. For example, rather than having the user provide category estimates from data, the system might be used to provide those estimates. In the case of determining "increasing," a computer estimate of the slope might be used.

5 Uniqueness Properties of Design Decision Rules

An important property of designing expert systems is that the decision rules for adding rules results in unique systems. This section provides uniqueness proofs for two such decision rules.

5.1 The Evidence Rule

The evidence rule can be characterized as follows: If $P(H|E) \geq P(H|E')$ then add the rule "If E then H". The use of the evidence rule might occur in those situations where it is felt there may be no ambiguity of interpretation or where there is no typical data that would be associated with the evidence. The evidence rule may be used in those situations where there are a set of heuristic rules or departmental rules, since those rules are generally coded without reference to specific occurrences (data).

The evidence rule will result in a unique set of rules (excluding ties at equality). There will be at most one rule with either E or E' and H. Similarly, there will be at most one rule with either E or E' and H'. Further, each of E, E',H and H' will be in at most one rule, with respect to those variables. This is guaranteed by the following theorem.

Theorem 1 -- Uniqueness

$P(H|E) \geq P(H|E')$ iff $P(H'|E) \leq P(H'|E')$.

Proof

$P(H|E) \geq P(H|E')$, implies that $1 - P(H|E) \leq 1 - P(H|E')$. But that implies that $P(H'|E) \leq P(H'|E')$. The other direction has a similar proof.

5.2 The Data Rule

The data rule can be characterized as follows: If $P(H|D) \geq P(H|D')$ then add the rule "If E then H". This approach might be used in those situations where the knowledge acquisition approach employs data to capture the concepts associated with the evidence. In this case the evidence categories may not be understood, but the data may have clear implications, e.g., in the situation of case-based reasoning. For example, bankrupt firms may have similar data characteristics that are arbitrarily labeled as a type of evidence, such as "liquidity" or "available cash."

The data rule also will result in a unique set of rules (excluding ties at equality). There will be at most one rule with either D or D' and H. Similarly, there will be at most one rule with either D or D' and H'. This is guaranteed by the following theorem.

Theorem 2 -- Uniqueness

$P(H|D) \geq P(H|D')$ iff $P(H'|D) \leq P(H'|D')$.

6 Summary and Extensions

This section provides a brief summary of the paper and a discussion about some of the possible extensions of the research presented in this paper.

This paper developed a model of semantic interpretation and studied the impact of that interpretation on deterministic models. Both empirical and analytical approaches were used to study the problem. The empirical portion of the paper presented evidence for the existence of semantic ambiguity. In one case 50% of subjects categorized data as E, while 50% categorized that same data as E'.

The analytical analysis pursued the differences between systems due to a single interpretation assumption and a multiple interpretation assumption. The use and development of expert systems each seem to require a different one of those assumptions. As the gap between those assumptions increases it appears important to shift the evidence categorization process from the user to other sources.

The approach used in this paper can be extended in a number of ways. First, only a single piece of evidence and a single hypothesis were considered. The results presented here can be extended to the integration of multiple pieces of evidence.

Second, the results can be extended to probabilistic models. Bayesian systems, such as AL/X [2,3] can be extended to account for ambiguity. In addition, the results can be extended to an the use in influence diagrams.

Third, the results presented in this paper indicate that it is critical for the development of approaches other than rules, in the design of expert systems. In particular, it is apparent that dialogues between the system and the user are probably necessary to mitigate the impact of semantic ambiguity.

References

1. Davis, R. and Buchanan, B., "Meta Level Knowledge," in Buchanan, B. and Shortliffe, E., Rule-based Expert Systems, Addison-Wesley, Reading, Massachusetts, 1985.

2. Duda, R., Gaschnig, J., and Hart, P., "Model Design in the Prospector Consultant System for Mineral Exploration," in D. Mitchie, (Ed.) Expert Systems for the Microelectronic Age, Edinburgh, Edinburgh University Press, 1979.

3. Duda, R., Hart, P. and Nillsson, N., "Subjective Bayesian Methods for Rule-based Inference Systems,"National Computer Conference, pp. 1075-1082, 1976.

4. Michaelsen, R., "A Knowledge-based System for Individual Income and Transfer Tax Planning," Unpublished Ph. D. Dissertation, University of Illinois, 1981.

A Deduction Rule for the Approximated Knowledge of a Mapping

J.Casasnovas

University of the Balearic Islands
Crra. Valldemossa Km. 7'5, 07071 Palma de Mallorca, Spain
e-mail: dmijcc8@ps.uib.es.

Abstract. The partial knowledge of a valuation, whose values are in the boolean algebra $\{0,1\}$ may be represented by the utilization of a set of four elements([1]). The partial or approximated knowledge of a valuation or a possibility or necessity measure, whose values are in the real interval $[0 \quad 1]$ may be represented by the set of "subintervals" and it is possible to define operations that also generalize the structures of algebra defined by Belnap. In this paper we propose the formulation of the "deduction rule" that allows us to deduce valid approximations from the available data.

1 Introduction

Valuations and possibility or necessity measures are mappings defined over sentences algebras and range in certain algebras of values. Valuations are *morphisms* with respect to each operation defined in the sentences algebra,but the measures only *transfer* the structure correspondent to the *join* (possibility) or the *meet* (necessity). The general cases where such algebras of values are boolean($\{0,1\}$, for instance) or the real interval $[0 \quad 1]$ [6] will be considered.

For a mapping, we shall consider(*instead of an exact knowlwdge*) *approximations* that assign to each element of the sentences algebra a subset of the algebra of values, to which (according to the available information) the value of the mapping over that element belongs to. Moreover, given that the algebras of values are totally ordered, it will be considered the case in which the approximation assigns to each sentence a *subinterval*. If the algebra of values is precisely $\{0,1\}$, then the set of subintervals coincide with the power-set $P(\{0,1\})$ and an approximation $[1 \quad 1]$ (respectively $[0 \quad 0]$) means that we know that the value of the mapping is precisely 1 (resp. 0), but an approximation $[0 \quad 1]$ means that *we don't know* the value of the mapping. Finally, an approximation $[1 \quad 0] = \emptyset$ means that the available information don't allow any value for the mapping(we have a *contradictory case*). We present in this paper a study of the *deduction* in the framework of the approximations. More concretely, if we know an approximation to the value of the mapping over an element, how can we obtain approximations to the value of the mapping over other elements? We present the solution of this problem by stating a *deduction rule* in the algebras of approximations introduced in ([3]), that are a generalization of the Belnap's ones([1])

2 Preliminaries

If the algebra of sentences is represented by A, the algebra of values by B, the power-set by $P(B)$, the set of intervals in B by $I(B)$,the approximated mapping by $f : A \rightarrow B$ and the approximation to f by $F : A \rightarrow P(B)$, then two kinds of operations in P(B) may be considered:

The first of them is composed by the usual set-operations: ***union, intersection and complementation*** of subsets of B and with which $P(\{0,1\}) = I(\{0,1\})$ results isomorphe to the algebra $A4$, used by Belnap ([1]), Driankov ([2]) and Casasnovas ([3]) with the aim to make ***accumulations*** of several approximations. For $I([0 \quad 1])$ or more general cases, $I(B)$ results only a ***partial algebra*** which will be named $A(B)$ and it may be used to accumulate and to order too.

The second kind of operations is composed by the ***induced operations*** by the ones of B on $P(B)$ and, even, on $I(B)$ by the ordinary form:

$$S\#S' = \{x\#x' \mid x \in S, x' \in S'\}$$

with which $I(\{0,1\})$results isomorphe to $L4$, also used by Belnap and, somehow modified, by Driankov, whereas, for the other algebras of values,it results a ***quasi-boolean.***algebra([6])that will be named $L(B)$ in this work.

If $I = [I_1 \quad I_2]$ $\quad I' = [I'_1 \quad I'_2]$ are intervals, the induced operations by the ***least upper bound(l.u.b.)*** and the ***greatest lower bound(g.l.b.)*** of B are the l.u.b. and the g.l.b. of the induced order defined by:

$$I \leq I' \text{if and only if both} I_1 \leq I'_1, I_2 \leq I'_2 \text{ hold}$$

with the maximal element $[1 \quad 1]$ and the minimal one $[0 \quad 0]$

The ***implication*** induces the following operation([6]):

$$Imp_i(I, I') = [Imp(I_2, I'_1) \quad Imp(I_1, I'_2)]$$

and it is an implication which doesn't satisfy the ***identity principle***, i.e.:

$$Imp_i(I, I) = [Imp(I_2, I_1) \quad Imp(I_1, I_2)] \neq [1 \quad 1]$$

and, consequently, it doesn't satisfy the ***modus ponens principle*** ([4]).

It is possible to define another "implication," also related with the order of the lattice $L(B)$, as follows:

$$IMP(I, I') = [Imp(I_1, I'_1) \quad Imp(I_2, I'_2)]$$

where $Imp(x, y)$ is the implication defined in B and it satisfies the identity and the Modus ponens principles. The order in $L(B)$ becomes related with the function "IMP" by means of: $I \leq I'$ if and only if $IMP(I, I') = [1 \quad 1]$

3 A Deduction Rule

If it is possible to state a *modus ponens* for the approximations:

$$\frac{\begin{array}{l} F(a) \longrightarrow F(b) \\ F(a) \end{array}}{F(b)}$$

then we would have a *deduction rule* absolutely analogue to the one that exists in B. But there we find some difficulties: the value of the implication between intervals is not generally an available information. The relation ship between the known approximation to the value $f(a)$ and the unknown approximation to $f(b)$ it is not generally known itself.

Often it is known an approximation of the relation that exists between $f(a)$ and $f(b)$, or, more frequently, the existent relation between the elements a and b in A *carried* by the approximated mapping $f : A \rightarrow B$ to the values $f(a)$ and $f(b)$ in B. Even, in a real information it is frequent enough to know only an approximation of the value $f(a \longrightarrow b)$, i.e. the deduction rule will be stated:

$$\frac{\begin{array}{c} F(a \longrightarrow b) \\ F(a) \end{array}}{F(b)}$$

and the problem will be *to define the "modus ponens function"*([4]) such that:

$$F(b) = MP(F(a), F(a \longrightarrow b)$$

So, the main proposition is the following one:

Proposition 1. *If the approximated mapping,f, is a morphism with respect to the implication (like valuations),i.e. if* $f(a \longrightarrow b) = Imp(f(a), f(b))$, *then we can assure:*
If the approximations:

$$F(a \longrightarrow b) = [F_1(a \longrightarrow b) \quad F_2(a \longrightarrow b)], F(a) = [F_1(a) \quad F_2(a)]$$

are valid, then the approximation $F(b) = [F_1(b) \quad F_2(b)]$ *is valid if it is defined as follows:*

$$F_1(b) = x_0 = min\{x \in B \mid F_1(a \longrightarrow b) \leq Imp(F_1(a), x)\}$$

$$F_2(b) = y_0 = max\{y \in B \mid Imp(F_2(a), y) \leq F_2(a \longrightarrow b)\}$$

where the operations "Imp" and " $\leq$ *" are defined in B and the "max" and "min" also defined in B and with respect to the order "*$\leq$*"*

Proof. The proof is based in the the following property of the considered operation *implication* in a totally ordered lattice:

$$\text{if } x \leq x', \text{ then} : x \longrightarrow y \geq x' \longrightarrow y$$

$$\text{if } y \leq y', \text{ then} : x \longrightarrow y \leq x \longrightarrow y'$$

Let x_0 be the minimum value that satisfies the proposed first inequality. Then we would have: if $f(b) < x_0$:

$$F_1(a \longrightarrow b) > F_1(a) \longrightarrow f(b) \geq f(a) \longrightarrow f(b) = f(a \longrightarrow b)$$

but this is *contradictory* with our supposition that $F(a \longrightarrow b)$ is a valid approximation of $f(a \longrightarrow b)$

In the same way, if we suppose that y_0 is the maximum value that satisfies the proposed second inequality, and we also suppose that $y_0 < f(b)$, then we can assure the following contradictory inequality:

$$F_2(a \longrightarrow b) < Imp(F_2(a), f(b)) \leq Imp(f(a), f(b)) = f(a \longrightarrow b)$$

But, also it is possible to calculate other valid approximations:

Proposition 2. *If we know the valid approximations:*

$$F(a \longrightarrow b) = [F_1(a \longrightarrow b) \quad F_2(a \longrightarrow b)]$$

$$F(b) = [F_1(b) \quad F_2(b)]$$

then the approximation $F(a) = [F_1(a) \quad F_2(a)]$*, defined as follows, is valid:*

$$F_1(a) = z_0 = min\{z \in B \mid Imp(z, F_1(b)) \leq F_2(a \longrightarrow b)\}$$

$$F_2(a) = t_0 = max\{t \in B \mid F_1(a \longrightarrow b) \leq Imp(t, F_2(b)\}$$

Proof. Let's suppose that:

$$f(a) < z_0$$

then, we can assert:

$$F_2(a \longrightarrow b) < Imp(f(a), F_1(b))$$

from where:

$$f(a \longrightarrow b) \leq F_2(a \longrightarrow b) <$$
$$< Imp(f(a), F_1(b)) \leq Imp(f(a), f(b)) = f(a \longrightarrow b)$$

In the same way, if we suppose that $t_0 < f(a)$, then we can assert:

$$Imp(f(a), F_2(a \longrightarrow b)) < F_1(a \longrightarrow b)$$

from where:

$$f(a \longrightarrow b) = Imp(f(a), f(b)) \leq$$
$$\leq Imp(f(a), F_2(a)) \leq F_1(a \longrightarrow b) \leq f(a \longrightarrow b)$$

which result contradictories in the same sense that we have denoted in the proposition 1.

Examples:

Let U be a set and let $P(U)$ and $P^{\sim}(U)$ be the *power-set* and the *fuzzy power-set*([5]), respectively.

1. Let $v : P^{\sim}(U) \longrightarrow [0 \quad 1]$ be a valuation over the fuzzy power-set and let's suppose that the *implication* is defined in the real interval as follows:

$$Imp(r, s) = min\{1, 1 - r + s\}$$

then, if H,S are fuzzy-subsets of U, we can assert.

$$v(H \longrightarrow S) = min\{1, 1 - v(H) + v(S)\}$$

Assume further that we know an approximation:

$$F(H) = [0.6 \quad 0.9]$$

$$F(S) = [0.1 \quad 0.9]$$

$$F(H \longrightarrow S) = [0.7 \quad 0.8]$$

to the values: $v(H)$,$v(S)$ and $v(H \longrightarrow S)$, respectively
If we want to apply the previous propositions, we calculate:
The minimal solution of the inequality:

$$F_1(H \longrightarrow S) \leq Imp(F_1(H), x)$$

is the minimal solution of the inequality:

$$0.7 \leq min(1, 1 - 0.6 + x)$$

i.e.

$$x_0 = 0.7 + 0.6 - 1 = 0'3$$

For the other inequalities:
The maximal solution of the inequality:

$$min(1, 1 - 0.9 + y) \leq 0.8$$

is the value:

$$y_0 = 0.8 + 0.9 - 1 = 0.7$$

The minimal solution of the inequality:

$$min(1, 1 - z + 0.1) \leq 0.8$$

is the value:

$$z_0 = 1.1 - 0'8 = 0'3$$

Finally, the maximal solution of the inequality:

$$0.7 \leq min(1, 1 - t + 0.9)$$

is the value:

$$t_0 = 1$$

From the above it follows that the first Proposition allow us to build the appoximation:

$$G(S) = [0.3 \quad 0.7]$$

and, therefore, we have *improved* the available approximation: $F(S) = [0.1 \quad 0.9]$
However, the second proposition only allow us to build the approximation: $G(H) = [0.3 \quad 1]$, that is evindentely *worse* than the available approximation: $F(H) = [0.6 \quad 0.9]$

2. Now, let's suppose that we have the following approximation:

$$F(H) = [0.2 \quad 0.9]$$

$$F(S) = [0.3 \quad 0.5]$$

$$F(H \longrightarrow S) = [0.8 \quad 0.9]$$

Then, if we apply the proposition 2, we have:

$$max\{t \in B \mid F_1(H \longrightarrow S) \leq Imp(t, F_2(S)\}$$

is the maximal solution of the inequality:

$$0.8 \leq min(1, 1 - t + 0.5)$$

i.e.:

$$t_0 = 1.5 - 0.8 = 0.7$$

and the minimal solution of the inequality:

$$Imp(z, F_1(S)) \leq F_2(H \longrightarrow S)$$

is the minimal solution of the inequality:

$$min\{1, 1 - z + 0.3)\} \leq 0.9$$

i.e.:

$$z_0 = 1.3 - 0.9 = 0.4$$

and we have obtained a new approximation to the value $v(H)$:

$$G(H) = [0.4 \quad 0.7]$$

which is an *improvement* of the available approximation:

$$F(H) = [0.2 \quad 0.9] \ .$$

However, if we apply the proposition 1 to this case , we have:

$$x_0 = min\{x \in B \mid 0.8 \leq min\{1, 1 - 0.2 + x\}$$

$$y_0 = max\{y \in B \mid min\{1, 1 - 0.9 + y\} \leq 0.9\}$$

and, therefore:

$$x_0 = 0$$

$$y_0 = 0.9 - 0.1 = 0.8$$

and the new approximation $G(S) = [0 \quad 0.8]$ is *not an improvement* of the available approximation $F(S) = [0.3 \quad 0.5]$

Remark. 1. It is possible to state this propositions by means of the implication "*IMP*" defined in the quasi-boolean algebra of subintervals $L(B)$ and the sets implication ($\subset$ defined in $P(B)$:

The following approximation is valid:

$$F(b) = Max\{[x \quad y] \in I(B) \mid IMP(F(a), [x \quad y]) \subset F(a \longrightarrow b)\}$$

where "Max" is in P(B)

2. If the approximated mapping is a *valuation* onto $\{0,1\}$ we can state:

$$F(b) = max(inA4)\{[x \quad y] \in P(\{0,1\}) \mid$$

$$\mid IMP(F(a), [x \quad y]) \leq (inA4)F(a \longrightarrow b)\}$$

where the operation IMP is the defined one in $L4$

Finally, in the case of approximations to a *possibility measure* or, in general to a mapping that satisfies :$F(a \vee b) = f(a) \vee f(b)$, but that doesn't satisfy $f(a \wedge b) = f(a) \wedge f(b)$ neither $f(\neg a) = \neg f(a)$ we don't have the condition $f(a \longrightarrow b) = f(a) \longrightarrow f(b)$ and we cannot apply directly the previous propositions .

In this type of mapping we have the following property: If $a \leq b$ in the algebra A(that is equivalent to: *for each valuation* the sentence $a \longrightarrow b$ is always *true*), then we can assure:

$$Imp(f(a), f(b)) = 1$$

and we can state:

$$\frac{\begin{array}{l} a \longrightarrow b \\ F(a) \end{array}}{\qquad F(b)}$$

where:

$$F(b) = Max\{[x \quad y] \mid IMP(F(a), x \quad y]) \leq [1 \quad 1]\} =$$
$$Max\{[x \quad y] \mid IMP(F(a), [x \quad y] = [1 \quad 1]\}$$

The proof of the corresponents propositions is absolutely analogue to the propositions 1 and 2.

References

1. Belnap,Jr,N.D.: A useful four-valued logic. Modern uses of Multiple-Valued logic(1977),pp 8-40.Boston
2. Driankov D. : Towards a Many-valued logic of quantified belief :he information lattice. IJIS vol 6 pp135-166(1991)
3. Casasnovas J. : Contribucin a una formalizacin de la inferencia directa (Thesis D.PH.)(1989).U.I.B.Palma de Mallorca
4. Valverde L.:Deduction rules in Fuzzy Sets. (Thesis D.PH.)(1982)U.P.C. Barcelona
5. Dubois D. and Prade H. : Fuzzy Sets an Systems, theory and applications.Academic Press(1980)
6. Rasiowa E.: An algebraic approach to Non-clasical Logicas. North Holland, Amsterdam(1974)

On Knowledge Base Redundancy under Uncertain Reasoning

Gabriel Valiente Feruglio

Universitat de les Illes Balears
Dept. de Ciències Matemàtiques i Informàtica
E-07071 Palma (Balears) Spain

Abstract. Current notions of redundancy and subsumption for knowledge bases under boolean reasoning are extended in this paper to approximate reasoning. The extension is based on the folding of rules under uncertain reasoning as the basic operation for computing rule trees. In this way global subsumption can also be detected under approximate reasoning. A new method for the detection and removal of all redundant and subsumed rules under approximate reasoning, based on graph transformations, is also presented.

Keywords: Rule-based expert systems, approximate reasoning, knowledge base verification, rêdundancy, subsumption, graph grammars, algebraic graph transformations.

1 Introduction

Rule-based formalisms offer the user a great freedom for writing knowledge bases, although at the expense of almost unlimited possibilities for introducing structural deficiencies in the knowledge base. These structural deficiencies are the subject of knowledge base verification, and are very different in nature from problems of correspondence to the real-world problem domain being modeled by the knowledge base, that is the subject of knowledge base validation.

The main problems addressed by knowledge base verification have been the detection of inconsistencies, redundancies, and incompleteness. Informally, if a knowledge base is viewed as a logical theory, then it is inconsistent if it has no model and it is redundant if it contains rules that follow from the other rules.

Actually no precise definition of redundancy can be found in the knowledge base verification literature, that has been mainly devoted to consistency issues [1, 5]. This comes as no surprise, as consistency is a more stringent problem than redundancy, which is considered to be of less importance. Inconsistent knowledge bases cannot be used at all without the risk of obtaining conflicting results, while redundant knowledge bases can be used at merely some additional computational expense.

The real problem with redundancy is to be found during knowledge base maintenance. Let us agree that the main operations allowed on a knowledge base during maintenance are the addition, removal, and modification of rules, and that the expert tries to achieve a certain change in behavior (a certain change in the models of the knowledge base) when maintaining a knowledge base. Although elementary changes in behavior could be achieved in principle by making unitary changes in an irredundant knowledge base, the presence of redundant rules obscures the maintenance task.

2 Redundancy under Boolean Reasoning

Research in knowledge base verification has shown that the complexity of verification procedures is exponential when the semantics of the knowledge base is taken into account. Many efforts are then being directed towards syntactic notions of redundancy, independent from the control embodied in the expert system but in direct correspondence with the semantic notion of redundancy. While at the semantic level expert system control aspects play a central role, thus guaranteeing that only actual redundancy problems are being treated, at the syntactic level all potential redundancies are treated, although many of them will not actually occur in practice because expert system control can occasionally prevent the firing of redundant rules. Although the syntactic approach is more conservative in nature, it has the advantage that the resulting redundancy notions for knowledge bases are invariant with respect to expert system control. This means that once a knowledge base has been verified and all the potential sources of redundancy have been eliminated, no redundancy can be introduced by eventually modifying control aspects. Independence of structural verification with respect to control aspects is then a sign of system ***robustness***.

Knowledge base redundancy is a generalization of subsumption. Assuming the usual definition of valuation or interpretation from propositional logic and the usual definition for a formula to be true in an interpretation, subsumption in propositional knowledge bases is just a restriction of general subsumption [2] in Horn clausal logic to propositional logic [8]. The notion of *covering* is also borrowed from logic programming [2]. For a rule to be fireable under certain conditions producing some result is equivalent to saying that the rule covers that result under these conditions. That is, rule $r : A_1, \ldots, A_n \rightarrow C$ covers proposition symbol C in interpretation $\mathcal{I}$ if $A_1 \wedge \ldots \wedge A_n$ is true in $\mathcal{I}$.

Definition 1. Rule $r \in K$ subsumes (or is more general than) rule $s \in K$ if $rhs(r) = rhs(s)$ and for any interpretation $\mathcal{I}$ such that K is true in $\mathcal{I}$, $lhs(r)$ is true in $\mathcal{I}$ whenever $lhs(s)$ is true in $\mathcal{I}$.

Example 1. Rule r_2 subsumes rule r_3 with respect to a knowledge base containing the rules

$$P, Q \rightarrow R \quad (r_1)$$
$$R, S \rightarrow T \quad (r_2)$$
$$P, Q, S \rightarrow T \quad (r_3)$$

because in any interpretation in which the knowledge base is true and r_3 covers T, the proposition symbols P, Q, S and T are true, the proposition symbol R is also true, and r_2 also covers T in that interpretation.

Subsumption can be either local to the involved rules or global to the knowledge base. In the latter case, a rule subsumes another rule through some rule tree, where a rule tree in a knowledge base K is a set of rules $\{r_0, \ldots, r_k\}$ in K ($k \geq 0$) such that for all i there is a j for which $rhs(r_i) \subseteq lhs(r_j)$, with $0 \leq i < j \leq k$.

Example 2. The set of rules $\{r_1, r_2, r_3, r_4\}$ forms a rule tree

$$P, Q \rightarrow R \quad (r_1)$$
$$S, T \rightarrow U \quad (r_2)$$
$$U, V \rightarrow W \quad (r_3)$$
$$R, W \rightarrow X \quad (r_4)$$

$$P, Q, S, T, V \rightarrow X \quad (r_5)$$

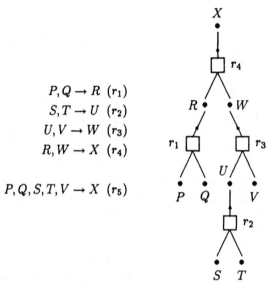

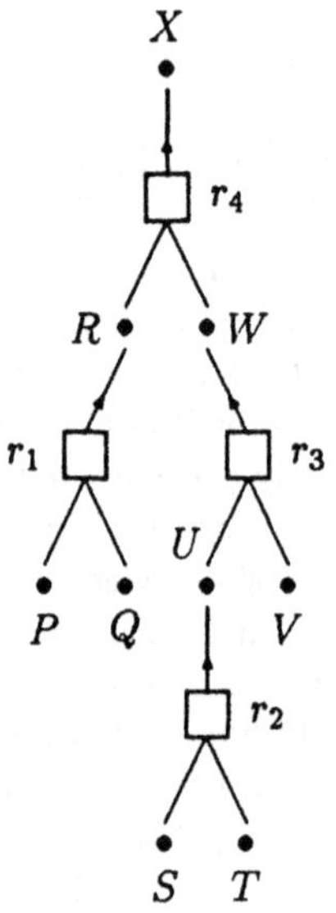

where rule r_4 subsumes rule r_5.

A syntactical characterization of subsumption for propositional and acyclic knowledge bases can be given that is based on the *cut* of a rule tree. The cut of a rule tree $\{r_0, \ldots, r_k\}$ in K ($k \geq 0$), noted $cut(r_0, \ldots, r_k)$, is the set of proposition symbols $lhs(r_0) \cup \ldots \cup lhs(r_k) \setminus rhs(r_0) \setminus \ldots \setminus rhs(r_k)$, where $\cup$ and $\setminus$ denote set union resp. set difference. The cut of an (elementary) rule tree $\{r\}$ is then $lhs(r) \setminus rhs(r)$ and this is equal to $lhs(r)$, because of the absence of cycles.

Example 3. The cut of the rule tree $\{r_1, r_2, r_3, r_4\}$ in example 2 above is the set of proposition symbols $\{P, Q, S, T, V\}$.

Theorem 2. *Rule $r \in K$ subsumes rule $s \in K$ if and only if $rhs(r) = rhs(s)$ and there is a rule tree $\{r_0, \ldots, r_i\}$ in K ($i \geq 0$) with $r_i = r$ such that $cut(r_0, \ldots, r_i) \subseteq cut(s)$.*

Proof. ($\Leftarrow$) Make $tree ::= r$. Take $\mathcal{I}$ to be the smaller interpretation in which $lhs(s)$ is true: $\mathcal{I}_{min} = lhs(s) \cup \{rhs(x) \mid x \in K \wedge lhs(x) \subseteq \mathcal{I}_{min}\}$. Note that $\mathcal{I}_{min}$ always exists, even if there is no such $x \in K$. For every $f \in lhs(r)$ to be true in $\mathcal{I}_{min}$ it must be either $f \in lhs(s)$ or there must be some rule $x \in K$ such that $\{f\} = rhs(x)$ and $lhs(x)$ is true in $\mathcal{I}_{min}$. In the latter case, make $tree ::= tree \cup \{x\}$ and proceed recursively with every $f \in lhs(x)$. When no further expansion of the tree is needed, that is, when every $f \in lhs(s)$, all the leaves of the tree belong to $lhs(s)$. Then $cut(tree) \subseteq lhs(s)$, and because $rhs(s) \not\subseteq cut(tree)$ it follows that $cut(tree) \subseteq cut(s)$.

($\Rightarrow$) Let $\mathcal{I}$ be any interpretation such that K is true in $\mathcal{I}$ and s covers $rhs(s)$ in $\mathcal{I}$. $cut(r_0, \ldots, r_i)$ is true in $\mathcal{I}$, because $cut(r_0, \ldots, r_i) \subseteq cut(s)$ and $lhs(s)$ is true in $\mathcal{I}$. For every rule $x \in \{r_0, \ldots, r_i\}$, $rhs(r)$ is true in $\mathcal{I}$, and in particular for those rules $y \in \{r_0, \ldots, r_i\}$ such that $rhs(y) \subseteq lhs(r)$. $lhs(r)$ is therefore true in $\mathcal{I}$. Then r covers $rhs(r)$ in $\mathcal{I}$. □

Redundancy is defined to be a generalization of subsumption, namely subsumption *in both directions*.

Definition 3. Rule $r \in K$ is redundant to rule $s \in K$ if r subsumes s and s subsumes r.

It follows that no global form of redundancy is possible, as stated in the following lemma.

Lemma 4. *Rule $r \in K$ is redundant to rule $s \in K$ if and only if $rhs(r) = rhs(s)$ and $cut(r) = cut(s)$.*

Proof. ($\Leftarrow$) There is a rule tree $\{r\}$ in K such that $cut(r) \subseteq cut(s)$. Then r subsumes s. In the same way, there is a rule tree $\{s\}$ in K such that $cut(s) \subseteq cut(r)$. Then s subsumes r. Therefore r is redundant to s.

($\Rightarrow$) $rhs(r) = rhs(s)$, by theorem 2. For rule $r \in K$ to be redundant to rule $s \in K$ there must be rule trees $\{r_0, \ldots, r_i\}$ and $\{s_0, \ldots, s_j\}$ in K $(i, j \geq 0)$ with $r_i = r$ and $s_j = s$ such that $lhs(r_0) \cup \ldots \cup lhs(r_i) \setminus rhs(r_0) \setminus \ldots \setminus rhs(r_i) \subseteq lhs(s) \setminus rhs(s)$ and $lhs(s_0) \cup \ldots \cup lhs(s_j) \setminus rhs(s_0) \setminus \ldots \setminus rhs(s_j) \subseteq lhs(r) \setminus rhs(r)$, by theorem 2. Then it must be $i = j = 0$. Therefore $cut(r) = cut(s)$. □

3 Redundancy under Uncertain Reasoning

The previous definitions of redundancy and subsumption under boolean reasoning can be extended to approximate reasoning based on the natural requirement that the certainty of the subsumed rule be less than or equal to the certainty of the rule subsuming it, besides being subsumed under boolean reasoning.

The cut of a rule tree can can be a very complex operation under approximate reasoning. It is easy to show, however, that it is equal to the composition of elementary *folding* operations [8], in such a way that computing the cut of a rule tree $\{r_0, \ldots, r_k\}$ can be realized by k folding operations.

Definition 5. The folding of rules $r : B_1, \ldots, B_m, \ldots, B_n \rightarrow A_1\ (L_r)$ and $s : B_1, \ldots, B_m \rightarrow A_2\ (L_s)$ is the new rule $r \uparrow s : A_2, B_{m+1}, \ldots, B_n \rightarrow A_1\ (L_{r\uparrow s})$, where L_r, L_s and $L_{r\uparrow s}$ are measures of rule uncertainty.

Theorem 6. *Rule folding preserves the semantics of the knowledge base if $L_r = \Delta(L_{r\uparrow s}, L_s)$, provided that the conjunction operator Δ is associative, idempotent and identical to the implication operator $\triangleright$ and that no other rule for A_2 exists in the knowledge base.*

Proof. The certainty for A_1 obtained through r is $V(A_1) = \triangleright(L_r, \Delta(V(B_1), \ldots, V(B_n)))$. On the other hand, the certainty for A_1 obtained through s and $r \uparrow s$ is $V'(A_1) = \triangleright(L_{r\uparrow s}, \Delta(V(A_2), V(B_{m+1}), \ldots, V(B_n)))$, where $V(A_2) = \triangleright(L_s, \Delta(V(B_1), \ldots, V(B_m)))$. It follows that $V'(A_1) = \triangleright(L_{r\uparrow s}, \Delta(\triangleright(L_s, \Delta(V(B_1), \ldots, V(B_m))), V(B_{m+1}), \ldots, V(B_n)))$. In order to be $V(A_1) = V'(A_1)$, it must be $\triangleright(L_r, \Delta(V(B_1), \ldots, V(B_n))) = \triangleright(L_{r\uparrow s}, \Delta(\triangleright(L_s, \Delta(V(B_1), \ldots, V(B_m))), V(B_{m+1}), \ldots, V(B_n)))$. Because $\triangleright = \Delta$, it follows that $\Delta(L_r, \Delta(V(B_1), \ldots, V(B_n))) = \Delta(L_{r\uparrow s}, \Delta(\Delta(L_s, \Delta(V(B_1), \ldots, V(B_n)))$. By associativity of Δ, $\Delta(L_r, V(B_1), \ldots, V(B_n)) = \Delta(L_{r\uparrow s}, L_s, V(B_1), \ldots, V(B_n))$. Therefore $L_r = \Delta(L_{r\uparrow s}, L_s)$. □

The additional requirement that no other rule for A_2 exists in the knowledge base is common to rule folding under boolean reasoning [7]. Idempotency is required for simplifying duplicated proposition symbols during rule folding. Because $L_{r\uparrow s}$ is, in general, not unique, we take the supremum $L_{r\uparrow s} = max\{L \mid \Delta(L, L_s) = L_r\}$. In those systems where the conjunction operator is taken to be the minimum function, for instance, the equation also states that folding can only be done if $L_s \geq L_r$.

Example 4. The cut of the rule tree $\{r_1, r_2, r_3, r_4\}$ is the set of proposition symbols $\{P, Q, S, T, V\}$ and can be obtained by the three folding operations $r_1 \uparrow r_4$, $r_2 \uparrow r_3$ and $r_3 \uparrow r_4$ in any order, in particular as follows:

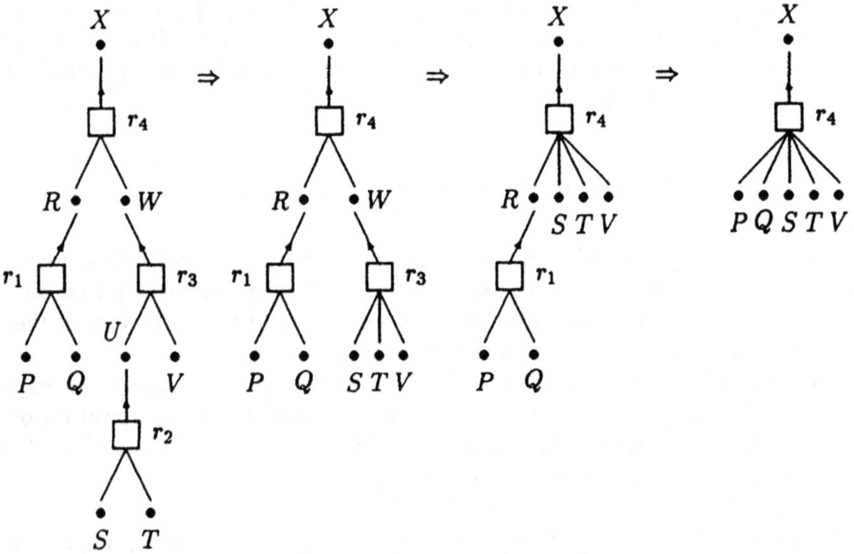

Theorem 7. *Rule $r \in K$ subsumes rule $s \in K$ under approximate reasoning if and only if $rhs(r) = rhs(s)$ and there is a rule tree $\{r_0, \ldots, r_i\}$ in K $(i \geq 0)$ with $r_i = r$ such that $cut(r_0, \ldots, r_i) \subseteq cut(s)$ and $L_{r_0\uparrow \ldots \uparrow r_i} \geq L_s$.*

Proof. The proof is trivial for the if part. Rule r subsumes rule s under boolean reasoning, because $rhs(r) = rhs(s)$ and there is a rule tree $\{r_0, \ldots, r_i\}$ in K $(i \geq 0)$ with $r_i = r$ such that $cut(r_0, \ldots, r_i) \subseteq cut(s)$. Furthermore, the certainty obtained through r (actually through $r_0 \uparrow \dots \uparrow r_i$) is always greater than or equal to the certainty obtained through s. Therefore r subsumes s under approximate reasoning. The only if part has been already proved for boolean reasoning (theorem 1). Case r local-subsumes s (that is, it subsumes s in a knowledge base consisting solely of r and s) it also subsumes s through the trivial rule tree $\{r\}$ with $r_0 = r_i = r$. Otherwise it global-subsumes s through some rule tree $\{r_0, \dots, r_i\}$ with $r_i = r$. In both cases it must be $L_{r_0\uparrow\dots\uparrow r_i} \geq L_s$ for the certainty obtained through r to be greater than or equal to the certainty obtained through s, that is, for the subsumption to hold under approximate reasoning. □

4 Verification Using Graph Transformations

A knowledge base transformation system for detecting redundancy and subsumption under approximate reasoning can be realized as a graph transformation system, as it has been already done for boolean reasoning [8].

Graph rewriting techniques are specially suited for describing the transformation of structures represented by graphs. The verification method is based on translating the knowledge base to be verified into a hypergraph representation, detecting and removing all redundant and subsumed rules by application of *graph productions*, and translating back the resulting hypergraph representation into a knowledge base, now free from redundancies and subsumptions.

We assume that the reader is familiar with the basic notions of graph grammars and algebraic graph transformations that are given in the appendix. Intuition should suffice, however, to understand the verification method. A graph production can be seen as describing a transformation of any graph (or hypergraph) that "contains" the left-hand side of the production. The transformation consists in essence of *cutting* the left-hand side from the graph and *pasting* the right-hand side onto the graph. A graph production can be applied to a graph whenever the left-hand side of the production *matches* some part (subgraph) of the graph.

The first step of the method consists of transforming the knowledge base to be verified into a hypergraph representation. Any (propositional) knowledge base K can be represented as a labeled, directed hypergraph by first creating a node for each distinct proposition symbol used in the rules, labeled with the proposition symbol itself, and then creating a hyperarc of the form

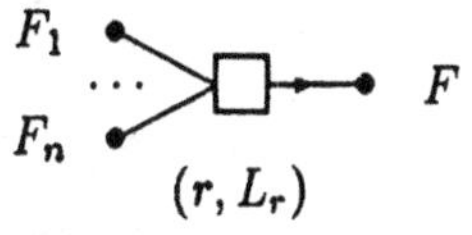

for each rule $r \in K$ of the form $F_1, \dots, F \to F\ (L_r)$, where $F_1, \dots, F_n, F$ are node labels and (r, L_r) is the label of the hyperarc.

Once the knowledge base has been translated into a hypergraph, the second step of the verification method permits the detection and removal of all redundant and subsumed rules by application of a set of graph productions.

Graph productions p_1 and p_2 below allow the detection and removal of all locally redundant resp. subsumed rules. The correspondence of L and R in the graph productions is obvious due to the similar arrangement of nodes and hyperarcs in L

and R. Moreover, all these graph productions are in fact ***graph production schemata***, where ellipses stand for zero or more nodes. Schemata are nothing more than syntactic sugar that avoid having to write down identical graph productions for different number of nodes.

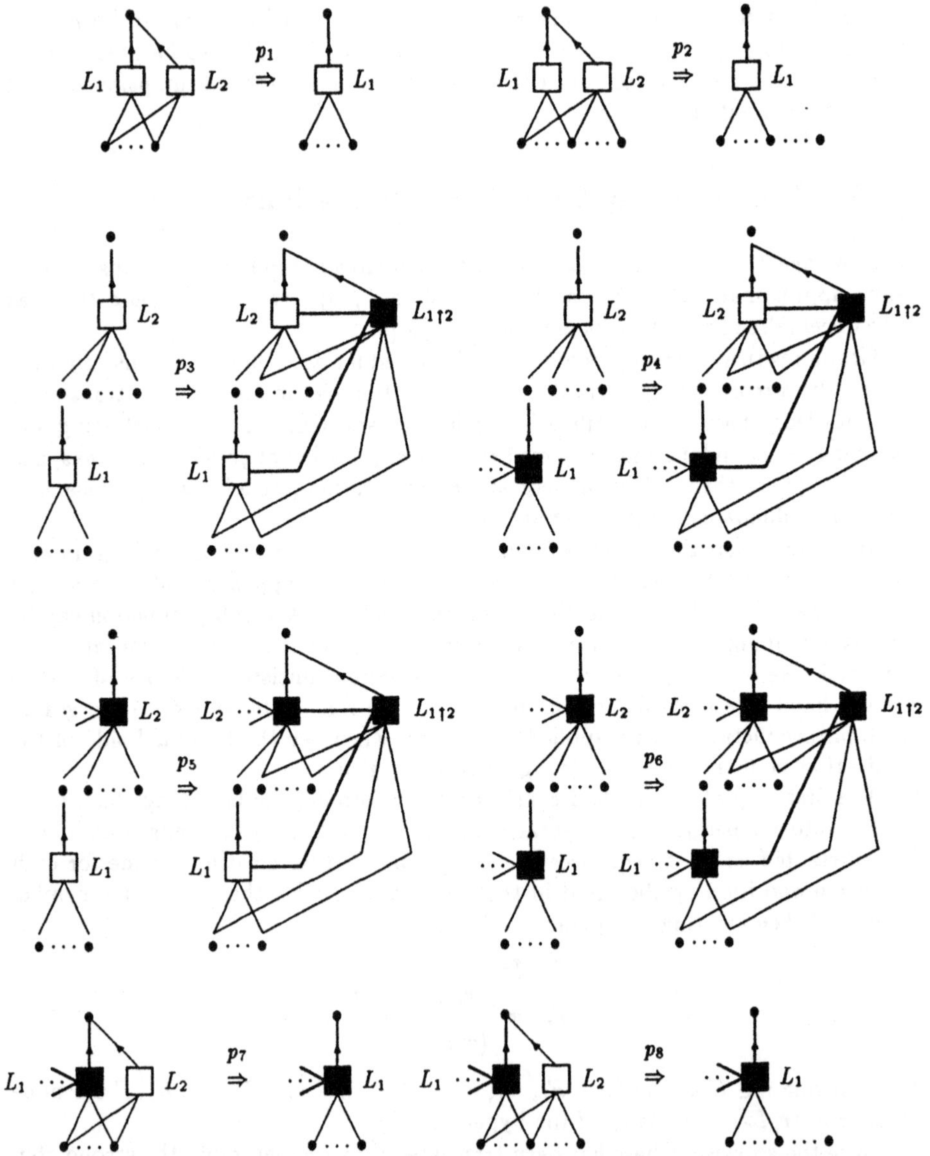

Graph productions p_1 and p_2 are subject to the application condition that $L_1 \geq L_2$. This application condition guarantees that the certainty of the redundant or subsumed rule be less than or equal to the certainty of the rule subsuming it.

Removal of globally subsumed rules requires an auxiliary construction. The graph-based representation of the knowledge base has to be extended by making explicit all rule trees (of depth ≥ 2), and this can be achieved by application of graph productions p_3 to p_6 above. The resulting, auxiliary hyperarcs are called black hyperarcs and are distinguished from rule (white) hyperarcs by having a special label (a filled square in the pictures) attached to them.

Graph productions p_3 to p_6 are subject to three application conditions: (a) that the black hyperarc being added by the production does not already exist in the graph, (b) that no other hyperarc incident on the node common to the two left hyperarcs exists in the graph, and (c) that $L_{1\uparrow 2} = max\{L | \triangle (L, L_2) = L_1\}$. Without the first application condition, graph productions p_3 to p_6 would be always applicable after they are applied once, resulting in a non-terminating computation. The second application condition corresponds to the requirement for semantics-preserving rule folding stated in theorem 2, while the third one computes the certainty of the folded rule.

Graph productions p_7 and p_8 allow the detection and removal of all globally subsumed rules, and are also subject to the application condition that $L_1 \geq L_2$. This application condition guarantees that the certainty of the (globally) subsumed rule be less than or equal to the certainty of the rule subsuming it.

Note that as a side effect of such graph transformations all black hyperarcs related to the removed rule (white) hyperarc are also removed. The removal of (the representation of) a rule originates then the removal of (the representation of) all rule trees to which the removed rule belonged, in descending tree depth, much like in a chain reaction.

Although we have suggested some order of application for the graph productions, no control flow needs to be specified for graph transformation systems. If a hypergraph representation of the knowledge base to be verified is taken to be the start graph of a graph grammar whose productions are graph productions p_1 to p_8, the verified knowledge base is a member of the language generated by the graph grammar, that is, it is always derivable from the start graph by sole application of the given graph productions. Moreover, since no particular order of application for the graph productions has to be defined, the verification method based on graph transformations can exploit computer architectures supporting massive parallelism, that being of great importance due to the computational complexity of the verification problem.

The third step of the method consists of extracting the knowledge base, free from redundancies and subsumptions, from the graph-based representation. This is achieved by just translating back each white hyperarc into a rule and forgetting any remaining black hyperarcs.

5 Conclusion

Current notions of redundancy and subsumption for knowledge bases under boolean reasoning have been extended to approximate reasoning. The extension is based on the folding of rules under uncertain reasoning as the basic operation for computing rule trees. In this way global subsumption can also be detected under approximate reasoning. A new method for the detection and removal of all redundant and subsumed rules under approximate reasoning, based on graph transformations, has also been developed.

Acknowledgement

The extension of folding for uncertain reasoning has evolved through many communications with Lluís Godo. The research described in this paper has also benefited from many discussions with Andrea Corradini, Thomas Hoppe, Martin Korff, Jordi Levy and Michael Löwe. I am very grateful to all of them.

References

1. M. Ayel and J.-P. Laurent, editors. *Validation, Verification and Test of Knowledge-Based Systems*, Chichester, England, 1991. John Wiley & Sons.
2. W. Buntine. Generalized Subsumption and its Applications to Induction and Redundancy. *Artificial Intelligence*, 36(2):149–176, Sept. 1988.
3. H. Ehrig and A. Habel. Graph Grammars with Application Conditions. In G. Rozenberg and A. Salomaa, editors, *The Book of L*, pages 87–100. Springer-Verlag, Berlin, 1985.
4. H. Ehrig, M. Korff, and M. Löwe. Tutorial Introduction to the Algebraic Approach of Graph Grammars based on Double and Single Pushouts. In H. Ehrig, H.-J. Kreowski, and G. Rozenberg, editors, *Proc. 4th Int. Workshop on Graph-Grammars and their Application to Computer Science*, volume 532 of *Lecture Notes in Computer Science*, pages 24–37, Berlin, 1991. Springer-Verlag.
5. U. G. Gupta, editor. *Validating and Verifying Knowledge-Based Systems*, Los Alamitos, California, 1991. IEEE Computer Society Press.
6. M. Löwe. *Extended Algebraic Graph Transformation*. PhD thesis, Fachbereich Informatik, Technische Universität Berlin, 1991.
7. H. Tamaki and T. Sato. Unfold/Fold Transformation of Logic Programs. In *Proc. 2nd Int. Logic Programming Conference*, pages 127–138, Uppsala, Sweden, July 1984.
8. G. Valiente. Verification of Knowledge Base Redundancy and Subsumption using Graph Transformations. To appear in *The Int. Journal of Expert Systems: Research & Applications*, 1993.

Appendix

The algebraic approach to graph transformation provides an elegant theoretical framework to describe the transformation of graph structures [4, 6]. In operational terms, the application of graph production $r : L \rightarrow R$ to a graph G at redex $m : L \rightarrow G$ first builds the graph $L_r \subseteq L$ consisting of all objects that are to be preserved by the transformation. Then all objects in $L - L_r$ are removed from G. Finally, all objects in $R - L_r$ are added to the graph. The context in which these objects are added in provided by the graph L_r that is preserved by the transformation. The algebraic description provides an abstract notion for graph transformation, where the transformation of a graph G into a graph H by application of a graph production $r : L \rightarrow R$ at a redex $m : L \rightarrow G$ is given by the pushout of r and m in the category of graphs and partial graph morphisms. Application conditions can be specified for any graph production, where they are just restrictions on the (class of) redices at which the graph production can be applied [3]. The previous description applies not only to the transformation of graphs but also to hypergraphs and to the higher-order hypergraphs used in the verification method.

A Fuzzy Logic Approach for Sensor Validation in Real Time Expert Systems

Juan A. Aguilar-Crespo, Erik de Pablo, and Xavier Alamán

Instituto de Ingeniería del Conocimiento, Universidad Autónoma de Madrid
Cantoblanco, 28049 Madrid, Spain

Abstract. Data validation of the information coming from sensors is a fundamental problem when developing on-line real-time expert systems. In this paper an approach using fuzzy logic methods is presented. This approach has been originated during the development of the *MIP* project, a real-time expert system for assistance to petrochemical processes that is described in [1]. The *MIP* expert system is deployed and in production in a petrochemical plant of INH-REPSOL in Tarragona, Spain. The method presented in this paper complements the *MIP* expert system by preprocessing the incoming data and assigning confidence values to each measurement from the sensors. These confidence values can be used subsequently to enrich the conclusions obtained by the *MIP* system. The method is currently in field test in the plant.

1 Description of the problem

Several problems related with uncertainty management arise when developing on-line real-time expert systems, especially within the area of process control. One of the most important of these problems is the low reliability of the incoming data. Because of various technical reasons wrong measurements are very frequently obtained from sensors. Human experts acknowledge this fact by checking carefully the validity of all the measurements before making any diagnosis or taking any decision. If an expert system has to perform the same task, the validation step becomes essential: wrong input data has to be quickly pinpointed to avoid expensive mistakes.

Some approaches to sensor validation have been proposed in the literature. See for example [2, 3, 5, 6, 7]. Some common conclusions from these references are:

- The history of each variable has to be stored and processed somehow to obtain information about the confidence that the current value deserves.
- Redundancy in the information is a powerful tool for validating measurements. This may be achieved by using several sensors to measure the same physical variable or by measuring simultaneously several physical variables that are numerically related to each other.
- It is important to distinguish between normal and abnormal behaviors in each sensor. For example, if a sensor is measuring the temperature of a huge amount of material, quick changes in the value are not expected. On

the other hand, if the sensor is measuring the flow of material through a valve, steady values are suspicious.

Additionally, it has to be noted that two different sources of uncertainty are involved in the measurement process: the imprecision in the sensors because of technical limitations, and the inevitable presence of faults in the sensors and associated electronics because of the physical nature of the process (malfunctions, degradation, etc.).

Our proposed approach to sensor validation is described in the rest of the paper, taking into account these conclusions from previous work in the area.

2 Implementation

The implementation of this approach has been made using fuzzy logic methods. The reasons to choose fuzzy logic as opposed to other uncertainty management paradigms are:

- Fuzzy logic mechanisms deal naturally with imprecision in the measurements. For example, the concepts of two measurements being "equal" or a measurement being "steady" are essentially fuzzy.
- It is easy to express expert rules about the confidence deserved by measurements depending in fuzzy concepts such as "being equal", "changing together", "being steady", etc. It is important to note the significance of being able to implement non-linear correspondence between behaviors of the variables and confidence values deserved. Linear mechanisms would not be able to represent adequately this correspondence (for example, a steady behavior of a sensor is evidence for normality, however a completely steady behavior is evidence of abnormality).
- There are inference engines for fuzzy logic in the market that offer runtime efficiency capable of meeting the needs of real-time applications. Moreover, hardware implementations of the same algorithms are available if needed. This fact protects the investment in the development of the method in case of more strict runtime requirements.
- Fuzzy logic systems have proven to be easy to tune in real applications. This characteristic is fundamental for systems that have to be really deployed and put in production.

In our system ([1]), a modular approach to sensor validation has been used. Instead of doing the validation as part of the work of the expert system, a separate module preprocess the incoming data, and ascertains confidence values (values in the interval [0,1]) to each measurement. The module has been implemented by means of a fuzzy logic shell that generates C code. This code is fully portable and there is subsequently no problem to integrate the module into the system.

Thus, the expert system takes as input the sensor measurements *plus* the confidence values. Any posterior reasoning may take into account these confidence values as needed. This architecture presents several advantages:

- The diagnosis problem (faults in the process) is clearly separated from the sensor validation problem (faults in the measurements). Dealing with both kinds of problems separately improves greatly the communication with process experts at knowledge acquisition meetings and allows a clearer representation of the knowledge about process diagnosis.
- These two steps may be carried out simultaneously, in parallel, obtaining a significant speed-up of the system. This is fundamental for a system that has to work in real-time.

  The proposed preprocess-reason paradigm follows closely the scheme used by human experts: they first check for the validity of the data and then use these data for subsequent reasoning.
- The maintainability of the system is enhanced.
- Other modules apart from the reasoning module may use the confidence values. For example, a simulator module may choose among several methods to calculate a desired variable taking into account the confidence values of the input variables.

On the other hand, a disadvantage of this approach is that the confidence in any measurement is calculated in terms of the measurements themselves (and possibly their history), but not taking into account any evidence from further reasoning. For example, if a conclusion is drawn that is noticeably wrong, it would seem reasonable to tag the involved data as suspicious. This possibility is not allowed in our system. However, in our experience in real cases, human experts most of the time use the forward reasoning paradigm represented in our method.

3 A fuzzy logic approach to sensor validation

As explained in the previous section there is a separate module that complements the *MIP* expert system by preprocessing the incoming data and assigning confidence values to each measurement from the sensors, taking into account all the current measurements and their history. The module considers for calculating these confidence values the *individual behavior* of each sensor and the *collective behavior* of sets of related sensors.

3.1 Individual behavior

For each sensor its history is processed, several characteristics of its behavior being analyzed (for example the values of the sensor, the differences between two consecutive values, the second order differences,...). For each of these characteristics a histogram is constructed and from the histogram a possibility distribution is defined ([4]), that is interpreted as the fuzzy definition of *normality* for each of the behavior characteristics (see Fig. 1). When subsequently analyzing the behavior of the sensor, the current values of the characteristics are calculated and the "normality" grade of each estimated using the possibility distributions. From the several "normality" estimations a final individual confidence value for the sensor is calculated by a suitable t-norm (for example the product operator). This *individual confidence value* represents the "normality" of the current behavior of the sensor.

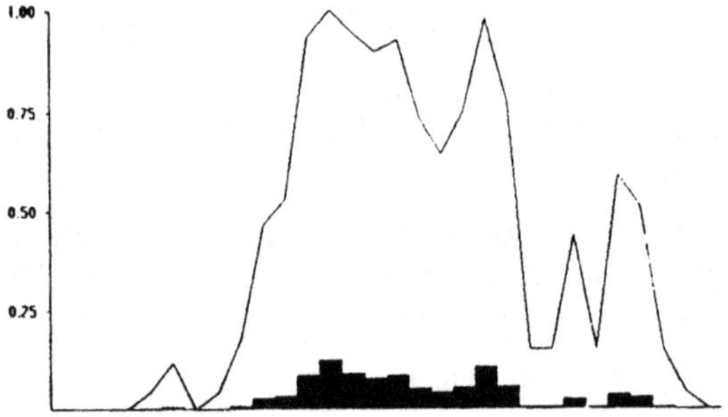

Fig. 1. Possibility distribution constructed from a histogram.

What interval of time has to be analyzed for the definition of the possibility distributions? The *MIP* system automatically generates 96 hours logs of each measurement. The possibility distributions obtained from two consecutive 96 hours logs are shown in Fig. 2. It can be seen that the distributions are very similar. If we take any 96 hours log from each month we can observe the distributions evolution for longer periods of time (Fig. 3). The final adopted solution is to take a 96 hours log to get an initial possibility distribution and then update it each 96 hours. This process can be carried out by the module in parallel with the assignation of confidence values.

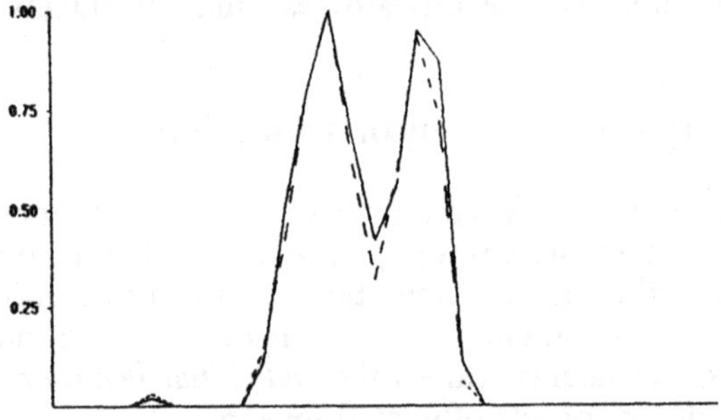

Fig. 2. Possibility distributions evolution.
Two consecutive 96 hours logs.

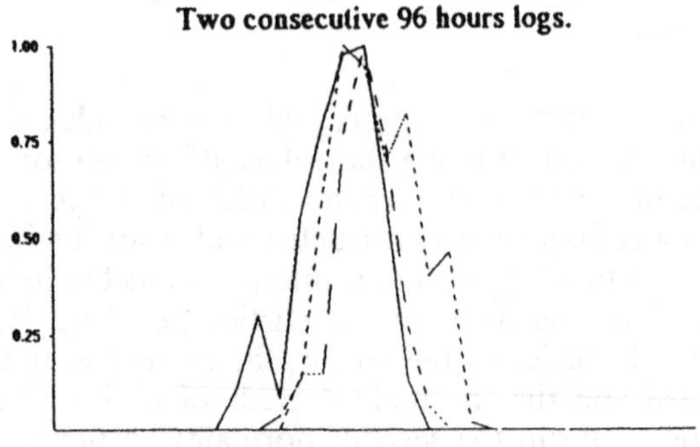

Fig. 3. Possibility distributions evolution.
— Jan 92 ---- Feb 92 ······ Mar 92

3.2 Collective behavior

Suppose we have several sensors, all of them measuring independently the same physical variable. In this case, we compare measurements in pairs, and depending on the "grade of coincidence" in their values and in the evolution of their values, ascertain pairwise confidence values to the measurements. This process may be repeated for threes, fours, etc.

On the other hand, suppose we have several sensors measuring simultaneously several physical variables numerically related to each other. Now, we analyze the evolution of the different related measurements. Depending on the "agreement" of this evolution with the relationships between the different measured variables, we ascertain a collective confidence value to each measurement.

For both cases a set of fuzzy rules is defined using "grade of coincidence" and "agreement" as fuzzy concepts to assign the *collective confidence values*. These fuzzy rules represent the expert knowledge available about the collective behavior of the sensors.

As a result of the previously described process we obtain several confidence values for each measurement, one of them individual, and several collective. The next step is to fuse this evidence into a single final confidence value. This can be done by means of the following function

$$\sqrt{w_1 a_1^2 + w_2 a_2^2 + \dots + w_n a_n^2}$$

where a_i are the confidence values obtained, and w_i are the weights of each confidence value in the final fusion ($0 < w_i < 1, w_1 + \dots + w_n = 1$). Expert criteria is used in this step, allowing the particular characteristics of each type of sensor and each actual location of the sensor to have an impact in the final confidence through the concrete knowledge of the process expert. Additionally it has been proved empirically that it is very easy to tune the impact of each confidence value.

We have chosen this function because it presents smoother changes in their values than, for example, a linear weighted average. The closer to 1 the confidence values are, the closer to 1 the final confidence value. This value is associated to the measurement, and can be used by other modules (i.e. expert system modules) for subsequent processing and reasoning.

We have selected two concrete cases to show the procedure followed in this approach. It has to be noted here that these examples can be easily generalized to any other set of sensor measurements.

4 Case studies

4.1 Case study 1: Oxygen Excess

The *MIP* expert system has three measurements for the value of oxygen excess in the output of the petrochemical plant. This is a critical variable for subsequent reasoning. Two of the measurements (A and B) come from field sensors with different sensibility and reliability factors. The third measurement (C) comes every five minutes from an automatic analysis from a mass spectrometer.

For each measurement three confidence values are obtained; one individual value and two pairwise values. The individual confidence value is obtained by comparing the current behavior of the sensor with its past behavior, as explained in the previous section.

The pairwise confidence values are obtained by comparing two sensors and deciding their "coincidence" rate. If "similar", the pairwise confidence is HIGH. If "different" the pairwise confidence is LOW. The case of "not very different" needs further processing. In this case, the recent changes in the values are used, by means of a set of fuzzy rules such as:

- If sensor A is STEADY and sensor B INCREASED-A-LOT, then pairwise confidence AB is LOW and pairwise confidence BA is MEDIUM.
- If sensor A INCREASED and sensor B DECREASED, then pairwise confidence AB is LOW and pairwise confidence BA is LOW.
- etc.

The rules are designed to cover all the cases with the knowledge of the expert about sensitiveness of each sensor, precision expected, reliability of the measurements, etc.

The final fusion of the individual and the two pairwise confidences for each sensor is made by the function shown in the previous section.

4.2 Case study 2: Ammonia Evaporator

This example shows the case of several sensors measuring physical variables numerically related. In the ammonia evaporator of the petrochemical plant considered in the *MIP* project there are three sensors (temperature, pressure and ammonia level) that are related as follows:

- If the level decreases a lot, temperature has to increase a lot and pressure has to increase (the opposite is not true).
- Changes in temperature and pressure have to occur in the same direction.
- Temperature has to change at least in the second decimal figure.
- etc.

This knowledge is encoded as fuzzy rules with linguistic concepts being represented as fuzzy sets. For example:

- If LEVEL is DECREASED-A-LOT and TEMPERATURE is INCREASED-A-LOT and PRESSURE is INCREASED, then collective confidence LEVEL is HIGH, collective confidence TEMPERATURE is HIGH, and collective confidence PRESSURE is HIGH.
- If TEMPERATURE is DECREASED and PRESSURE is DECREASED, then collective confidence TEMPERATURE is HIGH and collective confidence PRESSURE is HIGH.
- etc.

As in the former case, for each sensor an individual confidence value (by means of possibility distributions for several behavior characteristics), and a collective confidence value (using the knowledge encoded as fuzzy rules) are calculated, obtaining the final confidence value by a method similar to the one used in the previous example.

5 Results and conclusions

The method described in this paper has proven to be very effective in all the cases studied. Two characteristics that had a big impact in the success are the central role played by information redundancy and the easy tuning of the final system that allows to correct any undesirable behavior quickly and easily. The proposed approach can be applied to the case of several sensors measuring the same variable or to the case of several sensors numerically related.

The following problems have been identified during the development of the method:

- Is it necessary to filter out defective data before calculating the possibility distributions? If affirmative, how to identify automatically these defective data?.
- Would it be interesting to consider also utility values?. In other words, if some measurement is critical, how this fact will affect to the calculation of the confidence value?.

Ongoing research is addressing the solution of these problems.

The described method for sensor validation has been implemented as a pre-processing module for the *MIP* expert system. In a first stage the module was installed in the off-line version of the *MIP* system in July 91, in order to test it. The results obtained were quite satisfactory and the module is currently in field test in the plant. For this validation phase other sets of measurements have been added to the module. The results obtained in this project will be applied in the HINT project, an European ESPRIT project that will combine different Artificial Intelligence techniques in an integrated architecture with the goal of improving process control operation.

References

1. X. Alamán et al.: MIP: a real time expert system. 8th. Conference on Artificial Intelligence for Applications, CAIA-92, Monterrey, California, March 1992.

2. S.M. Alexander, C.M. Vaidya: An architecture for sensor fusion in intelligent process monitoring. Computers Ind. Eng. Vol. 16, No. 2, pp. 307-311 (1989).

3. B. Chendrasekaran, W.F. Punch: Data validation during diagnosis, a step beyond traditional sensor validation. AAAI 1987, pp. 778-782.

4. D. Dubois, H. Prade: Fuzzy sets, probability and measurement. European Journal of Operational Research Vol. 40, 135-154 (1989).

5. M.S. Fox et al.: Techniques for sensor-based diagnosis. IICAI 83, pp. 158-163.

6. D. Leinweber, K. Gidwani: Real-time expert system development techniques and applications. Western Conference on K.B. Engineering and E.S., pp. 69-77, (1986).

7. D.A. Rowan: On-line expert systems in process industries. AI EXPERT, Miller Ferman Publications, August 1989.

5. Neural Networks

Application of Neuro-Fuzzy Networks to the Identification and Control of Nonlinear Dynamical Systems

Pierre Yves Glorennec[1], Claude Barret[2] and Michèle Brunet[2]

[1] Département d'Informatique, INSA, 35043 RENNES CEDEX, France
E-mail : glorenne@irisa.fr
[2] Laboratoire de Robotique, IUT d'EVRY, 91025 EVRY CEDEX, France

Abstract. A Neuro-Fuzzy Network (NFN) is proposed, combining the merits of Artificial Neural Networks and Fuzzy Logic Systems. Most specifically, prior knowledge can be embedded in the synaptic weights of the NFN, speeding up the convergence.This NFN can be used for rule extraction or for identification and control of nonlinear dynamical systems.

1 Introduction

The abilities of Neural Networks to approximate sufficiently accurately large classes of nonlinear functions are now well-known [1]. The high nonlinearities in a net allow it to capture important features : with inputs split into previous historical data and previous net inputs, a Neural Network can be thought of as a generalized nonlinear ARMA model. Moreover, no assumptions are made about plant structure, so Neural Networks are prime candidates for use in dynamic models for the representation of nonlinear plants.

Unfortunately, prior knowledge cannot be embedded into network parameters. Therefore, the learning procedure begins from a random point in the parameter space. This leads to bad convergence properties and possible local minima.

On the other hand, if we have prior information concerning the input-output behaviour of the plant, we can convert the control knowledge of an operator into an automatic control strategy. Fuzzy modelling and fuzzy control appear very useful when the responses to change in manipulated variables are nonlinear and/or very sensitive or when there is a lack of well-posed mathematical model. However, fuzzy approach has weak points : lack of efficient systematic methods for extracting rules and for optimizing membership functions.

In order to reduce the respective drawbacks of Neural Networks and Fuzzy Logic, Neuro-Fuzzy Networks have been suggested to merge fruitfully the advantages of those two approaches, e.g. [5], [6], [13], [2].

2 The Proposed Neuro-Fuzzy Network

2.1 Motivations

We consider a Fuzzy Logic System performing a mapping from an input space $U \subset \mathbb{R}^n$, to $\mathbb{R}^p$. Therefore, such a Fuzzy Logic System can be thought of as a multilayered feed-forward neural network, with a different semantic for each layer :

1. An input layer (n inputs), feeding input patterns into the next layer of the network,
2. A first hidden layer, in which the neurons compute the membership value, μ of the inputs with respect to the fuzzy subsets defined on the respective universes of discourse. With m membership functions for each variable, we have $n.m$ neurons in this layer.
3. A second hidden layer, in which the neurons compute the truth values, *And*, of the rules : there are m^n neurons in this layer.
4. An output layer for the inference, I (p outputs).

The following figure shows the NFN structure for a two inputs-one output system, with two membership functions.

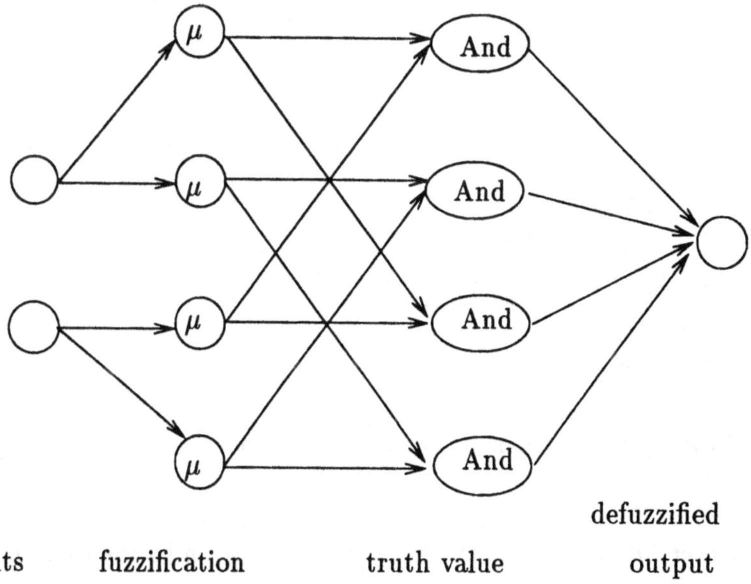

Fig. 1. Neural-like Structure of a Fuzzy System

This neuron-like structure puts a new light on Fuzzy Logic System and, thus, supervised learning methods are developped for rule extraction, see [5], [6], [13], [2], [10], [9].

But, this similarity between Fuzzy Logic Systems and Neural Networks can be taken even further, by expressing the membership functions and the logical operators of conjunction, disjunction and implication in a neural manner (with the usual definition of an artificial neuron : a processing unit which fires a function of the weighted sum of its inputs).

This leads to the possibility of implementation of Fuzzy Logic Systems on actual neural VLSI chip [3]. Our choices are the following :

a- Membership Functions. A smoothed form of the usual triangular functions can be given in a neural manner by one gaussian function or two sigmoidal functions [2].

b- AND Operator. Lukasiewicz's AND,

$$And(x, y) = Max(0, x + y - 1)$$

for x and $y \in [0, 1]$, is suitable for a neural implementation, with the activation function :

$$u \rightarrow Max(0, u), u \in [-1, 1]$$

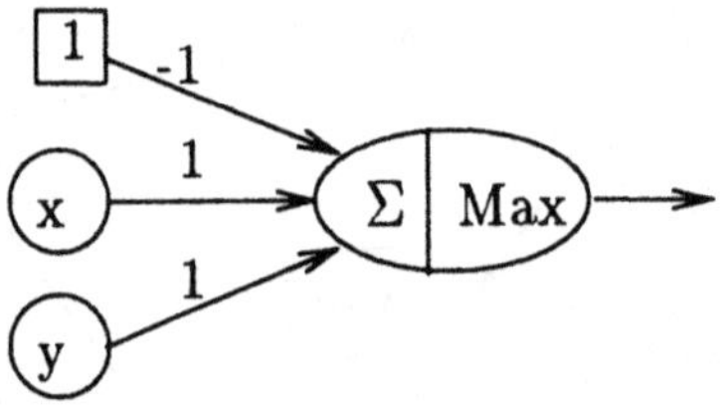

Fig. 2. Neural Implementation of Lukasiewicz's T-norm

Moreover, we can replace the Lukasiewicz's T-norm by the smoothed quasi T-norm :

$$And_b(x, y) = \frac{1}{1 + exp(-\frac{x+y-1.5}{b})} \tag{1}$$

with b chosen for minimizing $\mid And_b(x, y) - Max(0, x + y - 1) \mid$, x and $y \in [0, 1]$.

c- Inference Method. We choose Sugeno 's inference method, with crisp values in the consequent part of the rules. In this way, defuzzification is not necessary and the FLC output is given as follows :

$$z = \frac{\sum_i c_i \alpha_i}{\sum_j \alpha_j} \tag{2}$$

where α_i is the truth value of the rule i :

$$(R_i) : \textbf{if "premise part" then } z \textbf{ is } c_i$$

The c_i coefficients can be thougth of as the weights between the output layer and the previous one.

By these choices, the Fuzzy Logic System is a real Neural Network with sparse connectivity, and we call it a Neuro Fuzzy Network (NFN).

A learning algorithm, derived from BackPropagation, allows quick supervised learning, for both tuning the shape of membership functions and extracting fuzzy rules [2].

2.2 Initialization

We use, without loss of generality, the following multiple inputs-single output (MISO) system : two inputs with m fuzzy subsets for each input. Therefore, the system is driven by a set of m^2 fuzzy rules :

$$R_i : \textbf{if } x \text{ is } A_i \textbf{ and } y \text{ is } B_i \textbf{ then } z \text{ is } c_i \tag{3}$$

A_i and B_i are fuzzy subsets, c_i a crisp value.

With the proposed NFN structure, the synaptic weights are

1. the parameters of membership functions,
2. the c_i coefficients in the consequent part of the rules, for $1 \leq i \leq m^2$.

For initialization, we choose a set of membership functions with the following property :

Let $(x_i, y_i)_{i \in [1,m^2]}$ the points at which $\mu_{A_i}(x_i)$ and $\mu_{B_i}(y_i)$ achieve their maximum value, ($\mu_{A_i}(x_i) = \mu_{B_i}(y_i) = 1$ with gaussian membership functions). If we have :

$$\alpha_i(x_i, y_i) = And(\mu_{A_i}(x_i), \mu_{B_i}(y_i)) = 1 \tag{4}$$

$$\alpha_j(x_i, y_i) = And(\mu_{A_j}(x_i), \mu_{B_j}(y_i)) = \text{"very small"}, \text{ for } j \neq i \tag{5}$$

then, from (2), we see that :

$$z(x_i, y_i) = \frac{c_i + \sum_{j \neq i} c_j \alpha_j}{1 + \sum_{j \neq i} \alpha_j} \approx c_i \tag{6}$$

These points $(x_i, y_i)_{i \in [1,m^2]}$ form a lattice in the input space and we need only know the desired response for these points. In consequence :

1. if the rules are known, all the synaptic weights are approximatively known and, at this stage, the NFN performs a rough interpolation of the given input-output relationship. Better approximation properties will be given by the learning algorithm.
2. otherwise, the NFN performs 1) a fast rule extraction from a learning set to obtain the c_i parameters, with the given membership functions, and 2) a fine tuning of membership function parameters.

In both cases, learning starts from a point in the parameter space presumably near to the optimum.

3 Application for Identification of an Unknown Nonlinear Dynamical System

In this section, we present simulation results of non linear plant identification and control, using NFN.

3.1 Example 1

The first example is a system dealt with by Narendra and Parthasarathy [12] using a multilayered neural network. This system is defined by the following equation (model IV in [12]) :

$$y(t+1) = f[y(t), y(t-1), y(t-2), u(t), u(t-1)] \tag{7}$$

where $y(t)$ is the model output at time t, $u(t)$ is the control input and f is defined by :

$$f(a,b,c,d,e) = \frac{abce(c-1)+d}{1+b^2+c^2} \tag{8}$$

We use the series-parallel identification architecture :

1. for the model, in input : $u(t)$, $u(t-1)$, $y(t)$, $y(t-1)$, $y(t-2)$ and in output : $y(t+1)$
2. for the NFN, in input : $u(t)$, $u(t-1)$, $y(t)$, $y(t-1)$, and in output : $y_{NFN}(t+1)$

With 3 fuzzy subsets by input, we have to identify 81 fuzzy rules (105 parameters vs. 341 in [12]).

The identification procedure was carried out using a random input signal uniformly distributed in [-1, 1]. The backpropagation is used in two steps : firstly only the weights in the last layer (acting as the consequent part of fuzzy rules) are optimized ; and secondly all the weights in the whole network are adjusted. Ten presentations of 200 learning patterns, with weight adaptation after each pattern, are sufficient to obtain a residual identification error of 0.01 (with regard to the same problem in [12], the number of training iterations is reduced by close to a factor of 50). The NFN is now able to reproduce the behaviour of the plant for any kind of input signal in the range [-1,+1].

For study of performance, the control input to the model and the identified NFN was :

$$u(t) = (12 + 3t - 5.5t_2 + 7.2t_3)(1 + cos4\pi t)(1 + 0.8sin3\pi t)/25 - 0.6 \quad (9)$$

and the NFN inputs :

$$u(t), u(t-1), y_{NFN}(t), y_{NFN}(t-1) \quad (10)$$

The following figure shows the results of identification.

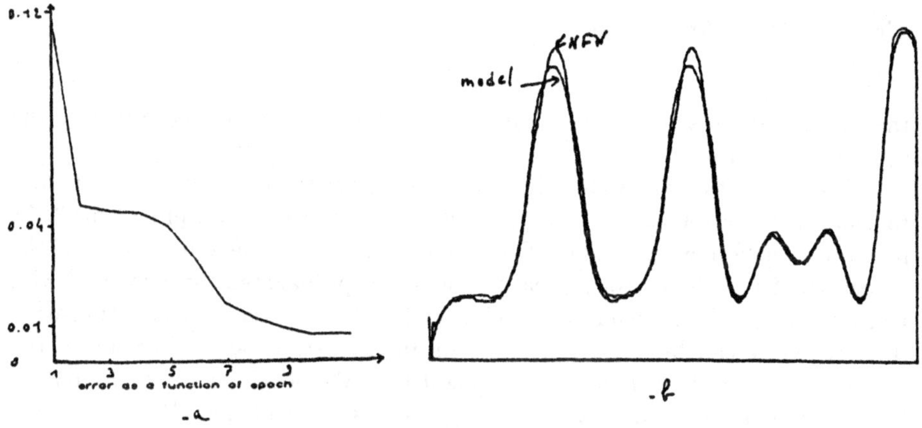

Fig. 3. a) Learning Error b) Actual and Identified Response

3.2 Example 2

This example deals with a DC motor described by the equation :

$$y(t+1) = y(t) + [u(t) - k_f sign(y(t))]\frac{\Delta t}{J} \quad (11)$$

In this equation, y is the motor speed, u the input torque, Δt the sampling period and J the moment of inertia. The non linear term, $k_f sign(y(t))$, represents a friction torque.

We use the adaptive control scheme represented in Fig. 4. This structure is derived from the one proposed by [7] or [11] with ordinary multilayered neural networks. Here we use two neuro-fuzzy networks : the Neuro Fuzzy Model (NFM) and the Neuro Fuzzy Controller (NFC). The role of the NFM is to reproduce

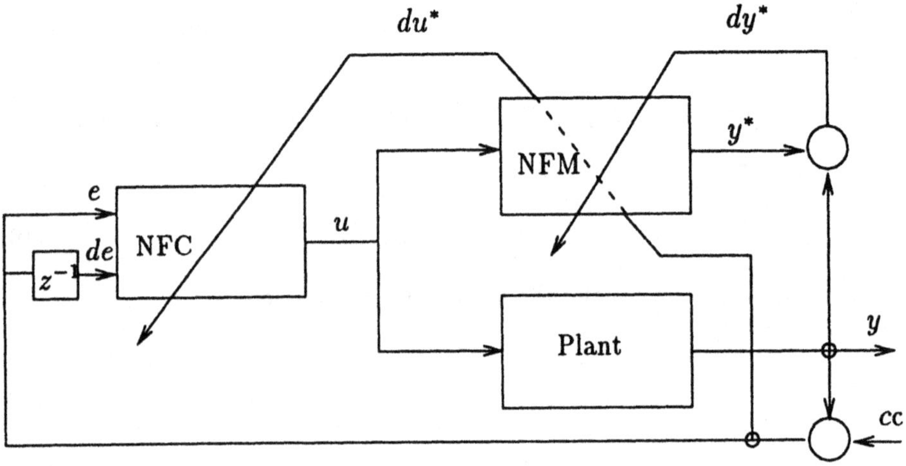

Fig. 4. Controller Architecture

the dynamical behaviour of the plant, and the role of the NFC is to furnish the right control command.

This architecture allows to solve a well known problem in neural control : how to evaluate the error du on the input u of the plant at each sampling time ? We proceed in the following manner. The difference e between the reference c and the actual speed y of the motor is measured and backpropagated through the NFM. During this step, the synaptic weights of NFM are locked. Backpropagation through NFM can be considered as a means to extract an estimation of the inverse of the Jacobian matrix of the plant [11]. We obtain the error du on the command, which is used to adjust the synaptic weights of the NFC.

By interleaving sequences of identification (backpropagation of dy^*) and control (backpropagation of du^*), true adaptive control can be obtained. As reported by [7], the control performance with this "distal teacher" system is right even if the accuracy of the model is not excellent.

a- Model Identification. To obtain the model, we use the same architecture as in Fig. 4. with the NFC replaced with a conventional PD controller, which only furnishes "reasonable" u values. The learning set is constituted of 200 tupples $y(k), u(k), y(k+1)$ from a periodic square wave input c. We use 5 fixed gaussian membership functions per input, leading to 25 fuzzy rules. After 25 presentations of the learning set, the average error is less than 4.510^{-4}, and the learning process is stopped. Fig. 5 shows the comparison between the system and model outputs, both being driven by the same PD controller submitted to a square wave input.

b- Controller Identification. Now the PD controller is replaced by the NFC with inputs $e(k) = c(k) - y(k)$ and $de(k) = e(k) - e(k-1)$. We take 5 membership gaussian functions per input, leading to 25 rules, but the weights in the

348

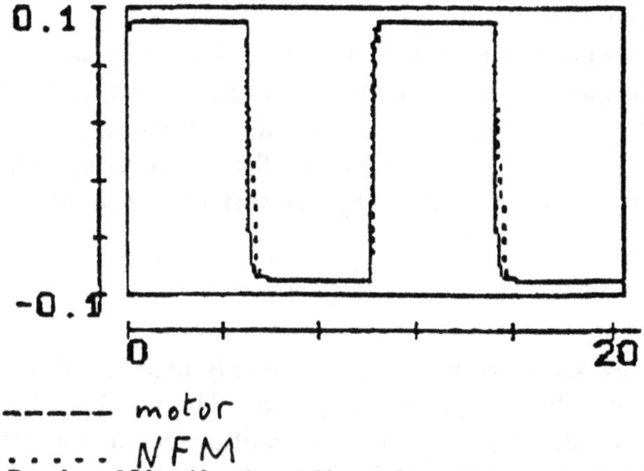

Fig. 5. Results of Identification : Closed Loop Behaviour of Motor and NFM

consequent part of these rules are initialized at zero. Tuning this weights is entirely performed in line, from $t = 0$. Results are given in Fig. 6. During the first transition, the plant output exhibits an overshoot of about ten percent, but this overshoot vanishes very quickly and a very satisfying output is obtained after a few periods.

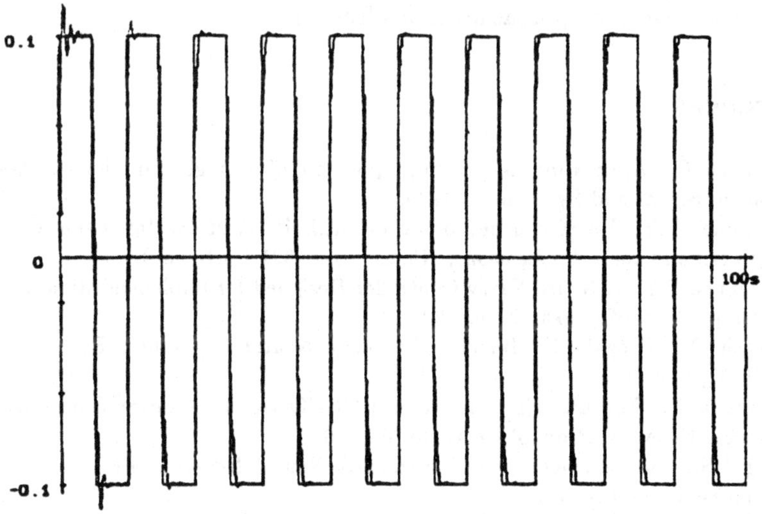

Fig. 6. Control of the Motor.

It is interesting to compare this result with those obtained by an ordinary neural network. In that case, the network is initialized with randomly distributed synaptic weights. So it is impossible to use the neural network directly in line.

This neural network has to be pre-tuned off line in order to avoid unacceptable commands to the system.

Conversely, it is quite possible to include more prior knowledge in the weights of the NFC, in order to speed up the training. For instance, the synaptic weights in the second hidden layer of the NFC can be initialized at values corresponding to the usual working of a PD (or a PI)-like controller. Work along this line as well as on the stability and robustness of NFC are currently in progress.

4 Conclusion

The neuro-fuzzy network structure has been successfully used for identification and control of highly non linear dynamical systems. The number of learning steps is greatly reduced with respect to classical multilayered neural networks. This opens the possibility to develop fast adaptive controllers with NFN. We are now working on improvements to NFN : rule extraction and simplification, constraints for membership functions and applications in control problems.

From a Neural point of view, fuzzy rules can initialize neural network weights and improve the convergence rate. Conversely, after learning, neural knowledge can be translated into fuzzy rules.

From a Fuzzy point of view, if we have a learning set, BackPropagation-like algorithm can be used for identification of both antecedent and consequent parts of fuzzy rules.

Merging these two approaches seems fruitful.

References

1. Cybenko G.: Approximation by Superposition of a single function. J. Math. of Control, Signal and Systems, **2**, 1989.
2. Glorennec P.Y.: Un réseau neuro-flou évolutif. Proc. of 4th Int. Conf. on Neural Networks and their Applications, Nîmes, nov. 1991 (in french).
3. Glorennec P.Y.: A Neuro-Fuzzy Controller Designed for Implementation on a Neural Chip. Proc. of Iizuka'92, july 92.
4. Hayashi Y., Czogala E., Buckley J.: Fuzzy Neural Controller. Proc. of FUZZ-IEEE'92, San Diego.
5. Horikawa S-I., Furuhashi T., Okuma S., UCHIKAWA Y.: A Fuzzy Controller Using a Neural Network. Proc. of Iizuka'90, july 90.
6. Jang J-S.: Rule extraction by Generalized Neural Network. Proc. of 4th IFSA Congress, Brussel, july 1991.
7. Jordan M.I., Rumelhart D.E.: Forward Models : Supervised Learning with a Distal Teacher. MIT Center occasional paper 40.
8. Keller J., Yager R., Tahani H.: Neural Network Implementation of Fuzzy Logic. Fuzzy Sets and Systems **45**, no 1, jan. 92
9. Kosko B.: Neural Networks and Fuzzy Logic. Prentice-Hall International Editions, IBSN:0-13-612334-1
10. Lin C-T., Lee C.C.: Neural-Network-Based Fuzzy Logic Control and Decision System. IEEE Trans. on Computers, **20** no. 12, dec. 1991.

11. Martinez J.M., Houkari M., Parey C., Barret C.: La rétropropagation sous l'angle de la théorie du contrôle. Proc. of 4th Int. Conf. on Neural Networks and their Applications, Nîmes, nov. 1991
12. Narendra K., Parthasarathy K.: Identification and Control of Dynamical Systems using Neural Networks. IEEE trans. on Neural Networks, **1** no. 1, march 90.
13. Nomura H., HAYASHI I., WAKAMI N.: A Self-tuning Method of Fuzzy Control by Descent Method. Proc. of 4th IFSA Congress, Brussel, july 1991.
14. Sontag E., Sussmann H.: BackPropagation can give rise to spurious local minima. Complex Systems **3** (1989), 91-106.

Comparison Between Artificial Neural Networks and Classical Statistical Methods in Pattern Recognition.

Hervás Martínez, C.; Romero Soto, E.J.; García Pedrajas, N.; Medina Carnicer, R.

**Unidad de Informática. Dept. Matemática Aplicada.
Universidad de Córdoba.
Avda. Menéndez Pidal s/n. 14071 - Córdoba. (España).**

Abstract. The main difficulty of any pattern recognition system is the great amount of fuzzy and incomplete information it has to deal with. Moreover, the classification problem does not allow an exact solution, so statistical and artificial neural network techniques must be used in order to obtain results that offer an optimum degree of reliability. This paper analyses the methodology used to compare some of these techniques. Our data are related to educational and biological environments.

1 Introduction

Given these features, there are two techniques that are widely used: statistical methods and artificial neural networks. Both are able to treat information of the kind described below. Now, we present the basis of these two methodologies:

1.1 Statistical Methods

This methodology uses the randomizing properties of the information. It is founded on finding decision functions that allow patterns to be classified. A minimization of the misclassification error probability is sought, applying Bayes Theorem.

The use of a specific type of decision function depends on the features of the data. The most important of these features is the probability distribution of the variables that characterize our environment.

Once the type of decision function has been selected, the next step is to obtain its coefficients. Training (or learning) algorithms are used to carry out this task.

The learning process is divided into two different classes (depending on the a-priori knowledge of the patterns): supervised and unsupervised learning. Supervised learning can be used when there is a set of patterns (the 'training pattern') of known classification. Otherwise, when the classification of any pattern, even the number of classes, is unknown, we must apply unsupervised pattern recognition. The latter is more complex because a-priori knowledge is poor, but it is more general.

We use Factor Analysis to study the intercorrelations of a large number of variables by clustering them into common factors such that variables within each factor are highly correlated, to interpret each factor according to the variables with high loadings belonging to it, and to summarize many variables by a few factor or summary scores. The assumption is that the number of factors will be appreciably less than the original number of variables ([AFI79], [VRC90], [OJA92]).

The learning algorithm we have used is the k-means algorithm and its variations, to make partitions of a set of cases into clusters. At the end of the run, each case belongs to the cluster whose center is closest in Euclidean distance to the case. It begins with user-specified clusters or with all the data in one cluster and repeatedly splits a cluster into two until it reaches the requested number of clusters. The cases are iteratively reallocated into the cluster whose center is closest to the case.

Finally, we need to perform a discriminant analysis between two or more groups; that is, to find the combinations of variables that best predicts the category or group to which a case belongs. We choose Stepwise Discriminant Analysis to obtain the combination of predictor variables: 'classification function' which can then be used to classify new cases whose group membership is unknown. We evaluate the number of cases correctly classified into each group, performing a jackknifed-validation procedure to reduce the bias in this evaluation, and when classifying cases which were not used in the computations, we obtain a test for our learning and results to compare the applicability of statistical treatment with neuronal networks in classification activities.

Our statistical analysis must consider the characteristics of the information we are managing in order to obtain a good result. So we have to correct previous errors in data, extract incomplete information from our model, compare results with expected ones to analyse differences and improve the method. This requires feedback changes to the system and to repeatedly begin with new calculations.

1.2 Artificial Neural Networks

Artificial neural networks are constructed imitating the human nervous system. They consist of a complex interconnection of simple units, called neurons. The artificial neural network handles information in such a way that when it receives an input it produces the desired output.

Each neuron behaves as an independent point of processing with very simple functioning. It carries out the weighted addition of the received signals from other neurons connected to it. If this sum is above a certain threshold the neuron activates its output that is connected to another set of neurons. These sets of neurons are set out in different layers.

A neural network must be trained by a 'learning algorithm'. This is the way in which the neural network learns.

Neural networks are applied to those activities in which the human brain works efficiently and this is the reason why they are applied to pattern recognition.

The neuronal network design is carried out using a series of steps: preprocessing and optimal input representation, choosing of the activation function, neuronal network structure and learning algorithms.

2 Preprocessing and optimal input representation.

In theory, a multilayered network should be able to produce the desired outputs from any input representation that encodes the relevant information. In practice, careful preprocessing of the inputs is usually required to obtain an efficient network.

To remove the unsignificant characteristics of learning patterns, we have carried out a Factor Analysis. Then a K-means analysis of the resulting factors is carried out.

Now, we may begin training our neural network based on the clusters obtained in the preceding analysis. The results using the original variables for training are worse than those using factors, moreover, the factors generalization capacity is more suitable for other pupil classifications. Definitively we use factors as input to the network and our learning patterns must be previously randomized.

In general, all inputs should be scaled to a common interval (usually 0 to 1, -1 to 1, or -0.5 to 0.5). In our case the training time increases very much.

In fact, there are different methods for processing input data, which depend on the type of problem. So, in the images and sounds treatment we need logarithmic and Fourier transformations ([WAI89], [ROS89]).

3 Choosing the activation.

The most commonly used activation function with backpropagation is the logistic or sigmoid function.

Stornetta and Huberman [STO87] described a simple method for improving the training characteristics of backpropagation networks. They said that the conventional output 0 to 1 is not optimum. Because the magnitude of a weight adjustment is proportional to the output level of the neuron from which it originates, a level of 0 results in no weight modification. The solution is to subtract 1/2 from the logistic function, thereby shifting the output range to the open interval -1/2 to +1/2.

$$OUT = -\frac{1}{2} + \frac{1}{1 + e^{-G * NET}}$$

In this way, Stornetta and Huberman reduced training times by 30 - 50 percent. Also, one must not neglect to change the output function derivatives from $x(1-x)$ to $1/4-x^2$.

When the outputs tend to be at the extremes of the sigmoid function, the derivate is near 0, so only a very small weight change may occur. Fahlman [FAH88] achieved an improvement in training time simply by adding 0.1 to the sigmoid derivative to prevent it from becoming 0.

$$OUT = 1/4 - x^2 + 0.1$$

We have used both functions. The standard function is better than the Stornetta and Huberman function with no scaled data, but with scaled data we have obtained the opposite result.

4 Neuronal network structure.

When using a backpropagation network, one of the most important configuration issues is to select the optimal number of hidden layer. Hecht-Nilsen [HEC87] proved that a network with one hidden layer can compute any arbitrary function of its inputs. This result is of dubious utility, because the neurons have different activation functions and do not give a constructive method for obtaining them.

Cybenko [CYB88] shows that one hidden layer, with homogeneous sigmoidal activation functions, is sufficient to compute arbitrary decision boundaries for the outputs, and that two hidden layers are sufficient to compute an arbitrary output function of the inputs. Since simple sigmoidal output functions are used, these results are much more useful. Lippmann [LIP87] has provided a very intuitive geometric argument which considers that two hidden layers are better than one to compute arbitrary decision boundaries.

Empirical tests using the backpropagation network for diagnosis have not demonstrated a significant advantage for two hidden layers over one in a relatively small and simple diagnostic network (Bounds and Lloyd, [BOU88]). The best advice based on current knowledge is probably this: for a classification (decision boundary) problem, where the output node with the greatest activation will determine the category of the input pattern, one hidden layer will be sufficient; and if the output needs to be continous functions of the inputs, you should use two hidden layers or different transfer functions, such as the radial basis function. Even for continuous outputs, a single hidden layer may be sufficient, depending on the nature of the problem. In linearly separable cases, no hidden layers may be required.

Another problem is the selection of the number of layer neurons. The input layer will have the same number of neurons as factors. The output layer will be coincident with number of clusters in the model. Choosing the right number of hidden nodes is the most interesting and complicated aspect of network configuring. There are different theories such as:

- 2N + 1 hidden nodes (Hecht-Nielsen) where N is the number of inputs.
- Lippmann said that the maximum number of hidden nodes is OP*(N+1), where OP is the number of output nodes and N is the number of input nodes.
- Kudrycki [KUD88] said that the maximum number is OP*3.
- Geometric mean of the number of inputs and outputs.

The best method is the empirical test. By using this method we have built a network with hidden nodes.

5 Learning algorithms.

The best working choice with networks for most pattern recognition, signal processing, and similar applications is a multilayered feedforward network with backpropagation ([WER74], [RUM86], [WAS90]).

Limitations of the backpropagation network include extensive training time for large networks (Waibel, [WAI89]), the network paralysis, and the local minimum. The basic backpropagation algorithm has been modified in a myriad of different ways, each attempting to circumvent one or more ot these limitations.

Wasserman proposed a method that combines the statistical methods of the Cauchy machine with the backpropagation to produce a system that finds global minima but tends to be slow to compute it.

In our analysis, we are using the momentum method, and the Sejnowski and Rosenberg [SEJ87] method.

6 Objectives

Our main objective is to compare the results obtained by these two methods when they face the same problem, in both supervised and unsupervised pattern recognition.

In order to carry out this study we will solve two different problems of classification. The first one implies a training set of very fuzzy data. It represents the worst situation we would have to face in any problem of pattern recognition. So the results obtained allow us to compare both classifiers when they are obliged to work in the toughest environment.

The second problem is somewhat simpler. We know the number of classes presented in the data and the classification of all the patterns. It is an excellent situation in order to evaluate neural networks and statistical methods in supervised learning.

We set out the characteristics of these two problems in Fig. 1.

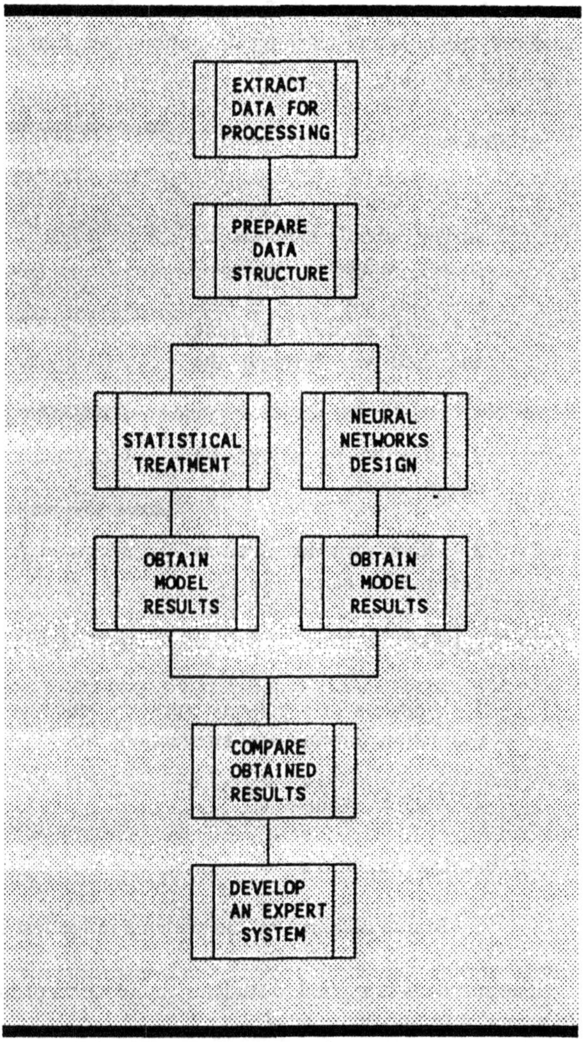

Fig. 1 *General Model Structure.*

7 Evaluation of an Educational System

We need to analyse the different aspects that influence an educational environment: students, teachers and teaching institutions (see Fig. 2). Each one of these elements is classified according to the following aspects:

a) Students:

1.- Answers to a personal survey about methods of study, subjects, teachers, etc. This survey is carried out both at the beginning and half-way through the year.

2.- Results of a test on subject level.

3.- Other variables, such as age, marks, etc.

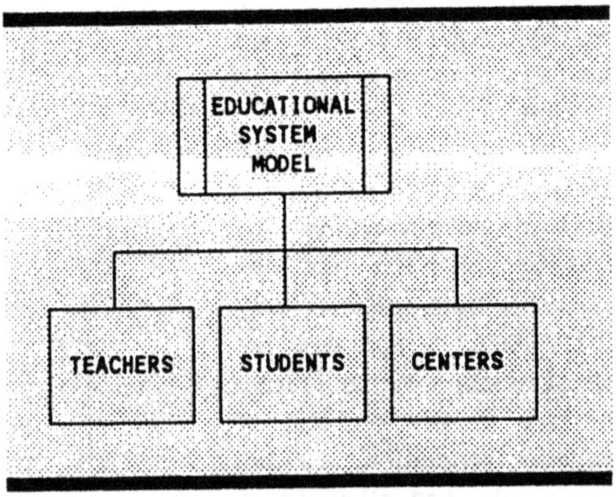

Fig. 2 *Model Elements*

b) Teachers:

1.- Answers to a personal survey about teaching methodologies, methods of evaluation, professional satisfaction, etc.

2.- Student evaluation.

c) Teaching institutions:

1.- Marks obtained by the students in the last few years.

The survey was applied to students and teachers of high schools. We have now begun to extend it to university level.

The information, very heterogeneous and fuzzy, ensures the comparison of both methodologies in working conditions of great difficulties.

Our analysis will treat two different environments of educational activity. The first one is the University educational model, and the second one is about teaching methodology in schools. It is not centered on only one geographic zone, but it studies models from several centers in many populations located far away from each other.

8 Cell Classification

It presents the results obtained from a form recognition process on cellular cycle phases. The system used consists of a citophotometer with a mobile platform, which may be remotely controlled, a computer with a real colour image analysis system, and a video camera incorporated into the citophotometer which allows the search of a random sample of the cells present in a preparation. Thereafter a classification is carried out, through the 'intelligent' extraction of the characteristics of the images obtained, when possible, and through citophotometric data, obtained by the system itself, when there is no possibility of discriminating by form or texture (differentiation of the interphase subphases).

This second problem presents different characteristics. We classify digitized images of cells into two groups, interphase and mitosis. Each cell is defined in two ways: by 64 Fourier descriptors and 7 statistical invariant moments.

We know the class to which each cell belongs; so we can apply supervised learning.

9 Pattern Recognition Process

The statistical treatment of the data is carried out using a series of steps. The most important ones are:

1.- Prior multivariate analysis of the data.

2.- Principal components analysis to reduce the amount of data with the minimum loss of information.

3.- Cluster analysis, using k-means algorithm.

4.- Obtaining and evaluating decision functions.

In order to carry out this process we have used statistical packages, BMDP and SAS, and we have developed a C library of functions that covers all of the steps described. The analysis via neural networks presents the following important aspects:

1.- Prior treatment of the data to randomize the sample.

2.- Supervised training of the neural network with retropropagation. We adjust the number of hidden layers, the number of neurons, the learning ratio, etc.

This process has been carried out using neuronal network packages for training and testing our networks. First we used BrainMaker [BRA90] in our analysis, but it is a closed package and it had many limitations for testing some properties of the neuronal networks. Later on we tried to design our own neuronal network for a microcomputer environment, but it needed a great amount of training time etc. Finally, we are working with Rochester [NIG90], designed for a minicomputer with optimal and faster results. It may be completely configured for our working environment, network structures, activation functions and it uses dynamic data structures: units, sites and links, for managing the training process and network architecture.

10 Conclusions

The process described seeks to compare the usefulness of both methodologies, and obtains information of the applicability of each according to the features of the pattern that we have to classify. We have obtained results about this methodology applied to educational systems (90-91 and 91-92 course data) and now we are working with 92-93 course data. Similar results are obtained using biological information.

Acknowledgements

This work has been financed by the national project of I + D TIC90-0648 CICYT (SPAIN).

References

[AFI79] Afifi, A. A., and Azen, S. P.. Statistical Analysis: A computer oriented approach. 2nd ed. New York: Academic Press. (1979).

[BOU88] ounds, D.J., and Lloyd, P.J. Proc. Second IEEE Int'l. Conf. Neural Networks. San Diego, C.A. (1988).

[BRA90] BrainMaker. Neural Network Simulator. California Scientific Software. (1990).

[CYB88] Cybenko, G. Continuous valued neural networks with two hidden layers are sufficient, preprint, Computer Science Dept., Tufts University. (1988).

[DIX83] Dixon W. J. BMDP Statistical Software. (1983).

[FAH88] Fahlman, S.E. An empirical Study of Learning Speed in Backpropagation Networks. Carnegie Mellon Technical Report. (1988).

[HEC87] Hecht-Nielsen, R. Proc. First IEEE Int'l. Joint Conf. Neural Networks. San Diego C.A. (1987).

[KUD88] Kudrycki, T.P. Neuronal Network Implementation of a Medical Diagnosis Expert System, Masters's Thesis, College of Engineering, University of Cincinnati. (1988).

[LEU90] Leung, M. Engeler, W.E., and Frank, P. Proc. Third Int'l. Joint Conf. Neuronal Networks. San Diego, CA. (1990).

[LIP87] Lippmann , R. P. IEEE ASSP Magazine. (1987).

[NIG90] Nigel H. Goddard. Kenton J. Lynne, Toby Mintz, Liudvikas Bukys. Rochester Connectionist Simulator. The University of Rochester. Computer Science Department. Rochester, New York. (1990).

[OJA92] Oja, E. Principal Components, Minor Components and Linear Neural Networks. Neural Networks. Vol. 5 pp. 927 - 935. (1992).

[ROS89] Rossen, M.L., and Anderson, J.A. Proc. First Int'l. Representational issues in a neural network model of syllable recognition. Joint Conf. Neuronal Networks. Washington D.C. June, 18-22, I-19-I26. (1989).

[RUM86] Rumelhart, D.E., Hinton, G. E., and Williams, R.J. Parallel Distributed Processing: Explorations in the microstructure of Cognition: Volume 1. Foundations, MIT, Cambridge, M.A. (1986).

[SAS87] SAS. Reference Manual. (1987).

[SEJ87] Sejnowsky, T. J. and Rosenberg C. R., Parallel networks that learn to pronounce English text. Complex Systems. Vol. 1 n° 1,145-168. (1987).

[STO87] Stornetta, W. S., and Huberman, B. A. An improved three layer, back-propagation algorithm. Proceedings of the IEEE First International Conference on Neuronal Networks, edt. M. Caudill and C. Butler. San Diego, C.A.: SOS Printing. (1987).

[VRC90] Vrckovnik, G. Chung, T., and Carter, C.R. Proc. Int'l. Joint Conf. Neural Networks, San Diego, C.A. (1990).

[WAI89] Waibel, A. , Sawai, H. Shikano, K. IEEE Trans. Acoustics, Speech, and Signal Processing. (1989).

[WAS90] Wasserman P.D. J. Neural Computing. Van Nostrand Reinhold. New York. (1990).

[WER74] Werbos, P. Beyond Regression: new tools for prediction and analysis in behavioral sciences, Ph.D. Thesis in applied mathematics, Harvard Univ. (1974).

Learning Methods for Odor Recognition Modeling

Amghar S. Paugam-Moisy H. Royet J.P.

URA CNRS 934
43 Bd du 11 Novembre 1918
69622 Villeurbanne

URA CNRS 1398
LIP ENS-Lyon
46 allée d'Italie
69364 Lyon Cedex

URA CNRS 180
43 Bd du 11 Novembre 1918
69622 Villeurbanne cedex

Abstract. This paper presents a phenomenon modeling of human odor perception. For a recognition test by discrimination, odors are presented in couples. Pair odors are separated by an arbitrary defined time interval. Individuals have to recognize if the odor which is presented the second time is the same as, or different to the odor which was smelt the first time. Recognition does not imply identification but only remains validated by success or check terms. For each tested odor, an evocation list is established by various individuals, hence a feature profil for each odor is available. From these data, the aim is to design a prediction model which determines the score for an individual uniquely from his odor evocation pattern. For modeling this phenomenon, we have applied learning methods especially neural networks. A process named "spy" was used to find the best architecture and the best parameters of a given neural network. This tool observes a net of neural networks, which all work in parallel, from the same sets of patterns, but which differ from one another in some of their parameters. In this communication, we also present a comparative study between neural network performances and those given by discriminant analysis which was applied to this odor memorizing problem.

1 Introduction

Connectionism is nowadays a promising and tempting approach, both by the increasing number of researchers and by the pluridisciplinary of its investigation fields. Based on the modelling of neurobiologic systems, neural networks have specific characteristics, especially those of learning and adaptation. Connectionist methods are known to be efficient in dealing with types of problems for which classical methods are far less adapted. In this paper, we present the application of this new approach in order to model the phenomena linked to olfactory memory in man.

The experimental procedure consists in presenting odors by couples. A fixed time interval of thirty seconds separates two presentations of odors of a same pair. Individuals must recognize if the odor which is presented the second time is the same as, or different to the odor which was smelt the first time. Therefore, the experimental procedure concerns a recognition memory test by discrimination without identification. This recognition is only validated by success or check terms. For each tested odor, pertinent evocations are selected from a list by several individuals, hence, a feature profil of an odor is available. We presume that an average profil of evocations, observed with approximately fifty individuals, leads to discrimination. Based on this hypothesis, it seems possible to predict recognition scores of individuals who have not been tested and whose we know the evocation pattern for a given odor. Practically, this application concerns a problem of Pattern Recognition (PR) which is formalized as follows:

from a finite sample W of individuals extracted from a population P, we know:

- the state of p variables $X_1, X_2, ...X_p$ called "exogenous" or explanatory variables (for this example, these variables concern evocation patterns);
- the state of a variable Y, called "endogenous" or to explain, considered as qualitative having modalities called labels (which in this case characterize the recognition score).

The objective is to establish a prediction rule F which determines $Y(w) = F(X(w))$ from available $X(w) = (X_1(w), X_2(w), ..., X_p(w))$ for an w Œ $P - W$ of which $Y(w)$ is unknown.

Generally, the F rule building needs two stages: first, the learning stage during which the model is elaborated, and second, the test or generalization stage which is necessary and which allows to estimate the system performances. This system can extend its power to non-learned examples and therefore increases its own capabilities.

In order to carry out the F rule, the connectionist approach has been used and a comparison was established with discriminant analysis. Multi-layer neural networks, with gradient back-propagation learning, were retained as network model type (1), (2). One of the major drawbacks of back-propagation remains the computing time of the learning phase. To solve this problem, a method based on a process named "spy" (3) has been applied in order to explore and choose the best architecture and the best parameters for an artificial neural network with regards to a given application. This spy runs in a parallel architecture environment. It observes and evaluates the results of several neural networks, and it adjusts parameters of new neural networks, depending on the previous results.

This paper is structured as follows. Section 2 continues describing this approach. In section 3, we briefly recall discriminant analysis principle. Finally, in section 4, we illustrate experimental results through a comparative array emphasizing the contribution of the connectionist approach.

2 Connectionist approach

The multi-layer networks involved in this application, are characterized by one input layer, by one or several intermediate layers called hidden layers, and by one output layer. Signals of a same layer are only sent to following layer units. By their excitatory or inhibitory effects, weights have an impact on network ability to acquire knowledge and on network performances. Therefore, most learning algorithms will act on their variations.

The main problem of supervised learning consists of carrying out a treatment which modifies weights, in order to reduce error between the calculated value by network and the value to be learned. The back-propagation algorithm offers such a possibilty (4), (5). Several hundreds, even thousands of iterations are necessary for learning ; this is due to network architecture, difficult adjustment of parameters and, sometimes, weight initialization (6).

With regard to this application,we use a new device called the "spy" (3, 4) to explore and choose the best architecture and the best parameters. The spy observes a set of neural networks (NN) [Figure 1], which all work in parallel, from the same set of patterns, but differ from one another in some of their parameters. This system is implemented on a T-node of 32 transputers disposed according to a linear topology.

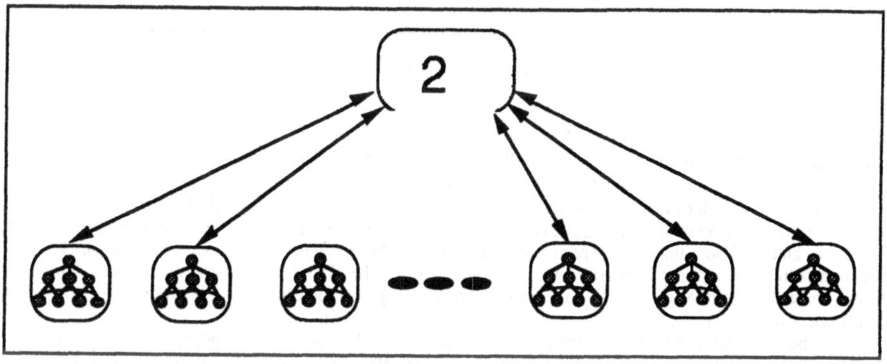

Fig. 1: The spy-process and its farm of neural networks

The spy process computes an optimization algorithm for automatically selecting the neural networks which provide good performances. For this application, the parameters to be optimized are :

- the number of hidden units, on one or two hidden layers,
- a constant coefficient denoted by Kalpha , defined by : learning rate = Kalpha/fan-in, where fan-in is the number of input links of each unit. The learning rate is the coefficient of weight updating in back-propagation algorithm (1, 2).

3 Discriminant analysis

In spite of available numerous methods, we have preferred using discriminant analysis. This technique (7) is based on class separation hypothesis which considers that individuals having distinct labels are represented in different areas which are separated by geometric borders of linear or ellipsoidal types.

After a learning phase which permits searching surfaces on the whole set of representation, surfaces such as hyperplane separating different classes as best they can. These areas obtained will be used to classify non-labelled individuals. A step by step algorithm was used (8).

4 Application

Until now, little interest has been shown in olfactory memory. However, previous researches attempt to show the non negligible role of olfaction in the mnesic process and the impact that it could have on the cognitive area (9, 10).

Nine odor pairs have been used in the experimental tests. They are presented in a random order which is previously defined and in an identical manner for all individuals. In order to allow an individual to familiarize himself with the protocol, a preliminary test odor couple (numbered 0) is presented. A delay of thirty seconds separates two presentations of odors of a same pair. For this experiment, three classes of odor couples have been used: odors of the same pair are either identical, slightly different or very different. The table 1 illustrates the list of odors.

Pair	Odor A	Odor B	
0	Anisole	Anethole	very different
1	Eugenol	Limonene	very different
2	Hexenol	Hexenol	identical
3	Coumarin	Coumarin	identical
4	Geraniol	Phenylethyl Alcohol	very different
5	Naphtalene	Naphtalene	identical
6	Aldehyde C8	Aldehyde C10	slightly different
7	3,3-Dimethyl-2-butanone	2,3-Dimethyl-2,3-butanediol	slightly different
8	Menthone	L-Carvone	very different
9	b-Hexenyl Acetate	Iso-Amyl Acetate	slightly different

Table1: List of nine odor pairs and a preliminary pair(numbered 0)

For each odor couple, the individual task is to recognize if the odor which is presented the second time is the same as or different to the odor which was smelt the first time. The recognition is validated in terms of success or check. This is a short-term recognition memory test without identification.

Recognition of an odor means establishing an identical relation between the actual olfactory experiment and the remembrance of previous experiments. On one hand, this recognition is constrained by the properties of the perception, and we know that odors are encoded holistically. On the other hand, olfactory sensations generate evocation patterns which are memorised by individuals and can be classified in distinct categories. These are hedonic sensation, familiarity, intensity, memories of places, objects, non-olfactory sensations (acid, hot, sweet, ...), generic term (fruity, spicy ...).

Except the active part of souvenir during this recognition test, olfactory performances also vary according to the characteristics of each individual, for instance : age, sex, olfactory experience, smoking habits, education level, birthplace,...

4.1 Model from odorant descriptors

For each pair odor, the individual supplies his evocation pattern concerning the second odor (odor B), from a descriptor list which is presented to him. This list is arranged in 8 categories:

- intensity,
- familiarity,
- hedonic sensation,
- generic term,
- non-olfactory sensation,
- veridical term,
- memorie,
- place.

The sample used during the olfactory test is made up of 105 individuals. For all treatments carried out, a set of 84 individuals (among the whole sample) constitutes the data base for the learning stage. The remaining constitutes the test set.

On the basis of these data, we attempt to build a network model which computes the recognition score of an individual based on his evocation pattern for a given odor.

For each odor, various multi-layer neural networks are tested, in parallel, under the control of the "spy" process (section 2). By fixing the iteration number, the best architecture of the model is obtained. For illustration, the neural network architecture which was designed for the more difficult odor to discriminate among the ten odors: ALDEHYDE C10 is shown in Figure 2.

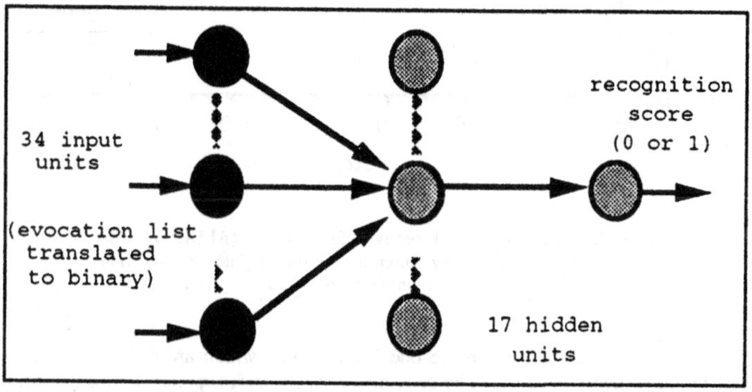

Fig. 2: Network architecture for ALDEHYDE C10.

Furthermore, Figure 3 (a and b) shows the behavior of the two networks which were choosen for predicting th recognition score of odors 6B and 8B respectively. This was permormed by recording the learning an generalization success rates after each serie of 10 steps. For these two odors, we remark that the learning succes rates are nearly 100% after about 50 iterations in stable stages. However, we note that their generalizatio performances are nearly 67% for odor 6B and 73% for odor 8B after the same number of iterations. However, le us note that for the other odors, the neural networks have given satisfying results more easy.

a)

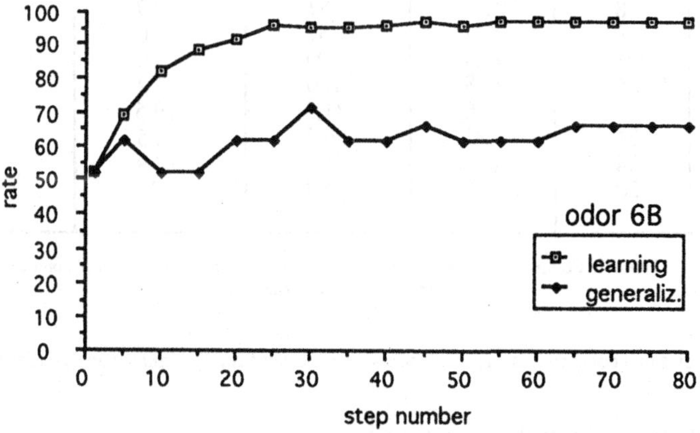

b)

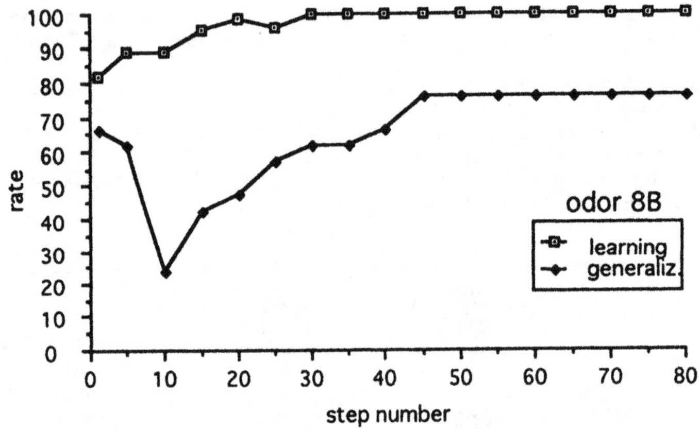

Fig. 3: Illustration of network behavior for odors 6B (ALDEHYDE C10) and 8B (L_CARVONE) by presenting the success rates as a function of the number of iterations.

The table below (Table 2) summarizes, on the one hand, results which are obtained by the connectionist approach and, on the other hand, those given by discriminant analysis. It supplies, for each odor, the best model regarding the spy and resumes the different success rates for learning and generalization stages.

Odors	Connectionist approach performances			Discriminant analysis performances	
	Number of units in hidden layer	Learning (%)	Generalization (%)	Learning (%)	Generalization (%)
2	8	96,4	81	60,7	43
3	9	100	81	70	57
4	3	98,8	100	90	95
5	6	98,8	100	72	66
6	17	97,6	71,4	79,5	56
7	21	100	90,5	65	52
8	34	100	71,4	69	54
9	20	100	85,7	72	45

Table 2: Comparative array between results obtained from connectionist approach and discriminant analysis.

This array shows that connectionist approach offers results better than discriminant analysis for any odor.

4.2 Model from individual characteristics

The second aim of this application is to study if a correlation exist between the different recognition scores of individuals and some of their characteristics such as:

- age,
- sex,
- olfactory experience,
- smoking habits,
- education level,
- birthplace.

For this olfactory test, the recognition scores which are collected are between 5 and 10 meaning that each individual has recognized 5 odors at least among the 10 odors which have been presented to him. As with odorant descriptors, several networks are tested. The spy allows us to retain the best model of which the learning and generalization curves are illustrated in figure 4. Let us remark that a learning success rate of 100% is obtained after 220 iterations. However, the generalization success rate is only about 30%. This result is due to a difficulty to model the correlation between recognition scores and individual characteristics.

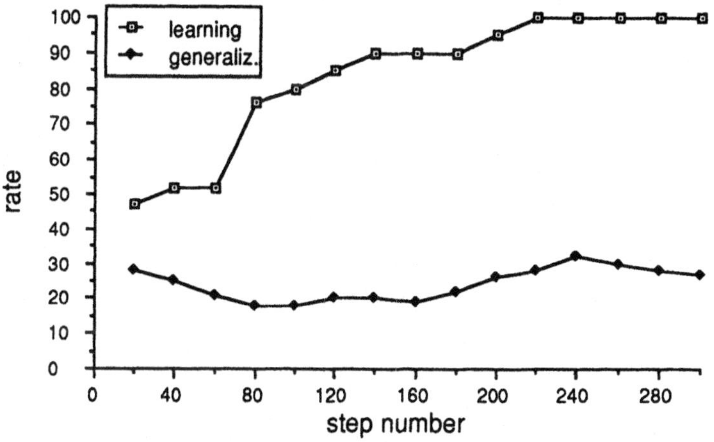

Fig. 4: Temporal behavior of the neural network from individual characteristics.

5 Conclusion

According to experimental results of the different tests with the aim of modelling this olfactory perception phenemonon, the connectionist approach seems promising, especially when applying the spy device. This tool helps to rapidly evaluate and compare the learning capabilities of a large number of NN. Therefore, we can obtain vast quantities of results, which would under sequential programming, require seven or eight months of work.

Neural networks have shown an efficiency with the first objective of our application (score recognition from odorant descriptors) but have checked with the second aim, at the generalization level particularly. However, this first experience is necessary. Studies about characteristics should lead us to choose pertinent informations.

6 References

1. Y. Lecun, "Une procédure d'apprentissage pour réseaux à seuil asymétrique", Proceedings of Cognitive 85, p599-604, Paris, Juin 1985.

2. D.E. Rumelhart, G.E. Hinton, and R.J. Williams, "Learning Internal Representations by Error Propagation", in Rumelhart & McClelland, 318-362, 1986.

3. H. Paugam-Moisy, "Selecting and parallelizing neural networks for improving performances", in : Artificial Neural Networks [ed. Kohonen & al.], North-Holland, 659-664, 1991

4. H. Paugam-Moisy, "Optimisation des réseaux de neurones artificiels. Analyse et mises en oeuvre sur ordinateurs massivement parallèles", Thèse de Doctorat, ENS LyonI, 1992.

5. Y.H. Pao, "Adaptative Pattern Recognition and Neural Networks", Addison-Wesley, Reading MA, 1989.

6. S. Fogelman, P. Gallinari, "Neural networks : from theory to industrial applications", tutorial 7, pp.2-10, neuro-nîmes 91, Nîmes (France), (nov 4-8, 1991).

7. R.A. Fisher, "The Use of Multiple Measurements in Taxonomic Problem". Ann.Eugenics, N°7, p179 - 1936.

8 J.M. Romader, "Méthodes et programmes d'analyse discriminante", Dunod, 1973.

9. T. Engen, B. Ross, "Long-term memory of odors with and without verbal description", J. Exp. Psyhol, 100:221-227, 1975.

10. J.T.E. Richardson, G.M. Zucco, "Cognition and Olfaction/ A review", Psychol. Bull., 105:352-360, 1989.

Springer-Verlag and the Environment

We at Springer-Verlag firmly believe that an international science publisher has a special obligation to the environment, and our corporate policies consistently reflect this conviction.

We also expect our business partners – paper mills, printers, packaging manufacturers, etc. – to commit themselves to using environmentally friendly materials and production processes.

The paper in this book is made from low- or no-chlorine pulp and is acid free, in conformance with international standards for paper permanency.

Lecture Notes in Computer Science

For information about Vols. 1–615
please contact your bookseller or Springer-Verlag

Vol. 616: K. Jensen (Ed.), Application and Theory of Petri Nets 1992. Proceedings, 1992. VIII, 398 pages. 1992.

Vol. 617: V. Mařík, O. Štěpánková, R. Trappl (Eds.), Advanced Topics in Artificial Intelligence. Proceedings, 1992. IX, 484 pages. 1992. (Subseries LNAI).

Vol. 618: P. M. D. Gray, R. J. Lucas (Eds.), Advanced Database Systems. Proceedings, 1992. X, 260 pages. 1992.

Vol. 619: D. Pearce, H. Wansing (Eds.), Nonclassical Logics and Information Proceedings. Proceedings, 1990. VII, 171 pages. 1992. (Subseries LNAI).

Vol. 620: A. Nerode, M. Taitslin (Eds.), Logical Foundations of Computer Science – Tver '92. Proceedings. IX, 514 pages. 1992.

Vol. 621: O. Nurmi, E. Ukkonen (Eds.), Algorithm Theory – SWAT '92. Proceedings. VIII, 434 pages. 1992.

Vol. 622: F. Schmalhofer, G. Strube, Th. Wetter (Eds.), Contemporary Knowledge Engineering and Cognition. Proceedings, 1991. XII, 258 pages. 1992. (Subseries LNAI).

Vol. 623: W. Kuich (Ed.), Automata, Languages and Programming. Proceedings, 1992. XII, 721 pages. 1992.

Vol. 624: A. Voronkov (Ed.), Logic Programming and Automated Reasoning. Proceedings, 1992. XIV, 509 pages. 1992. (Subseries LNAI).

Vol. 625: W. Vogler, Modular Construction and Partial Order Semantics of Petri Nets. IX, 252 pages. 1992.

Vol. 626: E. Börger, G. Jäger, H. Kleine Büning, M. M. Richter (Eds.), Computer Science Logic. Proceedings, 1991. VIII, 428 pages. 1992.

Vol. 628: G. Vosselman, Relational Matching. IX, 190 pages. 1992.

Vol. 629: I. M. Havel, V. Koubek (Eds.), Mathematical Foundations of Computer Science 1992. Proceedings. IX, 521 pages. 1992.

Vol. 630: W. R. Cleaveland (Ed.), CONCUR '92. Proceedings. X, 580 pages. 1992.

Vol. 631: M. Bruynooghe, M. Wirsing (Eds.), Programming Language Implementation and Logic Programming. Proceedings, 1992. XI, 492 pages. 1992.

Vol. 632: H. Kirchner, G. Levi (Eds.), Algebraic and Logic Programming. Proceedings, 1992. IX, 457 pages. 1992.

Vol. 633: D. Pearce, G. Wagner (Eds.), Logics in AI. Proceedings. VIII, 410 pages. 1992. (Subseries LNAI).

Vol. 634: L. Bougé, M. Cosnard, Y. Robert, D. Trystram (Eds.), Parallel Processing: CONPAR 92 – VAPP V. Proceedings. XVII, 853 pages. 1992.

Vol. 635: J. C. Derniame (Ed.), Software Process Technology. Proceedings, 1992. VIII, 253 pages. 1992.

Vol. 636: G. Comyn, N. E. Fuchs, M. J. Ratcliffe (Eds.), Logic Programming in Action. Proceedings, 1992. X, 324 pages. 1992. (Subseries LNAI).

Vol. 637: Y. Bekkers, J. Cohen (Eds.), Memory Management. Proceedings, 1992. XI, 525 pages. 1992.

Vol. 639: A. U. Frank, I. Campari, U. Formentini (Eds.), Theories and Methods of Spatio-Temporal Reasoning in Geographic Space. Proceedings, 1992. XI, 431 pages. 1992.

Vol. 640: C. Sledge (Ed.), Software Engineering Education. Proceedings, 1992. X, 451 pages. 1992.

Vol. 641: U. Kastens, P. Pfahler (Eds.), Compiler Construction. Proceedings, 1992. VIII, 320 pages. 1992.

Vol. 642: K. P. Jantke (Ed.), Analogical and Inductive Inference. Proceedings, 1992. VIII, 319 pages. 1992. (Subseries LNAI).

Vol. 643: A. Habel, Hyperedge Replacement: Grammars and Languages. X, 214 pages. 1992.

Vol. 644: A. Apostolico, M. Crochemore, Z. Galil, U. Manber (Eds.), Combinatorial Pattern Matching. Proceedings, 1992. X, 287 pages. 1992.

Vol. 645: G. Pernul, A M. Tjoa (Eds.), Entity-Relationship Approach – ER '92. Proceedings, 1992. XI, 439 pages, 1992.

Vol. 646: J. Biskup, R. Hull (Eds.), Database Theory – ICDT '92. Proceedings, 1992. IX, 449 pages. 1992.

Vol. 647: A. Segall, S. Zaks (Eds.), Distributed Algorithms. X, 380 pages. 1992.

Vol. 648: Y. Deswarte, G. Eizenberg, J.-J. Quisquater (Eds.), Computer Security – ESORICS 92. Proceedings. XI, 451 pages. 1992.

Vol. 649: A. Pettorossi (Ed.), Meta-Programming in Logic. Proceedings, 1992. XII, 535 pages. 1992.

Vol. 650: T. Ibaraki, Y. Inagaki, K. Iwama, T. Nishizeki, M. Yamashita (Eds.), Algorithms and Computation. Proceedings, 1992. XI, 510 pages. 1992.

Vol. 651: R. Koymans, Specifying Message Passing and Time-Critical Systems with Temporal Logic. IX, 164 pages. 1992.

Vol. 652: R. Shyamasundar (Ed.), Foundations of Software Technology and Theoretical Computer Science. Proceedings, 1992. XIII, 405 pages. 1992.

Vol. 653: A. Bensoussan, J.-P. Verjus (Eds.), Future Tendencies in Computer Science, Control and Applied Mathematics. Proceedings, 1992. XV, 371 pages. 1992.

Vol. 654: A. Nakamura, M. Nivat, A. Saoudi, P. S. P. Wang, K. Inoue (Eds.), Parallel Image Analysis. Proceedings, 1992. VIII, 312 pages. 1992.

Vol. 655: M. Bidoit, C. Choppy (Eds.), Recent Trends in Data Type Specification. X, 344 pages. 1993.

Vol. 656: M. Rusinowitch, J. L. Rémy (Eds.), Conditional Term Rewriting Systems. Proceedings, 1992. XI, 501 pages. 1993.

Vol. 657: E. W. Mayr (Ed.), Graph-Theoretic Concepts in Computer Science. Proceedings, 1992. VIII, 350 pages. 1993.

Vol. 658: R. A. Rueppel (Ed.), Advances in Cryptology – EUROCRYPT '92. Proceedings, 1992. X, 493 pages. 1993.

Vol. 659: G. Brewka, K. P. Jantke, P. H. Schmitt (Eds.), Nonmonotonic and Inductive Logic. Proceedings, 1991. VIII, 332 pages. 1993. (Subseries LNAI).

Vol. 660: E. Lamma, P. Mello (Eds.), Extensions of Logic Programming. Proceedings, 1992. VIII, 417 pages. 1993. (Subseries LNAI).

Vol. 661: S. J. Hanson, W. Remmele, R. L. Rivest (Eds.), Machine Learning: From Theory to Applications. VIII, 271 pages. 1993.

Vol. 662: M. Nitzberg, D. Mumford, T. Shiota, Filtering, Segmentation and Depth. VIII, 143 pages. 1993.

Vol. 663: G. v. Bochmann, D. K. Probst (Eds.), Computer Aided Verification. Proceedings, 1992. IX, 422 pages. 1993.

Vol. 664: M. Bezem, J. F. Groote (Eds.), Typed Lambda Calculi and Applications. Proceedings, 1993. VIII, 433 pages. 1993.

Vol. 665: P. Enjalbert, A. Finkel, K. W. Wagner (Eds.), STACS 93. Proceedings, 1993. XIV, 724 pages. 1993.

Vol. 666: J. W. de Bakker, W.-P. de Roever, G. Rozenberg (Eds.), Semantics: Foundations and Applications. Proceedings, 1992. VIII, 659 pages. 1993.

Vol. 667: P. B. Brazdil (Ed.), Machine Learning: ECML – 93. Proceedings, 1993. XII, 471 pages. 1993. (Subseries LNAI).

Vol. 668: M.-C. Gaudel, J.-P. Jouannaud (Eds.), TAPSOFT '93: Theory and Practice of Software Development. Proceedings, 1993. XII, 762 pages. 1993.

Vol. 669: R. S. Bird, C. C. Morgan, J. C. P. Woodcock (Eds.), Mathematics of Program Construction. Proceedings, 1992. VIII, 378 pages. 1993.

Vol. 670: J. C. P. Woodcock, P. G. Larsen (Eds.), FME '93: Industrial-Strength Formal Methods. Proceedings, 1993. XI, 689 pages. 1993.

Vol. 671: H. J. Ohlbach (Ed.), GWAI-92: Advances in Artificial Intelligence. Proceedings, 1992. XI, 397 pages. 1993. (Subseries LNAI).

Vol. 672: A. Barak, S. Guday, R. G. Wheeler, The MOSIX Distributed Operating System. X, 221 pages. 1993.

Vol. 673: G. Cohen, T. Mora, O. Moreno (Eds.), Applied Algebra, Algebraic Algorithms and Error-Correcting Codes. Proceedings, 1993. X, 355 pages 1993.

Vol. 674: G. Rozenberg (Ed.), Advances in Petri Nets 1993. VII, 457 pages. 1993.

Vol. 675: A. Mulkers, Live Data Structures in Logic Programs. VIII, 220 pages. 1993.

Vol. 676: Th. H. Reiss, Recognizing Planar Objects Using Invariant Image Features. X, 180 pages. 1993.

Vol. 677: H. Abdulrab, J.-P. Pécuchet (Eds.), Word Equations and Related Topics. Proceedings, 1991. VII, 214 pages. 1993.

Vol. 678: F. Meyer auf der Heide, B. Monien, A. L. Rosenberg (Eds.), Parallel Architectures and Their Efficient Use. Proceedings, 1992. XII, 227 pages. 1993.

Vol. 679: C. Fermüller, A. Leitsch, T. Tammet, N. Zamov, Resolution Methods for the Decision Problem. VIII, 205 pages. 1993. (Subseries LNAI).

Vol. 682: B. Bouchon-Meunier, L. Valverde, R. R. Yager (Eds.), IPMU '92 – Advanced Methods in Artificial Intelligence. Proceedings, 1992. IX, 367 pages. 1993.

Vol. 683: G.J. Milne, L. Pierre (Eds.), Correct Hardware Design and Verification Methods. Proceedings, 1993. VIII, 270 Pages. 1993.

Vol. 684: A. Apostolico, M. Crochemore, Z. Galil, U. Manber (Eds.), Combinatorial Pattern Matching. Proceedings, 1993. VIII, 265 pages. 1993.

Vol. 685: C. Rolland, F. Bodart, C. Cauvet (Eds.), Advanced Information Systems Engineering. Proceedings, 1993. XI, 650 pages. 1993.

Vol. 686: J. Mira, J. Cabestany, A. Prieto (Eds.), New Trends in Neural Computation. Procedings, 1993. XVII, 746 pages. 1993.

Vol. 687: H. H. Barrett, A. F. Gmitro (Eds.), Information Processing in Medical Imaging. Proceedings, 1993. XVI, 567 pages. 1993.

Vol. 688: M. Gauthier (Ed.), Ada - Europe '93. Proceedings, 1993. VIII, 353 pages. 1993.

Vol. 689: J. Komorowski, Z. W. Ras (Eds.), Methodologies for Intelligent Systems. Proceedings, 1993. XI, 653 pages. 1993. (Subseries LNAI).

Vol. 690: C. Kirchner (Ed.), Rewriting Techniques and Applications. Proceedings, 1993. XI, 488 pages. 1993.

Vol. 691: M. Ajmone Marsan (Ed.), Application and Theory of Petri Nets 1993. Proceedings, 1993. IX, 591 pages. 1993.

Vol. 692: D. Abel, B.C. Ooi (Eds.), Advances in Spatial Databases. Proceedings, 1993. XIII, 529 pages. 1993.

Vol. 693: P. E. Lauer (Ed.), Functional Programming, Concurrency, Simulation and Automated Reasoning. Proceedings, 1991/1992. XI, 398 pages. 1993.

Vol. 694: A. Bode, M. Reeve, G. Wolf (Eds.), PARLE '93. Parallel Architectures and Languages Europe. Proceedings, 1993. XVII, 770 pages. 1993.

Vol. 695: E. P. Klement, W. Slany (Eds.), Fuzzy Logic in Artificial Intelligence. Proceedings, 1993. VIII, 192 pages. 1993. (Subseries LNAI).

Vol. 696: M. Worboys, A. F. Grundy (Eds.), Advances in Databases. Proceedings, 1993. X, 276 pages. 1993.

Vol. 697: C. Courcoubetis (Ed.), Computer Aided Verification. Proceedings, 1993. IX, 504 pages. 1993.

Vol. 700: A. Lingas, R. Karlsson, S. Carlsson (Eds.), Automata, Languages and Programming. Proceedings, 1993. XII, 697 pages. 1993.